Law and Economics

Alternative Economic Approaches to Legal and Regulatory Issues

Foreword by Warren J. Samuels

Editors
Margaret Oppenheimer and Nicholas Mercuro

Routledge
Taylor & Francis Group
LONDON AND NEW YORK

First published 2005 by M.E. Sharpe

Published 2015 by Routledge
2 Park Square, Milton Park, Abingdon, Oxon OX14 4RN
711 Third Avenue, New York, NY 10017, USA

Routledge is an imprint of the Taylor & Francis Group, an informa business

Library of Congress Cataloging-in-Publication Data

Law and economics : alternative economic approaches to legal and regulatory issues / edited by Margaret Oppenheimer and Nicholas Mercuro.
p. cm.
Includes bibliographical references and index.
ISBN 0-7656-1331-X (alk. paper)
1. Law and economics. I. Title: Law and economics. II. Oppenheimer, Margaret, 1947– III. Mercuro, Nicholas.
K487.E3L374 2004
340′.11—dc22

2004005951

ISBN 13: 9780765613318 (hbk)

Contents

List of Tables and Figures

Tables

Figures

Foreword

Some Thoughts on the Study of Law and Economics and on the Role of Government

Warren J. Samuels

The great University of Chicago economist Frank H. Knight told a class in 1933–34: "There is no established economic usage for anything in economics." Seventy years later the same description still applies to the whole of economics and to the field of law and economics (as well as to just the field of law). There is no more reason to expect one established usage than to seek one established policy in any area. Legal-economic "reality" is so complex and kaleidoscopic, and the standpoints from which it can be approached are so numerous, that multiple definitions of that reality, not one, are to be expected. Similarly, with legal-economic or regulatory issues, matters of static- and dynamic-evolutionary complexity, various analytical and normative standpoints, and competing judgments as to whose interests should count and the consequences thereof, are all to be expected—especially as varying "experiments" are tried in different jurisdictions. And, indeed, there are numerous different approaches, no one of which is itself homogeneous. This book recognizes the many contributions that these different approaches can make to the field of law and economics.

Neoclassical law and economics enjoys a hegemonic position. Actually, two different variants of the neoclassical approach exist, neither of which is homogeneous. One variant studies how the legal system/government operates. The other variant studies the results or impacts of the legal system/government. Each variant encompasses two modes of analysis: One mode is a positivist, neutral description and explanation; the other is subjective and normative. Each variant and its twin modes of analysis also pursue two different research protocols, or agendas. One seeks to generate unique determinate equilibrium results—the normative version seeking also the "optimum" result in each case—and typically works with pure, abstract a-institutional conceptual categories (such as "the market"). The other looks to identify the several or many tendencies that may emerge from any policy or institution and the conditions that help determine which tendency is likely to emerge—and typically works with actual markets and the institutions that form and operate through markets. Each also combines researchers with different psychological attitudes; some seek determinacy and closure, for example, applying a-institutional, purely conceptual analysis to selective existing institutions and policy problems; and some are comfortable with ambiguity and open-endedness, such as indicating the comparative likely performance consequences of different institutions. Each is also caught up in the situation that important facts are theory-laden and that theories tend to be derived from certain readings of facts. Circularity and cumulative causation are common—much maligned but inevitable—characteristics. *Substantially all legal-economic research is a mixture of each of the foregoing pairs.*

The range of work on the topic of law and economics is enormous, far beyond the range of a preface to even outline.[1] Instead, I shall make a number of points that I consider important. Scholars in the field of legal and regulatory issues tend strongly to seek—indeed, to often have felt a need for—specific and singular policy conclusions. Economic and legal scholars typically want to do so, and others also often want them to do so. There is no necessary reason for this to be the case. Moreover, empirical work—induction and deduction—have severe limits when deployed in policy analysis. Clearly, it seems to me, greater attention is needed for the study of what has been—describing and explaining how the legal system/government operates and the consequences of its results—and less than hitherto for the study of what should have been and what should now be the policy. Still, it is understandable that independent, open-minded researchers could become so immersed in the materials of a particular field, issue, or policy problem, that policy implications form in their minds that appear sensible and obvious but lack perspective.

Belief in comparative institutional analysis is the motivation behind many chapters in this collection. They look at structure, behavior, and performance, not necessarily all at the same time, seeking to understand how each influences, and is influenced by, the others. The premise is that institutions matter; their causes and consequences need to be examined. The consequences of particular institutions are, in part, a function of the institutions themselves and of the environment in which they operate. All aspects of those relationships exhibit the truth of the proposition that the story is in the details. Thus, one has to study the content and character of the decision-making structures, policies, and goods involved in human interdependence, such as high exclusion cost, information cost, social traps, and so on.

It must be clear that policy is a deeper and broader matter than that found in the incremental contribution made by particular pieces of legislation and particular court decisions. It must also be clear that the ostensible or apparent policy is not necessarily the actual policy. For example, a contest may exist between policy A and policy B. Policy A wins. But the group appointed to administer the institution created in the aftermath of policy A's victory, may believe—and be appointed because they believe—in policy B, so they adopt rules that for all practical purposes effectuate policy B. In another example, a policy may be proposed on the ground that it will diffuse power. However, under the conditions in which the policy would be executed, the effect would be to concentrate power in some hands and reduce the power of those hitherto in a more advantageous position—which is the actual motivating force.

One hurdle of clear thinking about legal-economic policy is the idea of laissez-faire. Both sentimentally and substantively, laissez-faire stands for an economic system based upon institutions of private property, free enterprise, competition, markets, meaningful private choice, and a presumption against government activism; markets govern resource allocation. Sentimentally, it is an idealization of the Western economic system, a projection of certain individualist sentiments. Compared to mercantilism and Soviet-type planning, it also has substantive meaning. While laissez-faire seems an attractive solution to social problems and escapes the burden of choice, and because movement toward an idealized image is perceived as neither government nor change, problems arise in its application within a market economy.

Market economies are usefully modeled as market plus framework systems. Markets operate within frameworks of moral and legal rules structuring and operating through markets they help form. This model gives effect to (1) private choice and (2) necessary social control. Problems arise over the substance of rules, mode of determining rules, relative reliance upon moral and legal rules, and changing legal rules. The model postulates a joint process: optimizing market resource allocation and reforming the framework. Regulation is a mode of revising rights; deregulation is the functional equivalent of regulation, only the protected interests are different.

Because the presumption against legal activism is easily rebutted, the substantive interpretation becomes ambiguous. Legal social control is necessary. The basic economic institutions are legal in character. People who believe they have problems in pragmatic, democratic regimes seek government's help. Working all this out is messy. Politicians seeking reelection must attend to citizen attitudes and perceptions of problems, problems likely to be very real. For this and numerous other reasons, changing the legal rules governing property rights and other institutions happens frequently—to the dismay of believers in strict laissez-faire.

Modern Western economies exhibit several practical models of laissez faire. First, government is projected as an evil intruder, with the emphasis on *evil,* to be removed from the backs of the citizens. Second, existing governmental activities are taken for granted, treated as natural. In the first two models, officials' principal function is to enforce the law, and neither to expand their scope nor to introduce change. Third, typically inexplicit in ordinary discourse, government is the object of reform, making government do the correct things for the right people. The first model minimizes government; the second minimizes change of law and of the interests protected by government; and the third minimizes control of the agenda by the wrong people.

This practical orientation faces fundamental problems. First, conflicts exist among the three models considered as agendas for government. Second, all three are applied selectively, therefore inconsistently, resulting in ambiguity and inconclusiveness. Third, economic policy is a function of contests among elites and between elites and nonelites to determine who are the right people to control and benefit from government. Fourth, a tension may exist between economic and social conservatives; the former want to enhance, and the latter to constrain the range of private discretion allowed by law, generally but not necessarily in different spheres of life.

Another problem is *governance,* defined as decisionmaking importantly affecting other people. Official government is one institution of governance; others include other governments, international organizations, domestic and foreign corporations, nonprofit organizations, organized religion, education, and customs. Government has formal responsibility for the division of power within the nominally private sector and between the private and public sectors. But government is an object of a ubiquitous contest over its control. Limiting government does not limit governance.

Common to much of the above is that government "interferes" in order to control "interference" by others. Freedom—freedom to manufacture and to trade—is a function of the total system of freedom and control. Legal rules both limit and enhance the individual's range of operative discretion, typically differently for different people. A historic example is the contest between labor and capital over the legal status of unions.

Private property is what it is because of government and because it is a check on the power of government—given suitable legislators and judges. During the period of transformation from the old to the modern state and economy, new forms and new meanings of property arose and old ones fell. Property was not protected because it is property; it was property because it was protected. But such did not prevent claims invoking the sacred character of property and the need to protect property against the claims of those who wanted government to protect their interests just as it had protected others, as property.

"Laissez-faire" was fiction, an exercise in wishful thinking and the language of those who opposed certain proposed changes, but not their own changes. The concept has mixed sentimental and existential or substantive meaning, suffused with selectivity in application and ambiguity of meaning. Certain sentiments are effectively expressed; yet fundamentally inconclusive with respect to the issues to which they are addressed, generally represented by the question, "What should government do?" The question is more complicated than the phrase and its underlying sentiment might lead one to expect. Laissez-faire is a simplistic and disengaging view of complex real-world problems, the dynamics of change, and the need for collective decisionmaking. Accordingly, no country could or has practiced laissez-faire, though much has been done in its name.

The chapters in this volume challenge mainstream neoclassical law and economics. The contributing authors have followed several different economic, legal, and philosophical approaches and have extended that challenge to numerous important legal-economic and regulatory issues. The contributions thus offer fresh perspectives on these many issues. The field of law and economics can only benefit from opening the discourse to these new ideas and applications.

Note

1. See, for example, Warren J. Samuels, ed. *Law and Economics.*

Reference

Samuels, W.J., ed. *Law and Economics.* 2 vols. London: Pickering and Chatto, 1998.

Part 1

Introduction: New Approaches to Law and Economics

1

Law and Economics

Making the Case for a Broader Approach

Margaret Oppenheimer and Nicholas Mercuro

> *If someone had predicted twenty years ago that law and economics would become a central organizing philosophy in U.S. legal education by the end of the century, he would have been dismissed as delusional. And yet that prediction has come to pass.*
>
> Robert D. Cooter and Thomas S. Ulen (2000)[1]

Over the last several decades the field of law and economics has expanded and matured beyond anyone's expectations. As Lawrence Lessig wrote, "We all are law-and-economists now."[2] Law and economics has developed into a rather substantial movement, certainly within economics but even more so within the law. Not only has the field helped to expose economics to the important implications of the evolving legal environment, but it has also brought to the forefront the fact that legal decisions often have important economic implications that can be uncovered with the application of economic theory. On the legal side, a key aspect of this process has been the incorporation of mainstream neoclassical economic theory into legal thought and, hence, legal education. The neoclassical approach now dominates research and writing in economics departments as well as in law schools, especially in the United States. The result has been extensive discussion and critique about what is now simply referred to as "*the* economic approach to law."

However, despite the popularity of neoclassical theory (and especially rational choice theory), in both economics and law, what critics (mainly within law) call *the* economic approach to law, is really a misnomer. A central flaw in much of their criticism is the tendency to equate all economics with the Chicago School of Law and Economics and, by extension, with its conservative—ubiquitous market-oriented—ideology. However, the growing field of law and economics is not a homogenous movement; it reflects several traditions, sometimes competing and sometimes complementary, and is actually far more inclusive than the critics recognize. *The* neoclassical economic approach is merely one of many economic approaches that can be applied to legal and regulatory issues.[3]

The contributing authors to this book provide alternatives to the mainstream approach. They utilize a variety of heterodox legal-economic approaches to address a broad range of legal issues. They demonstrate how these various approaches can lead to alternative theories and conclusions concerning the role of the law and legal intervention in a wide array of contexts. The legal and regulatory issues examined in this volume include antitrust and competition, corporate governance, the environment and natural resources, land use and property rights, unions and collective bargaining, welfare benefits, work-time regulation and standards, sexual harassment in the workplace, obligations of employers and employees and others, crime, torts, and even the structure of government. Given its scope and content, we believe that this volume will be of interest to lawyers, economists, and those in contiguous disciplines, indeed, anyone who has an interest in how various economic arguments can be used to better understand legal and regulatory issues, and to make better decisions and policies.

The motivation for compiling this volume came, in part, from the experiences of the editors at various conferences on law and economics and presentations at law schools on heterodox economics. These experiences have uncovered a widespread interest in economic approaches to legal-economic issues, but the search seems to be for an economics that is an alternative to mainstream neoclassical theory. Even among the legal scholars who accept and apply mainstream economic thought with accuracy and comfort, there was concern that applying it blindly would result in both bad economics and bad law. Moreover, Lessig's invocation notwithstanding, some law faculty and students have asserted that they do not accept the application of economics to legal issues at all. Upon further discussion, it became clear that what they rejected were some, although not necessarily all, of the implications of neoclassical economic thought in much of the current law and economics' literature; at the same time, these same individuals were simply not aware that economists had a wider range of ideas and models upon which to draw. The result was a rejection of economics as a resource for legal thinking, rather than an active dialogue of what economics could bring to legal debates. This volume, by providing concrete examples of various alternative economic approaches to legal and regulatory issues, is meant to broaden the debate over a wide range of legal issues and more generally about the application of economics to the law.

The neoclassical approach to law and economics, as it is typically applied to legal issues, claims to make positive (rather than normative) statements regarding proposed policy/legal changes or recommendations, hence the emphasis on efficiency and Pareto optimality. At the same time, the law to many scholars interested in policy is inherently and appropriately entwined with such issues as rights and responsibilities, equity, fairness, and distribution. The concerns over these latter issues affect attitudes by legal scholars, legal practitioners, and citizens as to the role of the individual and the role of the state. In a newsletter published by the Committee on the Status of Women in the Economics Profession (CSWEP), Susan Rose-Ackerman, an economics Ph.D. from Yale, and professor of law and political science at the Yale Law School, gives the following advice for lawyer/economists:

> They . . . need to be willing to entertain a broader set of normative concerns than just the achievement of Pareto optimality. Some prominent members of the field urge scholars to avoid any taint of normative analysis beyond a concern for efficiency. Those who follow that advice and refuse to engage the concerns of the legal academy risk becoming isolated from the broader range of legal scholarship and debate.[4]

It is hoped that this collection will demonstrate the richness of both positive and normative, nonmainstream economic thought and its application to this broader range of legal scholarship and debate.

There are many fruitful ways to catalog economic models. At one end of the spectrum are schools of thought that emphasize the attributes of markets, especially allocative efficiency; this is the mainstream neoclassical approach. At the other extreme are schools of thought that reject the market completely as a central organizing mechanism to allocate resources.[5] The chapters in this volume fall somewhere along this spectrum, rather than at either extreme. The schools of thought and methodologies represented here include institutional economics, new institutional economics, socioeconomics, social economics, behavioral economics, game theory, feminist economics, Rawlsian economics, radical economics, Austrian economics, and personalist economics. Although several of these approaches overlap, each author brings a different emphasis to the legal topic he or she has chosen. What they have in common, however, is that all provide thoughtful, provoking analyses and conclusions that depart in some way from the mainstream approach to their topics.

In his foreword, Warren Samuels recognizes that the premise of many chapters in this volume is that institutions matter and that their causes and consequences need to be examined. In order to understand the consequences of particular institutions, we need to study the structures of human interdependence, such as high exclusion cost, information cost, social traps, and so on. However, he goes on to point out that one of the hurdles to clear thinking about legal-economic policy is the sentimentality of the idea of laissez-faire. Many of these chapters ask the question, "What should government do?" Samuels believes that an answer to that question requires more than the agenda offered by neoclassical economics. We need to explore, at a deeper level, the role of government, the concept of governance, the meaning and uses of the concept of property, and so on. From this vantage point it becomes clear that laissez-faire is a far too simplistic and disengaging view of complex real-world problems and that it is necessary to draw on a much wider range of economic approaches to the law than has commonly been done.

The body of the book is divided into five sections. Accompanying this introduction to the volume in Part 1 is a chapter by Amitai Etzioni, presenting the broad contours of the foundations of socioeconomics as a viable alternative approach to the more conventional neoclassical approach to law and economics. His argument is presented on the belief that this new paradigm will, in time, prove to be more useful then existing paradigms that describe and analyze the law. The chapter first outlines the reasons he believes that the time has come to develop a shared disciplinary core for socioeconomics; he then outlines the guiding principles he thinks should be used to develop the core theory, and finally, suggests specific elements for such a discipline.

The chapters in Part 2 explore several legal and regulatory issues concerned with firms and market structure. Claude Menard's chapter utilizes and extends the theoretical framework provided by new institutional economics. From this theoretical base, he then proceeds to explore the implications of applying the theory to standard competition policies regarding vertical integration or deintegration as well as the case of the so-called hybrid arrangements. In this he shows how competition policies that ignore transaction costs can generate unexpected biases. Emphasizing the key role of transaction costs, both as a tool for analyzing the relevance of these policies and as a key factor that drives decisionmaking, he concludes the following. First, competition policies cannot be examined solely with respect to the cases to which they apply. Second, decisions about vertical integration or deintegration must take into consideration not only ex post consequences but also ex ante circumstances that determined the choices made by actors. Third, modern market economies are made of a complex set of interwoven arrangements, of which spot markets and integrated firms are only two cases among others. In addition, he demonstrates that competition policies cannot evaluate properly nonstandard arrangements of the hybrid type with the sole reference to markets and hierarchies as benchmarks. Fourth, competition policies are embedded in institutions. They are subject to bounded rationality, to the self-interest and opportunism of those in charge of designing and implementing these policies, and to lobbying from the parties concerned. All these factors generate transaction costs that are typically the costs of running the system, for example, a market economy. These costs need to be measured and evaluated comparatively.

Kellye Testy's chapter employs feminist economics to analyze corporate law and governance. It is premised on the belief that too little attention has been paid to the promising contributions of feminist economics in general and, with respect to law in particular. She demonstrates that the field of corporate law and governance has been quite insulated from feminist analysis and contends that this is both remarkable and unfortunate. Her quest then is to elevate a new vision of corporate law that can be furthered through an alternative form of analysis, one that is grounded in feminist economics. Hers is a three-part effort. First, she provides a brief summary of feminist economics, highlighting the key ways in which its methods and content differ from the dominant neoclassical approach. Second, she describes both the dominant model of corporate law and governance in the United States, as well as five significant counter-approaches, discussing how each approaches key corporate law issues such as the nature of the firm and the relative rights and duties of the corporation's constituents. She then concludes by explaining how a feminist economic analysis of corporate law would alter significantly one's view of an optimal corporate regulatory environment, and by outlining several avenues for future research that should be pursued, including the potential for a productive alliance between feminist economists and progressive corporate law scholars.

Patrick Welch and Thomas Greaney outline the three most recognized economic approaches to antitrust: the neoclassical approach, the Harvard School approach, and the Chicago School approach. The chapter includes an insightful analysis of the effects of these different economic perspectives on antitrust enforcement. In observing that there is no complete agreement on the goals and objectives of antitrust enforcement, they explore the several controversies over means and goals that arise with particular attention paid to (1) the relationship of efficiency and consumer welfare, (2) the protection of small sellers, and (3) the protection of democracy.

Part 3 looks at several of the legal-economic issues related to the environment, natural resources, and land use. Nicholas Mercuro's chapter sets forth a conceptual model of a comparative institutional approach to law and economics including the (1) constitutional, (2) institutional, and (3) economic impact stages of choice. The model focuses on four different means of social control, together with their respective property rights regimes that serve to allocate society's scarce resources—the market sector (private property rights), the public sector (status rights), the communal sector (communal rights), and the open-access resource sector (no property rights). Environmental, natural resource, and land-use examples are included in the analysis of each stage of choice and in exploration of the consequences of fashioning remedies within the market sector, the public sector, the communal sector, or leaving resources in the open-access resource sector.

In her chapter, Ann Davis observes that in the last few decades, the issue of property rights has become more contested with the increase in concern for the environment and the perceived decline of community. Davis adopts an institutional economics approach to document and detail the development patterns in New York State's Hudson Valley Region over the course of two centuries. The chapter defines and analyzes the institutional and historical contexts of what transpired with respect to property and land-use development in the area, using the notion of property as a heuristic device for tracing institutional change across a long period. This rich history traces the development of modern notions of "public" municipal corporations and "private" land markets, as both legal theory and republican government developed in the eighteenth and nineteenth centuries. This look to the past brings the reader an awareness of the wide range of land-use regimes, the relatively recent separation of public from private, and the implications related to the separation of governance from ownership. The central argument is that as one comes to understand the history of property—with its differential, shifting meanings over time, both ideological and institutional—that understanding helps make clear the forces that have recently led to scenery and farmland being consumed at a rapid rate in the Hudson Valley Region, all to the apparent dismay of local residents, policymakers, and local leaders.

The premise of Elizabeth Kruse's chapter on property rights and institutions is that over the past decade the analysis of property rights and institutions has continued to adhere and take place within the neoclassical economic framework. At the same time, she notes, there has been a growing consensus, even among mainstream economists, that such models are too limited to encompass adequately elements such as transaction costs, opportunism, subjectivity, limits on rationality, and real or historical time. She contends that what is needed are new economic models for property rights analyses and that these models should include not only the usual factors traditionally examined in neoclassical models of property rights, namely—resource characteristics, technology, and product markets—but also the contributions from new institutional economists including ideologies and existing institutions. She then goes further to argue that any serious consideration of these factors logically points to the need to incorporate concepts of power into the analyses. As a vehicle of analysis, Kruse explores the creation of property rights in the radio spectrum in the United States between 1899 and 1934. This case study illustrates her approach in attempting to provide a fuller understanding of the origin of property rights institutions. Her analysis demonstrates the necessity of considering the influences of institutions, ideologies, and power, in shaping and creating property rights in general, and in the radio spectrum in the United States in particular.

The chapters in Part 4 look at a variety of labor market and workplace problems. Kenneth Dau-Schmidt's chapter concentrates on the National Labor Relations Act of 1935 and American labor law, particularly those policies that foster unionization and regulate collective bargaining. He contends that the policy of fostering unions and regulating collective bargaining to promote equity and industrial peace makes no sense in the context of the traditional monopoly model of unions and collective bargaining. His argument is advanced on the belief that this monopoly model is inadequate in several regards. Specifically, under the monopoly model, unions cause inefficiency and inequity by establishing a labor cartel and prompting employers to cut production, inefficiently mix capital and labor, displace workers to unorganized markets, and raise prices to consumers. His chapter uses what he terms a "fortified bargaining analysis" of unions and collective bargaining in the United States in an attempt to provide a deeper analysis of the efficacy of American labor law. From this analysis he is able to conclude that the optimal public policy with respect to unions and collective bargaining would be for the government to try to maximize the social benefits of employee organization, while minimizing its social costs. That is, the policy implications that emerge from his alternative economic analysis is for the government to draft and enforce legislation that would foster and promote employee organization and its benefits of redistribution of employer rents, industrial democracy, and democratic pluralism. Such legislation would help minimize waste by regulating the conduct of collective bargaining to prohibit or discourage strategic behavior while at the same time require unions to allow workers to gain a greater share of the proceeds of the business and to make valuable contributions to the running of that business and society through the expression of their collective voice.

Edward O'Boyle examines the competing premises of neoclassical economics and what he terms "personalist economics." Personalist economics is based, not on the neoclassical concept of *homo economicus,* but instead on *homo socioeconomicus,* a conceptualization of economic agents that recognizes that all human existence is really coexistence. Personalist economics rests on four premises—the person, institutions, uncertainty, and inherent dignity—rejecting the more familiar premises of neoclassical economists: the individual, the law of nature, certainty, and instrumental value. The underlying argument for a personalist economics is that by making its premises clear and differentiating them from the premises of neoclassical economics, lawyers who rely on economics to inform their work can better understand how and why personalist economists observe, interpret, and represent economic affairs differently. Personalist economics goes beyond the traditional bounds of neoclassical economics, which claims to be value free. For personalist economics, economic justice is fundamental to any understanding of economic affairs. To this end personalist economics incorporates three principles of economic justice: equivalence, distributive justice, and contributive justice. The chapter explores these concepts in the context of affirmative action and violations such as redlining, insider trading, insurance fraud, dumping, harassment, price gouging, loan sharking, and sweatshops. Finally, the chapter focuses attention on the person acting as an economic agent in economic affairs and describes the nature of choices made by the acting person in three types of interaction in economic affairs: consumer and merchant (product market), worker and producer (resource market), and entrepreneur and financial agent (financial market).

An underlying fundamental premise of the American reforms dealing with welfare programs is that welfare recipients include many individuals who have become dependent on unearned income and who have opted for a life of leisure or even indolence. Morris Altman argues that this belief is fostered through conventional neoclassical economic modeling techniques of welfare programs. As a consequence, the conventional models have a significant impact on public policy by predicting that social welfare programs will have negative effects upon the economy in terms of labor supply, production costs, and employment. Specifically, the conventional models argue that the direct income payments and in-kind income associated with welfare, serves to increase unemployment by reducing the incentive of economic agents to search for and engage in either short- or long-term market employment. This chapter attempts to specify the assumptions underlying the conventional model of welfare payments and the manner by which they causally relate to the analytical predictions of the model. In addition, it addresses the question of the economic impact of welfare payments from an alternative and more realistic analytical framework, thereby providing an alternative theoretical construct of the underlying assumptions. This alternative theoretical framework—based on the target income approach—suggests that the conventional analysis of welfare can be highly misleading, generating policy recommendations that have welfare reducing effects on the economy as a whole, and especially upon the lowest income cohort of an affected population.

Morris Altman and Lonnie Golden argue that conclusions regarding the role of law, in particular, the welfare consequences of proposed reforms in the United States and European Union (EU) regulation of working hours, depend largely on whether the scope of analysis is broadened to include non-neoclassical perspectives. They argue that a behavioral economic approach is needed to improve our understanding of why individuals supply the number of hours of work that they do, why they may be rising in certain countries and how this may interact with labor law and regulation. To this end they present a behavioral economic model that considers individuals' supply decisions as a function of both target market income and target nonmarket time, which in turn are structured by individuals' hierarchy of needs. The model—whose origins lie in social economics and institutionalism—incorporates the notion that individuals' targets and needs derive in part from their social reference groups. They assert that welfare losses stem from both (1) overemployment, individuals working beyond their preferred hours, and (2) overwork, working hours sufficiently long, even voluntarily, to yield social spillover costs, and that these real economic impacts are not easily captured by conventional economic theory, nor addressed satisfactorily through the pay premium policy. They conclude that what may be needed is new legislation and regulations that provide institutional counterpressures to reduce the tendency toward over-supplied labor.

Toni Lester explores the topic of sexual harassment in the workplace, arguing that the Chicago approach to law and economics (especially the works of Judge Richard Posner and law scholars such as Richard Epstein, Gary Becker, and Marie Reilly) does not provide an adequate analytical lens through which the problem of sexual harassment can be viewed. While stipulating that it may be helpful in explaining some of the reasons why sexual harassment takes place, it neglects to address other important ones. That is, from the vantage point of feminist jurisprudence, Lester argues that the Chicago approach incorrectly frames the important issues and creates a dangerous moral vacuum in which women would be forever relegated to the low status, low paying, sexually hostile working conditions of the past, and, in many instances, the present. In its place, Lester sets forth a Rawlsian/feminist analysis to counter the Chicago interpretation and explores how such an approach can offer viable alternative solutions to the free-market approach. Lester argues that while many in the Chicago law and economics movement might find that sexual harassment is efficient from a free-market perspective (noting that this assertion has not been fully substantiated), it is not equitable from a Rawlsian/feminist perspective. She argues that, at a minimum, most feminists and Rawlsians would preserve the current legal scheme as an appropriate response to the problem—and indeed would even strengthen it.

The final section of this volume looks at three additional legal-economic issues. The first chapter, by Mark White, provides us with a new model of individual decisionmaking regarding criminal behavior. Consistent with the belief of the legal philosopher Jules Coleman, White contends that the application of neoclassical economics to crime is flawed and that the topic of crime in all of its forms is an inextricably moral enterprise. Thus, any attempt to study it within a determinedly amoral paradigm will be doomed to failure. As such, White's alternative approach to the more familiar neoclassical law and economics consideration of crime is one that incorporates a discussion of values and the ethics of Immanuel Kant, an initiative that has been embraced by social economists. He argues that this model, with the explicit incorporation of ethics, can better explain a wide variety of criminal behavior, particularly the so-called "irrational" law-abiding activity, and discusses the ramifications of the approach to the optimal enforcement of law.

The second chapter in this section, by Edward Stringham and Mark White, begins by outlining several of the positive criticisms of the neoclassical law and economics' approach to tort law from the viewpoint of Austrian economics. In particular, they explore the circularity problem of economic calculation with undefined property rights, contending that in a world with an unclear or uncertain allocation of rights, it is impossible for judges to gauge the economic effects of their decisions. Hence, the very process of using efficiency to determine tort law raises several issues that render it nonfunctional. However, they also point out that Austrian economics, as a positive endeavor, does not offer or recommend particular normative ends, but it can help identify the deficiencies in certain normative proposals. Because economists in the Austrian tradition must rely on a normative theory of property rights from outside economics, they take that next step and try to fill this void by proffering an alternative doctrine for tort, one based on Kantian ethics. They argue that notions of hypothetical compensation, reciprocal causation, and the instrumental nature of rights, all essential to the neoclassical law and economics approach to tort law, are all inconsistent with a Kantian respect for the dignity of persons. They argue that when tort cases are decided by Kantian-like notions of justice rather than efficiency, judges would not be burdened with the thorny task of calculating all the economic consequences of their decisions.

Finally, as Fernando Toboso has observed, while many changes in policy governance have taken place since 1978 in Spain (including those resulting from Spain's membership in the EU), the institutional organization of government in Spain has experienced a radical transformation over the last twenty-five years. From a highly centralized and authoritarian political regime in which there were only two levels of government (central and local),

Spain has moved to a more democratic and three-level political system (central, regional, local). His chapter focuses on the process of institutional design by which the intermediate or regional level of government has been set in place. In this, he explores the impact of decentralizing public expenditures and tax responsibilities along with some of the regulatory functions of these regional governments. The analysis is conducted from what he terms a middle-way institutional perspective that, based on the principles of institutional individualism, allows him to pay attention to both the efficiency and the distributive impacts of the new institutional setting of this new multilevel governance structure. Toboso uses the Länder in Germany as a benchmark to make qualitative and quantitative comparisons. In his analysis, he uncovers how the new legal rules, together with some other informal institutions, have influenced the behavior of government agents and, in turn, have affected the surprising path of economic and social growth of Spanish regions since 1980.

Each chapter in this book, then, uses one or more alternative economic approaches to improve our understanding of a legal issue and to develop implications for improving law and regulatory policy. Taken together, these chapters provide ample evidence that there are many economic approaches that can be applied to legal and regulatory issues. It is hoped that these chapters not only provide new insights into the issues they address, but also will stimulate further analysis and discussion of alternative economic approaches and their application to the law.

Notes

1. Robert D. Cooter and Thomas Ulen, *Law and Economics,* ix.
2. Lawrence Lessig, "The Prolific Iconoclast: Richard Posner," 109.
3. Economists disagree among themselves about many, if not most, important issues. It should not be a surprise if they also disagree about what economics can say about the law and regulation. In fact, the very notion that there should exist *one* generally accepted economic approach in the "law and economics movement" runs counter to the well-known reputation for disagreement among economists, particularly over policy issues. For a scholarly analysis of the degree of disagreement see Victor R. Fuchs, Alan B. Krueger, and James M. Poterba, "Economists' Views about Parameters, Values, and Policies: Survey Results in Labor and Public Economics." As they put it, "The image of economists in disarray about economic policy is firmly embedded in the popular mind." Further, they find "a great deal of disagreement among economists about policy proposals in their areas of specialization," suggesting that "policy positions are usually more closely related to differences in values than to differences in estimates of what we judge to be relevant economic parameters." Generalizing, they observe that "economists, like experts in many fields, reveal considerable overconfidence in their estimates of the economic parameters" (1387–89).
4. Susan Rose-Ackerman, "Law and Economics," 4.
5. Economists may group models in several different ways, depending, in part, on

the applications being considered. For the applications to legal intervention being considered here, microeconomic models of individual behavior and models of how markets work are generally emphasized, rather than macroeconomic theory. See, for example, Susan Feiner, "The Conservative/Free Market, the Liberal/Imperfectionist, and the Radical/Exploitation Schools," 22–27. She describes three major paradigms: the conservative/free market; the liberal/imperfectionist; and the radical/exploitation schools. See also David L. Prychitko, ed., *Why Economists Disagree: An Introduction to the Alternative Schools of Thought,* for comparisons among various schools of thought within macroeconomics and microeconomics. See Nicholas Mercuro and Steven G. Medema, *Economics and the Law: From Posner to Post-Modernism* for a thorough review and analysis of a range of current approaches to legal thought as it intersects with economic theory. For an historical time line of economic approaches as applied to labor issues, see Bruce E. Kaufman, 145–88. For an analysis of how a socioeconomic approach can be applied to legal issues, see Lynne L. Dallas, *Law and Public Policy*.

References

Cooter, R., and T. Ulen. *Law and Economics*, 3rd ed. Reading, MA: Addison-Wesley, 2000.

Dallas, L.D. *Law and Public Policy: A Socio-Economic Approach,* Durham, NC: Carolina Academic Press, 2004.

Feiner, S. "The Conservative/Free Market, the Liberal/Imperfectionist, and the Radical/Exploitation Schools." In *Race and Gender in the American Economy: Views from Across the Spectrum,* ed. S. Feiner, 22–27. Englewood Cliffs, NJ: Prentice-Hall, 1994.

Fuchs, V.R., A.B. Krueger, and J.M. Poterba. "Economists' Views about Parameters, Values, and Policies: Survey Results in Labor and Public Economics." *Journal of Economic Literature* 36 (September 1998): 1387–425.

Kaufman, B.E., "The Evolution of Thought on the Competitive Nature of Labor Markets." In *Labor Economics and Industrial Relations: Markets and Institutions,* ed. C. Kerr and P.D. Staudohar, 145–88. Cambridge, MA: Harvard University Press, 1994.

Lessig, L. "The Prolific Iconoclast: Richard Posner." *The American Lawyer* (December 1999), 109.

Mercuro, N., and S.G. Medema. *Economics and the Law: From Posner to Post-Modernism.* Princeton, NJ: Princeton University Press, 1997.

Prychitko, D.L., ed. *Why Economists Disagree: An Introduction to the Alternative Schools of Thought.* Albany, NY: New York Press, 1998.

Rose-Ackerman, S. "Law and Economics." In *Committee on the Status of Women (CSWEP) Newsletter)* Winter 2000: 4. Available at www.cswep.org/ackerman.html.

2

The Foundations of Socioeconomics and Its Relation to the Law

Amitai Etzioni

Introduction

This chapter depicts the broad foundations of socioeconomics. It is presented in the belief that this new paradigm would prove more useful than the existing models that describe and analyze the law. The chapter has three parts. The first part outlines the reasons I believe the time has come to develop a shared disciplinary core for socioeconomics. It then turns to the principles that ought to guide us in developing such a core, and, finally, it suggests several specific elements needed for such a discipline. Together, these principles and elements offer a more promising way to examine the formation, structure, processes, and economic impact of law and legal institutions.

A Disciplinary Core

Socioeconomics has come a long way over the last decade. Energetic and dedicated leadership and fine executive directors have put the International Society for the Advancement of Socio-Economics on a sound footing. Attendance at annual meetings is solid. Colleagues attend because they find the meetings stimulating. (They hardly provide a job market, a reason why many feel that they ought to attend the meetings of other disciplinary associations.) The executive council is much stronger than it used to be. Several new books have been published that cover socioeconomic topics.

With all of this in mind, three steps are suggested: (1) Socioeconomics ought to become institutionalized, in the sense that we need to find or form some graduate departments or schools to train students in socioeconomics and to accord degrees in this field. There is a steady demand for socioeconomists, especially by CEOs and heads of nongovernmental organizations (NGOs), but not enough supply. (2) We need a journal in which to publish solid socioeconomic works, rather than one that is a grab bag of papers that happen to come in over the transom, many of which should not have been published in the first place, and most of which do not have a socioeconomic bone in them. (3) Both of the first two developments are conditioned on the third one, that socioeconomics develop a limited core of shared principles. Neoclassical economics, for instance, is built around the perfect competition model and all that it entails. Law and economics, seen as a composite discipline that now command the loyalty of a third of the legal scholars in the United States, is, in turn, based on the neoclassical model. Biology long took one form or another of Darwinism as its core. As a result, members of that discipline can take certain core assumptions for granted. These serve to define what is part of the discipline and what belongs elsewhere; to allow members of the discipline to build on elementary terms and the basic approach, rather than continually to reexamine them; and—most important—to provide a base for the accumulation of knowledge generated by different scholars. This is what socioeconomics appears to be ready for, and indeed requires, if it is to grow significantly as a discipline beyond its current level.

A New Paradigm

To develop the said shared socioeconomic core, my argument is that we must make a paradigm shift—a basic change in perspective. There are now two fundamentally different paradigms, or models, of social science, which in turn have deep connections to distinct bodies of social philosophies, ethics, social values, and even political ideologies.

One paradigm is centered around the individual, who is assumed to be the agent, the choice maker, the foundation of liberty. (Among those who speak in this mode are classical liberals, contemporary classical liberals, laissez-faire conservatives, and libertarians.)

When economics is formulated in the terms of this paradigm, as neoclassical economics is, we find that consumer sovereignty is a core concept, the examination of which here will stand for many others. This is the notion that the direction of the economy in toto arises out of an aggregation of individual choices and transactions. This cardinal assumption guides much of the work done in the neoclassical approach. Thus, if a neoclassical economist is studying how to make people save more, she will "naturally" think about increasing the incentives for people to save (e.g., increase the amount one may contribute to an IRA) or the disincentives for not saving (e.g., introduce a tax on consumption). She is much less likely to start an analysis by considering increasing the budgetary surplus and/or paying off more of the national debt, both much more effective ways to boost saving than trying to affect the choices of millions of individuals. Of course, there are macroeconomists who study national budgets, but they cannot find in their paradigm the principles and concepts that nourish analysis that are not based on aggregating individual choices.

One should also note that the neoclassical approach has clear normative and political roots and consequences. Granted, it would be wrong to imply that all or even most neoclassical economists—those who build on the individualist paradigm—are laissez-faire conservatives or libertarians, Thatcherites or Reaganites. It would be accurate, though, to observe that certain basic assumptions are shared by neoclassical economics and by these ideologies. They nourish each other.

Socioeconomics, as I see it, best draws on a different paradigm, one that builds on different core assumptions and implicit normative content. So far it has been much less well articulated than the individual-centered model, but, nevertheless, it has been and remains very influential. One may refer to it as a societal-historical, institutional, or cultural approach.[1] Because it focuses on factors that affect the preferences and choices of millions of individuals—such as the epoch in which people live and the culture that surrounds them—I will refer to it for short as a macro approach. And just as the individualistic paradigm does not reject macro factors (although it has a hard time accommodating them), so too socioeconomics has room for the study of aggregations of individual choices, although this is not at its core. Note that an overwhelming majority of the topics listed in the *Madison Declaration on the Need for Socio-Economic Research and Theory*, concern macro elements.[2] (Robin Stryker correctly points out that further sophistication requires a multilayered approach that goes beyond that macro/micro dichotomy, a point not further discussed here.)[3]

If one accepts, for the sake of discussion, that socioeconomics requires a different paradigm than neoclassical economics, two insights follow. First, it is counterproductive to try to convince neoclassicists that they are making wrong assumptions, or to chastise them for not incorporating societal, cultural, and historical factors into their paradigm. It is futile because once a discipline has acquired a definite core, its members' "job" is to defend it, to try to work within it, and to try to incorporate into it pesky challenges, rather than abandon the paradigm. (See, for instance, the way social norms have recently been treated by neoclassical scholars.)[4]

Moreover, if one examines how paradigms have historically shifted, one finds that new paradigms have emerged not because followers of the old, obsolescent paradigms were won over to new ways of approaching the world. Rather, a group peels away from an old tradition or a new group is formed, giving rise to legitimate conflict between the old and new paradigms. Then the "market" decides which paradigm has more evidence and is more compelling, although often both the old and the new coexist for long periods of time. The main contest is over attracting new followers rather than converting the old-timers.

Ergo, if there is to be a socioeconomic disciplinary core, it will rise out of the work of socioeconomists, not neoclassical ones, and most neoclassicists—at least the deeply entrenched—will not be won over. New generations and those who have not previously committed themselves to any particular paradigm (including many students of law and economics) are going to be the bearers of the new one.

It follows, then, that socioeconomics, by definition, is an interstitial discipline; it is a bridging discipline. In that sense, it is similar to biochemistry and social psychology, rather than to biology or chemistry, sociology or psychology. Its variables are derived from two or more social science disciplines rather than from any one. (The term "socio" in socioeconomics does not stand for sociology alone; it includes major segments of psychology and anthropology, history, and political science—the whole complex of disciplines that examine the relationships between society and the economy.)

Moreover, the paradigm at the foundation of socioeconomics points to the "location" of causality (or independent variables). Socioeconomics requires, on the face of it, that one deals with one or more social variables and one or more economic variables. If one deals only with economic variables—for instance, if one studies whether low levels of unemployment and high rates of inflation are correlated—one is not in socioeconomics. It is a fully legitimate subject for study, but an intra-economic one. And if one explores the question of the effects of fundamentalism on science, this study, too, is not part of socioeconomics, because all the variables there are social and none are economic. Socioeconomics arises when analysis starts with the independent variables in the social realm, and then moves to economically dependent variables. For instance, do people who are more conservative in their political ideology save more than those who are not? Do people who are alienated make for less productive workers? Does lobbying affect prices and to what extent? What social and political conditions impel higher economic growth? And so on.

Next, and on the same point, it is a grave error to treat the economy as a self-sustaining system, to view the market as separate from society (and its polity). The starting point of socioeconomic analysis is that the economy is a subsystem of the societal system. Much of what is occurring within the economy is best explained by looking at attributes and processes that occur outside of it. One very well-known and compelling example is Max Weber's study of the social (and religious) conditions under which capitalism arises and thrives.[5]

To make the difference between neoclassical economics and socio-economics less abstract, here is a specific example. George Stigler wanted to provide an example of the governing assumption of neoclassical economics, that the market (an aggregation of the choices of all participants) ultimately sets the context in which individual choices must be made.[6] Thus, if a manager reads the market correctly in terms of what will sell at what price, then that manager's corporation will stay in business; if the manager misreads the market's signals and persists in not responding to its dictates, the firm will soon be bankrupt.

To illustrate this point, Stigler focused on wheat farmers. Individual farmers cannot decide what to charge for a bushel of wheat; they can charge only what the market will bear. The market decides. The core assumption is that the market works like an anonymous box into which suppliers throw in their bids and buyers throw in theirs, and out of this invisible hat the "correct" price drops out.

A socioeconomist, not bound by the aggregate individualist paradigm, will note that in the United States, farmers are not merely "in the market," but also in the polity; they are members of one of two political lobbies. These lobbies influence Congress to enact various legislations that greatly affect the price of wheat. While for the last forty years this has been changing, the price of wheat is not determined by an autonomous machine: It cannot fall below a certain level because the government protected the price. The details are a bit more complicated. To protect their egos, farmers did not want to take money directly from the government; handouts were for despised welfare recipients. Farmers, therefore, gave their wheat as collateral to the government, which in turn gave them loans. If the market price moved up, the government took the wheat out and sold it; if it fell, it left the wheat in the silos and kept it until it rotted. When all was said and done, the government had ensured that the price the farmers got did not fall below a certain level, as determined by politics and not the market.

The price reflected the fact that the farmers lived in both the polity and the economy, and they wore their lobbying citizens' hats to influence the economy. Farming is hardly the only sector in which this occurs. If you look at textiles, you will find that we have something called a multifiber agreement, with which the government controls how much textile is imported from what country and at what prices. For many years we had a trigger price for steel; reflecting pressure from Congress, we had a so-called voluntary quota limiting the importation of cars from Japan to 2.3 million per year. The same can be found in many other areas. About the only sectors in the United States that truly approximate the neoclassical model are Chinese restaurants and laundromats, and even they are regulated by a city when it tells them they cannot open one too close to another.

A Core Theorem: Self-Interest and Values

To reiterate, socioeconomics, by definition, is an interstitial science. To apply this essential observation—just illustrated on a macro, societal level—to the micro, individual level, the following core theorem might be considered as a cardinal building block of socioeconomics: Individuals' decisions and behaviors, far from following one unified principle of seeking to maximize pleasure and minimize pain or marching to one overarching utility, reflect empirically the conflict between two—at least two—irreducible utilities. The first is our desire for pleasure; the other, our moral obligations.

An extremely simple example to start with: When one says, "I would like to go to a movie, but I ought to visit my friend in the hospital," the statement contains both what is pleasurable and what is morally right. Indeed, most of our values are dedicated to pulling us against the pleasure principle. Whether religious or secular, they call on people to fast, to give to the church or a charity, to refrain from in sex, and so on. In other words, there are certain things that one is supposed to do that are virtuous for a variety of reasons, but the variable they share is that they pull us in directions that are counter to where the pleasure principle pushes us.

Our nature is to be conflicted between these two "utilities." Much of what we do reflects this inevitable tension between things we would like to do and things we ought to do. Many empirical observations support this generalization. Let us start with the question of why people vote. Economists find it surprising that people vote; such behavior does not fit the standard economic model. Individuals are expected to do things for a return, for profit, or for some other form of benefit. When someone votes, he cannot reasonably expect that his vote will make a difference. So the question economists ask is, "why do people expend the time standing in line and lose leisure or work time, when there will be no specific outcome for them"?

For a socioeconomist, this behavior is not puzzling. The number one variable that explains the difference between people who vote and those who do not is the sense of civic duty. Those people who do vote feel that they have an obligation to vote. To them, it is the right thing to do. Those who have this sense are much more likely to vote than those who do not have such a sense.[7] This is not to suggest that the length of lines, the weather, and so forth do not make a difference; they do affect behavior and the "costs" of voting. But the overriding factor explaining the variance is the relative strength of a person's sense of civic duty.

Another illustration: If people were to act only to maximize their pleasure, those who smoke would vote against taxes on cigarettes, and those who do not would favor these taxes. The fact, though, is that there are a large number of smokers who vote *for* taxes on cigarettes, because they are aware that they are damaging the public and ought to do something to compensate for that. And there are a fair number of nonsmokers who vote *against* these taxes because they are libertarians or they feel the government should not interfere. A study found that individuals who had been told that conserving energy during peak demand periods would be good for the community were likely to lower their electricity use during such periods if they felt that households as a group could make a difference.[8] People's moral concepts and their social philosophies are not the only factors used to make decisions, but they are important ones for understanding their social-political-economic behavior.

One last example: Neoclassical economists try to explain why people—most people—with spouses who have Alzheimer's disease stay with them. These economists treat marriage as an economic contract, in which income and services are exchanged. But with Alzheimer's patients, there is no payback because there is no reasonable hope that the afflicted person will recover and take care of the other person. One may say that the caregiving spouse does so because of the kudos he or she will receive from members of his or her extended family and neighbors and friends. However, tending to an Alzheimer's patient day-in and day-out is so taxing that all the kudos in the world could not compensate for it. Finally, economists use the notion of psychic income. But again, that explanation fails because the afflicted person does not respond with a warm appreciation for the service; indeed, they become ever more abusive as time goes on. So why do most spouses stay with their suffering husband or wife? In interviews with these people, one repeatedly hears the statement: "This is the right thing to do." The same sentiment is found in Roberta Simmons's studies of kidney donations.[9] People have a strong moral commitment, a powerful factor that outweighs the pain that they have to endure.

My thesis is not that values drive behavior, but that there is a continual conflict between self-interest and the pleasure principle on one hand, and powerful moral commitments on the other. It follows that socio-economists would benefit if they took as their starting hypothesis that people are conflicted, and if they then tried to understand people's inconsistencies and tendencies to zigzag as a result of their being subject to these two competing super-utilities.

The Socioeconomic Mind

No theory of human behavior can be developed without first accepting a core assumption about the intellectual capabilities of each person. I suggest that our deliberations use as their starting point the key observation that people are poor processors of information—just the opposite of what used to be the neoclassical economists' assumption that information flows instantaneously and is absorbed instantaneously, all without any costs. The economists wisely retreated from these suppositions, and they now recognize that information is not immediately absorbed and that the process has costs. In this and several other contexts they refer to "imperfect" systems. This is a tricky concept that is inadvertently misleading. The term implies that there is a speck of dust on the perfect scale. Actually, people's limitations in information processing are much greater. Indeed, strong evidence shows that people start with little knowledge and that they are slow and poor learners.

A simple case in point: Every day millions of people all over the world call their brokers and either ask their advice on which stock to purchase or they order them to buy one, on the presumption that these individual investors could beat the market averages. (Otherwise they would buy index funds and save costs.) Nevertheless, there is strong, consistent, robust data to show that this is an irrational act; one cannot consistently out-perform the market. Moreover, brokers have a conflict of interest with the callers; brokers benefit from high turnovers in their accounts, while investors benefit from low turnovers and infrequent transaction costs. Furthermore, despite the fact that studies supporting the use of index funds (rather than brokers) have been repeatedly publicized in the popular press, in classrooms, and on television, millions of people ignore this advice and persist in untutored behavior.

Many scholars interested in the interrelationships between economics and the law recognize that current attempts by economists to inform the law (or public policy generally) are wanting. They will remain so until we adopt an approach along the lines offered by socioeconomics.

Notes

In this article I have drawn on my book *The Moral Dimension: Toward a New Economics*. I am indebted to Rogers Hollingsworth for comments on a previous draft.

1. For a fine recent discussion of institutionalism in this context, see Robin Stryker, "The Future of Socio-Economics and of the Society for the Advancement of Socio-economics," 51–58.

2. Society for the Advancement of Socio-Economics, *Madison Declaration on the Need for Socio-Economic Research and Theory.*

3. Robin Stryker, "The Future of Socio-Economics and of the Society for the Advancement of Socio-Economics," 51–58.

4. Amitai Etzioni, "Social Norms: The Rubicon of Social Science," 163–85.

5. Max Weber, *The Protestant Ethic and the Spirit of Capitalism,* and *Economy and Society: An Outline of Interpretive Sociology.*

6. George J. Stigler, "A Competition," 181–82.

7. Brian Barry, *Sociologists, Economists and Democracy.*

8. J.S. Black, "Attitudinal, Normative, and Economic Factors in Early Response to Energy-Use Field Experiment."

9. Roberta G. Simmons, Susan D. Klein, and Robert L. Simmons, *Gift of Life: The Social and Psychological Impact of Organ Transplantation.*

References

Barry, B. *Sociologists, Economists and Democracy.* Chicago: University of Chicago Press, 1978.

Black, J.S. "Attitudinal, Normative, and Economic Factors in Early Response to Energy-Use Field Experiment." Unpublished Ph.D. dissertation, University of Wisconsin, 1978.

Etzioni, A. *The Moral Dimension: Toward a New Economics.* New York: Free Press, 1988.

———. "Social Norms: The Rubicon of Social Science." In *The Monochrome Society: Essays about the Good Society*, ed. A. Etzioni, 163–85. Princeton, NJ: Princeton University Press, 2001.

Simmons, R.G., S.D. Klein, and R.L. Simmons. *Gift of Life: The Social and Psychological Impact of Organ Transplantation.* New York: John Wiley, 1977.

Society for the Advancement of Socio-Economics. *Madison Declaration on the Need for Socio-Economic Research and Theory*, 1999. Available at www.sase.org/conf1999/declaration.html (August 5, 2000).

Stigler, G.J. "A Competition." In *International Encyclopedia of Social Science*, vol. 3, ed. D.L. Sills, 181–82. New York: Macmillan, 1968.

Stryker, R. "The Future of Socio-Economics and of the Society for the Advancement of Socio-Economics." In *Advancing Socio-Economics: An Institutionalist Perspective*, ed. J.R. Hollingsworth, K.H. Müller, and E.J. Hollingsworth, 51–58. Lanham, MD: Rowman and Littlefield, 2002.

Weber, M. *The Protestant Ethic and the Spirit of Capitalism*, trans. Talcott Parsons. New York: Scribner, 1958; and idem, *Economy and Society: An Outline of Interpretive Sociology*, trans. E. Fischoff, et al., ed. G. Roth and C. Wittich. New York: Bedminster Press, 1968.

Part 2

Legal Issues Concerning Firms and Market Structure

3

The Inadequacy of Competition Policies

A New Institutional Approach

Claude Menard

Introduction

New institutional economics has developed rapidly over the last twenty-five years.[1] Although the main concepts were already in the pioneering papers by Ronald Coase, we have had to wait for the efforts of Williamson and North to make these concepts operational, thus allowing the new research program to take off.[2] Hundreds of papers and books later, we are far beyond the simple acknowledgement that institutions and organizations matter. A set of analytical tools is now available, with transaction costs at the core, and the nature and role of diverse modes of organizations and of specific institutions are now being investigated.

A central component of new institutional economics is the analysis of the role of the legal system at the micro level, through its impact on the modes of organizations, and at the macro level, through its consequences as facilitator or inhibitor in the dynamics of transactions. Again, this was anticipated by Coase, who played a major role in the diffusion of the new approach, particularly as editor of the *Journal of Law and Economics* for two decades. But once more it was in the late 1970s and the 1980s that new institutional economists really began the exploration of how laws and regulations affect the way transactions are organized and how legal systems largely determine the volume of transactions and their costs. The analysis of regulation and competition policies played a key role in these developments.[3] On the occasion of the celebration of the fifty years of the National Bureau of Economic Research, Coase bitterly noted that "industrial organization has become the study of the pricing and output policies of firms," obsessed with the control of monopoly but deprived of "a theory that would enable us to analyze the determinants of the organization of the industry."[4] A few years later Williamson published his influential *Markets and Hierarchies* with a subtitle too often ignored: *Analysis and Antitrust Implications.*[5] This contribution, combined with North's insistence on the role of the institutional environment in shaping conditions for growth and innovation, generated a growing flow of studies about the impact of regulations and the legal systems on how transactions are organized and what determines the resulting performance.

It is the purpose of this chapter to review some of these issues, with special attention to how competition policies that ignore transaction costs can generate unexpected biases.[6] This chapter is organized as follows: The next section summarizes and extends the theoretical framework provided by new institutional economics. I then proceed to the review of some implications that have been exhibited when it comes to the application of standard competition policies to vertical integration or deintegration. The last section extends the analysis to the case of "hybrid arrangements," a mode of organization that has increasingly attracted attention over the last decade. The conclusion follows.

The upshot of the chapter is that in a world of uncertainties, in which most contractual arrangements are incomplete and plagued with hazards, all feasible forms of organizations are flawed. Economic efficiency therefore can be determined only comparatively, with trade-offs among alternative modes of organizations understood as a quest for forms that fit relatively better with the transactions at stake, thereby economizing on production and transaction costs. Competition policies built on the simplified alternative of pure forms of "markets," compared with fully integrated "firms," ignore the diversity of modes of organization, their respective transaction costs, and how they are embedded in their institutional environment. This tends to introduce biases that can severely hamper the functioning of market economies.

Theoretical Background

The point of entry in new institutional economics is an empirical observation: In a developed market economy and, more generally, in all economic systems, there is a vast array of modalities for organizing transactions. At least three fundamental questions follow: What is the theoretical explanation of that diversity? What factors determine the choice by economic agents of one form rather than another? Are there institutions more favorable than others to the efficient development of transactions?

Why Transactions?

As is now well known, the answer of new institutional economists to the first question lies in the concept of transaction. But why focus on transactions?

Many critiques have challenged this choice, arguing that it leads to the neglect of production costs.[7] I think this interpretation results from a deep misunderstanding of what is at stake. As emphasized repeatedly by Coase and others, the reason for looking primarily at transactions is quite simple: Beyond its technological constraints, production could not take advantage of the division of labor and of the specialization of investments (both capital and human investments) without the existence of devices for organizing the transfer of rights of usage among technologically separable activities.[8] This is precisely the definition of what a transaction is. These devices can be systemic, part of the institutional environment (e.g., laws governing property rights or contract law). Or they can operate at the micro level, characterizing the different arrangements available for monitoring transactions within the rules of the game defined by this institutional environment. They are all costly, so that a major issue is the comparative costs of these institutions and organizations.

The "Coasian World" Revisited

Here, we are back to the famous Coase theorem. There are many different interpretations of this so-called theorem. My take follows Coase's discussion of his own contribution.[9] In a world without transaction costs, institutions and organizations would not really matter from an economic perspective. Agents could choose different arrangements for trading their rights, and they would do so up to the point where they reach a mutually satisfying solution, and all this at no cost. In other terms, the choice of a specific legal system and of a specific mode of organization would be economically neutral. This is often called a "Coasian world," an interpretation that deeply irritates Coase.[10] Indeed, his "world" is one where transaction costs are positive.

This situation totally differs from the previous one in at least three aspects. First, "once transaction costs are taken into account, many of these measures will not be undertaken because making the contractual arrangements necessary to bring [transactions] into existence would cost more than the gain they make possible."[11] As a result, transactions that could be advantageous to partners may not happen. Second, there is no reason to believe that *all* contractual arrangements would involve the same costs. This is the fundamental argument developed already in Coase's "The Nature of the Firm"[12] (1937): Markets and firms differ with respect to their costs in organizing transactions. Third, "with positive transaction costs, the law plays a crucial role in determining how resources are used."[13] A consequence is that different laws, and different law regimes, generate differentiated transaction costs, thus creating comparative advantages and disadvantages.

When applied to the problem of the impact of regulations and competition policies, the "Coasian world" thus defined involves two important consequences. One is that neoinstitutionalists must pay special attention to the interaction between the rules of the game delineated by these policies and the ways the modes of organization operating within these rules are selected and behave. A second consequence is that it is essential to identify and measure the factors determining the respective transaction costs of different institutions and organizations, thus allowing comparison. This is where Williamson's contribution comes in.

Trade-offs: The Basic Model

The analysis developed by Williamson is well known, though not always well understood, and does not require a detailed presentation. However, a short reminder may help to better understand the extension I propose. The central idea of the model was introduced almost twenty years ago.[14] Three characteristics of transaction are considered to play a central role in determining transaction costs: the uncertainty surrounding a transaction, the frequency of that transaction, and, above all, the degree of specific investments required. The key relationship can then be expressed as follows:

$$TC = f(\underset{+}{U}, \underset{-}{F}, \underset{+}{AS})$$

where U, F, and AS stand for uncertainty, frequency, and asset specificity, respectively, while positive and negative signs represent the variation in transaction costs when the related variable increases.

The second step in the demonstration shows that agents confronted with these costs tend to search the best mode for organizing a specific transaction, that is, the mode that best fits the characteristics of that transaction and thus minimizes its costs. There are two underlying assumptions here: (1) Agents are assumed to search for a well-adapted solution because they are under competitive pressure; and (2) they are assumed to be rational and to be looking for solutions that minimize costs, although their calculative capabilities are limited so that choices made are rarely optimal. A third assumption is that agents are opportunistic, jockeying to take advantage of the many contractual hazards, so that safeguards are needed that can be provided either by the organizational mode itself (e.g., self-enforcing contracts) or by the institutional environment (e.g., contract laws).

Endowed with these properties and confronted with different possible ways of organizing transactions, agents make continuous trade-offs. In the 1980s

Figure 3.1 **Transactions Costs as a Function of Asset Specificity**

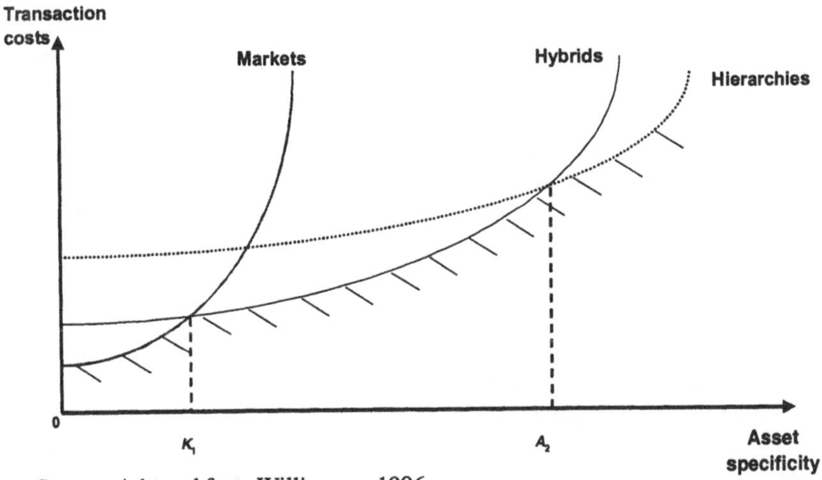

Source: Adapted from Williamson 1996.

and early 1990s, the attention mostly focused on the now paradigmatic trade-off between "make" or "buy": They had to decide whether or not to organize a transaction through markets, with the key role of the price system, or to proceed within the firm, through the allocation of resources by the hierarchical structure. But it rapidly became obvious that an entire set of arrangements did not fall within the two categories of "markets" and "hierarchies." Bilateral and multilateral agreements often tie up firms on subsets of their domain of decisions, although they remain autonomous, with distinct property rights. Examples are franchise systems, networks, and supply chain systems. These forms are often grouped under the label "hybrid forms": They share some characteristics of markets as well as of integrated organizations while keeping properties of their own. I will come back to these arrangements with more details in the last section. For the time being, let us assume that we have these three sets of organizational forms: markets, hierarchies, and hybrids. For the sake of simplicity, let us also assume that one of the three independent characteristics identified above is the major determinant of transaction costs. Because it is the variable that has been most tested in empirical studies, and abstracting from the controversies that this prioritization has provoked, let us consider the degree of specific investments required as this major determinant.[15] The rationale behind this choice is that the more specific investments are, the greater dependence there is among partners to the transaction and the more exposed they are to opportunistic behaviors. The trade-offs with which agents are confronted can be examined with the help of Figure 3.1.

When assets involved in a transaction are of a generic type ($k < k_1$), that is, there are substitutes available and the assets can easily be redeployed on alternative uses, agents will prefer to contract through markets, taking advantage of the powerful incentives that markets provide. On the opposite, when a very high level of specificity in the investments is involved ($k > k_2$), they can hardly be useful in alternative uses, thus creating dependence and increased contractual hazards, thus the hierarchical mode will be preferred; transactions will be integrated within the firm. Between these polar cases, when the investments required are moderately specific, agents will prefer interfirm agreements with more or less elaborated safeguards.[16]

The conclusion of this model is that, confronted with these alternative modes of organization, calculative agents tend to select the form that better fits the properties of the transaction at stake (in the variant above, the degree of specific investments the transaction requires). That is to say, they tend to remain on the lower boundary of the curves in Figure 3.1.

Extension of the Model: Impact of Competition Policies and Regulation

This heuristic model provides a very useful tool not only for analyzing the trade-off among modes of organization, but also for examining within a unified theoretical framework the consequences of regulations or competition policies (and, more generally, of institutional rules such as the regime of property rights, contract laws, etc.). Technically, this means looking at the effect of changes in the parameters defining the curves associated with the three modes of organization considered above.

Let us assume that in order to control quality in a supply chain system, a group of firms establishes a tight coordination through a list of specifications detailing the duties of the partners (e.g., characteristics of inputs to be used, characteristics of the production process, characteristics of the output, conditions of delivery of the product, etc.). Moreover, let us then assume that this network of firms implements an "authority," a "private government" in charge of monitoring this contractual arrangements and of disciplining parties to the agreement to guarantee the quality delivered to customers. This private government can penalize partners who behave opportunistically and also can represent the network in negotiating with, say, a large retailer. Such arrangements are routinely brought under examination by authorities in charge of competition policies.[17] Last, let us assume that existing regulations convey these authorities to make a decision unfavorable to the arrangement. Two polar decisions will illustrate the impact that rules of the game can exert on the way transactions can be organized.

Figure 3.2 **Effect of Prohibition on Governance**

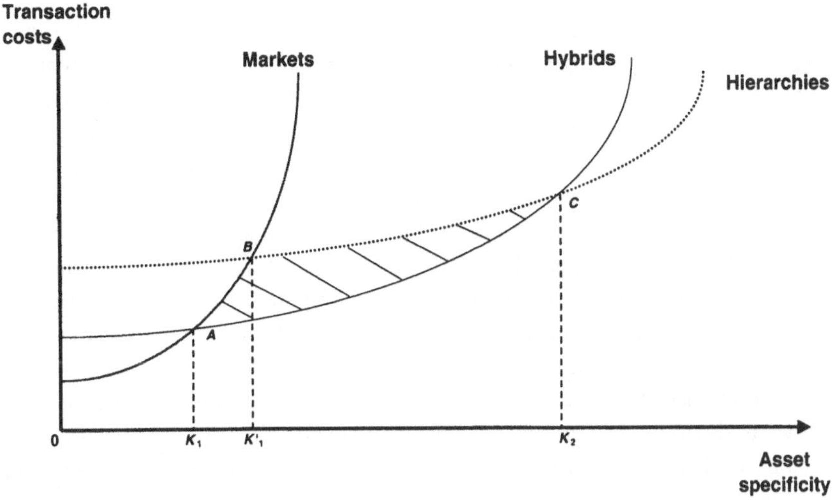

Case #1: The Arrangement Is Prohibited

One possibility for competition authorities is to declare that the arrangement described above is a coalition with anticompetitive goals that oppose antitrust laws, and that it must be prohibited. In this situation, our model predicts that the prohibition of the hybrid form leaves partners with only two choices: either they turn to spot market contracts or, more likely, because the hybrid arrangement was motivated by the necessity to coordinate in order to favor specific investments while reducing contractual hazards, they integrate within a unified firm.

Technically, the prohibition of the hybrid form means that the switching point shifts from k_1 to k'_1, with the elimination of the arrangement that corresponded to the lower envelope of the curves between k_1 and k_2 (See Figure 3.2). If the specificity of investments required by the initial arrangement is relatively low (smaller than k'_1), partners will switch to markets. But if the degree of mutual dependence is relatively high (superior to k'_1), there is a powerful incentive for partners to merge in a unified firm. They may be particularly inclined to do so if the industry is competitive, so that the risks that competition authorities block this solution are weak. Moreover, in the new situation transaction costs corresponding to the previous arrangement (the domain $[k'_1, k_2]$) are higher than they were with the hybrid form. The prohibition not only modifies the trade-off among modes of organization, but it also alters transaction costs, in our example making them higher, thus reducing the volume of transactions. The resulting social loss is measured by the area delineated by points *A*, *B*, and *C*.

Case #2: Restrictions Are Imposed on the Arrangement

A second possibility is that competition rules are such that the authorities can tolerate the hybrid arrangement, but conditional to constraints they impose on it. For example, they may prohibit some clauses of the contract that intended to limit the risk of opportunistic behavior among partners. Or they may require the dismantlement of the "private government" that was implemented to ensure that partners would respect the stipulations guaranteeing quality.

Under these constraints imposed by public policies, our model predicts that parties will have incentives to find other ways to attain the desired results and to obtain the required investments from each participant. Solutions can be more complex contracts with self-enforcing clauses that impose constraints previously managed by the "private government;" or, if costs of such arrangements become prohibitive while specific investments are still needed, they can decide to merge, thus escaping the accusation of coalition. In other terms, the implementation of rules of the game by competition authorities that did not take into account transaction costs moves the switching point from k_2 to k'_2 (See Figure 3.3). This change pushes partners toward adopting a new form of hybrid organizations with higher transaction costs if the degree of specificity of needed assets is moderate (to the left of k'_2), or to integrate their activities within a single firm if the specificity of investments is such that contracting with autonomous partners under the new rules would be too risky (the domain $[k'_2, k_2]$). The social cost of the arrangement is now delineated by A', B', C'.[18]

Some Lessons

These two polar cases illustrate how transaction costs matter for evaluating competition policies and, more generally, for estimating the impact of different rules of the game on organizational choices and, consequently, on welfare. Of course the comparative static exercise above can be extended. There are situations in which rules of the game, or their implementation, can lower transaction costs, favoring, for instance, the development of market relationships. More radical changes may affect the entire shape of the different curves representing transaction costs under the different arrangements, for example, the transition from a planned economy to a market economy. In a dynamic perspective, inadequate rules of the game that tend to increase transaction costs over time may push actors to look at new types of investment that are less specific and less prone to opportunistic behavior, such as standardization through technological innovation; or they may lobby for changing their institutional environment. What I want to emphasize with these examples is

Figure 3.3 **Effect of Restrictions on Governance**

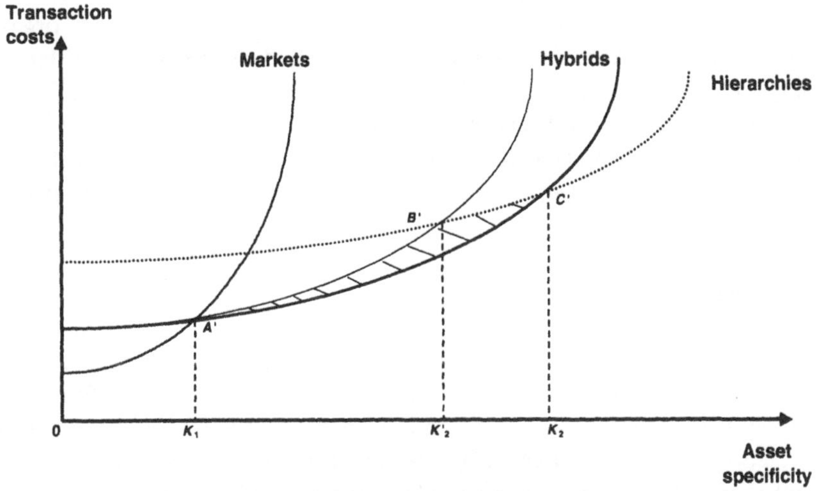

a basic lesson learned from new institutional economics: Ignoring transaction costs can lead competition policies and regulations to introduce major biases, translating into distorted trade-offs regarding the mode of organization chosen and/or solutions that increase global transaction costs, thus negatively affecting growth and social welfare. Let us now turn to the application of these lessons to more specific issues.

Vertical Integration and Disintegration

A paradigmatic application of the model developed by new institutional economists is vertical integration or, more precisely, the explanation of the trade-off between "to make" or "to buy." This is considered a "success story" because transaction cost analysis provides tools for making predictions about when a firm decides to produce inhouse rather than acquiring resources it needs through market contracts. These predictions have been tested in a huge number of empirical studies.[19] The underlying model was summarized at the beginning of the previous section. It predicts that incentives for integrating are rooted in the characteristics of the transactions at stake, with a special emphasis on the role of the specificity of assets. Simply stated, the theory predicts that with weak specific investments involved, which means that substitutes are easily available on the market, there are comparative advantages in buying rather than producing inhouse, thus taking advantage of the powerful incentives provided by market competition. But when the investments required for making a transaction possible are highly specific, the risk of opportunistic behavior and, more generally, of contractual hazards becomes so significant that integrating represents a more advantageous solution. Therefore, there is a continuous trade-off between acquiring on markets and organizing within the firm. The solution is determined by the incentive under competitive conditions to select the mode of organization that fits better the characteristics of the transaction, thus minimizing its costs. However, as emphasized by Joskow, the consequences of this approach for competition policies and regulation are far from being fully explored.[20] Let me review three important aspects here.

Full Integration

As early as 1972, Ronald Coase pointed out that the deterministic technological representation of the firm, subsumed under a production function, introduced a propensity to view firms' strategies that did not correspond to pure competition as motivated by the search for monopoly power. Coase went further: "One important result of this preoccupation with the monopoly problem is that if an economist finds something—a business practice of one sort or other—that he does not understand, he looks for a monopoly explanation."[21] Examining the Vertical Merger Guidelines from 1968 and 1982, Williamson later noted how the definition of the natural boundary of the firm based on technology fed a suspicious, "inhospitable" approach to mergers and acquisitions.[22] Although competition policies have evolved on this issue, less systematically viewing integration that is not justified by scale or scope economies as a move toward price discrimination and the creation of barriers to entry, antitrust policies remain spontaneously hostile to vertical integration. There may be more weight for efficiency considerations in recent mergers guidelines, in the United States as well as in the European Union, but suspicion continues to permeate their approach to integration, and particularly to horizontal integration.

Numerous examples have been provided by Williamson[23] and Joskow,[24] among others. There is no need to summarize and discuss these examples here. The main point they emphasize is how much competition policies regarding integration tend to focus on ex post consequences, looking essentially at how mergers and acquisitions not justified by technological determinants can generate market power. The burden of the proof that a merger is efficient continues to rely on the party wishing to expand, not on the entities in charge of implementing the policy. As noted by Joskow, it is extremely difficult for merging parties to show that integration will be cost saving, that savings will be passed to consumers, *and* that this efficiency could not be attained by other means.

Most of the time, however, market power remains the only relevant test, with a high concentration ratio combining with high barriers to entry. But this criterion is very difficult to implement. Market power is well defined in economic theory, with competitive models identifying it as a situation in which firms are not price takers because they deal with a downward sloping demand curve. But competition policies apply mostly to situations of imperfect competition, and therefore they develop a different approach because they need to define the relevant market in order to measure concentration and to determine barriers to entry. Examining the difficulties involved, Joskow pointed out two particularly important issues from a new institutional perspective.[25]

First, market power is usually approximated by market share, with criteria that are often vague ("workable competition," "significant market power") and hardly adequate for taking into account transaction costs involved in alternative arrangements. Second, a "relevant market" is often defined with a glance at the ex post consequences of integration. As a result, the focus tends to be on intrabrand competition (among wholesalers and/or retailers of a given brand), thus neglecting or ignoring the ex ante conditions that determined the decision to merge (particularly the possible existence of intense interbrand competition). A good example is provided by the decision made by Kodak to fully control the after-sale services of its copiers in the mid-1980s, and the subsequent long judiciary saga.[26]

What different perspective would a transaction cost approach develop? Basically, it looks at integration in a more "hospitable" way, first considering the possibility that, conditional to the existence of interbrand competition ex ante, the decision to merge may well be a cost-reducing response to transaction characteristics. In other terms, the first question that a transaction cost perspective raises when confronted with mergers or acquisitions is: Does this choice correspond to an effort of the buyer to align its organization to the attributes of the transaction at stake, in order to facilitate investments in specific assets, while mitigating contractual hazards and reducing the risk of opportunism? The motivation behind this approach, that puts more weight on the ex ante conditions of integration and that leaves open the possibility of a move based on an "economizing" strategy rather than a "monopolizing" strategy, lies in the acknowledgement of the transformation that happens in contractual arrangements between ex ante and ex post conditions. Indeed, a party planning highly specific investments may consider ex ante that the risks in contracting with partners prone to opportunistic behavior may be too high, or that the contract needed to implement adequate safeguards would be too complex and too costly to establish and implement. Under such expectations, integration may be the way to justify adequate investments, thus lowering costs and improving efficiency. In other terms, there are situations in which integration may be "collusion enhancing," as suspected by standard competition policies, but there are also cases in which it may well be "efficiency enhancing."[27]

Transaction cost economics therefore support a different approach to integration, with a view at the cost economizing strategy involved. In that respect, the evaluation of the costs and benefits of integration should examine two questions beyond looking at technological factors: (1) What is the specificity of the assets involved in the move, that is, can integration be motivated by the high risks that would pose contractual hazards if a market relationship was maintained? (2) What are the ex ante conditions in the industry? If competition prevails in the sector, can integration be motivated by the need to mitigate ex post holdup potential,[28] so that the relevant market that should be taken into account should be interbrand rather than intrabrand? There is yet another dimension to consider in a new institutional perspective. Antitrust legal rules should take into account benefits and costs for the specific firm that is the target of investigation, as suggested by the analysis above. But costs and benefits for "all firms and markets whose behavior and performance will be affected in the future by legal rules defined by decisions in specific cases" must also be evaluated.[29] Among these costs are those associated with the very existence of the institutions in charge of defining and implementing these rules. Economists still have a lot of work to do in this area.

Vertical Restrictions

Another nonstandard relationship that has attracted much attention from transaction cost economists is the imposition of vertical restrictions by a firm either on its upstream suppliers or, more often, on its downstream partners. Joskow recently characterized the competition policies toward nonprice vertical restraints as a particularly "depressing area of antitrust law."[30]

The problem is well captured by the issue of tying arrangements. As with vertical integration, competition authorities and courts tend to focus on ex post consequences, thus examining these agreements with a very narrow perception of the relevant market, reduced to intrabrand competition. This means substantial neglect of the ex ante incentives of firms imposing restrictions in the context of interbrand competition, that is, adopting restrictions to mitigate contractual hazards and to limit the risks of opportunistic behaviors from partners on which they depend.

A standard example, repeatedly developed by Williamson (but also often quoted by other transaction cost economists), is the case of *United States v. Arnold, Schwinn & Company* (388 US 365, 1967). At a time when its market share was only 22 percent, the Schwinn Company, which specialized in the production of quality bicycles, imposed restrictions on its exclusive distributors, namely, that their authorized dealers, who were required to provide quality services to their customers, were prohibited from reselling Schwinn bicycles to unauthorized dealers, particularly to discount stores. The motivation behind this decision was to occupy a niche based on the quality of the product and of its after-sale services, with exclusivity intending to signal clearly to buyers what they could expect from the authorized dealers.

Thus the restriction was designed as an insurance system for consumers, relying on the reputation of Schwinn bicycles, a reputation built on the exclusion of sellers who could behave as free rider (offering the same product but with no guarantee in regard to the quality of services). Williamson summarizes the issue as follows:

> Viewed through the lens of contract, vertical market restrictions often have the purpose and effect of infusing order into a transaction where the interests of the system and the interests of the parts are otherwise in conflict. For example, the Schwinn bicycle company imposed nonresale restrictions upon franchises. The concern was that the integrity of the brand, which was a system asset, would be compromised by franchises who perceived local opportunities to realize individual gain by selling to discounters, who would then sell a "bike in a box," without service or support.[31]

From a transaction cost perspective, the prohibition of tied arrangements imposed by one party, here the manufacturer on its authorized dealers, needs to be examined from an ex ante as well as an ex post perspective. At least two questions must be considered in order to make sound legal decisions: (1) Does the vertical restriction create or enhance market power as it exists ex ante? (2) Does the vertical restriction facilitate efficient transactions? As argued by Joskow, decisions against nonprice vertical restraints such as the one in the Schwinn case ignore this transaction costs perspective. They focus on intrabrand competition ex post while they neglect the interbrand competition that existed ex ante and often continue to exist ex post. For example, ten years after Schwinn implemented its restrictions, its market share had dropped to 13 percent. In neglecting the ex ante dimension, the analysis of vertical restrictions developed by competition authorities led to "single-brand market definitions, in which the supplier of the brand had a very high market share, and a resulting inference that the supplier of the brand had 'market power' of concern to the antitrust laws in its relationship with the firms that it had contracted with downstream ex ante."[32]

The lesson, again, is that ignorance of transaction costs issues may lead to biased decisions that interfere with potentially efficient modes of organization and to actually reduce competition rather than enhance it.

Restructuring: Deintegration and Divestiture

One last issue that deserves to be mentioned regarding the new institutional perspective on vertical integration and restrictions concerns the reverse of integration, that is, the imposition by competition authorities of deintegration and divestiture. Let me illustrate briefly with two aspects that have generated an extensive literature recently.

Public Utilities

The important deregulation movement of the last twenty-five years and the change in the status of previously publicly owned monopolies it initiated raises issues similar to those discussed above. Indeed, it rapidly became obvious in the 1980s that reforming public utilities by the simple transfer of property rights to private interests, through privatization, would not be a satisfying solution. It could often mean transferring monopoly power from a public entity to a private one. In order to introduce competitive pressure, it is the restructuring of previously integrated public utilities that was viewed as a potential source of renewed efficiency. Hence, hundreds of public utilities worldwide have been "reorganized" with very little concern for transaction cost issues. Deregulation was accompanied with deintegration. In many cases, the technological factor clearly dominated the decisions regarding the unbundling of previously integrated public utilities. In the electricity sector, for instance, an apparently simple way to restructure was to split production, transmission, and distribution. But in order to introduce real competition, usually more is needed that does not depend solely on technical factors: competitors should be introduced at each level. A significant and quite radical illustration is provided by the reform of the British rail industry, in which not only functions were deintegrated at quite a detailed level, but also several competitors were introduced in many of these functions (e.g., for passengers' transportation).[33]

From a transaction cost perspective, the introduction of competition in previously integrated public utilities requires taking into consideration the following question: How can deintegration be introduced and competition developed while preserving operating and investments efficiencies previously associated with integration, and how can this be done in a way that mitigates the costs of the transition? To answer this question, it is necessary to determine how formerly integrated public utilities will respond to changes and what can be expected, particularly with regard to investments, under the new regulatory conditions and competition environment. Part of the problem comes from characteristics of these sectors that are familiar to transaction cost economists: public utilities often involve highly specific investments; their activities require tight coordination, in some cases with almost instant capacity of reaction as in the electricity sector; and system failures may have very high economic as well as social costs.

As a consequence, a badly designed unbundling, that is, a deintegration that neglects the transactional aspects, may well create very substantial contractual hazards. Sound decisions must take into account the trade-off between the potential benefits of markets replacing regulated monopolies, and the potential costs of hazards arising from the splitting of a formerly integrated organization. The underlying rationale is that there may be reasons going deep beyond intended monopoly power and political consideration that explain why there was a high level of integration in many public utilities. From a transaction cost perspective, it is necessary to look at the transactions at stake, to consider their attributes with long-run efficiency considerations, and to explore alternative organizational arrangements before making a decision regarding how to change the existing arrangement. Unfortunately, not that many reforms have been designed and implemented with such a perspective in mind. Dramatic consequences may result, as with the spectacular accidents suffered by the British rail system or with the California energy crisis.[34]

Institutional Endowment

Another aspect that deserves to be mentioned, although I do not have space to develop it here, is the role of the institutional environment more broadly defined than the sole regulatory and legal systems. In many ways, the necessity—while studying vertical integration or deintegration—to take into account the interaction between the general rules of the game provided by institutions and the restructuring of an industry or a firm previously regulated and/or publicly owned is complementary to the necessity of examining not only the direct impact of legal rules and decisions about integration, but also their indirect effect on how other firms and other sectors will react. Indeed, unbundling or interfering through public authorities or courts' decisions on the organization of a firm or a sector requires considering the institutional endowments that can be mobilized to define and implement these policies.

By institutional endowments, we mean the administrative, political, and judicial resources on which public authorities depend. For instance, it may be desirable when deregulating and unbundling several public utilities involved in distinct activities (e.g., telecommunications, gas, electricity, water) to have different regulators in charge of the different sectors; but the administrative capabilities of the country may make such institutional design unfeasible. Another example is the lack of adequate laws allowing the development of an efficient financial market so that introducing competitors strong enough to challenge the historical monopoly may be idealistic.

Several studies by transaction cost economists have exhibited the importance of these institutional endowments when authorities intend to interfere with the organization of a sector. Levy and Spiller have shown the particular importance of checks and balances within the political power in the reform of the telecommunication industry in several countries.[35] Shirley et al. went a step further in demonstrating, through a set of case studies in the water sector, how unbundling firms and reorganizing a sector along the same type of contractual arrangement may be a success or a failure, depending on the institutional resources available, particularly the level of capacities (legal, administrative) to monitor the arrangement and discipline the partners.[36]

More generally, what such studies show is that two intertwined institutional questions must be taken into consideration when unbundling previously integrated public utilities and developing competition in a sector formerly highly regulated: (1) What new mode of organization should be implemented that can fit better the transactions this arrangement will have to organize? (2) How should regulatory governance and competition policies be designed that are feasible, considering the institutional endowment of the public authorities involved? Indeed, many organizational arrangements and many competition policies are chosen and implemented with radical flaws because institutional resources made them irrelevant.[37]

Convergences

Although much more development is obviously needed, the transaction cost approach to vertical integration/deintegration converges on three major points.[38] First, organizational changes are often motivated by economizing strategies and by the search for safeguards that parties need for mitigating contractual hazards and for keeping opportunistic behaviors under control. Hence, vertical integration and/or restrictions should be examined at their face value, without the prejudices too often underlying the standard approach that is obsessed with the risk of anticompetitive behaviors. Second, there are gains to be expected in adopting a gradualist approach when dealing with complicated issues of economic organization that are poorly understood. Interferences with decisions of firms regarding their structure and boundaries need to be manipulated with great caution. Third, the capacity to implement adequately decisions of competition authorities regarding divestitures or reorganizations imposed on projected mergers should also be taken into consideration.

These lessons from transaction cost economics regarding vertical integration/deintegration are even more relevant when it comes to nonstandard organizational arrangements that do not fall under the dichotomy between "markets" versus "integrated firm."

Hybrid Arrangements

"Hybrid organization" is a generic term for nonstandard contractual arrangements that are alternatives to vertical integration as well as to spot markets. Their qualification as "nonstandard" is what matters here. Indeed, it is the distinctive characteristics of hybrids that raise problems for competition policies deeply rooted in the dichotomy of markets compared with hierarchies. Before examining some of these issues, let me briefly clarify the nature of arrangements for which even the terminology remains fluctuant.[39]

What Are Hybrid Arrangements?[40]

The set of organizational forms falling neither under spot markets nor under integrated firms for arranging transactions covers a large domain. Let us qualify these forms more precisely as all arrangements that involved deliberate coordination of a subset of activities among partners who maintain autonomous property rights and who remain independent as decisionmakers in last resort. In other terms, they do not rely mainly on prices for their mutual adjustments; but they do not depend either on administrative decisions of the hierarchical type. A wide variety of agreements fall into this category.

Empirical Description

From an empirical standpoint, we can identify at least seven modes that correspond to the qualification above. First, we have subcontracting practices, with a "pilot" firm coordinating a group of suppliers. One important characteristic of subcontracting, as exemplified in the automobile industry or in the construction industry, is that it is usually based on durable relationships in order to coordinate more efficiently than markets while avoiding the bureaucratic burden and lack of flexibility of integration. Second, there are networks of firms positioned quite symmetrically, as in many supply chain systems. Coordinating quantity, quality, or both, appears as a major motivation here, with interdependence understood as a way to reduce costs while creating value to be shared. A third form is franchising. Usually built on a brand name, franchise systems generate agreements that must guarantee quality, provide visibility of services and/or goods offered, and implement devices for monitoring partners who have strong incentives for free riding. Formalized procedures, standardization of inputs and/or outputs, and centralization of several functions are part of the toolbox. Fourth, collective trademarks and their supportive mode of organization share many characteristics with franchises. One major goal here is to develop arrangements that reduce consumers' search costs while partners benefit from joint marketing. It differs from franchising in that it is usually an agreement among a group of peers, which makes enforcement particularly challenging. Fifth, partnership is a form that presents similar problems. Loosely defined, it mixes characteristics of an integrated firm and characteristics of a network. Links among partners can be more or less formalized, but usually involve coordination of complex services in situations in which human assets play a crucial role. Sixth, cooperatives also share characteristics of hybrids. They rely on decentralized decisions, with property rights and decisionmaking maintained distinct, but also on elaborate coordination needed for controlling quality, for imposing constraints on quantity, and so forth. One major issue with cooperatives relates to the ill-defined property rights, making rules for sharing rents a crucial problem. Last, alliances are closer to standard contractual practices among firms, although they tend to develop specific modes of coordination, particularly when the development or transfer of technologies is at stake, as with joint R&D projects. Anticipated coordination costs and contractual hazards play major roles in the choice of a governance structure that can be either close to market arrangements, when it relies almost exclusively on contractual clauses, or to integrated firms, as with joint equities.

Shared Properties

Notwithstanding this diversity of arrangements, all the forms above do share some common characteristics, the combination of which defines their "configuration," making them distinct from markets and from integrated firms. Let me emphasize three properties that are particularly consequential for competition policies.

First, hybrid arrangements pool resources. Whatever form they take, they are systematically oriented toward organizing subsets of activities through interfirm coordination and cooperation, so that key investment decisions must be made jointly. Hybrids develop because markets are perceived as unable to adequately bundle important resources, while integration would reduce flexibility and weaken incentives. But pooling requires cooperation and continuity, so that devices are needed to secure those elements at low cost without loosing the advantages of decentralized decisions.

Second, specific forms of contracts develop that play central roles in hybrids, providing means for regulating partners. But because the contractual relationship tends to be much longer than the technical duration of specific contracts, incompleteness of contracts is a major component, with unforeseeable revisions as a source of risks. Contractual hazards generated by the autonomy of partners who remain legally independent decisionmakers push toward the adoption of governing devices that can secure contracts while minimizing costs of adjustments.

Third, hybrids coordinate, but they also compete. Of course, competition also exists within integrated firms (and, obviously, on markets). However the fundamental difference with hybrids is that they are agreements in which partners remain independent residual claimants with full capacity to make autonomous decisions in last resort, while they simultaneously implement mechanisms for monitoring and controlling some of their activities. Competition operates in two directions. Partners may compete against each other, as when there is bidding at the renewal of the agreement or when they coordinate on some activities and compete on others. Hybrids also compete with other arrangements, including other hybrids. If specific investments are moderate, partners may therefore be tempted to switch among arrangements, as can be observed in franchising systems. A consequence is that the implementation of an internal mode of regulation and control becomes a key issue.

Hence, important regularities underline the apparently heterogeneous set of hybrid arrangements. Aspects of these regularities are present in markets or hierarchies, which may explain why hybrids are often viewed as "intermediate" forms. But the combination of these properties defines a genuine mix of competition and cooperation ("coopetition") that substitutes the key role played by prices on markets and by command in integrated firms. And these are precisely the characteristics that are problematic for standard competition policies.

Practices That Challenge Standard Competition Policies

Indeed, the properties identified above generate a set of behaviors that challenges representation beyond competition policies, which is fundamentally based on the alternative between markets and integrated firms. Competition policies tend to ignore the intermediate zone illustrated in Figure 3.1. When confronted with hybrids, such policies tend to make decisions that introduce biases of the type described in our cases 1 and 2, above. Let me illustrate on three issues.

Vertical Coordination and Restrictions

Hybrids develop because they need coordination. But the maintained autonomy of rights and of decision power challenges their stability, thus pushing them toward the adoption of mechanisms of control and regulation. Restrictive practices of four types result.

First, hybrids are selective. There are almost always barriers to entry and often to rights of control at exit (e.g., rights to control the sale of a unit). Standard competition policies view these as restrictions on supply. Second, hybrids develop mechanisms for controlling the risk of free riding by partners to the arrangement. The more specific the investments, the tighter the control over parties involved, the ultimate form being the implementation of a "private government" in charge of policing partners.[41] But this looks very much like a coalition or a cartel in the dichotomist view of markets compared with integration. It is even more so, and this is the third restrictive practice because hybrid arrangements tend to regulate quantities. Indeed, coordination among partners may be motivated by the search for more efficiency, but it also requires motivating partners through adequate incentives. In order to exist and to be stable, hybrids need to generate rents. They can do that by lowering their costs by sharing functions (e.g., centralizing and customizing the acquisition of inputs), or by expanding demand through joint marketing. But generating rent also involves regulating supply: No franchise system wants to have three franchisees of the same group on the same corner! Again, this is vertical restriction imposed on partners. Fourth, hybrids may also control transfer prices among partners. It is particularly so when joint investments are made that create interdependencies among the parties. If a group of producers is organized as a supply chain system and coordinates to buy inputs at a low price, to adopt standardized production process in order to control quality, and to impose standards on the products they deliver, can they regulate internal transfer prices? Strictly speaking, standard competition policies view such practices as anticompetitive.

Now, let us assume that all the strategies above are developed by an integrated firm with a relatively small market share. Would competition authorities even care, as long as the market share is small?[42]

Horizontal Agreements

Hybrid agreements are regarded even more suspiciously when they involve coordination among partners exercising the same type of activity. It is so even when this coordination develops in order for small businesses to compete efficiently with large integrated firms. Let me emphasize three aspects here.

The first type of agreement that represents a problem for standard competition policies is when a group of small partners organizes into a structure with "representatives" in charge of negotiating with their customers quantities to be delivered, conditions of delivery (including standards of quality), and even prices. For instance, in the 1980s the French Label System, which organized small producers of high-quality food products, coordinated through certifying organizations. Each organization associated a group of small producers, other partners (e.g., slaughterhouses in the poultry industry) and representatives of the government and of different associations. Each organization defined products submitted to very strict requirements and implemented them in the network, thus "certifying" the deliverables. Last, the organization was also able to negotiate with large retailers.[43]

For each type of product, several hybrid organizations were competing, beside integrated firms. In the early 1990s, for instance, thirteen certifying organizations were competing in the sector of high quality poultry ("red label"), with none of them dominating the market. Notwithstanding this highly competitive environment, the arrangement was challenged by competition authorities and a European Directive from 1994 considerably reduced the capacity of these organizations to coordinate.[44]

A second situation that also challenges standard competition policies is one in which a group of partners delivering the same type of goods (or services) decide to coordinate in order to lower their costs while financing joint advertising campaigns to compete with large integrated retailers. Coordination may operate through the creation of a specific organization in charge of buying inputs, a homogenized accounting system with shared services, an integrated computerized system, agreements for transferring goods in order to reduce stocks, an insurance system allowing customers to take advantage of after-sale services provided by all members of the chain, and so forth. In several cases, competition authorities have considered that type of arrangement as a cartel, particularly when several stores of the same hybrid organization were operating in the same area, even if they represented only a small part of the market.[45] Had it been an integrated firm, it is very unlikely that competition authorities would even have noticed.

A third and last situation that is also challenging has to do with price policies. It is well known that competition policies are particularly sensitive on this issue and that a substantial part of the activity of antitrust authorities is devoted to tracking and sentencing agreements on prices among independent firms. One puzzling issue that has come repeatedly under scrutiny in Europe, however, is the possibility of hybrid organizations promoting products through advertising campaigns that signal one single price for goods offered by different partners. Advertising availability at the same price of products offered in the different stores of an integrated retailer, even if this retailer commands a large share of the market (e.g., Wal-Mart in the United States; Carrefour in France), does not raise any question. But different cooperatives and groups of independent retailers intending to do the same thing have been repeatedly submitted to a suspicious if not hostile approach by competition authorities, even when they represented a very small part of the market. For instance, a group of small stationary stores that represent less than 5 percent of the French market was not allowed to advertise some of their products at a unique price while an integrated distributor with over 25 percent of the market had no problem in doing so. All that the hybrid form was authorized to do was to advertise selected products with the mention: "Maximum price recommended at the stores participating to this campaign." This is surely not the best marketing strategy one wants to develop for attracting the attention of consumers![46]

Coordinating Mechanisms

One last dimension of the hybrid arrangements that repeatedly collides with authorities in charge of competition concerns the mode of government that hybrids tend to implement in order to monitor their agreements and to discipline participating partners.

Indeed, a fundamental characteristic of hybrid arrangements, which distinguishes them from spot market contracts, is the continuity in their relationship, as needed by the mutual dependence that specific investments create. In a world of incomplete contracts, a way to make such arrangements stable is through the device of specific mechanisms for coordinating activities, organizing transactions, and resolving disputes. Beside the restrictive provisions analyzed above, many hybrids implement "private governments" as a core architectural element.[47] The authority, voluntarily deposited by partners in the hands of these "governments," involves both intentionality and mutuality. These entities are more or less formal and are endowed with more or less power (some have even an internal "court" for judging and sentencing free riders). The spectrum goes from coordination based on mutual trust to very formal arrangements, as illustrated by the certifying organizations mentioned above.

Beyond their diversity, these forms of governance do share one major property: they are mechanisms implemented to prevent predation by some partners, that is, to avoid the hold up of rents when bi- or multilateral dependence creates significant contractual hazards. These "private governments" can therefore be understood as multilateral enforcement devices endowed with significant disciplinary power. But the resulting private order is embedded in agreements with a coercion factor that once more represents a challenge for antitrust policies and that may push hybrid arrangements thus constrained to adopt extralegal solutions.[48]

Competition Policies Versus Hybrid Organizations

The basic message delivered in this section is relatively simple. Competition policies have largely been developed in ignorance of the nature and role of hybrid organizations. As a result, authorities in charge of implementing these policies tend to regard suspiciously at best, and adversely most of the time, the different coordination devices generated by these arrangements in their strategies to compete with integrated firms. They largely ignore the underlying rationale provided by a transaction cost perspective to the existence of hybrid forms, that is, that they are modes of organization adopted because they tend to better fit the requirements of the characteristics of transactions they organize. As a result, it may be that policies intending to favor competition end up eliminating a mode of organization that could actually maintain a competitive environment. Indeed, as shown by the model developed in the first section, transaction cost economics helps us predict that if specific investments are needed and if contractual hazards are significant, parties that are not allowed to coordinate properly through contractual arrangements will have no choice but to integrate.[49]

Conclusion

This chapter emphasized some contributions of the new institutional economics approach to the analysis of legal issues regarding vertical integration and nonstandard forms of organizations. Four major ideas structured the chapter. First, competition policies cannot be examined solely with respect to the cases to which they apply. Effects on decisions made by actors operating in the same industry or in other sectors must also be considered, with special attention to their impact on future transaction costs. Second, decisions about vertical integration or deintegration must take into consideration not only ex post consequences but also ex ante circumstances that determined the choices made by actors. Careful scrutiny must be given to the fitness of the arrangement chosen with the attributes of the transaction they intend to organize. Third, modern market economies are made of a complex set of interwoven arrangements, of which spot markets and integrated firms are only two cases—important cases for sure, but they are, nevertheless, only two cases among others. Competition policies cannot evaluate properly nonstandard arrangements of the hybrid type with the sole reference to markets and hierarchies as benchmarks. Fourth, competition policies are embedded in an institutional environment. Their efficiency depends not only on their relevance per se, but also on the institutional endowments available for designing and implementing them.

In examining these issues, I have emphasized the key role of transaction costs, both as a tool for analyzing the relevance of these policies and as an issue. Ignoring transaction costs introduces important biases and distortions in the organization of production and exchange, with significant consequences on welfare and innovation. We need to better understand how this interaction works. There are other dimensions that should be explored too. Competition policies are embedded in institutions. They are subject to bounded rationality, to the self-interest and opportunism of those in charge of designing and implementing these policies, and to lobbying from the parties concerned. All these factors generate transaction costs that are typically the costs of running a market economy. These costs need to be measured and to be evaluated comparatively. This part of the research program in new institutional economics is still in its infancy. Much remains to be done.

Notes

I would like to thank Margaret Oppenheimer for her very helpful comments on previous versions of this chapter.

1. Extensive surveys of these developments are provided in Claude Menard and Mary Shirley, eds., *Handbook of New Institutional Economics.*

2. Ronald H. Coase, "The Nature of the Firm" and "The Problem of Social Cost"; Oliver E. Williamson, *Markets and Hierarchies*; Douglass C. North, *Structure and Change in Economic History.* Coase himself noted in "Industrial Organization" that "The Nature of the Firm" was "an article much cited and little used" (62). The same surely applied to "The Problem of Social Cost" at that time.

3. Of course this is a two-way street: changes in laws (e.g., the emerging deregulation movement) and changes in organizations (e.g., the development of franchising) also stimulated new ideas (and led to pressure for new laws as well).

4. Coase, "Industrial Organization," 61 and 62, respectively.

5. This is on the cover. The inside title page is expanded: *Markets and Hierarchies: Analysis and Antitrust Implications. A Study in the Economics of Internal Organization.*

6. For reasons that should become rapidly obvious in what follows, this chapter makes no distinction between new institutional economics and transaction cost economics. Indeed, I understand the latter as the core analytical apparatus of the former.

7. See among others, William Dugger, "The Transaction Cost Analysis of Oliver E. Williamson"; and Ernest J. Englander, "Technology and Oliver Williamson's Transaction Cost Economics."

8. Coase, "The New Institutional Economics, " 73.

9. Coase, *The Firm, the Market, and the Law*, 174.

10. Ibid.

11. Ibid., 175.

12. Coase, "The Nature of the Firm", 33–55.

13. Coase, *The Firm, the Market, and the Law,* 178.

14. Michael Riordan and Oliver E. Williamson, "Asset Specificity and Economic Organization."

15. A good review of the elements of the controversies is provided in the April 2000 issue of *The Journal of Law and Economics* (see particularly the papers by Ronald Coase and by Benjamin Klein et al.).

16. An analysis of these safeguards and their governance mechanisms is provided in Claude Menard, "The Economics of Hybrid Organizations."

17. Examples are provided in the last section of this chapter. The stylized case developed here is "inspired" by the organization of the high-quality segment of the fresh food industry in France (the "red label" system). For details, see Menard, "On Clusters, Hybrids, and Other Strange Forms."

18. As with the previous case, we assume again that the industry is competitive, so that public authorities will not ban this solution. The motivation behind this assumption is not only the necessity to make the point as clear as possible, but also that hybrid arrangements tend to develop in very competitive environments (hence the incentive to coordinate). Would integration be prohibited, then the model predicts that a certain degree of specific investments would not be developed, which also involves social costs.

19. Partial surveys are provided in Paul Joskow, "Asset Specificity and the Structure of Vertical Relationships"; and Howard Shelanski and Peter Klein, "Empirical Research in Transaction Cost Economics: A Survey and Assessment."

20. Joskow, "Transaction Cost Economics," 95.

21. Coase, "Industrial Organization," 67.

22. Williamson, *The Economic Institutions of Capitalism,* 26 and chap. 4.

23. Williamson, *The Mechanisms of Governance,* chap. 11, provides a good summary of his analysis.

24. See particularly Joskow, "The Role of Transaction Cost Economics in Antitrust and Public Utility Regulatory Policies," "Restructuring Competition and Regulatory Reform in the US Electricity Sector," and "Transaction Cost Economics, Antitrust Rules and Remedies."

25. Joskow, "Transaction Cost Economics, Antitrust Rules and Remedies," particularly sections 3 and 4.

26. Joskow, op. cit.,105–11.

27. Williamson, *The Mechanisms of Governance,* chap. 11, 292.

28. In a transaction cost perspective, holdup occurs when one party to an agreement takes advantage of specific investments made by the other party to rip off the quasirent generated by these investments. For example, in a contract linking a producer of electricity and a distributor, the latter may take advantage ex-post of the investments made by the former in building generator plants to capture the benefits. The classic papers on holdup are from Williamson, "Francise Bidding for Natural Monopolies"; and Benjamin Klein, Armen A. Alchian, Robert G. Crawford,"Vertical Integration, Appropriable Rents, and the Competituve Contracting Process."

29. Joskow, "Transaction Cost Economics, Antitrust Rules and Remedies," 98.

30. Joskow, "The Role of Transaction Cost Economics in Antitrust and Public Utility Regulating Policies,"section 2.2.

31. Williamson, "Transaction Cost Economics"; forthcoming in Menard and

Shirley, *Handbook of New Institutional Economics*. Details of the Schwinn case, of the arguments developed by the Department of Justice, and of the transaction cost perspective on them are developed in Williamson, *The Economic Institutions of Capitalism*, 183–89.

A somewhat similar and more recent type of argument was developed by the French Conseil de la Concurrence et des Prix about a tying arrangement between a group of oyster producers and transporters. See Decision 95-D-78, in *Bulletin Officiel de la Concurrence, de la Comsommationet de la Répression des Fraudes*, February 28, 1996.

32. Joskow, "Transaction Cost Economics, Antitrust Rules, and Remedies," 103.

33. A detailed analysis is provided in A. Yvrande-Billon and C. Menard, "Institutional Constraints and Organizational Choices."

34. Joskow has analyzed these issues extensively for the electricity sector, often anticipating problems that became apparent years later. See particularly the synthesis he provided in "The Role of Transaction Cost Economics in Antitrust and Public Utility Regulatory Policies,"and "Restructuring, Competition and Regulatory Reform in the US Electricity Sector."

35. Brian Levy and Pablo Spiller, "The Institutional Foundations of Regulatory Commitment."

36. M. Shirley, ed., *Thirsting for Efficiency.* See particularly chap. 1, by Menard and Shirley, "Cities Awash."

37. Detailed examples are provided in Paul Joskow and Richard Schmalensee, "Privatization in Russia"; and in Claude Menard and George Clarke, "A Transitory Regime, " chap. 8, 273–316. Even in a well-developed country with rich institutional endowments, results can be very mixed when transaction costs are ignored, as suggested by a study from the Federal Trade Commission on divestiture (see Joskow, "Transaction Costs,Antitrust Rules, and Remedies," 114).

38. Williamson, *The Mechanisms of Governance,* chap. 11.

39. We use the term hybrid, following the approach by Williamson. But terms like "networks," "clusters," "symbiotic forms," "supply chain systems," and "administered channels" are often used to designate basically the same empirical objects.

40. Extensive developments are provided in Menard, "The Economics of Hybrid Organizations."

41. Examples are provided in Menard, ibid.

42. To illustrate: In 2001, the Swiss Competition Commission challenged the set of agreements linking thousands of participants to the supply chain producing and transforming Gruyère cheese, although it represents a very small share of the market. Meanwhile, one of the two food retailers that dominate the Swiss market (the two of them total 80 percent of the purchase of food production in Switzerland) was able to absorb a small independent retailer detaining 2 percent of the market without questions from competition authorities.

43. Contrary to a common belief abroad, distribution in France is extremely concentrated. In 1999, the five leading retailers represented over 80 percent of total sales in the food sector.

44. Details are provided in Menard, "The Maladaptation of Regulation to Hybrid Organizational Forms."

45. A good example is provided by the condemnation of KRYS, a group of independent opticians, by the French Competition Commission. See Decision 97-D-49, *Bulletin Officiel de la Concurrence, de la Consommation et de la Répression des Fraudes*, September 17, 1997.

46. For instance, see French Competition Commission, "Recommendation 99-A-18," *Bulletin Officiel de la Concurrence, de la Consommation et de la Répression des Fraudes*, March 31, 2000.

47. A detailed analysis of such organisms is provided in Menard, "The Economics of Hybrid Organizations," section IV.

48. See Lisa Bernstein, "Opting Out of the Legal System."

49. An early example was provided by Thomas M. Palay who, in "Avoiding Regulatory Constraints: Contracting Safeguards and the Role of Informal Agreements," showed how forms of contracts—prohibited among partners involved in transactions that needed tight coordination—displayed informal ways to get around the regulatory constraints.

References

Bernstein, L. "Opting Out of the Legal System: Extralegal Contractual Relations in the Diamond Industry." *Journal of Legal Studies* 21 (1992): 115–57.

Bulletin Officiel de la Concurrence, de la Consommation et de la Répression des Fraudes, February 28, 1996; September 17, 1997; March 31, 2000.

Coase, R.H. "The Nature of the Firm." 1937. In Coase 1988, 33–56.

———. "The Problem of Social Cost." 1960. In Coase 1988, 95–156.

———. "Industrial Organization: A Proposal for Research." 1972. In Coase 1988, 57–74.

———. *The Firm, the Market, and the Law*. Chicago: The University of Chicago Press, 1988.

———. "The New Institutional Economics." *American Economic Review* 88, no. 2 (1998): 72–74.

———. "The Acquisition of Fisher Body by General Motors." *Journal of Law and Economics* 43, no. 1 (2000): 15–32.

Dugger, W. "The Transaction Cost Analysis of Oliver E. Williamson: A New Synthesis?" *Journal of Economic Issues* 17, no.1 (2000): 95–114.

Englander, E.J. "Technology and Oliver Williamson's Transaction Cost Economics." *Journal of Economic Behavior and Organization* 10, no. 3 (1988): 339–53.

Joskow, P. "Asset Specificity and the Structure of Vertical Relationships." *Journal of Law, Economics and Organization* 4, no. 1 (1988): 95–117

———. "The Role of Transaction Cost Economics in Antitrust and Public Utility Regulatory Policies." *Journal of Law, Economics and Organization* 7 (1991): 253–83.

———. "Restructuring, Competition and Regulatory Reform in the US Electricity Sector." *Journal of Economic Perspectives* 11, no. 3 (1997): 119–38.

———. "Transaction Costs Economics, Antitrust Rules and Remedies." *Journal of Law, Economics and Organizations* 18, no. 1 (2002): 95–116

Joskow, P., and R. Schmalensee. "Privatization in Russia: What Should Be a Firm?" *International Journal of the Economics of Business* 2, no. 2 (1995): 297–327.

Klein, B. "Fisher-General Motors and the Nature of the Firm." *Journal of Law and Economics* 43, no. 1 (2000): 105–41.

Klein, B., A.A. Alchian, and R.G. Crawford. "Vertical Integration, Appropriable Rents, and the Competitive Contracting Process." *Journal of Law and Economics* 21, no. 2 (1978): 297–326.

Levy, B., and P. Spiller. "The Institutional Foundations of Regulatory Commitment." *Journal of Law, Economics and Organization* 9 (Fall 1994): 201–46.

Menard, C. "On Clusters, Hybrids and Other Strange Forms." *Journal of Institutional and Theoretical Economics* 152, no.1 (1996): 154–83.

———, ed. *Transaction Cost Economics. Recent Developments*. Cheltenham, UK: Edward Elgar, 1997.

———. "The Maladaptation of Regulation to Hybrid Organizational Forms." *International Review of Law and Economics* 18, no. 4 (1998): 403–17.

———. "The Economics of Hybrid Organizations." *Journal of Institutional and Theoretical Economics* 160, no. 3 (2004): 1–32.

Menard, C., and G. Clarke. "A Transitory Regime: Water Supply in Conakry, Guinea." In *Thirsting for Efficiency: The Economics and Politics of Urban Water System Reform,* ed. M. Shirley, chap. 8, 273–316. New York: Pergamon-Elsevier, 2002.

Menard, C., and M. Shirley."Cities Awash." In *Thirsting for Efficiency: The Economics and Politics of Urban Water System Reform,* ed. M. Shirley, chap. 1, 1–42. New York: Pergamon-Elsevier, 2002.

———, eds. *Handbook of New Institutional Economics*. Norwell, MA: Kluwer Academic Press, 2004.

North, D.C. *Structure and Change in Economic History.* New York: Norton, 1981.

Palay, T.M. "Avoiding Regulatory Constraints: Contracting Safeguards and the Role of Informal Agreements." *Journal of Law, Economics, and Organization* 1, no. 1 (1985): 155–75.

Riordan, M., and O.E. Williamson. "Asset Specificity and Economic Organization." *International Journal of Industrial Organization* 3, no. 4 (1985): 365–78.

Shelanski, H., and P. Klein. "Empirical Research in Transaction Cost Economics: A Survey and Assessment." *Journal of Law, Economics and Organization* 11, no. 2 (1995): 335–61.

Shirley, M. ed. *Thirsting for Efficiency: The Economics and Politics of Urban Water System Reform.* New York: Pergamon-Elsevier, 2002.

Williamson, O.E. *Markets and Hierarchies: Analysis and Antitrust Implications*. New York: Free Press, 1975.

———. "Franchise Bidding for Natural Monopolies—In General and with Respect to CATV." *Bell Journal of Economics* 7 (1976): 73–104.

———. *The Economic Institutions of Capitalism.* New York: Free Press-Macmillan, 1985.

———. *The Mechanisms of Governance*. Oxford: Oxford University Press, 1996.

———. "Transaction Cost Economics." In *Handbook of New Institutional Economics,* ed. C. Menard and M. Shirley (forthcoming).

Yvrande-Billon, A., and C. Menard. "Institutional Constraints and Organizational Choices. The Case of the British Rail Industry." *Journal of Economic Behavior and Organization* (forthcoming).

4

A Market Path to Liberation?

Feminism, Economics, and Corporate Law

Kellye Y. Testy

Just as an economic approach to law began its ascendancy in the United States in the 1980s, a growing feminist analysis began to emerge in the discipline of economics.[1] The economic analysis imported to law, however, did not—and for the most part, still does not—contain those feminist insights; instead, the economic approach to law has remained a decidedly neoclassical one.[2] Indeed, it is fair to say that among many lawyers and legal academics, there is too little awareness that just as the meaning and purpose of law is contested, the discipline of economics is at the same time a vigorously challenged ground. Accordingly, rather than resist or embrace an economic analysis of law outright, it is important to understand first that there are many versions of economics and that each does or could bring varying strengths and weaknesses to the task of legal analysis.[3]

Though many schools of economic thought receive minimal attention in law, this chapter seeks to remedy what is arguably one of the most glaring instances of neglect. Considering the substantial influence that feminist thought has had upon many areas of law, together with law's enthusiastic embrace of economic reasoning, the lack of attention to feminist economics in law is both remarkable and unfortunate. One possible dynamic behind this neglect is that economic reasoning has had more influence in business-related areas of law; not coincidentally, feminist legal theory has had the least influence in these areas. Thus, economics and feminism have rarely been in the room at the same time, so to speak, in legal edifices. To probe that dynamic and the scholarly disregard of feminist economics it has produced, this chapter deploys feminist economics in the context of corporate law and governance, a legal arena that is perhaps most wedded to a neoclassical model of economic thought and that has been quite insulated from feminist analysis.

At least since the 1980s, the corporate regulatory environment in the United States has been dominated by a neoclassic economic approach, one that is radically privatized and dedicated to the norm of shareholder wealth maximization. That model's dominance, both in the United States and as a common export to other nations, led two prominent corporate law scholars to declare the "end of history for corporate law."[4] That claim was easier to defend before September 11, 2001, and the terrorists' attack that destroyed the World Trade Center, sending an anti-American corporatism message heard 'round the world.[5] It became even more difficult as 2001 ended with the Enron bankruptcy; then 2002 exploded with an alarming display of corporate malfeasance disclosures, fraud and self-dealing investigations, and lawsuits.[6] For some corporate law scholars, however, Enron was less a surprise than it was an example. A minority of writers have been critiquing the dominant model of the corporation as well as the regulatory climate flowing from it for some time, though those efforts have not succeeded in bringing about significant legal change.[7] As a result, the neoclassical economic model of the corporation retains its hegemony in the United States and is rapidly being exported to other nations as well.[8]

This chapter argues that a new and sorely needed vision of corporate law can be furthered through an alternative form of analysis, one that is grounded in feminist economics. To do so, the chapter has three sections. Part 1 offers a brief summary of feminist economics, highlighting the key ways in which its methods and content differ from the dominant neoclassical approach. Part 2 describes both the dominant model of corporate law and governance in the United States, as well as five significant counterapproaches, discussing how each addresses such key corporate law issues as the nature of the firm and the relative rights and duties of the corporation's constituents. Part 3 concludes by explaining how a feminist economic analysis of corporate law would alter significantly one's view of an optimal corporate regulatory environment, and by outlining several avenues for future research that should be pursued, including the potential for a productive alliance between feminist economists and progressive corporate law scholars.

Feminist Economics

Feminist insights into economic matters have long and varied histories that are commonly marked by a disappointing marginalization from dominant intellectual paradigms and institutional configurations that have been constructed largely by men, about men, and for men.[9] For instance, Paul Samuelson's classic text, *Economics,*[10] made no reference whatsoever to "women" and just two to "females," both of which were contained in a short segment on "minorities."[11] Rather than comprising a central subject of economic inquiry, subjects particularly salient for women frequently have been relegated to the study of constraints or treated as exogenous factors.[12] Indeed, of the many social sciences, economics has been among the most impervious to feminist inquiry, owing, among other things, to its dogged quest for status as a hard science that claims to be objective at all times but often reflects biases and limited perspectives.[13]

Beginning in the mid-1980s, and gaining significant momentum into the 1990s, however, a growing number of feminist approaches to economic matters coalesced into a distinct school of economic thought. These scholars seek to understand and to challenge historical and contemporary resistance to feminist economic thought. Though there are of course differences among those who identify as feminist economists, it is already possible to outline several major themes in this growing and promising body of work. These major themes are outlined below by highlighting three categories of feminist contributions to the advancement of economic thought: (1) theoretical innovations, which seek to redefine economic analysis; (2) methodological applications, which seek to address gender bias in methodological approaches and applications; and (3) institutional reconfigurations, which seek to remedy the historical and continuing exclusion of gender-based inquiry from the discipline of economics.

Theoretical Innovations

Like feminist analyses in other disciplines, a feminist approach to economics has enhanced the theoretical rigor of the field. It does so at the most fundamental level by bringing the postmodern critique of objectivity to bear upon economics. For feminists, economics, like all scientific method, is itself permeated with value judgments and expressions of power relations.[14] Feminists seek to reveal the ethical and political questions that are often elided in the field's epistemological and methodological choices. Economics is thus conceived of as a social institution or a "state of affairs" rather than as an abstraction separate from people and culture.[15]

For starters, feminist economists probe the underlying purposes of economic inquiry. Feminist economists insist that the field of economics be accountable not just to itself or to particular segments of society, but to humanity more fully.[16] Social welfare, or the long-term well-being of humans, is privileged over short-term measures of utility, including productive output. Notably, a key objective of feminist economists is to free "economics from the straitjacket of constrained optimization and formal mathematical modeling."[17]

One of the key theoretical insights of feminist economists is that the human subject at the center of much economic thought has been imbued with certain attributes that may inaccurately describe much of the world's population.[18] For instance, at the core of neoclassical economics is *homo economicus,* or economic man. Economic man is a self-interested individual, characterized by rational and autonomous decisionmaking. Feminists have critiqued this model on several grounds. First, it does not account for the limited autonomy that is experienced by many persons, such as that which can stem from physical or mental disability, from age (both children and the elderly), or other sources.[19] Moreover, it fails to consider that structural circumstances may severely limit the ability of people to make choices. Those circumstances can include such systemic inequalities as race and gender discrimination, specific issues of violence and coercion, and cultural norms that are embedded in both social and institutional structures.[20] Accordingly, feminists argue that reliance on a model of economic man is distorting, obscuring focus on conditions that may or may not permit choice to be exercised.[21]

Refining yet further the critique of economic man, as feminist economics has matured, scholars have also sought to take antiessentialist critiques of feminism to heart in advancing alternative theories of economic life. Thus, for feminist economists, gender is understood as a socially constructed phenomenon, the effects of which vary across factors including sex, race, age, ethnicity, class, and sexuality. So while gender "underlies economic processes," it does so only in "culturally specific, path-dependent ways."[22] Gender is, therefore, both an important and a complex area of economic inquiry; although it is always implicated in economics, it is not always entangled in the same ways or to the same degrees.

While rejecting the model of economic man, feminist economists do not posit a singular replacement for that model. The complexity of a feminist approach to economics, as well as its intellectual commitments to situated knowledge, leads to rejection of the idea of one supreme explanatory model of economic behavior. Though it is common for the economic intellectual community to refuse to take challenges to existing models seriously until a viable alternative model has been formulated, feminist economics resists that mode of thought.[23] A defining feature of feminist critique is that knowledge is not an abstract universality, but rather that it is contextual and contingent. Thus, feminist inquiry seeks to expand models of economic thought, not to articulate a dominant model, because any alternative model that feminists might offer would remain open to their own charge that the vantage point of the observer will have biased her or his conclusions. Recognizing the contingency of knowledge is a strength, not a weakness, of the critique, as paradoxical as is it may seem. By recognizing that all models are incomplete and by striving to include the experiences of those who are currently marginalized or even excluded from the intellectual marketplace in which economic models are judged, economic models are apt to be more useful than traditionally has been the case in explaining and predicting patterns of economic behavior in society.

Methodological Applications

While many feminist economists have concentrated on challenging the dominant neoclassical model and building alternative visions of economics, others have focused their attention on more intermediate concerns. One such strain in feminist economic thought concentrates on highlighting methodogical approaches that are seen as more likely to achieve the richer view of economic life that feminists seek to mine from economic studies. In this vein, feminists often call for a broadening of methods, asking that economics not prioritize one method, such as mathematical modeling, but instead embrace a multiplicity of methods for the various insights each can offer to the discipline of economic study.[24]

In particular, feminist economic inquiry has privileged empiricism, caring much more about what really happens in economic life than what a model might predict could or should happen.[25] As part of its commitments to empiricism, feminist economists study the distributional effects of economic policies. Attention to demographics is important because the distribution of well-being matters in feminist inquiry into quality-of-life indicators.[26] Thus, developing richer assessments of both total well-being, as well as the relative well-being of various groups, is a research priority.

To achieve that research goal, an abundant array of feminist economic inquiry is based on the common feminist method of asking the "woman question." Asking the woman question in economics means, for instance, inquiring how a study would be different if women were included as subjects or as designers. Through this method, feminist economists have also exposed bias errors in the application of mainstream theory and methods, in addition to critiquing the mainstream model itself and theorizing new models. By pointing out poor assumptions and neglected areas of study, feminist economists have succeeded in curing many gender-based flaws in economics. In particular, the subject of labor has been a fruitful area of inquiry for feminists. Feminist economists have demonstrated how the failure to consider issues of gender has led to errors in the study of such issues as occupational segregation, wage gaps, unpaid labor, and employment discrimination.[27]

In addition to labor, the family has been a further area of productive inquiry for feminist economists. Mainstream economics has tended to characterize the family either as an economic agent that is internally controlled by norms of cooperation and altruism, or as a bargaining site controlled by consent.[28] These formal models trouble feminist economists for several reasons. First, and arguably the most serious, the bargaining model of the family fails to address disparities in power that render reliance on abstract notions of consent unsustainable and thus undermine the explanatory efficacy of the model.[29] Further, feminists have exposed the failure of either model to capture anything but a narrow slice of domestic arrangements by presuming a traditional nuclear family rather than addressing families in their multivarient forms.[30]

Institutional Reconfigurations

As an important component of its efforts, feminist economics has consciously sought to unearth the important contributions that feminist thinkers have made to economics, many of which have been obscured and neglected.[31] In so doing, these scholars have made important links between institutional developments and configurations in the field of economics and the marginalization of feminist thought. Along these lines, writers have pointed to such matters as the historical exclusion of home economics from the general field of economics. With women relegated to the home, or to the study of it in educational fields, the discipline of economics remained a largely male enclave. Furthermore, disciplinary conventions in publication practices that obscured contributions of women, employment practices that marginalized work by and about women, and teaching texts that largely ignored the female half of the population contributed to the maintenance of a discipline considerably isolated from feminist advances occurring in other intellectual areas.[32]

Accordingly, feminist economists have labored to build institutions to support feminist inquiry into economics in order to encourage and sustain their work. One significant advancement was made in 1992 with the formation of the International Association for Feminist Economics. Other significant institutional achievements include a journal, *Feminist Economics,* devoted to publishing feminist economic thought that is often marginalized by more mainstream publications. While it is safe to say that no feminist economist would consider his or her work complete, the theoretical, methodological, and institutional advancements made by this diverse group of scholars are ones that hold much promise for enhancing the field of economics and the society it serves.

Corporate Law and Governance

In the United States, corporate law and governance has been increasingly seen through the lens of economics. The model dominating this growing economic approach is a neoclassical one, though too often that important issue is obscured through discourse that fails to specify that defining fact. In order to analyze how a feminist economic approach to corporate law might alter current regulatory regimes governing corporations, this section first surveys both the dominant view of corporate law in the United States, as well as several key critiques of that model.

The Dominant Model: Shareholder Primacy

The dominant model of corporate law in the United States stems from its underlying conception of the nature of the firm. Known as contractarianism, the firm is viewed as a private nexus of contracts rather than as a public entity.[33] That is, it is viewed as an aggregate of various inputs acting together to produce goods and services. The firm is thus a legal fiction representing the set of implicit and explicit contractual relationships between and among participants, including employees, shareholders, creditors, and managers.

Under this view of the firm, state corporate law is relegated to enabling the explicit and implicit bargains that comprise the firm. Serving as an off-the-rack standard form contract, it allows participants efficiency gains as they need only to vary those provisions that do not suit them. Law for the most part is thus not mandatory, as it might be commonly assumed, but is instead a series of default rules that can be either accepted or bargained around as suits the participants in the firm.[34]

At least since Berle and Means's classic exposition,[35] to the extent that corporate law has a substantive thrust, it is aimed at solving agency problems.[36] Created by the separation of ownership (shareholders) from control (managers and directors) in the public corporation, agency issues include managers who might run the corporation incompetently or in their self-interest rather than in the shareholders' best interests. Moreover, agency issues also concern the free-rider and other collective action impediments to widely dispersed shareholders' abilities to hold managements' feet to the fire on their own.[37] Accordingly, in order to address these agency issues, corporate law's role is to assure that the corporation is indeed run in the interests of its shareholders, leading to what many commentators refer to as the shareholder primacy norm in corporate law.

Shareholder primacy vests the shareholders, however, with the ultimate monitoring authority. The directors are charged first and foremost with protecting the shareholders' interests. As the firm's residual claimant, the shareholder is thus encouraged to detect and punish shirking by the other constituents in order to enhance the residual claim. So shareholder wealth maximization becomes the board of directors' polestar.

To carry out its duties, corporate law vests the board of directors with the power and the responsibility to manage the corporate enterprise. All powers and duties reside in the board as a whole.[38] Because it is charged with managing the enterprise, and because it is elected by shareholders (owners), the board is said to owe fiduciary duties to the shareholders, who own the corporation and elect the directors. These duties are usually characterized as the twin duties of care and loyalty, in addition to the obligation of good faith.[39]

The duty of care can be likened to the scrupulous management of the corporation. Although formally described as the requirement that a director must employ such a degree of care that a reasonably prudent person would employ in similar circumstances, the dominant version of corporate law has rendered the duty of care a largely procedural construct rather than one with substantive bite.[40] The duty of loyalty can be likened to the obligation to not be selfish, including the duty to not divert corporate opportunities for personal benefit or to engage in transactions where the director has a conflict of interest. Again, the formal statement of that responsibility is significantly lessened in practice, where directors enjoy substantial protections from liability for breach of these duties, including the business judgment rule, indemnification, exculpatory provisions in the articles of incorporation, good faith reliance on expert advice, and insurance contracts.[41]

Significant Critiques of Shareholder Primacy

Like all hegemonic discourse, however, the shareholder primacy model of corporate law and governance has generated a bevy of significant critiques. Many commentators have taken issue with the shareholder primacy and wealth maximization model, seeking to describe alternative visions of corporate law. While these counterapproaches surely are not new, most have gained additional purchase in post-Enron America as concerns over misuses of corporate power continue to escalate. While some of the individual characteristics of these efforts will no doubt be lost for the sake of simplicity and brevity, there are presently five broad categories of counterapproaches that can be identified in the literature on corporate governance: the team production model, corporate accountability, stakeholder theory, corporate social responsibility, and progressive corporate law.

Team Production Model

A team production theory of corporate law is a relative newcomer to the field of corporate governance. Drawing on Alchain and Demsetz's classic work on economic organization,[42] as well as upon more recent and innovative attention to power in the firm by Rajan and Zingales,[43] Professors Margaret Blair and Lynn Stout[44] developed an alternative model of corporate law and theory that they have termed the team production model (TPM). As its name implies, the TPM conceptualizes corporate participants—including managers, shareholders, employees, creditors, and local communities—as a team. The team forms because the members perceive that each will obtain more from the cooperative endeavor than from individual action. The resulting team production (or rents) then must be distributed through an allocative method.[45]

After rejecting several ex ante and ex post possibilities due to their suboptimal efficiency, Blair and Stout's model vests allocational authority in the corporation's board of directors, which they describe as an independent third party or "mediating hierarch."[46] Accordingly, rather than viewing directors as beholden to shareholders, the TPM posits that directors are beholden to the team and responsible for allocating corporate rents through a bargaining process among the firm's participants. Blair and Stout present the TPM as both a better description of current corporate governance, as well as a superior normative theory of what corporate governance should be once unyoked from slavish devotion to shareholder interests.

Owing to the recentness of this new model, corporate law scholars are uncertain whether the TPM has power to disrupt the dominant model of shareholder primacy. Some writers have praised the TPM's revisionist potential because it takes on economic theory on its own terms, and thus may penetrate the neoclassical discourse of shareholder primacy in ways that the other counter-hegemonic discourses cannot. Moreover, because TPM envisions the corporation as a collective enterprise, it holds substantial potential for recasting the duties the stewards of that enterprise might owe to those nonshareholder constituents affected by its reach.[47] Finally, this new model of the corporation more pointedly reveals the allocation of corporate rents as a political power question. Even so, concerns remain that because the model is fundamentally a bargain-based one, its ultimate effect may be a reinforcement of shareholder primacy because of shareholders' power advantage over other corporate participants under present law.[48]

Corporate Accountability

The accountability approach to corporate law is essentially one of disclosure, adopting the core animating principle of the federal securities laws.[49] Under this view, corporations will be penalized for bad deeds and rewarded for good ones, provided they disclose these to the investing and consuming public. In order to encourage this dynamic, proponents of corporate accountability advocate increasing the kinds of materials subject to disclosure, so that both financial and social information are put into the public realm.[50] Because large public corporations are already under substantial duties of disclosure under the federal securities laws, this does not add a duty as much as it expands the list of items that are subject to it.

The accountability approach to corporate governance is an indirect one and is faithful to efficient market creeds. For accountability to work, the information must make its way to the market in a manner that allows for its incorporation and dissemination there. Moreover, market participants must be willing and able to access that information and to act upon it. Thus, this approach does not limit managers' power to bring down negative consequences or to be punished directly for doing so. Rather, it leaves the task of judgment to the shareholders, the targets of disclosure rules.[51] As a result, accountability proponents leave existing shareholder power largely in place, and therein do little to alter the dominant corporate model of shareholder primacy.

Stakeholder Theory

Stakeholder theory proceeds on the premise that there are a number of related but separable interests in the manner in which a corporation exercises its power, and that managers should consider all of those interests in its decision-making processes, not just one.[52] Stakeholder (or other-constituency) theory was born in the takeover boom of the 1980s, as managers struggled to find a legitimate reason to "just say no" to an acquirer offering a substantial share-price premium. Although usually resistant to entreaties to consider nonshareholder interests, managers seized upon the idea of stakeholders as a reason to reject a premium bid and thereby remain in control of their enterprise and, arguably, their jobs. Over thirty states now have legislation permitting corporate directors to consider interests of other groups, in addition to shareholders, when making decisions. Only one (Connecticut) of those statutory schemes, however, makes that broader consideration mandatory; the rest are merely permissive.[53]

Not surprisingly, the permissive nature of other-constituency statutes has limited their effect in corporate decision-making processes. Outside of the hostile takeover context, evidence of directors willingly adding other constituencies into the decision-making mix under the permissive statutes is nil. Moreover, the definitional and operational difficulties of a stakeholder approach to corporate governance have been well documented and discussed elsewhere.[54]

Chief among those critiques is that the ambiguity in defining who is and who is not a stakeholder will actually increase the power and discretion of management, because it will be beholden to no one in particular. With shareholder primacy, the managers are clear on whom they should be serving; that clarity, even if it does no more, at least offers more constraint than an amorphous responsibility to an ill-defined group of corporate stakeholders.

Despite their hypocritical origins, permissive nature, and practical difficulties, these statutes nonetheless have succeeded in stepping up discourse around the concept of the corporate stakeholder. For instance, communitarian discourse concerning stakeholders is increasingly common today in business school classrooms, where future managers are taught that it is good for the corporation to consider all stakeholders and that such inclusiveness is part of a corporation's best practices. Accordingly, the stakeholder approach to corporate governance has had substantial effect and promises to continue to thrive, at least at the levels of business norms and practices.

Corporate Social Responsibility

Corporate social responsibility is a long-standing legal and activist debate that takes many forms: "Theories of corporate social responsibility cast a potentially broader net, emphasizing all of the social costs of corporate activity, and therefore embrace, for example, environmental or political concerns as well as stakeholder interests."[55] Proponents of corporate social responsibility characterize the corporation as a public entity rather than a private one, and most generally concentrate reform efforts on enhancing regulation of the corporate form. Concern over the increasing concentration of wealth in society that the relentless pursuit of shareholder profit has facilitated, and how the power that wealth creates is deployed, animates the growing chorus of corporate social responsibility advocates.[56]

While it is safe to say that this movement has been effective at the level of discourse about corporate law, for the most part it has yet to claim any significant victories at the level of legal doctrine or public policy, though the post-Enron flurry of legislative action and other denouncements of corporate greed has spurred hope that further change in corporate regulation is forthcoming. Although there is much talk in business about social responsibility, most commitments to that idea are increasingly cast in terms of improving profits rather than improving the societal conditions that launched the corporate social responsibility movement. There is real concern that corporate social responsibility will become just another commodity that businesses sell in the service of short-term shareholder wealth maximization, rather than the basis for any substantive change in the way business is done.[57]

Progressive Corporate Law

Like many discourses, particularly emergent ones, progressive corporate law is not amenable to easy definition. At this juncture, however, it is fair to say that what arguably unites progressive corporate law scholars with one another are the deep concerns they share over concentrations and antidemocratic uses of corporate power, both domestically as well as globally.[58] More specifically, these scholars are motivated by profound anxiety over corporate illegality and immorality; the rampant increase of wealth disparities both domestically and globally that undermine economic democracy; concentrations of corporate power and corporate influence in political processes that undermine political democracy; and environmental degradation and other externalities visited upon workers, consumers, and communities.[59]

Rather than focus exclusively on potential solutions to these issues that lie outside of what is traditionally characterized as "corporate" law, as earlier corporate social responsibility advocates primarily did, progressive corporate law scholars today view corporate law itself as a large part of the problem.[60] Moreover, these scholars believe it unlikely that any single change to corporate law and governance will have a significant effect. Thus, while they would agree that corporate transparency (accountability) and stakeholder recognition are important, most think that neither of those two approaches carry enough weight standing alone. Accordingly, the work of progressive corporate law scholars has thus far zeroed in on some of the fundamental tenets of corporate law, especially ones on which the dominant, shareholder-centered conception of corporate law rests.

Specifically, in contrast to the contractarian view of the firm, many progressive corporate law scholars view the corporation as an (at least) quasi-public entity.[61] Given its public dimensions, these scholars suggest that, like other public institutions, the corporation should be operated and regulated in accordance with the public interest. In this regard, the corporation is somewhat more than the sum of its parts, and individuals acting within the corporate structure cannot be assumed to act as individuals do outside such a structure.[62] Moreover, law has a much more substantive job to do. Rather than enable private bargaining, law constrains and compels the corporation to serve the public interest, not only the shareholders' interests.

Furthermore, progressive corporate law scholars resist the hegemony of shareholder primacy. In its place, they posit a web of stakeholders, each of which has an interest in the affairs of the corporation, and each of which should be considered in managerial decision making. Stakeholders variously include, in addition to shareholders, workers, creditors, the community, and society as a whole. For progressive corporate law scholars, norms of long-term enterprise wealth maximization and fair divisions of corporate rents predominate over short-term shareholder wealth maximization goals. Thus, rather than being beholden to one constituent, corporate boards and managers are seen more as trustees for the entity and for the society in which it is situated.

Progressive corporate law scholars have not yet reached consensus on issues concerning the role, duties, and composition of the board of directors, though significant energy has been directed toward its appraisal.[63] Some issues presently under exploration include an assessment of Blair and Stout's team production model[64] of the firm and whether it furthers or impedes a progressive vision of corporate law, the role and meaning of "outside" directors in corporate decisionmaking, and the role and meaning of the director duties of care and loyalty in order to constrain managerial self-interest without overly deterring entrepreneurship and beneficent risk taking.[65]

Though the contours of the progressive corporate law critique are still emerging, it is also important at this point to spend some time making clear what progressive corporate law is not. Though often mistakenly so categorized, progressive corporate law is not a rejection of market economies. Instead, properly regulated markets are viewed by most progressive corporate law scholars as a superior means of resource allocation than are bureaucratic governments of nation-states. Thus, progressive corporate law is not antimarket. Similarly, neither is it an anticorporate, though again it is often misjudged as such, particularly by those who, for political gains, would reject out of hand any critique of the corporation as inherently "anticapitalist," even unAmerican. Progressive corporate law scholars recognize positive benefits of the corporate form, being far more concerned with dangers perceived in large-scale corporations—particularly multinationals—than in smaller, more closely held entities. It is thus not the corporate form per se that concerns progressive corporate law scholars; rather, it is particular incantations of that form and its effects upon its many constituents that rivets their attention.

Corporate Governance Through a Feminist Economic Lens

The feminist critique of economics discussed above bears a striking resemblance to the critiques of the shareholder wealth maximization norm in corporate law and governance. This overlap is not coincidental. Both the feminist critique of economics and the mounting critiques of corporate law and governance take aim at the same concerns: the regulatory and policy results of continued adherence to neoclassical economic thought. This is particularly true of the overlap between feminist economics and progressive corporate law, both of which seek to further the value of equality and to enhance societal well-being across lines of race, gender, class, and other markers of difference. Nonetheless, in the disciplines of both economics and corporate law, neoclassical models continue to hold sway, albeit amid varied and vigorous scholarly critiques.

Furthermore, in both disciplines, social realities are pressing in on the dominant model as much as, if not more than, the scholarly critiques. For most of the world's population, economic life is a source of stress and discontent, not a source of sustenance. Wealth disparities are widening to such an extent that much of the world's population lives not just in poverty, but in total or near-total deprivation. Models of rational choice have increasingly little to offer such a state of affairs. *Homo economicus* may have always been a rather pale fellow, but what is left of any lifeblood is quickly draining.

What is more, that state of affairs is intimately entwined with increasing concentrations of economic power in corporate hands. Many of the world's largest economies today are corporate domains, not the domains of nation-states. Those who work in the field of corporate law cannot continue to ignore the fact that the regulatory environment of the corporation presents questions rivaling the urgency of questions regarding the role of the state. The tremendous scale and extreme concentration of global corporations stifle democratic processes, overpower market competition, and subvert environmental justice values. Corporate law has become the new constitutionalism, defining and determining the individual's relationship to society to a far greater extent than other factors.

The economic difficulties plaguing society are complex and interdisciplinary ones. They will not be resolved easily or quickly. The argument here is not otherwise, though it does suggest that applying feminist economics to questions of corporate law and governance can be part of the solution. The contributions that feminist economics can make to current regulatory debates in corporate law are many and varied and will benefit from further development of feminist economics itself, as well as from greater exploration of points of intersection. This section offers preliminary thoughts on ways that feminist economics can assist with corporate reform efforts and suggests a number of avenues for further research.

To begin, one of the key contributions that feminist economists can make to the study of corporate law and governance is in helping to understand and describe the conditions that the present corporate regulatory environment creates. While there are significant numbers of citizen action groups that are, and have been for some time, sounding alarm bells about the role of corporations in society, their claims are often long on hyperbole and short on data.

As a result, it is easier to shrug them off as "anticorporate" or "activist" and to claim either that there is "no alternative" to the existing regulatory climate or to reject proffered alternatives as "radical" or "unworkable." What feminist economists can bring to the task of assessing the effect of the current regulatory climate are their methodologies of study, particularly their preferences for empiricism.

Consider that one of the key insights that feminist economists bring to the table is the important question of distributional consequences. As corporate law scholars consider regulatory reform, one of the key questions they should be regarding is who is bearing the costs and benefits of the current regulatory regime and what distributional impact will reforms make. For the feminist economist, demographics and distributional consequences matter. As a result, they have the tools and desire to understand not only whether a particular category of corporate constituent is being harmed or helped by corporate law and policy, but precisely who is in which category. For example, while it would be helpful to know whether it is workers as a group that are suffering from laws concerning corporate control transactions, it would be most helpful to know which workers are hit hardest. If, extending the example, it were women with children that bore the brunt of particular laws or practices, then that needs to be known. From a policy standpoint, it is one thing for hardship to fall; it is another for it to fall repetitively along lines of systemic inequality.

Feminist economists' emphasis on distributional consequences also would be quite useful in debates over the nature of the firm in corporate law. As noted above, the dominant model of the corporation conceives of it as a nexus of contracts, which has been criticized as an abstract bargaining model that does not take account of disparities in bargaining power. Feminist economics' emphasis on distributional consequences can shed light on which corporate constituents benefit from this model and which do not. Likewise, the norm of shareholder wealth maximization can also benefit from distributional analysis. Share ownership has changed dramatically in the United States in recent years, moving increasingly into institutional ownership structures. These changes, both alone and in combination with changes in the labor force and pension fund structures, demand more rigorous distributional analyses.

Feminist economic insights can be deployed further to study the multitude of corporate configurations that exist in society. Critiques of corporate law and policy too often proceed as if all corporations are similarly situated, when this is clearly not the case. Corporations vary tremendously in size, ownership structure (public/private), and internal culture. Again, policy prescriptions need to be tailored to these various contexts once it becomes clear the differences those contexts actually make for corporate activity. As an example, it is common for the large publicly held multinational corporations to be the targets of the most criticism. After the latest round of regulatory change post-Enron, many corporations have completed, or are considering, going-private transactions so that the new legal requirements for public corporations will no longer apply. Study is warranted on whether it is public firms or private firms that are of the most concern to advocates of increased accountability.

When questions of accountability arise, one of the most pressing issues is the question of corporate externalities. Feminist economists, who privilege a wide lens on the costs of activity—thinking not just in financial terms, but also in terms of such harms as gender and race discrimination—have much to offer this debate. Efforts to study and to quantify all the costs of corporate activity are needed to proceed within the purview of a feminist economic approach to corporate law.

Just as measurements of the costs of corporate activity are important, so, too, is increasing sophistication about measurement of the benefits of corporate activity. The present measurement of economic progress is the gross domestic product, which came of age in the time of World War II when measurements of productive capacity of goods and services were sought. Today this measure is not a reliable one for social health. Some commentators have likened it to measuring an individual's physical health by his waist size. The kinds of goods and services produced and who they serve are not factors; nor is the unpaid labor that feminist economists have revealed that remains the job of most women. Accordingly, devising more thorough methods for studying the benefits of economic activity is likewise a task for which a feminist economic approach to law is well suited.

Finally, feminist economic insights can be brought to bear on many of the questions being raised by progressive corporate law scholars about corporate activity. Because both feminist economics and progressive corporate law seek to achieve a normative vision of society that is premised on equality and human flourishing, both lines of investigation would profit from more explicit collaboration. Questions remain about more meaningful duties of directors, enhanced diversity in director ranks, more stringent controls on corporate political activity, appreciation for workers' firm-specific investments, and a richer view of the meaning of efficiency as a goal of corporate activity.

Conclusion

Feminist economics has much to offer to questions of corporate regulation. Like economics more generally, it brings to the task a skill set that is particularly appropriate for assessing an institution, the corporation created by law for economic purposes. But unlike the dominant model of economics deployed in law, it brings to that project a richer view of the underlying purposes of economic study, as well as a more rigorous insistence on understanding the social consequences of models and the policy prescriptions that flow from them. In short, feminist economics recognizes that economic questions are also normative political questions. As a result, it is a beckoning field of inquiry that can assist both legal scholars and regulators in calibrating the regulatory environment to assure that corporations work for the long-term good of society, rather than against it.

Notes

Professor Testy thanks Deans Rudolph Hasl and Janet Ainsworth of the Seattle University School of Law for research support.

1. Francine D. Blau and Marianne A. Ferber, *The Economics of Women, Men, and Work*; Marilyn Waring, *If Women Counted: A New Feminist Economics*.

2. Henry Hansmann and Reinier Kraakman, "The End of History for Corporate Law."

3. Nicholas Mercuro and Steven G. Medema, *Economic Analysis of Law from Posner to Post-Modernism.*

4. Hansmann and Kraakman.

5. Faith Stevelman Kahn, "Bombing Markets, Subverting the Rule of Law: Enron, Financial Fraud, and September 11, 2001."

6. For example, William W. Bratton, "Enron and the Dark Side of Shareholder Value."

7. For example, Lawrence E. Mitchell, *Progressive Corporate Law.*

8. Lawrence E. Mitchell, *Corporate Irresponsibility: America's Newest Export.*

9. Michéle Pujol, *Feminism and Anti-Feminism in Early Economic Thought.*

10. Paul Samuelson, *Economics.*

11. Marianne Ferber and Julie Nelson, *Beyond Economic Man: Feminist Theory and Economics,* 4–5.

12. Gillian Hewitson, *Feminist Economics: Interrogating the Masculinity of Rational Economic Man*; J. Still, *Feminine Economies.*

13. Marianne Ferber and Michelle L. Teiman, "The Oldest, the Most Established, and the Most Quantitative of the Social Sciences—and the Most Dominated by Men: The Impact of Feminism on Economics," 125–39; Edith Kuiper and Jolande Sap, *Out of the Margin: Feminist Perspectives on Economics.*

14. Sandra Harding, *The Science Question in Feminism;* idem, "Can Feminist Thought Make Economics Objective?"

15. Drucilla K. Barker and Edith Kuiper, *Toward a Feminist Philosophy of Economics*, 3.

16. Diana Strassman, "Feminist Economics."

17. Barker and Kuiper, 3.

18. Hewitson, *Feminist Economics: Interrogating the Masculinity of Rational Economic Man*.

19. Diana Strassman, "Not a Free Market: The Rhetoric of Disciplinary Authority in Economics," 54–68.

20. Bina Argawal, "Bargaining and Gender Relations: Within and Beyond the Household," 1–51; Kimberly Christensen, "Economics Without Money; Sex Without Money; Sex Without Gender: A Critique of Philipson and Posner's *Private and Public Health:* The Aids Epidemic in an Economic Perspective," 1–24.

21. Hewitson, *Feminist Economics: Interrogating the Masculinity of Rational Economic Man.*

22. Eiman Zein-Elabdin, "The Difficulty of a Feminist Economics," 337.

23. Strassman, "Feminist Economics."

24. Argawal, "Bargaining and Gender Relations"; Diana Strassman, "A Special Issue: Expanding the Methodological Boundaries of Economics," *Feminist Economics.*

25. Joyce P. Jacobsen, "Some Implications of the Feminist Project in Economics for Empirical Methodology," 89–104.

26. Maria Floro, "Women's Well-Being, Poverty, and Work Intensity," 1–25; Julie Aslaksen and Charlotte Koran, "Explorations on Quality of Life Indicators."

27. Janice Madden, *The Economics of Sex Discrimination*; Myra H. Strobe, "Toward a General Theory of Occupational Sex Segregation: The Case of Public School Teaching," 144–56; Francine D. Blau and L. Kahn, "Rising Wage Inequality and the US Gender Gap," 23–28; Jacobsen, "Some Implications of the Feminist Project in Economics for Empirical Methodology," 89–104.

28. Strassman, "Feminist Economics."

29. Newburg Tot, "Fertility and the Division of Work in the Family: A Game Theoretic Model of Household Decisions," 23–36; Argawal, "Bargaining and Gender Relations," 30.

30. Strassman, "Feminist Economics."

31. Pujol, *Feminism and Anti-Feminism in Early Economic Thought.*

32. Ferber and Teiman, "The Oldest, the Most Established," 125–39; Susan Feiner and Bruce Roberts, "Hidden by the Invisible Hand: Neoclassical Economic Theory and the Textbook Treatment of Women and Minorities," 159–81; Strassman, "Feminist Economics."

33. For example, William W. Bratton, "The Nexus of Contracts' Corporation: A Critical Appraisal," 407; Frank H. Easterbrook and Daniel R. Fischer, "The Corporate Contract."

34. Easterbrook and Fischer, "The Corporate Contract."

35. Adolph A. Berle and Gardiner C. Means, *The Modern Corporation and Private Property.*

36. Michael C. Jensen and William H. Heckling, "Theory of the Firm: Managerial Behavior, Agency Costs and Ownership Structure," 305.

37. For example, James D. Cox, Thomas Lee Hazen, and F. Hodge O'Neal, *Corporations.*

38. For example, Model Business Corporation Act, § 8.01 (1984).

39. For example, Model Business Corporation Act, § 8.01 (1984).

40. For example, Smith v. Van Gorkom, 488 A.2d 858 (1985).

41. Model Business Corporation Act § 8.01 (1984).

42. Airmen A. Alchian and Harold Demsetz, "Production, Information Costs, and Economic Organization."

43. Rathdrum G. Rajan and Luigi Zingales, "Power in a Theory of the Firm."

44. Margaret M. Blair and Lynn A. Stout, "A Team Production Theory of Corporate Law."

45. Ibid, 264–71.

46. Ibid, 270–79.

47. Kellye Y. Testy, "Liking Progressive Corporate Law with Progressive Social Movements," 1227–52.

48. David Million, "New Game Plan or Business as Usual? A Critique of the Team Production Model of Corporate Law"; K.Y. Testy, "Linking Progressive Corporate Law."

49. Louis Loss and Joel Seligman, *Securities Regulation*, 171–80.

50. Cynthia A. Williams, "The Securities and Exchange Commission and Corporate Social Transparency."

51. Ibid.

52. Stephen M. Bainbridge, *Corporation Law and Economics*, 414–17.

53. Ibid.

54. For example, Symposium, "Corporate Malaise—Stakeholder Statutes: Cause or Cure?"

55. Million, "New Game Plan," 1001, *n*5.

56. Douglas M. Branson, "Corporate Social Responsibility Radix," 1207–26.

57. Peter Simon, "Crisis of Conscience, B1.

58. Mitchell, *Corporate Irresponsibility*.

59. Mitchell, *Progressive Corporate Law;* Testy, "Linking Progressive Corporate Law."

60. Branson, "Corporate Social Responsibility Redux."

61. Testy, "Linking Progressive Corporate Law."

62. Mitchell, *Progressive Corporate Law*.

63. For example, Lynne L. Dallas, "The New Managerialism and Diversity on Corporate Boards of Directors."

64. Blair and Stout, "A Team Production Theory of Corporate Law."

65. For example, Cheryl L. Wade, "Racial Discrimination and the Relationship Between the Directorial Duty of Care and Corporate Disclosure"; Janis Sarra, "The Gender Implications of Corporate Governance Change"; Marleen O'Connor, "The Enron Board and the Perils of Groupthink"; Kent Greenfield, "September 11 and the End of History for Corporate Law."

References

Alchian, A.A., and H. Demsetz. "Production, Information Costs, and Economic Organization." *American Economic Review* 62 (1972): 777.

Argawal, B. "Bargaining and Gender Relations: Within and Beyond the Household." *Feminist Economics* 3 (Spring 1997): 1–51.

Aslaken, J., and C. Koren, eds. "Explorations on Quality of Life Indicators." *Feminist Economics* 5 (July 1999).

Bainbridge, S.M. *Corporation Law and Economics*. New York: Foundation Press, 2002.

Barker, D.K., and E. Kuiper, eds. *Toward a Feminist Philosophy of Economics*. London: Routledge, 2003.

———. "Introduction: Sketching the Contours of a Feminist Philosophy of Economics." In *Toward a Feminist Philosophy,* ed. Barker and Kuiper, 1–18.

Berle, A.A., and G.C. Means. *The Modern Corporation and Private Property.* 3d ed. New Brunswick, NJ: Transaction Publishers, 1991.

Blair, M.M., and L.A. Stout. "A Team Production Theory of Corporate Law." *Virginia Law Review* 85 (1999): 247.

Blau, F.D., and M.A. Ferber. *The Economics of Women, Men, and Work.* Englewood Cliffs, NJ: Prentice-Hall, 1986.

Blau, F.D., and L. Kahn. "Rising Wage Inequality and the US Gender Gap." *American Economic Review* 84 (May 1994): 23–28.

Branson, D.M. "Corporate Social Responsibility Redux." *Tulane Law Review* 76 (2002): 1207–26.

Bratton, W.W. "The 'Nexus of Contracts' Corporation: A Critical Appraisal." *Cornell Law Review* 74 (1989): 407.

———. "Enron and the Dark Side of Shareholder Value." *Tulane Law Review* 76 (2002): 1275–361.

Christensen, K. "Economics Without Money; Sex Without Gender: A Critique of Philipson and Posner's *Private and Public Health: The Aids Epidemic in an Economic Perspective.*" *Feminist Economics* 4 (Summer 1998): 1–24.

Cox, J.D., T.L. Hazen, and F.H. O'Neal. *Corporations.* New York: Aspen Law and Business, 1997.

Dallas, L.L. "The New Managerialism and Diversity on Corporate Boards of Directors." *Tulane Law Review* 76 (2002): 1363–407.

Easterbrook, F.H., and D.R. Fischel. "The Corporate Contract." *Columbia Law Review* 89 (1989): 1416.

Feiner, S., and B. Roberts. "Hidden by the Invisible Hand: Neoclassical Economic Theory and the Textbook Treatment of Women and Minorities." *Gender and Society* 4 (June 1990): 159–81.

Ferber, M., and J. Nelson, eds. *Beyond Economic Man: Feminist Theory and Economics,* Chicago: University of Chicago Press, 1993.

Ferber, M., and M.L. Teiman. "The Oldest, the Most Established, and the Most Quantitative of the Social Sciences–and the Most Dominated by Men: The Impact of Feminism on Economics." In *Men's Studies Modified: The Impact of Feminism on the Academic Disciplines,* ed D. Spender, 125–39. New York: Pergamon Press, 1981.

Floro, M. "Women's Well-Being, Poverty, and Work Intensity." *Feminist Economics* 1 (Fall 1995): 1–25.

Greenfield, K. "September 11 and the End of History for Corporate Law." *Tulane Law Review* 76 (2002): 1409–31.

Hansmann, H., and R. Kraakman. "The End of History for Corporate Law." *Georgetown Law Journal* 89 (2001): 439–60.

Harding, S. *The Science Question in Feminism.* Ithaca, NY: Cornell University Press, 1986.

———. "Can Feminist Thought Make Economics More Objective?" *Feminist Economics* 1 (1994): 7–32.

Hewitson, G. *Feminist Economics: Interrogating the Masculinity of Rational Economic Man.* Aldershot, UK: Edward Elgar, 1999.

Jacobsen, J.P. "Some Implications of the Feminist Project in Economics for Empirical Methodology." In *Toward a Feminist Philosophy,* ed. Barker and Kuiper, 89–104.

Jensen, M.C., and W.H. Meckling. "Theory of the Firm: Managerial Behavior, Agency Costs and Ownership Structure." *Journal of Financial Economics* 3 (1976): 305.

Kahn, F.S. "Bombing Markets, Subverting the Rule of Law: Enron, Financial Fraud, and September 11, 2001." *Tulane Law Review* 76 (2002): 1579–643.

Kuiper, E., and J. Sap, eds. *Out of the Margin: Feminist Perspectives on Economics.* London: Routledge, 1995.

Loss, L., and J. Seligman. *Securities Regulation.* 3d ed. Frederick, MD: Aspen Law and Business, 1989.

Madden, J. *The Economics of Sex Discrimination.* Lexington, MA: Lexington Books, 1973.

Mercuro, N., and S.G. Medema. *Economic Analysis of the Law from Posner to Post-Modernism.* Princeton, NJ: Princeton University Press, 1997.

Millon, D. "New Game Plan or Business as Usual? A Critique of the Team Production Model of Corporate Law." *Virginia Law Review* 86 (2000): 1001.

Mitchell, L.E., ed. *Corporate Irresponsibility: American's Newest Export.* New Haven, CT: Yale University Press, 2001.

———. *Progressive Corporate Law.* Boulder, CO: Westview Press, 1995.

O'Connor, M. "The Enron Board: The Perils of Groupthink." *University of Cincinnati Law Review* 71 (2003): 1233.

Pujol, M. *Feminism and Anti-Feminism in Early Economic Thought.* Aldershot, UK: Edward Elgar, 1992.

Rajan, R.G., and L. Zingales. "Power in a Theory of the Firm." *Quarterly Journal of Economics* 113 (1998): 387.

Samuelson, P. *Economics.* New York: McGraw Hill, 1948.

Sarra, J. "The Gender Implications of Corporate Governance Change." *Seattle Journal for Social Justice* 1 (2003): 457–502.

Still, J. *Feminine Economies.* Manchester, UK: Manchester University Press, 1997.

Strassman, D. "Not a Free Market: The Rhetoric of Disciplinary Authority in Economics." In *Beyond Economic Man,* ed. Ferber and Nelson, 54–68.

———. "Feminist Economics." In *The Elgar Companion to Feminist Economics,* ed. J. Peterson and M. Lewis. Cheltenham, UK: Edward Elgar, 1999, 360–73.

———, ed. "A Special Issue: Expanding the Methodological Boundaries of Economics," *Feminist Economics* 3 (1997).

Strober, M.H. "Toward a General Theory of Occupational Sex Segregation: The Case of Public School Teaching." In *Sex Segregation in the Workplace,* ed. B. Reskin, 144–56. Washington, DC: National Academy Press,1994.

Symposium, "Corporate Malaise–Stakeholder Statutes: Cause or Cure?" *Stetson Law Review* 21 (1991): 3.

Testy, K.Y. "Linking Progressive Corporate Law with Progressive Social Movements." *Tulane Law Review* 76 (2002): 1227–52.

Wade, C.L. "Racial Discrimination and the Relationship Between the Directorial Duty of Care and Corporate Disclosure." *University of Pittsburgh Law Review* 63 (2002): 389.

Waring, M. *If Women Counted: A New Feminist Economics.* San Francisco: Harper and Row, 1988.

Williams, C.A. "The Securities and Exchange Commission and Corporate Social Transparency." *Harvard Law Review* 112 (1999): 1197.

Zein-Elabin, E. "The Difficulty of a Feminist Economics." In *Toward a Feminist Philosophy,* ed. Barker and Kuiper, 319–38.

5

Alternative Economic Approaches to Antitrust Enforcement

Patrick J. Welch and Thomas L. Greaney

Recognition of the problems created by monopolization and conspiracy in restraint of trade—the focus of antitrust enforcement—far predates the Sherman Act of 1890, when the federal government formally entered the arena. Adam Smith, for example, voiced his concern in *The Wealth of Nations:* that "Monopoly . . . is a great enemy of good management. . . . People of the same trade seldom meet together, even for merriment and diversion, but the conversation ends in a conspiracy against the public, or in some contrivance to raise price."[1] In fact, recognition of antitrust-type problems dates back at least to Old Testament times.[2]

Given this long history, is it reasonable to expect a consensus on the goals and procedures of antitrust enforcement? Hardly. The Sherman Act and other antitrust legislation have been described as broad and imprecise, with key terms like unfair competition, conspiracy, and monopolization lacking clarity and definition.[3] This breadth and imprecision led one commentator to describe the statutes as "a social Rorschach test, on which courts and commentators can project a variety of perspectives and goals."[4] For example, at one extreme, the Supreme Court in *United States v. Trans-Missouri Freight Association* (1897) held that the language in the Sherman Act stating that "Every contract . . . in restraint of trade . . . is . . . illegal" is so broad that it makes all contracts run foul of the law because, by their nature, they restrain trade.[5] At the other extreme, one commentator recently complained that the shapers of today's antitrust policy adhere to a philosophy that "if it is in the best interest of a manufacturer to frustrate competition among retailers, then it should be perfectly kosher under the U.S. antitrust laws."[6]

One consequence of this breadth and imprecision is that it has opened the door for economics to play a major role in interpreting and enforcing antitrust issues. It has been argued that economists' case for competition as the preferred mechanism for controlling the economy has had a significant impact on antitrust analysis and enforcement, and that this impact is demonstrated by the general acceptance of economic efficiency as antitrust's primary goal.[7] Further, an exclusively economic approach to antitrust has been ranked as more coherent than other approaches that emphasize interest group protection, fairness, and other noneconomic objectives.[8]

While all this may be true, the fact remains that the legal reasoning economics supports is not simply a value-free, analytical construct described by:

$$(\text{facts} \times \text{rules}) = \text{decision.}$$[9]

For one thing, the relevant facts may be limited or unavailable. For another, and appropriate to an inquiry into the implications for law of differing economic perspectives, applying rules requires choices about which economic assumptions to endorse.[10] Because of these choices, the presence of alternative, sometimes contradictory, economic perspectives from which antitrust issues can be viewed can lead to significant controversies over economics' contribution to antitrust analysis and enforcement. As Flynn and Ponsoldt put it: "Today, instead of economic analysis assisting antitrust analysis by illuminating some aspects of reality, a narrow brand of economic analysis is used to the exclusion of broader economic and other insights. . . . Antitrust policy cannot avoid confronting the intellectual reality that every legal decision is unavoidably a moral one."[11]

Flynn and Ponsoldt's closing remark points directly to a problem inherent in having several economic approaches to choose from when analyzing and implementing antitrust policy: Each approach rests on (often implicit) value judgments regarding whose interests should be served.[12] Consequently, there is ample room for disagreement over which approach is most appropriate.

Here we explore the three most recognized economic approaches to antitrust: The neoclassical approach, the Harvard School approach, and the Chicago School approach.[13] We begin with a brief description of each approach's main tenets. Next is an overview of what generally are regarded as the primary goals of antitrust enforcement. This is followed by a discussion of controversies surrounding the different approaches' rankings of those goals.

Alternative Approaches to Antitrust Enforcement

Certainly, an Aristotelian, mercantilist, Marxian, or other economic perspective on antitrust can be, or has been, constructed. However, today these alternatives get little, if any, recognition. Attention focuses mainly on the three approaches listed above.[14]

The Neoclassical Approach

While it is an interesting coincidence that the Sherman Act and Alfred Marshall's groundbreaking neoclassical text, *Principles of Economics*, both appeared in 1890, it would be overreaching to suggest that, from the outset, neoclassical economics directly and significantly impacted antitrust enforcement. For one thing, this theory was apparently largely unknown when the major antitrust laws were introduced. For another, leading economists of the day, who tended more in the longer-established classical direction, are said to have ignored or opposed the laws' adoption.[15] However, over time, the neoclassical approach gained momentum.

Although neoclassical economics goes far beyond considerations of free markets, choice, and other matters at the heart of antitrust enforcement, its theories and underlying assumptions are now widely accepted and are seen as providing coherent answers to most of the questions central to antitrust policy. As the argument goes, while there are disagreements over matters such as the significance of entry conditions into markets, they tend to be technical and more often than not at the periphery of antitrust concerns.[16]

Several facets of neoclassical economics, a precursor of the Chicago School, discussed below, have implications for how antitrust enforcement is approached. First, like much of modern economics, it tends toward formal, deductive arguments and away from induction and specific institutional considerations. Second, it emphasizes the role of markets and focuses largely on the comparison of idealized, purely competitive markets to monopolized markets. These two facets, one can argue, comport nicely with an approach to antitrust enforcement that seeks to minimize discretion by judges and government enforcers, and favors "certain" (and at the extreme, per-se) rules. Third, neoclassical economics recognizes categories of efficiency; notably, allocative efficiency where resources are directed toward uses most valued by consumers, and productive efficiency in how businesses use those resources. Finally, neoclassical economics is built on the assumption that individuals are rational maximizers. These last two considerations lend support to the argument that antitrust laws should not inhibit rational, efficient behavior that benefits both producers and consumers.[17]

The Harvard School Approach

It is instructive to begin a discussion of the Harvard and Chicago Schools by reviewing what are called the "structural" and "nonstructural" approaches to antitrust enforcement. These two approaches describe different positions on how three key elements for antitrust analysis are related, and provide a useful framework for differentiating between the two schools' perspectives.

The key elements in the structural–nonstructural approaches are market structure, the behavior of sellers in the market, and the performance of those sellers; or, as more commonly labeled, "structure," "behavior," and "performance." Structure is concerned with the number of sellers in the market and their relative sizes (otherwise known as "concentration"), as well as such factors influencing the number and sizes of those sellers as scale economies, product differentiation, mergers and acquisitions, and conditions of entry into the market. Behavior focuses on decisions by sellers in a market that relate to matters such as pricing policies and their objectives, predation (e.g., below-cost or discriminatory pricing to injure a rival), and the interrelatedness of those sellers' decisions—ranging from independent to collusive. Performance addresses the welfare effects of sellers' activities measured in terms of efficiency (e.g., their impact on costs and technological change), distribution (e.g., whether they lead to wealth transfers from consumers to producers), and other broader considerations (e.g., their effects on consumer choice and the political process).

The structural approach sees the relationship between these three elements as described by:

Structure → Behavior → Performance.

That is, structural elements are the prime movers behind the performance, or welfare, effects of sellers' behaviors. Accordingly, if sellers in a market are creating deadweight losses, are x-inefficient, or are conspiring against the interests of the consumer, the appropriate remedy is not to attack the sellers' policies (i.e., the behavior elements).[18] Rather, it is to restructure the market by, for example, disallowing mergers, forcing sellers to divest assets, and lowering entry barriers. Obviously, such a remedy is likely to be more threatening and costly to a seller than being told to adjust "behavior" by developing an alternative pricing, distribution, or other policy.

The nonstructural approach sees structure, behavior, and performance related in this way:

Structure → Performance ← Behavior
↑
Government

Here structural elements are still acknowledged as affecting sellers' performance, but they no longer hold the status of prime movers. Rather, when there is a problem with, for example, pricing, the presumption is not that its most efficient remedy is found in restructuring the market. Instead, something like a redesign of specific agreements between the seller and its suppliers or buyers might be seen as a superior remedy. Also according to the nonstructural position, a merger between two competitors that significantly raises concentration in a market need not necessarily lead to a net decline in performance.

An additional feature often associated with the nonstructural approach is doubt about the likely net benefit to performance from government intervention into market processes. All other things equal, this doubt leads to a preference for market-heal-thyself solutions over intervention. Accordingly, a nonstructuralist would be expected to prefer a less aggressive formal pursuit of antitrust enforcement than would a structuralist.

Given this distinction, Harvard School-type economic arguments are seen as tending to lean in the structuralist direction.[19] Relative to the Chicago School approach, greater emphasis is placed on market structure and the effects of product differentiation, entry barriers, vertical restraints, mergers, monopolization, imperfect information, and other departures from purely competitive environments. As a result, the Harvard School approach is seen as more aggressive than the Chicago School approach in its pursuit of monopolization, mergers, vertical restraints, and other structural issues.

Also, the Harvard School position may appear less doctrinaire than the Chicago School attitude because it is not as obviously grounded in a specific political/economic philosophy as is the Chicago School with its signature free market position. As a result, the Harvard School attitude may be seen as more accepting of real world departures from theory and willing to acknowledge the complexity of specific situations.

The Chicago School Approach

Several widely recognized names are associated with the Chicago School, for example, Robert Bork, William Posner, and George Stigler. Stigler and his followers played a major role in attacking the structuralist approach by questioning whether firms in any market can effectively agree on prices, the likelihood that a seller with a large market share would necessarily exercise monopoly power, and other structural positions.[20]

Contrary to the structuralist approach, the Chicago School starts from the premise that markets are strong and tend to have efficient outcomes if left unrestricted because consumers are well-informed maximizers. Also, well-operating capital markets help offset start-up costs for potential entrants attracted to markets offering excess profits. As a result, the Chicago School sees concerns about market imperfections as exaggerated. They also see the possibility that there might be welfare-enhancing efficiency effects resulting from high concentration, mergers, vertical arrangements, and other factors presumed destructive to welfare using the structural approach.[21] Consequently, the Chicago School can be described as favoring a less aggressive approach to antitrust enforcement than the Harvard School: An approach that can be characterized as "don't intervene if the conduct of sellers is not provably inefficient."[22]

There are two aspects of the Chicago School focus on efficiency that bear mention. First, and as will be discussed shortly, efficiency ranks ahead of inhibiting wealth transfers from consumers to producers in the school's list of antitrust's goals. Second, and related to the nonstructuralist concern over the effect of government intervention on performance, followers of the Chicago School are skeptical about the extent to which government intervention and private lawsuits improve efficiency in markets. Government interveners might face pressure from special interest groups; judges might not have the resources to effectively and accurately second-guess the market, and private plaintiffs might sue to recover damages resulting not from predatory use of monopoly power, but from active competition by an efficient competitor with a large market share.[23] Such a noninterventionist view, it can be argued, comes down to the position that private monopoly can be superior to public regulation, and is supportive of a libertarian or conservative position.[24]

In closing this section it should be noted that while there are clear differences between the Harvard and Chicago School approaches to antitrust, over the last twenty years those differences have lessened as both sides have moderated their positions. The courts have tended to follow the Chicago School on some matters, such as dealing with vertical nonprice restraints, while siding more closely with Harvard School analysis in areas such as merger law. In a few instances, courts have also recognized post-Chicago principles, such as the impact of imperfect information on the analysis of market definition and power. A recent review of the two schools by Hovenkamp concludes that judicial doctrine has tracked the Harvard position somewhat more closely than the Chicago position, though the two have moved closer together on many issues.[25]

Goals of Antitrust Enforcement

Judge Robert Bork observed that if antitrust policy is to be rational, there must be a clear understanding of its goals. Unfortunately, the list of goals in antitrust enforcement is not cast in stone. Some argue that both Congress and the courts have supported a variety of goals. Others argue that the only goal Congress had in mind when passing the Sherman Act was maintaining allocative efficiency, and even if this was not Congress's sole intent, it should be the primary goal when interpreting the law.[26]

For those in the multiple-goals camp, several classifications have been offered. Legal scholar Eleanor Fox has suggested dispersion of economic power, freedom and opportunity to compete on merits, consumer satisfaction, and protection of the competitive process governing markets. The historian Richard Hofstadter grouped goals into three categories: producing efficiency through competition (an economic goal), blocking the accumulation of power and protecting democratic government (a political goal), and supporting the development of people's character and competitiveness (a social/moral goal).[27] For our purposes, goals will be placed within two broad categories: economic and noneconomic. Within the economic category are three subcategories: maintaining interfirm competition, efficiency, and consumer welfare.

Economic Goals

Maintaining Interfirm Competition

Some have argued that the goal of antitrust enforcement is to protect and maintain competition among firms in markets. On close inspection, however, maintaining competition appears to be more of an intermediate goal, or means to an end, than an end in itself. This is because competition-as-goal arguments tend to go on to say that its importance rests in its role in increasing society's material welfare or, more specifically, promoting efficiency and consumer welfare.[28] Thus, the lion's share of attention toward economic goals is devoted to efficiency and consumer welfare, unfortunately, according to some observers, without there being a clear consensus as to what each means.[29]

Efficiency

At the extreme, and associated largely with the neoclassical and Chicago School approaches, is the position that efficiency is all that matters in antitrust enforcement. Often accompanying this position is the argument that maintaining efficiency and controlling distributional effects on consumer welfare from sellers' behavior are separate goals, and that distributional effects of actions that increase efficiency should be ignored.[30]

The earlier discussion of the neoclassical approach to antitrust introduced two subcategories into which efficiency can be placed: Allocative efficiency, where goods and services go to those who value them most; and productive efficiency, where goods and services are produced using the least-cost method of production. To these can be added a third category: innovative efficiency.

Figure 5.1 **Monopolization and Consumer Surplus**

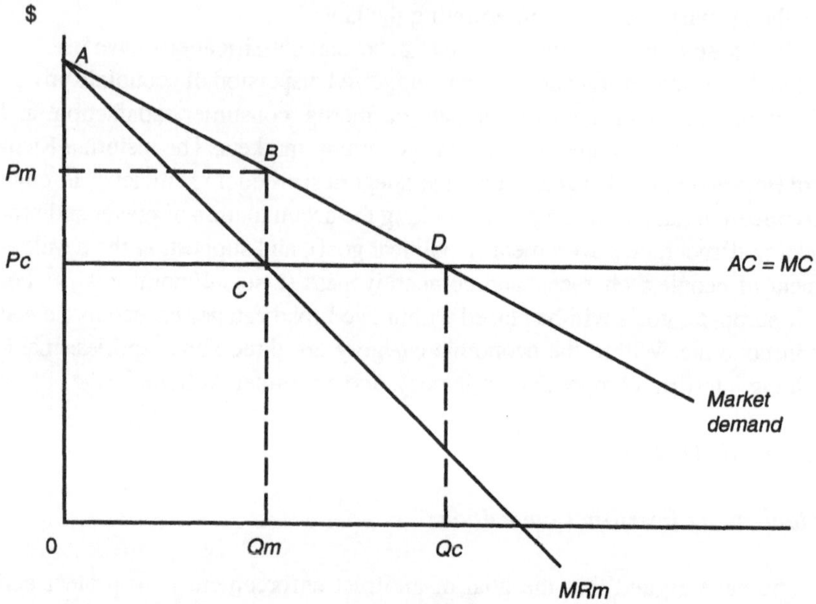

Here the focus is on increasing social wealth through the invention, development, and diffusion of new products.[31]

Of the three categories, economists have tended to pay most attention to allocative efficiency.[32] The loss of allocative efficiency resulting from the movement of a market from competitive to monopolized is measured by the deadweight loss of consumer surplus as a result of that transition. Briefly, consumer surplus is the difference between how much consumers *value* a particular amount of a product and how much they *pay* to acquire that amount. Typically, consumer surplus and its loss due to monopolization is illustrated in a manner similar to that in Figure 5.1.[33]

The figure assumes sellers' costs are constant, so that at any level of output average cost (*AC*), equals marginal cost (*MC*). If the market is competitive, it goes into equilibrium at an output of *Qc* and a price of *Pc* because, at this output, *Pc* = *MC*. But because *MC* = *AC* with constant costs, *Pc* also equals *AC* at this level of output. Consequently, the sellers' revenues cover all costs (including opportunity cost), normal profits are earned, and there is a consumer surplus shown by the area *PcAD*.

Were the sellers to form a monopoly, its profit maximizing output would be *Qm*, where *MRm* (the monopolist's marginal revenue) = *MC*. At this output, price is *Pm* and the consumer surplus is reduced to *PmAB*. The lost consumer surplus shown by the area *BCD* is the allocative inefficiency, or deadweight loss of the transition from a competitive to a monopolized market. It is deadweight in the sense that it is not a redistribution of a surplus from consumers to the monopoly seller as a result of the price increase. Rather, it is the consumer surplus that had been generated by the outputs from Qm to Qc, which are no longer produced as a result of the transition to monopoly.

While economists' primary focus may be on allocative efficiency, it has been argued that this focus is misdirected. For one thing, empirical research suggests that deadweight losses are relatively small. Harburger, in 1954, conducted a study that concluded that removing deadweight loss would lead to a less than one-tenth of 1 percent gain in total output.[34] Other more recent studies have come to similar conclusions. Building on that research, Scherer argues that antitrust enforcement is of little consequence if the only concern is allocative efficiency. Rather, the focus should be on productive and technological efficiency.[35]

Consumer Welfare

According to Brodley, "The term consumer welfare is the most abused term in modern antitrust analysis." It has been made synonymous with efficiency. It has been used to refer to particular consumer interests without defining what those interests are. It has been used rhetorically to support one position over another.[36] Here we focus on two dimensions of consumer welfare: distributional effects of anticompetitive acts and consumer choice.

The appropriate treatment by the antitrust laws of distributional effects of anticompetitive acts is open to debate. On one side is the view, associated with Bork and others, that Congress's intent in passing the antitrust laws was to maximize consumer welfare by maximizing efficiency. According to this position, consumer welfare excludes any concern over the distribution of wealth, and wealth redistribution is not an appropriate focus of antitrust because to argue for a particular distribution requires a value judgment whose basis can be challenged.[37] On the other side is the view that the main concern of Congress in passing the antitrust laws was unfair transfers of wealth. Its objective was not to define a "fair" distribution or to aid the poor but, rather, to prevent a type of wealth transfer seen as inequitable and to promote a distribution that would result from the operation of competitive markets.[38]

A typical mechanism for evaluating the distributional effects of anticompetitive acts is to construct a social welfare function along the following lines:

$$\text{Social Welfare} = (\text{consumer surplus} + \text{producer surplus}),$$

where producer surplus equals total revenue minus total cost, or economic profit from producing.

The distributional effect of going from a competitive to a monopolized market can be seen by returning to Figure 5.1. Following the price increase from *Pc* to *Pm*, there is a deadweight loss of consumer surplus equal to the area *BCD*. But this is only part of the loss the consumers incur. Prior to the market reorganization, consumer surplus was *PcAD*. Following the reorganization, it is *PmAB*. In addition to the deadweight loss is a loss of consumer surplus equal to the area *PcPmBC*. This represents the transfer of consumer surplus to profit following the now combined sellers' ability to raise price from *Pc* to *Pm*. While the social welfare loss from the reorganization is relatively small (the consumer surplus that became deadweight loss rather than profit), the redistributional effects appear to be significant, having gone from (*PcAD* [consumer surplus] + 0 [producer surplus]), to (*PmAB* [consumer surplus] + *PcPmBC* [producer surplus]). In the case in Figure 5.1, consumer surplus drops by approximately 75 percent.

Consumer choice, the second approach to consumer welfare, has as its objective that buyers be free to choose from among real options. Its aim is to ensure that consumer demand, not government directives or the preferences of individual business people, guides the economy. The consumer choice approach is argued to be superior to the efficiency or distribution approaches for guiding antitrust because efficiency and price analyses are not well designed for dealing with nonquantitative considerations, such as the value placed by buyers on having options.[39] Also, the consumer choice approach is broader in its perspective on consumer welfare than is the distribution approach because it embodies notions about individual rights in society. The approach has been described as an implicit part of the Western response to Marxism and other twentieth-century totalitarian viewpoints, which moves us to an analysis of noneconomic goals of antitrust enforcement.[40]

Noneconomic Goals

Noneconomic antitrust goals are those not focused on maintaining competition for its own sake, efficiency, or consumer welfare. They have been described as "populist," and include fairness, dispersion of economic power (and through that, support of democratic society), and protection of small businesses.[41] Like the distributional effects of anticompetitive acts, the place of noneconomic goals in antitrust enforcement is open to debate. On one hand, Lande holds that one purpose of Congress in passing the antitrust laws was to support decentralized economic, social, and political decisionmaking to ensure that private interests not prevail over the public good resulting from competition.[42] Also, Averitt and Lande characterize the pre-1975 period of enforcement as one where big business was suspect and the short-term welfare of small businesses and decentralized decisionmaking were prioritized above economic efficiency.[43]

On the other hand, Areeda and Hovenkamp describe noneconomic goals as incoherent and indefensible. An example of this argued incoherence is the question of whether an interest group such as "small sellers" can be defined with enough precision to prevent policies designed to benefit the group from harming some of its members. For instance, should a defendant with a substantial market share be sanctioned if its cost-reducing strategy weakens the competitive positions of small, relatively inefficient rivals? Also, what if the defendant's low-cost operation allows its small buyers to lower their costs and prices because of reduced input prices?[44]

As with the Harvard and Chicago School approaches, the above should not be taken to suggest that there are two, irreconcilable sides to the debate over the role of noneconomic goals in antitrust enforcement. There is also a middle ground that acknowledges that the pursuit of economic goals might also result in the attainment of noneconomic goals. For example, antitrust policies that attack monopolies resulting from something other than improved efficiency, scale economies, or superior skill stand to benefit small competitors.[45]

The Effects of Economic Perspective on Antitrust Enforcement

The existence of alternate economic approaches to antitrust enforcement, combined with a lack of agreement on which specific goals should be pursued or how they should be ranked, gives rise to several controversies. Here we focus on three controversies involving the relationship of efficiency and consumer welfare, the protection of small sellers, and the protection of democracy.

Efficiency and Consumer Welfare

The question of how efficiency and consumer welfare are to be ranked is a frequent source of debate in the literature on the economic goals of antitrust enforcement. One's position on this debate can be largely anticipated if he or she is an acknowledged supporter of the neoclassical approach or, especially, the Chicago School approach.

Consider, for example, the Chicago School. As noted at different points in the preceding discussion, its position is that efficiency matters most and distributive effects on consumer welfare from antitrust violations matter less, if at all. Also noted were several arguments on which this position rests: first, that Congress's intention in passing the antitrust laws was to protect consumer welfare by maximizing efficiency; second, that wealth distribution should not be a concern when pursuing consumer welfare because such a concern presupposes a challengeable value judgment on how wealth should be distributed; third, that a focus on efficiency does protect consumers because practices harmful to consumers, such as price fixing and cartels, would be condemned on grounds of their inefficiency.[46]

To these can be added arguments such as the neoclassical view that consumers are rational maximizers who do not need an intervener deciding distributional matters on their behalf; that economists typically do not judge the desirability of alternative income or wealth allocations among different groups; and that a focus on redistribution is inappropriate because there is nothing in the statutory language or history that gives criteria for making decisions concerning allocations.[47]

Perhaps the relative importance given to wealth redistribution in antitrust enforcement by the Chicago School is best summed up by Scherer, who writes:

> The maintenance of price above cost . . . redistributes wealth from consumers to producers. . . . In the standard analysis of efficiency, this redistribution is of no concern. It merely reflects a robbing of Peter (the consumer) to pay Paul (the producer), and since Paul might be more deserving than Peter, who knows whether society is worse off as a consequence? . . . So why all the furor about antitrust?
>
> There are several answers. One is that antitrust should be concerned with wealth redistribution, not just with deadweight loss triangles. This is a sufficiently unfashionable view that I put it to the side.[48]

Do redistribution concerns deserve little or no attention in antitrust enforcement? Under what circumstances would an exclusive focus on efficiency have positive or neutral redistributive effects for the consumer? In theory, such circumstances can be found.

One is illustrated in Figure 5.2, which builds on the deadweight loss analysis in Figure 5.1. Here $ACc = MCc$ represents sellers' average and marginal costs when the market is competitive. As in Figure 5.1, in this competitive situation, market supply and demand are equal at a price of Pc and quantity of Qc, consumer surplus is $PcAB$, and, because price equals average cost, sellers earn only a normal profit.

Suppose now that the sellers form a monopoly, and because of efficiencies resulting from scope economies or other operational improvements, the monopolist's average and marginal costs fall to $ACm = MCm$. Here the mo-

Figure 5.2 **Where Monopolization Increases Efficiency and Consumer Surplus**

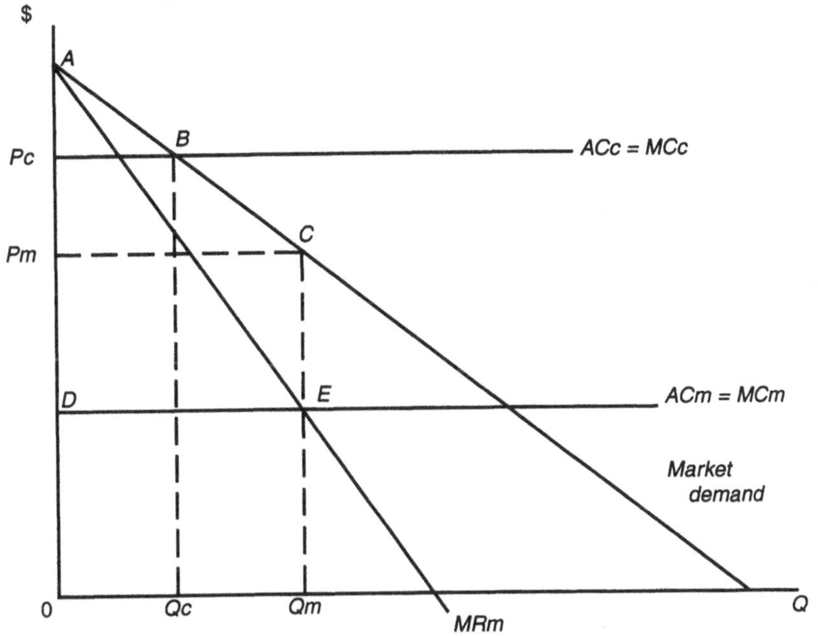

nopolist maximizes its profit by selling *Qm* units of output at a price of *Pm*.

The monopolist clearly benefits significantly from the reorganization and resulting efficiency gain. Whereas the firms comprising the monopoly were previously earning only normal profits, following the reorganization there is excess or economic profit shown by the area *DPmCE*.

But the gain to the monopolist in no way comes at the expense of consumers. In fact, the efficiency gain increases consumer welfare. For one thing, there is no conversion of consumer surplus into deadweight loss because the efficiency gain allows the output to increase from *Qc* to *Qm*. Also, and more directly related to the efficiency/distribution question, the efficiency gain allows the price to fall from *Pc* to *Pm*, with a resulting increase in consumer surplus from *PcAB* to *PmAC*.

While such a gain is possible in theory, the question remains, is it certain to occur? If the answer is no, a follow-up question is: Then what is the effect on consumer surplus of smaller gains in efficiency? Consider the situation in Figure 5.3.

As before, in Figure 5.3, *ACc* and *MCc* represent sellers' average and marginal costs before the market transitions from competitive to monopolized, and *ACm*, *MCm* represent their average and marginal costs after the

Figure 5.3 **Where Monopolization Increases Efficiency but *Not* Consumer Surplus**

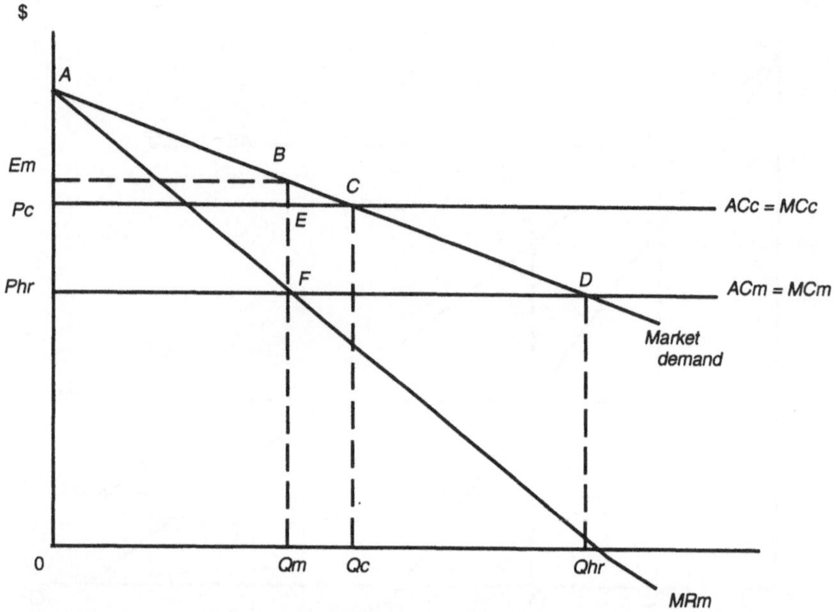

transition. *Pc* and *Qc* represent the price and quantity offered in the competitive market, and *PcAC* represents consumer surplus. Following the reorganization, the market price is *Pm* and the output is *Qm*. As shown by the relative positions of the competitive and monopoly average and marginal cost curves, the market has become more efficient as a result of the transition.

At first glance it appears that consumer welfare has been hurt in two ways by this transition to an efficient monopoly. First, unlike the case in Figure 5.2, the improvement in efficiency is not enough to allow output to increase, or even stay at *Qc*. Rather, output falls to *Qm*, with the consequent appearance of a deadweight loss of consumer surplus equal to *BCE*. Second, and again unlike the case in Figure 5.2, there is a redistribution of wealth from consumer surplus to profit equal to the area *PcPmBE*. The combined effect of these consequences of the transformation is that consumer surplus falls from *PcAC* to *PmAB*. Consumer welfare could improve from this level, however, if the market were contestable.[49]

A contestable market is one that is susceptible to "hit-and-run entry." That is, barriers to entry into and exit from the market are not sufficient to keep potential competitors from entering, capturing excess profit, and leaving. If the market were contestable, price would fall from *Pm* to *Phr* (where *hr* stands for hit-and-run), and output would increase from *Qm* to *Qhr*. As a result, the deadweight loss and all excess profit would disappear and consumer surplus would increase to *PhrAD*. Thus, in theory, even an efficient reorganization of a market that initially leads to a deadweight loss and redistribution from consumers to sellers has the potential ultimately to create a net benefit for the consumer. But to this argument can be responded, what is the likelihood of a monopolized market being vulnerable to hit-and-run entry?

Additional issues can be raised about an exclusive efficiency focus. For one, the pro-efficiency critique that intervention aimed at distributional effects of monopolies or mergers requires value judgments can be countered with the argument that focusing on efficiency also requires a value judgment because it calls for a ranking of consumers' and sellers' rights when establishing criteria for when to intervene against an efficient monopolist.[50] Another issue is that while the efficiency model is based on there being a rational consumer, that consumer may be hampered in responding to a monopolist because of sunk costs, imperfect information, and other market failures.[51] Finally, the Chicago School definitions of efficiency and consumer welfare are said to be based on a notion of *social* wealth equal to consumer surplus plus profit, rather than the more narrow definition of consumer welfare illustrated in Figures 5.1 through 5.3. This notion of social wealth supports a position that antitrust enforcement is called for only in cases where market conduct is provably inefficient and *aggregate* welfare is decreased.[52]

While there are clear arguments to be made against the neoclassical/Chicago School prioritizing of efficiency above consumer surplus and clear alternatives to these two approaches, several questions demand consideration before recommending that the approaches be modified. First, what are the different balances between efficiency and consumer surplus from which to choose? For example, do we take an extreme neoclassical/Chicago School stance and dismiss consumer welfare for the sake of efficiency? Do we go to the other extreme and treat near-term interests of consumers as the primary or sole objective of antitrust enforcement? Do we find a middle ground between the two extremes, and, if so, what is it to be?[53] Second, what criteria do we use when choosing among the options, and how are these criteria informed by explicit or implied values on matters such as whose rights are to be honored? Third, will moving to an alternative approach from what currently prevails end the debate, or simply reframe it?

Protecting Small Sellers

The noneconomic antitrust goal of protecting small sellers had statutory support from the 1930s through the 1970s. In 1937 Congress passed the Miller-Tydings Act, which amended the Sherman Act by allowing vertical price fixing, or "resale price maintenance," where manufacturers would set minimum prices below which independent distributors could not sell their products. This, in principle, would keep these distributors from underpricing their small competitors and driving them out of business. In 1952 the McGuire Act further amended the Sherman Act by holding that once a resale price maintenance agreement had been made between a manufacturer and a distributor, competing distributors were bound by its terms regardless of whether or not they too entered into such an agreement. In 1975 both amendments to the Sherman Act were repealed.[54]

Why this move away from protecting the small seller? One explanation traces back to the neoclassical/Chicago School preference for efficiency. Specifically, there could be significant adverse welfare effects from allocative inefficiencies and deadweight losses resulting from an enforcement policy that tolerates agreements to keep prices at or above designated minimum levels to protect relatively inefficient firms?[55] Another explanation builds on Joseph Schumpeter's metaphor of "creative destruction," wherein innovating firms enrich the standard of living through the introduction of new products and processes that have destructive effects on the businesses whose products or processes they replace. This too comes down to an efficiency/consumer welfare argument against protecting smaller sellers from larger firms that are vehicles for change that benefits the consumer.[56]

A third explanation is that to give priority to protecting this group is consistent with Marxian doctrine, and to speak of the Marxian foundations of antitrust enforcement would likely be seen by most as an oxymoron. Specifically, Marx describes the ultimate undoing of capitalism as resulting from capitalists seeking to lower their costs by replacing workers with machines. The result is that the released workers are forced into the "reserve army of the unemployed," causing total spending to fall because of their reduced earnings from which to make purchases. This, in turn, causes smaller businesses to fail—sending their workers and owners alike into the reserve army of unemployed as well. The process continues in a series of worsening crises until the capitalist system finally collapses.[57]

Providing antitrust protection to the small seller presumes that a value can be placed on that seller's presence in the market. That value could stem from something unique about the individual seller, such as his or her hard work or devotion to community service. More likely, though, the value would stem from a conviction that protecting the small seller is necessary for the attainment of broader economic, political, or social stability goals. If the latter is the case, one can argue that enforcement of the antitrust laws in a way that acknowledges the need to protect small sellers is sympathetic to Marxian doctrine.

Protecting Democracy

As noted above, a defining feature of the Chicago School is its skepticism about the efficiency of government intervention into markets.[58] This view, with its consequent preference for restraint in antitrust enforcement, at first appears consistent with the Chicago School's larger laissez-faire stance on the role of government in general. But is it?

One consequence of accepting mergers or other moves toward monopoly justified on efficiency grounds is that there will be a smaller than otherwise group of individuals with a larger than otherwise store of economic resources with which to pursue agendas of their choosing. On this, Justice William O. Douglas remarked:

> Power that controls the economy should be in the hands of elected representatives of the people, not in the hands of an industrial oligarchy. Industrial power should be decentralized . . . so that the fortunes of the people will not be dependent on the whim or caprice, the political prejudices, the emotional stability of a few self-appointed men. The fact that they are not vicious men but respectable and social-minded is irrelevant. That is the philosophy and command of the Sherman Act.[59]

Likewise, Senator John Sherman warned: "[I]f we will not endure a king as a political power, we should not endure a king over the production, transportation, and sale of any of the necessaries of life. If we would not submit to an emperor, we should not submit to an autocrat of trade, with power to prevent competition and to fix the price of any commodity."[60] Thus, the question can be asked: Why should a monopolizing businessperson's power to limit consumers' choices be tolerated when similar power in the hands of a government official is not?

One response to this question is that a tolerance for efficiency-increasing monopolies is not a license allowing businesses to exercise power over consumers that would be condemned were it exercised by government officials. For one thing, mergers or monopolies that do not lead to or result from economies of scale or other efficiency-enhancing opportunities would continue to be attacked. Also, if the goal of dispersing economic power were taken literally, it would lead to the condemnation of mergers and other activities that increase a firm's market share, regardless of their effects on efficiency and consumer choice. Finally, it can be asked whether a policy enforcing the dispersion of economic power would lead to a class of businesses whose survival depends on legislative or judicial protection. If so, would the effect be to increase the government's role in the operation of markets?[61]

Conclusion

In 1988, F.E. Banks wrote: "The difference between science and economics is that science aims at an understanding of the behaviour of nature, while economics is involved with an understanding of the behaviour of models—and many of these models have no relation to any state of nature that has ever existed on this planet, or any that is likely between now and doomsday."[62] It appears that this opinion, or one similar, has had an impact on the acceptability of economic input into antitrust proceedings. The Supreme Court, in *Daubert v. Merrell Dow Pharmaceuticals* established standards for the admissibility of expert testimony. Based on these standards, and the 1999 Supreme Court decision in *Kumho Tire Co., Ltd v. Carmichael*, federal district courts have been excluding what they perceive to be unreliable economic testimony. In the years immediately following *Kumho*, virtually every district court's exclusion of an economist's testimony in an antitrust matter has been affirmed on review by the circuit court.[63]

Does this imply that economics no longer has anything to contribute to antitrust analysis and enforcement? Clearly, this is not the case: History suggests that economics' impact on analysis and enforcement is felt far beyond the presence or absence of an expert witness. Rather, what it infers is that there may be a reaction to the fact that economic analysis is not separable from specific perspectives, and that those perspectives play a key role in determining how that analysis is used in arriving at legislative or judicial responses to antitrust problems. This further suggests the need for a greater awareness and understanding of alternative economic viewpoints on antitrust enforcement and their implications for that enforcement.

Notes

1. Adam Smith, *The Wealth of Nations*, 147, 128.

2. For example, see Robert Lande, "Wealth Transfers as the Original and Primary Concern of Antitrust: The Efficiency Interpretation Challenged," 877, *n*24.

3. See William Kovacic and Carl Shapiro, "Antitrust Policy: A Century of Economic and Legal Thinking," 43; Lande, 886.

4. Jonathan Baker, "A Preface to Post-Chicago Antitrust," 2.

5. Richard Posner and Frank Easterbrook, *Antitrust: Cases, Economic Notes and Other Material*, 18, 93.

6. Ken Rankin, "'Modernized' Antitrust Policies Could Affect American Retail," 14.

7. William Kovacic and Carl Shapiro, 43, 58; Andrew Rosenfield, "The Use of Economics in Antitrust Litigation and Counseling," 52.

8. Phillip Areeda and Herbert Hovenkamp, *Antitrust Law*, 118–19.

9. John Flynn and James Ponsoldt, "Legal Reasoning and the Jurisprudence of

Vertical Restraints: The Limitations of Neoclassical Economic Analysis in the Resolution of Antitrust Disputes," 1145.

10. Lande, 953.

11. Flynn and Ponsoldt, 1151, 1152.

12. Warren Samuels, "Normative Premises in Regulatory Theory," 101.

13. Areeda and Hovenkamp, 133–34. See also Kovacic and Shapiro, 55, and Flynn and Ponsoldt, 1130–31. There is also what is called the Post-Chicago Synthesis that follows the earlier approaches but is not covered here. See Kovacic and Shapiro, 55–58.

14. See Walter Adams and James Brock, *Antitrust Economics on Trial*, for a cleaver treatment of the neoclassical and Chicago School approaches to antitrust; and Ross Singleton, *Industrial Organization and Antitrust*, for a treatment of alternative views on economic perspectives on antitrust.

15. Flynn and Ponsoldt, 1137, including *n*50.

16. Warren Samuels,, "Can Neoclassical Economics Be Social Economics?" 1–2; Areeda and Hovenkamp, 119–20.

17. Samuels, "Can Neoclassical Economics Be Social Economics?" 3–4; Flynn and Ponsoldt, 1130–31, 1131, *n*20, 1135, 1137.

18. Deadweight loss is the disappearance of consumer surplus (rather than its redistribution to the seller) following an increase in price and decrease in output of the good being consumed. Deadweight loss is explored more fully below. X-inefficiency refers to a business not producing up to the potential of its set of resources. There is some discussion of the relationship of x-inefficiency to the degree of competitiveness in the market in which an x-inefficient firm resides. For more on x-inefficiency, see Donald Hay and Derek Morris, *Industrial Economics and Organization*, 44–47, 585–86.

19. The comments on the Harvard School approach are based on Areeda and Hovenkamp, 135–37.

20. Baker, 11–13.

21. Areeda and Hovenkamp, 133–34; Kovacic and Shapiro, 53–54.

22. Eleanor Fox, "What Is Harm to Competition? Exclusionary Practices and Anticompetitive Effects," 377–78.

23. Areeda and Hovenkamp, 135.

24. Fox, 379; Ingril Rima, "Can Neoclassical Economics Be Social Economics?" 9–10.

25. Herbert Hovenkamp, "Book Review: The Rationalization of Antitrust," 917–44.

26. Flynn and Ponsoldt, 1136–37; Lande, 873, *n*2, 910–11; Rosenfield, 49.

27. Flynn and Ponsoldt, 1138; Lande, 873, *n*5.

28. Joseph Brodley, "The Economic Goals of Antitrust: Efficiency, Consumer Welfare, and Technological Progress," 1023; Walter Adams and James Brock, "Antitrust and Efficiency: A Comment," 1116.

29. Brodley, 1120–21.

30. Neil Averitt and Robert Lande, "'Consumer Price' Becomes 'Consumer Choice': Antitrust Moves Toward a New Model," 6; Lande, 873, *n*2; James Ponsoldt, "Letters to the Editor: On the Docket: Robert Bork," 3.

31. Brodley, 1025.

32. Ibid., 1025; Rosenfield, 52; F.M. Scherer, "Antitrust, Efficiency, and Progress," 998.

33. See, for example, Scherer, 998–99; Oz Shy, *Industrial Organization*, 68–69; Jean Tirole, *The Theory of Industrial Organization*, 66–68.

34. Arnold Harburger, "Monopoly and Resource Allocation," 84, 87. Questions have been raised about how Harburger's methodology might have biased his results. See Tirole, 68, *n*5.

35. Scherer, 1002.

36. Brodley, 1032.

37. Flynn and Ponsoldt, 1131–32; Lande, 873, *n*2, 892.

38. Lande, 875.

39. Averitt and Lande, 9–18; Robert Lande, "Consumer Choice as the Ultimate Goal of Antitrust," 503.

40. Lande, "Consumer Choice as the Ultimate Goal of Antitrust," 503.

41. Areeda and Hovenkamp, 107–8; Flynn and Ponsoldt, 1138; Lande, "Wealth Transfers as the Original and Primary Concern of Antitrust," 873, n.2, 892–93.

42. Lande, "Wealth Transfers as the Original and Primary Concern of Antitrust," 911.

43. Averitt and Lande, 4–5.

44. Areeda and Hovenkamp, 100–2.

45. Ibid, 107–8; Brodley, 1021.

46. Averitt and Lande, 6; Flynn and Ponsoldt, 1131–32, 1136; Lande, "Wealth Transfers as the Original and Primary Concern of Antitrust," 873, *n*2, 892–93.

47. Areeda and Hovenkamp, 116; Lande, "Wealth Transfers as the Original and Primary Concern of Antitrust," 892; Rosenfield, 52.

48. Scherer, 998–99.

49. See William Baumol, John Panzer and Robert Willig, *Contestable Markets and the Theory of Industry Structure.*

50. See Samuels, "Normative Premises in Regulatory Theory," 108–10.

51. Lande, "Consumer Choice as the Ultimate Goal of Antitrust," 505–06, *n*9.

52. Fox, 377–79; Ponsoldt, "Letters to the Editor," 3.

53. Brodley, 1035–38.

54. S. Chesterfield Oppenheim, Glen Weston, and J. Thomas McCarthy, *Federal Antitrust Laws*, 548–49.

55. Averitt and Lande, 4–5.

56. Joseph Schumpeter, *Capitalism, Socialism and Democracy*, 82–83.

57. Robert Friedman, ed., *Marx on Economics*, 185, 193, 200–1.

58. Areeda and Hovenkamp, 135; Flynn and Ponsoldt, 1135.

59. Adams and Brock, 1117, *n*2.

60. Lande, "Wealth Transfers as the Original and Primary Concern of Antitrust," 904, *n*136.

61. Areeda and Hovenkamp, 104, 107–8.

62. F.E. Banks, "Learned Sophistry," 74.

63. Robert Badal and Edward Slizewski, "Economic Testimony Under Fire," 56.

References

Adams, W., and J.W. Brock. "Antitrust and Efficiency: A Comment." *New York University Law Review* 62, no. 5 (November 1987): 116–24.

———. *Antitrust Economics on Trial.* Princeton, NJ: Princeton University Press, 1991.

Areeda, P.E., and H. Hovenkamp. *Antitrust Law.* Vol. I. New York: Aspen Law and Business, 1991.

Averitt, N.W., and R.H. Lande. "'Consumer Price' Becomes 'Consumer Choice': Antitrust Moves Toward a New Model." Unpublished manuscript.

Badal, R.G., and E.J. Slizewski. "Economic Testimony Under Fire." *ABA Journal* 87 (November 2001): 56. ABI/Inform (Proquest).

Baker, J.B. "A Preface to Post-Chicago Antitrust." In *Post-Chicago Developments in Antitrust Law,* ed. R. van den Bergh, R. Pardolesi, and A. Cucinotta. Northampton, MA: Edward Elgar, 2003.

Banks, F.E. "Learned Sophistry." *Adbusters* 1, no. 3 (May 1990): 74.

Baumol, W.J., J.C. Panzer, and R.D. Willig. *Contestable Markets and the Theory of Industrial Structure.* San Diego: Harcourt, Brace, Jovanovich, 1988.

Brodley, J.F. "The Economic Goals of Antitrust: Efficiency, Consumer Welfare, and Technological Progress." *New York University Law Review* 62, no. 5 (November 1987): 1020–53.

Flynn, J. J., and J. F. Ponsoldt. "Legal Reasoning and the Jurisprudence of Vertical Restraints: The Limitations of Neoclassical Economic Analysis in the Resolution of Antitrust Disputes." *New York University Law Review* 62 (November 1987): 1125–52.

Fox, E.M. "What Is Harm to Competition? Exclusionary Practices and Anticompetitive Effects." *Antitrust Law Journal* 70, no. 2 (2002): 371–411.

Friedman, R., ed. *Marx on Economics.* New York: Harvest Books, 1961.

Harburger, A. "Monopoly and Resource Allocation." *American Economic Review* 44, no. 2 (1954): 77–87.

Hay, D.A., and D.J. Morris. *Industrial Economics and Organization.* New York: Oxford University Press, 1991.

Hovenkamp, H. "Book Review: The Rationalization of Antitrust." *Harvard Law Review* 116, no. 3 (January 2003): 917–44.

Kovacic, W.E., and C. Shapiro. "Antitrust Policy: A Century of Economic and Legal Thinking." *Journal of Economic Perspectives* 14, no. 1 (Winter 2000): 43–60.

Lande, R.H. "Wealth Transfers as the Original and Primary Concern of Antitrust: The Efficiency Interpretation Challenged." *Hastings Law Review* 50 (April 1999): 871–957.

———. "Consumer Choice as the Ultimate Goal of Antitrust." *University of Pittsburgh Law Review* 62, no. 3 (Spring 2001): 503–25.

Oppenheim, S.C., G.E. Weston, and J.T. McCarthy. *Federal Antitrust Laws.* St. Paul, MN: West Publishing, 1981.

Ponsoldt, J.F. "Letters to the Editor: On the Docket: Robert Bork." *The Wall Street Journal*, September 24, 1987, 2–3.

Posner, R.A., and F. H. Easterbrook. *Antitrust: Cases, Economic Notes and Other Materials.* St. Paul: West Publishing, 1981.

Rankin, K. "'Modernized' Antitrust Policies Could Affect American Retail." *DSN Retailing Today,* October 28, 2002, 14. ABI/Inform (Proquest).

Rima, I. "Can Neoclassical Economics Be Social Economics?" *Forum for Social Economics* 26, no. 1 (Fall 1996): 5–13.

Rosenfield, A.M. "The Use of Economics in Antitrust Litigation and Counseling." *Columbia Business Law Review* 1 (1986): 49–82.

Samuels, W.J. "Can Neoclassical Economics Be Social Economics?" *Forum for Social Economics* 26, no. 1 (Fall 1996): 1–4.

———. "Normative Premises in Regulatory Theory." *Journal of Post Keynesian Economics* 1, no. 1 (Fall 1978): 100–14.

Scherer, F.M. "Antitrust, Efficiency, and Progress." *New York University Law Review* 62, no. 5 (November 1987): 998–1019.
Schumpeter, J.A. *Capitalism, Socialism and Democracy.* New York: Harper and Brothers, 1947.
Shy, O. *Industrial Organization.* Cambridge, MA: MIT Press, 1995.
Singleton, R.C. *Industrial Organization and Antitrust.* Columbus, OH: Publishing Horizons, 1986.
Smith, A. *The Wealth of Nations*. New York: Modern Library, 1937.
Tirole, J. *The Theory of Industrial Organization.* Cambridge, MA: MIT Press, 1988.

Part 3

Legal Issues Concerning Natural Resources, the Environment, and Land Use

6

A Comparative Institutional Approach to Law and Economics

Theory and Applications—The Environment, Natural Resources, and Land Use

Nicholas Mercuro

> *Man, as a social being, has a degree of control over his future destiny. Today and yesterday are* irretrievably gone. *But the future can be of his own making. If one were to take a purposeful, a moral look at the future and ask himself, ask his generation, "What do we want to do with it?" he would find that meaningful alternatives were available. But only if we make a clearly defined choice regarding the moral assumption we choose to use. And* that *is the moral imperative for members of the economics profession. The only alternative is one of laissez-faire indifference. And the consequence of that moral position, for laissez-faire is equally a moral position, will be that meaningful alternatives are not made available and known to society.*
>
> —Kendall P. Cochran, "Economics as a Moral Science"[1]

Introduction

It is with respect to a desire to predict the potential consequences of a proposed public policy—here, environmental, natural resource, and land-use policies—that a need arises for a comparative institutional approach to legal-economic analysis. The purpose of this chapter is to explore how a comparative institutional approach to law and economics can help make the meaningful alternatives known to society. The driving force behind such an approach is the need to come to grips with the interrelations between legal and economic processes and, thus, consistent with the thrust of old and new institutional economics, institutional structure cannot merely be assumed away or taken as given.[2] Rather, it must be the subject of study involving a comparison of the effects of institutional alternatives on our environment, natural resources, and use of land—on our social well-being.

Stages of Choice

The selection or establishment of a specific set of institutions, and thus the character of life in a society, is the product of choice. Nobel Prize laureate James M. Buchanan emphasized this fact years ago when he observed that:

> Man must look to *all* institutions as potentially improvable. Man must adopt the attitude that he can control his fate; he must accept the necessity of choosing. He must look on himself as a man, not another animal, and upon civilization, as if it is of his own making.[3]

In contemplating the structure of its governing institutions, a nation must be concerned with (1) those institutional structures that will help promote cooperation among parties of interest, (2) those that will help channel conflicts among individuals and interest groups in society, and (3) those that will help accomplish change. The focus here will be on three different stages of choice.

First, it becomes necessary to describe and understand the emergence of the most basic social contract. This can be termed the *constitutional stage of choice*, the laying out of the fundamental behavioral rules that bind people together, based, in part, on the society's values and morals. The behavior rules are subject to both reinterpretation and incremental revision. Second, it is essential to describe and understand both the structuring and the restructuring of the decision-making processes of the political-legal institutions—the so-called *institutional stage of choice*. Here the focus is on the adoption of or the revision of the working rules and legal doctrines. Finally, the consequent impacts of altering the legal relations governing society must be analyzed—what is here termed the *economic impact stage of choice*.[4] This involves describing the economic impacts of revised legal relations governing society, be they in the form of private property rights, status rights, communal property, and/or open-access resources. In the process of formulating environmental, natural resource, and land-use policies, most of those advocating for a comparative institutional approach have divided their labors across three different stages of choice (see Figure 6.1).

The comparative institutional approach consists of describing and analyzing

Figure 6.1 **Stages of Choice**

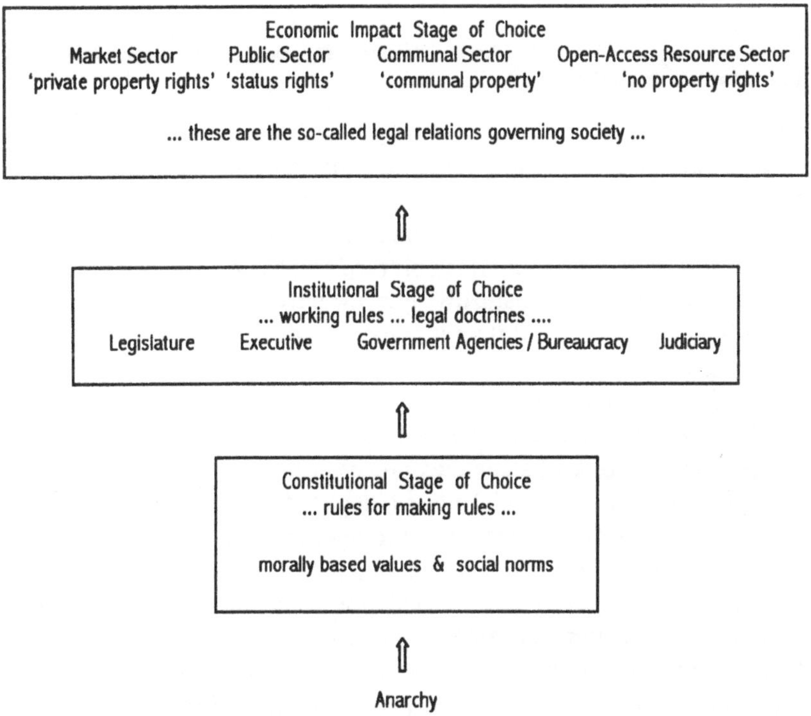

the systematic relationship between (1) the structure of political-legal-economic institutions, focusing on the rights, rules, and doctrines by which they operate; (2) the conduct or observed behavior in light of the prevailing social norms as well as the incentives (penalties and rewards) created by the structure of institutions; and (3) the consequent economic performance specific to those norms and institutions. Within this familiar structure-conduct-performance paradigm, the object, then, is to explain and compare the outcomes that will occur under real, discrete, alternative institutional structures. The underlying logic inherent in the conceptual model portrayed by Figure 6.2 is that public policy involves altering the law, that is, changing the constitution, altering working rules or legal doctrines, or refashioning the various legal relations governing society and thereby deciding which resources will come under which system of social control—the market sector using private property rights, the public sector using status rights, the communal sector using communal property, or just leaving resources as open-access resources. The belief is that the goals of public policy being sought—in particular here, environmental, natural resource, and land-use policy—will not

Figure 6.2 **Legal Centralism**

Δ *law* Δ *rights*
Δ *working rules* Δ *legal doctrines* → Δ *incentive structure* → Δ *behavior* → Δ *economic performance*
Δ *legal relations governing society*

come about by changing law or drafting regulations willy-nilly or in an ad hoc manner, but by structuring and adopting those laws, rights, rules, and doctrines for which there is a known nexus between the said change in law and the consequent outcome. This nexus constitutes the so-called *legal centralist* line of reasoning where it is observed that a change in law (as broadly defined above) will systematically alter incentives, which alters behavior, and with that, results in a different outcome—that is, a different economic performance.[5]

Of course, in reality, the logic of causation described above is more complex than the legal-centralist approach indicates (see Figure 6.3). First, law is, in part, the outcome of a complex process whose evolution is inspired by morally-based values and social norms (depicted by the vertical arrow going from social norms and values up to the law) that are embedded in a long tradition of political and legal thought that help form law. Second, behavior is affected by technology that expands the choice set for production and consumption.[6] And third, behavior is also a function of both (a) the structure of societal norms, customs, and mores that induce certain patterns of preference formation that impact economic performance, and (b) the morally-based values that influence or regulate conduct, either working independently of social norms, working together with social norms, or by giving rise to an array of social norms, customs, and mores. For example the socialization process (broadly conceived as the combined impacts of education, religion, the ongoing absorption of family and cultural values, peer behavior, etc.) may also explain why some may not pollute the environment, why others do not waste resources, or why some do not use their land in an exploitive manner. Consequently, proponents of the social norm literature argue for the inclusion of social norms to develop more robust explanations of behavior and to predict more accurately the effects of changing law (this literature is outlined briefly below in the section titled, "Preference Determining Social Norms, Customs, and Mores").

From the vantage point of Figure 6.3, not only are social norms and technology incorporated into the analysis, but so too is the recognition that as economic performance unfolds, as consumer demand shifts, as technologies change, as new resources are discovered and/or old ones move toward depletion, and as competition ensues, as new opportunities arise while past successes dwindle . . . the economy changes over time. In a dynamic economy

Figure 6.3 **Legal Centralism-Extended**

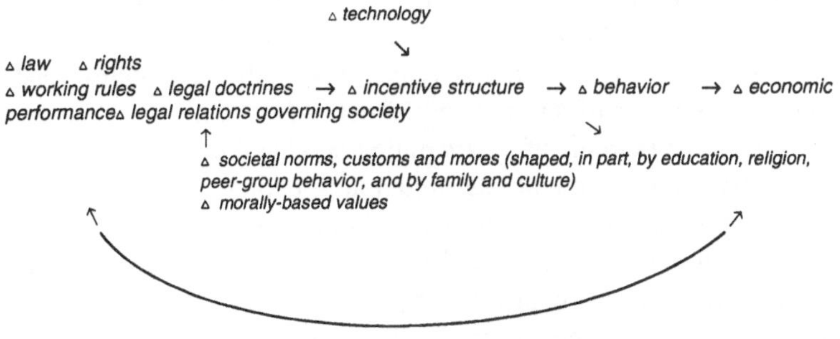

there is a reverse link going from economic performance back to the law; that is, new economic circumstances will invite new calls for additional changes in law-policy initiatives. The following section describes more fully what is involved in the three stages of choice described in Figure 6.1 above.

Constitutional Stage of Choice

At the most general level, a society is confronted with questions as to what will be the nature of its underlying constitution—the constitutional stage of choice—recognizing that the social contract that binds people together is always subject to reinterpretation and revision. In order to understand the nature of the choices necessary at the constitutional stage, it is useful to start by thinking about a society in a conceptual state of anarchy. In such a state individuals will contemplate the opportunity costs associated with the protective-defensive resource diversions that are necessary and essential for life under a system of anarchy. Once they recognize the potential prospects for improvement in the character of their economic life that would become possible by establishing a social contract or constitution, they will enter into some form of social contract or formally adopt a constitution. In so doing, the individuals will seek to spell out the behavioral limits of what is and what is not mutually acceptable conduct by laying out the so-called *rules for making rules*.[7]

Because constitutions are not immutable, the methods by which constitutional rules can be revised are also developed at this level of choice. Although altering an established constitution is typically thought to have only a subtle effect on the allocation and distribution of resources; as subtle as it may be, the impact cannot be ignored. Further, the relationships among emergent political-legal institutions are also partially resolved at the constitutional stage of choice. Society must know which institutions will prevail over others in the making of public policy or changing law, for example, and which particular system of checks and balances is in effect. Of course, a constitution is not typically thought of as a primary vehicle for implementing public policy. Nonetheless, some courts have included the U.S. Constitution in the policy mix. For example, Judge J. Rendlen in *Eyerman* argued that public policy has no one, unique origin and wrote: "Public policy may be found in the Constitution, statutes, and judicial decisions of this state or the nation."[8]

An interesting example of public policy making through the Constitution was over the issue of judicial interpretation in takings issue cases. Unsatisfied with the direction of court decisions in takings litigation, the Mackinac Center for Public Policy located in Midland, Michigan, argued that the judiciary can and should be controlled, by providing it with clearer guidance, particularly in land-use cases. While the state of Michigan could have followed the lead of several other states and passed a state statute, the Center, instead, drafted and offered a constitutional amendment to Article X, Section 2 (of the Michigan Constitution) in an attempt to limit the judiciary's power to ignore private property rights and to combat the courts' unwillingness to compensate partial or regulatory takings.[9] One revision would have altered the clause to read that the property shall not be "taken or damaged" without just compensation. Including "damaged" would have made restrictions on uses of property compensable, recognizing that while property is not actually transferred to the state in regulatory takings, the bundle of rights inherent in property is damaged by restrictions on its use. Another proposed change was to revise the clause to read property shall not be "taken, in whole or in part," thus ensuring that partial takings are compensable under the Constitution. Similarly, a separate section was to be added to explicitly deal with regulatory takings and deprivations of uses of property thereby trying to prevent deprivations of property uses without compensation and to ensure that individual property owners are not forced to bear the full cost of a regulation or action intended to benefit all of society.[10] This example serves only to make the point that the constitution may be used as a vehicle to pursue public policy goals.

Once a constitution is framed, it will then provide the basis for the emergence of a broad assemblage of political-legal-economic institutions that will more directly affect the allocation of resources in society. The structuring of these institutions constitutes the institutional stage of choice.

The Institutional Stage of Choice

The second stage of choice—the institutional stage of choice—centers on the structure of the *state,* by which is meant a nation's political-legal-economic institutions. At this stage of choice, it is the inner workings of the several branches of government that are at center stage, including the institutional working rules of government and the judicial legal doctrines. The rules and doctrines can and do have a direct bearing on the environment, natural resources, and land use.

Evolving Working Rules

The *working rules*—the complex set of rules that give rise to the institutional decision-making processes—adopted in (1) the executive branch, (2) the legislature, (3) the judiciary, and (4) across government agencies, departments, and commissions help shape the character of life in society. More often than not the decision-making processes of an institution are formally worked out by the institution itself in developing its own working rules (e.g., an institution's or agency's bylaws).

Two examples will help make clear the public policy nature of working rules. The first concerns a decision under the Clinton administration to significantly tighten wetlands regulations by phasing out the expedited permit procedure (under the purview of the Army Corps of Engineers). This permit procedure had allowed developers to drain tens of thousands of acres of wetlands, ten acres at a time.[11] Expedited permits, in effect, provided blanket approval for qualifying projects and allowed developers to avoid a prolonged application and burdensome review processes. Environmentalists and other federal agencies had complained that the quick procedure for getting the Corps' permission to develop wetlands, known as Nationwide Permit 26, had allowed the destruction of wetlands that absorb floodwaters and provide habitat for wildlife. It was shown that, under Permit 26, many different kinds of activities (sometimes in wetlands as big as seven football fields) could be used to gain swift project approval. In addition, under the new rules, the corps also took measures to prevent the past practice of "stacking" quick permits, an abuse wherein developers divided projects into small steps, each of them justified under a separate permit without a comprehensive review of the whole project. Additional concerns were raised regarding the level of adverse effects caused by the quick permits for separate projects being considered for authorization, especially when many permits were approved for projects in the same watershed.

While doing away with the one permit, the corps set in place another new working rule for expedited permits that developers could instead use. Under the new rule, a permit must specify a certain type of activity in wetlands, as well as spell out the conditions under which each activity can be approved without additional review. The new substitute permits would have a narrower scope and would serve as quick permits available for people who want to build a single home, draining less than half an acre of wetlands.

Another example of a change in working rules concerns grazing lands and the then Interior Secretary Bruce Babbitt's decision to give local interests, including ranchers and environmentalists, far more influence over cattle grazing on public land—some 270 million acres of public range-land in the West.[12] Before the new working rule was instituted, the local panels advising the Bureau of Land Management regarding grazing permits had been dominated by ranching interests. The change in working rules was an attempt to broaden the public's involvement in grazing decisions by constituting regional and advisory councils on which conservationists and ranchers would sit with local government officials and recreational users of public land. The new regional councils' purpose was to recommend grazing policies on which all sides could agree. The newly constituted councils would advise the government on such matters as how much livestock to allow on specific tracts, how to control damage caused by livestock on stream banks, and how to use grazing fees to improve the land.

From a policy standpoint, the primary difficulty in promulgating working rules lies in trying to design political-legal-economic institutions so as to provide the decisionmakers the proper incentives to correctly channel behavior so as to attain the desired performance. That is, the new working rule should be structured so as to enable society to provide the desired public goods or efficiently internalize negative externalities or resolve other instances of market failure. In the simplest of terms, "all bureaucracies are not created equal." With respect to the fashioning or the redesigning of working rules, much work remains to be done to identify which institutional structures go toward enhancing the efficiency of political-legal institutions in accomplishing their stated goals. There is no spontaneous mechanism within bureaucracies for ensuring that the working rules adopted by decisionmakers will necessarily be efficient. This problem is partially offset by the extent to which the selection of working rules are subject to benefit cost calculations—in such cases, some rules may be found to better conform to Kaldor-Hicks efficiency than others.[13]

Evolving Legal Doctrines

In a like manner, in common law, *legal doctrines* emerge as the judiciary, over time, decides cases and produces judge-made law. The common law is replete with examples that support the case for recognizing that in revising legal doctrines, judges do indeed "make the law." This observation-assertion does not require a unique or nuanced interpretation of existing cases; it simply requires an understanding of the judge's written word. A synoptic review of three cases should make the point. (There is full recognition that not all of these example cases, directly or indirectly, relate to environmental, natural resource, or land-use issues).

Charlotte Rosenberg v. Saul E. Lipnick & Another, Executors

Supreme Judicial Court of Massachusetts 377 Mass. 666 (1979)
[Text edited from the case as reported.]

Charlotte Rosenberg, the plaintiff, brought an action in the probate court against the executors of the estate of Perry Rosenberg, her deceased husband. Mrs. Rosenberg was seeking to have an antenuptial agreement that had been executed by her and her late husband invalidated and, thereby, have the court declare that she was entitled to her statutory share of his estate and a widow's allowance.

After the death of her husband, the master (appointed to the case) made findings of fact and concluded that the prenuptial agreement was valid and that the plaintiff was not entitled to a statutory share of the estate or to a widow's allowance. The probate court judge confirmed the master's report and entered judgment for the defendants. Both the master and the judge relied on the settled law of the state—the Wellington decision that was the undisturbed law in the Commonwealth of Massachusetts for over half a century. Under the rule of *Wellington v. Rugg*, 243 Mass. 30 (1922), a plaintiff seeking invalidation of an antenuptial agreement could not prevail in the absence of proof that her deceased husband either misrepresented or fraudulently concealed the extent of his assets prior to execution of the agreement. That is, in Massachusetts, the court held that a husband's simple failure voluntarily to disclose the value of his property prior to executing an antenuptial agreement was not sufficient to invalidate the antenuptial agreement.

The supreme court, acknowledged the master, found that the plaintiff failed to establish that the decedent either misrepresented or fraudulently concealed the extent of his assets prior to execution of the agreement. Following the rule in *Wellington*, the court affirmed the judgment for the defendants and then stated:

> [W]e have reviewed this case for error under the law as it existed in 1959. We have discerned none and thus affirm the judgment for the defendants. However, we take this opportunity to delineate new rules that shall apply to antenuptial agreements executed after the publication date of this opinion. . . . Although we agree that the *Wellington* principles should be abandoned, we do not think it wise to act retroactively.

The court went on to change the legal doctrine, observing that Massachusetts stood alone in requiring the party seeking invalidation of an antenuptial agreement to show fraud. The court recognized that while the lower court followed the *Wellington* case in the instant matter, it decided that the extent to which *Wellington* negates any duty of disclosure, the court should abandon that precedent in favor of the more enlightened rules of other jurisdictions, stating: "In future cases involving antenuptial agreements drawn after the date of this opinion, this court stated its intention to abandon the rule in *Wellington v. Rugg*, to the extent it negates any duty of disclosure and to hold that the parties by definition occupy a confidential relationship and that the burden of disclosure rests upon both of them."

Molitor v. Kaneland Community Unit District No. 302

Supreme Court of Illinois 163 N.E.2d 89 (1959)
[Text edited from the case as reported.]

Thomas Molitor, the father of Peter Molitor, brought an action against Kaneland Community Unit School District for personal injuries sustained by his son Peter in a school bus accident. Peter sustained severe, permanent burns and injuries as a result of defendant's negligence. Molitor asked for a judgment in the amount of $56,000. The appellate court affirmed the decision of the trial court, both ruling on behalf of the school district under the doctrine of immunity. Upon appeal, the Supreme Court of Illinois noted that, while it had adhered to the old immunity rule in the past, it had not reconsidered and re-evaluated the doctrine of immunity of school districts for over fifty years. It also made clear that over the years, the immunity doctrine had received exhaustive consideration by legal writers and scholars in articles and texts and, for the most part, was almost unanimously condemned.

In the end, the Supreme Court of Illinois adopted a new legal doctrine in concluding that the rule of school district tort immunity is unjust, unsupported by any valid reason, and has no rightful place in modern day society. In its consideration the court noted that the school district strongly urged that if the doctrine of immunity was to be abolished, it should be done by the legislature, not by the court. To this, the Supreme Court of Illinois stated:

> With this contention we must disagree. The doctrine of school district immunity was created by this court alone. Having found that doctrine to be unsound and unjust under present conditions, we consider that we have not only the power, but the duty, to abolish that immunity. . . . "We closed our courtroom doors without legislative help, and we can likewise open them." *Pierce v. Yakima Valley Memorial Hospital Ass'n*, 43 Wash.2d 162, 260 P.2d 765, 774. We have repeatedly held that the doctrine of *stare decisis* is not an inflexible rule requiring this court to blindly follow precedents and adhere to prior decisions, and that when it appears that public policy and social needs require a departure from prior decisions, it is our duty as a court of last resort to overrule those decisions and establish a rule consonant with our present day concepts of rights and justice (95).

Abraham Sommer v. James A. Kridel, Jr.

Supreme Court of New Jersey 74 N.J. 446 (1977)
[Text edited from the case as reported.]

The issue raised in this case was whether an apartment rental contract is binding on both parties, thereby not requiring the owner of the apartment unit to try to mitigate damages by re-renting the unit in the event a renter wants to "back out" of the contract. On March 10, 1972, the defendant, James Kridel (the renter), entered into a lease with the plaintiff, Abraham Sommer, to rent an apartment at the Pierre Apartments in Hackensack, New Jersey. The term of the lease was for two years starting from May 1, 1972. Although defendant had expected to begin occupancy around May 1, his plans were changed. Sommer sued and the trial judge ruled in favor of Kridel; thereafter the Appellate Division reversed and ruled on behalf of Sommer, concluding that the lease had been drawn to reflect *Joyce v. Bauman*—the "settled law" of the state of New Jersey.

The Supreme Court of New Jersey observed that this state has supported the rule that a landlord is under no duty to mitigate damages caused by a defaulting tenant (see *Joyce v. Bauman*). . . . The rule is based on principles of property law which equate a lease with a transfer of a property interest in the owner's estate. Under this rationale the lease conveys to a tenant an interest in the property which forecloses any control by the landlord; thus, it would be anomalous to require the landlord to concern himself with the tenant's abandonment of his own property. However, the Supreme Court of New Jersey then made new law holding that:

> [The] antiquated real property concept which served as the basis for the pre-existing rule, shall no longer be controlling where there is a claim for damages under a residential lease. Such claims must be governed by more modern notions of fairness and equity. . . . We now reverse and hold that a landlord does have an obligation to make a reasonable effort to mitigate damages in such a situation. We therefore overrule *Joyce v. Bauman* to the extent that it is inconsistent with our decision today.

Source Unknown

It has been written that:

> Ours is not a closed system of existing precedent. The law is not such a formal system at all. We [the United States Supreme Court] are not, as a court of last resort, absolutely bound by our own decisions. We legitimately made the law in question and can legitimately change it. *Courts must make*

> *law* [emphasis added]. Indeed courts are major policy makers in our system of government. We must be wary of petrifying the common law into a rigid system, utterly behind the times and totally at odds with the progress of science and social change.[14]

Thus, it is clear that specific public policy outcomes can be fought over at the institutional stage of choice either by altering working rules and/or by altering legal doctrine.[15] Of course, in an attempt to resolve environmental, natural resource, and land-use problems, one need not only rely solely on these two policy options; one could instead devote resources to alter social norms in an attempt to change behavior. This initiative is described more fully in the section titled "Preference Determining Social Norms, Customs, and Mores." But for now, it should be clear, as in the case of the constitution, the working rules and legal doctrines that undergird political-legal institutions are not set in stone but, rather, are themselves a response to economic needs and, as such, can and do undergo structural revisions. Such changes revise the decision-making processes of those institutions and alter institutional choices. These evolving institutions and the choices that emanate therefrom, directly impact the *legal relations governing a society*—the private property rights (within the market sector), the status rights (within the public sector), communal property (within the communal sector), and open-access resources. It is the choices as to the legal relations governing society to which we now turn by exploring the economic impact stage of choice inasmuch as it is this stage of choice that comprises the most prominent interface between economics and the law and has the greatest impact on environmental, natural resource, and land-use policy.

The Economic Impact Stage of Choice—The Legal Relations Governing Society

Conceptually, it is useful to begin with the notion of four distinct property right systems or regimes for organizing and controlling the allocation of society's scarce resources: (1) the market sector, (2) the public sector, (3) the communal sector, and (4) the open-access resource sector. Each one of these four sectors can be thought of as a distinct system of social control chosen to allocate society's scarce resources. Taken together, they comprise the legal relations governing society that define the limits of social behavior and, in so doing, determine what can and cannot be done by individuals and institutions in society. Initially here, each sector is treated as if it exists separate and apart from the other sectors. As will be seen, typically, all four systems operate contemporaneously to allocate resources in Western industrialized societies.

The Market Sector

In the pure market sector, all property rights are held privately as bundles of fee simple absolute rights. According to the conventional legal-economic definition of property rights, what is owned by individuals is not goods or resources but the rights to use goods and resources. Armen A. Alchian and Harold Demsetz stated, "What are owned are socially recognized rights of action."[16] Thus, as outlined by Tom Tietenberg in the pure market sector, property rights must have four characteristics.[17] They must be:

> *Universal:* All resources are privately owned and all entitlements completely specified.
> *Exclusive:* All benefits and costs accrued—as a result of owning and using the resources—should accrue to the owner and only to the owner, either directly or indirectly by sale to others.
> *Transferable:* All property rights should be transferable from one owner to another in a voluntary exchange.
> *Enforceable:* Property rights should be secure from involuntary seizure or encroachment by others.

When individuals in a society, acting through their political-legal institutions, make the choice to use the market as the preferred system of social control, they must, antecedently, use the state to define, assign, and enforce a structure of private property rights. Once this is accomplished, it is then possible for individuals to further enhance their welfare by specializing and engaging in exchange through trade or realigning the use of resources in production. This process of trade is conventionally viewed as a purely voluntary endeavor and, as characterized here, it is what transpires in the market sector. The voluntary nature of this market process is such that no individual will engage in a trade that leaves him worse off. The final allocative outcome will be arrived at once all the gains from trade have been exhausted in both exchange and production. Thus, given a set of defined private property rights and some given initial distribution of rights, barring externalities and the problem of public goods, one can expect, consistent with the duality theorem, the market outcome to provide a Pareto-efficient allocation of resources.[18]

It is important to emphasize that a market-sector allocation of resources is predicated upon the government-established and -enforced regime of private property rights; without government-sanctioned property rights to resources and goods, there would be no incentive to realign resource use and nothing to exchange on the market. The government selected and sanctioned structure of private property rights (hence the market) gains its legitimacy through the active role of government, *not* by government forbearance (this is more fully explored below in the section titled "Avoiding 'Single Institutionalism'").

The three examples offered here help to demonstrate that the market sector is being used as the preferred system of social control for some resources typically not thought of as "marketable"—air, water, and wetlands. The first and most widely known is that of the trading program for sulfur dioxide (SO_2) emissions. It is a clear example of a legislative initiative that is both an environmental and an economic success. The centerpiece of Title IV of the 1990 amendments to the Clean Air Act was the allowance trading program for SO_2. It has reduced annual emissions of SO_2 by nearly 50 percent and is doing so for about one-half to one-third of the cost that would have been incurred using the approach taken throughout the first twenty years of federal air pollution control. As observed by Dallas Burtaw, "The success of the SO_2 program comes as no surprise to many scholars. They predicted that the largest share of economic benefits from a trading program would come not from the trading of allowances per se, but from what economists call 'dynamic efficiency'—innovation, competition, and discovery of new ways of compliance."[19]

The second example concerns the growing market for water. Subsidized water storage and distribution systems and irrigation projects have contributed to a ninefold rise in water withdrawals from 1900 to 1970. They also contributed to the loss of tens of thousands of miles of once free-flowing streams. Water is becoming increasingly scarce in the United States. Demand is rising along with a growing population, larger incomes, and an enhanced appreciation for the services and amenities that streams, lakes, and other aquatic ecosystems have to offer. Market forces, however, have been slow to develop as a means of adapting to water scarcity.[20]

More recently, in the arid and semiarid West, where most of the senior water rights are held by farmers and irrigation districts, there is a growing impetus to move from lower to higher value use; this impetus serves as the driving force for water banks and water transfers (sometimes temporary, short-term leases, or options to purchase during dry periods, and one-time purchases through water banks). A water bank provides a clearinghouse to facilitate the pooling of surplus water rights for temporary rental. If well defined, its rules and procedures can reduce the costs and uncertainties associated with a transaction and increase the opportunities for both buyers and sellers.

Finally, the third example is that of wetland mitigation banking. Wetland mitigation is generally defined as off-site wetland restoration, creation, enhancement, and, in exceptional circumstances, preservation undertaken expressly for the purpose of mitigating unavoidable adverse wetland losses in advance of development actions.[21] The goal of the mitigation bank is to provide for the replacement of the chemical, physical, and biological functions of wetlands and other aquatic resources that are lost as a result of authorized impacts. This is accomplished through the sale of mitigation credits to permit applicants who are seeking off-site mitigation to offset on-site development activities. It is viewed as a flexible method for balancing the competing needs of private developers (ameliorating development impacts) and government regulators (promoting the government's no-net-loss policy). Essentially, the concept combines the mitigation needs of many permit applicants into one large off-site area. This area is developed as a wetland mitigation bank to compensate for wetland impacts from numerous development projects. For purposes of a comparative institutional approach, all three of these examples make clear that the market constitutes one possible system of social control in implementing environmental, natural resource, and land-use policies.

Public Sector

The public sector is yet another arena for organizing and controlling the allocation of resources in a society. In this idealized sector the allocation and distribution of all resources will be determined by the state. That is, when individuals in a society, acting through their political-legal institutions, make the choice to use the public sector as the preferred system of social control, they must then define and assign *status rights,* which are, in effect, eligibility requirements for individuals to gain access to goods and resources. Status rights are rights to goods and resources that are exclusive and nontransferable, and are provided to individuals at the discretion of either the local, the state, or the federal level of government (or typically, some combination thereof).[22] Thus, the state's promulgation and establishment of status rights for certain goods and service or factors of production may be conceived of as "government provision" in its broadest sense. As such, political-legal institutions are understood to make a broad spectrum of decisions that give rise to status rights—essentially that which transpires throughout today's modern administrative state.

Over the past thirty years most of the nation's environmental and natural resource policies have been implemented as status rights through the public sector—that is, society chooses to use the public sector as the dominant system of social control to allocate much of our nation's air, land, and water resources. In most instances this manifested itself in the so-called command and control/permit approaches. As a consequence, much of current environmental, natural resource, and land-use law constitutes, in one form or another, status rights or eligibility requirements that stipulate the exact procedures, requirements, and regulations that allow private, public, industrial, or commercial entities to use our air, land, and water resources.

With the public sector as the system of social control, the emergent structure of status rights has a direct impact on the allocation of society's scarce resources. However, unlike the market-sector resource allocations, there are no spontaneous mechanisms for ensuring that government decisionmakers will formulate public policies that yield economically efficient public-sector allocations. As was the case with working rules, this problem is partially offset by the extent to which public-sector decisions are based on benefit cost calculations—in such cases, public sector decisions can be said to approach a Kaldor-Hicks efficient allocation of resources.

Communal Sector

Individuals in a society, acting through their political-legal institutions, may decide that commodities or resources will be communally owned (*res communes*). In essence, common-property resources are private property owned by a group of co-owners. Under communal ownership a group of individuals would have the rights to use and transfer the resource.[23] Typically, a management group oversees the manner by which a common property resource can be used and reserves the right to exclude nonmembers. Depending upon the group rules used to manage the resource, communal property can result in an efficient allocation of resources.

The three examples offered here help to demonstrate where the communal sector has been used at the system of social control to allocate three scarce natural resources—lobsters, fish, and coral reefs. One species that lends itself well to common property control is the lobster.[24] In the Maine lobster fishery, lobstermen have formed so-called "harbor gangs" that mark territories and turn away outsiders. These gangs are often composed of members of a particular family or are long-standing members of the local community. As a result of this private group management, the lobstermen in these fisheries have higher catches, larger lobsters, and larger incomes than lobstermen who fish outside controlled areas. In two regions in Mexico—around Cozumel and Punta Allen—some fishery cooperatives have created common property regimes that limit access to the lobster fishery and assign rights to specific areas to specific fishers.[25] Members of these cooperatives set rules and restrictions on lobster harvests and enforce territorial boundaries called campos that are divided within the cooperative. Within these campos many lobstermen create artificial habitats for the lobsters. These habitats have made fishing easier and more productive by concentrating the lobsters and by reducing nonhuman predation.

Second, a very good fisheries example can be found in New Jersey. During the late 1970s and early 1980s, the Fishermen's Dock Cooperative of Point Pleasant developed a complex system of catch limits for two species that were critical to the fishery during the winter months and were subject to sharp price declines when the market was glutted.[26] The system met all of the criteria thought necessary for success in a common property regime: (1) only members of the cooperative were eligible; (2) they met regularly to make decisions and air grievances; (3) rights to sell through the cooperative were not transferable; (4) complex ways of administering the catch rules were created to handle differences in capital and skill while rewarding both and yet maintaining a sense of fairness; and (5) both monitoring and enforcement were relatively easy. The boats had to land their catches and follow the rules to stay in the co-op. The fishermen were effective in excluding outsiders and in limiting the fishing rights of insiders so that fish stocks were sustainable, prices were maintained, and the fishery was viable.

The third example concerns coral reefs in the South Pacific. In the past these reefs had suffered from destructive fishing practices such as fishing with dynamite or cyanide. However, these destructive practices are often proscribed in places where fishing rights are group-owned, for example, where reef tenure takes the form of ownership by a clan or family.[27] Under this rights structure, ownership often extends from the beach to the outer edge of the reef, sometimes even miles out to sea. It has been determined that village control over local marine resources is the surest indicator of reef health, suggesting that one of the most important attributes of successful common property management of marine resources is secure tenure.

Open-Access Resource Sector

Finally, individuals in a society, acting through their political-legal institutions, may decide that commodities or resources will be owned by no one, equally available to all (*res nullius*), and thus, will belong to the party to first exercise control over the resource. In this case there are no property rights to the resource. The resulting open-access allocation of the resource would be allocatively efficient only if supply exceeds demand at a zero price. If supply does not exceed demand at a zero price and society nonetheless retains the resource in open access, the resource will be overused.[28] There are only a few resources for which no rights formally exist—the atmosphere, the oceans (beyond stipulated boundaries from land), the international seabeds, outer space, and the Antarctica.[29] All of these resources, except the extent to which all-inclusive treaties are established and enforced, are subject to the 'tragedy of the commons.'

Typically, Western industrialized societies are structured so that resources are allocated, and the character of life is determined by all four systems of social control; that is, some of a nation's resources are channeled through the market sector, the public sector, and the communal sector, and some are left as open-access resources. The final combination of sectors selected is a result of individuals working through government to advance their individual and/or group interests with the relative scope and content of each of the systems of social control being the result of a collective determination of those who prevailed in choice-making processes in the political-legal arena.

Preference Determining Social Norms, Customs, and Mores

The contemporary study of social norms has become an important element of modern law and economics and, thus, must be incorporated into any study of comparative institutional analysis. While its inception is often attributed to Robert Ellickson's path-breaking book *Order Without Law* (1991), many other legal-economic scholars have contributed to the field.[30] Proponents of social norm literature argue for the inclusion of social norms into their analysis so as to develop more robust explanations of behavior and to predict more accurately the effects of changing law. Recall from Figure 6.2 the legal-centralist position primarily hinges on the recognition that law alters incentives and thereby channels the behavior of individuals in society through the threat of legal sanctions. For example, the prospect of higher civil fines or longer criminal jail sentences raises the "price" of conduct that violates the prevailing laws; this increased price reduces the frequency of various forms of undesired conduct, for example, polluting the environment. But as was alluded to earlier in the discussion of Figure 6.3, such behavior may also be induced by altering social norms.

For purposes of the brief exposition here, we will use Richard A. Posner's definition of a norm as "a rule that is neither promulgated by an official source, such as a court or a legislature, nor is enforced by the threat of legal sanctions, yet is regularly complied with."[31] That is, the literature identifies norms as informal social regularities that individuals feel a compulsion to follow either because of an internalized sense of duty or obligation, or because of a fear of external nonlegal sanctions, or both. Social norms signal to us what we should do under a given set of circumstances, and they are therefore obligatory upon those who wish to participate in the society that is at least partly constituted by such norms. Much of the legal-centralist approach distinguishes between social norms and law in terms of the subjects' compliance. That is, in the case of law, subjects comply under the will or sanction of the sovereign; in the case of norms, subjects comply under the will or sanction of the community. Thus, on this view, an individual complies with the law because the sovereign has told him to do so and will punish him if he does not; and will comply with social norms because the community has told him to do so—with a felt sense of obligation—because of the threat of punishment if he does not comply (e.g., by experiencing some psychic cost through a sense of "letting down the community").

Social norms appear to matter in legal analysis for many reasons—they can matter because (1) sometimes norms control individual behavior to the exclusion of law (e.g., the property norms ranchers seemed to follow in Shasta County[32]), (2) sometimes norms and law work together to influence behavior (e.g., to obligate tax paying or not to steal), and (3) sometimes norms and law influence each other (e.g., legally restricting public smoking may strengthen an antismoking norm, or antilittering laws may strengthen the norm to not litter).

An interesting application of "policy by social norming" once again concerns the proposed constitutional amendment intended to reform the takings law in the state of Michigan (described previously). That amendment was to be accompanied by a legislative bill that "would require *property-rights sensitivity training* (emphasis added) for the employees of the DNR [Michigan Department of Natural Resources] and the DEQ [Michigan Department of Environmental Quality]" in an attempt to alter the norms and, thus, their subsequent behavior and ultimately performance.[33]

In summary, from the logic of the conceptual model portrayed in Figure 6.3, it is clear that not only does the structure of rights, rules, and doctrines as well as technology affect behavior and thus economic performance, so too do societal norms, customs, and mores, by inducing certain patterns of preference formation that directly affects behavior (behavior that comports with the societal norms), and, in turn, affects economic performance. Those who confront environmental, natural resource, and/or land-use problems may sometimes fall victim to relying solely on one of these three factors in proposing remedies. For example, it is not all that unusual in policy debates to confront (1) proponents of "the technological fix," or (2) advocates of the market remedies favored by the supporters of Chicago Law and Economics, or (3) the social norm, nongovernmental organization (NGO) preachers calling for us to "do the right thing." Perhaps it is best to keep in mind what Garret Hardin reminded us in his seminal article:

> If the word responsibility is to be used at all, I suggest that it be used in the sense that Charles Frankel uses it. "Responsibility," says this philosopher, "is the product of definite social arrangements." Notice that Frankel calls for social arrangements—not propaganda.[34]

Further, once the roles of social norms are introduced into the equation, members of society confronting a variety of environmental, natural resource, and land-use problems cannot rely merely on "doing-the-right-thing" social norm propaganda. Here we must keep in mind what Cass Sunstein warns, that "a reference to social norms will become a conclusionary response to any apparently anomalous results."[35] This must be rejected. Within a comparative institutional approach, the quest must be to understand the role that social norms play in helping to order society (or social groups within the society) together with the role played by incentives promulgated by the state-sponsored legal change and with the impact brought on by changing technology and the ways in which the triad of law, social norms, and technology interact.

The Role of the Individual in the Complex Legal-Economic Arena

In the conceptual model depicted in Figure 6.3, the individuals within society are assumed to work to advance their interests within a pluralist democracy. Consequently, public policy (especially environmental, natural resource, and land-use policy) is determined, in large part, through the bargaining, negotiating, and, ultimately, compromising by various individuals and interest groups in society. Although the behavior of interest groups is not the sole force influencing the policy-making process, according to many scholars of American politics, individuals working through interest groups do have a significant impact on the policy outputs of American democracy. As V.O. Key once observed: "At bottom, group interests are the animating forces in the political process; an understanding of American politics requires a knowledge of the chief interests and their stake in public policy."[36] Indeed, in his book *The Governmental Process*, David Truman observed: "[Interest groups] are so intimately related to the daily functioning of those constitutionalized groups—legislature, chief executives, administrative agencies, and even courts—that make up the institutions of government that the latter cannot adequately be described if these relationships are not recognized as the weft of the fabric."[37]

Interest groups vary significantly in terms of their goals, size, organization, assets, and knowledge of what they are doing and how to reach their goals. In a pluralistic democracy the relative difference in the ability of interest groups' ability to prevail in the choice-making processes centers on several factors. Four are highlighted here. First, is the soundness of what they are trying to accomplish. Second is their ability to "make their case," which is a two-part process: (1) to clearly articulate the nexus between the proposed legal change, or new rule, or the public policy being sought and the specific goal they seek to attain; and (2) to persuade both their advocates and the skeptics that the implementation of the said legal change, rule change, or new public policy will not fall victim to "the law of unintended consequences." Third, not unrelated to the first, centers on each interest group's ability to raise the funds and garner many different types of resources to advance their cause. And, fourth, is their ability to access and use government (including all branches of government relevant to the policy goal being pursued) by lobbying the political structure and/or engaging in strategic litigation. Based on these four factors, different interest groups will have different levels of strength and influence as they attempt to impact the policy-making process at the constitutional, institutional, and economic-impact stages of choice.

Consistent with the options inherent within a pluralistic democracy, members of society, in attempting to promote their economic welfare or to pursue environmental, natural resource, or land-use policies, do not only promote different technologies and/or change social norms, but (as I hope the examples in each section helped to make clear) also act, both individually and collectively through interest groups, to revise the constitution, to structure and restructure the institutional working rules and legal doctrines, and to alter the legal relations governing society in the market, public, communal, or open-access resource sectors. All this is accomplished under the recognition that none of the norms, laws, rights, or rules are given immutably by nature but are themselves a response to economic needs and flexible in response to changes in those needs.

This recognition brings to the forefront the question, How should we think about the individual, the government, the economy, and property and their mutual impact on each other? The role of government in fashioning public policy (including environmental, natural resource, and land-use policy) involves much more than merely protecting private property and enhancing the role of markets. In all policy making there is an inevitable necessity of choice at all three stages of choice—in the legislature, in government agencies, and in the courts—where people have a say and where discretion is exercised in consideration of consequences. Constitutional provisions, working rules of the state, legal doctrines of the courts, and property rights are *not* rules, doctrines, and rights because they are preexisting but, rather, are rights and rules because they are advanced and protected through and by government (as the examples made clear). Law is not something that is given or to be discovered, but is instead a human artifact marked by deliberative and nondeliberative human choice at all three stages of choice where specific political-legal-economic outcomes are seen as an expression of the values of those who have participated and prevailed at each stage of choice in the political-legal-economic arena. In sum, they are an expression of those who were able to most effectively use government to further their own ends. The real world in which public policy is worked out was clearly described by Ralph Miliband. He wrote:

> More than ever before men now live in the shadow of the state. What they want to achieve, individually or in groups, now mainly depends on the state's sanction and support. But since that sanction and support are not bestowed indiscriminately, they must, ever more directly, seek to influence and shape it altogether. It is for the state's attention, or for its control, that men compete.[38]

Daniel Bromley characterized the essence of the choice to be made in environmental, natural resource, or land-use conflicts. He contends that it is wrong to take the view that government is somehow "interfering" with the wishes of the individual (or group) in the name of some nebulous concern for the "public interest." These disputes, he argues, are not between an individual or a group versus the government. The fact is, these "disputes [are] between the private interest of one party (Alpha) as against the private interest of another (Beta). Either the interests of Alpha will prevail, or the interests of Beta will prevail. . . . Both parties to a dispute will make a claim which they hope to have given protection as an entitlement by the state."[39] In this regard, he asserts that environmental, natural resource, or land-use "conflicts are more properly regarded as triadic matters; Alpha, Beta, and the state. To protect the interests of Alpha is to interfere with Beta, while to protect the interests of Beta is to interfere with Alpha. The state must do something, for to do nothing is to side with the party protected by the status quo property arrangement. One party's government interference is another party's liberation."[40]

Government thus becomes an object of control for those seeking either private or group legal-economic gain or advantage. As a consequence, the question is not, then, one of more versus less government but, rather, of whose interests government gives effect to through law. Such was the case when the conservative columnist (and now a Sunday morning "talking-head") George Will counseled conservative political operatives within the Reagan administration—Will's comments were in response to President Ronald Reagan's first address to the U.S. Congress, where the president had stated that "the taxing power of government must not be used to regulate the economy or bring about social change." Will observed:

> The choice of any tax program is a choice from a large universe of alternatives. Any tax program has special social consequences; it raises some

> revenues rather than others, encourages and discourages particular behavior. And rarely has there been a clearer, bolder, more self-conscious attempt than Reagan's to use the tax system as a lever for moving society in the direction of desired change. But American conservatives are addicted to the pose of hostility to government power, so they systematically misdescribe their own attempts to use government energetically. . . . When, Oh Lord, shall we be delivered from the conservatives' pretense that they, unlike liberals, do not believe in using government to promote their values through social change? If that were true, there would be no point in electing conservatives.[41]

Avoiding "Single Institutionalism"

A comparative institutional approach to law and economics must not fall victim to the tendency toward "single institutionalism."—narrowly advocating for public sector remedies or for private sector remedies. This is especially true in today's public policy environment where the call for privatization and for markets to allocate our environmental and natural resources is ubiquitous. To affirm solution by market as opposed to government, narrowly frames the issue *as if* the market was an alternative to government. This rhetorical device of framing the choice to be "the market versus the government" is a false dichotomy and is misleading in that government is omnipresent in all of the market's manifestations. Two points deserve attention.

First, an efficient market is predicted on well-defined, assigned, and enforced private property—hence property is a public fact. This has been clearly advanced by the philosopher John Taylor, arguing that property in anything depends not on Alpha's interests or claims but on the acknowledgment and forbearances of others; that is, property in a thing depends not upon Alpha's claim to it, but precisely upon others' readiness to admit Alpha's claim as privileged. He wrote:

> There lies the paradox of all property . . . for we have property only because first we consent to have community, and there is no greater mystification of human understanding than the belief that men establish community in order to preserve rights of property which they had apart from it. . . . Apart from [community] they have no property, and can have none. Outside of the bond of community a man owns nothing. . . . Private property is a public fact or it is no fact at all.[42]

Second, as I hope the examples made clear, the market sector remedies can exist only within the context of the constitutional laws, the surrounding working rules of the state, the prevailing legal doctrines and the rights structures sanctioned by government (as was evidenced in Figure 6.1). It makes little sense to speak of private-property based efficient market remedies as if devoid of government when the government is the predicate for the market sector and, hence, the market remedy. In fact, it is the government-selected, government-sanctioned, and government-enforced structure of private property rights that give rise to markets—the market sector is *niched within* a nation's political-legal institutions. The government is the means by which the market gains its status and legitimacy; the market exists through the active role of government, *not* by government forbearance. Indeed, to the extent that one is interested in advocating the market as the preferred system of social control, the real allocation mechanism is the *institutionalized market*. That is, within a comparative institutional approach, the focus must be on actual institutionalized markets and on describing the consequences of legal changes inherent therein.[43] Institutionalized markets are a function of the institutions (including the right and rules) and power structures that form and operate through them. From this vantage point the state stands as an essential complement to the market—the latter not an assumed superior substitute for the former. As George Will has counseled his fellow conservative travelers:

> [I] will remind everyone—some conservatives, painfully—that a mature capitalist economy is a government project. A properly functioning free market system does not spring spontaneously from society's soils as dandelions spring from suburban lawns. Rather *it is a complex creation of laws and mores* [emphasis added].[44]

Along the same lines, James Boyd White observed:

> From the point of view of the market and its proponents, the government is . . . an alien force, not expressing the judgment of the people, not constituting them as a polity, but interfering in their affairs. To talk about "governmental intervention," for example, is to implicitly assume that there is a pre-governmental state of nature called the market, into which government intrudes. *But this is obviously silly* [emphasis added].[45]

Indeed, the Institutionalist Clarence Ayres recognized this long ago in arguing that it was the organizational structure of society (read, the various stages of choice especially the economic-impact stage of choice) that determined the allocation and distribution of resources—not only the market. He wrote:

> The object of dissent is the conception of the market as the guiding mechanism of the economy, or more broadly, the conception of the

> economy as organized and guided by the market. *It simply is not true that scarce resources are allocated among alterative uses by the market* [emphasis added]. The real determinant of whatever allocation occurs in any society is the organizational structure of that society—in short, its institutions [at all three stages of choice]. . . . By focusing attention on the market mechanism, economists have ignored the real allocation mechanism.[46]

Thus, the issue is not, in the abstract, that the market sector (however institutionalized) is always to be the preferred system of social control over either the public sector, the communal sector or leaving resources in open-access. Little is learned by looking at instances of public sector failure and deciding that "the market sector" is the solution simply because market advocates think it may make matters better (what one may term *policy by conjecture*). As Ronald Coase has taught us, society bears high opportunity costs by "just looking at the market sector" or "just looking to the public sector" and conjecturing that its respective alternative is the policy to pursue.[47] Daniel Bromley concurred, writing that "conflicts over environmental policy arise whenever over-zealous economists claim that ubiquitous markets will solve all environmental problems, or when self-righteous planners and bureaucrats claim to know best about what should be done."[48] In fact, the issue is, Who is able to use government for what ends?—whether it is the natural resource and environmental interests or the land-use planners or the private and commercial developers. Whose opportunities are to be expanded (while others are diminished) by altering working rules or legal doctrines or by enhancing/diminishing the scope of the market, public, communal, or open-access vis-à-vis the other sectors?

A comparative institutional approach is dedicated to understanding the impact of new technologies, the impact that evolving social norms play, and the impact of changing incentives brought on by changing law in helping to order society, and the ways in which the triad of technology, social norms, and law interact with each other. Institutional alternatives are available whatever the public policy goal and the array of alternatives to be considered includes (1) the potential for constitutional change, (2) substituting new institutional working rules and legal doctrines for old ones, or (3) altering property rights (be they private, status, communal, or open-access resources) in the market, public, communal, or open-access resource sectors, respectively. A comparative institutional approach recognizes the multiplicity of potential solutions and underlying value premises; it attempts to flesh out what is actually going on by making clear the alternative possibilities that are open to society.

Notes

This chapter builds on and extends two earlier works—Nicholas Mercuro and Warren J. Samuels, "A Retrospective Interpretive Essay on the Diverse Approaches to the Fundamental Interrelationships Between Government and Property," 269–88; and Nicholas Mercuro, "Towards a Comparative Institutional Approach to the Study of Law and Economics," 1–26.

1. Kendall P. Cochran, "Economics as a Moral Science," 194.

2. For concise overviews of institutional economics, see Karl Pribram, *A History of Economic Reasoning;* and Henry William Spiegel, *The Growth of Economic Thought.* For overviews of new institutional economics, see Erik G. Furubotn and Rudolf Richter, *Institutions and Economic Theory;* and Erik G. Furubotn and Rudolf Richter, *The New Institutional Economics.*

3. James M. Buchanan, "Law and the Invisible Hand," 136.

4. The term *legal relations governing society* will be used throughout this chapter to collectively connote all four property rights' regimes: private property rights, status rights, communal property, plus open-access resources. The four rights regimes are presented in Daniel Bromley, *Environment and the Economy: Property Rights and Policy*, 14–40; Nicholas Mercuro, "The State & the Integration of Ecology, Law and Economics," 72–80. The four property rights' regimes are also described and applied in both Joanna Burger and Michael Gochfeld, "The Tragedy of the Commons 30 Years Later," 4–13 and 26–27; and in Elinor Ostrom et al., "Revisiting the Commons: Local Lessons, Global Challenges," 278–82.

5. The logic of *legal centralism* is inherent in A. Allan Schmid, *Property, Power, and Public Choice: An Inquiry into Law and Economics*; and A. Allan. Schmid, "Institutional Law and Economics," 33–51; see also Neil K. Komesar, "In Search of a General Approach to Legal Analysis: A Comparative Institutional Alternative," 1350–592; and Neil K. Komesar, *Imperfect Alternatives: Choosing Institutions in Law, Economics, and Public Policy.*

6. The role and impact of changing technology is not explored in this chapter.

7. Richard McKenzie and Gordon Tullock, *Modern Political Economy*, 75–90.

8. Judge Rendlen in *Eyerman v. Mercantile Trust Co.*, 524 S.W. 2nd 210 (1975), 217.

9. The account of this initiative relies entirely upon the description provided by Donald J. Kochan, *Reforming the Law of Takings in Michigan*, 19–20.

10. The proposed change, as recounted by Donald Kochan (ibid.) read: *Constitution of the State of Michigan of* 1963—*Article* X, *Section* 2:

> [P]rivate property shall not be taken for public use without just compensation therefore being first made or secured in a manner prescribed by law. Compensation shall be determined in proceeding of a court of record.
>
> *Suggested Constitutional Amendment*
>
> Article X, Section 2, shall be deleted. The following section shall be added to *Article I, The Declaration of Rights:*
>
> (a) Private property shall not be taken or damaged for public use without just compensation therefore being first made or secured in a manner prescribed by law. Compensation shall be determined in proceeding of a court of record.

(b) No owner shall be deprived of a use of property, or any part thereof, by governmental regulation or action that results in a non negligible reduction in fair market value without full compensation determined by a jury. No prior resort to administrative remedies shall be required. The court shall award reasonable attorney fees and costs to any prevailing owner.

11. The facts of this example are taken directly from John H. Cushman, "Corps Is Tightening Rules on Wetlands To Curb Developers," section A, 1.

12. The facts of this example are taken directly from John H. Cushman, "A Consensus Approach on Land Use," section 1, 8.

13. Kaldor-Hicks efficiency—the so-called compensation principle in economics—implies that society should adopt those legal changes that as a result of the change (1) income could have been redistributed after the change in the law so as to make everyone better off than before, and also, that (2) it was not possible to improve welfare before the legal change took place simply by redistributing income. A straightforward analysis is provided in Catherine M. Price, *Welfare Economics in Theory and Practice,* 19–30. This theory is the foundation of what is referred to as benefit-cost analysis and has recently manifested itself in U.S. Senate Bill 981—cited as the "Regulatory Improvement Act of 1997 with sponsors Senator Levin, Michigan (D) and Senator Thompson, Tennessee (R).

14. The source of the quote remains in question. It is cited twice in the legal literature, both incorrectly. As of this writing, I am still unable to locate the original source.

15. As to the evolution of legal doctrines in the common law, there is some evidence proffered by advocates of the Chicago School of Law and Economics that the common law tends to be efficient over time, though the matter remains unsettled; see Todd Zywicki, "The Rise and Fall of Efficiency in the Common Law."

16. Armen A. Alchian and Harold Demsetz, "The Property Right Paradigm," 17.

17. Tom Tietenberg, *Environmental and Natural Resource Economics*, 41.

18. The duality theorem—the proof that a perfectly competitive economy will yield an efficient allocation of resources—is concisely explained in Alan M. Feldman, *Welfare Economics and Social Choice Theory*, 1–4.

19. Dallas Burtraw, "Trading Emissions to Clean the Air," 3–6.

20. Kenneth D. Frederick, "Marketing Water: The Obstacles and the Impetus," 7–10.

21. Mark S. Dennison and James A. Schmid, *Wetland Mitigation: Mitigation Banking and Other Strategies for Development and Compliance.*

22. The use of the term status rights was first introduced by John H. Dales, "Rights in Economics," 149–55.

23. Bonnie J. McCay, "Common and Private Concerns," 111–26.

24. Michael DeAlessi, *Fishing for Solutions*, 18.

25. Ibid., 18–19.

26. McCay, "Common and Private Concerns," 118–19.

27. DeAlessi, *Fishing for Solutions*, 19–20.

28. This was the essence of the seminal article by Garrett Hardin, "The Tragedy of the Commons."

29. These several examples are described in Marvin S. Soroos, "Preserving the Atmosphere as a Global Commons."

30. Some recent books and articles that incorporate the analysis of social norms into the law and economics' literature include Eric Posner, *Law and Social Norms*;

Lawrence E. Mitchell, "Understanding Norms"; Robert D. Cooter, "Expressive Law and Economics"; Robert C. Ellickson, "Law and Economics Discovers Social Norms"; Richard M McAdams, "The Origin, Development, and Regulation of Norms"; Richard A. Posner, "Social Norms and the Law: An Economic Approach"; and Lawrence Lessig, "Social Meaning and Social Norms."

31. The law and economics literature often uses the term social norms as synonymous with ethical rules and moral rules; see Posner, ibid., 365.

32. This example is fully explored in Robert C. Ellickson's *Order Without Law.*

33. Described by Kochan, *Reforming the Law of Takings in Michigan*, 2.

34. Hardin, "The Tragedy of the Commons," 1247.

35. Cass Sunstein, "Social Norms and Social Roles," 945.

36. V.O. Key, *Politics, Parties, and Pressure Groups*, 17.

37. David Truman, *The Governmental Process*, 51.

38. Ralph Miliband, *The State and the Capitalist Society*, 1.

39. Bromley, *Environment and the Economy: Property Rights and Policy*, 19.

40. Ibid.

41. George Will, "Reaganism Is Not Quite Thatcherism," C7.

42. John Taylor, *The Masks of Society*, 108–9.

43. A discussion of institutionalized markets is contained in Steven G. Medema, Nicholas Mercuro, and Warren J. Samuels, "Institutional Law and Economics," 448–49 and is more fully developed in Nicholas Mercuro and Michael D. Kaplowitz, "Performance Indicators for Natural Resource and Environmental Policy: Contributions from American Institutional Law and Economics," 167–68.

44. George Will, "It's Time Bush Showed Anger Over Enron," 3.

45. James Boyd White, "Economics and Law: Two Cultures in Tension," 183.

46. Clarence E. Ayres, "Institutional Economics: Discussion," 26.

47. As Ronald Coase wrote in "The Problem of Social Cost," 18: "Satisfactory views on policy can only come from a patient study of how, in practice, the market, firms and governments handle this problem of harmful effects."

48. Bromley, *Environment and the Economy*, 20.

References

Alchian, A.A., and H. Demsetz. "The Property Right Paradigm." *Journal of Economic History* 33 (1973): 16–27.

Ayres, C.E. "Institutional Economics: Discussion." *American Economic Review* 47, no. 2 (May 1957): 13–27.

Bromley, D.W. *Environment and the Economy: Property Rights and Policy*. Cambridge, MA: Blackwell, 1991.

Buchanan, J.M. "Law and the Invisible Hand." In *The Interaction of Economics and the Law*, ed. Bernard H. Siegan, 27–38. Lexington, MA: Lexington Books, 1977.

Burger, J., and M. Gochfeld. "The Tragedy of the Commons 30 Years Later." *Environment* 40, no. 10 (December 1998): 4–13 and 26–27.

Burtraw, D. "Trading Emissions to Clean the Air." *Resources* (Winter 1996): 3–6.

Coase, R.H. "The Problem of Social Cost." *Journal of Law and Economics* 3 (1960): 1–44.

Cochran, K.P. "Economics as a Moral Science." *Review of Social Economy* 37, no. 2 (October 1974): 186–95.

Cooter, R.D. "Expressive Law and Economics." *Journal of Legal Studies* 27 (1998): 585–608.

Cushman, J.H. "Corps Is Tightening Rules on Wetlands to Curb Developers." *New York Times,* December 11, 1996, sec. A, 1.

———. "A Consensus Approach on Land Use." *New York Times*, February 19, 1994, sec. 1, 8.

Dales, J.H. "Rights in Economics." In *Perspectives on Property,* ed. G. Wunderlich and W.L. Gibson, 149–55. University Park, PA: Institute for Research on Land and Water Resources, Pennsylvania State University, 1972.

DeAlessi, M. *Fishing for Solutions*. London: Institute of Economic Affairs, Studies on the Environment, No. 11, 1998.

Dennison, M.S., and J.A. Schmid. *Wetland Mitigation: Mitigation Banking and Other Strategies for Development and Compliance*. Rockville, MD: Government Institutes, 1997.

Ellickson, R.C. "Law and Economics Discovers Social Norms." *Journal of Legal Studies* 27 (1998): 537–52.

———. *Order Without Law.* Cambridge, MA: Harvard University Press, 1991.

Feldman, A.M. *Welfare Economics and Social Choice Theory*. Boston: Martinus Nijhoff, 1980.

Frederick, K.D., "Marketing Water: The Obstacles and the Impetus." *Resources* (Summer 1998): 7–10.

Furubotn, E.G., and R. Richter. *Institutions and Economic Theory: The Contribution of the New Institutional Economics.* Ann Arbor: University of Michigan Press, 1998.

———. *The New Institutional Economics.* College Station: Texas A&M University Press, 1991.

Hardin, G. "The Tragedy of the Commons." *Science* 162 (1968): 1243–48.

Key, V.O. *Politics, Parties, and Pressure Groups.* New York: Thomas Y. Crowell, 1964.

Kochan, D.J. *Reforming the Law of Takings in Michigan.* Midland, MI: Mackinac Center for Public Policy, 1996.

Komesar, N.K. "In Search of a General Approach to Legal Analysis: A Comparative Institutional Alternative." *Michigan Law Review* 79 (1981): 1350–92.

———. *Imperfect Alternatives: Choosing Institutions in Law, Economics, and Public Policy.* Chicago: University of Chicago Press, 1994.

Lessig, L. "Social Meaning and Social Norms." *University of Pennsylvania Law Review* 144 (1996): 2181–89.

McAdams, R.H. "The Origin, Development, and Regulation of Norms." *Michigan Law Review* 96 (1997): 338–427.

McCay, B.J. "Common and Private Concerns." In *Rights to Nature,* ed. S. Hanna, C. Folke, and K.G. Maler, 111–26. Washington, DC: Island Press, 1996.

McKenzie, R., and G. Tullock. *Modern Political Economy*. New York: McGraw-Hill, 1978.

Medema, S. G., N. Mercuro, and W.J. Samuels, "Institutional Law and Economics." In *Encyclopedia of Law & Economics*, ed. B. Bouckaert and G. De Geest, 418–55. Cheltenham, UK: Edward Elgar, 1998.

Mercuro, N. "The State & the Integration of Ecology, Law and Economics." In *Ecology, Law and Economics*, ed. N. Mercuro, 71–94. Lanham, MD: University Press of America, 1997.

———. "Towards a Comparative Institutional Approach to the Study of Law and Economics." In *Law and Economics*, ed. N. Mercuro, 1–26. Boston: Kluwer Academic, 1989.

Mercuro, N., and M.D. Kaplowitz. "Performance Indicators for Natural Resource and Environmental Policy: Contributions from American Institutional Law and Economics." *Duke Environmental Law and Policy Forum* 11, no. 1 (Fall 2000): 139–72.

Mercuro, N., and W.J. Samuels, "A Retrospective Interpretive Essay on the Diverse Approaches to the Fundamental Interrelationships Between Government and Property." In *Fundamental Interrelationships Between Government and Property*, ed. N. Mercuro and W.J. Samuels, 269–288. Stamford, CT: JAI Press, 1999.

Miliband, R. *The State and the Capitalist Society.* London: Weidenfeld and Nicolson, 1969.

Mitchell, L.E. "Understanding Norms." *University of Toronto Law Journal* 49 (1999): 177–248.

Ostrom, E., J. Burger, C.B. Field, R.B. Norgaard, and D. Policansky, "Revisiting the Commons: Local Lessons, Global Challenges." *Science* (April 1999): 278–82.

Posner, E. *Law and Social Norms.* Cambridge, MA: Harvard University Press, 2000.

Posner, R.A. "Social Norms and the Law: An Economic Approach." *American Economic Review* 87 (1997): 365–69.

Pribram, K. *A History of Economic Reasoning.* Baltimore: Johns Hopkins University Press, 1983.

Price, C.M. *Welfare Economics in Theory and Practice.* London: Macmillan Press Ltd., 1977.

Schmid, A.A. *Property, Power, and Public Choice: An Inquiry into Law and Economics.* 2d ed. New York: Praeger, 1987.

———. "Institutional Law and Economics." *European Journal of Law and Economics* 1 (1994): 33–51.

Soroos, M.S. "Preserving the Atmosphere as a Global Commons." *Environment* 40 (March 1998): 7–13 and 32–35.

Spiegel, H.W. *The Growth of Economic Thought.* Durham, NC: Duke University Press, 1971.

Sunstein, C.R. "Social Norms and Social Roles." *Columbia Law Review* 96 (1996): 903–68.

Taylor, J.F.A. *The Masks of Society.* New York: Appleton, Century, Crofts, 1966.

Tietenberg, T. *Environmental and Natural Resource Economics.* New York: Harper Collins, 1996.

Truman, D. *The Governmental Process.* New York: Knopf, 1951.

White, J.B. "Economics and Law: Two Cultures in Tension." *Tennessee Law Review* 54 (1986): 161–202.

Will, G. "It's Time Bush Showed Anger Over Enron." *Jewish World News*, January 16, 2000, 3.

———. "Reaganism Is Not Quite Thatcherism." *Washington Post,* March 1, 1981, C7.

Zywicki, T.J. "The Rise and Fall of Efficiency in the Common Law." Law & Economics Working Paper, George Mason University School of Law, 2002, 1–82.

7

Property and Politics in the Hudson Valley

Continuity and Change in the Corporate Form

Ann Davis

Introduction

The original impetus for this chapter was the observation that scenery and farmland are being consumed at a rapid rate in the Hudson Valley, to the apparent dismay of local residents, policy makers, and leaders. Even a region so rich in cultural and historic assets appeared to be helpless in the onslaught of "suburban sprawl." The objective in this chapter is to define and analyze the institutional and historical contexts and to clarify the forces that lead to such an undesirable outcome. There is considerable irony in that 400 years of institutional development for the purposes of protecting property has led to loss of control of property in its most immediate sense, the land.

To begin, I propose the notion of property as a useful heuristic device for tracing institutional change across long periods of history.[1] I suggest that there is a history of property, with differential, shifting meanings over time, both ideological and institutional. Further, property is a convenient nexus with links to other key institutions, such as the state, the family, the market, and even personality.

A broad definition of property is a set of (social, legal, and market) relationships that represent (both valuation and jurisdiction), exchange, regulate, produce, and transmit across generations well-defined objects (which include labor, land, finance, and natural resources, as well as skills and ideas).

In the feudal period, the various dimensions of property were tightly woven into a coherent tapestry. Over time the threads have loosened into more of a web, with a single thread related to an entirely distinct, specialized institution. By starting with the quasi-feudal institutions in colonial New York, each strand can be more clearly identified and traced.

For example, the notion of land and sovereignty was once of a whole cloth, so to speak, which can be illustrated by Wesley Mitchell's discussion:

> Capitalism evolved slowly out of feudalism by the rise of novel practices, the exfoliation of concepts, and the formulation of new working rules by the courts. . . . Under William the Conqueror, the king's property was not distinguished from his sovereignty. . . . The idea of property in land was gradually separated from the idea of sovereignty by commuting the obligation of rendering military service to the king into the obligation of making money payments to him.[2]

The colony of New York was founded in the midst of this transition, and so provides a useful laboratory for exploring these changing relationships of sovereignty and property. In tracing the evolution of property institutions, I propose to follow the course of both land and sovereignty, since both are aspects of the organized collective action associated with property. In addition, the founders of the United States also placed significant weight on land and property in establishing rights of representation in formal governmental institutions, as in the bicameral legislature. I would argue that this type of "representation" of property in government is a significant aspect of the institution of property.

I shall analyze the change in property forms in one place, the Hudson Valley Region in New York State, where colonial corporations were reminiscent of feudalism and where the global market of the twenty-first century is still symbolized by "Wall Street" nearby. A discussion covering such a time span must be broad brush, but such a long-term view may be necessary to highlight key institutional transformations, which tend to emerge very slowly.

Property Institutions

The term "property" is often used as if the definition were precise and commonly understood. In fact, the types of property have been in flux continually, along with associated forms of governance and the economy. For example, the medieval town was a corporation encompassing common ownership of land as well as membership. According to Gerald Frug, the medieval town was

> a complex economic, political, and communal association. Rather than being an artificial entity separate from its inhabitants, the medieval town was a group of people seeking protection against outsiders for the interests of the group as a whole. . . . The idea of the autonomy of the town and of its citizens merged. . . . The distinctions we recognize as fundamental—between personal

property rights and town sovereignty rights, between the town as a collection of individuals and the town as a collective whole—were absent.[3]

At times, property has been used as an institutional base from which to *oppose* government, as the gentry used landed property as a buttress of independence in the struggle for the prerogatives of parliament versus the crown in the Glorious Revolution of 1688. In this context, land represented subsistence and military power. At other times, the interests of property have helped to shape and *form* government, as in the ferment leading up to the American Revolution and the ratification of the U.S. Constitution.[4] The rhetoric of property as freedom helped mobilize the support for the American Revolution. From *Federalist Papers #10*, James Madison writes "The diversity in the faculties of men, from which the rights of property originate, is not less an insuperable obstacle to a uniformity of interests. The protection of these faculties is the first object of government."[5]

In later developments, the presumed neutrality of the market helped suppress this language of property, as the progressive separation of law and politics, and politics from economics rendered the issues mute.[6]

In the colonial period, semifeudal forms of the municipal corporation and Hudson River manors and patents contained elements of governance, including political representation, access to resources, skills, occupations, production, distribution, marriage, jurisdiction, and intergenerational transmission. The founding mercantile corporations were responsible for governance of the colony, with rights of representation associated with membership, based on "freemen" status. The New York State General Assembly was formed in 1683 with representation for some manors as well as individual freeholders, by county. After the revolution, the several New York State constitutions established a legislature, but its role, powers, suffrage, apportionment, and methods of electoral representation were subject to continual revision.

The definition and separation of the public from the private occurred in the nineteenth century. Municipal corporations like Albany and New York City divested themselves of land ownership in the early decades, and Dillon's widely accepted legal treatise of 1872[7] argued for the formal subordination of these originally independent municipal corporations to the superior authority of the state. The passage of general incorporation laws transferred responsibility for economic development initiatives in the public interest from state-funded entities to private corporations.[8] The subsequent expansion of private corporations led to reregulation of price (Interstate Commerce Commission) and competition (Federal Trade Commission), along with the development and expansion of the private financial market.[9] In a dramatic reversal, by the early twentieth century, private financiers had accumulated sufficient resources to rescue the federal government.

What is commonly understood in the twenty-first century as individual private property, the personal exclusive right to use and dispose of a particular object, is a relatively recent creation. Access to the commons was understood as included in the rights of tenants and the landless poor as recently as the first half of the nineteenth century. The celebrated independence of the yeomanry and the proprietor was understood as based on a wide and equal distribution of land.[10] While the founding fathers of the revolutionary period and the authors of the constitution were dedicated to the protection of property, the meaning of this term has shifted dramatically as different types of property have emerged, with altered governance structures at the same time.

Colonial Corporations

The settlement of North America occurred during the period of the formation of global mercantile empires, reflected in the Dutch and English interests in colonial New York. The formal mechanism of colonization was the joint stock company chartered by the crown. Although English colonies had founding charters with a mission to establish representative local government forms, as well as to provide for religious freedom in the Massachusetts Bay Colony, for example, the colonies of New Netherlands and later New York were established primarily for commercial motives. In spite of New York's strictly commercial origins, nonetheless, the ideas of representative government and local autonomy were in wide circulation. The New York settlers (first as Dutch, then as English, colonists) observed, and perhaps participated indirectly in, the political struggles of their day. For example, their namesake, the Duke of York, was first crowned James II, and then deposed, in the Glorious Revolution of 1688, along with the struggle for independence of Dutch municipalities in the same period.[11]

Henry Hudson discovered the Hudson River in 1609, sailing for the Dutch East India Company. A new entity, the Dutch West India Company, was formed in 1621 to explore, trade, and colonize the region. New Amsterdam received its charter in 1653. As a national joint stock company, the interests were more commercial than settlement or nation building.[12] As a result, settlements were widely scattered, operating more like trading and military outposts along river routes, to defend the colony against competing European powers and Native Americans.

For the early seventeenth century Dutch settlers, the rivers facilitated ease of navigation, providing settlements with access to the Indian fur trade, as well as the seaport. Albany was strategically situated at the juncture of two rivers, the Mohawk and the Hudson, and was located well into the hinterland, where pelts were abundant. This extensive territory, and the need for settlers, led to the granting of large manors and feudal privileges by a series of Dutch and then English colonial governors. The only lasting patroonship from the Dutch period was Rensselaerwyck, in the Albany area, but the English governors continued to grant large patents and manors. Following English conquest in 1664, the English Governor Thomas Dongan renewed the charters for New York City and Albany in 1686, and granted additional patents and manors from 1672 to 1688, with Governor Benjamin Fletcher granting more from 1692 to 1698.[13]

While some historians glorify the municipal corporations as citadels of medieval democracy, a unified corporate body, others emphasize the hierarchy and the closed nature of these corporations.[14] Both elements can be found in the examples in the Hudson Valley. The municipal corporations of New York and Albany exercised control of the land within their borders by virtue of royal charters under both Dutch and English rule. These municipal corporations held monopolies themselves, in fur in Albany until 1726, and in export in New York City, and both were also able to commission chartered monopolies for the purposes of development. Suffrage was held by males with freehold tenure in land, or freeman status in trades, and the corporation exercised control over prices, land use, and occupation, similar to medieval forms.

New York City received grants from the English governors of the colony in 1665, 1686, and 1730 by Governor John Montgomerie. The mayor, the aldermen, and the commonalty, including the freemen and freeholders of the city, were one body corporate and politic. Suffrage was held by licensed tradespersons and holders of land. A Common Council, made up of elected aldermen and an appointed mayor, had the power to pass ordinances and bylaws, as well as to lay out and open streets, to operate the markets of the city, and to regulate and license tradesmen.[15] The "private property" of the corporation as granted in its charter included the land, the economy, and the courts, protected vis-à-vis the crown. Property was an inclusive concept, including life, liberty, religion, and conjugal affection, as well as wealth, all aspects of which may be required for personal independence. The common lands, essentially including Manhattan Island, were leased and regulated for the purposes of conserving their value.[16]

By mid-eighteenth century, the Albany and New York City corporations relied less on exclusionary provisions, monopoly, or price regulations to restrict the practice of the trades. In 1784 the New York City corporation began the sale of its land for revenue purposes. By 1806 the corporation began to adopt the more "liberal" view, that property was more properly held by private owners. After the War of Independence, Albany and New York City formed separate judicial authorities distinct from the corporation, and the freeman status, granted by the alderman, was no longer considered necessary for suffrage.[17]

The colonial manors and patents in the Hudson Valley also illustrated some feudal obligations, as well as emerging market relations and republican government structures. Manorial courts, landlord access to tenant services, inheritance restrictions, representation, production, employment, and distribution were all associated with the place of residence on a particular family estate. There were divergent policies among the landholding families regarding sale as opposed to lease. For example, Madame Brett, a widow on the Rombout patent, dispersed her holdings, while the Philipse and Verplanck families did not, leading to unrest among tenants in the colonial period. The gradual tendency toward longer leases, commutation of feudal in-kind obligations, and money rents affected suffrage within Dutchess county. Such families as the Schuylers converted to more capitalist relationships in the 1780s. In other places manorial relationships persisted as late as 1865, and remnants have lasted into the present, from the Rensselaerwyck patroonship, the site of protracted anti-rent struggles in the nineteenth century, located in present day Albany and Rensselaer counties. Rules and practices of inheritance affected land parcelization. Robert Livingston divided his land among five heirs in his will of 1790, contrary to his family tradition. By contrast, Stephen Van Rensselaer III divided his estate among two heirs in 1839, who then resisted sale of land to tenants.[18]

With intermarriage and elite social networks, New York State politics was dominated by a few families, including the Livingstons, the Clintons, and the Schuylers. For example, there was considerable intermarriage between the Livingston and the Beekman families, whose founders had arrived in the Hudson Valley in the mid-seventeenth century. There were strategic marriages among the Beekman, Livingston, Schuyler, Van Cortlandt, and Van Rensselaer families, as well. Among the manor elite, politics was personal and based on family ties and family loyalties, often including tenants.[19]

The self-governing towns in New England and Long Island provided alternate models, along with Whig politics in England, and the labor shortage provided leverage to the tenants relative to the lords of the manors. The New York General Assembly was formed in 1683, in response to demands for self-governance. While some of the manors had representation in the General Assembly, the form of land tenure was extended to make the tenants eligible for suffrage, by extending leases to twenty-one and ninety-nine years, or in perpetuity, in some examples. Town lines were drawn by the General Assembly in 1691, and town supervisors were elected to facilitate tax collection. While formal feudal privileges were revoked by the General Assembly (and again in the New York State Constitution of 1846), the established pattern of respect, wealth, and social position allowed well-placed families to retain prestige and political office.[20]

This political model of landed independence was predicated nonetheless on male heads of households, with a reliance on household division of labor, bound labor, and slavery in the colonial period.[21]

Federal Structure and Governing Institutions

While New York State was not strictly necessary for the ratification of the U.S. Constitution, it was certainly an important staging ground for the formulation of the issues. The conflict over ratification of the federal constitution of 1787 raised many issues, which still resound in contemporary politics, regarding the role of property and the size and degree of centralization of government.[22] The historiography surrounding the Federalists/Anti-Federalists debates tends to reveal distinct trends regarding reference to the role of property and class. The Anti-Federalists discourse included an explicit consideration of property and class, and even the Federalists divided immediately after the ratification into factions reminiscent of the court versus gentry. Hamilton represented the court element, with an explicit ambition for a strong mercantile state, while Jefferson and Madison extolled the virtues of the independent yeomanry. The legacy of strict construction of the Constitution originated in the efforts to limit Alexander Hamilton's centralizing and state-building tendencies, in the early formation of the Republican party. While the rhetoric of class is less effective in contemporary public debate, the Anti-Federalist and "country" legacy has resurfaced again to legitimate the attack on big government since the 1980s.[23]

According to Pocock, property was an indicator and a training ground for virtue in the Republican tradition, a view that was challenged by Anti-Federalists. Debate leading up to the American Revolution and the ratification of the Constitution took place in various "voices," many appealing to the ordinary person in various guises. While there was some violence and mob unrest,[24] legitimate interests were most often cast in terms of those who owned modest property, whether farmland or skill, and to appeal to their common interests in improving it. Landlords who supported the Revolution became Federalist after the Revolution, opposing their previous allies among the Anti-Federalists. Those in privileged positions sought to co-opt extreme views, restrict the range of issues subject to debate, and to moderate the challenge to existing authority.

The positions taken by various authors in the Federalist/Anti-Federalist debate resonated with persons and issues first encountered in the tenant unrest in the Hudson Valley, where the positions of George Clinton and Alexander MacDougall against Alexander Hamilton and John Jay were already familiar. While class position was one indicator of one's stance in this early debate, with merchants and large landowners typically Federalist, it was not always decisive. For example, Federalists and Anti-Federalists both agreed on respect for the law and property. George Clinton, the future Anti-Federalist, helped put down Shays' Rebellion in Massachusetts, and future Anti-Federalists in Dutchess county helped put down the tenants' rebellion in 1766. The Livingston family, although large landholders, tended to be Anti-Federalist. The sale of Royalist lands helped to enfranchise some, to isolate others, and to burden still others with financial debt instead of feudal duties.[25] The dissenting voice of the Anti-Federalists helped to legitimate an oppositional discourse and ultimately to strengthen the American constitutionalism. While property was still a qualification for voting, the Federalist Party was essentially abandoned in 1800 when it seemed too dedicated to the interests of the aristocracy.[26]

After the American Revolution, one of the central issues of the new republic was the power and authority of the central government. Arguably, this is the issue upon which stable political alignments were first observed, continuing the debate surrounding ratification of the Constitution in the 1780s into the formation of the first political parties in the 1790s. While there was considerable expression of small government as the best protection of democracy, often the positions on the size of government were related to issues of property. For example, Hamilton was a principal spokesperson for centralized government, for the explicit purposes of finance, military, and trade. As Edward Countryman points out, the conservatives raised the issue of national government and the degree of centralization. The terms small, local, and legislative became proxies for "the people," and the value of democracy was expressed in terms of property forms, such as "landed democracy" versus "moneyed aristocracy." Similarly, the Federalist party was controlled from New York City, with a base among wealthy merchants, and was more likely to represent those with more affluence and a college education.[27]

By all accounts, the figure of Alexander Hamilton was a formative influence in the state-building projects. As an immigrant from the British West Indies, Hamilton benefited from the care of his employer, Nicholas Cruger, in a merchant firm on the island of St. Croix. Cruger's New York connections helped Hamilton to obtain an education and to gain aristocratic connections by marriage into a prominent Dutch Hudson Valley family with extensive landholdings, the Schuylers. Hamilton was a pamphleteer for the Revolution while still in college, gaining attention and influence. With his own law career in New York City, Hamilton was also able to gain extensive contacts among New York City merchants. During the revolutionary period, Hamilton was able to represent a middle course between Tories and democrats. As an aide to Washington during the war, Hamilton also developed close ties to the first president.[28]

According to Huston, Hamilton's "conservative nationalist" politics in the 1780s helped to preserve the manorial land system in the Hudson Valley into the nineteenth century, along with the service of the manor lords in the patriot cause. Hamilton helped to consolidate the conservative resurgence after the Revolution. Hamilton, along with Madison, also played a central role in the call for the Constitutional Convention and in its ratification. Not only was Hamilton a significant contributor to the Federalist Papers, he was also likely a key organizer of this project.[29]

It has been said that Hamilton organized the project of the Federalist Papers in order to counter the strength of Governor Clinton and the Anti-Federalists in the Hudson Valley. The rising class of freeholders gave the Anti-Federalists their best source of political leadership. One example is Melancton Smith, an Anti-Federalist member of the New York State ratifying convention from the Hudson Valley who changed his vote to support the ratification. His Anti-Federalist tracts, written under the pseudonyms of "Federal Farmer" and "A Plebian," were widely circulated throughout the colonies. Without the four crossover votes from Dutchess County, including Smith, New York would not have ratified the constitution. From the west bank of the river was George Clinton, a lawyer with yeoman roots and substantial connections among the landlords, with service in the Revolutionary War, and increasingly radical positions in his seven terms as governor of New York State. Leading politicians from New York State like Martin Van Buren also acknowledged their debt to Anti-Federalism.[30]

What has been called "Hamiltonianism" is characterized by a reliance on centralized government, a strategic role of the merchant class, and a strong fiscal authority. Hamilton saw finance as a form of property, to be protected as a "highest mandate." Hamilton also articulated a role of government for and by the propertied classes. Hamilton wished to concentrate finance into the hands of the mercantile class and to use the funded national debt as a capitalization of the national tax capacity. Hamilton's proposal for a national bank became one of the first issues regarding interpretation of the constitution.[31]

Later, in the 1790s, Jefferson and Madison split with Hamilton over the degree of centralization of the federal government, which they interpreted as unduly favoring the mercantile class. Former Hamilton allies and supporters like Albert Gallatin and James Madison became alienated. The issue of the national bank was one of the reasons for the schism with Madison and the formation of parties, so that the Federalist coalition was split by 1791, only three years after ratification of the Constitution. The split between the Hamiltonians and the Jeffersonians led to the development of formalized party politics, and states' rights and strict construction as the method of preserving autonomy and democracy. Hamilton's idiosyncrasies may have given Jefferson and the Republican party its margin of victory in the presidential election of 1800. Arguably, the issues that appeared in the debate about ratification of the Constitution re-emerged as the Republican-Federalist schism took place. The issue of the national bank remained central to partisan politics, in the careers of Andrew Jackson and Martin Van Buren, regarding the charter of the Bank of the United States and the independence of the Treasury Department.[32] Hamilton's explicit move toward the enlistment of the merchants as government financiers may have appeared as the formation of a consolidated faction, threatening the influence of the small property owners, the independent proprietors.

Property and Party

As the formal structure of government became consolidated, as distinct from the founding municipal corporations, one of the separate threads to become differentiated was the form of association of political party. As inhabitants began to view themselves as separate from governing bodies, those members formed autonomous associations that were no longer tied to a particular geographic locality or a specific form of property. Further, within a federal structure, there was a need for an aggregating device, and a form of outreach to organize constituencies for electoral gain. In both cases, political parties emerged as playing a significant role, especially as suffrage was extended to include all white men after the New York State Constitution of 1821.[33]

Madison suggested that property was the anchor for political parties, in the formation of alliances as well as the subject and substance of those coalitions. To quote Madison in *Federalist Papers #10*:

> From the protection of different and unequal faculties for acquiring property, the possession of different degrees and kinds of property immediately results; and from the influence of these on the sentiments and views of the respective proprietors ensues a division of the society into different interests and parties.[34]
>
> But the most common and durable source of factions has been the various and unequal distribution of property. Those who hold and those who are without property have ever formed distinct interests in society. . . . The regulation of these various and interfering interests forms the principal task of modern legislation and involves the spirit of party and faction in the necessary and ordinary operations of government.[35]

As can be observed in New York State, these alliances and their positions change in both form and substance as types of property shift. Political parties in turn play a significant role in shaping property institutions, both legislative and constitutional. The history of party achieved significant milestones in New York, beginning with the Federalists and the subsequent split with the Republicans. Further, the origin of the spoils system is attributed to New York, with DeWitt Clinton and Martin Van Buren making disciplined use of their appointment powers. The New York Constitution of 1777 provided for a council of appointments, which facilitated the distribution of position based on partisan alliances. Others argue that the spoils system was actually invented even earlier, by the John Jay administration. New York has certainly been prominent in the history of machine politics, such as Van Buren's Regency, and the machine politics of Tammany Hall.[36] After the extension of manhood suffrage in 1821,

> Politics . . . had evolved from a gentlemanly exercise in the exchange of personal favors for power to a struggle among disciplined parties. . . . Personal relations had given way to party programs behind which citizens sorted themselves out. Political agendas, partisan discipline, and governmental spoils rather than influence, deference, and personal favors now informed political behavior.[37]

At the same time, political parties become increasingly well organized and influential in order to affect rules and regulations that altered economic prospects for particular firms and industries, what Logan and Molotch call "structural entrepreneurship"[38]

Shifting and Contested Nature of Property

Corporations

One of the most significant changes in the form of property was related to the formation of corporations. During the colonial period the corporation of the city of New York could grant a special franchise to a company to build water lots[39] or operate ferries for the purposes of the corporation as a whole. Another example of direct government initiative was the Croton Water Aqueduct, constructed in 1842 to provide New York City with fresh water.[40]

The state of New York also initiated economic development projects directly, as with the construction of the Erie Canal from 1827 to 1835, a government project financed at public expense. This effort served the political ambitions of DeWitt Clinton, nephew of George Clinton. The Erie Canal was also consistent with the national issue of internal improvements, in the context of the Embargo of 1807 and the War of 1812, which cut off international trade. At this juncture in the early nineteenth century, states themselves were an instrument of economic development, with internal improvements like the Erie Canal and railroads leading to the development of a national market. The Erie Canal is an early example of growth coalition and advanced New York State in competition with other states into its role as the "Empire State." New York attained prominence in exports and finance relative to its competitor cities Boston and Philadelphia.[41]

The transformation of corporations from instruments of public governance to private entities depended on a series of Supreme Court decisions. One of the issues surrounding the national bank controversy was the power of the federal government to establish corporations. The Marshall court settled this issue in 1819, in the case *McCulloch v. Maryland*, along with the inviolability of corporate charters in the Dartmouth College case. In these rulings, Marshall's career can be viewed "as a process of reading Hamilton's state papers into the Constitution."[42] With these 1819 rulings, corporate charters were viewed as explicitly protected by the Contract Clause of the Constitution, making corporate charters even more valuable. The legislature was increasingly occupied with the consideration of these special charters, the granting of which were seen as special privileges, prone to legislative deal making and logrolling.[43] Responding to the growing backlog of these requests, along with political pressure from both critics of monopoly and those seeking to acquire the powers of incorporation, the New York State Constitution of 1846 enabled the legislature to establish general incorporation laws by type of corporation.

The nature of the corporation shifted from a combination of public and private, to distinctly private, along with the provisions of general incorporation. For example, New York City as a municipal corporation in the colonial period was both public and private; that is, nothing distinguished public from private. In the early nineteenth century the New York City property was protected from the state as "private." As early as 1806, the Common Council decided to transfer corporate-owned land to private hands as expeditiously as possible. By the mid-nineteenth century the New York City corporation was considered as having no private property of its own (Darlington case of 1865).[44] For example, the status of the Brooklyn Ferry shifted from an exclusive franchise of the colonial corporation of the city of New York in 1708, as granted by Lord Cornbury, to the freehold right of the corporation in 1850, to a part of public authority in 1865.[45]

The public/private distinction was instituted as a distinction between types of corporations. Dartmouth (1819) explicitly protected the contracts of private corporations, but not the public corporation.[46] New York State institutionalized Dartmouth (1819) in its Constitution of 1821. The New York State Constitution of 1846 "completed the radical separation of the state government from all business corporations," that had been begun with the general incorporation of manufacturers in 1811 and free banking in 1838. The general incorporation law constitutionalized laissez-faire in the private corporate form.[47]

During this transition there was, as well, a shifting nature of contracts. In moving from the privileged chartered monopoly to general incorporation, corporations were more responsible for their own competitive context. Rather than be assured of clientele from an exclusive grant of monopoly, the private corporation was increasingly responsible for assuming risk for changes in the valuation of its property, and was less frequently shielded from competition from other entrants. The doctrine of "vested rights" in the value of existing property and franchises was substantially revised, and eminent domain frequently used without compensation to the original property owner. Courts began to adopt instrumental reasoning to support economic growth, rather than rely on custom and precedent. Instead of assuring that contracts were based on the exchange of equal value, the court developed the will theory of contract, in which exchange was enforced based on the specified terms of the transaction. These practices served to progressively undermine the traditional economic regulation of the colonial period.[48]

With the development of general incorporation laws in the early nineteenth century, the role of corporations changed, from "body politic" to depoliticized private entity. The general incorporation laws helped to legitimate the corporation, and to provide uniform and neutral procedures, open to all applicants equally. The ultimate result, however, was the decline in the authority of the state. Initially corporations were authorized by special charters approved by the state legislature to accomplish public purposes. The new distinction between public governance corporations and private economic corporations was accomplished with laws of general incorporation. This split expanded the authority of the private corporation and streamlined the development of the private economy but led to an impoverished government.[49] The local municipal corporation became the vehicle of governance but was separate from the private economy, Referring to Dillon's Rule of 1872, Hartog said: "American courts do not usually regard a municipal corporation as the embodiment of a local political community. To the contrary, a municipal corporation is said to be a public corporation created by a state legislature solely for the purposes of providing subordinate administration."[50]

With the privatization of corporations and the professionalization of government, the new model of the administrative state emerged. Political parties competed for majority status, with alternating patronage within the civil service system, based on the winner-take-all majority party.[51]

Real Estate Markets

The quintessential notion of property is land, although the role of land in national cultures has varied. For example, in the Dutch culture, land was simply the locus of trading relationships, while in England, land represented status.[52]

The operation of land markets in the Hudson Valley was the result of a long and contested process. On colonial manors, rights to work the land were exchanged for rent and for service to the landlord. Leases were for years, or lives, or perpetuity, but the tenants were not owners. The anomalous concept of "lease in fee" was a contradictory combination of freehold and lease. Tenants were able to sell the land, after first giving the lord the option to buy and a share of the proceeds, called quarter sales. That way, tenants could reap the returns for their improvements to the land. When landlords began to call in overdue rent, and to enforce quarter sale terms, to charge for timber cut on the commons, and to impose fees for mills, the tenants began to raise the issue of property rights in a collective form. From 1830 to 1850, difficult economic times, falling prices, and competition from western lands intensified the conflict between landlord and tenant. Deference on the part of the tenant and benevolence on the part of the landlord were strained under these more difficult circumstances. For example, Stephen Van Rensselaer III founded Rensselaer Polytechnic Institute in 1824, but his son was financially unable to sustain his philanthropic tradition.[53]

Using the rhetoric of property, tenants claimed the rewards of their own labor, in a form of the labor theory of value. These ideas were disseminated by such organizations as the National Reform Association, modeled on land reform organizations in New York City. Tenants viewed their "freedom" as threatened by the landlords' claim to the land that they inhabited and worked. Tenants formed voluntary associations, conducted rent strikes, organized mass rallies, perpetrated physical intimidation of law enforcement officials and compliant tenants, enlisted in political parties, and challenged the landlords' titles in court. While some of their proposed legal strategies were constitutional, such as eminent domain with compensation, the bill that was ultimately passed in 1860 was judged in violation of the contract clause of the U.S. Constitution and vested rights. According to this ruling, the existing leases were protected by "freedom of contract" language, construing the tenants as voluntarily entering these agreements, even though the perpetual lease constituted an obstruction on market alienability. This argument left in effect the preexisting feudal leases from the colonial period, a type of legal restriction on land in Republican America that had been outlawed in England in 1290.[54]

Partisan politicians like William Seward and Martin Van Buren strove to address tenants' grievances, but shifted their demands into terms that could be met by capitalist economic development strategies. The tenants' agitation helped form the political impetus for the New York State Constitutional Convention of 1846 and for the U.S. Homestead Act. The legislation of the period of the American Revolution recognized two land systems, one feudal and one alodial. Although this duality was resolved in the New York State Constitution of 1846 (Article I, section 12), which prescribed alodial forms of landholding for all future leases,[55] the existing specific leases in the Hudson Valley remain in effect even at present, restricting sale or types of use.

The transition from manor to real estate thus took several centuries. Once reframed in liberal terms, laissez-faire helped form the coalition between the middle class and farmers against manorial lords, even though their visions remained very different.[56] According to Bruegel, "While the entrepreneurial middle-class adversaries of manorial estates saw land as a commodity best subjected to the abstract laws of supply and demand within an economic system in which capital flowed freely, . . . antirenters conceived of landed property as the foundation of working farmers' independence and dignity."[57]

With this transformation the real estate market developed, along with the role of rentier in growth coalitions in both New York City and upstate New York, and tenant movements in the cities.[58]

Free Labor

As immigrant labor become more available, landlords and factory owners could avoid the cost of maintenance of slave and bound labor. From the patriarchal household labor system, both farm and crafts, to separation of work and home, there was a gradual development of a wage labor market. New York State outlawed slavery in 1827,[59] and was part of the free labor coalition to eliminate slavery nationally. Married women's property rights were also increasingly recognized, with a provision in the New York State Constitution of 1846.[60]

Public/Private Split

Definition of the Public

After the separation of public from private corporations in the early nineteenth century, the definitions and uses of the "public" were still open to alternate interpretations and practices. The tenant legal strategy of acquiring land from their landlords was still considered private. The interpretations surrounding the New York State Private Road Act of 1843 prevented the use of eminent domain for the acquisition of land by the tenants in the Hudson Valley. The transfer of property was considered justified only if it served the public purposes. The transfer of property in the Hudson Valley manors from landlords to tenants was considered private, and redistribution was not considered in the public interest. A few years later legislation was enacted by New York State to acquire land in New York City for use as a public park in 1851, but a private board was appointed to manage its design, construction, and access.[61] While the doctrine of eminent domain allowed the acquisition of private property for public purposes, the definition of "public" was still to be interpreted.

The separation of public and private was part of the challenge to the New Deal by the judiciary. The post-Depression policy model assigned to public jurisdictions the responsibility for the private economy, while preventing direct economic operation by a public jurisdiction.[62]

Finance, Public and Private

As finance began to be considered property, along with land, the distinction between public and private also became relevant. While colonial finance was family-based, government debt helped develop private financial markets, as Hamilton understood. For example, Wall Street first developed as the financial vehicle for government securities before corporate securities, beginning with the Revolutionary War debt and Hamilton's "funding and assumption" scheme in 1790. Under this scheme, the federal government assumed the states' debt, in exchange for relocating the capital in Washington, D.C., in a deal between Jefferson, Madison, and Hamilton. Treasury Secretary Albert Gallatin returned to Wall Street to finance the War of 1812 in the years in which there was no national bank.[63]

When New York City made the transition to a public municipality instead of autonomous corporation, there were implications for finance as well.[64]

> The change was especially acute in New York. Governance in early nineteenth-century Manhattan was largely defined by the city's status as a proprietary corporation with extensive land grants. . . . The "privatization" of urban land was mirrored by a "publicization" of civic authority: municipal government recast itself from a proprietary grantee with particular estates and resources to an agency of the liberal state with general duties and power. The transformation was both fiscal and institutional. Public spending

> ballooned in the mid-nineteenth century, as did New York's reliance on taxes, rather than rents, to pay for it.[65]

To finance public improvements such as streets and parks, New York City bonded debt increased from $12.2 million in 1850 to $97.3 million in 1872, at the peak of the Tweed regime.[66]

> The Empire City, in short, was a debtor's paradise. . . . In the most literal sense, borrowing appealed to boosters . . . debt financing forced propertied New Yorkers to replace local interests with metropolitan ones; it required collective decision making about the spatial and aesthetic needs of the city as a whole. Moreover, it embodied a confidence that the present and future could rely on each other: . . . destiny."[67]

Morgan and Rockefeller interests developed along with the formation of railroads, where growth of large corporations led to initial efforts at regulation, such as the Railroad Commission in New York State in 1853. J.P. Morgan operated in both public and private finance. In the nineteenth century, Morgan used the trust as a private financial instrument to avoid ruinous competition, an effort which was followed by public regulation. Morgan's financial resources were then sufficient to rescue the U.S. financial system in 1907.[68]

The U.S. national bank system, which finally emerged in 1913 with the Federal Reserve Act, was a complex combination of both public and private. The question of the regulation of finance is still an issue, with recent scandals regarding financial information, insider trading, and conflict of interest in stock analysts' advice.[69]

Planning

As Keith Revell observes:

> Although it had long been something of a national conceit that Americans considered government a "necessary evil" and strove for minimal public interference in private affairs, cities generally, and New York especially, had an almost unbroken heritage of public activism—as evident in three of the most significant infrastructure achievements of nineteenth century government: the Croton waterworks, Central Park, and the Brooklyn Bridge.[70]

What may have been forgotten by such scholars is the history of New York City as an independent corporation with autonomy and authority over its own property. Even in the late nineteenth and the twentieth century, New York City retained a leadership role among urbanized areas.

New York's urbanists in the late nineteenth century, a blend of elite, reformers, and real estate boosters, between 1850 and 1870, had many accomplishments to their record in public spaces, culture, transportation, and architecture. Prominent leaders such as Frederick Law Olmstead and Andrew Green influenced such achievements as Central Park and the consolidation of New York City in 1898. Professional planners sought to solve the interdependencies of the large metropolis by expertise, in the country's first zoning laws, in 1916, affirmed by *Euclid v. Ambler* in 1926.[71] These zoning regulations had the support of real estate interests, in order to rationalize land use and to protect property values, in spite of their exclusionary impact, and this approach to land-use control was later promoted nationwide by Herbert Hoover as secretary of housing.

Governmental Corporations

Almost as soon as the corporation of New York City was integrated into the modern economy in the mid-nineteenth century, public corporations, owned and operated by the government, were reinvented. In 1921 the Port of New York Authority again combined public power with authority to issue revenue bonds and to charge tolls and fees. The Port Authority proceeded to build bridges and tunnels, bus stations and rail connections, and provided a model for the Tennessee Valley Authority and other public-works agencies during the New Deal.[72]

Recurrent Fiscal Crises of Local Governments

Between 1820 and 1860, municipalities relinquished their role as regulators of the local economy and divested themselves of property. At the same time, they acquired additional public functions, such as the provision of education, fire protection, police, and welfare, which had been private and voluntary. Even though the towns and cities in the Hudson Valley had been created before the state, they were no longer considered autonomous. Dillon's Rule of 1872 assumed that cities and towns were only creatures of the state, and therefore derived their powers from the state, and only as enumerated. With the nineteenth century legacy of the separation of public from private, the consideration of corporations as private "individuals" to be protected from the state, and the subordination of the local public government to the state and federal, the freedom of association and right to self-government were no longer recognized.[73] These were accomplishments of the Marshall Court in the early nineteenth century, a legacy consistent with Hamiltonianism. Local governments were no longer owners of property and had no independent authority to tax, yet they were still "responsible" for the fiscal integrity and economic vitality of each local jurisdiction. That is, the public/private distinction served effectively to socialize the costs and privatize the rewards of economic development. This combination of responsibility with no authority has led to an irrational competition for ratables and a chronic fiscal crisis of the local areas, both cities and towns, and even states.

The "home rule" provisions of the late nineteenth century were enacted to help local governments deal with their loss of control of their economic fate, such as the home rule provision in the New York State Constitution of 1894. When the boroughs of New York were consolidated into one metropolitan government in 1898, it was an act of the New York State legislature, which the mayor could veto by his home rule authority. In Howard McBain's view, the home rule provision of New York State "gives freedom from interference, but almost no measure of independent opportunity for constructive local action." The strategy of local government incorporation allowed the formation of multiple, overlapping layers of government, in the futile search for local autonomy.[74]

This effort to facilitate representative government may have resulted in the opposite, as fragmented local government became overpowered by integrated finance capital. Yet the legacy of home rule complicates land-use and fiscal planning, frustrating both developers and regionalists.

Municipal fiscal crises have a long history, beginning at least in the early twentieth century. The prominent example of New York City's fiscal crisis in 1970s has left a large literature. The recurrent state and local fiscal crises in 2003 are also beginning to receive widespread national attention.[75]

Hudson Valley Redux

Like the colonial period, the large bulk of the New York State economy is still predominantly located in the corridor between New York City and Albany, including the Hudson Valley. The politics of New York State at this writing are also triangular, between Governor George Pataki, originally from the Hudson Valley, Senator Joseph Bruno from Albany, and Representative Sheldon Silver from New York City. Deals regarding the budget are made among these three behind closed doors, and then passed by the legislature, and the New York State budget is always late, months after its April 1 deadline every year. The exception was the 2003 budget, for which the legislature overrode the governor's veto, to raise taxes rather than undergo draconian cuts, due to the national recession of 2001 and the impact of the terrorist attack on the World Trade Towers on September 11, 2001.

The Hudson Valley is studded with spectacular evidence of its manorial history, notably in its numerous state and federal parks. Currently managed by the National Park Service, the homes of Franklin and Eleanor Roosevelt are located in Hyde Park, and the mansion of the Vanderbilts, whose family riches were made in steamship and rail transportation, has majestic river views. Nearby Locust Grove in Poughkeepsie is the home of Samuel B. Morse, inventor of the Morse code, located on an estate that was part of the original Rombout patent. Clermont, the remaining estate of the original Livingston manor, is a state park in Columbia County, immediately adjacent to the Hudson River. The home of Martin Van Buren in Kinderhook is a state historic site. Vassar College, founded by a prosperous Poughkeepsie brewer in 1861, stands as a lasting tribute to his foresight and interest in higher education, along with Rensselaer Polytechnic Institute to the north in Troy, a direct legacy of patroonship.

Many of the current local controversies surround land-use conflicts. A real estate transfer tax to protect open space preservation in the village and town of Warwick in Orange County was denied by the state legislature, because local government is subject to state legislative authority. The tax is opposed by the local and state real estate interests, even though their land values would rise as a result of the open-space amenities.[76] A major upscale, gated, residential development at the base of the Schawangunk Mountains is opposed by a citizens' movement, Save the Ridge. To save it from development, Sterling Forest, a large forest tract near New York City, was purchased by the U.S. and New York State governments, with the assistance of a long-standing New York City nonprofit group, Regional Planning Association, in a deal brokered by Newt Gingrich. Environmental groups, like Clearwater and Scenic Hudson, save parcels up and down the river for public access, and bring lawsuits against General Electric to clean up PCBs from its plants by dredging the Hudson River, involving the Environmental Protection Agency of the U.S. government. The redevelopment of the river city Beacon has occurred with the initiative of entrepreneurs, arts institutions, and developers, with access to private finance far exceeding the fiscal capacity of the local municipality.

The leading multinational corporation, IBM, has its world headquarters in Westchester County, with sites at Yorktown Heights, Armonk, and Somers. In Dutchess County, two IBM manufacturing sites remain, at Poughkeepsie and at East Fishkill, while the plants in Kingston and Endicott were closed during the corporate downsizing in 1993. What had been a corporate policy of "full employment contract" was ended, with IBM as one of the last U.S. corporations to implicitly guarantee lifetime employment. Embracing an alternate form of labor, IBM has been a leader in support for the open-source software code, Linux, the product of a voluntary, self-organized, Internet-based, global cooperative in software development.

As an affordable enclave in the vicinity of a major metropolis, home prices in the Hudson Valley rose rapidly in the late 1990s, from the economic expansion and then as an alternative investment once the stock market bubble had burst in 2000. The scenic beauty and local arts venues have attracted press attention, promoted as the next big thing after the Hamptons.[77] Rising home and land prices intensify land-use conflict, as proposed industrial sites like St. Lawrence Cement in Hudson, Columbia County, and new power plants, in Athens, Ulster County, threaten to block the scenic views and recreational ambiance that attracts second-home residents. Suburbanization, as well as gentrification, drive out both agriculture and manufacturing. Like Hamilton's investors in the early republic, home owners and stockholders have a stake in the financial markets and have become participants in, if not also supporters of, the regime.

Twenty-First Century Corporate Forms

Private corporations, seen as fictional "individuals" and protected from governmental interference, have grown very large. Rather than view this phenomenon as a threat to freedom, the pejorative moniker related to size has been attached to "big government" by the neoliberal movement, ascendant since 1980.

Eminent domain was used in the nineteenth century by the growth coalition to support internal improvements, when state and local governments supported emergent corporations with subsidy and legal privileges. In the twentieth century, this same power of eminent domain is characterized as "takings," a term meant to suggest a violation of the due process protection of property in the U.S. Constitution, by the law and economics movement.[78] Arguably, the law and economics movement is making use of issues formulated by the Anti-Federalists in the eighteenth century, along with the pseudonyms and rhetorical postures of that period ("Cato" for example, may have been the pen name of George Clinton or Abraham Yates, both of the Hudson Valley, now the name of a conservative think tank). In the early twentieth century, it was progressive historians who tended to claim the legacy of the Anti-Federalists.

> But with the rise of conservative populism [in the 1970s and 1980s] . . . the democratic localism of the Anti-Federalists had taken on a decidedly conservative appeal. Ronald Reagan became the quintessential Anti-Federalist.[79]

There is considerable irony that Franklin Delano Roosevelt's strong centralized government resonates more with the positions that Hamilton espoused.[80] With globalized finance and privatized corporate power, neoliberals currently advocate small government instead, particularly eschewing the role of a strong federal government in income redistribution, land-use regulation, and in the provision of economic security. The mission of providing everyone with the right to acquire and protect property, so important to the founders, now applies only to "private" property.[81] While protecting property from the majority of propertyless was an explicit objective of the Federalists, the public/private distinction, and the relative downsizing of the public, is the institutional form that now serves that same purpose more discreetly, while property is no longer an explicit part of public discourse.

Now the threads of property, which had been woven into a whole cloth, have become a finely grained mesh of parcelization covering the entire globe. Because of the legacy of the public/private split, the political party and the private corporation are the most powerful aggregators, while the territory of local government is merely subdivided into lots for sale in a global "real estate game."[82]

Notes

1. I am applying the Commons' concept that an institution is "collective action in control of individual action," as quoted in Wesley C. Mitchell, "Commons on Institutional Economics," 1935. Specifically, I am starting with the institution of property as central to economic activity. This concept of property has immediate links to judicial aspects, valuation, and representation, as well as physical characteristics. This definition of an institution is close to Reeve Huston's definition of politics as "public, collective action that aims at shaping the terms of collective life . . . encompass[ing] not just electoral politics, but also rioting, civic ritual, ethnic and reform associations, and the labor movement" (Huston 2000, 265, *n*58). This suggests an interpenetration of politics and institutions, by which stable social forms are also viewed as in flux, in process. In a sense, property is both a type of relationship and a substantive issue with which that sort of relationship is concerned, both structure and process.

Mark Gottdiener, *The Decline of Urban Politics*, 1987, develops a theory of local government based upon the notion of property (168–69, 179–81, 195–98, 273–85), but he does not consider how the specific forms of property and government are both in flux historically.

2. Mitchell, 140–41.

3. Gerald E. Frug, *City Making*, 27, 30.

4. J.G.A. Pocock, *The Machiavellian Moment*, 1975, discusses landed property of the gentry as a basis for independence and virtue, compared with the corruption of patronage by the crown. He sees a parallel in the debate between Jefferson and Hamilton in the U.S. revolutionary period. See Pocock, 407–14, 421, 427, 478, 486, 508, 525–29, 529–35; See also Stanley Elkins and Erie McKitrick, *The Age of Federalism*; Gordon S. Wood, *The Creation of the American Republic*; and Staughton Lynd, *Anti-*

Federalism in Dutchess County, New York, and *Class Conflict, Slavery, and the United States Constitution,* among others, in the lively literature that discusses the role of property in the American Revolution.

5. Alexander Hamilton, James Madison, and John Jay, *The Federalist Papers,* 46.

6. Jennifer Nedelsky, *Private Property and the Limits of American Constituionalism,* 230–31, 239–40. See also Morton J. Horowitz, *The Transformation of American Law, 1780–1860,* and *The Transformation of American Law, 1870–1960,* regarding the separation of law and politics.

7. John F. Dillon, *Treatise on the Law of Municipal Corporations, 1872,* in Frug.

8. See Frug, 45–47, for a discussion of Dillon's treatise. The transition from the public to the private corporation is discussed in Jon C. Teaford, *The Municipal Revolution in America*; Horowitz, 1977, 1992; and L. Ray Gunn, *The Decline of Authority.* Frug discusses the rendering of local municipalities entirely "public," 46.

9. Howard Wachtel, *Street of Dreams,* discusses the development of financial markets and the role of Wall Street.

10. R. Huston, *Land and Freedom,* 38–44, 47, 129.

11. Regarding Dutch independence struggles, see Donna Merwick, *Possessing Albany, 1630–1710,* 220–21; see Hendrik Hartog, *Public Property and Private Power,* 21–32, and Allan Tully, *Forming American Politics,* 13–16, 21–27, 47–48 regarding the New York City corporation and the Glorious Revolution.

12. Oliver Rink, *Holland on the Hudson,* describes the settlement of the Dutch colony, 50–53.

13. See Sung Bok Kim, *Landlord and Tenant in Colonial New York,* for a description of the settlement patterns, 20–22, 67–60.

14. Hartog and Frug seem more sympathetic to the medieval corporation, while Teaford is more critical.

15. In *City and Surburb,* Teaford describes the operation of the colonial corporation of New York City in both political and economic functions, 19–20, 27–28, 30–31, 33.

16. Hartog also provides an indepth analysis of the New York City corporation, 14–19, 23–24, 27–28.

17. For descriptions of this transition, see Hartog, 104, 109; and Teaford, 1975, 29, 49–53, 66, 74–76.

18. For the varieties of landlord practices in lease provisions, see Lynd, 39–46, 53–54; Huston, 13, 45–46; Edward Countryman, *A People in Revolution,* 264–65; Charles W. McCurdy, *The Anti-Rent Era,* 15–18, 316, 330–31; Elizabeth Blackmar, *Manhattan for Rent,* 24–25.

19. For intermarriage and social networks, see Evan Cornog, *The Birth of Empire,* 24; Carl Becker, *The History of Political Parties,* 13–14, 16–17; Lynd, 1962; Huston, 11, 17–18, 28–32; McCurdy, 10. For politics based upon landlord family-based coalitions, see Tully, 126–45.

20. For the influence of the New England model on New York politics, see Rink, 228; Kim, 115–118; Huston, 23, 28–33; Patricia Bonomi, *A Factious People,* 33–35.

21. For the reliance on patriarchal forms of household labor, see Blackmar, 1–2, 21–23, 16–21, 36, 51–58; Martin Bruegel, *Farm, Shop, and Landing,* 52–54; Huston, 6, 38–40, 125–29.

22. See David Greenberg, "Debunking America's Enduring Myths," for a discussion of the ongoing interest by well-regarded historians such as Bernard Bailyn, *To Begin the World Anew,* and Leon Ferling, *A Leap in the Dark.*

23. Hamilton viewed the federal, centralized state as necessary to integrate the

dual ambitions of the republic as well as empire; see Pocock, 529–31. For a discussion of the role of class in the historiography of the Federalist period, see David J. Siemers, *Ratifying the Republic*, 5–9, 20–21, 215–22; Lynd, 1962, 5; Huston, 6–7; Saul Cornell, *The Other Founders*, 12–13, 34–50, 305. For the issue of class in contemporary politics, see Rick Lyman, "Every Four Years Blue Bloods Put on a Blue Collar."

24. See the discussion of property, class, and violence in Cornell, 40–44, 35–42, 49–51; Lynd, 1962, 59–64, 71; Becker, 79, 82–83, 108–11.

25. Regarding the character of revolutionary politics, see Lynd, 1962, 18–19, 46–51, 70, 79–81; Donald Cole, *Martin Van Buren and the American Political System*, 15; Countryman, 77–78; Becker, 16–17, 28–31, 49–51, 59–60, 75, 108–19, 163–65, 275; Lynd, 1962, 18–19, 46–52, 59, 70, 73–81; Siemers, 12–13; Cornell, 8–9; Cole, 15; Cornog, 24–25.

26. Regarding the issue of constitutionalism, see Siemers, 24, 77, 132, 144, 160–63, 222.

27. Regarding the debate over centralized government within the Federalist Party, see Siemers, 124–28, 139–41, 160–63; Gerald Leonard, *The Invention of Party Politics*, 33–35, 39–41; Tony A. Freyer, *Producers Versus Capitalists*, 4–8; Cornell, 1–15; Countryman, 266; Cole, 8–9, 21–25.

28. On Hamilton's career, see Elkins and McKitrick, 94–100; and Cole, 15. There is also an extensive literature on Alexander Hamilton, and most recently, Ron Chernow, *Alexander Hamilton*.

29. On Hamilton's influence on the conservative consolidation and the *Federalist Papers*, see Huston, 13–14; McCurdy, 10; Countryman, 252–59, 263–65; Samuel J. Konefstky, *John Marshall and Alexander Hamilton*, 22–31; Cornog, 19, 21; Wachtel, 5, 6–8; Siemers, 77–78; Elkins and McKitrick, 102–5; frontispiece to Hamilton, Madison, Jay; Cornog, 19.

30. Regarding the class origins of the Anti-Federalists, see Lynd, 1962, 9, 15–16, 22, 27, 52, 57, 61, 65, 82–88; Countryman, 197, 221–22, 234–38; Cornell, 25–26, 28, 36, 38–39, 83–95, 298–302; Cornog, 13, 298–302; David Ellis et al., *A History of New York State*, 119–33; Siemers, 206–7, 211–12.

31. On what has been called Hamiltonianism, see Cornell, 7, 174–87, 278–88; Countryman, 256–59; Konefsky, 54–58, 165–91; J.R. Nelson, *Liberty and Property*, 19, 31–33; Elkins and McKitrick, 115–19, 258–63; Siemers, 109–12; Leonard, 12–13, 193, 232, 266–67.

32. Regarding the partisan split between the Federalists and the Republicans, see Leonard, 28–29, 33; Nelson, 29–33, 38–50, 70–73, 77–79, 98, 101–6, 111, 113–14; Elkins and McKitrick, 257–63; Wachtel, 14–15, 20–24, 29–30; 34; Siemers, 17, 24, 106–7, 112–16, 140–41, 154–55; Cornell, 170–73, 190–94; Dixon Ryan Fox, *The Decline of Aristocracy in the Politics of New York*, 2–4; McCurdy, 34–35.

33. On the role of political parties, see Siemers, 136, 155–56; Amy Bridges, "Rethinking the Origins of Machine Politics," 64–69.

34. Hamilton, Madison, and Jay, *The Federalist Papers*, 46.

35. Ibid., 47.

36. On the origins of the spoils system and the political machine in New York State, see Cornog, 5, 37–38, 77–78, 82; Gunn, 61–67, 95–96; Cole, 6 and *n*2; Bruegel, 203–4; Dennis R. Judd, *The Politics of American Cities*, 55–56; T. Judd and D.R. Swanstrom, *City Politics*, 54–68. See also Amy Bridges, *A City in the Republic* and "Rethinking the Origins of Machine Politics."

37. Bruegel, *Farm, Shop, Landing*, 203–4.

38. John Logon and Harvey Molotch, *Urban Fortunes*, 30–34.

39. The term "water lot" describes the right to make improvements such as wharves, piers, and docks, along with the right of access, from a designated portion of the river. See Hartog, 46–68.

40. For discussions of New York initiatives prior to the public/private distinction, see David M. Scobey, *Empire City*, 125; Hartog, 224–30; Teaford, 1975, 105; Wachtel, 87; Edwin Burrows and Mike Wallace, *Gotham*, 625–28.

41. For references on these specific ventures, see Cornog, 112; Gunn, 114–18, 144–46; and Wachtel, 46–48.

For a general discussion of dual elements of such public initiatives, see Logon and Molotch. With the development of the market, the dual aspects of property, use value, and exchange value become related to different interests (Logan and Molotch, 17–24). The residents of a place appreciate its qualitative aspects, while the owners and real estate interests may only care for the sale price.

I further suggest that this distinction between use value and exchange value is assigned to different institutional actors. The economic model in the United States has been typically based upon public policies that rely on the private market, rather than government ownership (Judd, 5; Wachtel, 160, 187–90). The local government is responsible for the infrastructure functions that affect the attractiveness and competitiveness of the place, while the private economy makes investment and allocation decisions that affect its economic production. That would imply that the use value/exchange value distinction is related to the split between public and private, between nonprofit associations and market transactions. The "growth coalition" and structural entrepreneurship make use of public/private partnerships to enhance the exchange value of the entrepreneur's own property (Logan and Molotch, 30–34, 53, 63). This is portrayed at times as the "externality" of growth, in which all benefit. It is also liable to exploitation and corruption, as in machine politics, for one owner's benefit or one politician's career and power base, as in the notorious example of Tammany Hall in New York City. The growth machine will only support certain types of politicians (Logan and Molotch, 66–69), while political parties are arguably an important organizing device for the formulation of growth policies. A case can be made that the costs of development are the responsibility of the public, and the rewards of development are reaped by the private.

42. See John Marshall in Kermit L. Hall et al., *The Oxford Companion to the Supreme Court the United States*, 523–26.

43. Many of these points are made in Konefsky, 68–81, 146–91, with the direct quote on 13. See also Gunn, 106–13.

44. *Darlington* v. *The Mayor of New York* 31 N.Y. 164, 166 (1865). See discussion in Hartog, 259–60.

45. Hartog describes this transition for the New York City corporation, 14, 16–18, 26, 109–10, 185–86, 240–42, 257–61. See also Burrows and Wallace, 825–826.

46. *Dartmouth College* v. *Woodward* 17 U.S. 518 (1819). See Hall et al., 217–18.

47. The direct quote is from Ronald Seavoy, *The Origins of the American Business Corporation*, 183, along with other points, 96, 180–82, 184–86, 213, 238–41, 266–74; Frug, 39–51; Konefsky, 146–64; Teaford, 1975, 89–90; Hartog, 226–39

48. These observations on legal changes can be found in Horowitz, 1977, 23–29, 47–53, 63–66, 111–39, 173–88; Wachtel, 15; Cornell, 181; Gunn, 132–35; Nedelsky, 226–27; W.E. Nelson, *The Roots of American Bureaucracy*, 32–34.

49. These assessments of the impact of general incorporation laws can be found in Gunn, 106–107, 222–223, 241–244; Frug, 31.

50. Hartog, 2, referring to Dillon's Rule of 1872.

51. This view of the administrative state is from W.E. Nelson, 2–3, 5, 15–30.

52. For the changing role of land, see Merwick, 216–17, 282–85, 293, 295.

53. For this analysis of Hudson Valley leases, see McCurdy, 13, 22–30; Huston, 26–28, 33, 42, 45–48, 55–56, 58–61, 75, 85–86, 77–80, 90–92.

54. *Quia Emptores* of 1290 in England forbade subinfeudation and provided for free alienation of land. This law was not enacted in New York State (McCurdy, 25–26, 273–74). For tenants organizing strategies, see McCurdy, 25–30, 33–34, 37–38, 56, 111–13, 138–40, 285–86, 327–28, 333; Huston, 56, 91–92, 137, 214, 261, *n*10.

55. Regarding political impact of the anti-rent movement, see Huston, 34, 83–84, 172–73, 183–85, 214; McCurdy, 28–28, 32–35, 121–27, 327.

56. Regarding this long-term transition, see Bruegel, 71, 209–221, 223–226; Blackmar, 30–36.

57. Bruegel, 224–25.

58. For the growth of the real estate market, see Seavoy, 168; McCurdy, 121–27, 260–61, 327; Huston, 158–61; Blackmar, 24–26, 28–30, 32–40, 42–43; Logan and Molotch, 33–34, 69; Scobey, 93–133. For the development of the twentieth century tenant movement, see Ronald Lawson, *The Tenant Movement in New York City*.

59. For changes in the household labor system, see Blackmar, 26–28, 35–37, 43–51, 56–62. For the abolition of slavery in New York State, see Anthony Gronowicz, *Race and Class Politics in New York City*, 56.

60. For married women's property rights, see Norma Basch, *In the Eyes of the Law;* Bruegel, 123; McCurdy, 312.

61. McCurdy has a detailed discussion of the legality of the tenants' strategies, McCurdy, 110–16. See Roy Rosenzweig and Elizabeth Blackmar, *The Park and the People*, for discussion of Central Park as a "public" space, 18–29, 96–99.

62. The post-Depression model is from Judd, 5.

63. The development of financial markets on Wall Street is discussed in Wachtel, 6–7, 37–38, 46–48, 136–38, 141–42, 171–72; and Cornog, 23.

64. For a comprehensive treatment of New York City finances, see Scobey, 200–4.

65. Scobey, 200–1.

66. Scobey, 202.

67. Scobey, 203–4.

68. The topic of railroads and the stimulus to finance in summarized in Wachtel, 136–41, 144–46, 160, 164–70,187–90; and Seavoy, 200–1, 209, 211–12, 242–52.

69. For the formation of the Federal Reserve, see Wachtel, 173–77, 184–85. There have been conflicts of interest in advice given by stock analysts. Prominent cases include Frank Quattrone from Credit Suisse First Boston, in terms of analysts' conflict of interest. See, for example, Andrew Ross Sorkin, "Corporate Conduct: The Overview; Wall St. Banker Is Found Guilty of Obstruction," *New York Times*, May 4, 2004, A-1.

70. Keith Revell, *Building Gotham,* 9.

71. The innovations of urbanists in New York City is detailed in Scobey, 227–40, 255–57, 227–40; Wachtel, 49–51, 54–55, 79, 81, 86–89,136–38, 145–46; Cornell, 37, 45; Cornog, 20; Teaford, 1975, 106–7. For the development of zoning, see Revell, 185–226; Judd, 182–94; Randall Bartlett, *The Crisis of America's Cities*, 131–38; Martin Shefter, "Political Incorporation and Containment," 137.

72. See Jameson W. Doig, *Empire on the Hudson*, 1–3.

73. Frug has many observations of the impact of the public/private divide on public municipalities, including 38–39, 43–45, 48–50, 53, 56–58. See also Bridges 1–3, 5–6, 10–11, 85–87.

74. The topic of municipal home rule is found in Howard Lee McBain, *The Law and the Practice of Municipal Home Rule*, 101–6; Revell, 1; Frug, 50–51; Judd, 179; Logan and Molotch, 181–87; Gottdiener 30–35. The direct quote is from McBain, 105. The power for counties to create new towns was granted by an 1849 law, Gunn, 202–3. For a discussion of the ultimate impact, see Robert Wood, *1400 Governments*.

75. See Shefter for the New York City fiscal crises of 1907 and 1932–33, 143. There is a large literature on the fiscal crisis of local governments, including Joe Feagin and Robert Parker, *Building American Cities*, 264–68; Judd and Swanstrom, 324–34; Roger Alcaly and David Mermelstein, *The Fiscal Crisis of American Cities*. See L. Uchitelle, "Red Ink in States Beginning to Hurt Economic Recovery," and A. Murr and J. Ordonez, "Tarnished Gold," for the recent period. In the recent period of austerity, the state and local governments of the Hudson Valley are reevaluating tax breaks for nonprofit organizations (D. Shapley, "Nonprofit Tax Breaks Get Look").

76. According to Brad Kendall, Chair of the Dutchess County Legislature, in an interview on August 20, 2003, the realtors and builders made a deal with the chambers of commerce to oppose the sales tax increase if the chambers would oppose the real estate transfer tax. For a flavor of local land-use disputes, see www.savethegunks.org, www.scenichudson.org, and www.awostingreserve.com.

77. See Shyama Patel, "The Call of the Catskills"; and David Leonhardt, "Around U.S., a House Is a Home but Not a Bonanza" for a perspective on the recent appeal of the Hudson Valley to second-home and weekend clientele from New York City, as well as rising real estate prices. See also Ann Davis, *Hudson Valley Quarterly Report*, for data on home prices and disappearing farmland in the Hudson Valley, which has declined by 70 percent between 1940 and 1998.

78. For the use of eminent domain, see Nedelsky, 231–40.

79. Gordon Wood, "The Fundamentalists and the Constitution."

80. For the hypothesis that "Cato" was George Clinton, see Cornell, 37, 45; and Cornog, 20. For the consistency of Franklin D. Roosevelt with Hamilton's views of the centralized state, see Konefsky, 10, 73–76.

81. Since the late nineteenth century, there is no recognized right to association or to group self-government, and cities are no longer able to have both public and private functions (Frug, 44–47). In the eighteenth century there was no public/private distinction and no separation of governance from property.

82. Feagin and Parker, *Building American Cities*.

References

Alcaly, R., and D. Mermelstein, eds. *The Fiscal Crisis of American Cities*. New York: Random House, 1977.

Bailyn, B. *To Begin the World Anew: The Genius and Ambiguities of the American Founders*. New York: Alfred A. Knopf, 2003.

Bartlett, R. *The Crisis of America's Cities*. Armonk, NY: M.E. Sharpe, 1998.

Basch, N. *In the Eyes of the Law: Women, Marriage, and Property in Nineteenth-Century New York*. Ithaca, NY: Cornell University Press, 1982.

Becker, C.L. *The History of Political Parties in the Province of New York, 1760–1776.* Madison: Bulletin of the University of Wisconsin, 1909.
Blackmar, E. *Manhattan for Rent, 1785–1850.* Ithaca, NY: Cornell University Press, 1989.
Bonomi, P.U. *A Factious People: Politics and Society in Colonial New York.* New York: Columbia University Press, 1971.
Bridges, A. *A City in the Republic: Antebellum New York and the Origins of Machine Politics.* Cambridge, UK: Cambridge University Press, 1984.
———. "Rethinking the Origins of Machine Politics." In *Power, Culture, and Place: Essays on New York City,* ed. John Hull Mollenkopf, 53–73. New York: Russell Sage Foundation, 1988.
Bruegel, M. *Farm, Shop, Landing: The Rise of a Market Society in the Hudson Valley, 1780–1860.* Durham, NC: Duke University Press, 2002.
Burrows, E.G., and M. Wallace. *Gotham: A History of New York City to 1898.* Oxford, UK: Oxford University Press, 1999.
Chernow, R. *Alexander Hamilton.* New York: Penguin Press, 2004.
Cole, D.B. *Martin Van Buren and the American Political System.* Princeton, NJ: Princeton University Press, 1984.
Cornell, S. *The Other Founders: Anti-Federalism & the Dissenting Tradition in America, 1788–1828.* Chapel Hill: University of North Carolina Press, 1999.
Cornog, E. *The Birth of Empire.* Oxford. UK: Oxford University Press, 1998.
Countryman, E. *A People in Revolution: The American Revolution and Political Society in New York, 1760–1790.* New York: W.W. Norton, 1981.
Davis, A. *Hudson Valley Quarterly Report, First Quarter, 2003.* Poughkeepsie, NY: Marist College, 2003.
Doig, J.W. *Empire on the Hudson: Entrepreneurial Vision and Political Power at the Port of New York Authority.* New York: Columbia University Press, 2001.
Elkins, S., and E. McKitrick. *The Age of Federalism.* Oxford, UK: Oxford University Press, 1993.
Ellis, D.M., J.A. Frost, H.C. Syrett, and H.J. Carman. *A History of New York State.* Ithaca, NY: Cornell University Press, 1967.
Feagin, J.R., and Parker, R.E. *Building American Cities: The Urban Real Estate Game.* 2d ed. Washington, DC: Beard Books, 2002.
Ferling, L.E. *A Leap in the Dark: The Struggle to Create the American Republic.* Oxford, UK: Oxford University Press, 2003.
Fox, D.R. *The Decline of Aristocracy in the Politics of New York.* New York: Columbia University Press, 1919.
Freyer, T.A. *Producers Versus Capitalists: Constitutional Conflict in Antebellum America.* Charlottesville: University Press of Virginia, 1994.
Frug, G.E. *City Making.* Princeton, NJ: Princeton University Press, 1999.
Gottdiener, M. *The Decline of Urban Politics.* Beverly Hills, CA: Sage, 1987.
Greenberg, D. "Debunking America's Enduring Myths." *New York Times,* June 26, 2003.
Gronowicz, A. *Race and Class Politics in New York City Before the Civil War.* Boston: Northeastern University Press, 1998.
Gunn, L.R. *The Decline of Authority: Public Economic Policy and Political Development in New York, 1800–1860.* Ithaca, NY: Cornell University Press, 1988.
Hall, K.L., J.W. Ely, Jr., J.B. Grossman, and W.M. Wiecek. *The Oxford Companion to the Supreme Court of the United States.* New York: Oxford University Press, 1992.

Hamilton, A., J. Madison, and J. Jay. *The Federalist Papers,* ed. Clinton Rossiter. New York: Penguin, 1961.

Hartog, H. *Public Property and Private Power: The Corporation of the City of New York in American Law, 1730–1870.* Chapel Hill: University of North Carolina Press, 1983.

Horwitz, M.J. *The Transformation of American Law, 1780–1860.* Cambridge, MA: Harvard University Press, 1977.

———. *The Transformation of American Law, 1870–1960: The Crisis of Legal Orthodoxy.* New York: Oxford University Press, 1992.

Huston, R. *Land and Freedom, Rural Society, Popular Protest, and Party Politics in Antebellum New York.* Oxford: Oxford University Press, 2000.

Judd, D.R. *The Politics of American Cities: Private Power and Public Policy.* Boston: Little, Brown, 1979.

Judd, D.R. and T. Swanstrom. *City Politics: Private Power and Public Policy.* New York: HarperCollins, 1994.

Kim, S.B. *Landlord and Tenant in Colonial New York: Manorial Society, 1664–1775.* Chapel Hill: University of North Carolina Press, 1978.

Konefsky, S.J. *John Marshall and Alexander Hamilton: Architects of the American Constitution.* New York: Macmillan, 1964.

Lawson, R., ed. *The Tenant Movement in New York City, 1904–1984.* New Brunswick, NJ: Rutgers University Press, 1986.

Leonard, G. *The Invention of Party Politics.* Chapel Hill: University of North Carolina Press, 2002.

Leonhardt, D. "Around U.S., a House Is a Home but Not a Bonanza." *New York Times,* August 6, 2003, A-1.

Logan, J.R., and H.L. Molotch. *Urban Fortunes: The Political Economy of Place.* Berkeley: University of California Press, 1987.

Lyman, R. "Every Four Years, Blue Bloods Put on a Blue Collar." *New York Times,* October 5, 2003, Week in Review, 14.

Lynd, S. *Anti-Federalism in Dutchess County, New York.* Chicago: Loyola University Press, 1962.

———. *Class Conflict, Slavery, and the United States Constitution.* New York: Bobbs-Merrill, 1967.

McBain, H.L. *The Law and the Practice of Municipal Home Rule.* New York: Columbia University Press, 1916.

McCurdy, C.W. *The Anti-Rent Era in New York Law and Politics, 1839–1865.* Chapel Hill: University of North Carolina Press, 2001.

Merwick, D. *Possessing Albany, 1630–1710: The Dutch and English Experiences.* Cambridge, UK: Cambridge University Press, 1990.

Mitchell, W.C. "Commons on Institutional Economics." *The American Economic Review* 25: 4 (December 1935), as reprinted in W.J. Samuels, ed. *Institutional Economics.* Vol. I, 135–152. Hants, UK: Edward Elgar, 1988.

Murr, A., and J. Ordonez. "Tarnished Gold." *Newsweek,* July 28, 2003, 33–36.

Nedelsky, J. *Private Property and the Limits of American Constitutionalism.* Chicago: University of Chicago Press, 1990.

Nelson, J.R., Jr. *Liberty and Property: Political Economy and Policymaking in the New Nation, 1789–1812.* Baltimore: Johns Hopkins University Press, 1987.

Nelson, W.E. *The Roots of American Bureaucracy, 1830–1900.* Cambridge, MA: Harvard University Press, 1982.

Patel, S. "The Call of the Catskills." *New York,* August 4, 2003, 16–23.
Pocock, J.G.A. *The Machiavellian Moment: Florentine Political Thought and the Atlantic Republican Tradition*. Princeton, NJ: Princeton University Press, 1975.
Revell, K.D. *Building Gotham: Civic Culture and Public Policy in New York City, 1898–1938.* Baltimore, MD: John Hopkins University Press, 2003.
Rink, O.A. *Holland on the Hudson: An Economic and Social History of Dutch New York.* Ithaca, NY: Cornell University Press, 1986.
Rosenzweig, R., and E. Blackmar. *The Park and the People: A History of Central Park.* Ithaca, NY: Cornell University Press, 1992.
Scobey, D.M. *Empire City: The Making and Meaning of the New York City Landscape.* Philadelphia: Temple University Press, 2002.
Seavoy, R.E. *The Origins of the American Business Corporation, 1784–1855*. Westport, CT: Greenwood Press, 1982.
Shapley, D. "Nonprofit Tax Breaks Get Look." *Poughkeepsie Journal,* October 6, 2003, A1.
Shefter, M. "Political Incorporation and Containment: Regime Transformation in New York City." In *Power, Culture, and Place: Essays on New York City*, ed. J.H. Mollenkopf, 135–57. New York: Russell Sage Foundation, 1988.
Siemers, D.J. *Ratifying the Republic: Antifederalists and Federalists in Constitutional Time.* Stanford, CA: Stanford University Press, 2002.
Teaford, J.C. *The Municipal Revolution in America, Origins of Modern Urban Government, 1650–1825*. Chicago: University of Chicago Press, 1975.
———. *City and Suburb, The Political Fragmentation of Metropolitan America, 1850–1970.* Baltimore, MD: Johns Hopkins University Press, 1979.
Tully, A. *Forming American Politics: Ideals, Interests, and Institutions in Colonial New York and Pennsylvania*. Baltimore, MD: Johns Hopkins University Press, 1994.
Uchitelle, L. "Red Ink in States Beginning to Hurt Economic Recovery." *New York Times,* July 28, 2003, D-1.
Wachtel, H.M. *Street of Dreams—Boulevard of Broken Hearts: Wall Street's First Century.* London: Pluto Press, 2003.
Wood, G.S. *The Creation of the American Republic, 1776–1787*. Chapel Hill: University of North Carolina Press, 1969.
———. "The Fundamentalists and the Constitution." *The New York Review of Books,* February 18, 1988. Available at: www.nybooks.com/articles/4534.
Wood, R.C. *1400 Governments, The Political Economy of the New York Metropolitan Region.* Cambridge, MA: Harvard University Press, 1961.

8

Prior Questions

Endogenous Property Rights in Economics and the Case of the Radio Spectrum

Elizabeth Kruse

> *Questions addressed to the emergence and mix of the components of the bundle of rights are prior to those commonly asked by economists.*
>
> —Harold Demsetz, "Toward a Theory of Property Rights"

Introduction: The Search for New Models

Understanding the origins of diverse property rights systems is important both for the insight it gives into how economic life has been shaped and because theories about the origins of property rights influence social and economic life by legitimating certain economic choices. Yet the questions of how property rights originate, and why, have been largely ignored by mainstream economists. Most economists have taken property rights as exogenously given and have failed to acknowledge the existence of forms of property other than the polar cases of state and private property. This limits the study of economics by erasing from view much of the activity involved in creating and shaping markets, economic actors, and the distribution of the costs and benefits of economic activities. Where economists have acknowledged the importance of property rights structures, their focus usually has been on the consequences of these structures for the allocation of resources, rather than on their origins. These theories often assume,

Elizabeth Kruse currently works as an economist at the Office of Program Evaluation of the Internal Revenue Service. The Office of Program Evaluation of the Internal Revenue Service is not responsible for any of the opinions expressed or material contained in this chapter implicitly or explicitly, that the consequences of property rights structures explain their existence, although the mechanism by which this happens usually is not examined.[1]

This neglect of questions related to the origins of property rights is slowly being remedied by economists, variously referred to as Neoinstitutionalists, New Institutional Economists, or Induced Innovation theorists, who are searching for new models in which the creation and change of property rights, and other institutions, are endogenous to the economy. Such studies most often are justified, especially by economic historians, by describing the importance of property rights to economic growth. Distributional issues have received less attention overall, but are the focus of some work in the field of economic development, where the study of institutional change arose out of efforts to understand variations in the adoption of new technologies.[2]

While some of this recent work on property rights and institutions continues to adhere to a neoclassical economic framework, there is growing consensus, even among mainstream economists, that such models are too limited to encompass adequately elements such as transaction costs, opportunism, subjectivity, limits on rationality, and "real" or historical time; and that new models are needed.[3] In particular, the introduction of transaction costs into economic theory has been a major influence in moving economic theories of property rights beyond the standard neoclassical model. Once transaction costs are recognized, the precept that market processes yield Pareto-optimal outcomes is undermined, because transaction costs can block the trading on which Paretian results are based. This was one theme in Douglass North and Robert Paul Thomas's 1973 book, *The Rise of The Western World*. North has since emphasized that economic pressures can lead to institutional changes that may not maximize social output in the short run, and advocated a shift to definitions of efficiency based on long-term growth. In doing so, he attempted to graft theories of ideology and the state onto the neoclassical model. More recently North has explicitly abandoned the neoclassical model as too narrow, criticizing it for missing several essential ingredients including time, a focus on the nature of institutions and organization, and a critical evaluation of the rationality postulate.[4]

This chapter is intended to contribute to the search for new economic models for property rights analyses. I argue that the three factors traditionally examined in neoclassical models of property rights—resource characteristics, technology, and product markets—and the two additional factors that are the focus of work by new institutional economists—ideologies and existing institutions—are all necessary theoretical elements of analyses of the origins of property rights. These five factors constrain the shape that property rights can take, although in particular cases not all of these constraints are equally important. I further argue that serious consideration of these five factors logically points to the need to incorporate concepts of power into economic analyses. I use the creation of property rights in the radio spectrum in the United States between 1899 and 1934 as a case study to illustrate this approach to understanding the origin of property rights institutions.

Property rights in the radio spectrum are rights to use or control a given wavelength or band of wavelengths, together with rights or restrictions pertaining to the nature of the signals that may be sent on those wavelengths.[5] These rights or restrictions include the content of messages; the strength, timing, and place of origin of signals; the nature of transmitting equipment; the identity of operators and station owners; and the methods of financing such communications. The creation of property rights in the radio spectrum in the United States provides a case study of institutional innovation that is unusual on several levels. The beginning of the deliberate use of radio waves, which occurred at the end of the nineteenth century, is recent compared to that of most natural resources. This allows study of the initial creation of property rights in a resource that had no historically recognized claimants and no existing investment in institutions and technology specific to radio. The radio spectrum is not changed by use, eliminating resource depletion or change as a factor in the evolution of institutional arrangements. However, the spectrum is a scarce resource because signals sent simultaneously over the same or adjacent wavelengths in one geographical area interfere with each other, preventing intelligible reception. Because the original exploitation of this resource occurred relatively recently, there is a record of contemporary concerns over usage, allowing consideration of how politics and ideology interact with other factors in the evolution of property rights.

The process of establishing a stable law to govern the spectrum in the United States was protracted, lasting from the creation of the first wireless firms in 1899 until the passage of the Radio Act of 1927. The United States was exceptional in the length of time it took to develop a stable set of spectrum property rights and in the extensive property rights accorded to private interests.[6] Radio communications in Europe, by contrast, have been either state-owned and -operated, or heavily regulated in terms of content, financing, and ownership almost since the beginning of the radio era. Yet the factors usually emphasized in economic analyses of property rights—resource characteristics, technology, and product markets—were similar in Europe and in the United States. In contrast, the existing institutions and ideologies important to the development of spectrum property rights were quite different. This pattern of similarities and differences underscores the importance of existing institutions and ideologies, and of the political and economic power of interested groups, in the creation of property rights systems.

The second part of this chapter discusses the three factors emphasized in neoclassical models of endogenous property rights. The next part considers the factors emphasized by new institutionalist models of endogenous property rights. The fourth segment examines the role of power in economic theory and history. I conclude by summarizing the process of creating spectrum rights in the United States.

The Neoclassical Contribution

Basic Framework

Property rights in the neoclassical model are founded on technology, product markets, and resource characteristics. This theoretical framework explains institutional change in general as the result of activities undertaken by maximizing individuals in response to new profit opportunities. These new profit opportunities are in turn attributed to shifts in cost-benefit tradeoffs due to technological change, changing product markets, or changes in relative factor availability. The structure of the institutions resulting from this maximizing process is attributed to transaction costs, which also are assumed to be shaped by resource characteristics and technology. This body of work extended transaction costs analyses beyond the costs of exchange, which were the focus of Coase's work in 1937 in "The Nature of the Firm" and 1960 in "The Problem of Social Cost," to include the creation and enforcement of the property rights that underlie exchange.

Given the constraint of transaction costs, neoclassical economists usually hold that the process of changing institutions, and the institutions themselves, are efficient. These models of institutional change have been criticized for not explaining the *process* of change; delivering only an efficiency rationale instead.[7] The efficiency rationale is the result of a prior assumption that economic processes lead to Pareto-optimal outcomes. This approach explains inefficient changes as the result of interference from noneconomic processes. In a Pareto-optimal world only institutional change that adjusts to new cost-benefit possibilities is endogenous to the economy, so this model of economically induced institutional change ignores change that results from struggles over existing income streams. North described this simple model as the basis both for his own early work and for a substantial and continuing amount of the property rights literature.[8]

Resource Characteristics

Resource characteristics of interest to economists are scarcity; excludability, the degree to which access to the resource can be limited; subtractability, the degree to which consumption or use of the resource diminishes the contemporaneous benefit available to others; and renewability, the degree to which use of the resource reduces its long-term potential to provide benefits. Excludability is related to the costs of enforcement of rights to the resource, which depends upon the geography of the resource and available technologies, as well as institutional factors. Resource characteristics are due to the interaction of the physical properties of a resource and the dominant technologies in use at any given period.

Common property theorists have highlighted the difference between resource characteristics and property management regimes. Variations in the characteristics of excludability and subtractability place resources along a continuum from pure public goods through common-pool resources to pure private goods. Pure public goods have the characteristics that any number can use them at the same time, with no reduction of benefits; open-access without subtractability. Pure private goods can be used by only one individual at a time, and that use consumes them. Common-pool resources share with public goods the characteristic that many can use them at the same time, and with private goods the characteristic that use by one reduces benefits available to another; they are nonexclusive and subtractable.[9] The radio spectrum is a common-pool resource with global access and subtractable benefits due to signal interference. The technology used in accessing the spectrum is widely available, creating a large pool of potential users and making the measurement, monitoring, and enforcement costs of any property rights system high.

Resources can be held under four types of property regimes: open access, communal, state, and private property. Neoclassical economists have held that property regimes other than private property lead to mismanagement, overuse, and degradation of resources.[10] In fact, this bias among many neoclassical economists is so strong that they recognize only private property as property, lumping all other forms under the rubric of "no property." Recent work on common-property systems from the field of economic development has challenged the view that private property rights always provide the best use of resources on both theoretical and empirical grounds. This literature criticizes restrictive assumptions about information and inflexible models of adaptive choice that underlie neoclassical conclusions and describes cases of long-term, nondestructive community management of resources. It also emphasizes equity in judging economic outcomes in contrast to simple Pareto-optimality criteria.[11]

Neoclassical claims that private property is the most efficient form of rights have rested in part on ignoring or downplaying the costs involved in establishing or maintaining private property systems. Harold Demsetz assumed in his influential 1967 article "Toward a Theory of Property Rights," that a shift to private property involves an internalization of both the costs and benefits of such change, an assumption that allows the conclusion that such change only occurs when it increases efficiency. In contrast, Ford Runge pointed out the considerable social costs of private property regimes: "Private rights—individual rights to exclude others—must be based on clear definition and assignment in connection with the thing owned, together with a mechanism to adjudicate disputes when they arise. The more things for which exclusive rights are assigned and defined, the greater must be the social investment in assignment, definition, and adjudication. . . ."[12]

While a system of court-enforced laws is often viewed by economists as a public good, the costs and benefits of which are evenly distributed, this is an ideal. The fact that congestion limits a court system's usefulness gives it aspects of a common-pool resource when the number of users rises above a certain threshold. The physical characteristics of the radio spectrum make the transaction costs of enforcing any system of exclusive property rights in this resource particularly expensive. These costs are ignored by most theorists who call for a system of full, court-enforced private property rights to the spectrum, as Ronald Coase did in 1959. These enforcement costs were very clear to early users of the spectrum in the United States, however, and shaped their attitudes toward federal regulation of the spectrum.[13]

While the resource characteristics of interest to economists are simple in the abstract, in reality they are the result of a complex interaction between the physical characteristics of the resource, the dominant technologies in use, and the practices of users, all of which affect such aspects as scarcity, quality, and use value. Resource characteristics are subject to change as knowledge, technology, and patterns of common use change due to changes in economic, legal, and other institutions. Resource characteristics are thus flexible constraints on the forms that property rights in a natural resource can take.

Technology

Although the terms "technology" and "technological change" show up frequently in the economic literature on property rights in lists of factors that influence institutional change, property rights, and transaction costs, there is often little attention paid to this factor outside of the field of development economics. This has been particularly true for the fields of economic history and law and economics, in part due to the belief that the role of technological change has been overemphasized in explaining historical change.[14] Institutionalists' extensive work on the ways in which institutions structure technological change has provided an important corrective to technological determinism, but has left the role technology plays in shaping property rights relatively unexplored. While technological change is a major theme in development literature, technology is usually not seen as a "binding constraint" because this literature is often concerned with the ability of poor countries to "borrow" technology already available in other countries. Instead, this work examines institutions as a barrier to importing existing technologies.[15]

However, one area where institutionalists have examined the role of technology in shaping property rights is the influence of technologies on enforcement costs. The costs of enforcing property rights include those due to monitoring, measuring, protecting, and policing. Anderson and Hill stressed that laws alone do not create a desired property rights structure. They showed that technological change—the invention of barbed wire in 1874—was required to enable the creation of clearly defined private property rights to land and cattle in the nineteenth century American West. Before 1874 available methods for fencing were too expensive to make attractive attempts to enforce private property rights to land and cattle, even where laws provided for such rights and settlers already were ideologically oriented toward them.[16]

The measurement component of transaction costs has been emphasized by Douglass North and Yoram Barzel. North pointed out that most of the literature on transaction costs takes enforcement as a given, assuming either that it is perfect, or constantly imperfect in that the fact and degree of deviation is fixed and known. If enforcement were either, there would be no cost of detecting or measuring deviations from the standard set by a property rights structure. Because enforcement is imperfect and varying, measurement costs are a major component of transaction costs, and transaction costs depend heavily on measurement technologies.[17]

Technologies shape institutions by influencing resource characteristics, product markets, the costs of enforcing property rights, and the transaction costs associated with the process of institutional change. But technological change is itself influenced by existing institutional arrangements that influence the nature of the problems that inventors and innovators seek to solve. Power relations in a society also influence which technique is chosen for use from an available array of techniques, which in turn influences further technological change through learning-by-doing and technical interdependencies.[18]

Technology played a dramatic role in the creation of property rights in the radio spectrum. Technological breakthroughs in the last decades of the nineteenth century allowed the use of the spectrum for communications purposes, suddenly giving economic value to the physical properties of areas of the electromagnetic spectrum that lie outside the range of human senses. The new technology was fairly indiscriminate in its use of electromagnetic radiation for the first decades of wireless communication, making the spectrum an extremely scarce resource. Before the development of tuning—the transmission and reception of radio waves on particular wavelengths—in the first decade of the twentieth century, only one message at a time could be transmitted by wireless within wide geographic areas.[19] The scarcity of the spectrum resource was, and still is, a strong influence on research and development efforts in radio technology, as well as on the development of property rights in the spectrum. Throughout the twentieth century, some innovations in wireless technology allowed more efficient use of the spectrum for given uses, while other innovations increased demand for spectrum products, so that scarcity remains a concern.

While wireless technology required many decades of effort to achieve, once invented, many were able to duplicate it. And the "pool" of spectrum that is accessible in common has had a large geographical extent since the first decade of wireless, when signals began to reach for hundreds and then thousands of miles. Potential sources of interference can originate at numerous points over wide geographical areas. The physical nature of the spectrum resource makes "fencing" of wireless frequencies impossible.[20] This means that enforcement of spectrum rights depends entirely on measurement and monitoring technologies to detect and trace unauthorized use, along with social sanctions to deter it. While unauthorized uses of the spectrum often result in easily detectable interference with the signals of authorized users, interference is not always intentional and is, in any case, often hard to trace to its source. Trespass and responsibility for trespass are not obvious and are even harder to prove than detect. Measuring and monitoring of spectrum use require specialized equipment operated by trained personnel. All these technical factors have influenced the shape of property rights in the radio spectrum in the United States.

Product Markets

Neoclassical models of the impact of product markets on property rights start with an initial situation where full private property rights to a resource do not exist and describe a movement toward such rights. Usually the products markets being considered are for private goods, although this is not always stated explicitly. In these models, product markets influence property rights in a straightforward manner: Increasing demand for a private product increases the value of the inputs used for its production. This increasing value, in turn, stimulates individual activity to create better-defined property rights in inputs. In such models, changing demand in a product market disturbs an economy at rest at a Pareto-optimal equilibrium, and introduces movement to another optimal equilibrium position through changes in property rights.

Demsetz's discussion of the "theory relating privacy of land to the fur trade" is the canonic neoclassical description of the impact on property rights of changes in a product market for a private good, and was meant to be a demonstration of the broad applicability of neoclassical economic theory to property rights. In Demsetz's view, the original situation of Native Americans, in what is now southeastern Canada, was one where there were no property rights in land because it was not worthwhile for any individual to create them in a society where hunting for food and fur was done only for local use. In his view, a change in product markets—the advent of the fur trade with Europeans—increased the value of furs and led to overhunting on open-access lands, thereby increasing the importance of the externalities associated with lack of property rights in land. In response, land rights began to evolve in the direction of private property in order to allow conservation of fur-bearing animals. This evolution went through several stages, the first of which was the exclusive assignment of hunting lands to particular family groups.[21]

However, Demsetz's description of the progression of property rights from nonexistent toward private as a result of price signals from fur markets is not correct in some essential details. Hunting lands in what is now the northeastern Unites States and eastern Canada were not open-access before European settlement, but were held in common by tribal groups, or even used exclusively by family groups.[22] Therefore, what Demsetz sees as the first stage in the evolution of private property in response to the increased value of furs, in fact existed before the European fur trade penetrated North America. Often these lands came to be treated as open-access as a *result* of increasing European power in North America, because Europeans refused to recognize native sovereignty, property rights, and usage customs. Open access to land was a stage in the process of European colonization. Private rights to land were then allocated according to European-derived laws and customs, which usually did not recognize native claims as a basis for private rights. Private property rights to land that developed in North America after the advent of European trade and colonization arose as a result of the collision of two very different social and economic systems, one of which was far more powerful than the other. New property rights to land in North America were the result of the wholesale transformation of local ecologies and the social and economic relations of native peoples, not the result of individual choices in response to price signals.

A second problem with the Demsetz story is that the changes in property rights that took place after the fur trade became important did not prevent exhaustion of the resource in question. Instead, "[o]ne of the signal features of the trade was its rapid movement westward as one beaver population after another was hunted out, and the fur traders had to push farther inland in search of untapped beaver grounds."[23] Of course, neoclassical theory does not predict that private property will lead to stability in resources, only that it will lead to an optimal rate of use of such resources. But this result rests on the assumption that private property internalizes both the costs and the benefits of the use of resources and thereby brings social and private costs closer together.[24] Only a small measure of the costs of the fur trade was borne by those who benefited from it, whether native or European. Most externalities were not internalized by the movements toward private property; social and private costs were not brought into closer alignment.[25] Instead, the relative power of social groups played a large part in determining which would bear the costs or gain the benefits of the fur trade. Even product markets for private goods cannot be isolated arbitrarily from other social factors affecting property rights. They also cannot be examined without reference to the role economic and political power plays in determining which demands are met by the market and which are ignored.

Most of the economic literature on property rights has ignored the issue of public goods or argued that more complete definitions of private property rights to all economic resources can eliminate problems in the provision of what are currently considered public goods. Economic theories of public goods hold that market mechanisms cannot produce optimal amounts of all types of goods, particularly public goods. Generally, it also is assumed that the utility (satisfaction) of each individual using the public good increases with the quality or quantity supplied. In this model, if the decision to supply the good is left to the market, such goods will not be provided, or will be provided in less than optimal amounts, because individuals cannot exclude others from the benefits, so they cannot charge for providing the good. This leaves the provision of such goods to the state, which is held to improve on market-based allocations of resources by redirecting some to the production of public goods. The military, police, and court system are the most widely approved examples of public goods supplied by the state. Education, information, noncommercial broadcasting, parks, and highways are more controversial examples of public goods. The concept of public goods has provided the rationale for the existence of the state in many theories based on selfish individuals as far back as Thomas Hobbes's social contract and is one of the major justifications for regulation of markets in mainstream economics.

Critics of state intervention in the economy have argued that governments are subject to more inefficiencies than are markets, so they do not improve the allocation of resources to the production of goods and services.[26] These critics argue that the real solution to problems of public goods lies in the extension of private property rights. This solution ignores the fact that a system of property rights is a public good in itself. Also, as Demsetz and Barzel have argued, complete delineation and protection of property rights would be inefficient, even if it were possible, because of the high costs of establishing and enforcing such a system.[27] Some critics of regulation also argue that, in fact, public goods often will be provided by the market. Market-based solutions to public goods problems include mergers to internalize externalities and bundling of products, of which a prime example is commercial broadcasting with its combination of programs and advertising. The question of whether government provision of a good or service does cause improvement over the situation where such provision is left to private sources is a valid one, but most critics of governmental provision of goods or regulation of markets simply assume that markets are efficient rather than actually making a comparison.

While the neoclassical assumption that private property leads to optimal outcomes is unwarranted, these theories are correct in designating product markets a major influence on the evolution of property rights. This influence is particularly striking in the case of the radio spectrum. Demand for a system of wireless communication that would allow contact with isolated or moving points existed long before any technology capable of enabling it. This demand stimulated extensive experiments for fifty years before the first practical wireless communications systems were developed. Development of wireless technology in turn gave economic value to the radio spectrum and set off a long struggle in the United States for control of the spectrum. Analysis of the role of product demand in the creation of spectrum rights is, however, complicated because the products created by use of the radio spectrum—communications and information—do not fall into simple economic categories. That is, they can be private goods, public goods, producer goods, and consumer goods, sometimes simultaneously.

Historically, the first recognized product of a wireless communications system was point-to-point communications on the telegraph model, for which there was considerable private demand. Widespread point-to-point communications systems also have public good aspects due both to "network effects"—the fact that the value of the communications system to an individual is increased by the use of the system by others, until saturation of the existing infrastructure occurs—and to information and education effects. For these reasons, any widespread point-to-point communications network is often regarded as a public good, as witnessed by the special status of the federal post office in the U.S. Constitution. The importance of a second wireless product, broadcasted ship distress calls, was recognized shortly after some ships began carrying wireless equipment, which added weight to the public good concerns surrounding use of the spectrum. In the years before 1920, arguments in favor of government control or regulation of the spectrum were supported by three major claims about the public good aspects of a wireless network. The first was the importance of such a network for marine safety in general. The second was the importance of wireless to the U.S. Navy, which was widely held to be a public good in itself. And finally, government intervention was called for to prevent a restrictive commercial wireless monopoly by the Marconi Wireless Telegraph Company of America, a subsidiary of the British-based Marconi organization that was engaged in a largely successful attempt to control commercial wireless worldwide. It was feared that such a monopoly would limit the reach of the wireless network. These public good concerns, together with concerns about interference, played a role in the adoption of the Radio Act of 1912, the first legislation directed at controlling use and allocation of the radio spectrum in the United States.

After 1920 the rise of broadcasting as a form of mass entertainment and communications brought new public goods aspects of radio to the fore in debates over control of the spectrum. Broadcasting is a public good in the sense that access to it is open to everyone with the appropriate receiver. Because listeners could not be forced to pay for broadcasting directly, commercial networks developed a "bundled" product, in which advertising was interspersed with programming. But the broadcasting of programs can also be a public good in another sense if it provides information and education. The quality of broadcast programs is often viewed as a classic case of a public "good" problem, while advertising can be seen as a case of a public "bad" problem, with negative externalities that effect society in many ways. Broadcasts of advertisements are a special case, a private product in the sense that the benefits from advertising are appropriated privately, a public good or bad, in the sense that consumption of the product is widespread, and the costs of advertising are only partially internalized. The practice of bundling advertising and programming gives advertisers great control over programming content.[28] Proponents of commercial broadcasting argue that these bundled products have evolved in response to consumer choice, while opponents argue that they evolved as a result of the economic and political power of broadcast corporations, or in response to advertiser demands.[29] Public good concerns about mass communications networks were dominant in the development of property rights in the radio spectrum in European countries, while they have played a much smaller role in the United States, although they were responsible for the Public Broadcasting Act of 1967. In the United States commercial firms have shaped most of the use of the spectrum for both point-to-point communications and broadcasting. These differences in outcomes between the United States and Europe illustrate that the role of product markets in shaping property rights cannot be considered in isolation from other social structures that determine which demands are met, as did the case of the European fur trade and property rights in colonial America. New Institutional analyses of two additional factors shaping property rights—ideologies and institutions—provide the beginnings for an examination of the larger social context that structures product markets and property rights more generally.

New Institutional Extensions

Ideology

Consideration of the role of ideology as a factor in the creation of institutions has played a major part in the search for new economic models of institutional change. Douglass North has provided the theoretical foundation in mainstream economics for analyzing the influence of ideology on economic history. His theory of ideology, which is central to his overall theory of institutions, attempts to reconcile a methodology based on self-interested individuals with social cooperation of various forms. North views ideologies as rooted in human biology: Individuals with bounded rationality require patterns of thought and behavior that help them cope with environments that are too complex to permit every choice to be analyzed completely. In his theory, ideologies are literally "economizing device[s]" that allow individuals to function in the face of limited information and intellectual capacity.[30] Ideologies are acquired first from families and then from such other social institutions as schools and religion. North argues that individuals alter their acquired ideologies when their experiences diverge sufficiently from them, but because the information needed to develop new ideological frameworks is costly, ideologies tend to persist until some threshold of accumulated discrepancies is reached.[31]

North accounts for both stability and change in institutions with his theory of ideology. North believes concepts of equity are crucial to the way individuals make choices, as shown throughout history by the immense investment of resources in convincing individuals about the justice or injustice of various institutions. In his view, stability in social institutions is enhanced by widely held views that a system is fair or just. Investments in ideology by ruling groups contribute to institutional stability by making individuals believe that existing arrangements are fair, thereby reducing enforcement costs for the property rights institutions that make particular economic systems viable. Ideologies also explain the persistence of inefficient institutions because individuals often lack motivation or ability to replace their mental models of the world with more accurate ones. But the moral and ethical components of ideologies can lead to the simultaneous existence of conflicting ideologies within political entities. North believes that judgments about fairness also play a role in institutional change by overcoming the free-rider problem when private returns to action are negligible or negative.[32]

North makes a convincing case for the importance of ideology for economic theories of institutional change. Yet he has not analyzed its role in a concrete historical fashion, focusing instead on reconciling the concept with methodological individualism. And despite his theoretical recognition of the possibility of competing ideologies, his historical work has treated a single national ideology as a vague high-level factor in the long-run growth of national economies.[33] His idea that elites invest in ideology as a tool to help enforce property rights also needs to be considered in more depth. Ideologies play two roles in North's theory: They function both as individual belief systems that influence individual and group behavior and as tools consciously used to influence the behavior and economic choices of others. In the second case they are not *individual* economizing devices, but are related to Marxist analyses of ideology and to theories of power from political science literature that will be considered later in this chapter.

In the Marxist tradition, ideology plays an important role in the workings of the economy, although not always as an independent factor in the creation of property rights. In classical Marxist models, ideology, as well as law, is part of the social superstructure determined by the forces of production, rather than an independent force in shaping economic institutions.[34] This base-superstructure dichotomy has been abandoned by most current Marxist-influenced scholars in favor of theories that emphasize interaction between law, ideology, and the economy.[35] The classical Marxist theory of "false consciousness," holds that the dominant social ideology shapes choices made by individuals and classes by distorting knowledge and understanding of the world through education and other environmental influences. This does have some relationship to current Marxist and mainstream theories of the role of ideology in the economy. The implication that a "true" or "undistorted" or even a "dominant" consciousness can be found usually is rejected in recent economic theories of institutions, but otherwise this description of the role of ideology in the economy is compatible with a wide array of current scholarship.[36]

Approaches that emphasize the interconnectedness of ideology, legal institutions, and the economy offer the best description of the role of ideology at the level of whole societies over time. However, even from this perspective, ideology may be seen as an independent factor in economic analysis, depending on the level of examination and the length of historical time being considered. The novelty of the spectrum as a resource at the end of the nineteenth century allows ideology to be considered an exogenous factor in the shaping of spectrum property rights, at least initially. Yet part of the lasting significance of the structure of property rights in the radio spectrum that evolved between 1899 and 1927 has been, and is, the effect of that structure on mass communications and therefore on what Americans know, do not know, and believe.

The ideological context for the introduction of wireless technology into the United States contrasts sharply with that of European countries at the end of the nineteenth century. The right of European central governments to determine who could operate mass communications systems, how they would be financed, and what their content would be, was generally accepted at the time of the invention of the first wireless communications systems. In the United States the context was one of competition among ideological strands, which differed in views of the proper role of a federal government and of mass communications systems in a democracy. This ideological competition was exhibited in public debates over spectrum control and use, and helped delay achievement of a stable allocation system for thirty years in the United States. These ideological conflicts shaped property rights in the radio spectrum in two ways. First, the delay until 1927 in creating a stable system of property rights in the spectrum allowed the development of powerful economic actors with interests in allocation of the spectrum, such as commercial wireless firms, the Commerce Department's radio bureaucracy, and later the broadcasting networks. Second, these conflicting ideological views left their traces in the mixed property rights system in the radio spectrum, with its extensive de facto commercial rights, and its de jure concern with the standard of the public interest in deciding between competing claims to the spectrum.[37]

Existing Institutions

Early property rights theorists such as Thomas Hobbes and John Locke tried to ground their theories of property rights in a "state of nature" where there were no property rights and all things were held in common. Barzel however, has pointed out that it is "not possible to endow a pre-property rights state of affairs with meaning. In order to gain a toehold on the evolution of property rights, one must start with a world where some rights are already in place, resorting to something less dramatic than, but similar to, the physicists' 'Big Bang.'"[38] While few economists have made the case that existing institutions must be considered a factor in shaping property rights so directly, many have been more receptive to the idea that existing institutions shape the economy than they have been to the concept of ideology as an economic factor.[39]

Economists define institutions as the rules of society

> that facilitate coordination among people by helping them form expectations which each person can reasonably hold in dealing with others. They reflect the conventions that have evolved in different societies regarding the behavior of individuals and groups relative to their own behavior and the behavior of others. In the area of economic relations, institutions have a crucial role in establishing expectations about the rights to use resources in economic activities and about the partitioning of income streams resulting from economic activity.[40]

The importance of a society's existing institutions in shaping the creation or evolution of new property rights has been emphasized in the works of Douglass North and Gary Libecap. North accounts for the continuing influence of historical institutions on economic choices by their creation of vested interests, opportunities for organizational and entrepreneurial activities, and individual knowledge, skills, and expectations of the world. In his view, institutions, together with the standard constraints of economic theory, determine economic opportunities, and organizations are created to take advantage of these opportunities. The close fit between organizations and a given institutional structure creates vested interests in the perpetuation of that structure.[41]

Libecap also emphasizes the creation of vested interests and expectations by a society's institutional arrangements in his theoretical discussions of the creation of property rights in common-pool resources. He holds that institutions shape knowledge and expectations because they are created to reduce uncertainty and the costs of production and exchange. Institutions provide structures for interpreting and responding to economic events for individuals with limited information and calculating abilities. He also sees institutions as structuring economic opportunities through legal precedents, distributional norms, and individual expectations by influencing the costs faced by economic actors, and the available institutional responses to changes in relative prices or technology.[42] Libecap even argues that existing institutions create economic actors themselves: "Past political agreements on property institutions create the framework for responding to new common pool losses, the identities of agents for and opponents of change, their effectiveness in political bargaining, and the range of feasible alternatives."[43]

The most important preexisting institutions that affected the development of spectrum rights in the United States were the Congress, the Navy Department, and the wire telephone and telegraph industries, which were dominated by private companies. These soon were joined by the Department of

Commerce and Labor, created in 1903. These institutions created or supported various conflicting parties with an interest in shaping spectrum rights. Competition among these parties was the major cause, along with ideological conflicts, of the long delay in achieving a stable system of spectrum allocation. When that stable system was finally achieved with the Radio Act of 1927, the historical institutional context within which radio technology had been introduced was reflected in a number of ways. Federal civilian and military use of the spectrum was not made subject to the same authority as was that of state, local, and private entities. However, private use of the spectrum was not made subject to military authority either, and private rights to portions of the spectrum were institutionalized.

Power and Economic Theory

While the five factors discussed so far are all necessary theoretical elements of economic analyses of the origins of property rights, and together constrain the shapes that property rights can take, economic theories of property rights, and of institutions generally, are incomplete without an examination of the role of power in the economic sphere. Power relations between economic actors are involved in the original creation of property rights in resources, in the definition of externalities, in redistributional struggles over rights, in confrontations between the rights systems of different societies, in the choice of technologies and ideologies underpinning property systems, and in the determination of the distribution of costs and benefits of institutional change.

Most economists do not deal with issues of power, except the limited case of monopoly power, and define power as exogenous to the realm of economic analysis.[44] Where mainstream economists have dealt with the concept of power, their work usually has been divorced from institutional considerations, while the New Institutional economists have ignored power.[45] Inconsistent references to power in some forms do occur in the work of mainstream institutional economists, including references to violence, coercion, and even power itself.[46] In addition, references to enforcement of property rights are widespread in the property rights literature, although this is often assumed to be unproblematic. References to the monopoly of violence or coercion by the state are primary among the buried power references in the neoclassical literature on institutional change.[47] In the basic neoclassical model, the state, viewed as a maximizing individual, or a collection of agents of such an individual, is the source of property rights because of this monopoly on violence. Issues of power that might be raised by even brief mentions of violence, such as the process of establishing these property rights originally, and the difficulty and cost to both ruler and populace of enforcing them, are subsumed under social contract theories.

Modern social contract theories trace their origins to Hobbes's *Leviathan*, first published in 1651. Hobbes argued that the state originated in an agreement, or contract, among presocial, perfectly free individuals, existing in a "state of nature," to surrender their freedom and obey a government in exchange for guarantees of rights and security enforced by the state. All exercises of power, including violence, were surrendered to the state. This social contract was freely entered into by all who were subject to it because all benefited from it. All social contract theories hold that the constitutive elements of the state of nature, and therefore society, are individuals, who are actually or substantially equal.[48] Hobbes argued that all men in a state of nature were substantially equal, despite differences in strength or other faculties, because even the weakest could find a way to murder the strongest. This assertion of equality is what rules out the use of power in the creation of a state. The possibility of violence exists in a state of nature, but does not give one individual greater power than another—it merely serves as a spur to all to enter freely into the social contract.[49]

Social contract theorists after Hobbes have differed on the nature of the social contract, including the form of government thus created, but the contract theories of neoclassical economics usually are characterized as Hobbesian because of a number of similarities. These are that individuals are selfish; that under a social contract all power, and all use of violence, are monopolized by the state; and that enforcement of rights is not a problem. The Hobbesian ideal of a single ruler also fits well with methodological individualism in neoclassical economics. Many neoclassical economists, however, do not recognize the necessity, or even the existence, of Hobbes's argument for substantive equality, which is necessary to save social contract theories from circularity. Instead, many rely on the neoclassical definition of contract as voluntary in excluding concepts of power from their models. Buchanan and Tullock did this explicitly: "The early theorists (Hobbes, Althusius, Locke, and Rousseau) did assume consensus in the formation of the original contract. They did so because the essence of any contractual arrangement is voluntary participation, and no rational being will voluntarily agree to something which yields him, in net terms, expected damage or harm."[50] Thus, neoclassical economic theories of property rights do not recognize exercises of power because such rights are a form of contract, and contracts, by definition, cannot involve exercises of power. This view is so widespread among neoclassical economists that many rely on unelaborated references to contracts, or contracting, to rule out discussions of power in the creation of property rights or other institutions.

However, even inclusion of the argument for the substantive equality of "rational beings" in a state of nature does not remove issues of power from the creation and change of institutions for several reasons. First, social contract theories only posit rational status and equality for some individuals—those who qualify as the constitutive elements of a state of nature or society. Until recently these "rational beings" were always adult men, and usually only those from dominant social or ethnic groups. And social contract theories have always separated consideration of relations within families, defined as including servants, from relations between the adult male representatives of families and the state. These theories recognize the exercise of power within families, between husband and wife, father and child, and master and servant, as legitimate.[51] Thus social contract theories have relied on the prior existence of some institutions, including property institutions, to define rational beings, who are then assumed to be equal. Expansion of the definition of the constitutive elements of the social order to include all humans, or adult humans, removes the logical inconsistency of property institutions that precede society but asserts a much broader conception of equality than did Hobbes, one that is difficult to defend in historical terms.

Demsetz, whose 1967 article is often used as the starting point for mainstream economic theories of property rights, began his theoretical discussion of the creation of private property rights with an example of the evolution of property rights in land from "communal" ownership to private property. In his view, communal property has associated externalities, most importantly those connected with an overuse of resources and attempts to mitigate overuse are subject to prohibitively high transaction costs—those of negotiating and policing—due to the large number of people who must be involved in decisions; thus he effectively defined communal property as open access. Private property rights first arise to internalize the externalities found in this original state when changes in knowledge, technology, and markets make it cost effective to do so. These changes may either raise benefits available to those who undertake this change, or lower the costs of transacting the change. The assumption that both the costs and benefits of private resource ownership are internalized leads Demsetz to the conclusion that private property is more efficient than other forms of property, and thus raises overall social welfare. Some externalities continue to exist after this initial creation of private property because the costs of creating property rights to remove them are greater than the benefits of doing so. Later changes in knowledge, technology, and markets also lead to further increases in private property rights.[52] Following this approach, most mainstream theories of institutional change have assumed, either explicitly or implicitly, that in "market-oriented" societies there is a trend over time to increased internalization of externalities, due to increases in private property, which increases efficiency.

Demsetz did not explain why the dispossessed accept the new property arrangements. Fair recompense would surely be blocked by the same negotiation costs that block wise use of communal resources, so we are left with the idea that the costs of dispossessing others have become lower than the benefits *for the individuals* who undertake creation of the new property rights, but no proof that there has been any overall increase in benefits or improvement in use of resources. In other words, creation of property rights can be merely cost shifting instead of efficiency enhancing, and can involve an exercise of power.[53] And even if overall benefits increase, there is no reason to assume that the losers have been compensated by the winners, as is required by the assumption that both costs and benefits of the change are internalized. Outside of the fairly unrealistic and uninteresting world of the strict neoclassical model, the opposite conclusion is more valid, that in struggles to create property rights the winners appropriate all the benefits they can, and accept only the costs they cannot avoid.

James Boyce's study of the introduction of green revolution agricultural technologies in the Philippines illustrates this point about struggles over the distribution of costs and benefits of institutional change. Boyce found that the benefits of the new technologies were highly concentrated, while the costs were disproportionately borne by the poorest segments of the population. This result contradicted the expectations of the international agencies promoting these new technologies, which were that the new rice technology would have a positive distributional impact on the poor. The adverse results of the green revolution strategy in the Philippines were due to a failure to introduce changes, such as land reform, in institutions that governed the production of food and its distribution. Boyce found that interactions between wealth and power set in motion a cumulative process of economic and political polarization, in which initial inequalities between groups were widened because the wealthy were better able to prevail in contests over rights to land, water, and other endowments; to impose negative externalities on others; to exercise price-making power in credit, input, and rice markets; and to influence government policies and their implementation.[54] So there are questions prior to those posed by Demsetz in 1967: What determines the costs and benefits associated with changes in property rights and who will bear them? Considerations of power are central to a search for answers to these questions.

Institutionalist approaches to economics have logical relationships to a number of behavioral and structural theories of power, however unrecognized these links may be by most economists. In the social sciences outside the realm of neoclassical economics, the starting point for many current discussions on the meaning of power is still the "faces of power" debate, an extended exchange from the political science literature of the 1960s and 1970s.[55] This debate evolved around a number of issues, including definition of the social entities involved in an exercise of power, the role of behavior in the exercise of power, and what elements must exist or be observed to find an exercise of power. It began with Robert Dahl's *Who Governs? Democracy and Power in an American City*, which examined power from a methodological individualist viewpoint and defined power as a successful attempt by one individual to get another to do something he or she would not otherwise do. The work of Peter Bachrach and Morton Baratz, and that of Steven Lukes, further defined the debate.

Bachrach and Baratz, and Lukes, generally presented a behavioral model of power based on individual or group actions and decisions, but included elements in their overall discussion that alluded to structural determinants of power. Bachrach and Baratz described the importance of institutions, ideologies, and vested interests for the choices available to members of a society in ways that are similar to the mainstream economic literature on institutional change, particularly the work of North and Libecap. Bachrach and Baratz went beyond the economic literature by recognizing that individuals can exercise power through the medium of institutions and ideologies by shaping options—the "second face of power." Bachrach and Baratz described "a set of predominant values, beliefs, rituals, and institutional procedures ("rules of the game") that operates systematically and consistently to the benefit of certain persons and groups at the expense of others. Those who benefit are placed in a preferred position to defend and promote their vested interests."[56]

In Lukes's view, the study of power must extend beyond behaviorism to the structuring and patterning of group and individual behavior and to the practices of institutions. The exercise of power can be present, unrecognized by those affected, in situations where people are unaware either that alternatives to their perceived menu of choices exist or where their perceived wants are opposed to their "real" interests. Lukes went further than Bachrach and Baratz by recognizing that institutions and ideologies influence people's desires as well as their choices, through control of information, the mass media, and the process of socialization. He saw this process of socialization as the result of individually chosen acts, group action, collective policies, and the influence of "organizational forms."[57] Organizational forms seem to correspond to economists' definitions of institutions. If institutions cannot be assumed to be efficient or to evolve in that direction, as is the case in the models of North and Williamson, then there is room for the exercise of power by some individuals and groups in the processes by which institutions and ideologies shape endogenous preferences.

More recently developed structural theories of power, particularly those of Jeffrey Isaac and Thomas Wartenburg, also have important parallels to the work of institutional economists. Isaac argues for a realist theory of power in which "social power" is understood in terms of the underlying relations that structure behavioral interaction. He emphasizes that purposive human activity, such as is observed by behavioral theorists of power, has social preconditions that are relatively enduring relations such as marriage, employment, and citizenship. Isaac defines social power as the capacity to act, which results from enduring structural relationships in a society, and which is exercised by individuals and groups based on their location in a given structure. Isaac further argues that a structural theory of power does not detach the concept of power from human agency. While the exercise of social power always is shaped and constrained by underlying relational structures, it also is determined by the way particular individuals and groups choose to deal with their circumstances. In his view, the powers to act are part of the nature of socially structured relationships, but the successful exercise of these powers is not predetermined.[58]

Wartenberg's theory of "situated social power" sees power as the result of social arrangements, rather than the attributes of individuals. He describes a power relation between dominant and subordinate individuals as the result of the actions of others who are in control of desirable resources, and who respond in a coordinated fashion to the actions or signals of the dominant individual. It is the difference in the responses of others to the dominant and subordinate individuals in the power relationship that make it one of power, because these responses make threats by the dominant individuals effective.[59] Wartenberg argues that power operates through the structuring of human skills, desires, and expectations, as well as in more direct ways. Wartenberg also makes the point that power is often "a factor in a social situation because of human beings' expectations about what might happen to them. Power can be a significant factor in social relationships even when it exists as a set of complex anticipated reactions to the assumed actions of remote social agents."[60] These ideas echo accounts by North and Libecap of the continuing influence of historical institutions on economic choices due to their creation of vested interests, of opportunities for organizational and entrepreneurial activities, and of individual knowledge, skills, and expectations of the world. North and Libecap prefer to view these effects as an expanded set of constraints on individual choice rather than to discuss them in the language of power. Randall Bartlett's *Economics and Power* provides an extended discussion of why this approach cannot be used to remove power from economic models. He argues that the constrained-decisionmaking-in-market-setting model does not logically eliminate the exercise of power because property rights have historically been created without compensation or universal accord. Therefore the foundations of market economies involve the exercise of power while their ongoing support involves state enforcement of particular types of rights. Further, these foundations are constantly being renewed and renegotiated, in a process that involves further exercises of power.[61]

An expanded approach to institutional economics, which acknowledges a role for economic and political power in the economy, allows the separate consideration of structural and behavioral aspects of power without downplaying the importance of either. The structural theories of power considered above are related to the roles played by existing institutions and ideologies as factors in the creation of property rights and other institutions. Behaviorally based concepts of power are related to the exercise of power by economic actors, whether individuals or groups. It is the ability to act, and not the success of the action that defines an exercise of economic or political power. Exercises of economic and political power directed at the creation of property rights or other institutions can fail to achieve their desired ends. However, power is obviously transmitted through (operates through) institutions and ideologies and finds partial expression through the creation of economic actors.[62]

The exercise of political and economic power by various economic actors engaged in struggles over spectrum rights in the United States before 1927 included a broad range of investments, lobbying, and use of the spectrum aimed at shaping access and rights, as well as the distribution of the costs of enforcement of these rights and the nature of associated externalities. These activities included research and development, patent battles, technical demonstrations, network building, organization building, the provision of equipment and service to customers below cost, use of the spectrum to establish claims or prevent use by others, lobbying Congress and the public over legislation and regulation, attempts to shape debates and agendas, competition and/or cooperation with other interests, and attempts to develop norms for acceptable use of the spectrum.

Conclusion

Radio Spectrum Property Rights

Three of the five factors constraining property rights were similar in the United States and Europe at the end of the nineteenth century when wireless communications technologies were first developed. The radio spectrum is a globally accessible common-pool resource, making the measurement, monitoring, and enforcement costs of any system of spectrum rights high. While the original development of a reliable wireless communications technology was a lengthy, difficult, and expensive process, once the basic technology was invented, many were able to duplicate it, making the pool of potential users large, and creating the possibility of severe problems of interference and scarcity. Scarcity has continued to be a concern because technological improvements that save on spectrum use have been balanced by innovations that increase demand for spectrum products. The same range of technological options for wireless communication was available in the United States and Europe because knowledge of new wireless innovations was widely circulated in scientific and hobby journals and lectures on both sides of the Atlantic. The radio spectrum is everywhere an input to communications and information products and services with many public goods aspects. Despite these similarities, the establishment of property rights in the radio spectrum in the United States took a very different form than in European countries. In the United States, the development of a stable set of property rights took far longer and granted more rights to private interests. Public good concerns played a dominant role in the development of property rights in the radio spectrum in European countries, while they had a much smaller role in the United States. These differences were due to the ideological and institutional contexts within which spectrum rights developed in each area.

In the United States this context was one of competing ideologies and institutions. These conflicts shaped spectrum rights by delaying the creation of a stable property rights system, which allowed the development of varied economic actors who struggled over spectrum rights. Until 1912 the radio spectrum was an open-access resource in the United States. This situation was unstable because the spectrum was a scarce resource—especially in the neighborhood of important ports—while the public goods aspects of marine wireless communications were widely seen as both of national importance and essential to safety at sea. The communications branches of the military services, the Commerce Department, private wireless communications companies, scientists, inventors, and amateur enthusiasts all competed to use the spectrum and to influence the creation of property rights in the spectrum.

Competing ideologies concerning the proper role of the federal government and private business in a democracy also influenced the evolution of rights in the radio spectrum. Three views of the proper role of government in the economy and society were important: first, that the government's role was to provide for the health and safety of its citizens, including, in some versions, the creation of a strong military; second, that the government's most important function was to encourage and support private business activities; and third, that the government should provide essential services for its citizens, such as mass communications. Ideas on the proper role of private businesses ranged from the view that unfettered private business provided the best foundation for the well-being of the country, to the view that some goods and services were too important to be trusted to self-interested profit seeking.

The U.S. Navy, at the height of its power and influence after the Spanish-American War, offered one ready alternative for providing marine communications and controlling the spectrum at the beginning of the radio era. The naval network of wireless stations expanded more rapidly than that of any of the commercial firms before World War I and provided service to private ships as well as its own fleet. The Navy attempted to create a unified system under its control in which its network would be the primary provider of marine wireless, and regulatory authority over all users would be vested in the secretary of the navy. Under this system, commercial wireless firms would be primarily research, development, and manufacturing concerns, with limited rights to use the spectrum. The Navy's claim to the spectrum was made on the grounds that naval control of wireless was necessary to insure safety at sea and the national defense.

Competition between champions of government control and commercial rights hindered passage of any legislation controlling use of the spectrum before 1912. This period of delay in regulating the spectrum was crucial in allowing commercial wireless networks to develop. By 1912 commercial wireless firms had built up networks of stations and clients, and thereby created vested interests on the part of investors, employees, and customers that led these parties to participate in struggles over how the spectrum would be used and allocated. Use of the spectrum by these commercial wireless companies also helped validate their claims to rights in the spectrum. Initially, the private wireless communications firms were opposed to any form of government regulation of the radio spectrum, but by 1912 some supported the idea of a regulated industry with power vested in the Commerce Department, in large part due to concerns over unfettered amateur use of the spectrum interfering with their businesses. The activities of commercial wireless companies before 1912 established a strong base for commercial claims to property rights in the spectrum in later periods, including the 1920s when broadcasting became widespread.

Congress finally passed the Radio Act of 1912, which had an enforcement mechanism that drew on the Commerce Department and the Navy. The allocation methods of this act worked for a time, in part because one wireless company, American Marconi, had gained a near-monopoly of the commercial wireless market, largely internalizing the issue of sharing the spectrum for commercial use. The 1912 act also specified a time-sharing arrangement for cases where civilian and naval stations interfered with each other. The Commerce Department policed civilian use of the spectrum, concentrating on controlling amateur use of the spectrum. Most use of the spectrum was still for wireless telegraphy (code signals), which limited mass interest in its use outside of marine communications. While the Navy Department considered the Radio Act of 1912 a major advance on an unregulated spectrum, it had not abandoned its attempts to gain control of spectrum allocation. The act worked temporarily to control use of the spectrum, because some conflicts were muted in this period.

The Radio Act of 1912 granted the Navy right to control the spectrum in times of war, and this clause took effect when the United States entered World War I. The period from 1917 to 1919 was also temporarily stable. Commercial radio companies profited greatly from wartime manufacturing, commercial shipping fell off, and what remained used wireless only in emergencies. Many amateur and commercial wireless operators enlisted in the military, where they were in high demand. All this combined to make military use of the spectrum the primary demand for wireless. But civilian claims to spectrum rights and ideological opposition to government control were only temporarily suspended, not overcome, and the Navy was not able to retain control of the whole spectrum after the war. Wireless technology developed rapidly under naval oversight, and the pool of people familiar with the technology grew, factors that destabilized spectrum allocation after the war.

After World War I the large firms involved in the telecommunications industry attempted, with the support of the Navy and Commerce Departments, to return the wireless industry to its prewar configuration, with the Radio Corporation of America (RCA) taking the place of American Marconi as a commercial wireless monopoly. The focus of these actors was still long-distance point-to-point communications. However, new radio technology, based on the vacuum tube, was now cheaper and much more powerful, and many people had learned about its possibilities during the war. This created a new product market, broadcasting, and brought new actors into struggles over the radio spectrum. Some of the new broadcasters challenged Secretary of Commerce Hoover's attempts to allocate the spectrum based on the Radio Act of 1912, damaging his claim to legal authority by 1923.

The period between 1923 and 1926 was again one of instability, without a spectrum allocation system that was widely recognized as legitimate. Between 1923 and 1926, a sharp increase in the number of broadcasting stations, most small and individually run, made broadcasting the focus of public concerns about use of the spectrum, which now was widely viewed as public property. Large communications firms such as RCA and American Telephone & Telegraph (AT&T) responded to new product demands by moving into broadcasting, with support from Secretary Hoover. Opposition to domination of the spectrum by large firms came from both small broadcasters and the new mass audience, reinforced by the widespread antimonopoly sentiment of the time. The primary public good concerns of this period shifted from the safety, emergency, and military issues of previous periods to questions of how broadcasting would be supported, what kinds of programs would be aired, and how to ensure different regions of the country equitable access. The instability of this period led Congress to consider many bills on the subject, but final agreement took another four years until the passage of the Radio Act of 1927.

Between 1927 and the passage of the Communications Act of 1934, a stable system of property rights in the radio spectrum was defined and secured. The first piece was the 1927 act itself, which addressed several weaknesses of the Radio Act of 1912. The 1927 act explicitly stated that the spectrum was public property and that licenses and use of frequencies did not create private property rights. The right to transfer a license also was limited. The 1927 act created a Federal Radio Commission (FRC) with full authority to grant or refuse licenses and assign wavelengths—powers that had not been granted explicitly to the secretary of commerce in 1912. The 1927 act balanced some of the powerful competing interests in the spectrum by providing for separate allocation methods for military and civilian use, mandatory time sharing for shore stations that interfered with government stations, commercial service by naval stations in underserved areas, government control of the spectrum in times of war, and "equitable" regional allocation of broadcasting licenses. Monitoring of operators and equipment was left with the Radio Division of the Commerce Department, which also carried out all field work for the FRC. The 1927 act explicitly revoked earlier radio legislation but reenacted provisions of the 1912 act giving distress signals priority and mandating intercommunication among all marine stations. The 1927 act contained several antimonopoly provisions that addressed public resentment against monopolies without creating any real obstacles to use of the spectrum by RCA and AT&T.

The next piece of the property rights structure to be put in place was the assignment of use rights to frequencies through licensing, which was done by the FRC. The assignment of licenses for marine communications was not very controversial, as this area of use was dominated by a few large companies and the Navy, who had worked out methods of coexistence before and after World War I. The assignment of broadcasting licenses was highly controversial, even though it was supposed to be primarily a technical matter of working out optimum combinations of frequencies, transmitter locations, power levels, and allowed times of broadcast. The technical and engineering standards adopted by the FRC favored large, economically and politically powerful broadcasters, and forced smaller broadcasters, including educational, municipal, church, and labor groups off the air. Most of the decisions of the commission supported the growth of large commercial broadcasters linked by networks.[63] Despite its stated aim of extinguishing private property rights in the spectrum, the Radio Act of 1927 was in fact the basis for secure private rights for some favored entities, which allowed the development of a market for commercial broadcast licenses to develop.

During the period from 1927 to 1934, both the legality of the 1927 act, and the fairness of the Radio Commission's allocations were challenged. Courts upheld the constitutionality of the act, and challenges to the spectrum assignments made by the FRC that favored commercial interests over nonprofits were unsuccessful. The passage of the Communications Act of 1934, which incorporated the provisions of the Radio Act of 1927, marked the end of widespread challenges to federal regulatory authority over spectrum allocations and to commercial domination of broadcasting. Thus, after a long period of struggle over property rights in the radio spectrum, a stable property rights structure was constructed, one that could easily incorporate further changes in factors such as technology and product markets, as seen with the development of television. This system of spectrum property rights has had far-reaching consequences for many aspects of life in the United States, from politics to education, and even has been exported as a model to other countries. While the 2003 Supreme Court decision in the *NextWave* spectrum license case may indicate that this long period of stability is over, future arrangements will continue to be strongly influenced by the current system.[64]

In particular, the structure of costs, benefits, and externalities that has evolved under the current system of spectrum rights remains largely unquestioned. The structure and assignment of transaction costs associated with rights to the spectrum is a central, although often overlooked, element of the United States system. The system of property rights that was developed over the first three decades of the twentieth century provides for commercial rights that are close to de facto private rights, with the important exception that most of the associated costs of enforcing commercial rights, as well as the other recognized claims to the spectrum, is borne directly by the federal government. These costs include the extensive monitoring, measuring, and legal enforcement efforts of the Commerce Department in the past and the Federal Communications Commission (FCC) since 1934. Due to the open-access nature of the spectrum, an alternative system of court-enforced private rights would place higher enforcement costs on those assigned rights in the spectrum, considerably reducing commercial profits. Economic actors who favored private rights to spectrum use in the first three decades of the twentieth century were keenly aware of these characteristics that eventually led them to accept federal regulation of spectrum use. The concept of public ownership and federal control of the spectrum also received support from military interests concerned with maintaining control over at least some portions of the spectrum, and the deeply rooted beliefs of some actors that mass communications systems were an essential element in a democracy, too important to be left entirely to commercial incentives. But the primary objective of federal regulation, then and now, is enforcement, largely of commercial rights.[65]

Endogenous Property Rights

The enduring importance of Demsetz's 1967 article, "Toward a Theory of Property Rights," is that it reintroduced the issue of endogenous property rights into mainstream economics, even though many economists have been reluctant to acknowledge it. This reluctance is characterized by Abba Lerner's 1972 definition of the domain of economics as that of "solved political problems."[66] Lerner's domain is only one sphere of economic action, however, that of choice within stable property rights structures. The process of creating property rights is another sphere of economic action, one that converts varied initial possibilities into the stable, orderly situation of Lerner's domain. Stable property rights systems do limit the range of choices available to economic actors, as well as the range of economic actors themselves, and make economic choices seem regular and well ordered. The process of creating these stable property rights structures is as important to economic theory as the analysis of behavior within them. And the key role of property rights in shaping economic opportunities makes the process of creating property rights institutions central to analyses of economic history as well as to theory.

Before property rights in a resource stabilize, economic actors work to establish a system of rights assignments, enforcement, and externalities they think will be favorable to their interests. In doing this they are creating and shaping markets. Property rights structures are created through the actions of various institutionally defined actors using what economic and political power is available to them, which is also socially defined. Property rights structures in a given resource can take many forms, which distribute the costs and benefits associated with use of the resource differently. Private property rights are merely one form of such rights, and do not automatically internalize both the costs and benefits associated with ownership and use of a resource. Struggles over property rights are often attempts to appropriate the benefits of economic resources for some groups, while shifting the costs of use or enforcement to others. However, the forms that property rights can take are not infinite. Instead they are constrained by the five factors examined in this chapter: resource characteristics, technology, product markets, existing institutions, and ideologies. The long-run stability of a property-rights structure depends on the way that socially chosen forms of property interact with these five factors. The process of creating property rights in the radio spectrum in the United States provides a particularly strong illustration of the necessity of considering the influences of institutions and ideologies, along with those of resource characteristic, technology, and product markets, in shaping property rights structures. It also illustrates the need to integrate concepts of power into economic analyses.

Notes

I would like to thank James K. Boyce, John Brigham, and J. Mohan Rao for their comments on earlier versions of this chapter.

1. Examples of work that focuses on the consequences of property rights structures rather than their origins include Ronald H. Coase, "The Federal Communications Commission"; idem, "The Problem of Social Cost"; Oliver E. Williamson, *The Economic Institutions of Capitalism*; Oliver Hart, *Firms, Contracts, and Financial Structure*; and Robert D. Cooter, "Economic Theories of Legal Liability."

2. For work on economic growth, see Douglass C. North and Robert Paul Thomas, *The Rise of the Western World*; Douglas C. North, *Structure and Change in Economic History*; idem, *Institutions, Institutional Change, and Economic Performance*; idem, "Institutions and Credible Commitment"; idem, "The Evolution of Efficient Markets in History"; idem, "The Historical Evolution of Polities"; Gary D. Libecap, *Contracting for Property Rights*; and Thomas S. Ulen, "Law's Contribution to Economic Growth." For work on the adoption of new technologies, see Hans P. Binswanger, "Induced Technical Change"; Vernon W. Ruttan, "Induced Institutional Change"; idem, "Institutional Innovation and Agricultural Development"; and James K. Boyce, *Agrarian Impasse in Bengal*. For work on distributional issues, see Boyce, *Agrarian Impasse in Bengal*; idem, *The Philippines*; Daniel W. Bromley, *Economic Interests and Institutions*; Robert Wade, "The Management of Common Property Resources"; Pranab Bardhan, "Symposium on Management of Local Commons"; and Elinor Ostrom and Roy Gardner, "Coping with Asymmetries in the Commons."

3. Ronald H. Coase, *The Firm, the Market, and the Law*; Ieuan Williams, "Rationality and Human Nature in Economics and Law"; Jason Scott Johnston, "Law, Economics, and Post-Realist Explanation"; Williamson, *The Economic Institutions of Capitalism*; Dieter Schmidtchen, "Time, Uncertainty, and Subjectivism"; North, "Institutions and Credible Commitment"; idem, "The Evolution of Efficient Markets in History"; and idem, "The Historical Evolution of Polities."

4. North, "Institutions and Credible Commitment."

5. The radio spectrum is a region of the electromagnetic spectrum. The physical properties of regions of the electromagnetic spectrum vary by wavelength, measured as the distance between two crests of the wave, through progressively shorter sonic waves, radio waves, microwaves, infrared, visible light, ultraviolet, x-rays, and gamma rays. Any given wavelength has a corresponding frequency that varies inversely with

its length, so the term frequency also is used to indicate a particular area of the spectrum. Radio waves can travel long distances rapidly through the atmosphere, but they are not detectable by human senses until converted by a receiver to sound waves. This makes radio waves ideal as a means of long-distance, wireless communication.

6. These are private rights in the economic rather than legal sense. Private licenses for the use of the spectrum are issued for limited periods, must be renewed, are revokable, and cannot be transferred without permission of the regulatory commission. In addition, licensees must waive any claim to ownership of the portion of the spectrum they use as a condition of receiving the license. Yet, in effect, most private business users have been granted some property rights in portions of the spectrum that include an ability to sell the license with the expectation of approval, and an expectation of indefinite occupancy otherwise. Technically, the station and equipment are being sold, subject to FCC approval of transfer of the license, but a large part of the purchase price actually reflects the value of the license. Coase noted this fact in his 1959 article "The Federal Communications Commission." For an illustration of the viewpoint that private rights to the spectrum do not exist, see Stephen Sewell, "Assignments and Transfers of Control of FCC Authorizations under Section 310(d) of the Communications Act of 1934."

7. Schmidtchen, "Time, Uncertainty, and Subjectivism," 65–66.

8. North, *Institutions, Institutional Change, and Economic Performance*, 51.

9. Wade, "The Management of Common Property Resources"; Daniel W. Bromley, "The Commons, Property, and Common-Property Regimes"; Elinor Ostrom, "The Rudiments of a Theory of the Origin, Survival, and Performance of Common-Property Institutions"; and Ostrom and Gardiner, "Coping with Asymmetries in the Commons."

10. Harold Demsetz, "Toward a Theory of Property Rights," 357; North and Thomas, *The Rise of the Western World*, 1–3; and Libecap, *Contracting for Property Rights*, 1–2, 12.

11. Bonnie J. McCay and James M. Acheson, "Human Ecology of the Commons"; David Feeny et al., "The Tragedy of the Commons: Twenty-two Years Later"; Bromley, *Economic Interest and Institutions*; Ford C. Runge, "Common Property and Collective Action in Economic Development"; Ostrom, "The Rudiments of a Theory of the Origin, Survival, and Performance of Common-Property Institutions"; and Ostrom and Gardiner, "Coping with Asymmetries in the Commons."

12. Runge, "Common Property and Collective Action in Economic Development," 19–20.

13. Elizabeth Kruse, "From Free Privilege to Regulation."

14. North and Thomas, *The Rise of the Western World*, 2; North, *Structure and Change in Economic History*, 165; and Williamson, *The Economic Institutions of Capitalism*, 2.

15. Yujiro Hayami, *Development Economics*, 4.

16. Terry L. Anderson and P.J. Hill, "The Evolution of Property Rights."

17. North, *Structure and Change in Economic History*, 26, 204; idem, *Institutions, Institutional Change, and Economic Performance*, 54; Yoram Barzel, *Economic Analysis of Property Rights*, 3–4.

18. Strict neoclassical economic models view technological change as a "black box" from which emerge exogenous influences which the economy then adapts to in a manner that leads to a new Pareto-optimal equilibrium. Early economic literature on property rights, such as Demsetz, "Toward a Theory of Property Rights," followed this approach, citing technological change as one of the exogenous influences leading

to the creation or change of property rights in resources. However, technological determinism, the idea that technologies are an independent factor to which the economy adapts, has been rejected by most economists who study technological change and the history of technology. This body of work has shown that economic interests are a strong influence on the direction and timing of technological change. See, for example, Nathan Rosenberg, *Technology and American Economic Growth*; idem, *Inside the Black Box*; Paul David, *Technical Choice, Innovation and Economic Growth*; Richard R. Nelson, "Institutions Supporting Technical Advance in Industry"; Thomas P. Hughes, "The Evolution of Large Technological Systems"; Boyce, *Agrarian Impasse in Bengal*; and Hayami, *Development Economics*; North and Thomas, in *The Rise of the Western World*, also rejected the idea of exogenous technological change on slightly different grounds, arguing that it is institutional change that facilitates technological change, rather than the reverse.

19. Kruse, "From Free Privilege to Regulation," 665.

20. Encryptation only fences the information content carried by the frequency. One purpose of wire communications is to contain and direct electrical signals. It is the difficulty or impossibility of extending these electrical "fences" (wires) everywhere that make wireless communication desirable.

21. Demsetz, "Toward a Theory of Property Rights," 351–3.

22. William Cronon, *Changes in the Land*, 58–68. However, later Cronon does give a description of the progression of property rights to hunting lands in one area of what is now Maine that is similar in part to that of Demsetz; although his views on property rights changes in general are not. Cronon does not see the developments in Maine as typical of the New England region as a whole, 105–6; also 194, *n*40.

23. Eric R. Wolf, *Europe and the People Without History*, 161.

24. Demsetz, "Toward a Theory of Property Rights," 348; North and Thomas, *The Rise of the Western World*, 2–3.

25. Eric Wolf discusses the impact of the expanding North American fur trade on successive groups of Native Americans in *Europe and the People Without History*, 158–94. He sums up the chapter thus:

> Wherever it went, the fur trade brought with it contagious illness and increased warfare. Many native groups were destroyed, and disappeared entirely; other were decimated, broken up or driven from their original habitats. Remnant populations sought refuge with allies or grouped together with other populations, often under new names and ethnic identities. A few, like the Iroquois, expanded at the expense of their neighbors. (193)

26. Gary S. Becker, "A Theory of Competition among Pressure Groups for Political Influence"; idem, "Public Policies, Pressure Groups, and Dead Weight Costs"; Dennis C. Mueller, *Public Choice II*, 4–5.

27. Demsetz, "Toward a Theory of Property Rights," and Barzel, *Economic Analysis of Property Rights*.

28. For more discussion of the public goods aspects of radio communications and broadcasting see Elizabeth Kruse, "Property From the Sky," 84–87, 176–82.

29. For more discussion of these issues, see Susan Douglas, *Inventing American Broadcasting, 1899–1922*; Robert W. McChesney, *Telecommunications, Mass Media, & Democracy*; and James T. Hamilton, *Channeling Violence*.

30. North, *Structure and Change in Economic History*, 49.

31. North, *Structure and Change in Economic History*, 48–51; idem, *Institutions, Institutional Change, and Economic Performance*, 16–20, 97; idem, "The Historical Evolution of Polities," 383–5.

32. North, *Structure and Change in Economic History*, 19, 31, 45–47, 51; idem, "Institutions and Credible Commitment," 13–6.

33. North and Thomas, *The Rise of the Western World*; North, "Institutions and Credible Commitment," 11–12, 16–17.

34. A.I. Ogus, "The Parameters of Law and Economics," 18–19, 26; Alan Hunt, "On Legal Relations and Economic Relations," 57.

35. The "Critical Legal Studies" movement and constitutive theories of the law provide examples of work that rejects the base-superstructure dichotomy. See Hunt, "On Legal Relations and Economic Relations," 58, 82; and John Brigham, *The Constitution of Interests.*

36. North, *Institutions, Institutional Change, and Economic Performance*; idem, "Institutions and Credible Commitment"; idem, "The Historical Evolution of Polities"; Nicholas Mecuro and Steven G. Medema, *Economics and the Law*, 157, 160–8.

37. For more discussion of these issues, see Kruse, "From Free Privilege to Regulation"; idem, "Property from the Sky."

38. Barzel, *Economic Analysis of Property Rights*, 62.

39. For example, in the introduction to *The Regulated Economy*, Claudia Goldin and Gary D. Libecap state that the volume explores "how particular ex ante institutional arrangements altered the form of government regulation," 1. Many of the papers in the volume discuss "prior" or "preexisting" institutions, while only one, Keith T. Poole and Howard Rosenthal, "Congress and Railroad Regulation: 1874 to 1887," discusses ideology.

40. Ruttan, "Institutional Innovation and Agricultural Development," 1376.

41. North, *Institutions, Institutional Change, and Economic Performance*, 7–8, 21–22; idem, "Institutions and Credible Commitment," 17.

42. Gary Libecap, "The Political Economy of Institutional Change," 255–56; idem, *Contracting for Property Rights*, 18.

43. Ibid., 116. In contrast to the way ideology has been handled in economic literature, the role of existing institutions in structuring further institutional change has been examined in concrete historical case studies. In these works, particularly those of North and Libecap, the activities of a variety of individuals and groups is examined. However, some of the theoretical implications of this work have been ignored even by its authors, while economists cling to the concept of economic actors as individuals, whether rational or not. Yet by explaining the lasting influence of institutions on economic choices by the creation of vested interests, organizations, and economic actors themselves, North and Libecap have introduced a variety of economic actors into their theoretical models of the economy, as well as their case studies, which can only partially be reduced to mere agglomerations of "economic man." For more discussion of definitions of economic actors, see Kruse, "Property from the Sky," 47–55.

44. See Abba Lerner, "Economics and Politics of Consumer Sovereignty," 259; and Samuel Bowles and Herbert Gintis, *Democracy and Capitalism*, 64–71. The school of economics known as "Institutionalist" or "Evolutionary" economics is the major exception to this generalization about economists and power. John Kenneth Galbraith took the power blindness of neoclassical economics as the subject of his presidential

address to the American Economics Association: "Power and the Useful Economist." However, Galbraith saw the development of economic power as a relatively recent phenomena, linked to the rise of modern corporate structures rather than as inherent in the creation of property rights. Concepts of power and property rights also are central to Hart's theory of firm structure set out in *Firms, Contracts, and Financial Structure*. However, this work focuses on the consequences of property rights structures rather than examining their origins. See Randall Bartlett, *Economics and Power*, for an economic theory of power built on "the restrictive foundations of neoclassical economics . . . the most hostile of foundations," 17. Bartlett argues that all economic models that acknowledge limited information and intellect should acknowledge the exercise of power at several levels, including the connection between rights and power and the exercise of power at the foundation of market exchange.

45. For examples of power analyses without institutions, see Gary Becker, "A Theory of Competition among Pressure Groups for Political Influence"; idem, "Public Policies, Pressure Groups, and Dead Weight Costs."

46. One tradition of theorizing power, including the work of Talcott Parsons, defines power in direct opposition to the use of violence and force. Parson's definition of power corresponds to the definition of property rights used by most scholars of law and economics and institutional change (allowing for differences of style). "Power . . . is generalized capacity to secure the performance of binding obligation by units of a system of collective organization when the obligations are legitimized with reference to their bearing on collective goals and where in case of recalcitrance there is a presumption of enforcement by negative situational sanctions—whatever the actual agency of that enforcement" (Parsons quoted in Steven Lukes, *Power*, 28). This "unviolent" definition of power sees power as arising from a social contract, and has the same limitations as neoclassical views of property rights. Lukes, rightly in my view, criticizes definitions of power that have it existing only where force does not, as out of line with traditional and common uses of the term. A better concept of power includes violence, or the implied threat of violence, as well as more indirect forms of control. Thomas Wartenberg in the Introduction to *Rethinking Power*, xix, makes the important point that power is often "a factor in a social situation because of human expectations about what might happen to them. Power can be a significant factor in social relationships even when it exists as a set of complex anticipated reactions to the assumed actions of remote social agents."

47. For examples, see North and Thomas, *Rise of the Western World*, 69; Anderson and Hill, "The Evolution of Property Rights," 168; and Gary D. Libecap, "Politics, Institutions, and Institutional Change," 32. There are also areas of "buried power" in the economic literature on work relations and the structure of firms. In this area, power usually is buried also by reference to contracts of one sort or another, see Ronald Coase, "The Nature of the Firm"; and Bartlett, *Economics and Power*, 5–7. I have borrowed the metaphor from Bartlett, 6, although my discussion of the problem does not parallel his closely.

48. Norberto Bobbio, *Thomas Hobbes and the Natural Law Tradition*, 2.

49. Thomas Hobbes, *Leviathan*, 183.

50. James M. Buchanan and Gordon Tullock, *The Calculus of Consent*, 251–52.

51. Bobbio, *Thomas Hobbes and the Natural Law Tradition*, 15–20.

52. Demsetz, "Toward a Theory of Property Rights," 354–58.

53. Boyce, *Agrarian Impasse in Bengal*, 28–30.

54. Boyce, *The Philippines*, 126–54.

55. Robert A. Dahl, *Who Governs?*; Peter Bachrach and Morton S. Baratz, "The

Two Faces of Power"; Lukes, *Power*.

56. Bachrach and Baratz, quoted in Lukes, *Power*, 17.

57. Lukes, *Power*, 21–26.

58. Jeffrey C. Isaac "Beyond the Three Faces of Power," 42–55.

59. Thomas E. Wartenberg, "Situated Social Power," 79–101.

60. Wartenberg, "Introduction," xix.

61. Bartlett, *Economics and Power*, 62, 149–64.

62. For example, some recent work on the economic theory of regulation highlights the institutional aspects of the exercise of economic and political power by individuals. Charles W. Calomiris and Eugene N. White, in their study of the origin of federal deposit insurance, state that "the power of the [Congressional] committee chairmen is difficult to exaggerate." See "The Origins of Federal Deposit Insurance." 153. This work, and that of Poole and Rosenthal, "Congress and Railroad Regulation," make it clear that the role of legislators in creating property rights and shaping markets cannot be modeled simply as an exchange between neoclassical individual legislators and constituents, or even between legislators and interest groups.

63. For detailed analyses of these allocation decisions, see Hugh Richard Slotten, "Radio Engineers, the Federal Radio Commission, and the Social Shaping of Broadcast Technology"; and McChesney, *Telecommunications, Mass Media, & Democracy*.

64. NextWave, a start-up telecommunications company backed by large firms, won 200 licenses for broadband spectrum communications services during a 1996 FCC auction with bids totaling almost 5 billion dollars. This fourth spectrum auction permitted payment over ten years for the licenses, on the condition that failure to pay meant automatic license cancellation. NextWave, after failing to make more than the first payment, entered bankruptcy in 1998. The FCC confiscated the licenses and tried to reauction them. NextWave sued the FCC on the grounds that its action violated federal bankruptcy law, and eventually the case made its way to the Supreme Court, which ruled in favor of NextWave in January 2003. The FCC argued that it had a valid regulatory motive for its action and that regulatory conditions like full and timely payment are not properly classified as "debts" under bankruptcy law. The majority decision found these arguments irrelevant. See *Federal Communication Commission v. NextWave Personal Communication Inc. et al.* 537 U.S. 293 (2003).

65. For more discussion of the creation of property rights in the radio spectrum in the United States, see Kruse, "From Free Privilege to Regulation" and idem, "Property from the Sky."

66. Lerner, "Economics and Politics of Consumer Sovereignty," 259.

References

Anderson, T.L., and P.J. Hill. "The Evolution of Property Rights: A Study of the American West." *Journal of Law and Economics* 18, no. 1 (1975): 163–79.

Bachrach, P., and M.S. Baratz. "The Two Faces of Power." *American Political Science Review* 56 (1962): 947–52.

Bardhan, P. "Symposium on Management of Local Commons." *Journal of Economic Perspectives* 7, no. 4 (1993): 87–92.

Bartlett, R. *Economics and Power*. New York: Cambridge University Press, 1989.

Barzel, Y. *Economic Analysis of Property Rights*. Cambridge, MA: Cambridge University Press, 1989.

Becker, G.S. "Public Policies, Pressure Groups, and Dead Weight Costs." *Journal of Public Economics* 28 (December 1985): 329–47.

———. "A Theory of Competition among Pressure Groups for Political Influence." *Quarterly Journal of Economics* 98 (August 1983): 371–400.

Binswanger, H.P. "Induced Technical Change: Evolution in Thought." In *Induced Innovation*, ed. Binswanger and Ruttan, 13–43.

Bobbio, N. *Thomas Hobbes and the Natural Law Tradition*, trans. D. Gobetti. Chicago: University of Chicago Press, 1993.

Bowles, S., and H. Gintis. *Democracy and Capitalism*. New York: Basic Books, 1986.

Boyce, J.K. *Agrarian Impasse in Bengal: Institutional Constraints to Technological Change*. New York: Oxford University Press, 1987.

———. *The Philippines: The Political Economy of Growth and Impoverishment in the Marcos Era*. Honolulu: University of Hawaii Press, 1993.

Brigham, J. *The Constitution of Interests: Beyond the Politics of Rights*. New York: New York University Press, 1996.

Bromley, D.W. "The Commons, Property, and Common-Property Regimes." In *Making the Commons Work*, ed. Bromley, 3–15.

———. *Economic Interests and Institutions*. New York: Basil Blackwell, 1989.

———., ed. *Making the Commons Work*. San Francisco: ICS Press, 1992.

Buchanan, J.M., and G. Tullock. *The Calculus of Consent: Logical Foundations of Constitutional Democracy*. Ann Arbor: University of Michigan Press, 1962.

Calomiris, C.W., and E.N. White. "The Origins of Federal Deposit Insurance." In *The Regulated Economy*, ed. Goldin and Libecap, 81–120.

Coase, R.H. "The Federal Communications Commission." *The Journal of Law & Economics* 2 (October 1959): 1–40.

———. *The Firm, the Market, and the Law*. Chicago: University of Chicago Press, 1988.

———. "The Nature of the Firm." *Economica* 4, no. 3 (November 1937): 386–405.

———. "The Problem of Social Cost." *The Journal of Law & Economics* 3 (October 1960): 1–44.

Cooter, R.D. "Economic Theories of Legal Liability." *Journal of Economic Perspectives* 5 (Summer 1991): 11–30.

Cronon, W. *Changes in the Land*. New York: Hill and Wang, 1983.

Dahl, R.A. *Who Governs? Democracy and Power in an American City*. New Haven, CT: Yale University Press, 1961.

David, P. *Technical Choice, Innovation and Economic Growth*. Cambridge, MA: Cambridge University Press, 1975.

Demsetz, H. "Toward a Theory of Property Rights." *American Economic Review* 57 (May 1967): 347–79.

Douglas, S. *Inventing American Broadcasting 1899–1922*. Baltimore: Johns Hopkins University Press, 1987.

Feeny, D., F. Berkes, B.J. McCay, and J.M. Acheson. "The Tragedy of the Commons: Twenty-two Years Later." *Human Ecology* 18, no. 1 (1990): 1–19.

Galbraith, J.K. "Power and the Useful Economist." *American Economic Review* 61, no. 1 (March 1973): 1–11.

Goldin, C., and G.D. Libecap. "Introduction." In *The Regulated Economy*, ed. Goldin and Libecap, 1–11.

———, eds. *The Regulated Economy*. Chicago: University of Chicago Press, 1994.

Hamilton, J.T. *Channeling Violence: The Economic Market for Violent Television Programming*. Princeton, NJ: Princeton University Press, 1998.

Hart, O. *Firms, Contracts, and Financial Structure*. Oxford: Clarendon Press, 1995.

Hayami, Y. *Development Economics: From the Poverty to the Wealth of Nations*. Oxford: Clarendon Press, 1997.

Hobbes, T. *Leviathan*, ed. C.B. MacPherson. New York: Penguin Books, 1968.

Hughes, T.P. "The Evolution of Large Technological Systems." In *The Social Construction of Technological Systems*, ed. W.E. Bijker, T.P. Hughes, and T.J. Pinch, 51–82. Cambridge, MA: MIT Press, 1987.

Hunt, A. "On Legal Relations and Economic Relations: A Critique of G.A. Cohen." In *Law and Economics*, ed. Moles, 57–82.

Isaac, J.C. "Beyond the Three Faces of Power: A Realist Critique." In *Rethinking Power*, ed. Wartenberg, 32–55.

Johnston, J.S. "Law, Economics, and Post-Realist Explanation." *Law & Society Review* 24, no. 5 (1990): 1217–56.

Kruse, E. "From Free Privilege to Regulation: Wireless Firms and the Competition for Spectrum Rights before World War I." *Business History Review* 76, no. 4. (2002): 659–703.

———. "Property from the Sky: The Creation of Property Rights in the Radio Spectrum in the United States." Ph.D. diss., University of Massachusetts at Amherst, 2002.

Lerner, A. "Economics and Politics of Consumer Sovereignty." *American Economic Review* 62, no. 2 (1972): 258–66.

Libecap, G.D. *Contracting for Property Rights*. New York: Cambridge University Press, 1989.

———. "The Political Economy of Institutional Change: Property Rights and the General Revision Act of 1891." In *Capitalism in Context*, ed. J.A. James and M. Thomas, 265–78. Chicago: University of Chicago Press, 1994.

———. "Politics, Institutions, and Institutional Change." *Journal of Institutional and Theoretical Economics* 149, no. 1 (1993): 29–35.

Locke, J. *The Second Treatise of Government*, ed. T.P. Peardon. New York: Macmillan, 1952.

Lukes, S. *Power: A Radical View*. London: Macmillan Press, 1974.

McCay, B.J., and J.M. Acheson. "Human Ecology of the Commons." In *The Question of the Commons: The Culture and Ecology of Communal Resources*, ed. B.J. McCay and J.M. Acheson, 1–34. Tucson: University of Arizona Press, 1987.

McChesney, R.W. *Telecommunications, Mass Media, & Democracy*. New York: Oxford University Press, 1994.

Mercuro, N., and S.G. Medema. *Economics and the Law: From Posner to Post-Modernism*. Princeton, NJ: Princeton University Press, 1997.

Moles, R.N., ed. *Law and Economics: Association for Legal and Social Philosophy Fourteenth Annual Conference*. Stuttgart: Franz Steiner Verlag Weisbaden GMBH, 1988.

Mueller, D.C. *Public Choice II*. New York: Cambridge University Press, 1989.

Nelson, R.R. "Institutions Supporting Technical Advance in Industry." *American Economic Review* 76, no. 2 (1986): 186–9.

North, D.C. "The Evolution of Efficient Markets in History." In *Capitalism in Context*, ed. J.A. James and M. Thomas, 257–64. Chicago: University of Chicago Press, 1994.

———. "Institutions and Credible Commitment." *Journal of Institutional and Theoretical Economics* 149, no. 1 (1993): 11–23.

———. *Institutions, Institutional Change, and Economic Performance*. New York: Cambridge University Press, 1990.
———. "The Historical Evolution of Polities." *Journal of Law and Economics* 14 (1994): 381–91.
———. *Structure and Change in Economic History*. New York: W.W. Norton, 1981.
North, D.C., and R.P. Thomas. *The Rise of the Western World: A New Economic History*. Cambridge, UK: Cambridge University Press, 1973.
Ogus, A.I. "The Parameters of Law and Economics: From Pashukanis to Posner." In *Law and Economics*, ed. Moles, 14–27.
Ostrom, E. "The Rudiments of a Theory of the Origin, Survival, and Performance of Common-Property Institutions." In *Making the Commons Work*, ed. Bromley, 293–318.
Ostrom, E., and R. Gardner. "Coping with Asymmetries in the Commons: Self-governing Irrigation Systems Can Work." *Journal of Economic Perspectives* 7 (Fall 1993): 93–112.
Poole, K.T., and H. Rosenthal. "Congress and Railroad Regulation: 1874 to 1887." In *The Regulated Economy*, ed. Goldin and Libecap, 81–120.
Rosenberg, N. *Inside the Black Box: Technology and Economics*. Cambridge University Press: New York, 1982.
———. *Technology and American Economic Growth*. New York: Harper and Row, 1972.
Runge, C.F. "Common Property and Collective Action in Economic Development." In *Making the Commons Work*, ed. Bromley, 17–39.
Ruttan, V.W. "Induced Institutional Change." In *Induced Innovation*, ed. Binswanger and Ruttan, 327–57.
———. "Institutional Innovation and Agricultural Development." *World Development* 17, no. 9 (1989): 1375–87.
Schmidtchen, D. "Time, Uncertainty, and Subjectivism: Giving More Body to Law and Economics." *International Review of Law and Economics* 13 (1993): 61–84.
Sewell, S.F. "Assignments and Transfers of Control of FCC Authorizations under Section 310(d) of the Communications Act of 1934." *Federal Communications Law Journal* 43 (July 1991): 277–389.
Slotten, H.R. "Radio Engineers, the Federal Radio Commission, and the Social Shaping of Broadcast Technology: Creating 'Radio Paradise.'" *Technology and Culture* 36, no. 4 (1995): 950–86.
Ulen, T.S. "Law's Contribution to Economic Growth." In *The Law and Economics of Development*, ed. E. Buscaglia, W. Ratliff, and R. Cooter, 59–80. Greenwich, CT: JAI Press, 1997.
Wade, R. 1987. "The Management of Common Property Resources: Collective Action as an Alternative to Privatisation or State Regulation." *Cambridge Journal of Economics* 11, no. 2 (1987): 95–106.
Wartenberg, T.E. "Introduction." In *Rethinking Power*, ed. Wartenberg, xi–xxvi.
———. "Situated Social Power." In *Rethinking Power*, ed. Wartenberg, 79–101.
———., ed. *Rethinking Power*. Albany: State University of New York Press, 1992.
Williams, I. "Rationality and Human Nature in Economics and Law." In *Law and Economics*, ed. Moles, 32–46.
Williamson, O.E. *The Economic Institutions of Capitalism*. New York: Free Press, 1985.
Wolf, E.R. *Europe and the People Without History*. Berkeley: University of California Press, 1982.

Part 4

Legal Issues Concerning Labor, Employment, and Unemployment

9

An Alternative Economic Analysis of the Regulation of Unions and Collective Bargaining

Kenneth G. Dau-Schmidt

Since the passage of the National Labor Relations Act (NLRA) in 1935, it has been the policy of American labor law to foster unionization and regulate collective bargaining for the purposes of promoting equity in bargaining power between employers and employees, and industrial peace.[1] By protecting employee collective action, the framers of American labor law sought to allow employees to achieve some degree of parity with employers in the adjustment of disputes and the division of the proceeds of their labor. This system of "industrial democracy" was intended to provide employees with a greater say in the workplace and perhaps in society at large. Although strikes are a necessary evil in this process for the private resolution of grievances, the framers sought to minimize industrial strife by providing a system of elections to determine exclusive representatives, requiring "good faith" bargaining between unions and employers, and making collective bargaining agreements enforceable.

This policy of fostering unions and regulating collective bargaining to promote equity and industrial peace makes no sense in the context of the traditional monopoly model of unions and collective bargaining. Under the monopoly model, unions cause inefficiency and inequity by establishing a labor cartel and prompting employers to cut production, inefficiently mix capital and labor, displace workers to unorganized markets, and raise prices to consumers.[2] Why would the government want to allow, let alone foster or promote, the establishment of such wasteful cartels? How does the establishment of a labor cartel promote equity in bargaining power? Moreover, under the monopoly model, employers respond to union wage demands merely by retreating up their labor demand curve without any bargaining over wages or employment. When strikes are discussed, they are explained as merely a means by which employers communicate lack of profitability in order to lower unrealistic employee expectations. What justification could there be for the array of legal doctrines in our system for selecting exclusive representatives, bargaining in good faith, and enforcing collective agreements that are purported to promote industrial peace?

The monopoly model of unions and collective bargaining is inadequate in several regards. First, the model fails to adequately account for the possible benefits of employee organization to workers and society. The model examines only the possibility that some workers achieve a labor cartel at the expense of other workers and consumers without examining the possibility of the redistribution of product market rents from employers to employees or the possibility that unions can raise employee productivity. In fact, empirical evidence suggests that the majority of union wage increases come at the expense of employer profits rather than consumer prices and that unionization often leads to increases in employee productivity. Moreover, the monopoly model ignores the beneficial impact of employee organization on law and social norms. Unionization changes employees from "one-shoters" into "repeat players" for the purposes of litigation, and encourages employee organization for the purposes of lobbying and social organization. As a result, unionization allows employees to act as an effective counterbalance to employer interests in the evolution of our case law, statutes, and norms for behavior. With such a limited analysis of the benefits of unions, it is not surprising that the monopoly model cannot be used to effectively evaluate the American labor policy of fostering unionization and promoting equity in bargaining power.

Second, the monopoly model fails to provide an adequate model of the costs of collective bargaining and strikes. The model assumes that unions set wages and that employers set employment according to their demand curve, without any bargaining or give-and-take over these parameters. In fact, logical arguments establish that it is Pareto optimal for unions and employers to negotiate agreements with lower wages and higher employment along a "contract curve" to the right of the employer's demand curve. Empirical evidence strongly supports this contract curve response over the demand curve response. Moreover, under the monopoly model, strikes are simple information costs without any strategic or opportunistic character. In fact, many behaviors in industrial relations (e.g., discriminatory firings, strikes, and resort to costly litigation rather than arbitration), are strategic behaviors undertaken to gain an advantage at the expense of the other party. Rather than being simple information or transaction cost, the costs of these behaviors are positional externalities that are individually rational, but collectively irrational, for the parties to incur. Without a more sophisticated model of collective bargaining and industrial warfare, it is not surprising that the monopoly model cannot be used to adequately evaluate American labor doctrine designed to promote industrial peace.

In this chapter, I attempt to outline an alternative economic analysis of unions and collective bargaining that addresses many of the inadequacies of the monopoly model. In doing so, I draw heavily on previous work I have done on the "bargaining model" of unions and collective bargaining,[3] as well as work from the law and society literature and behavioral psychology. By using this alternative economic analysis, a "fortified bargaining analysis" if you will, I hope to present a better analysis of the efficacy of American labor law in fostering unions and promoting equity in bargaining power and industrial peace.

The Benefits of Employee Organization: Equity in Bargaining Power, Industrial Democracy, and Democratic Pluralism

The proponents of the NLRA argued that fostering unionization would allow employees to gain a greater share of the proceeds of their labor and achieve some level of "industrial democracy" in the workplace, and in our larger society.[4] Promoting employee organization was seen as a redistributive policy in which employees would gain at the expense of their employers, hopefully stimulating consumer demand to help ease the ravages of the Depression. The organization of workers in unions was also viewed as beneficial because it would give them a greater say in the running of the workplace and perhaps the country. The analogy was made that if democracy was the most beneficial and fair way of running the government, then "industrial democracy" was necessary for the advantageous and fair running of the workplace.

These arguments find no support in the traditional monopoly model of unions and collective bargaining. As previously mentioned, the source of employee wage increases under the monopoly model is the establishment of a labor cartel. Once established, the labor cartel establishes a cartel wage and the unionized employers respond by accepting this wage and shedding workers according to each employer's demand schedule. The laid-off workers are displaced into nonunion markets, where they depress the market wage. The employer also responds by inefficiently substituting capital for labor and raising product price. Accordingly, union wage increases are inefficient, because they result in decreased production and the displacement of labor and capital, and inequitable, because they are borne by displaced workers and consumers rather than wealthy employers. Moreover, the monopoly model contains no account of the benefits of industrial democracy or democratic pluralism. Indeed, to the extent that proponents of the monopoly model consider the political nature of unions, they usually depict them as violent, antidemocratic, and narrowly self-interested.[5]

Equity in Bargaining Power: Giving Employees an Opportunity to Share Employer Rents

The monopoly model ignores other more likely sources of union wage increases such as employer product market power rents, Ricardian rents, and quasi rents.[6] If there are the requisite barriers to entry to support a labor cartel, it would seem much more likely that these barriers would be exploited by the employers rather than the employees. The employers are much more concentrated and can earn normal economic profits to maintain them while they organize their cartel or increase their market share. The fact that antitrust laws regulate employers' anticompetitive behavior is notwithstanding, since the antitrust laws allow tacit collusion and monopolization through legitimate means and have been notoriously ineffective.[7] Moreover, it seems much more plausible that unions could organize employers who enjoy product market power rents, Ricardian rents or quasi rents because such organization could be undertaken on the much more manageable basis of one employer at a time rather than across all employers in the relevant product market as would be required for a labor cartel. Although labor cartels undoubtedly exist in the American economy, the empirical evidence suggests that labor cartel power is less important than these other sources of union wage increases. Few product markets approach a percent of workers organized that might even be imagined a labor cartel.[8] Moreover, the best available evidence suggests that union wage increases come largely at the expense of employers and are strongly associated with the market power of the employing firm.[9]

Wage increases from these sources are largely redistributive, with minimal impact on efficiency. Although this assertion can be demonstrated more generally, it is perhaps easiest to see when considering contract negotiations between a union and an employer with rents from a product market monopoly. Assuming that, prior to the organization of the union, the employer was optimally mixing capital and labor in production and optimally pricing his product in order to maximize the value of his monopoly rent, when the employees form a union and demand a share of that rent, any inefficient substitution of capital for labor and any change in product price will serve only to decrease the total size of the rent to be divided between the employer and the employees. Assuming the employer and the union negotiate to maximize the monetary value of their agreement, they will negotiate to increase wages but maintain employment at the current level. Only wage increases from quasi rents have a significant impact on efficiency, discouraging future efficient investments in capital with appropriable quasi rents. Accordingly, union wage increases from employer rents have predominantly the redistributive impact from employers to employees envisioned by the framers of the NLRA.

Industrial Democracy: Giving Workers a Greater Say in the Workplace

Moreover, there are a variety of theories that suggest that "industrial democracy," or giving workers a say in the workplace, can be productivity enhancing.[10] Workers' long hours engaged in production often result in ideas as to how productivity can be enhanced. If employees are allowed to engage management on an equal basis concerning the methods of production, they can often contribute useful insights. Moreover, workers have an interest in the productivity of their firm, and, if protected from arbitrary discharge by a union, can act as a more effective monitor of management waste than absent shareholders. Some have argued that the mere appearance of a union in the workplace can "shock" management out of lethargy and on to greater productivity. Unions can enhance productivity by enforcing long-term implicit contracts in which individual workers are paid less than their marginal product when they are young, and more than their marginal product when they are old, for the purposes of allowing investment in human capital and efficient monitoring. By deferring a portion of his or her wages, an employee can share the burden of his or her training costs, and guarantee incentive to be productive with minimal monitoring so as not to get fired for slacking before the payment of the deferred wages. Unfortunately, wage deferral also gives employers incentive to discharge employees even if they are productive, merely to keep the deferred wages. Individually, workers cannot prevent employer opportunism in firing them to keep deferred wages, but through unions employees can collectively protect each other over the life cycle. Unions can also enhance productivity by negotiating efficient contract terms with respect to public goods in the workplace, such as the speed of the assembly line, the quality of plant air, or the safety of common equipment. Because other workers cannot be excluded from one worker's negotiated improvements in such terms, workers have too little incentive to negotiate for them in the absence of the collective voice of a union. Finally, unions raise productivity by promoting the efficient expression of a collective voice rather than the costly "exit" of individual workers dissatisfied with their job. In a competitive labor market the primary mechanism for expressing dissatisfaction with working conditions is for the worker to take another job or "exit."

However, exit is less efficient than "collective voice" in encouraging changes in working conditions because exit communicates little and results in relocation and retraining costs. Convincing empirical evidence exists that some industries enjoy significant productivity increases from unionism.[11] For example, Kim Clark compared the physical output of cement plants before and after organization and between different organized and unorganized plants, and found statistically significant productivity increases from unionization that ranged from 6 to 10 percent.

Democratic Pluralism: Giving Workers a Greater Say in the Rules that Organize Society

Theoretical work also suggests that industrial democracy can benefit workers, and society, by promoting the efficient and equitable evolution of case law. Marc Galanter has established that, in legal disputes with "have-nots," the "haves" will continue to relitigate an issue until the law favors their position.[12] Paul Rubin has derived this same insight in an economic model examining the incentives of parties *A* and *B* to settle or litigate a dispute in which *B* has suffered a loss *X* in some activity with *A*, and the law currently favors *A*, so *B* is taking precautions.[13] Under Rubin's model, when only *B* is a "repeat player" in that only he anticipates facing similar disputes again in the future, and thus only *B* has an interest in precedent, the value of litigating to *A* and *B*, respectively is:

$$V_A = R(-X) - C$$

and

$$V_B = R(X) + R(T_B) - C$$

where V_A is the value to *A* of the law suit; V_B is the value to *B* of the law suit; *R* is the probability *B* will win the suit, and *A* will be held liable to him; *X* are the damages *A* has to pay *B* if *B* wins the lawsuit; *C* is each party's costs of going to court; and T_B is the present value to *B* of winning the suit and establishing favorable precedent to him so that he no longer has to take precautions. The parties settle if the value to *A* of avoiding court ($-V_A$) is greater than the value to *B* of going to court (V_B). Thus, the parties will litigate only if $-V_A < V_B$, or only if:

$$R(T_B) > 2C$$

Unless *R* and T_B are very small relative to *C*, the repeat player *B* will continue to litigate the dispute with each new "one-shoter" until a court rules in *B*'s favor and precedent favors *B*'s position. This is true even though the resulting legal rule may be inefficient. Thus, one can reasonably expect that the law will tend to evolve in favor of repeat players such as manufacturers, banks, and employers at the expense of individual consumers and employees, regardless of the efficiency or equity of the resulting legal rule.

However, when both sides to a dispute have an interest in precedent, under Rubin's analysis, the value of litigating to *A* and *B*, respectively, in the above problem is:

$$V_A = R(-X) + R(-T_A) - C$$

and

$$V_B = R(X) + R(T_B) - C$$

where T_A is the present value to *A* of the current favorable precedent in forgone precautions. Again, the parties will settle if $-V_A > V_B$, or litigate only if:

$$-R(T_A - T_B) > 2C$$

where $(T_A - T_B)$ is the value of the current legal precedent in favor of *A*. Thus, as Rubin points out, when both sides have an interest in precedent, only inefficient rules in which $(T_A - T_B) < 0$ will be litigated and the court interpretations of the law will evolve toward efficiency.

Although individual employees may be "one-shoters" in litigation with no interest in precedent, when they bind together in a union, the union will have a collective continuing interest in precedent in labor and employment law. Accordingly, one can reasonably argue that employee organization will lead to a more efficient and equitable evolution of labor and employment case law. For example, in litigation against individual employees, employers managed to convince courts that promises of "permanent employment" actually meant that the employee could be discharged at any time, for any reason.[14] This would not seem to be the efficient default for interpreting this language because it is contrary to common usage, and employees would have to retain a lawyer in order to know to contract around this result. Job security provisions in collective bargaining agreements enforced by unions are not interpreted so perversely.[15]

Similar arguments concerning the benefits of employee organization for the drafting and enforcement of labor and employment legislation can be made on the basis of public choice theory.[16] Public choice theory posits that there is a market for legislation in which constituents demand certain laws, and legislators supply them with the objective of achieving reelection. Because there are time and information costs to evaluating and opposing or supporting legislation, small organized groups in which individual members enjoy high benefits from a certain legislative position will gain in the legislative process at the expense of large disorganized groups in which the cost of the legislative proposal are broadly dispersed. Even if the general citizenry rise up and demand a legislative position contrary to the interests of the small organized interest group, the interest group will have advantages in influencing the administration of the law. Employers, and especially large corporations, have long been well organized and effective lobbyists. Their hierarchical command structure, access to resources and organization by industry, state, and nation, have long allowed them to pursue their interests in the legislative and administrative arenas at the expense of less organized and more dispersed groups and the public at large.

To the extent that employee interests are at odds with employer interests, employee organization can act as a counterbalance to employer advantages in lobbying resulting in more efficient and equitable legislation. For example, prior to the beginning of the twentieth century, the common law defenses of "assumption of risk," "contributory negligence," and the "fellow servant rule" largely prevented employees injured on the job from collecting from their employers which, combined with inadequate compensating wages, had the result that employers had too little incentive to take safety precautions.[17] Unions countered employer interests by lobbying for the statutory repeal of common law defenses, and then settling for workers' compensation statutes–a much more efficient and equitable result than the old common law. The drafters of the NLRA endorsed the idea that, because capital was already organized, it was only fair to encourage labor to organize in order to provide industrial and political symmetry.[18]

Finally, unionization can help promote social norms that benefit employees and society as a whole. Norms are informal standards for behavior that are widely held among the relevant population and enforced by the populations' approval or disapproval. Because people are social animals, people's behavior is influenced by norms as well as laws. Indeed, it is possible to think of the legal system as a formal subset of the system of norms. Laws and norms are endogenously determined in that practices that are required by law can become routine or custom and accordingly develop into a norm, and important norms that are broadly held by a population have a high probability of being formalized into law. Economists have hypothesized that society will tend to develop useful or efficient norms as groups of people who hold these norms succeed at the expense of people who don't.[19] This evolutionary theory of norms has been used to explain the development of norms for cooperation and altruism. Behavioral-psychologists have also demonstrated that norms for "fair treatment" affect people's bargaining decisions.[20] In the "ultimatum game," where one party picks the division of some cooperative surplus while the other side decides whether or not to reject the division and both lose the entire surplus, parties typically reject divisions that are one-sided and "unfair," even though this is individually irrational.

Analogizing from the argument on the evolution of useful or efficient case law, it seems quite plausible that organized groups have advantages in the development of social norms. Organized groups can better lobby the beliefs of the population at large and have advantages in litigation and legislation that also, in turn, may establish norms. To the extent that employee interests differ from employer interests, organized employees can act as an effective counterweight to organized employer interests and facilitate the production of more efficient and equitable norms. As with litigation, legislation, and administration, organized groups have an advantage in the formulation of social norms. Examples of norms that organized labor has influenced to society's benefit through social advocacy and legislation include the norm against child labor, the norm in favor of the forty-hour workweek and the increasing value placed on worker health and safety by society at large.

The Costs of Employee Organization: Collective Bargaining and Strikes

The drafters of the NLRA also believed that it is necessary to regulate the process of collective bargaining in order to minimize disruption to the economy and promote "industrial peace." To this end they prescribed the following: a process for electing exclusive representatives in "appropriate units"; a prohibition against discrimination on the basis of union affiliation; a requirement that the parties meet "at reasonable times" to bargain in "good faith" concerning wages, hours, and other terms and conditions of employment; and a system for the enforcement of collective agreements.[21] Invoking the statutory purpose of promoting industrial peace, the National Labor Relations Board (hereafter, the Board) and the courts have elaborated on this statutory framework, developing the presumption of continuing majority status, requiring exchanges of information in bargaining, and requiring deference to agreements to arbitrate contract disputes.

The traditional monopoly model of unions and collective bargaining provides little basis on which to evaluate the efficacy of these policies. Under the model, unions unilaterally set wages while employers unilaterally set employment—without any negotiations. This characterization of collective bargaining effectively precludes any consideration of strategic behavior.

Accordingly, to the extent that they are considered at all, strikes are characterized as ordinary information costs—a really expensive but credible way to communicate that the employer cannot afford a wage increase. With no effective representation of collective bargaining and "industrial warfare," it is not surprising that the model offers no way to assess policies designed to promote "industrial peace."

The Contract Curve Response

It has long been known that the "demand curve response" of the monopoly model is not the Pareto-optimal result and that both the employer and the union can do better by negotiating a trade-off of lower wages for greater employment along a "contract curve" to the right of the demand curve.[22] The superior contract curve response is shown in Figure 9.1.

In Figure 9.1, D is the employer's labor demand curve; P_0, P_1, and P_2 are examples of the employer's iso-profit curves; U_0 and U_1 are examples of the union's indifference curves; and C is the "contract curve" between the employer and the union. The employer's iso-profit curves give combinations of wage and employment that yield equal profits. They descend down on both sides of the employer's labor demand curve and increase in profits from P_0 to P_2. The union's indifference curves give combinations of wage level and employment among which the union is indifferent. They are convex to the origin and increase in preference to the union from U_0 to U_1. The contract curve between the employer and the union, C, is made up of all of the points of tangency between the employer's iso-profit curves and the union's indifference curves. Any point on this contract curve is Pareto optimal in that, at these points, neither the employer nor the union can be made better off without making the other worse off.

The superiority of deals on the contract curve to points on the demand curve can be readily demonstrated using Figure 9.1. When employees organize, they initially increase their wage demand from the competitive wage, W_c, to W_u. The employer's demand curve response would be to move to point A and decrease the number of workers employed from N_c to N_u. However, by tracing to the right along the firm's iso-profit curve P_0, one can see that by agreeing to any point on P_0 between A and C' the firm achieves the same level of profits while allowing the union to achieve a higher level of utility. Similarly, by tracing to the right from A along the union's indifference curve U_0, it can be seen that, by agreeing to any point on U_0 between A and C'', the union achieves the same level of utility while allowing the firm to achieve a higher level of profits. Thus the employer's labor demand response is not Pareto optimal because one or both of the parties can be made better off by

Figure 9.1 **Demand Curve Response Compared With Contract Curve Response**

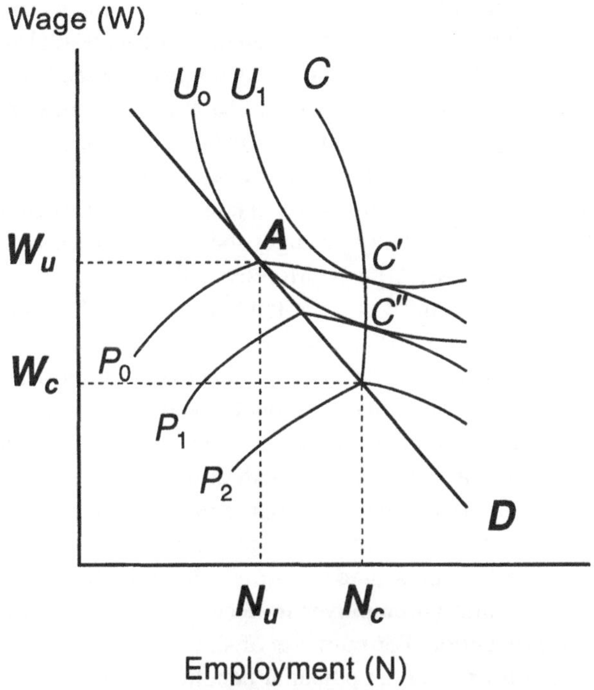

moving off the demand curve to a point in the area $AC'C''$. The tangencies between the firm's iso-profit curves and the union's indifference curves scribe the set of Pareto-optimal solutions to the parties' bargaining problem, C, known as the contract curve. Assuming the parties bargain to exhaust all benefits of trade, they will arrive at a wage and employment mix that is on the portion of the contract curve between C' and C''. Exactly where on the contract curve the parties will settle is an indeterminate bargaining problem. There is strong empirical work supporting the contract curve response over the monopoly model's demand curve analysis.[23]

The Costs of Collective Bargaining as Positional Externalities

By depicting collective bargaining as an indeterminate bargaining problem rather than a demand curve response, we can now take account of the fact that many of the costs of collective bargaining are properly characterized as positional externalities rather than ordinary time and information transaction costs. Such positional externalities occur when each side, on the basis of individual incentives, undertakes costly strategic behavior in order to gain a relative advantage in the division of the proceeds of production. In this situation, the behaviors tend to cancel each other out with respect to producing any advantage in collective negotiations, with the ultimate result being merely waste. Although some costs of collective bargaining are indeed ordinary time and information expenditures, it is evident that many activities of collective bargaining are strategic in nature and result in costs that are positional externalities. Organizational picketing, discriminatory discharges, recalcitrant bargaining, and resort to costly litigation in contract enforcement are all undertaken for the purpose of gaining a larger share of the proceeds of the firm at the expense of the passive party. Moreover, the rewards of each party, based on relative performance and the tendency for conflicts in collective bargaining to escalate into costly contests, are also evident. For example, "hard bargaining" can have its rewards in collective negotiations. However, if both sides follow this individually rational strategy, the result may be impasse and the waste of resources in a strike or lockout. As discussed below, similar examples of strategic behavior, with costs that are positional externalities, also occur in organizing campaigns and contract enforcement.

The problem of strategic behavior and positional externalities in collective negotiations can be represented in a simple dilemma game. Consider the problem of a union and an employer in deciding how to divide the joint benefits of their production. For purposes of simplicity, assume that the parties have already maximized the potential benefit of their agreement by including all efficient contract terms and are now bargaining over how to divide the total benefit of their production. Each party must receive at least the competitive rate of return on its investment or labor—otherwise they will pursue those options in the competitive market. In game theory this minimum payment is known as the "threat value" of the agreement. The benefit of the agreement in excess of these minimum values is the real subject of dispute and is known as the "cooperative surplus." As previously mentioned, in labor relations this cooperative surplus will be made up of rents and productivity increases associated with employee organization that are protected by barriers to entry. For the purposes of this negotiating game, assume that the total cooperative surplus to be divided by the parties over the term of the agreement is $10.

In this simple game, each side must decide whether to adopt a bargaining strategy of cooperation or of intransigence in its negotiations. As previously discussed above, intransigence constitutes a positional externality in negotiations because the parties are rewarded based on relative performance, and although such a strategy may yield individual benefits if only one side is intransigent, if both parties adopt this strategy, the result will be a strike and

Figure 9.2 **Possible Divisions of the Cooperative Surplus Between the Employer and the Employees**

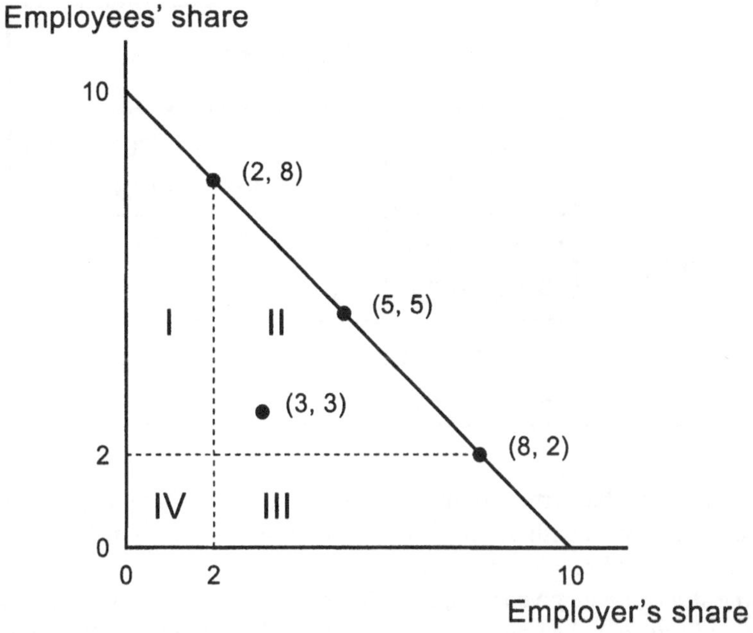

waste of some of the benefits of production. This can be seen by examining the common sense assumptions about the division of the cooperative surplus between the employees and the employer in Figure 9.2. The diagonal line in the figure shows all possible divisions of the cooperative surplus of $10 between the employees and the employer from $10 for the employees and none for the employer, to $5 for each, to none for the employees and $10 for the employer. Assume that if both parties bargain cooperatively over the division of the surplus, they will agree to divide it in half with $5 for both the employees and the employer. This "split the difference" assumption on the results of cooperative bargaining is simple, but consistent with much more sophisticated models of divisional bargaining.[24] If one side is intransigent while the other is cooperative, it is reasonable to assume that the intransigent side will achieve a larger share of the cooperative surplus. Thus, if the union is intransigent while the employer is cooperative, the employees will gain $8 while the employer gets $2, and that if the union is cooperative while the employer is intransigent, the employees will get $2 while the employer gets $8. However, if both sides are intransigent, the result is a strike that consumes $4 of the cooperative surplus in the form of $2 in lost profits and $2 in lost wages.

Figure 9.3 **Union and Employer Expected Payoffs for the Negotiations Game**

		Employer	
		Cooperative bargaining	Intransigent bargaining
Union	Cooperative bargaining	5 5	8 2
	Intransigent bargaining	2 8	3 3

After the strike the parties ultimately agree to equally share the remaining cooperative surplus with $3 for both the employees and the employer.

The union and employer payoffs for each possible combination of bargaining strategies are given in Figure 9.3. The employer payoff for each combination is given in the upper right-hand corner of the relevant cell, while the union's payoff is given in the lower left-hand corner of the cell. Examining the payoffs of this game, one can see the divergence between individual and collective interests that characterizes positional externalities and dilemma games. From the individual perspective of each party, the strategy of intransigence dominates because it yields a higher payoff regardless of what the other side does. From the union's perspective, if the employer decides to cooperate, the union does better by being intransigent ($8) than by being cooperative ($5), and if the employer decides to be intransigent, the union again does better by being intransigent ($3) than by being cooperative ($2). Similarly, from the employer's perspective, if the union decides to cooperate, the employer does better by being intransigent ($8) than by being cooperative ($5), and if the union decides to be intransigent, the employer again does better by being intransigent ($3) than by being cooperative ($2). Thus, if each party acts according to its individual interests, one would expect that both parties would be intransigent, reaching an equilibrium in the lower right-hand cell of Figure 9.3 ($3 each). However, from the collective perspective of both parties this outcome is clearly suboptimal because if both cooperated, they could avoid the costly escalation of the conflict into a strike and achieve the division represented in the upper left-hand cell of Figure 9.3 ($5 each). Therefore, to the extent the parties act individually rather than collectively, there is a tendency for the conflict to escalate into a costly strike despite the best interests of both parties to avoid a strike.[25]

Similar dilemma games can be constructed for organizing campaigns and enforcement of the collective agreement. With respect to organizing, the cooperative, or low-cost, strategy might be to merely provide pro- or antiunion information followed by an election while the recalcitrant, or high-cost strategies, correspond to discriminatory discharges and organizational strikes. It seems reasonable to assume that a party's payoff in organizing depends on its relative performance in that resort to the high-cost strategy by only one party will increase that party's chances of prevailing, while if both parties resort to the high-cost strategy, their efforts tend to cancel each other out. Thus, one would expect that organizing campaigns would have a tendency to escalate into costly affairs, wasting a portion of the cooperative surplus, in much the same way that negotiation conflicts can escalate. With respect to enforcement of the collect agreement, the cooperative, or low-cost strategy, is to resolve disputes over interpretation of the agreement through arbitration, while the recalcitrant, or high-cost strategy, is to resort to more costly litigation or strikes to resolve contract disputes. Again, it may be assumed that a party's chance of prevailing in an enforcement dispute depends on its relative performance in that resort to the high-cost strategy by only one party will increase that party's chances of prevailing, while if both parties resort to the high-cost strategy, their efforts will tend to cancel each other out. So one would expect that enforcement conflicts would have a tendency to escalate, wasting a portion of the cooperative surplus, in much the same way that organization and negotiation conflicts tend to escalate.

Maximizing Net Social Benefits: An Alternative Economic Analysis of American Labor Law

An Optimal Public Policy

The optimal public policy with respect to unions and collective bargaining would be for the government to try to maximize the social benefits of employee organization, while minimizing its social costs. Under the alternative economic analysis I have offered above, this would mean that the government should draft and enforce legislation that would foster employee organization and its benefits of redistribution of employer rents, industrial democracy, and democratic pluralism. If possible, the policy should seek to encourage the redistributive and productivity enhancing aspects of unionization, while discouraging the establishment of inefficient and inequitable labor cartels.[26] Moreover, the government should regulate the process of collective bargaining to minimize its social costs and the inevitable work disruptions that accompany this system for the private resolution of disputes. The government's regulation of collective bargaining should aim to promote cooperation in industrial relations and discourage opportunistic behavior and the escalation of industrial disputes into costly strikes.

What policies can the government use to encourage cooperation and discourage the escalation of the costs of collective bargaining? First, where it is easy to identify and prosecute strategic behavior, the government should prohibit that behavior and enforce its prohibition with suitable fines. For example, in the simple bargaining game presented above, if the government punished intransigent bargaining with a $4 fine, the game's expected payoffs would be such that the parties would find it in their collective *and* individual interest to bargain cooperatively. Although it is not always possible to determine when a party is bargaining intransigently and when he or she truly cannot afford the other side's demands, certain deleterious bargaining strategies such as lying, committing to third parties (such as creditors or customers) to achieve a certain bargaining outcome, and cutting off negotiations are more easily identified and should be prohibited and punished. The government may also want to discourage parties from taking hard stances on clearly inequitable positions, for example insisting on wage givebacks in the face of record profits, given the findings in behavioral psychology literature that parties commonly reject "unfair" deals. Other forms of strategic behavior such as discriminatory discharges or striking in violation of a no-strike clause are also identifiable and should be prohibited and punished.

Second, even where the government cannot readily identify and prosecute costly strategic behavior, it can formulate laws governing collective bargaining so as to promote the parties' ability to recognize and act on their collective interest in avoiding costly strategic behavior. Theoretical and empirical work in game theory suggests that there are a number of ways in which this can be done.[27] The government might promote union organization among employees with fairly homogeneous interests and limit the number of parties to negotiations in order to simplify the bargaining problem and prevent free riding on cooperation. The government might also require exchanges of information among the parties to promote their ability to determine the cooperative solution and to foster trust. Promoting repeat play among the participants to dilemma games, such as collective bargaining, has also been found to encourage cooperation by raising the possibility of future retaliation for current intransigence. Government enforcement of private armistices to refrain from strategic behavior encourages the formation of such armistices, leading to cooperation. Finally, where the government or some neutral party can determine the cooperative solution, the government can reduce strategic behavior by requiring the parties to adopt that cooperative solution or by mediating the dispute to encourage the cooperative agreement. Such mediation, fact-finding, or interest arbitration might help hold the parties accountable to social norms of fair treatment and promote cooperation consistent with those norms. The exact mix of the policies the government should adopt in addressing the problem of promoting cooperation between the parties is an empirical question and depends on the costs of implementing the policy and the efficacy of the policy in promoting cooperation.

The Policy Applied to American Labor Law

Paul Weiler has described American labor law as an "elegant tombstone" for the American labor movement, implying that, although it honors unions and collective bargaining with all of the appropriate doctrinal flourishes, ultimately it marks the demise of this great institution.[28] The alternative economic analysis of unions and collective bargaining that I have presented above provides abundant support for Professor Weiler's sentiment. Although most of the policies and doctrines expressed in American labor law find support in my economic analysis, the decline of the American labor movement under these laws would suggest that ultimately they have failed in their primary purpose of fostering unions and collective bargaining. Some of the reasons for this failure are discussed below.

The General Policies and Purposes of American Labor Law

The pervasive policy in American labor law of fostering unions and collective bargaining makes sense under this alternative economic analysis. Under the analysis, unions redistribute employer product market power and Ricardian rents to employees, thus allowing workers to gain a more equitable share of the proceeds from their labor. There is no productive reason why employers should not share these rents because they are payments in excess of what is necessary to call forth the employer's resources into employment. In addition, fostering unions may maximize wealth. Under this alternative analysis, inefficiency occurs only to the extent that the union is willing to trade employment for wages at the expense of maximizing the monetary value of the cooperative surplus and to the extent the union derives its wage increases from quasi rents or an effective labor cartel. However, unions can also promote efficiency in the workplace by spurring management to undertake greater efforts, allowing the enforcement of long-term implicit contracts, allowing the efficient negotiation of public goods, and decreasing turnover costs as workers exercise their collective voice to address dissatisfaction in the workplace. As previously discussed, empirical work suggests that in many industries the productivity-enhancing effects of unions outweigh their deleterious effects. Finally, unions give workers a greater say in the rules that govern our society. An effective labor movement can act as a counterbalance to employer interests in the litigation of disputes, the drafting of legislation, and the development of societal norms, thus promoting more efficient and equitable rules for the governance of our society.

Unfortunately, although it is the announced purpose of American labor law to foster unions and collective bargaining, the American labor movement has not done well under this law. Beginning approximately a decade after the passage of the Taft-Hartley amendments in 1947, the American labor movement has suffered a steady decline in membership from 40 percent of the private workforce in 1955 to about 9 percent of the private workforce today.[29] Although there are a variety of factors that have contributed to this decline, including the waning of the manufacturing sector, changing workforce demographics, international trade, and the unusually recalcitrant nature of American employers, it seems undeniable that American labor law has contributed to this decline. Among the shortcomings of American labor law are failures to provide a truly inexpensive method for employee organization, to require good faith bargaining over some "permissive" subjects of bargaining of great importance to unions, to prohibit employer strategic behavior in the permanent replacement of strikers, and the failure to provide adequate enforcement of and penalties for the developed doctrine.

The problem of inadequate enforcement and penalties in our labor law is pervasive. The Supreme Court has held that sanctions under the NLRA are merely remedial in nature and not punitive.[30] Accordingly, the Board can provide a remedy for an offense that attempts to correct the harm done, but it cannot punish a union or an employer to deter future misconduct. Even if society valued the benefits the parties received from violating the NLRA, economic theory would suggest that, to maximize social welfare, the penalties for such activities should be set so that the perpetrator's expected cost from engaging in the activity equaled the cost the activity imposed on other people. Because not all violators are caught and punished, this criterion suggests that penalties for violations of the labor law should be set higher than remedial damages so that the expected cost to the perpetrator equals the costs imposed on the victim. However, under my economic analysis, violations of the NLRA, such as discriminatory discharges and refusing to bargain in good faith, are merely wasteful rent-seeking of no social benefit. Accordingly, economic theory suggests that, to maximize social welfare, penalties for socially valueless activities should be set so high that the social benefits from increased deterrence equal the social costs of deterring marginally lawful activity and sometimes mistakenly imposing penalties on innocent defendants. The current remedial sanctions of the NLRA, which often do not even fully compensate the victim, clearly do not meet this standard.

The twin purposes of American labor law of promoting greater equity in bargaining power between employers and employees and of promoting industrial peace find ready recognition within the context of my alternative economic analysis. Employees can gain a share of the cooperative surplus from production only by binding together to negotiate. Individually, each will receive only the competitive wage for his or her services. In addition, it is only by binding together that the workers can achieve all of the productivity increases associated with such employee organization as the monitoring of management efforts, the enforcement of long-term implicit contracts, the efficient negotiation of collective goods, and the expression of collective voice. Thus, by fostering unions and collective bargaining, the law allows workers to elevate their bargaining position to one of rough parity with that of their employer and affords them the opportunity to make a productive contribution to the governance of the workplace. Similarly, under the bargaining model it makes sense for the government to attempt to minimize the amount the parties engage in strategic behavior. Such behavior is costly and, although it may be individually rational, from a larger societal perspective such behavior serves only to waste resources. So the purpose of promoting industrial peace finds direct translation into the bargaining model as society's desire to minimize wasteful strategic behavior on the part of unions and employers.

The record of American labor law on promoting equity in bargaining power and industrial peace is much more mixed. The inability of American workers to organize, of course, casts doubt on the success of American labor law at promoting equity in bargaining power. For the vast majority of workers, organization is a prerequisite to sharing in employer rents and participating in industrial governance. The doctrine of exclusive representation in section 9(a) of the NLRA, the prohibition on "yellow dog" contracts in the Norris-LaGuardia Act, and the limited provision for union security agreements in section 8(a)(3) of the NLRA facilitate workers in solving the free-rider problem in producing the public good of unionization. However, the allowance of state "right to work" laws under section 14(b) of the NLRA undermines the employees' ability to solve the free-rider problem of employee organization and the union's position of parity with the employer. At least where employees have successfully organized, American workers seem to have done well in gaining a share of employer rents and making productive contributions to the workplace. As previously mentioned, unionized American workers enjoy superior wages and benefits, largely at the expense of employer profits. Moreover, there is good empirical evidence that unionized workers increase the productivity of their workplace. American labor law also seems to have achieved some modest success in promoting industrial peace. In comparison with other industrialized countries, the United States ranks toward the lower end of the spectrum in terms of days lost to work stoppage per organized worker.[31] However, these efforts are undoubtedly hampered by inadequate penalties for strategic behavior.

The Law on Organizing

The basic outline of American labor law with respect to organizing makes sense under my alternative economic analysis of unions and collective bargaining. The most costly strategic behaviors on both sides have been restricted or prohibited in favor of the theoretically cheaper method of determining representation questions through a Board-supervised election. The NLRA severely limits recognitional picketing and strikes both as to their lawful circumstances and the length of time unions can engage in such activities.[32] These limitations, combined with the availability of the relatively inexpensive alternative of conducting an election campaign under section 9(a) of the NLRA, have led unions to rely on the election procedure as the primary method of resolving representation disputes. Similarly, employers are prohibited from undertaking discriminatory discharges, blacklisting employees, locking out employees, or relocating the plant in order to avoid union organization.[33] Unlike under the monopoly model, where such activities are useful because they undermine labor cartel power, within the context of my analysis, these activities are merely wasteful rent seeking on the part of the employer.

The provisions governing the conduct of representation elections are also supported by the analysis of the bargaining model. In contrast to the monopoly model, my model affirms the proposition that the government should facilitate a means by which the employees can make a reasoned decision as to whether it is in their interest to organize. A Board-supervised election is potentially an inexpensive procedure by which just such a decision can be made. Several provisions of American labor law seem aimed at minimizing the costs of elections. For example, there are a requirements that employers provide unions with an "Excelsior list" of the names and addresses of all eligible employees and that employers give employees access to the employer's property for purposes of union solicitation. These seem consistent with the objective of lowering election costs.[34] Similarly, the doctrine that employer predictions about the consequences of unionization must be based on objective facts and convey the employer's genuine belief as to demonstrable consequences beyond his control seems designed to limit the employer to conveying potentially useful information on the merits of organizing.[35] Employer threats or promises of benefits are appropriately prohibited because they are efforts to coerce or bribe the employees into sacrificing their collective interest in organization in favor of their individual interest of avoiding punishment or receiving a benefit. Such activities undermine collective bargaining by encouraging employees to act only on the basis of their individual interests and to free ride on others' collective action.

As previously mentioned, despite good intentions, it seems doubtful that American labor law has succeeded in providing employees with a genuinely low-cost method for deciding whether or not to organize. The lack of effective penalties makes retaliatory discharge a real possibility for any employee seeking to organize.[36] Moreover, the doctrine of allowing employers to exclude nonemployee organizers from nonwork areas on the employer's premises, even during nonwork time in areas available to the public, seems to raise the costs of elections merely to indulge the employer's strategic interest in resisting employee organization.[37] Similarly, the current doctrine that the National Labor Relations Board will not review campaign statements by employers or unions as to their truth or falsity seems contrary to the cost minimization objective.[38] Intentional falsehoods would seem to have no place in a system designed to allow employees, at minimum cost, to decide whether or not organization is in their collective interest. Several scholars have suggested ways to remedy the problem of costly organizing campaigns. These range from merely setting shorter deadlines for holding the election after the filing of the certification petition to doing away with the election procedure entirely and certifying unions just on the basis of representation cards.[39] Based on the current low rate of employee organization, it seems reasonable to believe that our law should be amended to lower the costs of employee organization.

The Law on Collective Negotiations

Many features of the law with respect to collective negotiations seem designed to discourage strategic behavior and promote industrial peace. The law requires that the parties bargain in "good faith" concerning "wages, hours and other terms and conditions of employment."[40] The existing standard for good faith, whether the party has subjective intent to reach agreement, seems aimed at precisely the problem of intransigence described in my simple negotiations game. Moreover, unlike the monopoly model, my alternative analysis provides a basis on which to evaluate strategies or conduct in collective negotiations that have been found to be in "bad faith." The prohibition against Boulwareism that exists under current law seems sound under the bargaining model because Boulwareism is basically a strategy under which the employer makes a strong commitment to the employees and the public not to change his bargaining position.[41] Committing yourself to a position favorable to yourself may be an individually rational bargaining strategy, but if both sides make such commitments, the result will be a deadlock and a strike. Similarly, the doctrine that employers are required to supply the employees with all relevant information for the purposes of collective bargaining finds support within the context of the bargaining model because such information allows the parties to see mutually beneficial cooperative solutions and engenders trust on both sides.[42]

Other provisions of the law prevent strategic behavior and promote industrial peace by facilitating the parties' ability to realize their collective interest in reaching cooperative solutions in bargaining. The limitation that employees can organize only in "appropriate bargaining units" of employees with sufficient "community of interest" seems designed to promote homogeneity in bargaining interests among the employees represented by the union.[43] Such homogeneity on the part of the employees simplifies the bargaining game and increases the chance that the parties will realize the cooperative solution. The doctrine of exclusive representation also facilitates cooperative solutions in bargaining by prohibiting individual and subgroup bargaining and limiting the number of players to the bargaining game.[44] In facilitating cooperative solutions, there is a trade-off between organizing employees in homogeneous groups and minimizing the number of players to the bargaining game. Finally, the presumption of the union's continuing majority facilitates cooperative solutions in bargaining by increasing the expectations of repeated play of the bargaining game.[45] By increasing the expectations that the union will be around for a while, the doctrine raises the expected costs of strategic behavior because such behavior not only threatens the success of current negotiations, but also future negotiations in which the other side might seek revenge.

One can raise legitimate questions about the efficacy of our labor law in promoting cooperative bargaining in industrial relations. Existing remedies for bad faith bargaining seem inadequate to discourage intransigence in bargaining. The typical remedy for a failure to bargain in good faith consists of an injunction and an affirmative order to bargain in good faith combined with the required posting of a notice. There is no penalty, nor even a make-whole remedy for wages or profits lost due to intransigent bargaining.[46] Based on the findings of the behavioral psychologists that people reject unfair deals, one might argue that the definition of good faith bargaining should go beyond mere intransigence to include some notion of fairness. There is no sign that the courts or the Board are inclined to interpret the act in this way. Under existing legal doctrine, unless the employer claims inability to pay, employers are only required to give unions data on wages and hours, but not on the profitability of the firm.[47] A rule on the sharing of information that sought to minimize the chances of strategic behavior and to maximize the parties' ability to realize cooperative solutions would require the full sharing of all relevant information. The Supreme Court has ruled that although economic strikers cannot be fired, they can be "permanently replaced."[48] This doctrine of "permanent replacement" seems to encourage costly strategic behavior on the part of employers and has been the subject of congressional concern. Finally, current doctrine only requires bargaining on "mandatory subjects of bargaining" and not "permissive subjects of bargaining." This might be all right, except that the Supreme Court has determined permissive subjects to include issues such as the employer's decision to partially or completely close the plant.[49] By excluding such issues of vital concern to the union from the requirement of good faith bargaining, the Court has failed to use the legislative system for encouraging the cooperative resolution of disputes on important industrial relations questions.

The Law on Enforcement of the Collective Agreement

The law on the enforcement of collective bargaining agreements also seems prudent under my alternative economic analysis. The Supreme Court has found that agreements to arbitrate disputes under collective bargaining agreements are enforceable as a matter of federal substantive law.[50] The courts can compel either side to comply with the agreement to arbitrate and can enjoin strikes or lockouts in contravention of that agreement.[51] Moreover the courts must show great deference to arbitrators both as to their jurisdiction under the agreement and their resolution of the dispute, forsaking the temptation to allow the parties to litigate such matters.[52] Agreements to arbitrate disputes under the collective bargaining agreement are the logical low-cost cooperative solution to the problem of contract enforcement. Resorting to economic warfare or costly litigation to resolve contract disputes is a positional externality that serves only to waste the cooperative surplus. Thus, it makes sense for the courts to enforce and encourage agreements to arbitrate while prohibiting or severely limiting the parties' recourse to economic or litigation weapons. American labor law seems to have scored an unqualified success with respect to its policy on the enforcement of collective bargaining agreements. On the whole our system of judicial deference to agreements to arbitrate and our system for the private arbitration of disputes under collective bargaining agreements seem to work quite well. Indeed, the strong current in the law is toward the private arbitration of all legal disputes between employers and employees, whether the employees are represented by a union, or not.

Conclusion

My alternative economic analysis of unions and collective bargaining confirms the basic logic of American labor law that the government should foster unions and regulate the conduct of industrial relations in order to promote equity in bargaining power and industrial peace. Under this analysis, unions allow workers to gain a greater share of the proceeds of the business and to make valuable contributions to the running of that business and society through the expression of their collective voice. Thus, by promoting workers to a more equitable bargaining position relative to their employer, unions can serve societal goals of redistributing wealth and giving workers a greater say in the workplace and society as a whole. However, despite these beneficial attributes of collective bargaining, both employers and unions have individual incentives for strategic behavior in the conflicts that occur in organizing, negotiations, and enforcement of collective agreements. Because of these incentives, the conflicts of collective bargaining have a tendency to escalate into costly affairs, wasting a portion of the potential proceeds of the enterprise despite the parties'—and society's—collective interest in avoiding such waste. The government can minimize this waste by regulating the conduct of collective bargaining to prohibit or discourage strategic behavior and promote industrial peace.

Many specific provisions of American labor law make sense within the context of this model. To resolve conflicts in organizing, the NLRA promotes elections as a relatively low-cost method by which the employees can decide whether to organize. Strategies or behaviors in collective negotiations that are likely to result in costly strikes, for example, intransigence in bargaining or Boulwareism, are prohibited or discouraged. Moreover, the law promotes the parties' ability to recognize their collective interests in cooperative bargaining by organizing the employees in relatively homogeneous units, encouraging repeat negotiations through the presumption of continuing majority status, and requiring exchanges of relevant information. Finally, to resolve conflicts in the enforcement of collective agreements, the law enforces agreements to arbitrate as the low-cost method of resolving such disputes.

However, my analysis also suggests several ways in which current American labor law could be improved. Perhaps chief among these improvements would be a substantial increase in penalties for violations of current law. The current remedial penalties of the NLRA do not adequately deter costly strategic behavior. In addition, it seems apparent that our labor laws have not succeeded in their objective of providing employees with a low-cost means of determining questions of representation. The lack of adequate penalties for discriminatory discharge and the ability of employers to exclude union organizers and resist organization have contributed to the decline of unions in America. Finally, my analysis suggests that a host of current legal doctrines—such as the Supreme Court decisions allowing permanent replacements and the court opinions determining that changes in the scope of a business are merely a permissive subject of bargaining—violate the basic purposes of the NLRA. Although my economic analysis demonstrates the consistent logic behind the core principles of American labor law, there are still many substantial changes that would allow workers to more fully enjoy the benefits of collective bargaining.

Notes

1. 29 U.S.C. § 151 (1988).

2. Milton Friedman and Rose Friedman, *Free to Choose*, 228–47.

3. Kenneth G. Dau-Schmidt, "A Bargaining Analysis of American Labor Law and the Search for Bargaining Equity and Industrial Peace."

4. Ibid., 420–22.

5. Friedman and Friedman, *Free to Choose*, 135–36.

6. "Product market power rents" are those profits earned by the employer in excess of the competitive rate of return because the employer enjoys a monopoly or participates in an oligopoly or cartel in the product market. Ricardian rents are those profits earned in excess of the competitive rate of return because the employer is fortunate enough to employ a particularly productive resource, such as mining a particularly rich vein of ore. The employees can share these employer rents without having a negative impact on production or price because such rents are in excess of the competitive return the employer requires to stay in production. "Quasi rents" are those profits earned on a resource in excess of what could be earned on that resource by transferring it to its next best use. For example, the profits earned on a steel mill are largely quasi rents because the large smelter and rollers are too heavy to transport to another market and can be used only in the production of steel. As the name implies, quasi rents are not true rents because, although employees can share in these rents without affecting the production of the employer in the short run, in the long run the employer will have inadequate incentive to continue to invest in the firm or location. Another source of employer rents that employees can share without adverse effect is employer monopsony rents in the labor market. Dau-Schmidt, "A Bargaining Analysis of American Labor Law and the Search for Bargaining Equity and Industrial Peace," 428–31.

7. Kenneth Elzinga, "The Antimerger Law."

8. Nationally, the proportion of private sector employees represented by a union is currently about 9 percent. The largest percent represented in any particular industry (transportation) is 24 percent, while the largest percent represented in any particular occupation (protective service) is 38 percent. The highest percent organized in any

state (New York) is 26 percent. U.S. Department of Labor Press Release, "Union Members in 2002."

9. Paula B. Voos, and Lawrence R. Mishel, "The Union Impact on Profits," 128–29, (found that on average union wage and benefit increases were 80 percent paid for out of company profits and 20 percent paid for by price increases to consumers); Nancy L. Rose, "Labor Rent Sharing and Regulation," 1175 (found that unions capture 75 percent of firm monopoly profits). See also, Barry T. Hirsch and John T. Addison, *The Economic Analysis of Unions,* 209–14; Richard B. Freeman and James L. Medoff, *What Do Unions Do?*, 52

10. Hirsch and Addison, *The Economic Analysis of Unions*, 188; Freeman and Medoff. *What Do Unions Do?*, 7–11; Orley Ashenfelter, P. Richard, and G. Layard, *Handbook of Labor Economics,* 789; Peter Kuhn, "Union Productivity Effects and Economic Efficiency," 229.

11. Hirsch and Addison, *The Economic Analysis of Unions,* 195–208; Freeman and Medoff, *What Do Unions Do?*, 162–80; Dale Belman, "Unions, the Quality of Labor Relations, and Firm Performance," in Lawrence Mischel and Paula B. Voos, eds., *Unions and Economic Competitiveness,* 41–107; Adrienne E. Eaton, "Unions and Contemporary Innovations in Work," in Lawrence Mischel, Paula B. Voos, eds., *Unions and Economic Competitiveness*, 173–215; Kim B. Clark, "The Impact of Unionization on Productivity"; Kim B. Clark, "Unionization and Productivity." Although significant, these productivity increases are still smaller than the typical union wage increase of 10–15 percent, leading to continued employer opposition to unionism.

12. Marc Galanter, "Why the 'Haves' Come out Ahead."

13. Paul Rubin, "Why Is the Common Law Efficient?"

14. See, for example, *Skagerberg v. Blandin Paper Co.*, 266 N.W. 872 (1936).

15. Frank Elkouri and Edna A. Elkouri, *How Arbitration Works*, 651–55.

16. Richard Posner, "Theories of Economic Regulation"; D. Lee, "Politics, Ideology, and the Power of Public Choice."

17. Matthew W. Finkin, et al., *Legal Protection for the Individual Employee*, 582–619.

18. James A. Gross, *The Making of the National Labor Relations Board,* 16. Of course, to the extent that employer and employee interests coincide in an industry, they can join forces to lobby at the expense of the public at large.

19. Kaushik Basu, "Notes on Evolution, Rationality and Norms."

20. W. Guth and R. Tietz, "Ultimatum Bargaining Behavior."

21. 29 U.S.C. § 158(a)(5) (1988).

22. Robert E. Hall and David M. Lilien, "Efficient Wage Bargains Under Uncertain Supply and Demand"; Ian M. MacDonald and Robert M. Solow, "Wage Bargaining and Employment"; Alison L. Booth, *The Economics of the Trade Union,* 128–34.

23. John M. Abowd, "The Effects of Wage Bargains on the Stock Market Value of the Firm"; David Card, "Efficient Contracts with Costly Adjustment."

24. John F. Nash, Jr., "The Bargaining Problem."

25. Although the results of a particular game can be changed by changing assumptions about the costs and benefits of intransigent behavior, the basic nature of collective negotiations as a dilemma game remains. Examining Figure 9.2, one sees that it can be divided into sectors I through IV according to the minimum payoff to the employees and employer for capitulating to the other side (the horizontal line at $2 for the employees and the vertical line at $2 for the employer in this game). If the expected settlement after a strike is in sector I, the employer will give in and not take a

strike because he will earn more by capitulating. Similarly, if the expected settlement after a strike is in sector III, the union will give in and not strike. However, if the expected settlement after a strike is in sectors II or IV, both sides will have individual incentives to undertake a strike. In sector II this is true because both sides will do better by striking than by capitulating. In sector IV a strike is also possible because, although each does better by capitulating, each may act recalcitrant and hope that the other side "chickens out" first. However, if in negotiations between the two parties the expected payoffs for a strike are consistently in sectors I or III, so that one side is always capitulating, the other side will have incentive to lessen the share they give for capitulation, expanding sectors II and IV and increasing the chances that the other side's expected payoffs recommend intransigence and a strike.

26. Freeman and Medoff, *What Do Unions Do?*, 248.

27. Dau-Schmidt, "A Bargaining Analysis of American Labor Law and the Search for Bargaining Equity and Industrial Peace," 485–86.

28. Paul C. Weiler, "Promises to Keep," 1769.

29. Weiler, *Governing the Workplace*, 105; United States Department of Labor Press Release, "Union Members in 2002," 8.

30. *Phelps Dodge Corp. v. NLRB*, 313 U.S. 177 (1941).

31. The United States, with an average of 110 days lost to work stoppage per year per thousand organized workers over the period 1978–94, ranks ahead of Canada (511), Australia (509), Italy (358), and the United Kingdom (252), but behind France (68), Germany (22), and Japan (13). Dau-Schmidt, "Labor Law and Industrial Peace."

32. 29 U.S.C. § 158(b)(7) (1988).

33. *Flora Construction Co.*, 132 N.L.R.B. 776 (1961), enforced, 311 F.2d 310 (10th Cir. 1962). *Local 57, Int'l Ladies Garment Workers' Union v. NLRB*, 374 F.2d 295 (D.C. Cir 1967).

34. *Excelsior Underwear, Inc.* 156 NLRB 1236 (1966); *Republic Aviation Corp. v. NLRB*, 324 U.S. 793 (1945).

35. *NLRB v. Gissel Packing Co.*, 395 U.S. 575, 618–19 (1969).

36. Weiler, "Promises to Keep," 1780 (the number of charges filed with the NLRB for employer discrimination on the basis of union affiliation in 1970, 1975, and 1980 were, respectively, 9,290, 13,426, and 18,315).

37. *Lechmere, Inc. v. NLRB*, 502 U.S. 527 (1992).

38. *Midland Nat'l Insurance*, 263 N.L.R.B. 127 (1982).

39. Weiler, "Promises to Keep," 1811.

40. 29 U.S.C. § 158(d) (1988).

41. *NLRB v. General Electric Co.*, 418 F.2d 736 (2d Cir. 1970).

42. *NLRB v. Truitt Manufacturing Co.*, 351 U.S. 149 (1956).

43. 29 U.S.C. § 159(b). *Continental Banking Co.*, 99 N.L.R.B. 777, 782 (1952).

44. Ibid.

45. Julius G. Getman, Bertrand B. Pogrebin, and Davis L. Gregory, *Labor Management Relations and the Law*, 36–42.

46. *Ex-Cell-O Corp.*, 185 N.L.R.B., 107 (1970).

47. *NLRB v. Truitt Manufacturing Co.*, 351 U.S. 149 (1956).

48. *NLRB v. Mackay Radio & Tel. Co.*, 304 U.S. 333 (1938).

49. *First National Maintenance Co. v. NLRB*, 452 U.S. 666 (1981).

50. *Textile Workers Union v. Lincoln Mills*, 353 U.S. 448, 449–56 (1957).

51. *American Manufacturing Co.*, 363 U.S. 564 (1960).

52. *Warrior & Gulf Navigation Co.*, 363 U.S. 574 (1960).

References

Abowd, J.M. "The Effects of Wage Bargains on the Stock Market Value of the Firm." *American Economic Review* 79, no. 4 (1989): 774–800.

American Manufacturing Co., 363 U.S. 564 (1960).

Ashenfelter, O., P. Richard, and G. Layard, eds. *Handbook of Labor Economics.* Amsterdam, New York: North Holland, 1986.

Basu, K. "Notes on Evolution Rationality and Norms." *Journal of Institutional and Theoretical Economics* 152 (1996): 739–50.

Belman, D. "Unions, the Quality of Labor Relations, and Firm Performance." In *Unions and Economic Competitiveness*, ed. L. Mischel and P.B. Voos, 41–107.

Booth, A.L. *The Economics of the Trade Union*. Cambridge, UK: Cambridge University Press, 1995.

Card, D. "Efficient Contracts with Costly Adjustment: Short-Run Employment Determination for Airline Mechanics." *American Economic Review* 76, no. 5 (1986): 1045–71.

Clark, K.B. "The Impact of Unionization on Productivity: A Case Study." *Industrial and Labor Relations Review* 33, no. 4 (1980): 451–69.

———. "Unionization and Productivity: Micro-Economic Evidence." *Quarterly Journal of Economics* 95 (1980): 613 -39.

Dau-Schmidt, K.G. "A Bargaining Analysis of American Labor Law and the Search for Bargaining Equity and Industrial Peace." *Michigan Law Review* 91, no. 3 (1992): 419–514.

———. "Labor Law and Industrial Peace: A Comparative Analysis of the United States, the United Kingdom, Germany and Japan Under the Bargaining Model." *Tulane Journal of International and Comparative Law* 8 (2000): 117–46.

Eaton, A.E. "Unions and Contemporary Innovations in Work." In *Unions and Economic Competitiveness*, ed. Mischel and Voos, 173–215.

Elkouri, F., and E.A. Elkouri. *How Arbitration Works*. Washington, DC: Bureau of National Affairs, 1985.

Elzinga, K. "The Antimerger Law: Pyrrhic Victories?" *Journal of Law & Economics* 12 (1969): 43–78.

Excelsior Underwear, Inc. 156 NLRB 1236 (1966).

Finkin, M.W., A.L. Goldman, C.W. Summers, and K.G. Dau-Schmidt. *Legal Protection for the Individual Employee*. 3d ed. Minneapolis: The West Group, 2002.

First National Maintenance Co. v. NLRB, 452 U.S. 666 (1981).

Freeman, R.B., and J.L. Medoff. *What Do Unions Do?* New York: Basic Books, 1984.

Friedman, M., and R. Friedman. *Free to Choose*. New York: Harcourt Press, 1980.

Galanter, M. "Why the 'Haves' Come out Ahead: Speculations on the Limits of Legal Change." *Law & Society Review* 9 (1974): 95–160.

Getman, J.G., B.B. Pogrebin, and D.L. Gregory. *Labor Management Relations and the Law.* New York: Foundation Press, 1999.

Gross, J.A. *The Making of the National Labor Relations Board: A Study in Economics, Politics and the Law*. Albany: State University of New York Press, 1981.

Guth, W., and R. Tietz. "Ultimatum Bargaining Behavior: A Survey and Comparison of Experimental Results." *Journal of Economic Psychology* 11, no. 3 (1990): 367–88.

Hall, R.E., and D.M. Lilien. "Efficient Wage Bargains Under Uncertain Supply and Demand." *American Economic Review* 69, no. 5 (1979): 868–79.

Hirsch, B.T., and J.T. Addison. *The Economic Analysis of Unions*. Boston: Unwin Hyman, 1986.

Kuhn, P. "Union Productivity Effects and Economic Efficiency." *Journal of Labor Research* 6 (1985) 229–54.

Lechmere, Inc. v. NLRB, 502 U.S. 527 (1992).

Lee, D. "Politics, Ideology, and the Power of Public Choice." *Virginia Law Review* 74 (1988): 191–98.

Local 57, Int'l Ladies Garment Workers' Union v. NLRB, 374 F.2d 295 (D.C. Cir 1967).

MacDonald, I.M., and R.M. Solow. "Wage Bargaining and Employment." *American Economic Review* 71, no. 5 (1981): 896–908.

Mischel, L., and P.B. Voos, eds. *Unions and Economic Competitiveness*. Armonk, NY: M.E. Sharpe, 1991.

Nash, J.F., Jr. "The Bargaining Problem." *Econometrica* 18 (1950): 155–80.

NLRB v. General Electric Co., 418 F.2d 736 (2d Cir. 1970).

NLRB v. Gissel Packing Co., 395 U.S. 575, 618–19 (1969).

NLRB v. Mackay Radio & Tel. Co., 304 U.S. 333 (1938).

NLRB v. Truitt Manufacturing Co., 351 U.S. 149 (1956).

Phelps Dodge Corp. v. NLRB, 313 U.S. 177 (1941).

Posner, R. "Theories of Economic Regulation." *Bell Journal of Economics and Management* 5 (1974): 335–58.

Republic Aviation Corp. v. NLRB, 324 U.S. 793 (1945).

Rose, N.L. "Labor Rent Sharing and Regulation: Evidence from the Trucking Industry." *Journal of Political Economy* 95 (1987): 1146–78.

Rubin, P.H. "Why Is the Common Law Efficient?" *Journal of Legal Studies* 6 (1977): 51–63.

Skagerberg v. Blandin Paper Co., 266 N.W. 872 (1936).

Textile Workers Union v. Lincoln Mills, 353 U.S. 448, 449–56 (1957).

U.S. Department of Labor Press Release. "Union Members in 2002." Available at: ftp://ftp.bls.gov/pub/news.release/union2.txt (2002).

Voos, P. B. and L.R. Mishel. "The Union Impact on Profits: Evidence from Industry Price-Cost Margin Data." *Journal of Labor Economics* 4 (1986): 105–30.

Weiler, P.C. "Promises to Keep: Securing Worker's Rights to Self-Organization Under the NLRA." 8 *Harvard Law Review* 96 (1983): 1769–827.

———. *Governing the Workplace: The Future of Labor and Employment Law.* Cambridge, MA: Harvard University Press, 1990.

10

Personalist Economics, Justice, and the Law

Applications to Labor, Product, and Credit Markets

Edward J. O'Boyle

For years Joseph Stiglitz and George Akerlof have been severely critical of some of the main tenets of conventional economics. In 2001 they received a joint Nobel Prize in Economics. In his Nobel lecture, Stiglitz[1] attacked the neoclassical paradigm for "seemingly precise models" that

- exclude information concerns and the possibility of involuntary unemployment;
- separate equity and efficiency;
- assume continuous market clearing and equilibrium;
- reduce economics to engineering;
- assert that markets are Pareto-efficient;
- hold fast to the invisible hand argument;
- fail to differentiate types of markets;
- break up action, information, and behavior;
- insist that privatization is always welfare enhancing; and
- treat supply and demand as constituting the whole of economic analysis.

Akerlof's Nobel lecture[2] put forward a shorter indictment: Neoclassical economics assumes that all economic behavior is maximizing, insists on strict rationality as opposed to near rationality, embraces the natural rate of unemployment hypothesis, asserts that saving too much or too little is impossible, excludes "reciprocity, fairness, identity, money illusion, loss aversion, herding, and procrastination," and does not recognize failure of credit markets and underdevelopment.

The problem, as Stiglitz[3] makes explicit, is that "the economists' traditional model of the individual is too narrow." However, neither he nor Akerlof offer a substitute for the individual and individualism that lies at the center of neoclassical thinking. In this chapter, we replace the individual and the individualism that are rooted in the Enlightenment and in what might be called the script stage of human communication with the concept of the person and personalism that emerged during the electronic stage of human communication. This difference matters importantly in our understanding of economic affairs, because the electronic stage has given rise to a new awareness of self and of others and, therefore, a new meaning to the concept of the economic agent.[4] We call this new approach "personalist economics." In this chapter we explore this new meaning in terms of three pairs of economic agents: consumer and merchant, worker and producer, and entrepreneur and financial agent.

The need for a new economics is best demonstrated in the deficiencies of the four premises of neoclassical economics: the individual, the law of nature, certainty, and instrumental value.[5] Personalist economics offers an alternative to each of these.

Premises of Personalist Economics

Individual Versus Person

By individual, neoclassical economics means a human being in whom individuality, inward directedness, autonomy, awareness of self, and self-interest are emphasized. The individual is intelligent, rational, utility-calculating and maximizing, and free to choose in all economic decisionmaking. *Homo economicus* is competitive, making use of his or her disposition to undertake certain tasks solely for the solitary reward. Though ever-changing, as accounted for conceptually by human capital, *homo economicus* nonetheless is predictable—a great convenience for economic analysis. Economic behavior is detached from any cultural influence because for *homo economicus* all existence is solitary existence. Finally, *homo economicus* is a living, breathing, existential actuality, though at times he is represented as a machine.[6]

Individualism provides the philosophical foundation for *homo economicus*, which is, today, the dominant way of thinking about economic agents in contemporary economics, because neoclassical economists are comfortable with individualism, and regard it as more than just a description of the way things are. For them, individualism is the ideal philosophy—proven superior for more than two centuries and validated most recently by the demise of *homo sovieticus* and the collectivist philosophy that supported a radically different characterization of economic agents. But individualism is not appropriate for the new economy in which economic affairs increasingly are centralized in supranational economic unions such as the World Trade

Organization and the European Union. *Homo economicus* fit well in a world and at a time when decentralization was taking place in political affairs, notably during the transition from royalty to free citizenry, from privilege to merit. Because the actual roles of economic agents have changed in the new economy, along with their personal characteristics, it follows that a new economics begins with a rethinking of *homo economicus*.

Personalist economics argues that there is much regarding economic agency today that is not accounted for by *homo economicus*. Personalist economics however, does not, discard that theory; rather, it adds characteristics not included in *homo economicus*.

A person is a human in whom both individuality and sociality are recognized and emphasized: inward-directed *and* outward-reaching, autonomous *and* dependent, and aware of self and self-interested *and* at the same time aware of others and concerned for their well-being. A person is a complex being whose decisionmaking in economic affairs often is a struggle between intelligence and intuition, reason and emotion, utility-maximizing and utility-satisficing, and individual freedom and social responsibility. In all economic affairs the person, *homo socioeconomicus*, is not only competitive, but also cooperative, making use of the human disposition to undertake certain tasks collectively for the gain that cannot be achieved so well or at all when those tasks are undertaken alone.

The economy may be compared to a twin-engine aircraft that is built through the efforts of human economic agents such as working, saving, innovating, and trading, and is powered by the engines of competition and cooperation. As with the aircraft, the economy performs better when both engines are synchronized in flight, though it can operate on just one alone.

The predictability of *homo economicus* means that his or her behavior is quantifiable and therefore can be incorporated in the mathematical models of neoclassical economics. *Homo socioeconomicus* is unique, one of a kind, valuing individuality and sociality differently, changing as an agent with changing economic conditions, a holistic, unified human being, not one part individual, one part social, an embodied spirit, a material body *inside* a human spirit, not one part body, one part spirit.

Scorning dead-end employment, the human spirit longs for a job that affords opportunities to put one's creative talents and energies to work. Further, humans need to be accepted by others on the job, need to experience a sense of belonging. As to consumption, humans need the goods and services required for physical well-being. Humans, however, are more than mere material beings who are concerned only with their physical well-being. The human spirit seeks goodness, truth, and beauty in music, art, drama, nature, literature, dance, and sports. In searching for these ideals, it normally is necessary to acquire certain goods and services. Humans may look for goodness through theater presentations that address the clash between good and evil, and truth may be pursued through educational institutions. Yearning for things of beauty, humans purchase the work of artists and buy tickets for access to the ballet and opera.

Human beings are different in countless ways. What may satisfy the spirit of one may be of no interest to another. Some are drawn to heavy metal, others to rap. One family member may find the beach the perfect vacation spot; another may prefer the mountains. Personalist economics thinks of the time set aside to purchase and use goods and services in this manner as leisure, an economic activity distinct from work and consumption. Leisure includes the rest that humans require on a daily basis due to embodiment, and to the longer breaks over weekends, holidays, and vacations needed to cope with the stress of daily living. Neoclassical economics, on the other hand, defines leisure in a negative sense: time spent not working.

Homo socioeconomicus is aware that community and a sense of belonging emerge not when humans avoid harm to one another, but when they participate in one another's economic existence; that economic community, notably in the form of companies that produce the goods and services vital to human well-being, requires positive contributions from the economic agents who form those communities, that all existence is coexistence, that the human spirit plays a major role in work, consumption, and leisure. Fairness, benevolence, trust, and generosity are necessary for a human being to develop from the individual *homo economicus* to the person *homo socioeconomicus*.

Adam Smith's *The Theory of Moral Sentiments* calls attention to these duties, and Alfred Marshall rejects competition as the fundamental characteristic of modern economic systems, affirming instead the importance of neighborhoods and collective action, of honesty, fidelity, unselfishness, and sympathy.[7] But neoclassical economics constructed *homo economicus* from Smith's *An Inquiry into the Nature and Causes of the Wealth of Nations*. In that sense, personalist economics and *homo socioeconomicus* return to Smith's and Marshall's original ideas about economic agency, and personalism becomes the new philosophical ideal.

Personalist economics sees culture—"a social force that encompasses individuals and welds them into communities [shaping] their prejudices, ideas, values, habits, attitudes, taste and priorities"[8]—as playing an important role in economic affairs. To embrace culture, neoclassical economics must yield on the solitary existence of the atomistic individual and admit that economic agents coexist as persons in communities. Culture relates to the specific ways in which the needs and wants of the human body and human spirit are addressed. To illustrate, across Europe the month of August is set aside for vacations. In the United States work is so highly valued that many Americans are workaholics and seldom take time off.

Culture relates to the economy the same way weather influences the twin-engine aircraft. A culture of life and hope, which is affirmed when human beings care for one another, enhances the performance of the economy just as the aircraft performs better in good weather. Personalist economics advocates such a culture for that very reason. In contrast, a culture of death and despair—which in the extreme is reinforced by a pervasive attitude that death is the answer to social problems—degrades economic performance just as the aircraft functions less effectively in bad weather. For over 100 years, we have witnessed the devastating economic consequences of genocide, ethnic cleansing, civil war, terrorism, drugs, slavery, and the like. By analogy, neoclassical economics admits of no role for the weather in aircraft operations. Neoclassical economists are in denial, doggedly holding on to *homo economicus* in the face of overwhelming evidence that it fails to represent human nature accurately in the electronic age.

Law of Nature Versus Institutions

By the "law of nature," neoclassical economics means that markets provide a forum for the interaction of economic agents and that those markets by their very nature function efficiently and effectively. The law of nature presumes that every economic agent is capable of representing his or her own best interest without assistance. However, individual freedom to act in markets does not justify bringing harm to others, and there is no need for any intervention on the part of private groups or public bodies unless that prohibition is breached. Drawing on the law of nature, neoclassical economics denies that community or culture truly matter in conditioning the behavior of economic agents and therefore neither one plays a role in shaping economic affairs.

Personalist economics argues, instead, that markets at times dysfunction, and *institutions* are needed to address that dysfunction. For example, some employers, left to their own devices, contaminate the air, soil, or water with their waste discharge. Therefore, it is necessary to limit the waste that they discharge and to fine them and shut them down whenever they exceed that limit. Another limit is the minimum wage, which forces some employers to pay more than they would otherwise. By analogy, intervention, whether by private group or public body, represents the control surfaces of the twin-engine aircraft such as the rudder and flaps that allow the pilot to control the economy during takeoff, flight, and landing. Loss of those control surfaces makes landing the aircraft extremely difficult.

Certainty Versus Uncertainty

Neoclassical economics relies on mathematical models and data sets to describe and understand economic affairs with certainty. This investigative methodology is grounded in the Enlightenment and the scientific method. Personalist economics contends that certainty is not possible because economic agents are complex, ever-changing human persons who remain, in part, a mystery even to themselves and therefore difficult to fully represent in mathematical models. Thus, the conclusions drawn from economic research must be couched in terms that reflect some uncertainty. For the research specialist, the problem is how to deal with uncertainty in an open and honest fashion, weighing the evidence to draw only those conclusions that the evidence supports. Achieving certainty today in the new economic order is an even greater challenge due to cultural differences and misunderstandings and, consequently, different and incompletely understood human behavior. What in one culture is unacceptable and illegal (bribery) may be acceptable in another (facilitating payment, a cost of business). In this regard, analogy can be a powerful model, though lacking in precision. However, when it is carefully crafted, analogy can be more deeply probing and instructive of economic affairs than a mathematical model.

Instrumental Value Versus Inherent Dignity

By instrumental value, neoclassical economics means that the worth of every economic agent is determined by the contract that sets forth the payment that an agent has accepted for labor services or other supplied resources. Worth ultimately depends on how useful an agent is as an economic instrumentality. Personalist economics takes exception to that premise. Humans have an inherent dignity that is central to their nature as persons and that everyone is duty-bound to respect. There is no philosophically valid way to rank order humans according to their economic productivity. Each is precious, each has the same worth, no one is to be valued more highly than anyone else because no human being has the wisdom to create such an ordering. *Homo socioeconomicus* embraces the social value of human equality. *Homo economicus* does not.

Integration of Economic Theory

Another major deficiency in neoclassical economics is that microeconomics and macroeconomics have not been integrated into a unified general theory. This predicament originates with the premise that the central unit of analysis is the atomistic individual. There is no such problem when economics proceeds from the premise that the central analytical unit is the person. To explain, microeconomics represents a description and understanding of economic affairs from the perspective of human individuality. Macroeconomics, on the other hand, sees the same economic affairs from the perspective of human sociality. An integration of these two branches is necessary because humans are fully integrated, so that it is impossible to separate the individual being from the social being. Personalist economics makes the unification of economic theory possible by construing all economic affairs—working, consuming, saving, investing, lending, borrowing, innovating, brokering, insuring, buying, selling, resting, hiring, dismissing, and the like—not in terms of the impersonal mechanical forces of the market, but in Marshall's personalist language of humankind "in the ordinary business of life." [9]

Freedom and Justice in Economic Decisionmaking

By their very nature humans are or should be: (1) free *to* be all that they can be, (2) free *from* coercion wherein freedom is equated with liberty, and (3) free *for* the purpose of meeting their obligations. *Homo economicus* openly embraces the first and second meanings of freedom. *Homo socioeconomicus* embraces all three.

Acting as economic agents, and given their free will and intelligence, human persons are capable of making choices. In many instances those choices are ethically neutral. For example, the decision to install white tiles in the bathroom floor rather than, say, brown tiles has no ethical content. However, the decision as to how much to pay a worker to install the tiles very likely has an ethical dimension. Deliberately withholding pay until the work has been completed and paying the worker less than what was agreed to even though the work was done fully and properly are unethical.

Are decisions regarding ethical issues in economic affairs entirely arbitrary, depending completely on the opinions, attitudes, and values of the persons making those decisions? Or are there objective standards that apply in economic affairs rendering ethical decisionmaking reasoned, defensible, and alike from one person to the next except in specific extenuating circumstances? The view from personalist economics is that there are certain objective ethical standards to be applied in economic affairs, ultimately originating in the human experience, and embodied in three principles of justice.

In economic affairs the three principles are equivalence, distributive justice, and contributive justice. There are three principles of economic justice because there are only three ways in which economic agents can interact: person to person, superior to subordinate, and member to group.[10]

Equivalence

The principle of equivalence states that buyer and seller in the product market, resource holder (including worker) and producer in the resource market, and creditor and borrower in the financial market have two duties that are ethically binding on both parties: to exchange things of equal value and impose equal burdens on one another. In many transactions, personal experience informs us as to what equal value means. By equal burdens we mean that the seller's burden is to give up possession of the good or service in question; the buyer's burden is to hand over the money necessary to acquire that good or service. For the worker, the burden is performing the work required by the employer. For the employer, it is paying the worker the agreed wage. For the creditor, the burden is surrendering use of the loaned funds, waiting for repayment, and taking on the risk of default. For the borrower, it is making payments on time as agreed.

At times, the things exchanged are not of equal value, such as when a house is sold, and the buyer takes possession but makes only partial payment in cash. To simplify this example, assume that the seller offers to lend the buyer the difference. Under those circumstances, the seller/lender faces the risk that the buyer/borrower may not be faithful with regard to paying down the balance. The seller/lender also must wait until payments are made and at closing forgoes the use of that money for other purposes. Consequently, the seller/lender is justified in charging interest to equalize the burdens. Though we would prefer to be certain with regard to the precise amount of interest that equalizes the burden, we cannot claim certainty except regarding the duty imposed by the principle of equivalence: Lender may not impose an undue burden on borrower. What is undue is case-specific and must be determined by the circumstances at the time the loan is negotiated.

In the product market, one common practice based on the principle of equivalence is the money-back guarantee. This guarantee is the seller's recognition that at times an honest mistake is made, and the things exchanged are not of equal value. Merchants who depend on repeat business understand that the money-back guarantee is good for their business, even though they might not understand consciously that they are being faithful to the demands of the principle of equivalence. In the resource market, the common expression "full day's *work* for a full day's *pay*" is a reminder of the worker's obligation under the principle of equivalence. Reversing the language to "full day's *pay* for a full day's *work*" underscores the employer's duty.

There are several ways in which equivalence is violated in the product market. We mention only two: shoplifting and price gouging. In the resource market there are several ways in which this principle is violated. We enumerate these two: sweating workers and embezzling. All violate equivalence regarding the duty to exchange things of equal value or to impose equal burdens.

Distributive Justice

Distributive justice requires the superior to distribute the benefits and burdens of the group under his or her supervision among its members in some equal fashion. This does not mean strictly equal because there likely are significant differences among subordinates, and it is appropriate to take those differences into account. For example, handicapped employees may require different parking and restroom accommodations than able-bodied employees. In assigning work and evaluating performance, distributive justice demands that the superior differentiate among subordinates when the differences among them are real and substantial. To illustrate, a supervisor may allow one employee to take time off to tend to a sick child, another to attend a funeral, but deny release time to shop for a sailboat or buy lottery tickets. Ultimately, this kind of decisionmaking turns critically on a judgment as to the need of the company for the employee's labor services and the need of the employee to attend to other matters. It is, strictly speaking, a value-laden and person-centered decision.

Discrimination occurs when the superior differentiates among subordinates for reasons that are insubstantial. In this regard, false stereotyping may be the device used to rationalize the different treatment. Sometimes people who are essentially alike are treated differently, as with older workers because they have "less upside potential" than younger workers,[11] women because it is assumed that work is of secondary importance, and immigrants, because they dress differently or speak with foreign accents.

"Equal pay for equal work" is required under distributive justice: Persons doing the same work, with the same on-the-job-performance of their assigned duties, are to be paid the same wages. "Equal opportunity" too is required under distributive justice, meaning that persons of equal experience and qualifications are to be afforded the same chance to be hired and promoted.

Under the 1964 Civil Rights Act, special protection has been accorded women, African Americans, Native Americans, Jews and persons of other faiths, and the foreign born. More recently, persons with disabilities have been included in the "protected class" along with those forty years of age or older. Discrimination and the government intervention required to address it are evidence that the law of nature at times is insufficient to resolve conflicts in economic affairs.

Distributive justice has application in the product market, too, but here the issues are not nearly as serious as in the resource market. In the product market, the merchant or shopkeeper is the superior when he or she enjoys some freedom to set the terms of trade and must decide how to deal with his or her customers without discriminating. A merchant who makes rain checks available is saying in effect that when an item is put on sale at a very favorable price, he or she will treat all customers alike, even those who come to the store after supplies have been exhausted. "Limit three to a customer" tells all customers that no one is free to buy the entire supply.

Contributive Justice

The principle of contributive justice lays down the obligation of the member to the group. Insofar as a person receives benefits from the group, that person has a duty to maintain and support the group. Paying dues is the usual requirement for persons joining a membership organization. Failure to pay dues reduces a person to inactive membership status, enjoying fewer membership benefits.

Of the three principles of economic justice, contributive justice is least familiar because Westerners think of themselves as individuals first and indeed have a high regard for "rugged individualism." For that reason, we have only weak examples of common expressions for this principle. In the resource market, where employees work in groups or teams, expressions such as "doing my fair share" and "paying my dues" are sometimes heard.

In the product market, there are certain expectations when persons come together, whether for a concert or sporting event or at a retail establishment. The last to arrive is expected to wait his or her turn. To do otherwise is disrespectful to those who have been waiting and sets an example for others to do the same, in which case a general loss of civility—pushing, shoving, trampling—may follow that is destructive of a sense of community. In like manner, paying dues is a condition of active membership in a professional association, and filing a tax return is the citizen's obligation to the state.

As to violations of contributive justice, there are several powerful examples. In the resource market, industrial spying and sabotage violate contributive justice because the person who appears to be a loyal member of one business establishment actually is faithful to a rival organization and seeks to undermine the effectiveness of the first establishment by stealing secrets and disrupting work. Insurance fraud violates contributive justice because, if a fraudulent claim is not detected, payment is made to the insured party, which drives up the costs of the insurer who then may pass those additional costs on to all policyholders in the form of higher premiums.

Justice, Neoclassical Economics, and Personalist Economics

Neoclassical economists assert that ethical problems in economic affairs are sorted out by the law of nature and the "invisible hand" of the market. They insist that economic agents pursue their own self-interest and, under conditions of perfect competition wherein Pareto optimality or allocative efficiency is achieved, each one receives his or her due. Justice, in other words, is served fully by allocative efficiency. This argument allows neoclassical economists to hold fast to the position that ethical matters are addressed fully through the self-interested behavior of economic agents, and thus to proclaim that their economic models are free of their own personal values and that economics more nearly is a hard science. In their world, because it is grounded in the objectivity of the scientific method and the certainty of mathematical models, positive economics is vastly superior to normative economics.

Personalist economics insists that pursuing self-interest alone is insufficient to establish the trust necessary for routine transactions. At the least, economic agents must be aware of their duties to others and must faithfully execute those duties. *Homo socioeconomicus* is trustworthy when he or she respects and protects the dignity of the other persons involved in a transaction and does not reduce them to mere instrumental value.

Personalist economics insists that ethics in economic affairs is necessary for building and maintaining trust—the willingness to accept another agent's promise to abide by the terms of a just agreement—between and among economic agents. Without trust, transactions tend to break down due to monitoring and enforcement costs.[12] The need for trust is heightened in "the new economy" and today's information age because decisionmaking often takes place over a shorter time period, giving less time to evaluate the trustworthiness of other economic agents. Trustworthiness is diminished whenever communications are less face-to-face, more at arm's length, indirect, and impersonal. It is enhanced whenever more or better information about other economic agents is readily accessible.

Justice functions in two modalities. In the activating modality, justice affirms what economic agents owe one another, and in that sense it functions like the oil in the engines of the twin-engine aircraft providing the necessary lubricant for "the ordinary business of life." In the limiting modality, justice condemns certain harmful business practices such as discrimination and exploitation, and in that sense functions like the oil filter removing impurities in the oil so that the aircraft's engines perform more efficiently. Just as any oil filter needs replacing, justice needs renewing to deal with abuses arising from new technologies such as stealing credit card and cell phone numbers.[13]

Reconstructing Economics

Following personalist economics, the reconstruction of economics begins with the *acting* person in economic affairs—the economic agent. Economic theory should be less about things such as prices, goods, natural resources, physical capital, and the like and more about human beings "in the ordinary business of life"—the *what* and the *why* of their actions as economic agents. Three agent pairs are especially important: entrepreneur and financial agent, consumer and merchant, worker and producer.

Entrepreneur and Financial Agent

The entrepreneur is the key economic agent because the entrepreneur precipitates change. By analogy the entrepreneur is the pilot of the aircraft.[14] The entrepreneur is the two-dimensional *homo socioeconomicus*, as opposed to the one-dimensional *homo economicus* of neoclassical economics, because the entrepreneur is a real, living, breathing person acting in economic affairs and not some totally self-interested, self-absorbed, completely rational calculating machine. There is a profound difference between the human pilot with a mind and a heart, possessing both intelligence and emotions, and the autopilot, which has neither mind nor heart, and for which intelligence is entirely machinelike and programmed.

According to Joseph Schumpeter, the entrepreneur triggers change in five ways.[15] In the marketplace, the entrepreneur introduces new goods and service and penetrates new markets. In the workplace, the entrepreneur utilizes different materials in the production process, innovates new production processes, and develops new ways of running the business. At times, more than one type of change is necessary for success. For example, introducing a new product also may require a change in the production process.

Schumpeter identifies persistence as the key personal trait of the entrepreneur, setting him or her apart from others. The entrepreneur is dogged in the pursuit of ideas. Entrepreneurs are visionary in that they see opportunities that other do not. Large established companies resist entrepreneurial change in a way that is reminiscent of Newton's third principle of motion: For every action, there is an equal and opposite reaction. Thus entrepreneurs often are associated with small companies, including firms that they themselves establish to implement their innovational ideas. They are driven at times by the survival needs of the company, though they are not always successful.

Culture can have a significant impact on entrepreneurial activity in the sense that entrepreneurs are more likely to accept failure and try again in a culture where business failure does not spell personal failure. Bankruptcy relief and "the golden parachute" are two ways in which American culture encourages the entrepreneur to try again.

The competitive/cooperative dimensions of human nature play a role in entrepreneurship. The competitive trait that rests on human individuality is vital to success in marketplace innovations because the marketplace is a competitive forum, whereas the cooperative trait that is grounded in human sociality is vital to success in the workplace because the workplace is a cooperative environment. Both traits frequently are vital to the successful implementation of innovational schemes. Some authors have correlated these traits directly with gender, with male and female. Our strong preference is to relate competitiveness to masculinity and the cooperativeness to femininity, which may be present in both men and women. This issue remains quite controversial.[16]

As stated previously, the entrepreneur is the pilot of the economy who decides where the economy is headed, following a flight plan, but capable of departing from that plan to avoid heavy weather. By making credit available to the entrepreneur through the loan process, the private commercial banker provides the fuel necessary to power the twin engines of cooperation and competition.

Successful entrepreneurs engage in a dynamic process that has two major effects. First, they create new business enterprises, new jobs, new resource requirements, which translate into new opportunities for workers, resource holders, suppliers, investors, and communities. At the same time, they destroy old business enterprises, old jobs, established supplier networks, which signify financial hardship or ruin for others. For good reason, Schumpeter called this process "creative destruction." [17]

As a matter of conscience, the successful entrepreneur should weigh the negative aspects of innovation against its positive aspects. In this regard, the principle of the double effect comes into play and sets two limits on what the entrepreneur should do. First, the destructive negative effects must not be greater than the creative positive effects. Second, the entrepreneur must not intend to use destructive effects as a way of singling out certain persons or organizations for punishment. Personalist economics argues that the entrepreneur has no right to act in ways that ignore the principle of the double effect. It also contends that philanthropy that was made possible by successful innovation may not compensate fully for abuses triggered by that innovation.

Though not the most important characteristic of capitalism, the private creation of credit is its *distinguishing* characteristic.[18] No other system operates with private commercial banks making loans without the money being saved beforehand. There are, of course, other sources of funds in which prior savings is a requirement, such as pension and venture capital funds. The central bank's function is to assure that there are adequate supplies of fuel for the economy and, in the extreme, to prevent an economic "crash." Subsidies, tax credits, and other forms of relief function like fuel additives, enhancing the power of the aircraft's twin engines.

According to *homo economicus*, by maximizing risk-adjusted returns on invested funds, financial executives also meet their public obligations. Personalist economics argues that there is considerable divergence between the social rate of return and the private rate of return—capital markets are not perfect. In making investment decisions, *homo socioeconomicus* cannot presume that every decision to serve the private good of investors will, at the same time, serve the common good. Instead, *homo socioeconomicus* is duty-bound to evaluate investment decisions in ways that take account of the difference between investments in such projects as gated communities and cosmetic surgery for the rich, and affordable housing and access to health care for the poor.

This obligation derives from the inherent dignity of all human beings as persons and their need for goods and services to sustain their lives and provision their well-being at some minimal level. The goods of this world are intended not for the exclusive use of those with the market power to command those goods, but for the general use of all humankind. It is the duty of financial executives to include the common good in their decisionmaking. They do so in a developed market economy by grounding their decisions in the love of virtue rather than the magic of the invisible hand.[19]

Intertemporal exchange introduces the risk of default, thus requiring reciprocal trust between the persons involved. This trust may be based on real reciprocal acquaintance, as happens in local finance, on reputation, with the resulting possible distortion of incentives on each side, or on some surrogate of trust such as contractual clauses that reinforce the borrower's incentive to honor his or her debt. In international financial contracts in particular, clauses often are introduced to make the problem of reciprocal uncertainty less difficult, but these contractual expedients often have undesired consequences. For instance, linking interest rates to the trustworthiness of the borrower or resorting in general to short-term loans may result in blocking loans for those projects where there are large social returns to the common good, but the expected private return is not high enough or is too far in the future.

The faithful practice of the principles of equivalence and distributive justice can contribute powerfully to (re-)establishing trust between financial agents. Under the principle of equivalence, both agents agree without coercion to the amount to be borrowed, the schedule for repaying the principal, and the interest rate that equalizes the burden for the creditor who must wait for repayment subject to the risk of default. Excessively high interest rates are condemned as usurious, and the creditor is labeled a "loan shark." Thus, there must be some upper limit to the interest rate that equates the borrower's burden to the creditor's. What that limit should be is determined by the specific financial conditions at the moment and by parties who are not driven entirely by personal gain but who understand that the creditor and the borrower are human beings whose dignity must be respected and who never are to be exploited. Otherwise, relying strictly on risk assessment, the powerful are able to deny the weak the credit they need, thereby perpetuating their weakness, or to take advantage of them by offering credit on terms that make repayment difficult or even impossible. Debt restructuring and debt forgiveness for nation-states as well as human persons are justified under the principle of equivalence whenever the burden to the borrower becomes unduly onerous or impossible to bear.

The creditor has a duty under distributive justice to treat as equals all prospective borrowers in similar financial circumstances, as determined by risk evaluation. Distributive justice demands that the lender not engage in price discrimination or "redlining" even when the opportunity presents itself. This requires transparency in credit transactions, which preferably is done by voluntary compliance or if necessary by some kind of private or public institutional oversight. The International Monetary Fund already has affirmed two codes on transparency: *Code of Good Practices on Transparency in Monetary and Financial Policies* and *Code of Good Practices on Fiscal Transparency*.[20] Voluntary agencies are preferred because they function closer to the day-to-day operations of the financial institutions requiring review. Locating the oversight agency as close to the actual lending institution, and therefore close to the specific conditions in which that institution extends credit, helps the oversight agency avoid supporting projects that have little prospects for economic success and long-term survival, and other projects that otherwise might be turned to personal rent-seeking activities. Senior executives and officials of financial institutions must make justice an everyday priority. What is most important for genuine justice in financial affairs is the integrity and courage of the human persons involved.

Consumer and Merchant

Our human bodily nature requires us to deal with two limits as consumers. Limit I, or maximum marginal utility, refers to the one unit consumed that produces the largest increase in utility. Limit II, or maximum total utility, refers to the last unit consumed that offers some increase in utility but beyond which disutility sets in. Though not given this expression by neoclassical economics, these two limits or maxima are at the heart of the principle of diminishing marginal utility. Putting the concept of the limit at the center of our understanding of consumer behavior in effect acknowledges the importance of moderation to assure that the goods and services sought after remain the means to satisfying human wants and meeting human needs and do not become ends in themselves.[21]

"Pigging out" is a common reference to having exceeded Limit II and afterward having some regrets. Consumers at times exceed Limit II because of peer pressure or because the product is available without charge. At times, the consumer is willing to challenge his or her own Limit II, thinking that the limit is higher than it truly is. Truth to tell, we do not always know the reason, because at times even the consumer does not know.

Every human faces these two limits as a consumer because everyone is embodied. Absent the body, the limits disappear. Personalist economics emphasizes that the limits are not the same for every consumer because each one has a body with its own metabolism and tolerances. And with age and experience, those limits change. The hyperactive body of the teenager requires more calories than the sedentary body of the same person much later in life.

The reason consumers buy more when the price is lower is that as they consume more, they eventually reach Limit I beyond which each additional unit consumed offers a smaller increase in utility than the preceding unit. They are willing to purchase those smaller increments beyond Limit I only when the price is lower. When it comes to consumer behavior, the principle of diminishing marginal utility probably best represents what neoclassical economics means by *homo economicus*.

Homo economicus is more than what is represented by diminishing marginal utility. Following neoclassical economics, the consumer is unique, solitary, autonomous, self-centered, and self-made, traits that never change, never conflict, and always accent the consumer's individuality.

The consumer behaves predictably in ways that are described as utility-maximizing, privacy-protecting, and commodity-acquiring. In Western culture, acquiring and accumulating goods are perceived as signs of success. As *homo economicus,* the consumer is free to choose whatever he or she is able to afford, to make those choices informed by reason for the purpose of satisfying some want, and to take into account not only experiences in the past, but also hopes and plans for the future. Adults are expected to plan years ahead for their retirement, rationally planning income and expenses to achieve that goal. Meeting need is rejected by neoclassical economics as a central determinant of consumer behavior because need is a value-laden concept, depending importantly on the person who uses the concept. In neoclassical economics, comparisons are made but they are intrapersonal or inward-looking, wherein consumers evaluate their own wants over time without any regard for others. Our language itself points to consumer behavior that is individualistic: the trendsetter is a consumer with much individuality; the conformist is one with little individuality.

In personalist economics, the consumer is a social being as well as an individual being. He or she often is forced to work out a compromise between sociality and individuality: between unique *and* alike, solitary *and* communal, autonomous *and* dependent, self-centered *and* other-centered, self-made *and* culture-bound. A husband may have to give up a fishing trip because his wife needs assistance in her donut shop. A teenager may have to wear clothes that are out of fashion because mother disapproves of what is fashionable at the moment. An elderly parent may have to change residence to allay the fears of adult children who are concerned for the parent's safety. The consumer at times must choose between self and other in ways that are not accounted for by neoclassical economics: between utility-maximizing *and* utility-satisficing, privacy-protecting *and* company-seeking, commodity-acquiring *and* gift-giving. A person may settle for less so that a friend might have more. A young woman eager to make friends in a new city may ask a neighbor to shop with her but discovers that whenever she wants to shop again, the neighbor insists on tagging along. A youngster must learn, sometimes with difficulty, that a friend's birthday is for giving rather than getting.

As *homo socioeconomicus,* the consumer is free to choose whatever he or she is able to afford but is morally accountable for the choices made. The buyer makes those choices informed by reason and emotion, both by mind and heart, for the purpose of satisfying a want or meeting a need. Even though it is a value-laden concept, need is embraced by personalist economics because it is a central determinant of consumer behavior. Fear drives some consumer choices, as at times with handguns and security systems. Some persons known as compulsive consumers or shopaholics are addicted to shopping. Their choices are not rationally determined, nor are they freely made. *Homo socioeconomicus* is not only hindsighted, but also foresighted, as when parents have to reduce current consumption to save for their children's future education. Human individuality prompts the consumer to make comparisons that are intrapersonal, but human sociality encourages interpersonal comparisons.

Personalist economics argues that poverty is primarily a microeconomic issue, not a matter of scarcity that an unrestrained market addresses through the price mechanism that automatically eliminates shortages and surpluses. It is a problem of unmet needs that often calls for intervention. From the very start, it is necessary to differentiate (1) those poor persons who use resources responsibly and still do not have enough to meet their needs, from (2) others who use resources irresponsibly. Personalist economics turns to the principle of subsidiarity to sort out society's response to the needy in these two groups. Subsidiarity states that the assistance should be located as close as possible to the persons/families in need in order to limit the abuse of (1) persons applying for assistance who are not needy at all or are irresponsible because by being closer, the agency likely is better informed and better able to identify the real abusers and to offer assistance in ways that address their irresponsibility; and (2) disrespectful program staffers because by being closer, applicants find it easier to complain to the supervisor about the abuse and to bring the problem to a successful resolution. Two benefits flow from organizing assistance in this manner. First, applicants are more likely to participate in reshaping the assistance program because they are closer to the administrative control of the program, thereby reinforcing the democratic principle. Second, a decentralized system allows for the development of many different programs and with the passage of time the emergence of a set of "best practices."

The social question raises a corollary question: What is the merchant to do in dealing with the poor? Neoclassical economics, which follows a libertarian philosophy, argues that even the poor should be free to make their own consumption decisions, and no one should intervene because the poor know what is best for them. If a specific consumer is wronged, it is a small price to pay for liberty. In any case, *caveat emptor*.

Personalist economics asserts that merchants have duties originating in the three principles of justice. First, merchants have an obligation to refrain from marketing and selling activities that worsen their customers' unmet needs. Second, retailers are admonished not to impose an unequal burden on their customers that derives from the customers' powerlessness in the face of a large, intimidating, or indifferent firm. Third, retailers may not force additional assistance costs on taxpayers who are required by law to come to the aid of needy people even when their unmet needs have been made worse by callous merchants. Fourth, and last, retailers are instructed to treat all of their customers as equals. A merchant with multiple locations may not charge inner-city customers a higher price than suburban customers unless there are higher costs in inner-city operations.

Neoclassical economics values liberty above all else. The free choices of *homo economicus*, especially when *homo economicus* is an adult, should not be preempted by others. Neoclassical economics asserts that customers and merchants alike should be free to see and use one another as the means by which self-interest is served. Personalist economics, while respecting liberty, values the inherent dignity of human beings above all else, and argues that *homo socioeconomicus* has a right to be protected from unscrupulous merchants. Further, personalist economics asserts that merchants have a duty to respect that right even when it adversely affects their profits. Personalist economics asserts that it is not in single-mindedly serving self that the merchant achieves success. Rather it is in respecting suppliers, employees, and customers as human persons, as ends in themselves, that the merchant transforms them into the means of his or her success.

In terms of the economy as a twin-engine aircraft, consumers are the passengers who board the aircraft in the expectation that it will carry them safely to their destination of a better standard of living both in terms of meeting their needs and satisfying their wants.

Worker and Producer

Work has two principal effects: on the goods and services produced and the persons who work. *Homo socioeconomicus* the worker has a dual character, at once both an individual being and a social being, capable of competing and cooperating. The worker is a real, living, breathing person, acting in economic affairs, and not merely a resource to be used in the production process. The worker, in other words, has dignity well apart from the instrumental value that attaches to his or her economic contribution.

Humans work in order to earn the income to buy the goods and services that meet bodily needs and satisfy bodily wants. Income from work depends in principle on the significance of the worker's total contribution to the production process. Thus, earnings are linked to the first main effect of work, and therefore are an implicit affirmation of the principle of private property. For personalist economics, the problem is that while an unrestrained labor market automatically eliminates shortages and surpluses, it does not necessarily meet workers' needs. Intervention at times is required to address those needs through measures such as limits to the length of the workday, bans on child labor, and inspections to assure worker health and safety.

Humans also work to meet the *need for work as such* that originates in the human spirit. This need for work is linked to the second main effect of work and is two-dimensional, conforming to the duality of human nature. Because he or she is an individual being, the worker has a need for job that provides opportunities for the application of his or her own special gifts and talents. This is done by incorporating into the worker's job specific tasks that require the use of those gifts and talents. The uniqueness of the worker is underscored here. Because he or she is a social being as well, the worker has a need for a job that makes that person a respected partner in the work process. The worker's need for acceptance and inclusion is underscored here.

Work is an opportunity for humans to develop more fully as persons by meeting (1) their need for self-expression through their own individual contributions and (2) their need to belong through the formation of integrated and inclusive workplace teams. Self-expression proceeds from and enhances the individual contribution of the worker, which flows from an authentic self-interest that is necessary for human survival. Belonging proceeds from and enhances teamwork, which flows from caring for others, which is rooted in a person's moral perceptivity, the ability to be aware of the needs of others.

Understanding producer behavior begins with the principle of supply. However, this principle, as in the case of the principle of demand, is strictly descriptive. It does not probe deeply into the behavior of the producer; it merely describes it in terms of price. Another principle—the principle of diminishing returns—is required to help explain producer behavior. The principle of diminishing returns explains producer behavior in terms of two limits: Limit III, or maximum returns, and Limit IV, or capacity. Whether the production process is capital-intensive or labor-intensive, these two limits originate in the plain truth that both workers and machines wear out with use, workers on a regular daily basis, machines less predictably.

Limit IV refers to the maximum output possible in a day by one worker with a given stock of capital. Before Limit IV is reached, each additional hour of work adds to total output. Beyond that limit, however, the worker's total output declines due to overuse of capital or physical exhaustion, because at that point he or she makes mistakes that, in turn, can lead to rework or accidents. Limit IV often is seen on the highway when exhausted truck drivers fall asleep, wreck their trucks, and destroy some of the goods they are carrying or, worse yet, injure or kill someone. Limit IV or capacity applies to everyone who works because every worker is embodied, and the human body requires daily rest.

Limit III (maximum returns or maximum marginal product) refers to the single hour of work in which the worker adds more to total output than any other. Before Limit III is reached, each additional hour of work adds more to total output than the preceding hour. After Limit III is attained, each additional hour adds less to total output than the preceding hour. Just as capital equipment usually does not break down without warning, exhaustion does not suddenly overtake us. Rather, we tire little by little, with hourly output declining as the work itself saps our strength until full exhaustion sets in and mistakes intrude.

The machines used in the production process are like human workers in that both are material in nature—the one animate, the other inanimate. Due to their materiality, both wear out under use and both require maintenance. Human maintenance means time away from work, in the form of a break, lunch hour, overnight rest, weekends, holidays off, and vacations. Machines cannot run indefinitely. They too require downtime, which the careful producer does not want to happen when the machines are most needed. For that reason, producers often schedule maintenance ahead of time to assure that the equipment is ready when it is called into use. Preventive maintenance is the advance scheduling of maintenance, and though it can be costly, it is undertaken for fear that in the absence of such procedures, the cost would be even greater.

Clearly, personalist economics does not dismiss either the principle of diminishing returns of neoclassical economics or the production function. However, personalist economics represents the production function in terms of two limits for two related reasons: Both machines and humans wear down with use and that wearing down effectively limits production. Simply put, whether it involves workers or machines, materiality is at the core of the production process and therefore matters critically when it comes to the cost of production and profitability.

With one possible exception, personalist economics represents the cost of production no differently from neoclassical economics. Unit cost and marginal cost are driven by the production function, and as output increases, average fixed costs tend to decline. However, the increase in average costs at capacity is interpreted by personalist economics in human terms rather than simply in financial terms: Human effort has limits and mistakes take off at Limit IV.

The observant production manager—*homo socioeconomicus*—is able to tell when capacity may be approaching when he or she notices that average costs are rising. Once production has been pushed beyond capacity, or Limit IV, mistakes take hold and workers are exposed to greater risk of injury or worse. Defective units are produced, requiring costly rework. *Homo socioeconomicus*, charged with the responsibility for supervising production, may subordinate output to the safety of the workforce in order to affirm the workers' inherent dignity as human beings. Additionally, reducing the rework that attends pushing production beyond Limit IV and assuring the safety of the workforce have the effect of cutting production costs and enhancing the company's competitiveness and profitability. Putting the concept of the limit at the center of our understanding of worker behavior acknowledges the need for restraint in the production process to avoid rework and protect workers, just as earlier we observed that moderation is required in consumer behavior to assure that the goods and services sought after remain the means to satisfying human wants and meeting human needs and do not become ends in themselves.

One of the most important responsibilities of the employer/producer is wage and salary administration, which involves two main tasks: evaluating performance and linking pay to performance. Three central questions must be addressed. How much does the worker contribute as an individual to the assigned tasks, and how much is that work worth? How much are others paid for the same work? How much does he or she contribute to the success of the group to which he or she is assigned, and how much is that contribution worth?

Performance evaluation involves the careful, honest, and comprehensive evaluation of the amount and quality of the work assigned. Evaluation should be quantifiable, but for some the nature of their work does not always lend itself to strict quantification. Inevitably, therefore, performance evaluation involves judgment. There are two procedures that help reduce arbitrariness in making judgments. First, the subordinate prepares his or her own performance evaluation and submits it to the supervisor. Second, the supervisor's performance evaluations are subject to review by the supervisor's own superior.

The best way to assure that performance evaluation is done properly is to select the right persons as supervisors and train them well. The mere fact that a supervisor may have done the very same assigned tasks is no assurance that performance evaluation will be conducted carefully, honestly, and comprehensively. The supervisor must be a person of integrity who understands that compensation is not reducible to labor market supply and demand only. Guided by justice and personalist economics, the employer/supervisor has two obligations. Under equivalence the employer/supervisor has a duty to the employee for "a full day's pay for a full day's work." Under distributive justice, the employer/supervisor has an obligation for "equal pay for equal work." Failing with regard to the first duty in effect breaks the employment contract and reneges on the wages and work specified contractually (either explicitly or implicitly). Failing with the regard to the second duty is discrimination.

The employee also has two obligations. A "full day's work for a full day's pay" is what the employee owes the employer/supervisor under equivalence, and as with the employer/supervisor, any failure effectively breaks the employment contract. The employee's second duty is to "do his or her fair share" and "pay his or her dues," that is, to contribute positively to the success of the group to which he/she has been assigned. This duty is less sharply defined than the first. Much depends on the circumstances at the moment in the workplace and the marketplace. More may be required of a person as a member of the team when the company is facing a difficult deadline, when necessary production materials are not readily available, or when someone on the team is sick or absent. Even more may be required when the company is on the brink of financial failure. In that sense, contributive justice requires a member to do all that is required for group success, provided what is required is reasonable. Thus, personalist economics recognizes that judgment inevitably is a part of any decision as to one's duty under contributive justice, and that duty involves an intensely personal commitment as to what is owed. Neoclassical economics and the law of nature, on the other hand, assert that what one owes to others is sorted out by the impersonal forces of the market, which are directed strictly by the self-interest of economic agents and the "invisible hand."

Workers are the ground crews, maintenance gangs, flight personnel, air traffic controllers, and regulatory agencies such as the U.S. Federal Trade Commission and the Antitrust Division who assure that the aircraft is safe to fly, that the passengers are properly attended during flight, and that the aircraft maintains a safe distance from other traffic on the ground and in flight.

Beyond Physical, Financial, and Human Capital

More than justice is required to forge human trust. Justice by itself can become cold and calculating if it is not tempered by caring or charity,[22] by a deep regard for the well-being of other humans with whom one interacts on a daily basis. Caring helps develop trust and solidarity by affirming that all humans are equal and never should be used strictly for personal gain. Charity helps develop this sense by insisting that all humans are precious, and before all else their well-being, not maximum efficiency, is the most important end of all economic affairs.

As with justice in its activating modality, caring lubricates the engine so that it can function safely at high temperatures. But caring is a higher-grade oil than justice, and charity—seeing in every human being a precious human person—works like an even higher-grade, longer-lasting oil, allowing the engine to function even more effectively and more efficiently. In real terms, caring and charity mean going beyond the demands of justice, such as when creditors renegotiate credit agreements to ease the burden on the troubled borrower, and merchants give their customers more than they have a right to expect. This additional value, which helps trust and solidarity grow and flourish, has a real economic component—the real though intangible business asset "good-will." Caring and charity thus become valued economic resources that uniquely acquire value only in the giving and not in the hoarding.

Neoclassical economics teaches (properly) that production increases with improvements in three types of capital: physical, financial, and human. Personalist economics adds a fourth type—personal capital—which refers to those sentiments and good habits of human beings such as sympathy and generosity, which students of economics have known about since Smith's *Moral Sentiments* but have been dismissed by neoclassical economics.

Human capital has value when it is put to use by the person who possesses it and who is free to adapt it to various uses, to misuse it, to neglect it, or to abandon it. Human capital is not depleted through use per se but can be rendered useless as the person ages, and the body and other human faculties decline. Personal capital, on the other hand, is not an asset to be owned, has no value when it is held as a possession, and is not depleted through use. Its value is not determined by the principles of ordinary marketplace exchange. Personal capital is not a commodity. It comes into existence and takes on value only when it is freely given. The generous merchant who gives freely transforms generosity into a *real bargain* for his or her customers, and the caring customer who is loyal to the merchant transforms caring into the merchant's *real asset goodwill.* Similarly, the unselfish employee who gives freely of his or her time and effort beyond what is required transforms that additional work into a *sense of community*, and the magnanimous employer who freely gives his employees more than what is required contractually converts that kindness into *goodwill.*

In both the workplace and marketplace the giving is self-reinforcing and contagious. The merchant who is known for bargains is rewarded by repeat business. Other merchants are inclined to embrace that practice in order to improve their own repeat business. The generous employer is rewarded by more productive and loyal workers. Other employers are apt to follow that example in order to improve their own productivity and the loyalty of their employees. Sadly, though, such bad habits as insensitivity, pettiness, incivility, prejudice, deceitfulness, and hostility also are self-reinforcing and contagious. And thus personal capital is dissipated and destroyed.

Human capital and personal capital are alike in that both reside in human beings, both can be learned, both can be altered by the very humans in whom the capital resides because humans are self-directed, are capable of acting on their own. Neither human capital nor personal capital necessarily requires physical capital to function effectively. They are like physical capital that exists only in the form of a material object in the sense that human and personal capital cannot exist outside the materiality of the human body. All four types of capital are alike in that they contribute to production and for that reason have instrumental value, but human beings most fundamentally have value beyond measure, have a dignity that does not derive from their instrumentality, are ends in themselves and not just means.

Without personal capital, the economic agent is an individual, a one-dimensional human who is self-absorbed. With personal capital, the agent becomes a person, a two-dimensional human who is at once an autonomous being and a social being who must balance and rebalance individuality and sociality as his or her functions as an economic agent change and as economic conditions change.

The individual and individualism as integrated into neoclassical economic theory are no longer an inadequate guide for the law because both originated in the seventeenth–eighteenth century Enlightenment when awareness of self and others was conditioned by the use of script in human communications, which in turn determined how the behavior of economic agents was understood and represented. It is time to recognize that the economic agent is not the same today as he or she was 200 to 300 years ago due, importantly, to the use of electronics in human communications, which has altered awareness of self and others in economic affairs, and which persuades us that the person and personalism as integrated into personalist economics are much better suited to the demands of teaching and practicing law and justice in the twenty-first century.

Notes

1. Joseph E. Stiglitz, "Information and the Change in the Paradigm in Economics," 460–501.

2. George A. Akerlof, "Behavioral Macroeconomics and Macroeconomic Behavior," 411–33.

3. Stiglitz, "Information and the Change in the Paradigm in Economics," 488.

4. See Walter J. Ong, *In the Human Grain: Further Explorations of Contemporary Culture,* for more on the three stages of human communications.

5. William R. Waters, "Social Economics," identifies the four premises of neoclassical economics and of personalist economics, 115–17.

6. Alan S. Blinder, "How the Economy Came to Resemble the Model," 18.

7. Alfred Marshall, *Principles of Economics*, 5–7.

8. Avery Dulles, "*Centesimus Annus* and the Renewal of Culture," 2.

9. Marshall, *Principles of Economics*, 1.

10. Edward J. Kane, "Justice and Welfare Economics," 105.

11. See Edward J. O'Boyle, "Salary Compression and Inversion in the University Workplace," for more on age discrimination in the university workplace in which disparate impact taking place over many years indicates disparate treatment, 959–79.

12. Federal Reserve Bank of Cleveland, 1.

13. See Kane, "Justice and Welfare Economics," for more on justice in economic affairs as seen from modern welfare (neoclassical) economics as compared to scholastic welfare (personalist) economics, 103–16.

14. In philosophical terminology, the entrepreneur is the efficient cause. Bernard W. Dempsey, *The Functional Economy: The Bases of Economic Organization,* asserts: "The economic function of the entrepreneur signalizes [the] irreducible paramount importance of the human person," 361.

15. Joseph A. Schumpeter. *Capitalism, Socialism, and Democracy*, 83, 132.

16. See Ong's work on human sexuality in *Fighting for Life* (45, 64–67ff) for a

supporting argument; and Robert Kabacoff, "Gender Differences in Organizational Leadership," 1–20, for evidence to the contrary. For a more recent report presenting both sides, see Rochelle Sharpe, "As Leaders, Women Rule," 75ff.

17. Schumpeter, *Capitalism, Socialism, and Democracy*, 81–86.

18. Joseph A. Schumpeter, "The Instability of Capitalism," 326.

19. Stephen T. Worland, "The Investment Decision as Moral Choice," 59–72.

20. *Trade and Development Report*, 81–82.

21. Peter L. Danner, *The Economic Person*, 124–25.

22. John Paul II, "From Justice for Each Comes Peace for All," §1.

References

Akerlof, G.A. "Behavioral Macroeconomics and Macroeconomic Behavior." *American Economic Review* 92 (June 2002): 411–33.

Blinder, A.S. "How the Economy Came to Resemble the Model." *Business Economics* 35 (January 2000): 16–25.

Danner, P.L. *The Economic Person: Acting and Analyzing*. Lanham, MD: Rowman and Littlefield, 2002.

Dempsey, B.W., S.J. *The Functional Economy: The Bases of Economic Organization*. Englewood Cliffs, NJ: Prentice-Hall, 1958.

Dulles, A. "*Centesimus Annus* and the Renewal of Culture." *The Journal of Markets and Morality* 2 (Spring 1999): 1–7.

Federal Reserve Bank of Cleveland. "The Economy in Perspective." *Economic Trends* (July 2002): 1.

John Paul II. "From Justice of Each Comes Peace for All." Catholic Information Network, January 1, 1998. Available at: www.cin.org/jp2/wdp98.html (April 14, 2001).

Kabacoff, R.I. "Gender Differences in Organizational Leadership: A Large Sample Study." Management Research Group. Available at: www.mrg.com/Publications (September 22, 2003).

Kane, E.J. "Justice and Welfare Economics: A Slightly Mathematical Approach." *Review of Social Economy* 21 (September 1963): 103–16.

Marshall, A. *Principles of Economics: An Introductory Volume*. New York: MacMillan, 1948.

O'Boyle, E.J. "Salary Compression and Inversion in the University Workplace." *International Journal of Social Economics* 28 (2001): 959–79.

Ong, W.J., S.J. *Fighting for Life: Contest, Sexuality, and Consciousness*. Ithaca, NY: Cornell University Press, 1981.

———. *In the Human Grain: Further Explorations of Contemporary Culture.* New York: The MacMillan Company, 1967.

Schumpeter, J.A. *Capitalism, Socialism, and Democracy.* New York: Harper and Brothers, 1950.

———. "The Instability of Capitalism." *The Economic Journal* 38 (September 1928): 361–86.

Sharpe, R. "As Leaders, Women Rule." *Business Week*, November 20, 2000, 75ff.

Smith, A. *The Theory of Moral Sentiments*, ed. D.D. Raphael and A.L. Macfie. Oxford, UK: Oxford University Press, 1976.

———. *An Inquiry into the Nature and Causes of the Wealth of Nations.* New York: Modern Library, 1937.

Stiglitz, J.E. "Information and the Change in the Paradigm in Economics." *American Economic Review* 92 (June 2002): 460–501.

United Nations. *Trade and Development Report, 2001.* New York: United Nations Conference on Trade and Development.

Waters, W.R. "Social Economics: A Solidarist Perspective." *Review of Social Economy* 46 (October 1988): 113–43.

Worland, S.T. "The Investment Decision as Moral Choice: The Perspective of *Centesimus Annus.*" In *Social Economics: Premises, Findings and Policies*, ed. E.J. O'Boyle, 59–72. London: Routledge, 1996.

11

The Efficiency and Employment-Enhancing Effects of Social Welfare

Morris Altman

Introduction

Conventional economic wisdom predicts that social welfare, specifically the direct income payments and in-kind income associated with welfare, serves to increase unemployment by reducing the incentive of economic agents to search for and engage in either short- or long-term market employment. In a word, welfare payments serve to reduce the opportunity cost of leisure, providing a cohort of individuals with the opportunity to realize their preference for leisure by making this preference affordable. This follows from the theory of income-leisure choice. In addition, to the extent that social welfare serves to increase the bargaining power of labor and thereby increases its reservation wage, resulting in higher market wages, average production costs are predicted to rise, further increasing unemployment and also reducing the competitiveness of the affected firms. The notion that increasing labor costs serves to increase production costs follows from the conventional model of the firm where it assumed that increasing labor costs cannot generate cost offsets in terms of increasing efficiency (increasing the level of x-efficiency) or by inducing technological change. Given these critical analytical predictions, the conventional model recommends the reduction if not the elimination of social welfare if the objective of society is to maximize labor force participation, minimize unemployment, as well as minimizing production costs. It is implicitly assumed in the conventional model that welfare recipients are unemployed largely due to their strong preference for leisure in the context of the availability of nonlabor income in the form of welfare payments and that the reduction or elimination of welfare will have no negative externalities in terms of reducing the level of human capital formation with regards to children and adults. In effect, the conventional modeling of social welfare predicts that there exists an unambiguous trade-off between social welfare and economic efficiency. Thus, if society deems it appropriate to establish social welfare programs or programs that provide supplements to or guarantees of certain levels of real income, it should be recognized that the opportunity cost of such programs is a lower level of real gross domestic product (GDP). There is, therefore, an unequivocal distributional effect of social welfare that is part and parcel of a subzero sum game. Social welfare represents a net income transfer to welfare recipients, which also serves to reduce society's level of aggregate and per capita GDP. Given their assumed preference for leisure, social welfare does not serve as an income safety net for the poor. Rather it serves to subsidize and foster the leisure preference of some at the expense of those with a veritable work ethic.

It is the conventional modeling of welfare that has underpinned the major revisions in welfare programs that transpired in the United States in 1996, which, in turn, have been among the most dramatic and substantive to be undertaken among developed economies. The American reforms are designed to force individuals off welfare by severely limiting lifetime years of eligibility and, additionally, to reduce income support, such as food stamps and health care, traditionally connected with the receipt of welfare payments.[1] A fundamental underlying assumption of the American reforms is that welfare recipients largely consist of individuals who have become addicted to unearned income and to a life of leisure or indolence. Once public support to this addiction is dramatically reduced, the erstwhile addicts will seek and find jobs, becoming productive members of society. It is assumed that reasonably well-paid jobs are there for the asking; well paid in the sense of at least yielding an income flow afforded to these individuals when in receipt of welfare payments. Thus a reduction or elimination of welfare payments should yield not only an increase in labor supply, but also no reduction in the material standard of well-being of the former welfare recipient. In addition, the upward pressures on the labor market induced by the traditional network of welfare and related payments will be relieved, making the American labor market more flexible and competitive in the long run.[2]

Such strong and stark analytical predictions and related policy recommendations flow directly from the assumptions underlying the conventional models. They are also made in the context of empirical studies that are, at best, ambiguous in terms of establishing a particular relationship between social welfare programs, broadly defined, and levels of per capita output, rates of growth of per capita output, and employment or unemployment. Thus, calls for cutting-back social welfare and the welfare state may be more a matter of political economy than of good economics.[3] Discussing various economic attributes of the welfare state Atkinson, argues:

> To understand the connection between the welfare state and economic performance, the theoretical framework needs to be set out explicitly. We cannot treat the relationship simply as a "black box." There are many mechanisms by which social transfers and possible reforms, may affect the working of the economy. We need to investigate the underlying microeconomic relationships.[4]

This paper seeks to open up the black box by specifying the assumptions underlying the conventional model of welfare payments and the manner by which they causally relate to the analytical predictions of the model. The focus of the discussion is on the economic consequences of income support payments be they in cash or in kind (such as food stamps or medical care). Such income support constitutes a critical dimension of the welfare state. We will not discuss here the impact of unemployment insurance that represents another important dimension of the welfare state.[5] In addition, we address the question of the economic impact of welfare payments from an alternative and more realistic analytical framework, thereby providing an alternative theoretical construct of the interior of the black box. This alternative theoretical framework suggests that the conventional analysis of welfare can be highly misleading, generating policy recommendations that have "welfare" reducing effects on the economy as a whole, especially upon the lowest income cohort of an affected population.

Applying the target income approach[6] to an analysis of the potential labor supply effects of welfare payments, I find that labor supply can be expected to fall only for those with very low real target incomes and for those with earning capacities below the target income or subject to a tax regime that taxes the earned income of welfare recipients at a 100 percent marginal tax rate. A very low target income need not be a product of a strong preference for leisure. It might very well be a product of other preferences, such as child care, being ranked above a higher level of real income. A very low target income might also be a product of a very low earning capacity. In this scenario, cuts to welfare payments yield an increase in labor supply, but at the cost of a deterioration in child care and a fall in real income. This, in turn, can have deleterious effects on the future earning capacity of both children and adults.

Applying a behavioral model of the firm[7] to an analysis of the labor and production cost impact of welfare payments, I conclude that increasing labor costs induced by welfare payments cannot be expected to increase unit production costs where increasing labor costs are expected to generate increases in the level of efficiency and technological change. In these circumstances, welfare serves to improve the overall level of material well-being in society by provoking higher levels of efficiency and higher rates of technical change. Moreover, welfare payments and related income supports serve to enhance the capacity of individuals to invest in human capital formation with regards to education and child care and to search for jobs that best match the needs of the job searcher.

This modeling of the economic agent and of the firm speaks in favor of developing an institutional framework designed to provide long-term economic benefits to individuals who are unable to work, inclusive of single parent families and of individuals with low real income earning capacities. This is in direct contrast to what is recommended based on the conventional worldview. However, the manner in which such benefits are structured will impact on work incentives and thus labor supply as well as on the degree of social acceptance of the provisions of such benefits by the long-term employed—those who ultimately must foot much of the bill for welfare payments and who also potentially have the largest political voice that can either make or break the existence and generosity of a social welfare system.[8]

The Traditional Model

Welfare programs in the form of income support are typically designed to assist individuals who are without work and not qualified for other sources of income support, such as unemployment insurance. Welfare programs also have been and can be designed to provide income supplements to individuals with low levels of market income. Such programs are often designed such that individuals on welfare need not work, search for work, or engage in skill upgrading. Thus welfare recipients consist of potential first-time workers, individuals who lost jobs but have been unable to find work, unemployed individuals who have ceased searching for employment (discouraged workers), single moms who choose to stay at home to provide child care to their children or do so because of the high cost of child care relative to prospective market income and the given level of welfare payments, individuals who do not have the physical or mental capacity to engage in market employment, and individuals whose prospective market income is less than welfare payments. Who gets welfare depends on the country and, indeed, often on the jurisdiction within a country wherein an individual resides. But from assessing the potential economic impact of welfare payments from either the conventional or alternative behavioral theoretical perspective, these finer institutional details are not of critical importance. What is critical is the basic modeling assumption of eligibility used when analyzing the economic impact of welfare payments.

A fundamental assumption of the conventional model is that welfare payments are an entitlement. It is further assumed that not working is equivalent to consuming leisure, which is assumed to be a normal good. In point of fact, not working on the market might very well mean engaging in nonmarket work, including household work and child care, in addition to engaging in leisure activities. However, given the assumed identity between not working and leisure and the assumption of leisure as a normal good, any increase in income can be expected to increase the demand for leisure time. Moreover, because to receive welfare requires, in most instances, that an individual not work at all, the objective choice facing an individual is between working and not working—a binary choice. In reality, for many welfare programs, if one works when on welfare, the earned income is taxed at a marginal rate of 100 percent. So, you can work when on welfare but only at a zero rate of net pay. Moreover, it is assumed that an individual, if he or she so chooses, can earn a net market income at least equivalent to the welfare-related income. The net market income is equivalent to the market income net of all expenses required to earn this income, inclusive of transportation costs and child care. It is typically assumed that such costs are zero. In this scenario, whether or not a person is on welfare is a product of an individual's relative preference for leisure. It is assumed in this conventional model that there will be a cohort of individuals who, because of the strength of their leisure preference, will choose not to work. But the model, per se, cannot predict a priori how many individuals, if any, would prefer not to work. Still, the conventional model assumes that society contains a cohort of individuals who, when faced with a choice of nonlabor income and leisure, will choose not to work. Moreover, it is often argued on the basis of the conventional model that because (and by assumption) people have a rather strong preference for leisure, welfare invariably reduces employment and increases the percentage of individuals who are voluntarily unemployed.

This argument is illustrated and further elaborated using Figure 11.1. The initial price or income curve is given by *AL*, the slope of which is determined by the market wage. The time available to spend on all activities is *L* hours per day. If one begins with a traditional convex indifference curve U_0, a utility maximizing individual chooses *0F* of nonmarket activities (assumed to be leisure) and *FL* of work. The introduction of entitlement-based welfare payments shifts the income curve to *BC*. If leisure is a normal good, our utility maximizing individual will choose the corner solution to the leisure choice problem, given at *C* for indifference curve U_1. This is so because the individual faces a choice between identical levels of income where this income, *LC* or *FG* in Figure 11.1, can be had by either working or not working. Because leisure is assumed to be a normal good, it is utility maximizing to choose not to work. In this scenario it is assumed that the marginal tax rate on market income to a welfare recipient is 100 percent. Thus, the slope of the price line at *C* is horizontal—the income constraint with a 100 percent tax on welfare becomes *CGA*. In other words, the after-tax market wage for an individual on welfare is zero. There exists no option of choosing a combination of work and welfare. In this model, therefore, welfare results in an unambiguous reduction in labor supply, albeit the size of this reduction can in no way be predicted by the model.

Also flowing from this model is the analytical prediction that if our individual is initially maximizing utility at *D* with an income given at *I*, the introduction of welfare payments of 0*H*, with an marginal tax rate of 100 percent on market work when an individual is on welfare, might still result in a corner solution at *C*, even while this results in a lower level of income of 0*H* (the welfare payment). An individual with a strong preference for leisure might chose not to work even at a lower level of income because with welfare he or she can obtain some income without any work effort. The utility gained in "leisure" more than offsets the utility lost with the fall in income. But the model cannot predict how strong this effect will be on the employed who earn more in employment than they can obtain on welfare. Even if the marginal tax rate was not 100 percent, the conventional model still predicts an increase in the demand for leisure time, although not necessarily as a great an increase as when the marginal tax rate is 100 percent. In this instance, the income curve or constraint is given by *CDA*, for example, as opposed to *CGA*, where the slope of *CD* is given by the net wage. The latter equals: (market wage)*(1 – tax rate). An individual who is initially at *G* can be expected to maximize utility given the existence of a welfare payment of 0*H* along income line *CD*, but to the right of indifference curve U_0. In other words, more of the normal good, leisure, would be demanded than in the no welfare scenario, but not necessarily as much as when the marginal tax rate is 100 percent for welfare recipients. A corner solution is possible but not necessary. The model cannot predict where along income line *JC* the individual's utility will be maximized, but only that more leisure will be demanded by a utility-maximizing individual.

It is important to note that our utility-maximizing individual need not choose welfare if leisure is not assumed to be a normal good, an assumption that is outside the realm of consideration in the conventional model. Indeed, individuals whose utility is enhanced by working might chose the work over the welfare option when both options yield the same level of income. Certainly without the assumption of leisure as a normal good, one cannot easily generate the prediction that welfare will yield an increased demand for leisure. And it is curious that this assumption has little empirical support.[9] Even with the assumption of leisure as a normal good, the conventional model

Figure 11.1 **Welfare Payments and Labor Supply**

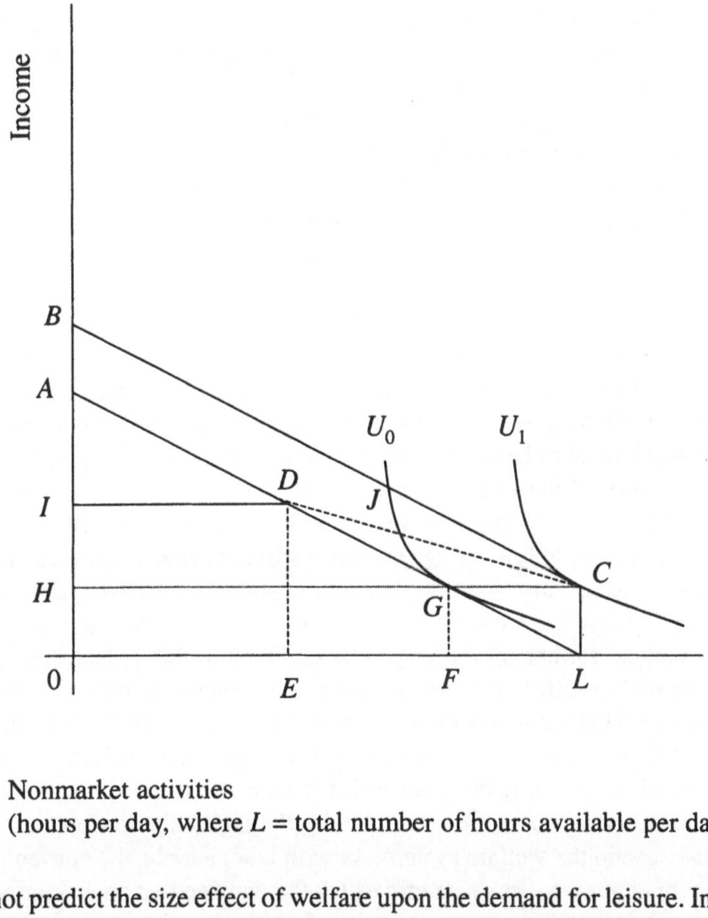

Nonmarket activities
(hours per day, where L = total number of hours available per day)

cannot predict the size effect of welfare upon the demand for leisure. In other words, the conventional model cannot, by itself, predict the elasticity of the demand for leisure to changes in welfare payments. The size effect is an empirical question. But the positive causal relationship between welfare and the demand for leisure underpins the model.

Given the assumptions of the conventional model, if we begin with a world of welfare and welfare recipients, the elimination of welfare payments has the predicted effect of increasing labor supply because the end of welfare serves to reduce the demand for leisure time. Individuals with a strong leisure preference would not long be able to indulge in this preference. The traditional model implicitly assumes that welfare recipients do not work because of their strong preference for leisure or their weak work ethic that is facilitated by the welfare system. The conventional model also predicts that modifying the welfare-related tax system, such that the market income earned while on welfare is not taxed at a 100 percent rate, serves to increase the supply of labor. Needless to say, the most effective mechanism of increasing labor supply is to eliminate welfare payments according to the conventional model. Apart from being unable to generate any substantive predictions with regards to the size effect of introducing, eliminating, or modifying welfare systems, the conventional model pays no heed to variables that might contribute to individuals choosing welfare, apart from the assumed demand for leisure. These variables include physical and mental incapacities that preclude an individual from working, child-care responsibilities, and the human capital limitations on the earning capacities of individuals. These issues will be addressed below, employing a target income model of labor supply.

The conventional model's prediction of a reduction in labor supply following the introduction of or improvements to a welfare system yields important secondary predictions with regards to the impact that such a reduction will have upon the price of labor and unit production costs. According to the conventional theory of the firm, because welfare payments serve to reduce the supply of labor and to increase the reservation price among, at least in the first instance, the cohort of lower wage earners, welfare payments generate higher wage rates that, in turn, yield higher unit costs of production. The higher wages among low wage earners might also positively affect the wage rates among workers further up the wage ladder. Overall, this reduces the competitiveness of the affected firms, damaging an economy's overall economic performance. This secondary effect is critical for it speaks to the damage that welfare is expected to have on the economy at large. Thus, welfare payments to individuals with strong preferences for leisure are financed not simply by taxing the working population, but also by damaging the market economy that must sustain the welfare system. As with labor supply, the conventional model cannot generate any size effects for the damage that an economy can be expected to sustain as a consequence of welfare.

In Figure 11.2 the prewelfare equilibrium is given by a wage rate W_1, with labor supply curve S_1 and the demand curve, based upon the marginal product of labor, given by D_1. However, the introduction of welfare shifts the supply curve to S_2, yielding a higher equilibrium wage, W_2. The higher equilibrium wage can also be expected to reduce employment from C to B, as firms cannot afford to employ as many workers, on the margin, at the higher wage rate. That such an increase in the wage rate can yield higher unit production costs is illustrated in Equation 1, where it is assumed for simplicity that labor is the only input into the production process:

$$AC = \frac{w * L}{Q} = \frac{w}{Q / L} \qquad [1]$$

AC s average cost, *w* is the wage rate, *Q* is real output, and *L* is labor inputs measured by hours worked, and *Q/L* is labor productivity. Because the conventional model of the firm holds that the wage rate and related labor costs have no positive impact on labor productivity, any increase in labor costs is assumed to increase average production costs. In this scenario, a 10 percent increase in the wage rate generates a 10 percent increase in unit production costs. This secondary effect of welfare payments can therefore have a substantive negative effect on the economy, all depending upon the size of the effect of welfare payments on the wage rate and the percentage of workers affected by the increased wage rate. But once again, the theory itself cannot predict the size of the wage effect. Moreover, it is critically important to note that unit costs increase in proportion to increases in wages only if labor represents the only input into the production process. This is typically not the case. When labor is not the only compensated factor input, unit costs increase less than proportionally to the increase in wage rates. This point is illustrated in Equation 2:

$$\frac{dAC}{AC} = (\frac{dw}{w}) * (\frac{w * L}{w * L + NLC}) \qquad [2]$$

where *dAC* is the change in average cost, *dw* is the change in the wage rate, and *NLC* is nonlabor costs. If, for example, the wage rate is increased by 10 percent *(dw/w)* and wage costs (*w* **L*) represent 100 percent of total costs, average costs increase by 10 percent. However, if wage costs represent only 50 percent of total costs, average costs increase by only 5 percent in this scenario. Still, according to the conventional model, welfare-related wage increases negatively impact upon the competitive position of the firm. To improve the competitive position of the firm, welfare payments need to be reduced or eliminated. But these rather strong analytical predictions, which speak against welfare, flow from the assumptions of the conventional model of labor supply and the conventional model of the firm.

Target Income and Labor Supply

The conventional model of income-leisure choice that underlies the conventional model of labor supply makes assumptions that are incorrect behaviorally

Figure 11.2 **Welfare Payments and the Labor Market**

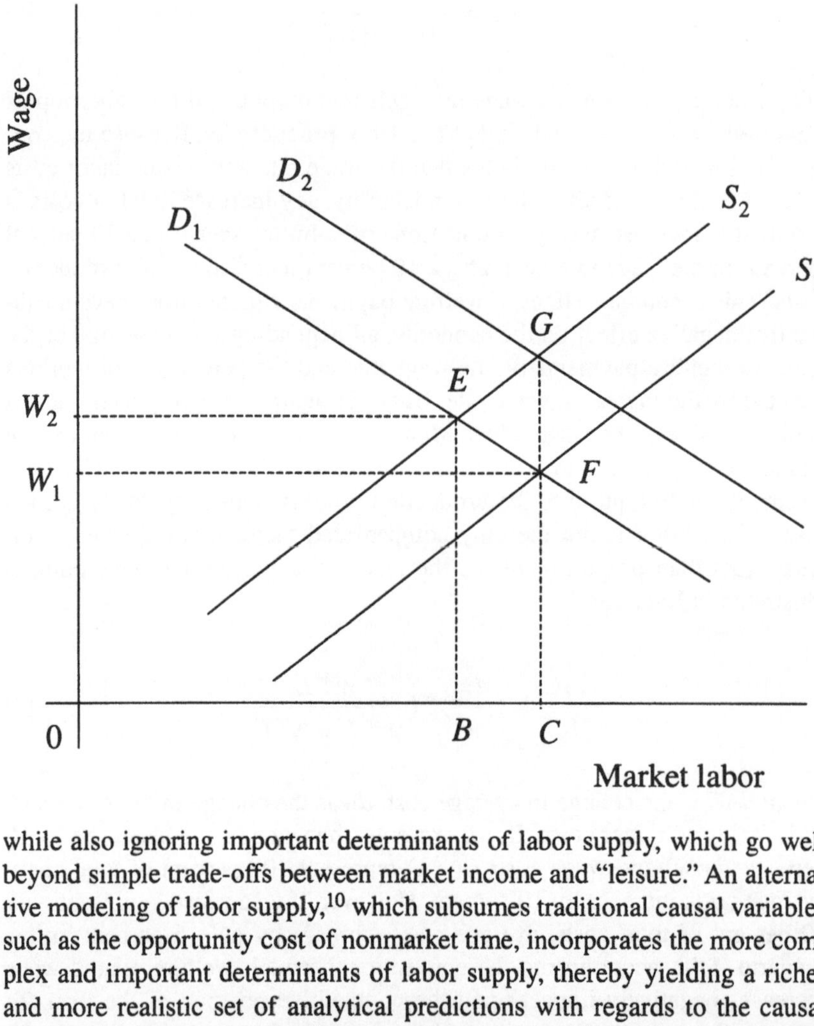

while also ignoring important determinants of labor supply, which go well beyond simple trade-offs between market income and "leisure." An alternative modeling of labor supply,[10] which subsumes traditional causal variables such as the opportunity cost of nonmarket time, incorporates the more complex and important determinants of labor supply, thereby yielding a richer and more realistic set of analytical predictions with regards to the causal relationship between market labor supply and welfare. This alternative model incorporates target levels of both income and of leisure time, or nonmarket activities, into an analysis of labor supply. Of overriding concern to the individual, according to this model, is the target level of market income in relationship to the nonmarket time desired by the individual. The latter is required, in combination with the market commodities derived from market labor, to produce the household goods and services that ultimately yields utility to the individual.[11] The quantity of required nonmarket time desired, for example, for child care, constrains the amount of time available for market labor.[12]

Thus, in this model, nonlabor time is not viewed as a normal good driving the supply of market labor, given the opportunity cost of this labor. Rather, the supply of labor is determined by the target income desired or required by the individual, constrained by her or his desire or need for a set of household goods and services, inclusive of leisure time and sleep. In this model, therefore, providing an individual with nonlabor sources of income, for example, cannot be expected to reduce the supply of market labor if income remains below the target level.

Of particular importance to this paper is the alternative model's assumption that the labor supply of utility maximizing agents is given by the individual's target income such that:

$$L = f(C_T) \qquad [3]$$

where L is market labor, and C_T is real target income or the real value of the commodities desired by the individual. As real target income increases, so does the supply of labor, ceteris paribus. More precisely the supply of market labor is given by

$$L = \frac{C_T}{w} - \frac{A}{w} \qquad [4]$$

where w is the real wage rate, and A is the real nonmarket income accruing to an individual over the relevant time frame. Given the wage rate and the level of nonmarket income, market labor supply is determined. In other words, once you know an individual's target income, his or her market wage and level of nonmarket income, you can determine the quantity of market labor required to realize the individual's target income. This level of labor supply need not be provided, however, if it exceeds what an individual is physically or psychologically capable of providing. As long as L does not exceed this constrained labor supply, L is what the individual will supply to the labor market.

This model predicts, for example, that, ceteris paribus, an increase in the wage rate yields a fall in market labor supply, as does any increase in nonmarket income if this reduction in labor supply is consistent with the realization of the target income. Such increases need not affect the supply of labor if the supply of market labor that can be provided by an individual is less than what is required to meet the target income. In this instance, any reduction in market labor supply would drive income even further below the target level. If for example, an individual can provide only ten hours of work per day at six days per week, but requires twelve hours per day at six days per week to meet the target income, increasing the wage or nonmarket income need not reduce the supply of labor as long as such increases will not yield an income in excess of the target income. Moreover, increases in either wages or nonmarket income need not yield a reduction in labor supply if target income increases along with increases in wages or nonmarket income. There is strong evidence to suggest that such increases in target income are typical of individual behavior.[13] On the other hand, as long as target income remains unchanged, a reduction in the wage rate will not yield a reduction in labor supply, in spite of this causing a reduction in the opportunity cost of leisure. Moreover, a reduction in nonmarket income will not yield an increase in labor supply if the prereduction supply of labor was at a maximum.

This modeling of labor supply is illustrated in Figure 11.3. If the target income is at Y_T, L_0L_1 of labor is required to achieve Y_T with a wage rate given by income constraint W_0. Less labor is supplied if the maximum labor that an individual can supply is given by L_0L_M, for example. In this instance, an income of $0F$, which is less than the target income, is obtained. Increasing the wage rate or increasing nonmarket income (which would shift the wage curves upward horizontally) will not reduce the supply of labor until L_M of labor supply suffices to achieve the target income Y_T or $0D$. Moreover, given a target income of Y_T and a labor supply of L_0L_1, if one begins with a wage rate less than what is given by W_0, such as W_2, increasing the wage rate will not reduce labor supply nor will labor supply be reduced by increasing the level of nonmarket income until such increases yield an income that is above the target level. Also, if target income increases with the wage rate, for example, one would also not expect any reduction in labor supply. An increase in the wage rate given by a movement from wage line W_0 to W_1 will not reduce the supply of labor if target income increases from Y_T to C. The potential impact of welfare payments on labor supply is modeled in Figure 11.4.

In a world without welfare and assuming no nonmarket income, such as interest-related income, market labor supply is at L_0L_1, given target income, Y_T and wage rate W_0 (at point E). The introduction of welfare payments of $0WP'$ or L_0WP, where market income for welfare recipients is taxed at a 100 percent rate, would not affect labor supply because accepting welfare would reduce income to below the target level. But we might we have another type of individual also with a target income Y_T, but with inferior human capital characteristics or bargaining power so that he or she can realize only a wage rate given by W_2 as opposed to W_0. This individual could realize only an

Figure 11.3 **Labor Supply and Target Income**

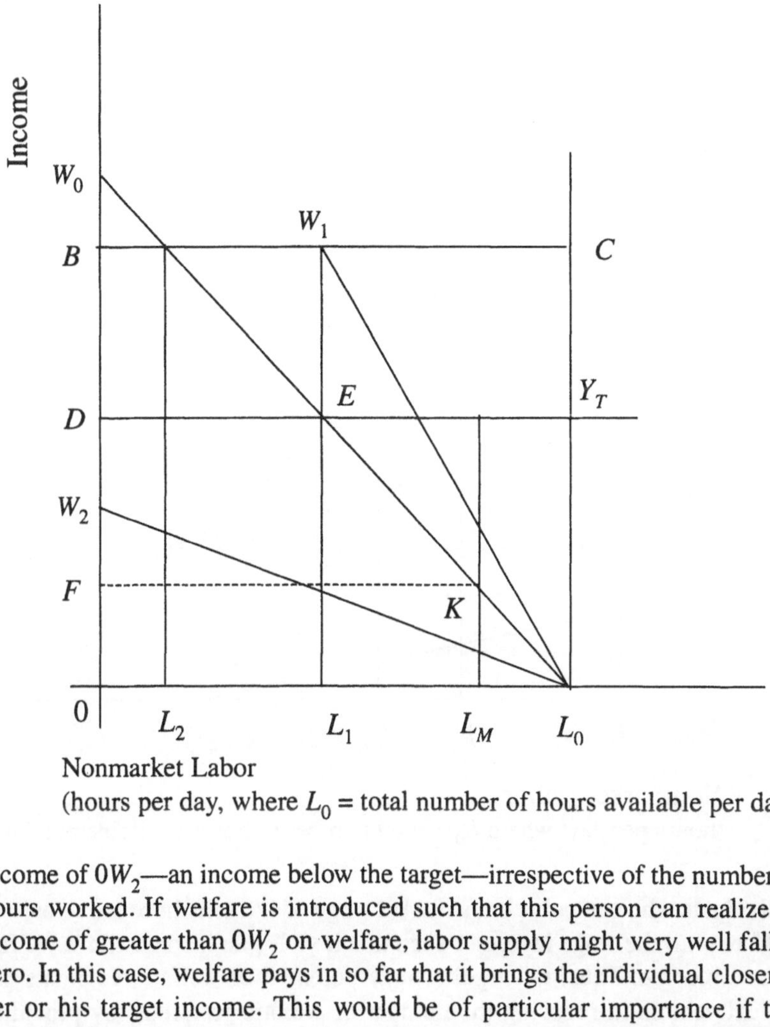

income of $0W_2$—an income below the target—irrespective of the number of hours worked. If welfare is introduced such that this person can realize an income of greater than $0W_2$ on welfare, labor supply might very well fall to zero. In this case, welfare pays in so far that it brings the individual closer to her or his target income. This would be of particular importance if this individual's market income yields a poverty line or below level of subsistence income. Welfare here serves to raise the individual above the poverty line. Moreover, for the individual with inferior bargaining capabilities, welfare serves to increase this individual's reservation wage and bargaining power by providing him or her with an income cushion to search for a better paying job or for a job where there is a better match between the individual's skill set and the skill set required by the job. In this case, the welfare system must be structured so that the individual has the option of choosing not to work even if relatively low-income job options are available. In this scenario,

Figure 11.4 **Impact of Welfare Payments on Labor Supply**

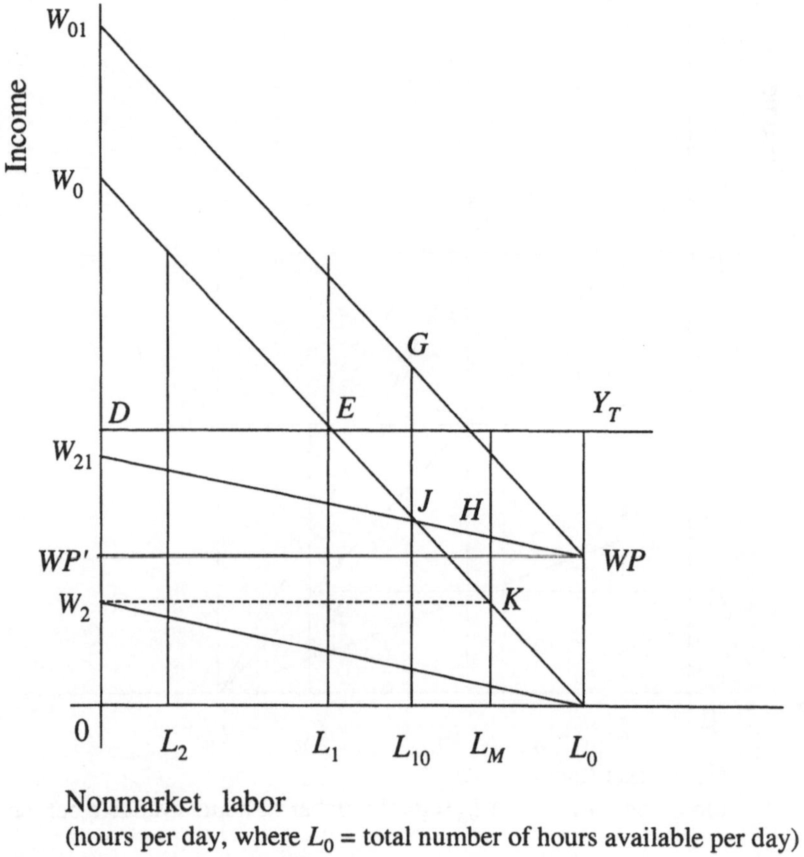

individuals who can only earn a market wage of W_2 will choose to remain on welfare until the wage increases such that it yields an income above welfare related income. Thus, raising the wage potential of welfare recipients is a critical vehicle in reducing the number of welfare recipients by providing job searchers with better matching jobs.

If welfare yields an income that simply equals $0W_2$, whether or not labor supply falls to zero depends, in part, on the utility that an individual garners from working and the stigma (disutility) attached to not working while receiving welfare. More concretely, if $0W_2$ is the poverty line and the individual concerned must sacrifice child care to earn this bare subsistence income, welfare payments affords the individual with the means to devote labor to child care without sacrificing any necessary income in the process. In this case, labor supply would fall to zero. Assume now that our individual is of a higher earnings capacity (W_0) but can only work L_0L_M for reasons of child care responsibilities, yielding a poverty rate income of $0W_2$. Welfare payments equaling $0W_2$ can be expected to reduce market labor supply to zero if more labor for child care is deemed necessary. In this case, increasing child care services will not drop the family below the poverty line. Welfare payments greater than $0W_2$ can also be expected to reduce labor supply to zero because welfare allows the individual and family to rise above the poverty line without sacrificing any child care. Indeed, in this case, under welfare more labor time could be devoted to child care without any sacrifice of income.

The typical modeling of the causation and motivation underlying the receipt of welfare payments focuses on the relationship of market labor supply and various possible causal variables, implicitly assuming that individuals will be fully employed in terms of the amount of labor they supply to the labor market. Of course this need not be the case, and the target income approach to labor supply facilitates incorporating this reality into an analysis of the relationship between labor supply and involuntary unemployment, as well as into an analysis of the determinants of the receipt of welfare payments. An individual's actual labor supply might well be above that individual's actual employment. Thus, an individual's labor supply might be at L_0L_1, but his or her employment might be at L_0L_M or even be zero at L_0, due to exogenous constraints such as the scarcity of jobs. In such exogenously constrained labor markets, an individual's income might be well below the target income of say, Y_T. In this case, the introduction of welfare payments increases the number of people on welfare, and it also serves to reduce the supply of market labor. Individuals turn to welfare as a means of increasing their income. In other words, welfare does not here attract people with a strong preference for leisure. Rather, it attracts individuals who are without work or are "underemployed" and who wish to approach their target income. The elimination of welfare, in this case, simply reduces the number of people on welfare and lowers such individuals' income, producing poverty, inclusive of defaults on mortgages or rents, and possible homelessness. Moreover, the elimination of welfare serves to increase the supply of market labor producing a drop in the wage rate.[14] In this scenario, the generation of more employment opportunities can be expected to reduce the number of welfare recipients when such employment yields an income greater than what is generated by the welfare payments. Moreover, increasing the market wage of the individual, ceteris paribus, can have the same effect.

When income-earning capacity is limited because of, for example, human capital constraints, bargaining constraints, child-rearing responsibilities, and employment constraints, welfare serves to raise individuals out of poverty and/or improve child care for children when parental provision of child care is the only affordable quality child care available. Thus the target model of labor supply predicts that welfare payments with an associated 100 percent tax on market income earned while on welfare, reduces the supply of labor for a particular cohort of the population who would otherwise live in poverty or be unable to take proper care of their children. Of course, welfare payments will also reduce the labor supply of those with a very low target income, those who place greater weight on nonmarket activities than on market work and derived market income. Overall, this model predicts that as long as welfare payments are less than the target income, they will reduce the supply of market labor of those with relatively low earning capacities and those with significant household and other nonmarket responsibilities. It follows that reductions to or the elimination of welfare will increase the market labor supply but at the expense of generating more poverty and reducing the quantity and quality of nonmarket activities such as child care.

Unlike in the conventional model, the target model of labor supply does not postulate that the key opportunity cost of cutting welfare is a reduction in the leisure time available to welfare recipients. This is a critically important point from the perspective of social policy and social welfare. Of course, individuals with a low target income—a strong preference for nonmarket activities—will also increase their labor supply with the elimination of welfare.

If the market income earned by welfare recipients is not taxed at a 100 percent, individuals whose market income is below the income derived from welfare payments will not face the binary choice of working and remaining at a relatively low income or not working and improving their income level. By working and receiving a market income the individual can only further improve her or his income toward the target level. Thus, unlike the conventional model of labor supply, the target income model predicts that reducing the marginal tax rate of market income of individuals receiving welfare will increase the supply of labor to what it would be in a world without welfare for most categories of welfare recipients. The conventional model predicts, as discussed above, that changes in the marginal tax rate are likely to improve the market labor supply, but the extent to which this is the case depends critically upon the affected individuals leisure preference. With respect to the target income model, only if the combined income accruing from welfare and market labor is above the target will market labor supply fall from what it would be in a world without welfare. This is unlikely in a world where target income tends to increase with increasing income-accruing opportunities.

In Figure 11.4, for example, if we apply this discussion to the individual constrained to work L_0L_M by child care responsibilities, and assume a market wage given by W_0 or W_{01} and a post-tax wage, for an individual on welfare, given by W_{21}, a target income Y_T, and welfare payments of WP, the welfare recipient continues to supply L_0L_M of market labor because welfare payments plus market income yield a total income of only L_MH, which is still below the target level of income. In another scenario, we assume that this individual is simply constrained by employment opportunities, effective labor supply remains at L_0L_1, and the individual searches for work until this level of employment is realized, yielding a target income of Y_T. Until L_0L_{10} of employment, welfare is received. At this point, the welfare wage tax generates tax revenues that suffice to cover the welfare payments (*GJ* equals WPL_0) and, therefore, the entire welfare payment is clawed back from employment income. As employment increases above L_0L_{10}, the wage line reverts to W_0 because it no longer pays to receive welfare payments. Given the welfare wage tax rate, net income would be less for the employed welfare recipients as compared to the nonwelfare-receiving employed, when employment increases beyond L_0L_{10}. This is so because the income of the employed who are off welfare does not face a welfare-related tax. In this case, welfare payments serve to supplement the income of the underemployed worker. This worker has the incentive to work under welfare, even when underemployed, because his or her take-home pay from market employment is positive.

But for certain categories of labor, it is quite possible that even the reduction in the tax rate to below 100 percent will not restore labor supply to prewelfare levels. The individual who takes advantage of welfare to reduce labor supply from a level that is greater than their desired number of hours is a good case in point. The change in the tax rate can be expected to increase labor supply from its 100 percent tax level however. A key social and economic question here is if one would want such an individual to work at this high number of hours if there exists, for example, no quality child care. Are the short- and long-term costs of such child neglect worth the related gains in labor supply? You might also have individuals involved in artistic pursuits that yield, in the short term, little or no market income. They might take advantage of welfare to devote a portion of their labor supply to such low-income activities. Reducing the tax rate makes market work pay, however, in a world of welfare. How much market labor is forthcoming critically depends on the target income of the artiste. In both of these scenarios note that labor market supply need not be restored to its hypothetical prewelfare state as the marginal tax rate on market income for welfare recipients falls, not as a consequence of any strong preference for leisure, but rather because of strong preference for certain types and quantities of nonmarket work.

Both the conventional and the target income models of labor supply predict that welfare yields some reduction in labor supply, albeit the target income model suggests a lesser reduction. Moreover, both models predict that welfare serves to increase the reservation wage of labor and, related to this, the bargaining power of labor. Thus both models predict that welfare has the important indirect effect of increasing the price of labor. To what extent it increases depends on the size and extent of welfare-related income flows, their impact upon the reservation wage, and the supply of labor. Welfare's effect on labor supply critically depends on whether, and the extent to which, market income earned by welfare recipients is taxed. Be this as it may, a critical question flowing from such a prediction is to what extent does increasing the price of labor damage an economy's competitiveness? The presumption that increasing wages must impact negatively and significantly on the economy is challenged by applying a behavioral approach to the firm, embedded in x-efficiency theory, to an analysis of the possible effects higher wages might have upon unit production costs.

X-Inefficiency, Welfare, and Wages

The conventional model of the firm presumes that firms are typically performing as well as possible in terms of the quantity and quality of effort inputs per unit of time and productivity maximizing technology. Market forces drive firms toward this efficient level of production and firms end up producing along the production possibility frontier.[15] As already discussed, these assumptions yield the prediction that increased wages increase unit production costs because no cost offsets exist to the increased wages in the face of ex ante efficiency in production. By how much, critically depends upon the percentage share of labor costs to total input costs (see Equations 1 and 2). The view that effort is maximized was challenged by Harvey Leibenstein[16] in his development of x-efficiency theory.

The key point made by Leibenstein is that when economic agents are not characterized by objective functions that are singularly focused upon cost minimization, requiring maximizing the effort inputs of all economic agents, effort need not be maximized. Owners and managers might also be more concerned about leisure activities that detract from effort maximization, and workers' need not have the incentive to do their best if they do not share the objectives of the firm's owners and managers. Workers, for example, can avoid maximizing their effort inputs when transaction costs exist in terms of monitoring and enforcing effort inputs. Thus, unlike in the conventional model, Leibenstein assumes effort discretion on the part of the economic agent. According to Leibenstein, ceteris paribus, less effort yields lower levels of labor productivity and thus higher unit production costs (see Equation 1). This deviation from maximum productivity is defined as x-inefficiency in production, which is assumed away in the conventional world of effort maximization. Firms can persist in producing x-inefficiently only where imperfect product markets exist. Otherwise, market forces would force x-efficiency in production upon firms and their employees, managers, and owners. In the contemporary efficiency wage literature, elaborated, for example in George Akerlof, George Akerlof and Janet Yellen, and Joseph Stiglitz,[17] effort discretion is also assumed. However, it is argued that given effort discretion, wages are employed by profit maximizing firms to induce cost minimizing quantity of effort inputs from the firm's economic agents. Diminishing returns to effort inputs are assumed with respect to wage changes. The cost-minimizing wage is denoted as the efficiency wage. Any deviation from this wage up or down serves to increase unit production costs. In equilibrium, all firms, irrespective of market structure, are expected to be characterized by their respective efficiency wages. Exogenous wage increases usually can be expected to increase unit production costs in both x-efficiency and efficiency wage theory, consistent with the analytical prediction flowing from the conventional modeling of the firm.

Building upon the theoretical insights of both x-efficiency and efficiency wage theory, I have constructed an alternative model of the firm wherein x-inefficiency can exist even in highly competitive product markets with profit maximizing firms. Moreover, there need not be some unique wage that yields economically efficient results.[18] Unlike in the x-efficiency models, making markets more competitive need not make markets more x-efficient, and, unlike in the efficiency wage literature, increasing the wage rate over some range need not increase unit production costs. With respect to the latter, in my model, some linearity is assumed in the relationship between wages, effort, and productivity. A basic assumption of this alternative model is that effort inputs are positively affected by the level of labor compensation, inclusive of wage rates, as well as by the entire industrial relations package of which labor compensation is but one component. This assumption is well documented, as is the fact that firms similar in technology and output adopt industrial relations structures ranging from low wage, poor working conditions to high wage, high quality working conditions of industrial relations.[19] Related to this, there does not appear to be a unique or efficiency wage that dominates the market. Finally, and more generally speaking, in a world of effort discretion higher wages pressure firms into becoming more x-efficient for evident cost reasons, whereas lower wages have the opposite effect. This has important implications for an understanding of the potential impact that welfare-induced wage increases might have upon the competitive position of the firm.

In modeling the firm in this fashion, unit production costs need not increase as wages increase as long as labor productivity increases to an offsetting extent, as is clear from Equations 1 and 2, above. Thus, to the extent that effort discretion and x-inefficiency exist, increasing wages need not generate higher unit costs. This point is illustrated in Figure11.5, where there exists an array of wage rates and related labor compensation that yields a unique average or unit cost of production *B* up to wage *W*. As labor compensation rises above *W*, average costs increase as diminishing returns to effort inputs set in and x-efficiency in production is achieved. This scenario is given by the average cost curve *BAC*. Thus, up to some point increasing wages do not negatively impact upon the firm's competitiveness. Moreover, lower wages yield lower levels of x-efficiency and a lower level of material well-being per person but do not affect average costs. Of course, in this model, it must be reiterated, some linearity in the relationship between wage rates and working conditions and labor productivity is assumed. This allows for a range of labor costs to be consistent with a unique average cost. In this scenario, firms can compete on the basis of either high or low wages. And firm decisionmakers have no immediate incentive to adopt the higher wage route in so far that the latter does not yield economic benefits to the firm per se in terms of lower production costs or higher profits. In contrast to this modeling scenario, in the efficiency wage literature, there is only one rate of labor compensation consistent with minimizing average cost. This is given by point *W* and average cost curve *ACAC*. Any wage deviating from the efficiency wage yields higher costs and lower profits.

An important implication of the behavioral model for assessing the economic effects of welfare payments is that to the extent that welfare payments generates the secondary effect of increasing the wage rate by reducing the supply of labor and by increasing the reservation wage and bargaining power of labor, this need not have the negative effects predicted by the conventional wisdom. Indeed, by forcing wages upward, welfare can have the positive effect of increasing the level of x-efficiency, which serves as the cost offset to the induced increase in wages. The flip side to this analytical prediction is that eliminating welfare payments or reducing them, by reducing wages, serves to reduce the level of x-efficiency and thus the average level of material well-being in the economy. Thus, from an efficiency and material welfare maximizing perspective, an appropriately structured welfare system is efficiency enhancing and efforts to eliminate welfare as opposed to restructuring and reforming it can be expected to have the opposite effect.

Another important implication of the behavioral model is that it suggests that to the extent that higher welfare-induced wages stimulate higher levels of productivity, such wage increases need not generate the fall in employment predicted by the conventional model. In Figure 11.2, if the availability of welfare decreases the supply of labor from S_1 to S_2, increasing wages

Figure 11.5 **Average Costs and Alternative Costs of Labor**

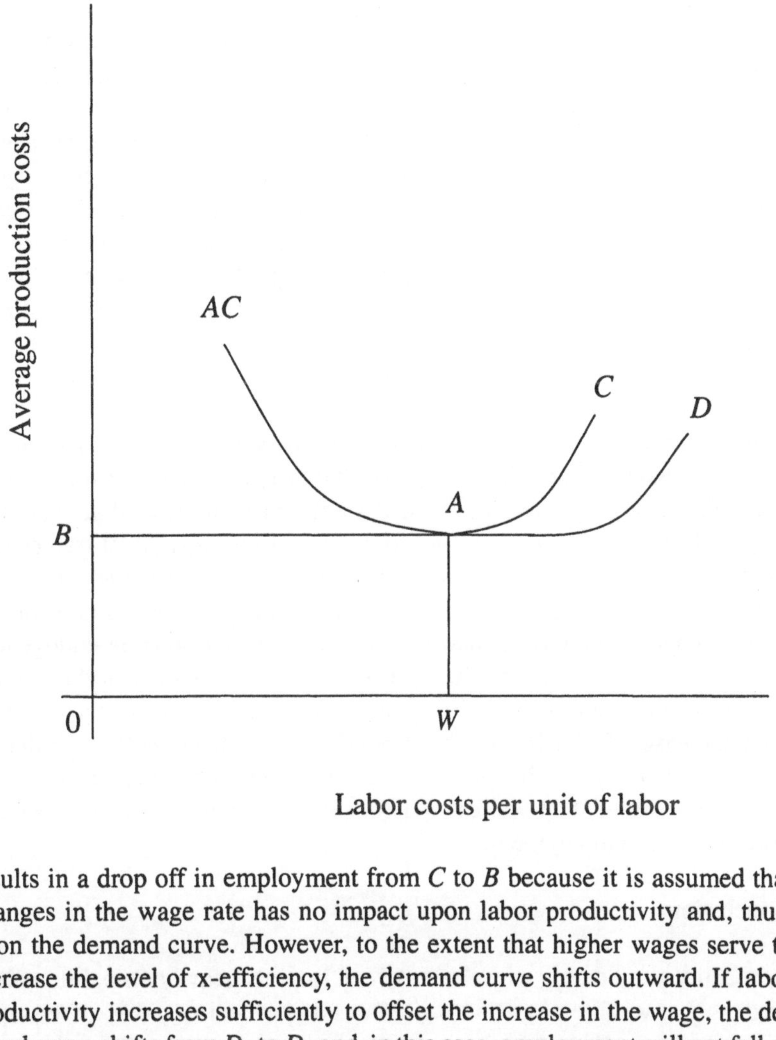

results in a drop off in employment from *C* to *B* because it is assumed that changes in the wage rate has no impact upon labor productivity and, thus, upon the demand curve. However, to the extent that higher wages serve to increase the level of x-efficiency, the demand curve shifts outward. If labor productivity increases sufficiently to offset the increase in the wage, the demand curve shifts from D_1 to D_2 and, in this case, employment will not fall as a consequence of welfare-induced increases to wages. The important point here is that the conventional model, at best, exaggerates the extent to which employment can be expected to fall as a result of increasing wages.

Thus far we have not considered the possibility of technological change as one consequence of wage changes. Analyses of welfare regimes typically assume no technological change. Moreover, the traditional modeling of technological change assumes it to be exogenous or at least not affected by movements in the wage rate or other factor prices. At best, a change in the wage rate induces firms to choose a more cost efficient factor input mix along the production isoquant and thus does not prevent average cost from rising as wage rates rise. An increasing wage is assumed not to have any causal effect on the position of the isoquant or production function, which, strictly defined, is what technological change is all about. In contrast, in a behavioral modeling of technical change developed in detail elsewhere, economic agents respond to increasing labor costs by either developing new technology or adopting known existing technology that becomes cost effective in the context of higher labor costs.[20] In this model, as labor costs increase, firms engage in technical change that increases labor productivity by more than it would otherwise be increased by simply raising the capital intensity of production. New technology is developed and adopted so as to keep unit costs from rising in the face of increasing labor costs. Such technical change complements increases in the level of x-efficiency induced by increases in these costs. To the extent that technical change is endogenous, as it is assumed to be in the behavioral model, one can expect that a given level of average costs would be consistent with an even wider array of labor costs than would be the case if one only brought effort discretion into the analytical framework. As illustrated in Figure 11.5, the average production cost curve shifts from *BAC* to *BAD* with technological change as firm decisionmakers respond to the challenge of increasing labor costs. Therefore, introducing endogenous technological change into the analysis provides firms with an additional degree of freedom with which to respond to the challenge of welfare-induced wage increases. That firms might respond to wage increases through the avenue of technological change further reduces the probability, from a theoretical perspective, that welfare must result in higher production costs and lower levels of employment.

Conclusion

Conventional modeling of welfare, which impacts heavily on public policy, predicts that welfare payments will have unequivocal negative effects upon the economy in terms of labor supply, production costs, and employment. But the conventional wisdom is predicated upon models that are built upon assumptions that are not appropriate and too restrictive given the questions being addressed. Of particular importance is the conventional model of labor supply that presumes that individuals have a strong preference for leisure (leisure is a normal good). Analysts often go one step further, assuming that individuals view leisure as a superior good and are willing to make significant sacrifices to obtain more leisure time. This analysis ignores the fact that nonmarket time is not simply leisure time and that an individual's choices with respect to nonmarket time are made in the context of the individual's market income requirements, as well as her or his obligations in terms of nonmarket time, net of true leisure activities. Moreover, the conventional wisdom typically assumes that full employment exists, thus individuals can obtain employment for the asking and at reasonable wages at that. Finally, the conventional wisdom is built upon a model of the firm wherein it is assumed that x-efficiency is the rule leading logically to the conclusion that higher wages induced by welfare programs yield higher production costs and less employment. Thus welfare programs are introduced and improved at a considerable cost to society at large, and these costs should be recognized at the get go. If such costs are to be avoided, the conventional wisdom recommends the effective dismantling of welfare programs and, in the absence of this, significant reductions of benefits.

The critical points made in this chapter derive from the application of alternative theoretical constructs, built upon more reasonable behavioral and related assumptions, to questions pertaining to the economic impact of welfare payments. Such alternative modeling of welfare benefits suggests that welfare payments need not negatively impact on the economy either in terms of labor supply or competitiveness. From the perspective of labor supply, a target income model suggests that labor supply is driven by concerns about target income and target nonmarket activities such as child care. From this perspective welfare payments can be expected to reduce labor supply only if individuals can earn more on welfare than on the market, given their target income and, related to this, their target nonmarket activities. For the cohort of the population where welfare tends to reduce labor supply, the traditional 100 percent tax rate on market income for welfare recipients only accelerates the negative effect of welfare on labor supply. If individuals can both work and collect welfare, it is unlikely that labor supply will diminish, unless target income is reached. One can expect labor supply to diminish in this scenario if certain nonmarket activities have priority over higher levels of income, and welfare payments make these nonmarket activities affordable. Overall, this alternative modeling of the relationship between welfare payments and labor supply suggests that the traditional model, by focusing on leisure preference, probably greatly exaggerates the reduction in market labor supply, which can be expected to follow from the introduction of or increases to welfare payments, as well as ignoring the possibility that nonmarket labor activities include much more than leisure and that market employment is not necessarily available for the asking at welfare or higher than welfare levels of income. Thus, this analytical framework also suggests that, ceteris paribus, eliminating welfare payments tends to reduce income to former welfare recipients (pushing individuals further into the web of poverty) and forces a reallocation of labor away from nonmarket activities, such as child care, to market activities. It is unlikely that eliminating or dramatically cutting welfare will serve to instill a work ethic into welfare recipients and thus increase labor supply, even at the cost of some short-term pain, when a weak work ethic in the form of a strong leisure preference is not the problem cause in the first instance.[21]

The available evidence suggests that the key to reducing the welfare rolls and reducing welfare payouts without eliminating or reducing welfare payments per recipient is to make market work pay.[22] Typically, individuals want to get off welfare. They do not have to be forced to work or to get job training or to improve their education. This is so because, contrary to the assumption of the conventional model, individuals are typically not out to increase their leisure time at every opportunity. Aggregate welfare payments can be reduced for example by increasing the rate of job creation, reducing the tax rate on market income earned by welfare recipients, increasing the income individuals can earn per hour in a particular job through skill formation, bargaining power or minimum wage legislation, and by making child care more affordable.[23] Otherwise, simply forcing people off welfare will increase poverty rates and levels, with a particular deleterious effect on children, and with the significant secondary effect of reducing the market price of labor and thus the income of those so affected.

The conventional model predicts that albeit such diminutions in wages might reduce income, they will increase the competitiveness of firms and increase employment, thus total per worker income may not fall after all. However, this model assumes that changes in wages have no effect on the efficiency of labor or upon the rate of technical change, and generally, and incorrectly, expects wages to be a very large component of total costs. In contrast, the behavioral model presented here suggests that it is unlikely that welfare payments will generate higher unit production costs or more unemployment predicted by conventional theory, given that there are cost offsets induced by welfare-induced wage increases in terms of increased efficiency and increased technical change. On the flip side, to the extent that policy is implemented, which serves to cut welfare benefits with the effect of reducing market wages, this cannot be expected to readily reduce unit costs or increase employment as such wage cuts serve to induce lower levels of efficiency and lower rates of technical change. Thus, overall, welfare payments, as part of an income safety net, can play an important role in poverty alleviation without necessarily having the negative effects predicted by standard economic theory. Much depends on how the system of welfare and related payments is designed in terms of the incentives and opportunities provided for individuals to search and accept market employment.

The modeling presented here is consistent with stylized facts already discussed that provide no clear support for the conventional hypothesis that social welfare, as currently practiced in advanced economies, must generate significant economic harm. Rather, the modeling presented here allows us to make sense of evidence suggesting that social welfare does not cause economic harm either in terms of reductions in employment, labor supply, or increases in production costs. It further allows us to contemplate and analyze the potential positive effects that social welfare can have upon socioeconomic well-being.

Notes

The author thanks Louise Lamontagne, Margaret Oppenheimer, and participants of the Business and Economics Society International Conference, Montreal, Canada, July 24–29, 2002, the International Association for Research in Economic Psychology/Society for the Advancement of Behavioral Economics Joint Conference, Turku, Finland, June 30–July 4, 2002, and the Association for Social Economics/Allied Social Science Association session on Law and Economics, January 2003, for their helpful comments and suggestions. Research for this paper was supported by a Law Commission of Canada/Social Science and Humanities Research Council grant.

1. The 1996 welfare reforms limit the time over which most families can receive welfare to five years. Moreover, the reforms have downloaded the responsibility of administrating and regulating the welfare system to the state, increasing the probability that former welfare recipients will be denied publicly provided medical care and food stamps that were critical supplements to welfare payments. See Peter Edelman, "The Worst Thing Bill Clinton Had Done"; Peter Edelman, "Reforming Welfare—Take Two"; and Pamela Loprest, "Families Who Left Welfare."

2. The results of the American experiment are clouded by the fact that welfare reform coincided with a period of dramatic reductions in the American unemployment rate due to substantial increases in employment opportunities that filtered down to the least skilled job seekers. Under these circumstances there would have been a major percentage cut in welfare recipients even in the absence of welfare reform. As it stands, welfare rolls have declined dramatically, as it must given the time restrictions of the new welfare rules. However, on average, the material level of well-being of the former welfare recipients has fallen. In addition, given the absence of affordable and quality day care for low-income families, the quality of child care has also fallen as mothers have now been forced out of their nonmarket job as child care providers into low wage market employees. See *Business Week* article, "From Welfare to Worsefare?" and Edelman, "The Worst Thing Bill Clinton Had Done."

3. Peter Lindert, ("Does Social Spending Deter Economic Growth?") in fact, finds that social welfare and growth are positively related where social welfare is measured in terms of its size, in terms of measured expenditures on social welfare programs relative to GDP. More specifically, low levels of social spending are not found to be a necessary condition to high growth rates or high levels of per capita GDP, nor are high levels of social spending found to be an obstacle to achieving high rates of growth or high levels of per capita GDP. High social spending economies can achieve high levels of growth and income by efficiently allocating social spending

and efficiently taxing income sources to finance relatively high target levels of social spending. On this, see also A.B. Atkinson, *The Economic Consequences of Rolling Back the Welfare State,* ch. 8; and Ian Gough, "Global Capital, Human Needs and Social Policies."

4. Atkinson, *The Economic Consequences of Rolling Back the Welfare State,* 184–85.

5. Morris Altman. "Economic Theory, Public Policy and the Challenge of Innovative Work Practices"; Morris Altman, "Why Unemployment Insurance Is Not Only Good for Soul, It's Also Good for the Economy"; Atkinson, *The Economic Consequences of Rolling Back the Welfare State.*

6. Altman, "Why Unemployment Insurance Is Not Only Good for Soul, It's Also Good for the Economy."

7. Morris Altman, "The Economics of Exogenous Increases in Wage Rates in a Behavioral/X-Efficiency Model of the Firm"; Morris Altman, "A High Wage Path to Economic Growth and Development"; Morris Altman, *Worker Satisfaction and Economic Performance.*

8. Recently resurrected and reconstructed by Philippe Van Parijs (*What's Wrong With a Free Lunch?),* there has long existed a case for a guaranteed income to be granted to all individuals irrespective of whether or not an individual is willing to work. The target income model of labor supply presented below suggests that such propositions need not have a large impact on labor supply. However, as pointed out by his critics (see comments to Van Parijs in his book), income grants to individuals who choose not work even when work is available can create a backlash from those with a stronger work ethic who ultimately must finance such a project. It also might undermine the notion of reciprocity and community between those who receive income support and those who finance income support programs.

9. Robert Solow, *Work and Welfare,* Lecture I.

10. Morris Altman, "Preferences and Labor Supply."

11. Gary Becker. "A Theory of the Allocation of Time."

12. See Altman, "Preferences and Labor Supply," for a detailed discussion of the target income theory of labor supply. See Bruce E. Kaufman, "Expanding the Behavioral Foundations of Labor Economics," for a discussion of the importance of developing an alternative theory of labor supply based upon more realistic behavioral assumptions.

13. Altman, "Preferences and Labor Supply."

14. An important point made by Solow (*Work and Welfare,* 23–32) in his critique of contemporary welfare reform in the United States is that the elimination of welfare will increase the supply of labor, driving down the wages not only of the least-skilled, lowest-paid workers, but also, through a ripple effect, of more highly skilled and paid workers.

15. Altman, "Preferences and Labor Supply; Milton Friedman, "The Methodology of Positive Economics"; and M.W. Reder, "Chicago Economics."

16. Harvey Leibenstein, "Allocative Efficiency vs. 'X-Efficiency'"; Harvey Leibenstein, "A Branch of Economics Is Missing."

17. George Akerlof, "Gift Exchange and Efficiency-Wage Theory"; George Akerlof and Janet Yellen, *Efficiency Wage Models of the Labor Market*; and Joseph Stiglitz, "The Causes and Consequences of the Dependence of Quality on Price."

18. Altman, "The Economics of Exogenous Increases in Wage Rates in a Behavioral/X-Efficiency Model of the Firm"; "A High Wage Path to Economic Growth and

Development"; *Worker Satisfaction and Economic Performance;* "Economic Theory, Public Policy and the Challenge of Innovative Work Practices."

19. Altman, "Economic Theory, Public Policy and the Challenge of Innovative Work Practices"; Casey Ichniowski et al., "What Works at Work."

20. Altman, A High Wage Path to Economic Growth and Development"; Altman, *Worker Satisfaction and Economic Performance.*

21. Gertrude Himmelfarb, "Comment on Work and Welfare," commenting on Solow's critique of American welfare reforms (*Work and Welfare),* which drastically reduces the level and extent of social welfare, argues that contrary to what Solow maintains, such reforms will serve to instill a work ethic among the American poor. The problem with welfare recipients, according to Himmelfarb, is not the lack of jobs and the tax structure relating market income earned by welfare recipients. Rather, it is that welfare has made the poor lazy—welfare has (Himmelfarb, 82), "lowered their [the poor's] morale and weakened their moral will." This type of assumption characterizes contemporary modeling of labor supply.

22. Greg Duncan and Lindsay Chase-Lansdale, *For Better and for Worse*; Christopher Jencks, *Rethinking Social Policy*; Loprest, "Families Who Left Welfare"; Charles Michalopoulos et al., "The Self-Sufficiency Project at 36 Months"; Michalopoulos, Robins, and Card, "When Financial Work Incentives Pay for Themselves"; Jane Pulkingham and Gordon Ternowetsky, "The State of the Art Review of Income Security Reform in Canada"; SRDC, "When Work Pays Better Than Welfare."

23. See Barbara Bergmann, *Saving Our Children from Poverty,* and David Blau, *The Child Care Problem,* for discussions of the importance of affordable day-care facilities for child development and of the positive incentive that subsidized child care has upon low-income earners' and welfare recipients incentive to engage in market employment. Bergmann focuses upon a French-American comparison whereas the Blau study deals with the American case specifically. With respect to increasing wages, Edmund Phelps (*Rewarding Work)* suggests wage subsidies. To the extent that this succeeds in increasing the earned income of the individual, this can result in the individual moving off welfare as his or her income rises above what can be earned on welfare. Related to this, earned income tax credits serve to increase the take-home pay from market work, thus possibly driving net earned income above what an individual might earn on welfare. In fact, earned income tax credits in the United States have increased average, single-parent income by 30 percent for those earning less than $6,000, and by 25 percent for those earning between $6,000 and $12,000 in 1999. This program had the related effect of reducing America's poverty rate by 13 percent (Bruce Meyer and Douglas Holtz-Eakin, *Making Work Pay.*

References

Akerlof, G.A. "Gift Exchange and Efficiency-Wage Theory: Four Views." *American Economic Review, Papers and Proceedings* 74 (1984): 29–83.

Akerlof, G.A. and J. Yellen, eds. *Efficiency Wage Models of the Labor Market.* New York: Cambridge University Press, 1986.

Altman, M. "The Economics of Exogenous Increases in Wage Rates in a Behavioral/X-Efficiency Model of the Firm." *Review of Social Economy* 50 (1992): 163–92.

———. "A High Wage Path to Economic Growth and Development." *Challenge: The Magazine of Economic Affairs* 41 (1998): 91–104.

———. *Worker Satisfaction and Economic Performance*. Armonk, NY: M.E. Sharpe, 2001a.
———."Preferences and Labor Supply: Casting Some Light into the Black Box of Income-Leisure Choice." *Journal of Socio-Economics* 31 (2001b): 199–219.
———. "Economic Theory, Public Policy and the Challenge of Innovative Work Practices." *Economic and Industrial Democracy: An International Journal* 23 (2002a): 271–90.
———. "Why Unemployment Insurance Is Not Only Good for Soul, It's Also Good for the Economy." *Review of Social* Economy 62 (2004): forthcoming.
Atkinson, A.B. *The Economic Consequences of Rolling Back the Welfare State*. Cambridge, MA: MIT Press, 1999.
Becker, G. "A Theory of the Allocation of Time." *Economic Journal* 75 (1965): 493–517.
Bergmann, B.R. *Saving Our Children from Poverty*. New York: Russell Sage Foundation (1996).
Blau, D.M *The Child Care Problem: An Economic Analysis*. New York: Russell Sage Foundation (2001).
Duncan, G.J., and P. Lindsay Chase-Lansdale, eds. *For Better and for Worse: Welfare Reform and the Well-Being of Children and Families*. New York: Russell Sage Foundation (2002).
Edelman, P. "Reforming Welfare—Take Two." *The Nation*, February 4 (2002).
———. "The Worst Thing Bill Clinton Had Done." *The Atlantic Monthly* 279, no. 3 (1997): 43–53.
Friedman, M. "The Methodology of Positive Economics." In *Essays in Positive Economics*, ed. M. Friedman, 3–43. Chicago: University of Chicago Press, 1953.
"From Welfare to Worsefare? Some Welfare Recipients Make Less Now That They Are Employed." *Business Week*, October 9 (2000): 103.
Gough, I. "Global Capital, Human Needs and Social Policies." New York: Palgrave, 2000.
Himmelfarb, G. "Comment on Work and Welfare." In *Work and Welfare*, ed. R. Solow, 77–84. Princeton, NJ: Princeton University Press, 1998.
Ichniowski, C., T.A. Kochan, D. Levine, C. Olson, and G. Strauss. "What Works at Work: Overview and Assessment." *Industrial Relations* 35 (1996): 299–333.
Jencks, C. *Rethinking Social Policy: Race, Poverty, and the Underclass*. New York: Harper Perennial, 1993.
Kaufman, B.E. "Expanding the Behavioral Foundations of Labor Economics." *Industrial and Labor Relations Review* 52 (1999): 361–92.
Leibenstein, H. "Allocative Efficiency vs. 'X-Efficiency.'" *American Economic Review* 56 (1966): 392–415.
———. "A Branch of Economics Is Missing: Micro-Micro Theory." *Journal of Economic Literature* 17 (1979): 477–502.
Lindert, P. "Does Social Spending Deter Economic Growth?" *Challenge: The Magazine of Economic Affairs* 39 (1996): 17–23.
Loprest, P. "Families Who Left Welfare: Who Are They and How Are They Doing?" Assessing the New Federalism Discussion Paper, 99–02. Washington, DC: Urban Institute, 1999.
Meyer, B.D., and D. Holtz-Eakin. *Making Work Pay: The Earned Income Tax Credit and Its Impact on America's Families*. New York: Russell Sage Foundation, 2002.
Michalopoulos, C., D. Card, L.A. Gennetian, K. Harknett, and P.K. Robins. "The

Self-Sufficiency Project at 36 Months: Effects of a Financial Work Incentive on Employment and Income." Ottawa: Social Research and Development Corporation, 2000.

Phelps, E.S. *Rewarding Work: How to Restore Participation and Self-Support to Free Enterprise*. Cambridge, MA: Harvard University Press, 1997.

Pulkingham, J., and G. Ternowetsky. "The State of the Art Review of Income Security Reform in Canada." Working Paper Series #4. Ottawa: International Development Research Centre, 1998. Available at: www.idrc.ca/socdev/pub/social/contents.html.

Reder, M.W. 1982. "Chicago Economics: Permanence and Change." *Journal of Economic Literature* 20: 1–38.

SRDC. "When Work Pays Better Than Welfare: A Summary of the Self-Sufficiency Project's Implementation Focus Group, and Initial 18-Month Impact Report." Ottawa: Social Research and Development Corporation, 1996.

Solow, R. *Work and Welfare*. Princeton, NJ: Princeton University Press, 1998.

Stiglitz, J.E. "The Causes and Consequences of the Dependence of Quality on Price." *Journal of Economic Literature* 25 (1987): 1–48.

Van Parijs, P. *What's Wrong With a Free Lunch?* Boston: Beacon Press, 2001.

12

Alternative Economic Approaches to Analyzing Hours of Work Determination and Standards

Morris Altman and Lonnie Golden

Introduction and Overview

A behavioral economic approach is needed to improve our understanding of why individuals supply the number of hours of work that they do, why they may be rising in certain countries and how this may interact with labor law and regulation. Our clinical focus is on the United States, where hours of work have increased and have done so relative to other developed economies.[1] The conventional, neoclassical labor supply model provides a useful starting point, but it is no more than a start. It assumes that workers form their desired number of work hours based on their market wage rate, nonlabor income sources, innate preferences for work and leisure, and that they may face exogenous, binding constraints, including fixed shift lengths imposed by employers. In contrast, the richer model of income-targeting behavior presented in this paper suggests that individuals first assume a predominant identity or role, leading them to seek market work sufficient to support their preestablished goals regarding consumption and nonmarket time. Goals reflect a hierarchical ordering of their physiological and unsatisfied needs.

Individuals face an opposing set of external economic, social, and cultural forces that may be making income a higher order need than nonmarket time, on balance. Desired hours of labor supply thus may be increasing voluntarily, flowing from the changing preferences of workers. More market work hours and eroding nonmarket time is manifested mainly through higher labor force participation rates and overtime (paid or unpaid), which are becoming less constrained by such institutions as government regulation or labor unions.

The possible contributing factors to this shift in preferences includes the stagnation in real hourly wage rates (among middle- and lower-income workers), the rise in relative income inequality, single parent families, consumer debt-to-income ratios, and shifting of work by employers to "exempt" jobs with unregulated hours. In addition, the improved flexibility of work schedules and other conditions of work that both diminish the "disutility" of work hours and the need for nonwork time have increased the capacity and desire of workers to work more hours. Moreover, desired labor supply can become endogenous, eventually increasing following a persistent inability to reduce their hours worked in line with a preference for shorter hours. Thus, a combination of forces is ratcheting upward workers' targeted income and thus preferred hours of market work

What we refer to as oversupplied labor, of which there are two forms, overwork and overemployment, are becoming more common. Overwork refers to the adverse consequences of long work hours on the health and safety of individuals, families, and the public, even if workers themselves desire the increase in hours worked. Overemployment refers to the situation where workers would be prepared to trade income proportionally for reduced work hours but cannot at their current job. Overemployment can, but need not, result in overwork. Surveys indicate an increased yearning among workers for additional time away from work. The crowding out of nonmarket time (of which there are six distinct types) creates a market failure either when voluntary overwork yields social costs not internalized by the worker or when the negative externalities generated by overemployment are not internalized by the employer. To resolve such market failures calls for new legislation and regulations that provide institutional counterpressures to reduce the tendency toward oversupplied labor.

The first part of the chapter, extending the work of Golden,[2] develops the notion of "oversupplied labor," distinguishing the sources of overemployment. The second part, building on the work of Altman,[3] develops an income-targeting model of labor supply that incorporates a comprehensive set of influences on workers' desired hours of market work. The third part sets up a framework to capture the potential economic and social welfare consequences of overwork, and the dynamic process by which an individual may start out either voluntarily overworked and only later become overemployed, or start out being overemployed and only later become overworked. The fourth section surveys recently adopted or proposed work hours legislation and regulation in the United States and the European Union (EU) and in light of the model, and derives implications for rising hours and the extent of oversupplied labor in the workforce.

Oversupplied Labor: Overemployment

Overemployment at the Microeconomic Level

The conventional neoclassical microeconomic model of labor-leisure choice and utility maximization recognizes the potential divergence of hours of labor demand and desired labor supply. Several economic factors may lead employers to establish a fixed or minimum hours that preclude downward adjustment of work hours. This includes a continuous production technology and fixed labor costs that increase with skill upgrading and structure of employee benefit contributions. The conventional labor supply model has been modified to emphasize the incentives for employers to establish minimum hours constraints, in the context of principal-agent, efficiency wage, and human capital investment.[4] A model is presented, below, that is designed to further explain the existence and persistence of overemployment.

"Overemployed" workers are defined as willing but unable to work shorter hours at their existing, primary jobs, even when willing to sacrifice proportionately either income or imminent raises.[5] An underlying inflexibility of work hours in the downward direction creates overemployment if a worker cannot refuse overtime work or voluntarily reduce it, or to shorten their work hours from standard hours to part-time. Exogenously fixed hours creates a "kinked budget constraint," driving a wedge between the market wage and a worker's marginal rate of substitution at their optimal hours choice. Actual hours worked can exceed desired hours, as a suboptimal but equilibrium state, with workers settling for a longer than optimal workweek. Overemployment is considered an economic and social problem not only because it creates a worker utility level that is suboptimal, but it is well documented as a source of costly worker absenteeism, tardiness, and excessive on-the-job leisure. In the extreme, the worker quits or suffers burnout that results in labor force withdrawal.

The inability of a sizable segment of the workforce to obtain their optimally desired hours is well recognized by virtually all labor supply models (e.g., Feather and Shaw).[6] However, while the literature has long acknowledged that there is a significant minority of workers dissatisfied with their current number of hours of work, it has not adequately explored whether and why the rate of overemployment may be increasing. In part this is so because the percentage of workers who are overemployed may pale in comparison to the proportion underemployed, particularly in the United States. Estimates of the overemployment rate range widely, from as little as 6 to 8 percent of the U.S. work force,[7] to over 50 percent. In a survey asking employed individuals whether or not they were free to choose their number of work hours, more than half of both wage and salary workers who work a fixed hourly schedule stated they were willing to work fewer hours for proportionately lower income.[8] Moreover, a 1997 survey revealed that over 28 percent of respondents would give up a day's pay for one fewer day of work per week.[9] A 1998 survey of U.S. workers found that overemployment had risen to encompass between 13 percent and 17 percent of the workforce.[10] About 17 percent would accept a 20 percent pay cut to get a four-day workweek, while over 50 percent would accept a 10 percent cut in their pay to get it. Even the most plausible estimates may vary greatly, because of the way the question is posed regarding the willingness to trade income for time and if the alternative to raise income through more hours of work is included. In addition, stated preferences might not match revealed preferences. Generally, however, it is safe to conclude that the rate of overemployment appears to be roughly on par with the rate of underemployment.

Overemployment at the Macroeconomic Level

Labor-leisure models portray overemployment as an individual, single labor market phenomenon, when it can also be viewed from a macroeconomic perspective. Categorizing the contributing sources of overemployment can be treated as analogous to the categorization of sources of unemployment. There are three distinct types: cyclical, structural, and frictional.

Cyclical overemployment occurs during cyclical booms, as aggregate demand (orders, customers) is surging, leading to longer hours demanded per worker by employers. Rising demand for hours may be rising faster than workers' desired hours (e.g., induced by rising wage rates if the substitution effect on labor supply is dominant). Structural overemployment occurs because of the existence of *structural* incentives inherent in labor market-related institutions and work organization. Labor market institutions include the inherently fixed costs of employment faced by employers. Their sources may be increasing skill shortages and escalating employee benefit premiums, which facilitate an upward push in demand for hours of work per employee or the imposition of minimum-hours constraints.[11] Such institutional practices also include the degree of willful compliance with and government enforcement of Fair Labor Standards Act (FLSA) overtime regulations. Changes in work organization include the spread of mandatory (forced) overtime practices and absence of quality part-time opportunities and job-sharing systems. It also includes the expansion of jobs that fall outside the purview of the FLSA and are thus more prone to uncompensated, extended hours.[12] Finally, frictional overemployment occurs due to the bundling of wage-hour in employment contracts and incomplete markets and information. A lack of knowledge among employers about their employees' preferences and among worker applicants about job requirements leads to mismatches. Lack of accessibility and barriers to full information regarding alternative jobs and work hours arrangements can be one source of frictional overemployment. Like unemployment, because such frictions cannot be entirely removed, it is unrealistic to expect that overemployment can ever reach a rate of zero. However, it would be socially optimal if overemployment were to decline toward zero, if overemployment spells could be made very short-lived. Similarly with unemployment, the degree of labor market hardship suffered from overemployment can be assumed to climb from frictional to cyclical to structural sources.

A Behavioral Labor Supply Model: Integrating Economic-Social-Cultural Factors

Q: How many neoclassical economists does it take to change a lightbulb?
A: It depends on the wage rate.

From a Web site, Jokes about Economists and Economics (http://netec.mcc.ac.uk/JokEc.html), this humor succinctly captures the neoclassical approach to explaining the quantity of labor. Note that it does not matter if the answer is assumed to come from the labor supply or the labor demand side. The question regarding the quantity of labor desired can be answered identically using either the supply- or demand-side reasoning. In the long run, the pure neoclassical conception of the "hedonic" labor market assumes the quantity of labor desired by employers will eventually equate with the quantity of labor desired by workers.[13] Thus, workers and firms will sort themselves in ways that match up desired and required hours of work. The wage rate, the only factor common to both functions, serves as the equilibriating force to align the quantity of labor demand and supply.

Perhaps because of this assumed convergence, neoclassical analyses tend to isolate and separate the demand and supply of hours of labor as independent forces. On the supply side, workers are assumed to adjust their labor supply until the unique point where the marginal rate of substitution (MRS), the relative preference for an hour of leisure vis-à-vis work, exactly equals the wage rate. At that point, the wage for the last hour worked is just sufficient to compensate workers for the disutility caused by that last hour of foregone leisure. In virtually all textbook presentations on the issue of labor supply, focus is placed on the price-quantity relationship. Primarily, the focus is on offsetting income and substitution effects of wage rate changes on the labor supply of men and women. That is, whether workers tend to reduce or increase labor supply when wages rise or when they fall. This has led to the creation of the well-known and useful backward bending labor supply curve. At relatively lower wages, the substitution effect is assumed to dominate, so that higher wage rates induce more hours of work. After some threshold level of wage is reached, further increases in wage rates induce a desire to work less and reap higher levels of nonmarket time.

There are two major weaknesses in applying the conventional labor supply model toward understanding trends in work hours. One is its inability to explain sufficiently the level and timing of changes in the course of average hours per worker over the twentieth century.[14] The other is its discounting of hours mismatches that can result in sustained overemployment or underemployment in the labor market. By focusing on work hours preferences and actual trends almost exclusively as a reflection of changes in wages that generate opposing income and substitution effects, it has paid insufficient attention to the importance of labor-supply "shifters" (other than "nonwage income"). The factors that shift the entire labor supply curve are typically relegated to the status of exogenous changes in preferences or constraints. This is not only unfortunate, because these shifters are crucial to understanding recent trends, but also perhaps mistaken because some of the shifters may become endogenous.

What Makes Average Working Time Rise?

A richer model is needed to account for the shifting trends in both labor supply and labor market mismatch (failure to equate actual with preferred hours). Such an approach would explicitly recognize the social and behavioral psychology basis of labor supply decisions, extending beyond the neoclassical preoccupation with responses to varying levels of wage rates. Individual decisions regarding desired work hours are made not only in the context of one's family or household situation, which is well recognized by neoclassical analyses, but in the context of other social groups and cultural influences and constraints.

Introducing income targeting and relative positioning behavior, in a variety of forms and contexts, contribute to a better understanding of the rising hours of labor supply and possible oversupply among individuals. Income targeting suggests that individuals supply the number of work hours they do in order to earn income sufficient to address their unsatisfied wants. Positional effects suggest that individuals seek work hours in order to enhance their relative status in at least three spheres—consumption, the workplace, and the household. What restrains desired hours from escalating ever-upward is that there is a hierarchy of needs, which includes the need for nonmarket time. But there may be a sequence of decisionmaking, with individuals prioritizing the achievement of their income target, then adjusting future preferences or behavior in order to seek their targeted amount of nonmarket time.

Income Targeting Behavior

Individuals may wish to supply more work hours because their current incomes are falling short of their predetermined wants.[15] *Intensified marketing and advertising* create tastes for more and more market goods and services. Wants may escalate over time, as they have over the past centuries, moving the income target ever further out, so that it is never actually reached or reachable.[16] Workers may start with "metapreferences" for a shorter working time, but the cumulative effects of intensifying product market promotional efforts eventually leads workers to prefer what were originally "unpreferred preferences" toward more income than leisure. However, marketing and advertising can also be providing more information that trigger the desire for more of these now familiar products or services. *Bandwagon effects* and interdependent utility function[17]: Individuals derive satisfaction out of consuming goods and services that others are consuming. As new commodities are introduced, new bandwagon effects are triggered, and what was once considered a luxury or amenity item gradually becomes a necessity, creating a new want to satisfy.

Relative Positioning in Consumption

Veblen effects in consumption mean that individuals may compete for higher status by acquiring or accumulating social status-conferring goods and services. Individuals seek to emulate the consumption patterns of the rich in order to enhance their own relative status. In the recent context of *rising income inequality*, this requires that less well-off individuals work more hours in order to gain the income to sustain their relative position in consumption levels.[18] Indeed, as the top income bracket pulls away from the rest, this goal may be unattainable. Those left behind, even with greater absolute income, may be no better off in welfare terms.[19] But much depends on the net effect of the positive welfare of increasing absolute income versus the negative effect of relatively lower income.

A rising "subsistence" level of consumption for low-income individuals suggests that what is considered a socially acceptable minimum material standard of living may be creeping higher over time. At very low levels of income, there may be a near zero marginal value of leisure. Leisure increasingly provides utility only if there is sufficient income to use during leisure time.[20] *Increased consumer debt-financed consumption*, which recently has led to record increases in consumer debt-to-income ratios and consumer-debt servicing on high interest rate credit cards, make longer work hours an option to avoid high interest balances or risk of personal bankruptcy. This debt might, of course, be a product of an increasing target income.

Relative Positioning in the Workplace and Income Spectrum

Rising job and income insecurity leads workers to prefer longer hours in order to build up an income to serve as a buffer against expected future job or income losses. If workers believe their employer is screening before a downsizing or reorganization, workers may view longer hours as an inoculation against the risk of future job loss, income loss, or demotion.[21] The *incentives of workplaces, occupations, and labor market* have heightened the incentive to strive for promotion. Working longer hours becomes a way to signal promotability to employers who interpret the "presenteeism" as an indication of an employee's level of effort and commitment. A greater dispersion of earnings, among occupations and industries as well as between racial groups, has served to "incentivize" workers to work relatively longer hours. The wider the gap between pay grades, the larger is the motivation to engage in such positive signaling tactics.[22] Workers may attempt to equal or perhaps exceed the hours worked of their fellow coworkers. Among those who expect to be in managerial positions, there is a clear positive empirical relationship between the number of work hours they "prefer" and the actual work hours of their coworkers (Eastman 1998).[23] Indeed, they are rewarded for their extra effort.[24] Similarly, there are *negative signaling effects for workers requesting shorter hours.*[25] Those expressing a wish to reduce work hours may be passed up for hiring, in an adverse selection model of hiring decisions. There is a *rising presence of professions that reward and valorize long hours*, which promotes a "rat race" with workers increasing their own work hours for reasons of long-term relative status, such as jobs in law and consulting.[26] With the apparent *rising amenities of the workplace relative to household work*, from on-site day care to a more stimulating, rewarding and less stressful environment, provides a growing allure of the office relative to the household.[27] Flexible schedules are increasingly valuable to workers, particularly those in dual-income households, and are relatively more available to those who work long hours rather than standard hours.[28] *More amenable working conditions*, which make more and more jobs less hazardous or unpleasant, may reduce the resistance to long hours, particularly among the higher educated.[29] If work activity is becoming more intrinsically rewarding, stimulating, safer, discretionary, and autonomous, then this implies something much different than if work is becoming more stressful, anxiety producing, onerous, routinized, and alienating. Work time might be yielding less disutility than it had historically.[30]

Relative Positioning in the Household

The member in the household with relatively greater earnings may attain a relative bargaining power advantage within the unit, owing to his or her superior income. Such leverage is not symmetrically derived from bringing home more "leisure" time, in the current culture. The individual with relatively greater income gains leverage in household decisionmaking, increasing the relative weight their preferences receive in decisions such as consumption purchases, leisure time use, and allocations among sons versus daughters.[31]

Endogenous Labor Supply Preferences

Oversupply creates time scarcity and a shift in household preference from self-produced to market-produced goods and services. Following a period of overemployment, workers may eventually shift their preferences from time-using toward more time-saving goods and services, which requires income. It also shifts preferences from time-intensive to income-intensive leisure activities. This ratchets up the individual's target consumption level and gradually dissipates the initial desire for shorter work hours.[32]

Overall, these various motivations yield the same predicted outcome—workers may be choosing to work longer than predicted by a model that assumes that individuals decide their hours in isolation from others, in a static climate. Moreover, actual hours worked might be greater than predicted by a model of income-leisure choice that pays no heed to the interpersonal aspects of decisionmaking, nor the importance of preferences and hierarchy of wants as core determinants.

Adverse Consequences: Overwork, Diminished Nonmarket Work Time and Labor Costs

Both overemployment and voluntarily chosen long hours of market work can yield overwork. Labor, like certain capital, can be overutilized to the point that it becomes unproductive or even counterproductive. Overwork occurs when the length of work hours begins to adversely affect the health and safety of individuals, families, organizations, and the public, even if workers themselves desire the increase in hours worked. (This point of overwork varies, of course, by the pacing and physical and mental demands of the job, workplace, and occupation and depends somewhat on the demands during nonmarket work time, such as commuting and household production responsibilities.) Even when externalities are generated, for example, on family members, voluntary overwork is sustained quite easily if the overworked individual does not internalize such externalities. The effects of voluntary overwork actually can be consistent with the overworked individuals maximizing their utility. Moreover, firms can sustain such inefficiencies in a competitive economy, even when they adversely affect the firm—through, for example, absenteeism, tardiness, on-the-job leisure, quits, and burnout—if firms are able to offset them by paying relatively lower rates of labor compensation.[33] In addition, to the extent that external costs are borne in employees' homes, inefficiencies are not imposed on the firm. When overemployment (beyond one's preferred hours) contributes to overwork, the divergence between profit maximization and worker well-being widens further.

But because overemployment is defined as a scenario wherein workers are willing to pay, through a reduction in income, for a shorter work day, work week, or work year, why would profit-maximizing firms refuse such an offer, which is consistent with profit maximization and actually serves to increase the welfare of workers? One possible explanation could be that firms have a status quo bias such that if a longer and shorter work period are both equally consistent with profit maximization, firms' decisionmakers might choose the tried and tested work hours duration as opposed to something new, at least in the absence of pressure. If dissatisfied workers react to an imposed unpreferred work schedule by actions that diminish firm productivity and thus increase unit costs, firms need not experience higher unit production costs if they can compensate for these with lower levels of pecuniary and nonpecuniary labor compensation. In this scenario, employers would be indifferent in terms of unit costs between a workplace with zero overemployment and overwork and some overemployment and overwork, even in a competitive environment. Thus, although reducing the level of overemployment and instances of overwork would yield higher levels of utility and material well-being among workers, firm owners and managers will not be forced into this option even by dint of market forces when there exists no perceived competitive advantage in so doing.[34]

Both excessive and involuntary hours of work can set into motion both direct and feedback effects that have both adverse individual and macroeconomic consequences. First, both overwork and overemployment generate adverse welfare effects[35] on individuals, although the former via fatigue and the latter via lost nonmarket time. Second, there are negative spillovers to family/marriage/children and social capital,[36] particularly with overemployment. Third, there may be potential negative effects on employment creation under certain circumstances,[37] although with overemployment this may be more direct than with overwork. Fourth, there may be negative effects on average productivity per hour,[38] although more directly and immediately due to overwork than to overemployment. Fifth, there are greater risks of accidents or mishaps that result in injury, illness, or adverse public health and safety problems,[39] particularly with overwork.

The dynamic process of oversupplying labor suggests that overemployment may be an important source of overwork if the involuntarily worked hours lead an overemployed worker to eventually become overworked. The model further suggests that even voluntary increases in hours of labor supply, if they eventually result in overwork, yield negative effects—economic, social, or psychological—upon the worker, her or his family, or society. The social costs of overwork and overemployment are similar but not entirely overlapping. An individual can be both overemployed and overworked, although an individual who is voluntarily overworked need not be overemployed. Moreover, most overemployed workers do not immediately quit or change jobs, "downshift," or even consider withdrawing from the labor force. Nor do they remain persistently overemployed. Rather, they are likely to adjust upward their consumption level, gradually raising their preferred hours up toward their actual hours.[40] But a social and economic problem remains if overwork is a consequence of longer hours of market work.

Overemployment prevents individuals from reaching their level of targeted nonmarket time. In the neoclassical model, leisure time is simply an end in itself, or, to their credit, is divided between leisure and household production activity. However, more specific uses and types of leisure can be identified to arrive at a richer model of individuals' hierarchy of needs and how time is needed to satisfy them. Even the parsing of nonmarket time to include household production is inadequate to explore deeply the issue of ideal work and nonwork hours. Nonwork or discretionary "leisure" time can be subdivided into at least six distinct categories.[41] This includes time involved in nonpaid activities that are (1) productive leisure, (2) recuperative leisure, (3) social reproductive leisure, (4) consumptive leisure, (5) nonproductive work-related leisure, and (6) nonproductive "pure" leisure.

Each subcategory of nonmarket time has a unique economic and social impact. Productive leisure includes activities that enhance such skills or knowledge related to one's job or career as reading for self-human capital investment, lifelong learning classes. The second includes rest and recuperative activities, such as recreation, that is either time-intensive or money-intensive, that facilitates achievement of maximum productive potential. The third, social reproduction, refers to child rearing, household chores, civic and volunteer work— activities that build future human and "social capital." The fourth, consumptive leisure, encompasses activities such as shopping. The fifth, nonproductive work-related leisure, reflects inactivity due to commuting time, and the sixth, nonproductive "pure" leisure, basic personal care or activities that disengage the mind and body (e.g., personal reflection or "channel-surfing." (There is, however, a risk that nonproductive leisure time can lead to counterproductive leisure activity, in the event it is used in ways that later impede effort during work, productive leisure, or social reproduction, such as excessive drinking.) The allocation of the six may confer a recursive, net economic benefit by affecting productivity during work time. This assumes that effort is a discretionary variable that is affected by both labor and nonlabor activities.[42]

Average hours (*H*) of work per individual determine the level of both market production and nonmarket activity *and* is determined by it, in a recursive process. The same process behind the determination of hours of paid work establishes a stock of nonwork time. Both the total and specific uses of this "leisure" time determine total output (*GDP*), via their effect on aggregate demand (*AD*) and aggregate supply (*AS*). Total output in a social economy is the summed value of market and socially productive nonmarket activity. The levels of both market and nonmarket production and time then feed back by influencing the hours of paid work demanded by employers and hours desired by workers.

When average hours of paid work are rising (assuming real wages constant), this boosts *AD* either by lifting disposable income (*DI*) or generating substitution of money-intensive leisure for time-intensive leisure activity. Longer hours increase *AS* by raising market output per worker, at least in the short run. However, longer hours of paid work clearly must come at the expense of at least one component of nonmarket time. Either it reduces the quantity (or quality) of productive leisure, such as lifelong learning activity, social reproductive leisure, such as time for effective parenting, or leisure time for prudent shopping (by limiting time for consumption-based leisure activities) and rest and relaxation. This in turn might curb either *AD* or *AS*, when the social costs of overwork and time-pressured "leisure" come back to haunt the macroeconomy, not only the particular individuals or family members bearing the brunt of it. Hours mismatches eventually feed back to impede macroeconomic performance. If better matches are made between employer-required and worker-desired work hours, the resulting reduction in overemployment and underemployment may raise *GDP*. This is because greater marginal productivity of hours (MP_H), productive and recuperative leisure, and potentially less overwork may stimulate average productivity, thus increasing *AS*. In addition, greater consumptive (money-intensive) leisure may raise the level of consumption and thus *AD*.

Implications of the Model for Legal and Regulatory Limitations on Hours and Reform

In a hypothetical, hedonic labor market that features perfect matching of employer demanded and employee desired hours of work, regulations that limit or deter long hours of work simply harm the welfare of workers and performance of firms. However, given that overemployment is created initially by the employer side of the labor market, its existence is not inconsistent with the assumption of firm profit maximization for overemployment to persist over time, even if this is incongruent with the preferences of workers. In this case, profit maximization per se is inconsistent with the maximization of workers' welfare. Thus, to the extent that longer hours create overemployment and social spillover costs of overwork, hours regulation may serve to enhance not only social welfare, but worker effort and productivity per hour as well, thus not harming firm performance.

A critical social dilemma arises when overwork increases, regardless of whether it is attributable to increases in overemployment or to more voluntary, income-targeting behavior. To what extent should hours be restrained? Every country or state places some sort of limitation on the duration of working hours. The extent of such regulation reflects a combination of not only working time preferences among men and women, but also the cultural, economic, and institutional context of the affected domain. National differences in preferred labor supply stem from not only individual-level, but country-level characteristics. The greater a country's *GDP* per capita, income equality, and well-developed policies to mitigate market risks, the greater the desire to reduce working hours in that country.[43] Thus, work time preferences might be at least partly endogenous to the national context and institutions in which they are embedded.

What are the existing and proposed reforms in working hours law? In the United States, the only restraint on hours of work is the Fair Labor Standard Act's (FLSA) overtime regulation, requiring premium pay for hours worked in excess of forty in a given one-week period, for those workers who are not exempt due to primarily having managerial, administrative, or professional duties. In EU countries, the desire to restrain or reduce working hours, even if voluntary, has been strong, serving the dual purpose of protecting the amount of nonwork time and spreading employment opportunities. The divergent directions taken in working hours policy in the United States vis-à-vis other countries reflect not only philosophical differences and power of political parties, but the differing degree to which governments view legislation and enforcement as a counterweight against the lengthening of work hours demanded and supplied (e.g., the EU Working Time Directive and France's new thirty-five–hour law). These standards not only reflect the consensus of work time preferences across countries in the EU, but the country-specific, higher standards appear to influence the work hours preferences themselves. This is evidenced by hours preferences being shorter in countries with shorter legal, standard hours and longer in those with longer standard hours.[44]

The EU Working Time Directive

The EU Working Time Directive, passed in 1993 and implemented in 1998, provides minimum standard protections for workers that limit hours to an average of forty-eight hours a week (although workers can choose to work more if they wish), an average of eight hours work in twenty-four hours for night-shift workers, and a right to eleven hours rest a day, a day off each week, and four weeks paid leave per year. EU member countries are free to legislate beyond these minimum standards. In addition, certain industries are permitted to apply for "derogations," an exemption from the strict standards of hours per week. A practice increasingly sought by employers across a variety of industries and countries is to allow hours of work limitations to be applied on an annual basis, which has spread the idea of annualization, where hours of work may exceed the standard during busier seasons provided they are reduced commensurately at some other point during the year.

France's Thirty-five Hour Workweek

France's most far reaching legislation was adopted to achieve the twin objectives of job creation and a better balance between work and personal life by improving working conditions, without sacrificing enterprises competitiveness. The 1998 law capped weekly hours at a fixed number of thirty-five. However, it was variable in the sense that the mechanics of reaching thirty-five was to be arrived at by negotiation, individually in each company or industry. The law later introduced flexible, annual time accounting (a total number of annual hours equivalent to an average thirty-five hours a week) and public subsidies for employers' social insurance payments, in order to serve the needs of both production and service businesses. The actual number of jobs saved or created by the law has been a source of much controversy. However, it is widely accepted that it reduced job insecurity, largely by facilitating mobility to voluntary part-time work and permanent hiring of temporary workers. The decreased job insecurity may temper the perceived need of labor suppliers to heighten their own hours as a protection device against potential layoff.

Britain's Flexible Working Regulations

The Employment Act 2002, coming into force in April 2003, provided 3.7 million employees with a new statutory right to request a contract variation to change the terms and conditions of their employment contract to allow for reduced hours of work. It is now the obligation of employers to honor formal requests for flexible working from parents of children under the age of six, provided the parents have worked there for at least six months. The Employment Act protects such working patterns from fear of dismissal or other detriment. Where requests are not accepted, there is provision for an appeal before an employment tribunal or external dispute resolution.

U.S. Congressional Proposals to Amend the Fair Labor Standards Act Overtime Rules

President George W. Bush has proposed sweeping changes in the rules that Department of Labor regulators apply to determine coverage under the exemption for executive, administrative, and professional jobs that would potentially remove millions of occupational classifications from the overtime pay premium requirement. In addition, Republican leadership in both houses of the U.S. Congress have engaged in piecemeal efforts to broaden the "exemption" status to include fewer and fewer occupations under the act's coverage. At the same time, Democrats have proposed bills that amend the FLSA to limit the number of mandatory overtime work hours, protect a worker's right to refuse overtime work, and fold the now separate "Hours of Service" regulations for truck drivers into the FLSA. It is clear that removing the deterrent of overtime pay rates, without a corresponding upgrade in the working conditions of jobs, is quite likely to ratchet up the hours requirements of such jobs. This is because the pay premium has effectively limited the hours of "nonexempt" workers.[45] Republican leadership in the Congress has promoted bills that permit a substitution of compensatory (comp) time for overtime pay, if employees waive their right to premium pay. In addition, the Senate version would permit the work period to be defined over two weeks, with a maximum of fifty hours in a given week before overtime premium is owed to employees. Under certain conditions, both these proposals of comp time and the more variable workweek might be applied by employers to alleviate both the problems of overemployment and overwork. However, it is more likely than not that over the course of a year, even with comp time earned, employees might easily end up working not only longer hours than previously in a given week, but over the year, as well when the initial overtime work is included.[46] That is because removing the immediate overtime premium penalty deterrent might lengthen the demand for hours per employee generally. Furthermore, the proposed regulatory reform legally grants to employers rather than employees the discretion over when comp time credits may be used for time off. Consequently, absent sufficient bargaining leverage and accommodating employers, workers would likely experience more rather than less involuntary hours of work in a given week or year. This is avoided only if both the timing of overtime work and the comp time off are ensured to be strictly voluntary, according to the preferences of employees. Thus, the proposed FLSA comp time and variable workweek reforms would make workers no less prone to overwork. The behavioral model of labor supply suggests that an initial condition of overemployment and then income-targeting behavior contribute to a preference for longer hours, regardless of the longer run risk of overwork, particularly among those who have less control over the duration of their hours and a lower rate of pay. This is supported by survey evidence suggesting the great majority of workers paid hourly and covered by the FLSA would much prefer pay over time off. The goal of curbing overemployment would be more likely to be accomplished if some sort of FLSA protection were extended to the white-collar, salaried employees who, particularly at certain points of their life cycle when nonmarket work time is most valuable, are disproportionately more likely to be overemployed.

Conclusion

The purpose of this chapter has been to refine traditional theoretical conceptions of labor supply and apply it toward market work hours law and regulation. Labor supply models should be enhanced to incorporate the microeconomic and macroeconomic forces that contribute to a perhaps growing incidence of overemployment and overwork and a resulting crowding out of nonmarket time. Overwork can be generated by targeted income behavior and relative positional concerns of individuals. Overwork may also start out as the result of inflexibility in jobs and workplaces that force workers to work more hours than desired. But longer hours can then become endogenous. Whether involuntary or voluntary, the oversupply of labor negatively impacts on both individual and social welfare, particularly over the longer run because the adverse effects may be cumulative. Oversupplied labor can occur even in the face of competitive circumstances yielding suboptimal stable socioeconomic results. The conventional modeling of labor supply and demand cannot easily model such persistent suboptimal results. This chapter attempts to steer future analyses of this important labor market and social issues in directions that conventional theory cannot negotiate but that are, nevertheless, important to an understanding of both labor market processes and the well-being or welfare of workers. The welfare consequences of labor law regarding working hours thus may be quite different from those suggested by a neoclassical, microeconomic labor demand and supply framework, when applying alternative models of work hours and effort determination.

Conclusions regarding the role of law in the case of working hours regulation depend largely on whether the scope of the model applied is purely neoclassical or widened to include contributions from behavioral and social economics. Applying the alternative framework, given the existence of overemployment, hours of work legislation can serve to enhance the welfare of workers by closing the gap between the work schedule and workers' preferences without damaging the competitive position of the firm. The social and economic benefits of hours of work legislation are accentuated if overemployment yields a greater risk and incidence of overwork. However, with respect to overwork, where workers are voluntarily working longer hours in spite of the negative externalities these yield, hours of work legislation might very well diminish the welfare of the individual worker while increasing the well-being of the wider community, including the worker's immediate family. In this case, there might be a welfare tradeoff between the worker and those affected by the worker's erstwhile choice of hours worked, and public policy in effect must come down on the side of one or the other individual or groups of individuals. To improve social welfare unambiguously, curbing voluntary overwork requires policies beyond the scope of traditional work hours regulation. It requires addressing the underlying social and economic sources behind increases in preferred hours of labor supply.

Notes

1. Michael Haut and Caroline Hanley, "Working Hours and Inequality, 1968–2001"; Lars Osberg, "Understanding Growth and Inequality Trends"; J. Jacobs and K. Gerson, "Who Are the Overworked Americans?"

2. L. Golden, "The Economics of Worktime Length, Adjustment and Flexibility"; "L. Golden, Flexible Work Schedules."

3. M. Altman, "Preferences and Labor Supply."

4. L.F. Dunn, "Loss Aversion and Adaptation in the Labor Market"; S. Kahn and Lang, "The Causes of Hours Constraints;" B. Kaufman, "Expanding the Behavioral Foundations of Labor Economics."

5. Overemployment is distinct from over*time*, which refers to working hours beyond some standard or norm. There is certainly much overlap between overemployment

and overwork, although it is less than complete. Overemployment may include those who work part-time or standard hours, if these actual hours exceed preferred work hours. Overwork may occur even if the excess work hours are partly or even wholly voluntary. Both, however, imply that work hours are crowding out time devoted toward other roles, uses, and pursuits.

6. P. Feather and D. Shaw, "The Demand for Leisure Time in the Presence of Constrained Work Hours."

7. S. Shank, "Preferred Hours of Work and Corresponding Earnings"; Kahn and Lang, "The Causes of Hours Constraints."

8. Feather and Shaw, "The Demand for Leisure Time in the Presence of Constrained Work Hours."

9. Jacobs and Gerson, "Who Are the Overworked Americans?" In the same survey, all hours worked at all jobs have risen markedly, from 43.6 hours in 1977 to 47.1 hours in 1997, with employees putting in six hours more than they are scheduled to work (E. Galinsky, S. Kim, and J.T. Bond, *Feeling Overworked*).

10. J. Schor, The Overspent American.

11. Such overemployment has had a long-standing, historical presence where, for example, the unregulated and highly competitive market for labor of the nineteenth century contributed to long hours of work per week tended to leave workers' desire for a shorter workday unfulfilled (M. Altman, "New Estimates of Hours of Work and Real Income from the 1880s to 1930"; J. Atack, F. Bateman, and R. Margo, "Productivity in Manufacturing and the Length of the Working Day.")

12. Daniel Hamermesh, "12 Million Salaried Workers Are Missing."

13. Hedonic labor market theory holds that if the hours demanded exceeds hours desired, employers would not be able to retain labor indefinitely, losing workers to other firms who offer shorter work hours in accordance with worker preferences, or to nonparticipation in the labor force (S. Rottenberg, "The Regulation of Work Hours and Its Externalities Defenses."

14. Altman, "Preferences and Labor Supply."

15. Ibid.

16. D. George, "Working Longer Hours"; I. Rima, "Involulntary Unemployment and the Re-specified Labor Supply Curve"; J.B. Twitchell, *Lead Us Into Temptation*.

17. Altman, "Preferences and Labor Supply"; H. Leibenstein, "Bandwagon, Snob, and Veblen Effects in the Theory of Consumers' Demand."

18. Samuel Bowles and Yongjin Park, "Emulation, Inequality, and Work Hours"; Robert Frank, *Luxury Fever*.

19. Schor, *The Overspent American*.

20. Altman, "Preferences and Labor Supply"; R. Prasch, "Reassessing the Labor Supply Curve"; M. Sharif, "Inverted 'S.'"

21. See R. Landers, J. Rebitzer, and L. Taylor, "Rat Race Redux."

22. L. Bell, "The Incentive to Work Hard."

23. W. Eastman, "Working for Position."

24. Jeanne Brett and Linda Stroh, "Working 61 Plus Hours a Week."

25. J. Rebitzer and L. Taylor, "Do Labor Markets Provide Enough Short-Hour Jobs?"

26. Landers, Rebitzer, and Taylor, "Rat Race Redux"; E. Yakura, "Billables."

27. A.R. Hochschild, *The Time Bind*.

28. Golden, "Flexible Work Schedules."

29. W. Gramm, "Labor, Work and Leisure."

30. J. Wisman, "Straightening Out the Backward Bending Supply Curve of Labor."

31. For evidence, see Blau, Ferber, and Winkler (2002), 46–47.

32. K. Rothschild, "A Note on Some of the Economic and Welfare Aspects of Working Time Regulations."

33. M. Altman, *Worker Satisfaction and Economic Performance*; G. Yaniv, "Burnout, Absenteeism, and the Overtime Decision."

34. This derives from the behavioral model of the firm, which builds upon the x-inefficiency theory developed in Altman, *Worker Satisfaction and Economic Performance*; and M. Altman, "Economic Theory, Public Policy and the Challenge of Innovative Work Practices."

35. Dunn, "Loss Aversion and Adaptation in the Labor Market"; Feather and Shaw, "The Demand for Leisure Time in the Presence of Constrained Work Hours."

36. R. Barnett, K. Gareis, and R. Brennan, "Fit as a Mediator of the Relationship Between Work Hours and Burnout"; Marin Clarkberg, "Understanding the Time Squeeze"; Virginia Major, K. Klein, and M. Ehrhart, "Work Time, Work Interference With Family, and Psychological Distress."

37. François Contensou and Radu Vranceanu, *Working Time*.

38. E. Shepard and T. Clifton, "Are Longer Hours Reducing Productivity in Manufacturing?"

39. K. Kogi, "Job Content and Working Time."

40. Altman, *Worker Satisfaction and Economic Performance*; Altman, "Economic Theory, Public Policy and the Challenge of Innovative Work Practices."

41. More formally, suppose each type of "leisure" activity is designated by $(L) = L$ $(L1, \ldots L6)$. If C is total consumption spending, then C/L = rate of "consumptivity." Thus, total consumption spending will not fall even with more leisure time if C/L rises proportionally to offset it.

42. Altman, *Worker Satisfaction and Economic Performance*; Altman, "Economic Theory, Public Policy and the Challenge of Innovative Work Practices"; Leibenstein, "Bandwagon, Snob, and Veblen Effects in the Theory of Consumers' Demand"; H. Leibenstein, "The Theory of Underemployment in Densely Populated Backward Areas"; and H. Leibenstein, "Allocative Efficiency vs. 'X-Efficiency.'"

43. Haya Stier and Noah Lewin-Epstein, "Time to Work."

44. See H. Bielinski, G. Bosch, and A. Wagner, *European Work Time Preferences*.

45. D. Hamermesh and S. Trejo, "The Demand for Hours of Labor."

46. Golden, *Comp Time Off Target*.

References

Altman, M. "Economic Theory, Public Policy and the Challenge of Innovative Work Practices." *Economic and Industrial Democracy* 23 (2002): 271–90.

———. *Worker Satisfaction and Economic Performance*. Armonk, NY: M.E. Sharpe Publishers, 2001a.

———. "Preferences and Labor Supply: Casting Some Light into the Black Box of Income-Leisure Choice." *Journal of Socio -Economics* 30 (2001b): 199–219.

———. "New Estimates of Hours of Work and Real Income from the 1880s to 1930: Long Run Trends and Workers' Preferences." *The Review of Income and Wealth*, Series 45 (1999): 353–72.

Atack, J., F. Bateman, and R. Margo. "Productivity in Manufacturing and the Length of the Working Day: Evidence from the 1880 Census of Manufacturers." Working Paper No. 317, Jerome Levy Economics Institute, 2000.

Barnett, R., K. Gareis, and R. Brennan. "Fit as a Mediator of the Relationship Between Work Hours and Burnout." *Journal of Occupational Health Psychology* 4 (1999): 307–17.

Bell, L. "The Incentive to Work Hard: Differences in Black and White Workers' Hours and Preferences." In *Working Time: International Trends, Theory and Policy Perspectives*, ed. L. Golden and D. Figart, 106-26. New York: Routledge, 2001.

Bielinski, H., G. Bosch, and A. Wagner. *Europeans' Work Time Preferences*, European Foundation for the Improvement of Living and Working Conditions, 2002.

Blau, F., M. Ferber, and A. Winkler. *The Economics of Men, Women, and Work.* 4th ed. Upper Saddle River, NJ: Prentice-Hall, 2002.

Bowles, S., and Y. Park. "Emulation, Inequality, and Work Hours: Was Thorsten Veblen Right?" SFI Working Paper #01–10–061 (2001).

Brett, J., and L. Stroh. "Working 61 Plus Hours a Week: Why Do Managers Do It?" Journal of Applied Psychology 88, no.1 (February 2003): 67–78.

Clarkberg, M. "Understanding the Time-Squeeze: Married Couples' Preferred and Actual Work-Hour Strategies." *The American Behavioral Scientist* 44 (2001.): 1115–36.

Contensou, F., and R. Vranceanu. *Working Time: Theory and Policy Implications.* Cheltenham, UK: Edward Elgar, 2000.

Dunn, L.F. "Loss Aversion and Adaptation in the Labor Market: Empirical Indifference Functions and Labor Supply." *Review of Economics and Statistics* 78 (1996): 441–50.

Eastman, W. "Working for Position: Women, Men, and Managerial Work Hours." *Industrial Relations* 37 (1998): 51–66.

Feather, P., and D. Shaw. "The Demand for Leisure Time in the Presence of Constrained Work Hours." *Economic Inquiry* 38 (October 2000): 651–62.

Frank, R.H. *Luxury Fever.* Princeton, NJ: Princeton University Press, 2000.

Galinsky, E., S. Kim, and J.T. Bond. *Feeling Overworked: When Work Becomes Too Much.* New York: Families and Work Institute, 2001.

George, D. "Working Longer Hours: Pressure from the Boss or from Marketers?" *Social Economy* 55, no. 1 (Spring 1997): 33-65.

Golden, L. *Comp Time Off Target*, Economic Policy Institute Briefing Paper, Washington DC, April 2003.

———. "Flexible Work Schedules: What Are Workers Trading Off to Get Them?" *Monthly Labor Review* 124 (2001): 50–67.

———. "The Economics of Worktime Length, Adjustment and Flexibility: Contributions of Three Competing Paradigms." *Review of Social Economy* 54 (1996): 1–44.

Gramm, W. "Labor, Work and Leisure." *Journal of Economic Issues* 21 (1987): 167–88.

Hamermesh, D. "12 Million Salaried Workers Are Missing." *Industrial and Labor Relations Review* 55 (2002): 649–75.

Hamermesh, D., and S. Trejo. "The Demands for Hours of Labor: Direct Evidence from California." *Review of Economics and Statistics* February (2000): 38–47.

Hochschild, A.R. *The Time Bind: When Work Becomes Home and Home Becomes Work.* New York: Metropolitan Books, 1997.

Hout, M., and C. Hanley. "Working Hours and Inequality, 1968–2001: A Family Perspective on Recent Controversies." Survey Research Center, University of California, Berkeley, 2003.

Jacobs J., and K. Gerson. "Who Are the Overworked Americans?" In *Working Time: International Trends, Theory, and Policy Perspectives*, ed. L. Golden and D. Figart, 89–105. New York: Routledge, 2001.

Kahn, S., and K. Lang. "The Causes of Hours Constraints: Evidence from Canada." *Canadian Journal of Economics* 28 (1995): 914–28.

Kaufman, B. "Expanding the Behavioral Foundations of Labor Economics." *Industrial and Labor Relations Review* 52 (1999): 361–92.

Kogi, K. "Job Content and Working Time: The Scope for Joint Change." *Ergonomics* 34 (1991): 757–73.

Landers, R., J. Rebitzer, and L. Taylor. "Rat Race Redux: Adverse Selection in the Determination of Work Hours in Law Firms." *American Economic Review* 86 (1996): 3229–48.

Leibenstein, H. "Bandwagon, Snob, and Veblen Effects in the Theory of Consumers' Demand." *The Quarterly Journal of Economics* 64 (1950): 183–207.

———."The Theory of Underemployment in Densely Populated Backward Areas." In *Economic Backwardness and Economic Growth: Studies in the Theory of Economic Development*, ed. H. Leibenstein, 58–76. New York: John Wiley, 1957.

———. "Allocative Efficiency vs. 'X-Efficiency.'" *American Economic Review* 56 (1966): 392–415.

Major, V.S., K. Klein, and M. Ehrhart. "Work Time, Work Interference With Family, and Psychological Distress." *Journal of Applied Psychology* 87 (2002): 427–36.

Osberg, L. "Understanding Growth and Inequality Trends: The Role of Labour Supply in the U.S.A. and Germany." *Canadian Public Policy* 28 (2002).

Prasch, R. "Reassessing the Labor Supply Curve." *Journal of Economic Issues* 34 (2000): 679–92.

Rebitzer J., and L. Taylor. "Do Labor Markets Provide Enough Short-Hour Jobs? An Analysis of Work Hours and Work Incentives." *Economic Inquiry* 33 (1995): 257–73.

Rima, I. "Involuntary Unemployment and the Re-specified Labor Supply Curve." *Journal of Post Keynesian Economics* 6 (1984): 540–50.

Rothschild, K. "A Note on Some of Economic and Welfare Aspects of Working Time Regulations." *Australian Economic Papers* 21 (1982): 214–18.

Rottenberg, S. "The Regulation of Work Hours and Its Externalities Defenses." *Journal of Labor Research* 16 (1995): 98–109.

Schor, J. *The Overspent American: Upscaling, Downshifting and the New Consumer.* New York: Basic Books, 1999.

Shank, S. "Preferred Hours of Work and Corresponding Earnings." *Monthly Labor Review* 109 (1986): 40–44.

Sharif, M. "Inverted 'S'—The Complete Neoclassical Labor Supply Function." *International Labor Review* 139 (2000): 409–35.

Shepard, E., and T. Clifton. "Are Longer Hours Reducing Productivity in Manufacturing?" *International Journal of Manpower* 21 (2000): 540–53.

Stier, H., and N. Lewin-Epstein. "Time to Work: A Comparative Analysis of Preferences for Working Hours." *Work and Occupations* 30, no. 3 (August 2003): 302–326.

Twitchell, J.B. *Lead Us Into Temptation: The Triumph of American Materialism*. New York: Columbia University Press, 1999.

Wisman, J. "Straightening Out the Backward Bending Supply Curve of Labor: From Overt to Covert Compulsion and Beyond." *Review of Political Economy* 1, no. 1 (March 1989): 94–112.

Yakura E. "Billables: The Valorization of Time in Consulting." *The American Behavioral Scientist* 44, no. 7 (March 2001): 1076–96.

Yaniv, G. "Burnout, Absenteeism, and the Overtime Decision." *Journal of Economic Psychology* (1995): 297–309.

13

Efficient But Not Equitable

The Problem with Using the Law and Economics Paradigm to Interpret Sexual Harassment in the Workplace

Toni Lester

Introduction

While Vivienne Rabidue worked as an administrative assistant at the Osceola Refining Company, one of her coworkers repeatedly called her a "fat ass" and referred to women as "whores" and "cunts."[1] Many of her male coworkers displayed pictures of nude women in their offices. When she complained to management, she was ignored and eventually fired because they said she had an "irascible and opinionated personality . . . [which made it hard for her] to work harmoniously with coworkers and customers."[2]

Rabidue sued her employer for sexual harassment and lost her case on appeal. Judge Krupansky, speaking on behalf of the majority, brushed aside her complaints. "[I]n some work environments, humor and language are rough hewn and vulgar," he said. "Sexual jokes . . . and girlie magazines may abound. Title VII was not meant to—or can—change this."[3] Thus, Rabidue should not have tried to get redress for something she should have known was going to happen. This was fairly predictable behavior for a male-dominated oil refinery. The judge also intimated that Rabidue was not forced to work at the refinery, and if she did not like what she found there, she could have looked elsewhere. He said: "[A] proper assessment . . . [of an harassment claim] would invite consideration of [a variety of factors]," including "the reasonable expectation of the plaintiff upon voluntarily entering that environment."[4]

Harvard sociology professor Orlando Patterson had an equally unsympathetic reaction to Anita Hill's sexual harassment allegations against Supreme Court Justice Clarence Thomas during his Senate confirmation hearings in

1991. Thomas's comments, Patterson argued, were simply a form of "Rabelaisian humor (possibly as a way of affirming their common [African-American and class-based] origins)," which consisted of a misguided "verbal style that carried only minor sanction in one subcultural context [but more severe ramifications when thrown] in the overheated cultural arena of mainstream, neo-Puritan America."[5]

A view similar to Professor Patterson's was held by the district court judge in *Ellison v. Brady*. The plaintiff in that case claimed that she feared a male coworker who had been asking her out for dates and sending her letters expressing a sexual interest in her over a four-month period.[6] The judge called the coworker's conduct "trivial" and ruled for the defendant.[7] Overturning the decision, the Ninth Circuit Court of Appeals said that the lower court judge incorrectly viewed the harasser as "a modern-day Cyrano de Bergerac wishing no more than to woo [the plaintiff] with his words"[8] At their worst then, in both the judge's and Professor Patterson's minds, Clarence Thomas's alleged words, and the harasser's letters in *Ellison*, were simply awkward yet innocent attempts at courtship or camaraderie.

This type of thinking reflects one of the basic premises of free market theory—that people are rational wealth maximizers who should be allowed to weigh the costs and benefits of their actions without having to worry about government or judicial intervention. Someone arguing from this perspective might say that male workers who direct unwanted sex-based verbal remarks at their female colleagues are rationally trying to maximize their prospects for friendship or sex. Moreover, firms who refuse to prevent such remarks are merely trying to appease the harassers because the costs of doing otherwise would be prohibitively high.

Thus, if a woman is offended or intimidated by this behavior, all she has to do is choose the course of action that brings her the biggest net gain. She can stay if she thinks her salary and other job-related benefits are greater than the costs of being offended or intimidated by the harasser, or she can find a new job where the harassment is less severe or nonexistent. Such views are also representative of the more conservative arm of the law and economics movement associated with people like federal court judge Richard Posner and law scholars Richard Epstein and Marie Reilly. I believe, however, that the law and economics paradigm does not provide an adequate analytical lens through which the problem of sexual harassment can be viewed. While it may be helpful in explaining some of the reasons why sexual harassment takes place, it neglects to address other important ones.

Those reasons have to do with the inherent power imbalance that exists between men and women in society and the desire that some heterosexual men in particular have to reinforce that dynamic in the workplace. They also have to do with the fact that harassment victims often lack meaningful choice with respect to more palatable job opportunities at commensurate skill and salary levels. Trying to find new employment can be reasonably costly at a time when victims are most vulnerable. These reasons have been addressed directly by feminist scholars and implicitly by the late philosopher John Rawls, especially in his writings about distributive justice. Any analytical model that interprets sexual harassment is therefore incomplete unless it incorporates these ideas.

Throughout this chapter, I refer to women as the harassment victims and men as the harassers. This is because numerous studies show that women are by far the most common targets of harassment.[9] It is important to note that harassment can and often does occur between people of the same sex. Much of that harassment is motivated by homophobia. Before 1998, however, most federal courts refused to consider harassment claims brought by gay employees. These courts concluded that gay men and lesbians were not entitled to Title VII's protections because, in their view, Title VII was designed to stop certain overt forms of misogyny, but not homophobia.[10] Eventually the Supreme Court ruled in the 1998 case *Oncale v. Sundowner* that Title VII should also be interpreted to prohibit same-sex harassment, as long as claimants could prove that the harassment took place "because of their sex."[11] Unfortunately, many lower courts have interpreted *Oncale* in a manner that still precludes gay harassment victims from suing, while at the same time allowing heterosexual claimants to sue their same sex harassers.

This chapter will focus only on examples of heterosexual male to female harassment, although I believe that most of its conclusions can be applied to any victim of harassment who is marginalized at work, and because of their social status, by the society at large. This would be especially true where group membership produces the same kind of unequal power relations and lack of choice that I will discuss below in the section titled "A Feminist Critique of the Law and Economics Paradigm." Thus, for instance, gay men, lesbians, the transgendered, and racial and ethnic minorities subjected to harassment in majority heterosexual or white work environments, respectively, should be covered by my analysis.

In order to support my assertions, I will show how sexual harassment can be viewed from the perspective of free market theory, with a particular emphasis on rational decisionmaking and cost-benefit analysis. Most law and economics writers talk about how their analysis can be used to interpret torts, contracts, Title VII discrimination in general, or crimes, but few have engaged in any in-depth analysis of sexual harassment. This article will address the implications of what these writers have said about the other mentioned topics for sexual harassment law. The law and economics paradigm will then be critiqued from the perspective of feminist theory, including a feminist reading of the work of John Rawls.

In the first section of the chapter, I discuss what sexual harassment is and briefly look at relevant statutory law, government guidelines, and Supreme Court rulings in this area. In the second section, titled "Using the Law and Economics Paradigm to Interpret Sexual Harassment," I will use the law and economics paradigm to explain why harassment takes place and why its targets respond to it in the ways they do. In the third section, titled "A Feminist Critique of the Law and Economics Paradigm," I will critique this explanation. Here, I will argue that while sexual harassment may be efficient in a neoclassical economic sense, it is not equitable in a feminist or Rawlsian sense. In the forth section, titled "Differing Perspectives on How the Problem of Sexual Harassment Can Be Solved," I will discuss proposals made by some proponents of the law and economics paradigm to eliminate or drastically reduce government regulation of sex discrimination and, by implication, sexual harassment. This section will also contain my assessment of how feminist theory and feminist interpretations of Rawls can offer viable alternative solutions to the free market approach. It should not be surprising that, at a minimum, most feminists and Rawlsians would preserve government regulation. Some, including myself, would even strengthen it.

Sexual Harassment Law

Statutory Law and Government Guidelines

Title VII of the Civil Rights Act of 1964 prohibits discrimination based on sex, race, color, religion, and national origin in employment.[12] The law was passed against the backdrop of the turbulent Civil Rights Movement of the 1960s, a movement largely associated with the advancement of rights for previously enslaved and oppressed African Americans. It is by now a famous story that a southern senator added the word "sex" to the proposed civil rights bill, hoping to stymie its passage. The senator believed that his peers would be so outraged by this that they would vote down the entire bill. The senator's calculations proved wrong, however, and workplaces across the country have not been the same since.[13]

Given this less-than-stellar start for the rights of working women, it should come as no surprise that for almost thirty years a mostly male judiciary did not make it easy for women to achieve the full promise of Title VII. This was especially true in the area of sexual harassment litigation. The fact is that Title VII never mentions the words "sexual harassment" and courts for many years refused to hold in favor of harassment victims who sought redress under the law.[14] It took the U.S. Supreme Court from 1964 until 1986 to finally say that sexual harassment was prohibited by Title VII, and that was only after the Equal Employment Opportunity Commission (EEOC), the government agency that enforces Title VII, adopted guidelines to that effect in 1980.

The EEOC guidelines say that sexual harassment occurs whenever (1) a supervisor demands sex from a subordinate in return for a job benefit (i.e., "quid pro quo harassment"), or (2) a coworker or supervisor engages in unwelcome conduct of sexual nature that "has the purpose or effect of unreasonably interfering with an individual's work performance or creating an intimidating, hostile, or offensive working environment" (i.e., "hostile work environment harassment").[15] Three key cases in which the Supreme Court took up these issues are *Meritor Bank v. Vinson* (1986), *Harris v. Forklift* (1993), and *Oncale v. Sundowner* (1998).

The Meritor, Harris, and Oncale Decisions

In *Meritor*, the plaintiff alleged that she was the victim of hostile environment harassment because she was forced to have sex with her supervisor. First the Court endorsed the notion that quid pro quo harassment is illegal under Title VII, but then found that the supervisor did not commit quid pro quo harassment because he did not overtly tie his requests for sex to any specific job benefit or detriment.[16] The Court did, however, find that the plaintiff's hostile environment claims had merit because she showed that the harassment was "sufficiently severe or persuasive to alter the conditions of [the victim's] employment and create an abusive working environment."[17]

The second time the Supreme Court addressed the issue of hostile environment sexual harassment was in the *Harris* case. Harris alleged that her former boss, the owner of the company she worked for, sexually harassed her by making inappropriate sexually-charged comments to and about her on a regular basis.[18] Some of the owner's comments included calling her a "dumb ass woman" and saying, "you're a woman; what do you know?"[19] Reversing the lower court's findings that Harris had to prove that she suffered severe psychological harm in order to win her case, the Court said that "[s]o long as the environment would reasonably be perceived, and is perceived, as hostile or abusive . . . there is no need for it also to be psychologically injurious."[20]

Finally, in the *Oncale* case, the Supreme Court decided for the first time that same sex harassment is a prohibited form of sex discrimination under Title VII. It overturned a lower court decision that refused to allow a male plaintiff, who had been taunted and threatened with rape by his male coworkers, to have his day in court.[21] "As we emphasized in *Meritor* and *Harris*," the Court said, "the prohibition of harassment on the basis of sex requires neither asexuality nor androgyny in the workplace, it forbids only behavior so objectively offensive as to alter the conditions of employment."[22] However, as I have written elsewhere, most post-*Oncale* lower courts believe that the Supreme Court's required "because of sex" standard described earlier, still only allows heterosexual, not gay or lesbian, harassment victims to sue.[23]

Using the Law and Economics Paradigm to Interpret Sexual Harassment

Law and economics proponents believe that the principles and methods used in economic analysis can be used to study both how laws get promulgated and the extent to which laws actually influence individual decisionmaking and behavior. One person who has been widely influential in this area is federal court judge Richard Posner. He believes "the exclusive goal of legal policy is economic efficiency, and that legal policies that cannot be justified on efficiency grounds are . . . inferior or at least unscientific."[24]

People like Posner are heavily influenced by the works of eighteenth century utilitarian thinker Jeremy Bentham and economics philosopher Adam Smith. Bentham believed that an action is "good" as long as it maximizes the pleasure (or minimizes the pain) of the person affected by it, and an action is good for society as a whole if it maximizes the pleasure of most of the people in society affected by it.[25] Smith, in turn, said that the free market, as manifested by what people spend their money on and what they decide to contract for, is the best place to look to determine what brings people the most pleasure. It is in the free market that Smith's "invisible hand" of economics is able to work its magic, with "economic actors [determining] . . . the way resources are to be allocated by 'voting' with their dollars."[26] Thus, what we spend our money on is a proxy for what brings us pleasure.

In order for the market to be truly free and generate efficient outcomes, however, certain conditions must be present. Those conditions relevant to the discussion at hand are that the parties to a transaction (1) have perfect, costless information about its nature and consequences and are aware of all the relative alternatives; (2) are rational maximizers of their own ends; and (3) are capable of choosing appropriate means to those ends. While free-market economists realize that these conditions will never be completely present in any given transaction, they do believe that they can be used to make fairly accurate predictions about how people will act.[27] Some law and economics writers have explored the above three conditions from the perspective of contract law; others have looked at them from the perspective of tort law. Relevant aspects of each of these two areas of law will be discussed throughout this chapter.

Perfect Information

So when do parties to a transaction have enough information to make it "perfect information" within the context of free market economics? Traditional contract law principles provide a useful framework for answering this question, because they were designed "to enforce efficient exchanges and to deny enforcement to other types of deals."[28] A contract can only be enforced if both parties understand the nature and consequences of the contract. For example, when someone defrauds another party (i.e., lies about or omits to reveal a relevant fact), the defrauded party is deemed to lack the level of information necessary to enter into the transaction. The defrauded party thus has the option of rescinding the contract and possibly suing for damages.[29]

Normally, however, unless they are asked a specific question about a fact that is relevant to the transaction at hand, neither side has a duty to disclose everything that they know during a negotiation.[30] In fact, each side has a responsibility to know about things that are obvious.[31] In such cases, if someone does not fulfill his responsibility, they will not be able to rescind the contract or sue for damages on the grounds that they were defrauded. Parallels to these contract law principles exist in Judge Krupansky's decision in the *Rabidue* case.

When the judge says that common knowledge dictates that rough humor and language would be present there, he is saying that it should have been obvious to Vivienne Rabidue that she would be harassed at the refinery. Thus, he believes that Rabidue had enough information to make a decision about whether or not she would take a job with the company. This view also presumes that there was no duty on the part of the company to provide her with that information. It also implies that had she decided after the fact to look for another job, she would have known that there would be "less harassment at those jobs [only] after [having] been at her present job . . . long enough to realize" what she faced.[32]

So far I have been talking about how the requirement for perfect information relates to the level of information that would be considered sufficient from the perspective of a female job applicant. But what about the employer's need for information about the applicant's qualifications, and how does the presence or lack of such information relate to sexual harassment?

It has been argued by some law and economics writers that if an employer has to choose between a white job applicant and a more qualified black job applicant, the employer would be justified in picking the white applicant because blacks as a group are believed to be statistically less productive than whites, and it would be unduly costly to make the employer have to research the qualifications of that particular black applicant. This form of discrimination is called "statistical discrimination."[33] Posner thinks statistical discrimination is justified.[34]

The same rationale has been used to explain and justify sex discrimination. According to this perspective, employers should be able to discriminate against women because women have the capacity to get pregnant and therefore tend to have higher turnover rates and take more sick leave than men.[35] Thus, women are less reliable, less productive, and more costly than men. Rather than having to do costly research on a case-by-case basis to determine if an individual female applicant actually plans not to get pregnant, it is much more efficient for employers to assume that *all* women applicants will get pregnant, in the same manner that it is efficient for them to assume that all black applicants are unqualified.[36]

The type of race and sex stereotyping inherent in statistical discrimination is not a valid defense to a discrimination claim under Title VII, but Posner thinks that it should be. "To the extent that race or some attribute similarly difficult to conceal (sex, accent, etc.) is positively correlated with desired characteristics," he says, "it is rational for people to use the attribute as a proxy for the underlying characteristic with which it correlated."[37]

Taking Posner's point one step further, it could be argued that sexual harassment happens when an employer decides to forego statistical discrimination against a female applicant, despite its misgivings about her. The employer can offset the costs of the woman's perceived lower productivity and reliability by allowing its male employees to harass her. This may be a conscious or unconscious decision, but the result is the same. I will elaborate more below on why the law and economics paradigm leads me to this conclusion. I should also note that it essentially justifies harassment, with which I strongly disagree. The third section of this chapter, "A Feminist Critique of the Law and Economics Paradigm," will contain my analysis of this point and other aspects of this perspective.

Rationality

Free market economic theory presumes that "human beings are rational; [and that] whatever they do is in their best interest, given their tastes, market opportunities, and circumstances."[38] The underlying assumption is that "everyone is doing as best he can . . . which, by definition, is 'good' for him."[39] Furthermore, "[a] corollary to the premise that benefit or loss reflects individual preferences is the notion that, at least at the outset of the inquiry, no conduct is inherently good or bad."[40] Thus, laissez-faire economics makes no moral judgments about the particular anathema tastes of certain kinds of individuals.

As Professor David Lyons has so kindly pointed out to me, John Stuart Mill, Bentham's disciple, did try to address the extent to which moral considerations should be tied to a person's quest for personal pleasure or happiness.[41] As D.G. Brown has said in a collection of essays edited by Lyons, Mill believed the following:

> When the agent considers his moral situation, the same principle continues to direct him to promote happiness, only the incidence of pleasure and pain is more widely surveyed, so as to take in the pleasures and pains of others on exactly the same terms. The transition, in this sense, from self to others is smoothed out to the point of invisibility, by the idea that pleasure, and the absence of pain regardless of whose, are in themselves simply desirable, and therefore ends (anyone's) rational action.[42]

Conservative law and economics scholars, however, tend to ignore this strain of utilitarian thought, and believe that moral factors should be treated as separate and distinct from efficiency concerns.

Rationality from Employer's and Harasser's Perspective

Is it "rational" in an economic sense when a male coworker harasses a female worker or when a supervisor harasses a female subordinate? Is it rational when a company decides to condone or ignore harassment? Apparently "yes," at least some of the time. To address these two answers in more depth, it is first necessary to talk about why labor economists believe that employment discrimination generally takes place. They believe that employment discrimination occurs because either (1) as I said earlier, companies have less than perfect information about individual women or minority applicants, and it would be too costly for them to get it; (2) employers, coworkers, or customers have an aversion to associating with women or minorities within a given job; or (3) members of the dominant or majority group want to make themselves better off at the expense of nondominant or minority group members.[43]

Gary Becker, in his seminal work *The Economics of Discrimination*, explains that people and firms have "tastes for discrimination" when they act like they are willing to pay something, either directly or in form of reduced income, to be associated with some persons instead of others. Because of this aversion to associate with nongroup members like blacks or women, group members incur "non-pecuniary, psychic costs" if they are forced to associate with nongroup members.[44] Also, because psychic costs actually have nothing to do with the productivity of African Americans or women, Becker says such an aversion lacks objectivity.[45]

Building on Becker's work, John Donohue has argued that if a company refuses to hire minorities or women whose marginal value is greater than their marginal cost, the company ultimately will be driven out of the market by other nondiscriminatory firms who refuse to discriminate in this manner. Because discrimination is essentially inefficient, Donohue contends, Title VII is an effective means of accelerating the market penalty on discriminating firms.[46]

Judge Posner, however, has chastised Donohue for neglecting to address the fact that the administration and enforcement of Title VII creates an additional cost for society that would not exist if the market were left to its own devices. In his opinion, Title VII produces a net loss to society that is not offset by the net gains experienced by individuals who are harmed by discrimination.[47] As I mentioned earlier, Posner also contends that because statistical discrimination is justifiable, the government should allow it to take place.

Usually statistical discrimination is only discussed in the context of disparate treatment in hiring, but it can also account for such posthiring conditions as lower salaries for women and the tendency for companies to put women in nonmanagerial positions.[48] Statistical discrimination thus holds important implications for sexual harassment, which, as has been noted by the Supreme Court, is an unreasonable altercation of a victim's posthiring terms and conditions of employment.[49]

For example, Judge Posner says that discussions about sex more appropriately lend themselves to a "bioeconomic" analysis, as opposed to a purely commercial one. Echoing comments made by Orlando Patterson and the district court judge in the *Ellison* case, he maintains that many men engage in sexually aggressive behavior at work in order to maximize their chances of getting a date.[50] Although Posner uses the term "harassment" without defining it, I am assuming that he considers the following types of conduct to fall within the range of possible date maximizing behaviors: (1) sexual teasing, jokes, remarks, or questions; (2) pressure for dates; or (3) suggestive letters and phone calls. All of these categories are taken from three of the most definitive studies on sexual harassment, which were conducted by the United States Merit Protections Board in 1981, 1988, and 1995. The first category, sexual teasing, was the most common form of harassment reported by female respondents in the 1995 study. The second category, pressures for dates, was the second most common form.[51] It should be noted that, contrary to what Posner thinks, there is very little actual research that indicates that most harassment is motivated by a desire to develop romantic relationships.[52]

Increased regulation of harassment, Posner warns, can thwart the efforts of men to get dates and could ultimately hurt both men and women looking to form romantic attachments at work.[53] Thus, in the tradition of judges who decided harassment cases in the early years of Title VII, Posner seems to think that the most common forms of harassment should be treated as private matters best resolved by the individual men and women involved. Following this logic, it could be argued that enhanced male manager and coworker prospects for dates or sexual gratification brought on by harassment simply increases the "psychic" wealth of male employees. This in turn translates into pecuniary gains for employers, because increased male worker morale could contribute to increased productivity. Thus, employers who allow harassment to occur are simply engaging in rational economic behavior because harassment helps offset the costs of hiring women who are expected to be less productive based on statistical discrimination. Taking this argument further, policing male employees would just increase the cost of hiring women, further discouraging such hires.

If my above analysis strikes some as a *reductio ad absurdum*, this is the very point I am trying to achieve. Law scholar Derrick Bell has used a similar technique to talk about the dangers of taking Richard Posner's and David Strauss's proposals to abolish Title VII to their logical conclusion. Bell argues that they can be read as advocating the creation of a licensing program that allows employers to buy permits to discriminate against blacks.[54]

The scandal at Astra, USA, in the 1990s is a case in point. In the largest settlement of a sexual harassment lawsuit ever at that time, Astra, a U.S. subsidiary of a Swedish drug manufacturer, agreed to pay $10 million to female employees who alleged that the company failed to prevent them from being subject to hostile environment harassment. They accused the president of the company of replacing mothers and older female employees with younger, single women so that the company executives could have access to sex with those women. The EEOC found that "at the initial training classes female employees were told that their performance evaluation depended upon their . . . socialization with senior management." [55]

Another reason why harassment against women occurs is that many men want to reinforce their feelings of male superiority by trying to subordinate women in the workplace. This could be because they fear that women are encroaching on their long-standing male monopolies in certain job sectors the same way that white males have felt threatened by African Americans in certain industries.[56] Furthermore, some sociologists believe that ideology is just as closely linked to intergroup intolerance as economic fear. With respect to white racism against African Americans, "even those whites who are unaware of the benefits they may receive act in accord with their self-interest, since they may adhere to a racial ideology shaped by interests of earlier generations of whites."[57]

Thus, many men harass women because they hold stereotypical notions about the role that women should play in society, and they want women to conform to that ideology.[58] These anxieties can only be placated if employers refuse to hire women altogether or assign them lower status or lower paying jobs. According to John Donahue and James Heckman, such an approach has been used by some employers, who get "positive utility from workers of a given racial group, if this conduct serves to brand the nonpreferred race as inferior."[59]

However, even when employers pay women less or assign them to low status jobs, this is still not enough for some men. In such cases they will try to reduce the psychic cost of having their sense of superiority over women threatened by engaging in the tactic of subordination. Basically, they will try to devalue women whenever they can because it makes them feel better about themselves. One of the most effective ways to make a woman feel devaluated at work is to treat her like a sex object.

Furthermore, because some white men have a desire to subordinate both women and African Americans in the workplace, this line of reasoning can be used to explain why a disproportionate amount of sexual harassment claims are brought by African American women.[60] Presumably, the net psychic gain to such men doubles when a black woman is the target of their overtures. This seems to have been the case in *Brooms v. Regal Tube*, where a white male supervisor harassed an African American industrial nurse by subjecting her to a combination of racial slurs and sexual vulgarities, including showing her racist pornographic pictures involving bestiality.[61] In doing so, the supervisor was able to make the nurse feel demeaned both as a black and as a woman.

The above perspective can also be used to explain—and some law and economics advocates even think justify—why so much harassment went unchecked before the sexual harassment laws were promulgated, and still does go unchecked despite the presence of those laws. A harasser, for example, may decide that the potential cost associated with getting reprimanded or fired for harassing someone are low, when compared to the psychic benefits he gains from being a harasser. On the other hand, an employer may believe that the costs of losing a harassment suit are low in contrast to the benefits it accrues for ignoring the harassment. This includes, in addition to the enhanced productivity benefits discussed earlier, an elimination of the costs associated with taking disciplinary action against employee-harassers, like the costs of defending a slander or wrongful discharge lawsuit brought by that person.

Gary Becker made similar findings about why people break our criminal laws. This occurs, he says, "not because their basic motivation differs from that of other persons, but because their benefits and costs differ."[62] Furthermore, there is a direct relationship between the number of crimes a person will commit and his or her likelihood of conviction and punishment.[63] Thus, according to Becker, people engage in criminal behavior when their expected utility is greater than the utility they can derive from legal activities.

Rationality from the Harassment Victim's Perspective

What about the harassment victim? Is it rational from an economic perspective for a woman to take a job where she knows she might be harassed or stay at one where she is already being harassed? Apparently Judge Krupansky thought it was rational for Vivienne Rabidue to do so. By arguing that most people would know that oil refineries are hotbeds of vulgar language, the judge suggests that Rabidue weighed the potential profit she would gain from her new salary against the potential psychological loss she might incur because of that language. She therefore concluded that the benefits of taking the job would be greater than the losses from the harassment. Under traditional tort law, such a plaintiff would be deemed to have "assumed the risk" of the injury in this situation and would not be able to recover damages from the tort-feasor. A similar conclusion was reached in *Barnes v. Train*, where the trial court judge ruled against a harassment plaintiff because it said she was fully aware of the employment climate when she went back to work.[64]

Female waitresses suing the Hooters restaurant chain in the 1990s faced similar arguments from the company that the women knew what they were getting into when they took their jobs. Some restaurants in the chain had signs saying things like, Men: No Shirt, No Shoes: No Service. Women No Shirt: Free Food.[65] The company argued that the waitresses assumed the risk that they would be touched and propositioned by male customers because they knew that the chain displayed this type of promotional material.

Of course, a woman like Vivienne Rabidue also might simply like the idea that she could get sex-based attention from her male coworkers and supervisors, perhaps because she thinks it will increase her prospects for sex. In fact, there have been numerous articles in the media lately about how work is fast becoming the only place for people to form romantic relationships. It is also possible that such a woman would not be offended or negatively affected by the conduct that took place at the Osceola Refining Company. In that case, she would be neutral toward the risk of encountering such behavior.

Free Choice

R.H. Coase, in his landmark article "The Problem of Social Cost," asserts that private individuals may have the ability to negotiate efficient compromise solutions without the need for government intervention. Coase says, however, that an ability to negotiate should be predicated on several factors, among them that both parties have equal bargaining power and that neither side has been forced to enter the transaction.[66] Again, we can look to traditional contract law to help us determine what types of conduct an economist would consider an unacceptable interference with someone's free contractual choice.

Under traditional contract law, force is usually equated with duress. Duress is defined as "conduct of a *coercive* nature," and typically entails such wrongful acts as physical threats, blackmail, or extortion.[67] Because "economic need is generally not sufficient to constitute duress," courts are reluctant to find that prospective job applicants are under duress when they agree to take a job.[68] As Richard Epstein has said:

> Markets offer a radical contrast [to force], for . . . each person now need look only to the other tail of the distribution—the people who make the best offers. . . . The victim of discrimination, unlike the victim of force, keeps his initial set entitlements—life, limb, and possession—even if he does not realize the gains from trade with a particular person.[69]

Judge Krupansky clearly thinks that this was the case when Vivienne Rabidue decided to work for the refinery. He says that a "proper assessment . . . [of a harassment claim] would invite consideration of [such factors as] . . . the reasonable expectation of the plaintiff upon *voluntarily* entering that environment."[70] This implies that had Rabidue decided to look for another job, she would have had "alternative employment opportunities (at *slightly* discounted wage) open to [her]."[71]

Richard Epstein would probably agree with Judge's Krupansky. He has complained that the type of government regulation embodied in our employment discrimination laws is "the antithesis of freedom of contract, a principle that allows all persons to do business with whomever they please for a good reason, bad reason, or no reason at all."[72] As is the case under traditional contract law, which does not provide a remedy where one person refuses to deal with another person, he says, "[s]o, too, when the contractual terms differ by race or sex it is a private matter. Those who believe . . . that they are worth more than they have been offered can search elsewhere."[73] Thus, if a woman thinks that she is worth more than the hostile and intimidating work environment that she enters, I suspect that Epstein would say that all she has to do is look for another place to work.

Free market theorists are conspicuously silent when it comes to making moral pronouncements about the reasons why people discriminate and the impact that discrimination has on its targets. The focus is almost exclusively on the right of individuals to maximize their wealth and well-being and the way that such behavior, best left unencumbered by the government restrictions, promotes market efficiency. As John Stuart Mill once said about Jeremy Bentham's utilitarian views, "the morality of actions depends on the consequence which they tend to produce, is the doctrine of rational persons of all schools; that the good or evil of those consequences is measured solely by pleasure or pain is all of the doctrine of the school of utility."[74]

Thus, people like Donahue and Heckman, for all their efforts to find a justification for Title VII, focus solely on whether or not the taste for discrimination leads to the furthering or diminishing of efficiently functioning markets. And when talking about race discrimination, Posner simply remarks, "[i]t might . . . be the case that the costs to whites being forced to associate with blacks are morally unworthy of consideration in the formulation of public policy. . . . But that should not be an *efficiency* justification in the wealth-maximization sense."[75]

Marie Reilly is even blunter about her disdain for making moral pronouncements about the pros and cons of efficiency. In her mind, regardless of the reasons why harassment occurs, the costs to women who are the targets of harassment should be given no more weight than the costs to men who have to refrain from it.[76] She would treat the harasser's desire to subordinate and demean as just another valid form of rational, utilitarian consumption.

As has been discussed above, those associated with the more conservative arm of the law and economics movement take a decidedly indifferent stance about the ethical implications of sexual harassment. Feminists argue, however, that this approach incorrectly frames the important issues and creates a dangerous moral vacuum in which women would be forever relegated to the low status, low paying, sexually hostile working conditions of the past and, in many instances, the present.

A Feminist Critique of the Law and Economics Paradigm

One of the basic premises of the feminist theory is that society is patriarchal because women are generally subordinate to men in a variety of contexts.[77] Furthermore, as social and political theorists have argued, "[o]ne of the prerogatives of the dominant class is that it gets to define what is real and what is good."[78] Feminists see the legal system as just one of many places where men have traditionally tried to justify their domination of women.[79] Critical race theorists have rightly argued, however, that white feminists have not always adequately addressed the important connection between racism, class, and sexism, especially as it relates to the privileged status that many white women legally, historically, politically, and socially, have occupied with respect to women of color.[80] Thus, for example, women of color can be the victims of both racial *and* sexual harassment, something made clear in the *Brooms* case discussed earlier. Also, many victims of *racial* harassment are men.[81] Furthermore, because of the dubious economic and social status they have occupied in this society, men of color who are accused of sexual harassment may face a higher level of scrutiny than their white male counterparts.[82]

Furthermore, in addition to heterosexually-based sexual harassment, there is harassment triggered by homophobic animus or religious intolerance.[83] I would ask that feminists and critical race theorists also examine the interlocking systems of domination that relate to class, race, sex, *and* able-bodied and religious intolerance, as well as homophobia. The focus of my inquiry, at least for the present, however, is on the ways that men, whatever their dominant or nondominant group status, engage in the harassment of women. I do recognize that this is a complicated issue involving a myriad of potential interpretations. To that extent then, my analysis here is incomplete. But I suggest that most of the arguments I make later for the adoption of a reasonable woman legal standard, could be extended to any member of a nondominant group who is the object of harassment. This standard has been called by a variety of scholars, the "reasonable victim" standard.

Feminists have many different ways of explaining why women have been treated less favorably than men in the courts. For example, "relational" or "cultural" feminists like Carol Gilligan say that men and women have very different moral perspectives. Men focus on abstract rules and rights, while women focus on an "ethic of care" that emphasizes relationships, concern for others, and responsibility.[84] Relational Feminists think that women's capacity for connectedness has been devalued in our culture and in the courts. Instead, they want the courts to celebrate that capacity.

"Radical feminists," according to legal scholar Robin West, believe that female connectedness should not be celebrated because it is that same attribute, especially as it relates to sex and pregnancy, that lies at the heart of women's subordination to men.[85] Radical feminism is associated with people like legal scholar Catherine Mackinnon, who has said that gender discrimination is based on the systematic social subordination of women and is not simply the result of irrational behavior.[86] "Postmodern feminists," on the other hand, reject the type of essentialist thinking inherent in relational feminism, and in contrast to radical feminists, believe that there is no single oppression of women, but only solutions tailored to the concrete experience of actual people. Regardless of their differing perspectives on the reasons why women are subordinated to men, most feminists agree that the law has a pivotal role to play in addressing the comprehensive bias against women that has been built into the legal system.[87] Thus, bias against women in the workplace is one area that feminists have sought to correct. I will discuss now a feminist perspective on perfect information, rationality, and free choice in markets as they relate to sexual harassment, and then discuss the feminist approach that supports the "reasonable woman test."

Perfect Information

Harassment victims "often have far from perfect information about a workplace, few viable alternatives, and there are high costs to switching" jobs.[88] To place those costs on the same level as the costs to male workers who refrain from harassment or the costs to employers who have to prevent it is extremely shortsighted. For example, the problem with the free market assumption that women have sufficient information about whether or not a prospective work environment will be particularly hostile to them is that (1) women usually do not have sufficient access to this type of information; (2) efforts to obtain such information would be unduly costly to them; and (3) assuming they could obtain the information at a nominal cost, most women do not have viable access to alternative job opportunities.

As I said above, most women have no way of knowing that they are about to enter a hostile work environment. This is because many companies handle internal harassment complaints confidentially, often leaving no public record that any problem took place. One of the reasons this occurs is because employers fear that if word gets out, a disgruntled harasser or harassment victim could sue them for slander. Such lawsuits are actually on the rise.[89] Also, other employees who know about the harassment may fear that they could be sued for slander if they were to tell anyone.

Many companies also choose to handle harassment cases informally, which can result in the absence of a record trail about problematic incidents.[90] One reason an employer might handle a complaint informally is because the company is so insensitive to a particular women's concerns that it refuses to give her the due that a formal process connotes.[91] Another reason a business might do so is because it is following the advice of the leading management consultants in this area, who recommend that companies honor a victim's requests to hold her complaints in confidence. While many consultants suggest that companies try to encourage the victim to seek redress through a formal fact-finding process, they also caution that "this option should not be pursued against her wishes."[92] Finally, it is widely known by trial attorneys that most companies choose to settle harassment lawsuits out of court, preferring to escape having their internal problems aired in public. Settlements usually require both litigants to remain quiet about the nature of the dispute. Additionally, victims are often reluctant to speak out because they do not want to be known as troublemakers.

Whatever the reasons are for why or how a company holds information about harassment close to its chest, the result is the same—a woman can end up taking a job where she unknowingly finds herself placed side by side with someone who has a track record of harassing other women. As has just been established, the probability of such a woman being able to get this type of information on her own, short of hiring a private investigator or enticing someone to risk a slander suit, is very low. Thus, from a purely economic perspective, any attempt to get this type or information would be unreasonably costly to her.

Rationality and Free Choice

Perhaps free market proponents would respond to my complaints by saying that women can sidestep these cost constraints by engaging in their own version of statistical discrimination. Using a perverse kind of logic, one could argue that because numerous studies show that sexual harassment is pervasive all around the world,[93] women can simply assume that there is a strong chance that they will be subjected to some form of harassment wherever they end up working. Armed with this knowledge, many women could simply choose to stay out of the workforce altogether, in the same way that a company refuses to hire individual women and minority applicants because it holds stereotypical assumptions about women and minorities as a group.

Presumably, Posner and Epstein would think that such decisions are justified because it is more efficient to make assumptions about the unreliability of individual women or minority applicants (in the case of employers) and potentially harassing environments at individual companies (in the case of female applicants) by equating both with perceived group norms. The main problem with employer statistical discrimination, however, is that while it may be efficient, it is a morally indefensible form of oppression. As University of Washington philosophy professor Kenneth Clatterbaugh has said, oppression "affect[s] individuals regardless of their character, merit, or moral standing. Oppression issues blanket judgments, often grounded in stereotypes, through which individuals are treated as a type rather than as an individual."[94]

The same can be said about a market that is indifferent to a woman who, based on her reliance on statistical evidence about harassment in general, supposedly "chooses" not to work for a particular company. This indifference merely helps perpetuate the type of gender-based job segregation that may be good for wealth-maximizing firms and their male employees, but is bad for women. As Yale law scholar Edward McCaffery has said:

> By focusing only on firms, on the institutional or demand side of the market, where he finds no monopoly power or irrational behavior, Epstein fails to see that individuals, on the supply side, are not being allowed to optimize, to pursue their vision of the good life as best as their endowments might allow. Where individuals are blocked by market failures from pursuing their life plans, efficiency talk loses much of its normative appeal.[95]

Of course, this may be the very result that free market proponents are hoping to achieve—a return to the days when women, or at least white middle-class women, were expected to stay at home, and minorities and working class members of both sexes were systematically relegated to low status, low paying jobs.

There is one last point I would like to make here. Even if a woman knows that harassment is common in a particular company, this should not be held against her later on grounds that she assumed the risk because she has the requisite information when she decided to work for that company. There are a wide variety of reasons why a woman might take a job where a work environment might be sexually hostile to her. The most obvious one is economic need. This human need should not, as the late writer and poet Audre Lorde once said, give way to a narrow definition of profit or gain.[96] The desire to subordinate or sex-stereotype should not be viewed as just another acceptable form of rational wealth-maximizing behavior best left to flourish in an unregulated market.

Furthermore, this type of thinking runs "the risk of reinforcing the prevailing level of discrimination. Harassers could continue to harass merely because a particular discriminatory practice was common, and victims of harassment would have no remedy."[97] The judge in *Robinson v. Jacksonville Shipyards* makes a similar objection: "A pre-existing atmosphere that deters women from entering or continuing in a profession or job is no less destructive to and offensive to workplace equality than a sign declaring 'Men Only.'"[98] Indeed, these are the very signs that the law should dismantle.

Mary Becker says that "racism and misogyny are deeply irrational emotions, based on hatred or a lack of empathy for 'the other,' often accompanied by the need to establish one's own importance by denying others' humanity."[99] The psychic gain that a misogynistic harasser might experience, or the net gain that an employer might incur by facilitating that experience, should never be given the same weight as the impact that the conduct has on its target.

Harassment, whether it consists of an outright physical assault, vulgar remarks, or requests for sex, can make a woman feel vulnerable, depressed, cause her to exhibit stress-related symptoms, seek counseling, and even quit her job in order to avoid it. Even Posner has recognized that harassment can be problematic for female employees because women are often afraid to complain for fear of jeopardizing their jobs.[100]

In one study of women harassment victims, "virtually all reported debilitating stress reactions affecting work performance and attitudes, psychological health, and physical health. The physical symptoms frequently reported . . . include[d] gastrointestinal disturbance, jaw tightness . . . headaches, inability to sleep, tiredness, nausea, loss of appetite, weight loss and crying spells."[101] Sometimes the harassment can be so troublesome that, as the *1995 Merit Report* indicated, many workers end up taking leave without pay in order to cope with it. Researchers in that report estimate that federal workers lost $4.4 million in wages from 1994 to 1995 alone because of unpaid leave taken in response to harassment.[102]

Furthermore, much of the sexual harassment that takes places in the workplace is the result of unequal gender-based power dynamics. As feminist law scholar Catherine MacKinnon says, "The presumption that sexual pressure in contexts of unequal power is an isolated idiosyncrasy to unique individual victims has been undermined both by the . . . [statistics] and by [the breakdown of these cases] by gender."[103] It is therefore unrealistic to rely upon the market to counteract these dynamics in any meaningful way, because, as Gary Becker has shown, many people will pursue their irrational tastes for discrimination even when it means they will incur a monetary loss.[104] Their psychic gain is so strong that even the threat of job loss will not stop them. That was certainly true in the *Brooms* case, where the supervisor continued to harass the nurse, even after he was warned that he would be fired if he continued.[105] Judge Keith in the *Rabidue* case believes that the law's purpose is to counteract these dynamics.[106] He also recognizes that women are not on equal ground with men at work because of the power differential that exists between them there and in society in general. Men have a special ability to exploit this dynamic in the workplace because women fear that if they complain about harassment they will lose their jobs. Such a dynamic holds able and talented women back.[107]

Is it fair to say that a woman who decides to stay and endure harassment has really "chosen" to do so? I think not. It seems a contradiction in terms to say that a woman who is being subjected to hostile, offensive, and intimidating behavior at work can weigh the costs and benefits of staying on or leaving in the cold, calm light of rationality. Barbara Gutek, a pioneer researcher on the psychological effects of harassment, says that, "Sexual harassment can . . . force a woman into an occupation which pays less well and/or offers fewer opportunities for advancement."[108] To my mind, the issue is not whether the victim is thinking rationally; the issue is how we can develop a definition of choice that fully addresses the range of difficulties a woman like this actually faces.

The Feminist Perspective and the Reasonable Woman Test

As I mentioned above, law and economics proponents have long recognized that a transaction that comes about because of force violates the requirement that parties are able to choose their own ends.[109] Such a violation has been traditionally regulated vis-à-vis traditional contract law prohibitions against duress, which I have already discussed. In addition, other forms of force recognized under the common law that might arise in the context of sexual harassment are intentional torts like assault, battery, invasion of privacy, or the intentional infliction of emotional distress. Richard Epstein has even suggested that sexual harassment laws are acceptable as long as they substantively parallel these common law prohibitions.[110] The problem is that his definitions of fraud and force are so narrow that most victims of the most common forms of sexual harassment would be unable to seek redress in the courts.

Epstein says the common law definitions for these torts are broader than the definition for sexual harassment that is articulated in the EEOC guidelines and in recent court cases. In the common law, he says, "it did not matter why the harassment took place . . . any motive will do. . . . [Thus,] the common law rules of the liability are broader than the analogous rules of Title VII, which are unnecessarily limited by an antidiscrimination norm to certain motive-based forms of conduct [like sex discrimination]."[111] Epstein neglects to acknowledge, however, one very important problem with the common law—that traditional common law definitions of duress, or the intentional torts just mentioned, do not provide an adequate standard for addressing the full range of negative experiences harassment victims are forced to endure. This is because the law has tended to see these torts, as well as harassment, solely from the harasser's perspective.

Much has been written about the failure of the courts to give due weight to the experiences of women victims in harassment cases, and many, including myself, have advocated that courts apply a "reasonable woman test" in order to render more just decisions in cases involving male on female harassment.[112] Just because an act does not meet the common law definition of force does not mean that the target of the harassment does not justifiably experience that act, in her mind, as force. The problem is not with the victim. It has to do with the fact that the individual victim's experiences, and the experiences of women as a group, have not been traditionally considered by the courts. For example, consider the tort of intentional infliction of emotional distress.

Generally, to win a common law claim for emotional distress, a plaintiff has to prove that the defendant's conduct was so outrageous that it was beyond the bounds of human decency. She also usually has to show that she suffered some kind of identifiable "emotional distress . . . evidenced by some physical symptom or illness or some emotional disturbance that can be documented by a psychiatric consultant or other medical professional."[113]

For example, in *White v. Monsanto*, a female worker, along with several coworkers, was told to handle containers holding hazardous materials. She could not begin the task, however, until someone brought her protective gloves and goggles. While she was waiting for that person to come, her foreman subjected her to a tirade of obscenities, and threatened to fire her for being lazy. Even though she responded to his treatment by having an acute anxiety attack, the woman was not able to win a claim for emotional distress because the court said that she had not proven that the foreman's behavior was sufficiently outrageous.[114] The conduct, the court said, "although crude, rough and uncalled for, was not tortuous. The brief, isolated instance of improper behavior . . . was the kind of unpleasant experience persons must expect to endure from time to time."[115]

On the other hand, relying on the rationale in *White*, the plaintiff in the *Brooms* case discussed earlier probably would have been successful had she decided to sue for intentional infliction of emotional distress. In *Brooms*, the supervisor physically threatened the plaintiff and showed her racist and sexist pornography, which caused her to experience psychological distress. At one point, the only way she could get him to refrain from restraining her was to throw hot coffee on him and run away.[116] Most likely, the judge in *White* would conclude that this supervisor's overtly threatening and obnoxious behavior was egregious enough to amount to the type of outrageous conduct needed to win an emotional distress claim. Richard Epstein would probably be satisfied with this result, because *Brooms* could have won for emotional distress or sexual harassment, and Epstein thinks that sexual harassment law should parallel the common law.[117]

But what happens when the conduct is less severe, but equally troubling because it intimidates and offends a female employee? That was the case in the *Harris* case discussed earlier in the chapter. There, the plaintiff's boss never threatened to hurt her or show her the type of vulgar pornography that the plaintiff in *Brooms* was forced to see. He engaged in the most common form of harassment—verbal harassment—by making sexist remarks to her and demeaning her abilities as a woman in front of others.[118]

The plaintiff in Harris admitted that she "experienced anxiety and emotional upset . . . did not want to go to work . . . [and] cried frequently,"[119] but she was never physically assaulted and did not experience severe psychological distress like the plaintiff in *Brooms*. Nevertheless, the Supreme Court was sympathetic to her situation, stating that:

> Title VII comes into play before the harassing conduct leads to a nervous breakdown. A discriminatorily abusive [hostile] work environment, even one that does not seriously affect employees' psychological well-being, can and often will detract from employees' job performance, discourage

employees from remaining on the job, or keep them from advancing in their careers.[120]

A similar set of circumstances was present in the *Ellison v. Brady* case discussed above. There the harassment consisted mostly of letters sent to the plaintiff, in which the harasser expressed his sexual desire and love for her. The harasser in *Ellison* did not physically assault the plaintiff, and the plaintiff never suffered a nervous breakdown, but the Ninth Circuit still felt she was entitled to recover for sexual harassment.[121]

I suspect that Epstein would not be pleased with the decisions in either *Harris* or *Ellison*. He would say that the courts in both cases inappropriately expanded the common law definition of force. Had there been no sexual harassment law at the time that either of the plaintiffs brought their claims, they would not have won their cases. I doubt that a court applying the common law would consider the type of behavior they were subjected to outrageous enough to meet the definition for intentional infliction of emotional distress.

Thus, while the common law, at least in theory, might protect a woman from outright rape or more severe forms of harassment, it would not protect her from the most common forms (i.e., the sexual teasing, jokes, remarks or questions, pressure for dates, or suggestive letters and phone calls that I mentioned above in the section titled "Using the Law and Economics Paradigm to Interpret Sexual Harassment"). And even here, I say, in "theory" because feminists have written extensively about how difficult it is for women rape victims to have their experiences taken seriously by the legal system as well.[122] Nevertheless, Epstein and Posner seem to be saying that women should only be able to seek help if they are subjected to the most extreme and least common forms of harassment. The broader definition of force that has been advocated by feminist scholars, however, addresses the fact that harassment, whether it is physical or verbal, can be tantamount to force in *the eyes of the victim*.[123] And it is her experience and the experience of women in general that need to be more appropriately acknowledged.

In fact, the views of Epstein and Posner reflect what has come to be seen as a significant gender gap in public attitudes about sexual harassment. Men, at least heterosexual men, are much more likely than women to think that the problem of sexual harassment is exaggerated.[124] Barbara Gutek says that this gender gap may exist because of "[w]omen's greater vulnerability and experience with sexual harassment . . . [because of the fact that men] are infrequent victims of sexual harassment and most sexual harassers are men . . . men may identify more with the harasser than the victim."[125]

Feminists have long argued about whether or not the incorporation of an essentialist approach to gender in the law, one which adapts the view that women are inherently different than men, is either accurate or appropriate with respect to furthering the rights of women. Such an approach, it has been contended, may help perpetuate stereotypes about women being weaker and less capable than men. Indeed, it could be said that I am advocating a basically essentialist approach, because I argue that women's unique experiences need to be given greater weight in the courts. I, too, however, am sensitive to the dangers associated with essentialism and recognize the need to "bring out the multicultural differences in women's life experiences by deconstructing the unitary quality and character of gender identity." [126] However, because numerous studies have shown that a significant number of women have reported experiencing the debilitating effects of sexual harassment, it is important that their experiences be acknowledged in a legal system that has traditionally belittled those experiences across the board.

For these reasons I endorse the use of a reasonable woman or victim standard in sexual harassment law. For, as Harvard law professor Martha Minnow has said, "refusing to acknowledge these differences may make them continue to matter in a world constructed with some groups but not others, in mind."[127] A feminist reading of Rawlsian philosophy will lead to the same conclusion.

A Feminist Reading of Rawlsian Philosophy and Its Applicability to Sexual Harassment Law

Rawls is known for his writing on equity and economic justice. One of his most well-known arguments is that if a group of people were put in a hypothetical "original position," one in which they are ignorant about their ultimate gender, class, or race status, they would develop a society in which no one in the group could be made better off unless there was some commensurate increase made in the well-being of the least well off among them. Rawls calls this "the difference principle."[128]

Rawls, who passed away in 2002, did not write any overtly feminist texts. In fact, political science professor Susan Moller Okin has said that "Rawls neglected to deal with the problem of gender in any meaningful way because he did not consider whether or in what form the family is a just institution . . . [even though] his own theory of moral developments rest centrally on the early experience of persons with a family environment that is both loving and just."[129] Nevertheless, feminists can find much in Rawls's work that can be used to support the rights of women.

For example, Okin postulates that once the veil is lifted for people in the original position, they may find themselves "feminist men or women whose conception of the good life includes the minimization of social differentiation between the sexes."[130] Thus, she argues, they would end up creating a society "in which men and women participated in more or less equal numbers in every sphere of life, from infant care to different kinds of paid work."[131]

Ethics writers Deborah L. Wells and Beverly Kracher have taken this logic and applied it to sexual harassment. They say that if employers imagined that they were in the original position, they would adopt policies and procedures in which employees are encouraged to recognize the other person's perspective.[132] This means that they would acknowledge that they have a duty to show mutual respect and that the victim's perspective *always* needs to be adopted. Such approach "promotes an individual's duty not to harm the innocent because it requires that people identify sexually hostile environments from the perspective of the innocents."[133]

I would take the Wells, Kracher, and Okin endorsement of Rawls one step further. As critical race scholar Mari Matsuda has said, rather than simply relying on Rawls's "*abstract* consideration of the position of the least advantaged . . . [we really need to study] the *concrete* experience of oppression."[134] In other words, we need to look at the *actual* experiences of women with respect to sexual harassment. I have outlined many of those experiences above. That the victim's perspective needs to be adopted in this manner is also advocated by Judge Keith in his dissenting opinion in *Rabidue* case.

Judge Keith argues that "unless the outlook of the reasonable woman is adopted, the defendants as well as the courts are permitted to sustain ingrained notions of reasonable behavior fashioned by the offenders, in this case, men."[135] Judge Krupansky on the other hand, in his majority opinion says that the test should be how the situation is viewed from the perspective of a reasonable *person*, a test that traditionally resulted in trivialization of a harassment victim's complaints.[136]

But reasonable women, Judge Keith replies, think very differently from men. While men might view verbal harassment as, in the words of Judge Krupansky, merely "annoying," women see harassment as a serious problem.[137] They often fear that it will escalate into physical violence. Keith argues that women should not be expected to work in places where they are subjected to the type of harassment described in the case simply because it is a "matter of prevailing male prerogative."[138] Keith thus sees the law as a vehicle for social change, one that can empower women as opposed to holding them back. His call for a more equitable approach is very much in keeping with Rawls's theory of the original position, as well as Matsuda's challenge that the real-life experiences of victims in these instances need to be recognized. As the above discussions show, free market theorists on one hand and feminist and Rawlsian theorists on the other hand have very different opinions about why sexual harassment occurs and what the appropriate standard of review should be for judges and juries who render decisions in such cases. They also have very different ideas about the role that the government should play in addressing the problem.

Differing Perspectives on How the Problem of Sexual Harassment Can Be Solved

The Law and Economics View—Limited or No Government Regulation

Free market advocates often criticize government regulation for both unduly interfering with competition and producing a variety of unintended and undesirable consequences.[139] They would agree with Judge Krupansky, who, criticizing the plaintiff's harassment claim, said, "Title VII *was not meant to*—or can—change this."[140] Someone who holds theses views would say that sexual harassment laws enable women to unfairly restrict the behavior and speech of men at work—something that Congress never intended when it adopted Title VII in 1964. This then, is just another form of sex discrimination—with men on the receiving end this time instead of women.

Furthermore, potential harassers will now simply find ways to harass women covertly so that they can get away with it. While in the past, some men might have simply said questionable things to women without worrying about being heard by others, now they will say things out of anyone else's earshot, or target women who are more passive and less likely to complain. And managers who suspect or know about harassment will simply look the other way.

People like Gary Becker, based on his criminology work, would probably say that harassers perform an internal cost benefit analysis and weigh their chances of getting fired against their desire to continue the harassing behavior. Managers who fail to investigate suspected problems or take preventive measures to prevent harassment also engage in an internal cost benefit analysis. They weigh their chances of getting sued for failing to prevent harassment against the benefits of maintaining the status quo discussed in the section titled "Using the Law and Economics Paradigm to Interpret Sexual Harassment." If EEOC statistics about the large increase in the number of harassment claims is any indication of whether or not the law is really working,[141] someone applying a law and economics analysis would say that the increase in claims actually means that harassment has increased, not decreased—definitely an unintended consequence of Title VII.

As said at the start of this chapter, most free market proponents have engaged in very little in-depth analysis of sexual harassment. Most of my analysis of the paradigm's relevance to sexual harassment has been based on applying what they have said about employment discrimination in general to this topic. This includes how their proposals for an alternative approach to the current regulation scheme under Title VII can be applied to sexual harassment as well.

Epstein and Posner believe that firms should be allowed to engage in discrimination as long as they see fit and that the market should be left alone to enable discrimination to reach its most efficient level. Probably recognizing the controversial nature of these arguments, Epstein does not propose that the market should have *complete* free reign when it comes to gender discrimination. He says that equitable issues should be taken into account, but only in a manner that produces the greatest net gain to society. To accomplish this, he suggests that Title VII be abandoned altogether and replaced with some type of redistributive scheme,[142] which would be applied to all of Title VII's protected categories, including color, religion, national origin, sex, and race.

Epstein argues that private companies should be allowed to discriminate against women freely. They would, however, be expected to pay a discrimination tax, the funds from which would be distributed to victims of discrimination in the form of welfare payments.[143] His ideas echo some of the debate taking place between environmentalists and manufacturers about whether or not the government should be in the business of offering pollution permits. Under this approach, separately identifiable government pollution permits would be created to allow companies to pollute (either by air or water or in waste dumps, etc.) up to some predetermined level. The government would then make an initial public offering of these permits on the free market and sell them to the highest bidders.[144]

Some argue that the advantages of marketable permits are that they enable the public to consume products that have a high social utility (i.e., they are products that are in great demand on the free market). Permits allow the government to control the production and use of such products and thereby manage the extent to which companies pollute, without outlawing the sale of those products altogether. For example, cars pollute, but we still allow people to drive. Some states, like California, however, have mandatory emissions inspections and require cars to be retrofitted with special pollution control devices.

Furthermore, many think that permits are a less costly and more effective remedial approach than the type of direct government intervention that takes place under a regulatory program. They believe that permits are cheaper to administer because once the permits are sold on the market, none (or at least much less) of the subsequent oversight and administrative costs associated with regulatory agency enforcement efforts are present. Posner, in a similar vein, has said that the costs of administrating Title VII are unreasonably high.[145] There is a great deal of similarity between the arguments in favor of pollution permits and Epstein's proposals for a discrimination tax. If this logic were applied to the most common forms of sexual harassment, companies would be allowed to purchase "harassment permits," which would enable them to allow harassment against female employees to take place without the risk of being taken to court. I suspect that such a permit scheme would have made people like the president of Astra, U.S.A., very happy. Posner and Strauss both endorse such an approach with respect to disparate treatment in hiring based on race and, I think, by implication, sex discrimination.[146]

A Feminist Solution to the Problem—Maintain or Increase Government Regulation of the Market

To a feminist, a proposal that would allow companies to pay a tax or get a permit to discriminate sounds very much like the type of "modest proposal" made by Jonathan Swift during the eighteenth century. Swift, in an effort to show how insensitive the British were to the plight of the starving Irish, proposed in a scathing satire that perhaps the solution to the problem would be for the Irish to eat their children.[147] Rather than condemning discrimination in all its forms, law and economics proponents say that the victims of discrimination should be left to their own devices in a market that is, at worst, violently hostile and, at best, indifferent to them.

And what would the funds from taxes or permits be used for? Perhaps Posner, Strauss, or Epstein might say that they could be used for improved educational opportunities for minorities, set-asides for the creation of minority- or women-owned businesses, or even courses in self-esteem for members of these groups. The latter, dare I say, especially if they have been subjected to harassment, will need it. I am not sure, however, what the benefits of such programs would be, because nothing in the scheme suggests that employers, or customers for that matter, would be forced to refrain from statistical discrimination. Thus, even if a former harassment victim (now not only qualified, but with a heightened sense of confidence bolstered by her subsidized classes in self-esteem) were to apply for a job, the employer would still be justified in not hiring her—or, in the alternative, in allowing her to be subjected to the most common forms of harassment. Thus, nothing really changes under the law and economics paradigm. And change is what is needed.

In my opinion, the only way to correct the inequities brought about by profit maximizing discriminating individuals is to keep Title VII and the EEOC guidelines in place, and to introduce the type of equitable corrective measures proposed by Judge Keith in his dissenting opinion in the *Rabidue* case. A scheme that would allow redistributive taxes or permits flaunts the very purpose of our civil rights laws. "Title VII's precise *purpose* is to prevent such behavior and attitudes from poisoning the work environment [for women]," says Judge Keith.[148] An approach that would allow the government to participate in the furtherance of harassment through the granting of permits or a tax scheme is neither administratively efficient nor morally sound.

First, regulatory prohibitions against sex discrimination—and, by implication, sexual harassment—serve as a strong disincentive for companies who may be contemplating engaging in discriminatory conduct. Second, contrary to what law and economics theorists say, the evidence suggests that Title VII is in fact working. The increase in EEOC sexual harassment claims really means that public awareness about the problem has increased and that more women are coming forward now that they know they have a right to redress.[149] Indeed, with the Supreme Court's more recent approval of same sex harassment claims, claims filed by male victims of same sex harassment are on the rise as well.[150] A company who is considering ignoring employee complaints about sexual harassment will also think twice if it knows that it could face up to $300,000 in punitive damages under Title VII, and potentially more under state law. That company also risks losing the goodwill of the public if it were to become known that it ignored the legitimate complaints of its female workers. All of these risks should influence such a company to "do the right thing."

Of course, some may take a more cynical "Beckerian" view and argue that an employer will simply weigh the potential cost of paying money damages versus the benefits of looking the other way when harassment occurs. If the benefits outweigh the costs, the employer will simply ignore the law and continue to fail to take steps to prevent harassment. This will especially be the case if an employer concludes that the odds of its actually getting sued and losing in the first place are low or nonexistent.

As more and more women become aware of their rights under Title VII, however, I think this view is naïve. Thus, as referenced earlier in this chapter, the EEOC reported that harassment claims filed with it increased by 50 percent right after the Clarence Thomas Supreme Court nomination hearings.[151] And in many states, like the state of Massachusetts, the number of sexual harassment claims filed has risen sharply over the past few years.[152] Thus, the argument that regulations are not an effective means of prohibiting harassment is a weak one.

In addition to the current regulatory scheme, which allows harassment victims to sue for up to $300,000 in punitive damages, employers would have even more of an incentive to take the law seriously if there were no caps on the amount of damages. I favor allowing harassment complainants to sue for the same level of unlimited damages that are available to those who bring race discrimination claims under section 1981 of the Civil Rights Act of 1966.[153] Such a proposal was made by Senator Ted Kennedy in 1993, but it has yet to be passed by Congress.[154]

Finally, as I said in my discussion about Rawls, the ethically correct approach to the problem of sexual harassment is to give more weight to the experiences of harassment victims through the adoption of the reasonable woman or victim test. Thus, maintaining current laws and EEOC guidelines, eliminating caps on punitive damages, and adopting a reasonable victim standard are much more effective and equitable solutions to the problem than those suggested by law and economics proponents.

Conclusion

John Stuart Mill once said of his mentor, Jeremy Bentham, the following:

> [Bentham] committed the mistake of supposing that the business part of human affairs was the whole of them. . . . Not that he disregarded moral influences when he perceived them. But his want of imagination, small experience of human feelings, and ignorance of the filiation and connexion of feelings with one another, made this rarely the case.[155]

In the same sense, as the title to this chapter suggests, a law and economics approach to sexual harassment may be efficient (and even that is questionable according to people like Gillian Hadfield), but it is not equitable. It is not acceptable, to paraphrase Audre Lorde, to put profit ahead of human need, or in the case of sexual harassment, to put the misogynist on equal footing with his victim. Or, as I said previously, it is not acceptable to put the dominant group's psychic gain from racism, homophobia, or religious or class intolerance ahead of the victim's loss. From an ethical perspective, a more appropriate approach would be to give the greater weight to the victim's experiences and perspective and to create and maintain laws that seek to honor both.

Notes

I owe thanks to Professor David Lyons of Boston University Law School for his helpful comments and to Professors Tom Koenig and Steven Nathanson of Northeastern University for inspiring me to make the connections between free market theory and sexual harassment. An earlier version of this chapter was published in the Spring 1998 volume of the *Vermont Law Review.*

1. *Rabidue v. Osceola Refining*, 611, 624. *Rabidue* is now almost twenty years old. Some of the rationale in *Rabidue* was overturned by the Supreme Court in *Harris v. Forklift*, 510 U.S. 17 (1993), dropping the *Rabidue* court's requirement that plaintiffs in harassment cases always have to show that they experienced severe psychological harm. The case is still very important, however, because it illustrates how certain aspects of free market economic theory are incorporated, either consciously or unconsciously, into the decisions of certain judges. This relevancy is made even more compelling by the fact that President George W. Bush, Jr. has the ability over the next few years to fill a large percentage of federal judgeships with conservative appointees who still adhere to certain aspects of the free market rationale adopted in the *Rabidue* case.

2. Ibid., 615.

3. Ibid., 620–21.

4. Ibid., 620.

5. Orlando Patterson, "Race, Gender and Liberal Fallacies," 15, Sec. 4.

6. *Ellison v. Brady*, 874. One of the letters said, "I cried over you last night, and I'm totally drained today." Another said, "Watching you. Experiencing you from O so far away. . . . [We are] striking off such intense sparks."

7. Ibid., 876.

8. Ibid., 880.

9. U.S. Merit Systems Protection Board, *Sexual Harassment in the Federal Workplace* 2, 13 (hereinafter "1995 Merit Report"). The report shows that out of the 8,000 federal workers who responded to the survey, 44 percent of the women and 19 percent of the men reported experiencing some form of unwanted sexual attention at work. See also Tom Weidlich and Charise K. Lawrence, "Sex and the Firms," 22–24, reporting that of the lawyers surveyed, 51 percent of the women and only 6 percent of the men said they had experienced sexual harassment at work.

10. Toni Lester, "Protecting the Gender Nonconformist from the Gender Police," 97–103.

11. *Oncale v. Sundowner*, 1002.

12. 42 United States Code Sec. 2000e (1991).

13. Charles and Barbara Whalen, *The Longest Debate*, 115–18.

14. For example, see *Barnes v. Train*, 123; and *Corne v. Baush & Lomb*, 161.

15. 29 Code of Federal Regulations, Sec. 1604.11 (a).

16. *Merito v. Vinson*, 57.

17. Ibid., 67.

18. *Harris v. Forklift*, 19.

19. Ibid., 14.

20. Ibid., 22.

21. *Oncale v. Sundowner*, 11.

22. Ibid., 10.

23. Lester, "Race, Sexuality, and the Question of Multiple, Marginalized Identities."

24. Herbert Hovancamp, "Law and Economics in the United States," 331–32.

25. Jeremy Betham, "An Introduction to the Principles of Morals and Legislation," 65–111.

26. Bailey Kuklin and Jeffery Stempel, *Foundations of the Law*, 30. See also, generally, Adam Smith, *The Wealth of Nations*.

27. Kuklin and Stempel, 33.

28. Werner Hirsch, *Law and Economics*, 30.

29. Michael B. Metzger et al., *Business Law and the Regulatory Environment*, 265–72.

30. Kenneth W. Clarkson and R. LeRoy Miller, *West's Business Law*, 282–83.

31. Ibid., 284. For example, in real estate law, "if the defects [to property being sold] are of the kind that would be obvious on inspection, the buyer cannot justify relying on the seller's [fraudulent] representations. If the defects are hidden or latent . . . the buyer is justified in relying on the seller's statements."

32. Mary Becker, "Needed in the Nineties," 1659.

33. David Strauss, "The Law and Economics of Racial Discrimination in Employment," 1619, 1622–23. For one of the earliest treaties on this topic, see Edmund S. Phelps, "The Statistical Theory of Racism and Sexism," 659.

34. Richard Posner, "The Efficiency and Efficacy of Title VII," 513, 516, quoting Phelps:

> Suppose that, because of past exclusion of blacks from equal educational opportunities or for other reasons, the average black worker is less productive than the average white, and suppose further that it is costly for an employer to determine whether an individual worker deviates from the average for the worker's group. Then an unprejudiced employer might nonetheless decide to pay blacks less than whites. This would be unfair to blacks who were in fact above average, yet it might still be an efficient method (in the presence of high information costs) of compensating black workers).

35. Edward J. McCaffrey, "Slouching Towards Equality," 595–675 (1993).

36. Posner, "An Economic Analysis of Sex Discrimination Laws," 1311, 1320. While "it would not be efficient to ascertain individual qualifications, it would be possible to do so—that is, the costs would not be infinite. But in the case of women, the cost would be infinite."

37. Posner, *Economic Analysis of Law*, 62.

38. Hirsch, *Law and Economics*, 5.

39. Ibid., 458.

40. Mary T. Reilly, "A Paradigm for Sexual Harassment," 427, 435.

41. D.G. Brown, "What Is Mill's Principal of Utility?" 9, 17, 19–20.

42. Ibid., 20.

43. Belton M. Fleisher and Thomas J. Kniesner, *Labor Economics: Theory, Evidence, and Policy*, 389–393.

44. Gary Becker, *The Economics of Discrimination*, 153.

45. Ibid., 39.

46. John J. Donahue III, "Is Title VII Efficient?" 1411–22.

47. Posner, "An Economic Analysis of Sex Discrimination Laws," 513, 515–16.

48. McCaffrey, "Slouching Towards Equality," 611.

49. Meritor v. Vinson, 57, 67.

50. Posner, *Sex and Reason*, 118. In comparing rape law to harassment law, Posner says that a man can get off the hook in a rape case because his belief that he had consent is reasonable. If such a defense were abolished, it would "increas[e] the cost of dating to men . . . [and] reduce the amount of dating, and heterosexual women would suffer. A similar objection can be lodged against proposals to strengthen the sanctions for sexual harassment in the work place." Ibid., at 395.

51. *1995 Merit Report*, 14, showing that nearly 37 percent of women surveyed reported experiencing sexual remarks, jokes, and teasing, 29 percent said that they were the object of unwanted sexual looks and gestures, and 10 percent said they received suggestive letters and phone calls.

52. Barbara A. Gutek, *Sex and the Workplace: The Impact of Sexual Behavior and Harassment on Women, Men, and Organizations*, 13–15.

53. Posner, *Sex and Reason*, 118f.

54. Derrick Bell, Faces at the Bottom of the Well, 55.

55. Kenneth Gilpin, "Firm to Pay $10 Million in Settlement of Sex Case," *New York Times*, A10.

56. Gutek, *Sex and the Workplace*, 15–18, 118–19; Mark A. Chesler, "Contemporary Sociological Theories of Racism," 21, 46.

57. Chesler, Ibid., 46.

58. David E. Terpstra and Douglas D. Baker, "Sexual Harassment at Work: The Psychological Issues," 179.

59. John J. Donahue and James J. Heckman, "Re-evaluating Federal Civil Rights Policy," 1713–35.

60. Kimberle Crenshaw, "Whose Story Is It, Anyway?" 402, 412; Nancy S. Ehrenreich, "Pluralist Myths and Powerless Men," 1177, 1228 *n*187 "The fact that a large proportion of the sexual harassment cases that have been litigated were brought by black plaintiff's begs for explanation. The history of slavery, in which African American women were constructed as 'fair game' for the sexual exploits of their white masters, would certainly seem a promising place to start."

61. *Brooms v. Regal Tube*, 412, 416–17.

62. G. Becker, "Crime and Punishment," 176.

63. Ibid., 177.

64. *Barnes v. Train*, 983.

65. Andrew Blum, "Assumption of Risk Tested In Hooters Suit," 7.

66. R.H. Coase, "The Problem of Social Cost," 1.

67. Clarkson and Miller, *West's Business Law*, 285.

68. Ibid., 286.

69. Richard A. Epstein, *Forbidden Grounds*, 30.

70. *Rabidue v. Osceola*, 620. Emphasis added.

71. M. Becker, "Needed In The Nineties," 1668 *n*55. Emphasis added.

72. Epstein, *Forbidden Grounds*, 3.

73. Ibid., 351.

74. John Stuart Mill, *Utilitarianism*, 171.

75. Posner, "An Economic Analysis of Sex Discrimination Laws," 516.

76. Reilly, "A Paradigm for Sexual Harassment," 435–36 "Scholarship that characterizes defendants in sexual harassment cases as 'injurers' and plaintiffs as 'victims' presupposes an ethic under which plaintiffs' values morally trump those of defendants. The choice of language obscures the ultimate question: When should one type of conduct yield to another?"

77. Gary Minda, *Postmodern Legal Movements*, 128.

78. John Hardwig, "Should Women Think In Terms of Rights?" 441, 449.

79. Patricia Smith, "Introduction," 3–15.

80. Bell Hooks, *Yearning*, 9, stating that it is important for white feminists to understand "the ways race and class status [also] determine the degree to which one can assert male domination and privilege." See also, generally, Midge Wilson and Kathy

Russell, *Divided Sisters*; Gloria T. Hull, ed, *All the Women Are White*; Julianne Malveaux, "Gender Differences and Beyond."

81. See, for example, *Daniels v. Essex Group*, 1264, 1266. African American man was routinely called "nigger" and "Buckwheat," and found a dummy at work simulating the lynching of a black man; Davis v. Monsanto Chemical, 345, 347. African American man alleged that he was subjected to racist graffiti and spat upon; and *Erebia v. Chrysler*, 1250. Mexican American man, on a daily basis over a three-year period, was called derogatory names like "wetback" and "tomato picker," and told that he should go back to Mexico .

82. See Henry Louis Gates, "The Naked Republic," 117, quoting feminist writer Naomi Wolfe, who asks: "Why could questions be put to Clarence Thomas about his sexuality in a way that such questions had never been put to a white man? Because black men are sexualized in a way that white men in power are not."

83. *Goldberg v. City of Philadelphia*, 1, Jewish man called "bagel" and a "fucking Jew" by his coworkers.

84. Smith, "Introduction," 7; and see, generally, Carol Gilligan, *In a Different Voice*.

85. Robin West, "Jurisprudence and Gender," 28–29.

86. Catherine MacKinnon, "Feminism, Marxism, Method, and the State," 137.

87. Smith, "Introduction," 6–7, 11–15.

88. M. Becker, "Needed in the Nineties," 668 *n*55.

89. Ruth A. Kennedy, "Insulating Sexual Harassment Grievance Procedures from the Chilling Effect of Defamation Litigation," 235, 237–38.

90. Stephanie Riger, "Gender Dilemmas in Sexual Harassment Policies and Harassment Procedures," 497–98.

91. See, for example, *Robinson v. Jacksonville Shipyards*, 1486, 1530, judge criticizing the company' informal handling of complaints.

92. Mary P. Rowe, "Comment," in David Niven, "The Case of Hidden Harrassment," 7.

93. See 1995 Merit Report, 55; International Labour Office, 285–89.

94. Kenneth Clatterbaugh, "Are Men Oppressed?", 289–305.

95. McCaffrey, "Slouching Toward Equality," 649.

96. Audre Lorde, *Zami; Sister Outsider; Undersong*, 114–15.

97. *Ellison v. Brady*, 872.

98. *Robinson v. Jacksonville Shipyards*, 1526. See also MacKinnon, *Feminist Jurisprudence*, 115: "If the pervasiveness of an abuse makes it nonactionable, no inequality sufficiently institutionalized to merit a law against it would be actionable."

99. M. Becker, "Needed in the Nineties," 1664.

100. Posner, *Sex and Reason*, 392.

101. Barbara A. Gutek and Mary P. Koss, "Changed Women and Changed Organizations," 28, 33.

102. *1995 Merit Report*, 26. See also Gillian Hadfield, "Rational Woman," 1151. She says that harassment "introduces a discriminatory factor into women's economic choice . . . [which can] lead women . . . as rational actors, to make employment decisions that differ from those made by men in otherwise similar circumstances." Ibid., 1167.

103. MacKinnon, "Sexual Harassment," 145–57.

104. G. Becker, "Crime and Punishment," 14.

105. *Brooms v. Regal Tube*, 416.

106. *Rabidue v. Osceola Refining*, 1041.

107. For a more extensive analysis of how this power dynamics work, see, generally, Toni Lester, "Should the Courts Penalize Victims Who Adopt Passive Coping Strategies?" 323–38.

108. Gutek and Koss, "Changed Women," 31.

109. Epstein, *Forbidden Grounds*, 75.

110. Ibid., 351–52.

111. Ibid., 353–54.

112. See, for example, Kathryn Abrams, "Gender Discrimination and the Transformation of Workplace Norms," 1183, 1206. "If these latter forms of employment discrimination against women are to be corrected, and if the norms that permit them to flourish are to be modified, then courts must employ a standard that reflects the women's perceptions of sexual harassment." See also, generally, Toni Lester, "The Reasonable Woman Test in Sexual Harassment Law," 227–62; and Kim Lane Scheppele, "The Reasonable Woman," 36–46.

113. Clarkson and Miller, *West's Business Law*, 107.

114. *White v. Monsanto Chemical*, 1205, 1211.

115. Ibid., 1211.

116. *Brooms v. Regal Tube*, 416–17.

117. Epstein, *Forbidden Grounds*, 351–52.

118. *Harris v. Forklift*, 19.

119. *Harris v. Forklift* , 1900 U.S. Dist. Lexis 20115, 6 (November 28, 1990) [hereinafter "Harris District Court"].

120. *Harris v. Forklift*, 22.

121. *Ellison v. Brady*, 874, 883.

122. See, generally, Susan Estrich, *Real Rape*.

123. It should be noted that the Supreme Court explicitly endorses the use of the reasonable person test in sexual harassment law. See *Harris v. Forklift*, 25 (Judge Ginsburg, concurring). While the Harris court did not overtly endorse the use of the reasonable woman test, it most certainly endorsed a broader standard than the standard used in *Rabidue*. Harris never would have won her case before the Rabidue court because it would have viewed her predicament as trivial, especially because she was not able to show that she had experienced severe psychological harm. The Supreme Court thus definitely gave more weight to the experiences of harassment victims, even though it said that it was taking a "middle path between making actionable any conduct that is merely offensive and requiring the conduct to cause tangible psychological injury" *Harris*, 21.

124. Barbara A. Gutek, "How Subjective Is Sexual Harassment?" 447, 454 (citations omitted); see also Weidlich and Lawrence, "Sex and the Firms," 1, 22, citing the 1993 *National Law Journal* survey of 800 men and women attorneys in large law firms, which showed that seven in ten women reported thinking that a problem exists, while only four in ten men reported thinking the same thing.

125. Ibid., 461.

126. Minda, *Postmodern Legal Movements*, 144, discussing postmodern feminists Mary Joe Frug, Joan Williams, and Zillah Eisenstein. See also Nancy J. Chodorow, *Feminism and Psychoanalytic Theory*, 115. "Feminist theories . . . based on the notion of essential difference . . . are doing feminism a disservice."

127. Martha Minnow, "Justice Engendered," 217. Even Barbara Gutek, who has

cautioned against making generalizations about what she says is inconclusive empirical data on the gender gap in perceptions about sexual harassment, says that "[t]he notion of reasonableness changes as we acquire new information. Perhaps what we hope to see is a standard of reasonableness that corresponds to the intent of the reasonable woman standard. Thus, in cases of sexual harassment, a reasonable person should adopt the point of view of the recipient." Barbara Gutek and Maureen O'Connor, "The Empirical Basis for the Reasonable Woman Standard," 151, 161.

128. John Rawls, *A Theory of Justice*, 75–78, 118–50.

129. Susan Moller Okin, *Justice, Gender, and the Family*, 108.

130. Ibid., 174.

131. Ibid., 171.

132. Deborah L. Wells and Beverly Kracher, "Justice, Sexual Harassment and the Reasonable Victim Standard," 423–31.

133. Ibid., 428.

134. Mari Matsuda, "Looking to the Bottom," 63. (Emphasis added, citations omitted.) Matsuda is talking here about the need to focus on the experiences of those at "the bottom," as she puts it, namely people of color. These ideas, however, are also relevant to feminist thought and are applicable to white women, women of color, and any other group that has occupied a position of powerlessness in relation to the mainstream society, like gays, the poor and the disabled. See also Mari Matsuda, "Public Response to Racist Speech," 2320.

135. *Rabidue v. Osceola Refining*, 623, 626.

136. See, generally, Lester, "The Reasonable Woman Test."

137. *Rabidue v. Osceola Refining*, 622.

138. Ibid., 627.

139. Epstein, *Forbidden Grounds*, 10, 12.

140. *Rabidue v. Osceola Refining*, 621 (emphasis added).

141. For example, from 1990 to 1995, after the Anita Hill-Clarence Thomas senate hearings, the number of sexual harassment claims filed with the EEOC more than doubled, rising from 6,127 to 15, 549. See Diane Lewis, "Women's Groups Target Limit on Sex Harassment Cases," 71.

142. Richard Epstein, *Forbidden Grounds*, 9, 12.

143. Ibid., 9, 12.

144. Derrick Bell, *Faces at the Bottom of the Well*, 57, *n*22–24.

145. Posner, "An Economic Analysis of Sex Discrimination Laws," 514.

146. Ibid., 516. "It might be that a tax on those whites for the benefit of blacks would be justifiable on grounds of social equity." See also Strauss, "The Law and Economics of Racial Discrimination in Employment," 1630. "Why would the objectives of compensatory justice and avoiding racial stratification not be better served, at less cost, if the legal system permitted statistical discrimination, captured the efficiency gains (and the gains from reduced administrative costs) through taxation, and transferred the proceeds to African Americans?"

147. Jonathan Swift, *A Modest Proposal*, 614–21.

148. *Rabidue v. Osceola Refining*, 626 (emphasis added).

149. Margaret Talbot, "Men Behaving Badly."

150. Ibid.

151. Lewis, 71.

152. Ibid. For instance, from 1990 to 1995, claims with the Massachusetts Commission Against Discrimination rose from 100 to just below 500.

153. 42 U.S.C. 2000e-5(g) (1991).

154. A Bill to Amend Section 1977A.

155. John Stuart Mill, *Utilitarianism*, 157.

References

Abrams, K. "Gender Discrimination and the Transformation of Workplace Norms." *Vandervilt Law Review* 42 (1989): 1183–1248.

Barnes v. Train, 13 Fair Employment Practice Cases (BNA) 123 (D.D.C. Aug. 9, 1974), rev'd. 561 F.2d 983 (D.C. Cir 1977).

Becker, G. *The Economics of Discrimination*. 2d ed. Chicago: University of Chicago Press, 1971.

———. "Crime and Punishment: An Economic Approach." *Journal of Political Economy* 78 (1968): 169–217.

Becker, M. "Needed in the Nineties: Improved Individual and Structural Remedies for Racial and Sexual Disadvantages in Employment." Georgetown Law Journal 79 (1991): 1659–93.

Bell, D. *Faces at the Bottom of the Well*. New York: Basic Books, 1992.

Bentham, J. "An Introduction to the Principles of Morals and Legislation." *In Utilitarianism and Other Writings*, ed. Mary Warnock, 33–77. New York: Meridian Books, 1962.

Blum, A. "Assumption of Risk Tested In Hooters Suit." *The National Law Journal* (May 14, 1993): 7.

Brooms v. Regal Tube, 881 F.2d 412 (7th Cir. 1988).

Brown, D.G. "What Is Mill's Principle of Utility." In *Mill's Utilitarianism—Critical Essays*, ed. D. Lyons, 9–24. Lanham, MD: Rowman and Littlefield, 1997.

Chesler, M.A. "Contemporary Sociological Theories of Racism." In *Towards the Elimination of Racism*, ed. Phyllis A, Katz, 21. New York: Pergamon Press, 1976.

Chodorow, N.J. *Feminism and Psychoanalytic Theory*. New Haven, CT: Yale University Press, 1989.

Clarkson, K.W., and R. LeRoy Miller, eds. *West's Business Law*, 6th ed. Minneapolis: West Publishing, 1995.

Clatterbaugh, K. "Are Men Oppressed?" In Rethinking Masculinity: Philosophical Explorations in Light of Feminism. 2d ed., ed. L. May, R. Strikwerda, and P.D. Hopins, 289–305. Lanham, MD: Rowan and Littlefield, 1996.

Coase, R.H. "The Problem of Social Cost." *Journal of Law and Economics* III (October 1990): 1–44.

Corne v. Bausch & Lomb, 390 F. Supp. 161 (D. Ariz 1975), rev'd. 562 F. 2d 55 (9th Cir. 1977).

Crenshaw, K. "Whose Story Is It Anyway? Feminist and Antiracist Appropriations of Anita Hill." In *Race-ing Justice, En-gendering Power: Essays on Anita Hill, Clarence Thomas, and the Construction of Social Reality*, ed. T. Morrison, 402–40. New York: Pantheon Books, 1992.

Daniels v. Essex Group, 937 F. 2d 1264 (7th Cir. 1991).

Davis v. Monsanto Chemical, 858 F 2d. 345 (6th Cir. 1988).

Donahue, J.J. "Is Title VII Efficient?" *University of Pennsylvania Law Review* 134 (1986): 1411–31.

Donahue, J.J., and J.J. Heckman. "Re-evaluating Federal Civil Rights Policy." *Georgetown Law Review* 79 (1991): 1713–1735.

Ehrenreich, N.S. "Pluralist Myths and Powerless Men: The Ideology of Reasonableness in Sexual Harassment Law." *Yale Law Journal* 99 (1990): 1177–1234.

Ellison v. Brady, 924 F.2d 874 (9th Cir. 1991).

Epstein, R. *Forbidden Grounds: The Case Against Employment Discrimination*. Cambridge, MA: Harvard University Press, 1992.

Erebia v. Chrysler Plastics Products Corp. 772 F. 2d 1250-1261 (1985).

Estrich, S. *Real Rape: How the Legal System Victimizes Women Who Say No*. Cambridge, MA: Harvard University Press, 1987.

Fleisher, B.M., and T.J. Kniesner. *Labor Economics: Theory, Evidence, and Policy*. Englewood Cliffs, NJ: Prentice-Hall, 1984.

42 United States Code Sec. 2000e (1991).

Gates, H.L. "The Naked Republic." *The New Yorker*, September 1, 1997, 117.

Gilligan, C. *In A Different Voice: Psychological Theory and Women's Development*. Cambridge, MA: Harvard University Press, 1982.

Gilpin, K. "Firm to Pay $10 Million in Settlement of Sex Case." *New York Times*, A10.

Goldberg v. City of Philadelphia, 1994 U.S. Dist. Lexis 8969 .

Gutek, B.A. "How Subjective Is Sexual Harassment? An Examination of Rater Effects." *Basic and Applied Social Psychology* 17, no. 4 (1995): 447–67.

———. *Sex and the Workplace: The Impact of Sexual Behavior and Harassment on Women, Men, and Organizations*. San Francisco: Jossey-Bass, 1985.

Gutek, B.A., and M.P. Koss. "Changed Women and Changed Organizations: Consequences of and Coping With Sexual Harassment." *Journal of Vocational Behavior* 42 (1993): 28–47.

Gutek, B., and M. O'Connor. "The Empirical Basis for the Reasonable Woman Standard." *Journal of Social Issues* 51 (1995): 151–66.

Hadfield, G. "Rational Woman: A Test for Sex-Based Harassment." *California Law Review* 83 (1995): 1151–89.

Hardwig, J. "Should Women Think in Terms of Rights?" *Ethics* 94 (1984): 441–5.

Harris v. Forklift, 510 U.S. 17 (1993).

Harris v. Forklift Systems, No. 3:89–0057, 1900 U.S. Dist. Lexis 20115, *6 (November 28, 1990).

Hirsch, W.Z. *Law and Economics, An Introductory Analysis*. 2d ed. Boston: Harcourt Brace Jovanovich, 1988.

Hooks, B. *Yearning: Race, Gender and Cultural Politics*. Boston: South End Press, 1990.

Hovancamp, H. "Law and Economics in the United States: A Brief Historical Survey." *Cambridge Journal of Economics* 19 (1995): 331–52.

Hull, G.T., P. Bell Scott, and B. Smith, eds. *All the Women Are White; All the Blacks Are Men, But Some of Us Are Brave: Black Women's Studies*. New York: Feminist Press, 1982.

International Labour Office. *Combating Sexual Harassment at Work*, Volume 11. Geneva, Switzerland: International Labour Office, 1992.

Kennedy, R.A. "Insulating Sexual Harassment Grievance Procedures from the Chilling Effect of Defamation Litigation." *Washington Law Review* 69 (1994): 235–53.

Kuklin, B., and J. Stempel. *Foundations of the Law: An Interdisciplinary Jurisprudential Primer*. Minneapolis: West Publishing, 1994.

Lester, T. "Protecting the Gender Nonconformist from the Gender Police: Why the Harassment of Gays Is a Form of Sex Discrimination." *New Mexico Law Review* 29 (1999): 89–118.

———. "Should The Courts Penalize Victims Who Adopt Passive Coping Strategies?" *Labor Law Journal* 46 (June 1995): 323–38.

———. "The Reasonable Woman Test in Sexual Harassment Law: Will It Really Make A Difference?" *Indiana Law Review* 26 (1993): 227–62.

———. "Race, Sexuality and the Question of Multiple, Marginalized Identities in U.S. and European Discrimination Law." In *Gender Nonconformity, Race and Sexuality: Charting the Connections*, ed. T. Lester. Madison: University of Wisconsin Press, 2002.

Lewis, D. "Women's Groups Target Limit on Sex Harassment Cases," *Boston Globe*, June 30 (1966), 71.

Lorde, A. *Zami; Sister Outsider; Undersong*. New York: Quality Paperback, The Crossing Press, W.W. Norton, 1984.

MacKinnon, C. "Feminism, Marxism, Method, and the State: Toward *Feminist Jurisprudence*." *Signs* 7, no. 3 (Spring 1982): 227–56.

———. "Sexual Harassment: Its First Decade in Court." In *Feminist Jurisprudence*, ed. Patricia Smith, 145–57. New York: Oxford University Press, 1993.

Malveaux, J. "Gender Differences and Beyond: An Economic Perspective on Diversity and Commonality Among Women." In *Theoretical Perspectives on Sexual Difference*, ed. D. Rhode, 226–38. New Haven, CT: Yale University Press.

Matsuda, M. "Looking to the Bottom: Critical Legal Studies and Reparations." In *Critical Race Theory: The Key Writings That Formed the Movement*, eds. Kimberle Crenshaw, et al., 63–79. New York: New Press, 1995.

———. "Public Response to Racist Speech: Considering the Victim's Story." *Michigan Law Review* 81 (1989): 2320–81.

McCaffrey, E.J. "Slouching Towards Equality: Gender Discrimination, Market Efficiency, and Social Change." *Yale Law Journal* 103 (1993): 595–675.

Meritor v. Vinson, 477 U.S. 57 (1986).

Metzger, M.B., et al. *Business Law and the Regulatory Environment*. 9th ed. Chicago: Richard D. Irwin, 1995.

Mill, J.M. *Utiliarianism*, ed. M. Warnuck. New York: Penguin, 1962.

Minda, G. *Postmodern Legal Movements: Law and Jurisprudence at Century's End*. New York: New York University Press, 1995.

Minnow, M. "Justice Engendered." In *Feminist Jurisprudence*, ed. Patricia Smith, 217–43. New York: Oxford University Press, 1993.

Okin, S.M. *Justice, Gender, and the Family*. New York: Basic Books, 1989.

Oncale v. Sundowner, 1998 U.S. Sup. Ct Lexis 1599.

Patterson, O. "Race, Gender and Liberal Fallacies." *New York Times*, October 20, 1991, 15 Sec. 4.

Phelps, E.S. "The Statistical Theory of Racism and Sexism." *American Economic Review* 62 (1972): 659–61.

Posner, R. *Economic Analysis of Law*. Boston: Little, Brown, 1986.

———. "The Efficiency and Efficacy of Title VII." University of. Pennsylvania. Law Review 136 (1987): 513–21.

———. "An Economic Analysis of Sex Discrimination Laws." *University of Chicago Law Review* 56 (1989): 1311–35.

———. *Sex and Reason*. Cambridge, MA: Harvard University Press, 1992.

Rabidue v. Osceola Refining, 805 F. 2d 611 (6th Cir. 1986).
Rawls, J. *A Theory of Justice*. Cambridge, MA: Harvard University Press, 1971.
Reilly, M. "A Paradigm for Sexual Harassment: Toward the Optimal Level of Loss." *Vanderbilt Law Review* 47 (1994): 427–75.
Riger, S. "Gender Dilemmas in Sexual Harassment Policies and Harassment Procedures." *American Psychologist* (May 1991): 497–505.
Robinson v. Jacksonville Shipyards, 760 F. Su1486 (M.D. Fla. 1991).
Rowe, M.P. "Comment." In D. Niven, "The Case of Hidden Harrassment." *Harvard Business Review*, March-April (1992): 7.
Scheppele, K.L. "The Reasonable Woman." *The Responsive Community* 1 (Fall 1991): 36–47.
Smith, A. *The Wealth of Nations*. New York: Modern Library, 1965.
Smith, P. "Introduction." In *Feminist Jurisprudence*, ed. Patricia Smith, 3–15. New York: Oxford University Press, 1993.
Strauss, D. "The Law and Economics of Racial Discrimination in Employment: The Case for Numerical Standards." *Georgetown Law Journal* 79 (1991): 1619–57.
Swift, J. "A Modest Proposal." *The Art Bin Origo*. Available at: http:art-bin.com/artomodest.html (August 2004).
Talbot, M. "Men Behaving Badly." *New York Times*, October 13, 2002, Sec. 6, 52+.
Terpstra, D.E., and D.D. Baker. "Sexual Harassment at Work: The Psychological Issues." In *Vulnerable Workers: Psychological and Legal Issues*, ed. Marilyn J. Davidson and Jill Earnshaw, 179, 1991.
29 Code of Federal Regulations, Sec. 1604.11 (a)
U.S. Merit Systems Protection Board. *Sexual Harassment in the Federal Workplace: Trends, Progress, Continuing Challenges*, 1995.
———. Sexual Harassment in the Federal Government: An Update, 1988.
Weidlich, T., and C.K. Lawrence. "Sex and the Firms: A Progress Report." *National Law Journal* (December 20, 1993): 1, 22–24.
Wells, D., and B. Kracher. "Justice, Sexual Harassment and the Reasonable Victim Standard." *Journal of Business Ethics* 12 (1993): 423–31.
West, R. "Jurisprudence and Gender." *University of Chicago Law Review* 55 (1988): 1–72.
Whalen, C.W., and B. Whalen. *The Longest Debate: A Legislative History of the 1964 Civil Rights Act*. Washington, DC: Seven Locks Press, 1985.
White v. Monsanto Chemical, 585 So. 2d 1205 (La. 1991).
Wilson, M., and K. Russell. *Divided Sisters—Bridging the Gap Between Black Women and White Women*. New York: Anchor Books, 1996.

Part 5

Other Legal Issues

14

A Social Economics of Crime

(Based on Kantian Ethics)

Mark D. White

The neoclassical economics of crime (NEC), stemming chiefly from Gary Becker's groundbreaking 1968 paper,[1] is perhaps the most ambitious undertaking within the larger program of law and economics. Property law and contract law are more obvious areas of the law to which economics can be applied, because their subject matter is to a large extent pecuniary to begin with. Even tort law, which deals with "private wrongs," often concentrates on damage to property or financial interests, which again can easily be stated in terms of money. Once the costs and benefits of various legal rules and institutions in these areas are put in terms of dollars and cents, the analyst can apply economic reasoning to maximize efficiency, wealth, or well-being, the standard policy goal of normative law and economics (and normative neoclassical economics in general).

But crime is a distinctly different area of law from those mentioned above (though the distinction is notoriously difficult to pin down). Legal philosopher Jules Coleman holds that economic theory "has no place for the moral sentiments and virtues appropriate to matters of crime and punishment: guilt, shame, remorse, forgiveness, and mercy, to name a few. A purely economic theory of crime can only impoverish rather than enrich our understanding of the nature of crime."[2] As Nicholas Mercuro and Steven Medema write, "The type of response that is predicted by economic analysis may well apply more accurately to more overtly economic areas of the law—property, contract, tort, and corporations, for example—than to family or criminal law, where noneconomic motivations might be expected to play a more critical role."[3] The current neoclassical paradigm in law and economics, based on brute utilitarian thinking and self-interested preference-satisfaction, does not seem appropriate for an institution based on such deontological precepts as rights and duties, and other-regarding behavior.

An alternative to neoclassical economics, one that may be better suited to an economic analysis of criminal behavior and law enforcement, is social economics.[4] One goal of social economics is to incorporate ethical thinking and behavior into economic theory, and therefore social economics has a special relevance to the economic study of crime. Mark Lutz, a prominent social economist, writes that a central problem of the neoclassical model of choice "is the exclusion of the moral dimension, or the denial of moral conduct *by assumption.*"[5] Another social economist, Christine Rider writes that "in contradistinction to the neoclassical paradigm, [social economists] explicitly include values and the process of value formation in the modeling of economic reality. . . . By including issues of morality, and the ways in which individual members of social groups learn to behave, social economists' paradigm provides a richer and more accurate explanation of economic reality than the neoclassical."[6] This property of social economics makes it uniquely applicable to analyzing criminal (immoral) behavior.

Social economists' commentary on the economics of crime, or on the broader field of law and economics, is not extensive, but it is significant. Most relevant for our purposes is the work of Sheldon Danziger and David Wheeler, who propose a new theory of individual choice regarding criminal behavior, one that has much in common with the model suggested here.[7] Reza Fadaei-Tehrani and Thomas Green have also commented on the economic study of criminal behavior,[8] and more generally, Mark Lutz, Kenneth Lux, and Steven Medema all critique law and economics from the viewpoint of social economics.[9]

To add to this literature, I will use the ethics of eighteenth century German philosopher Immanuel Kant to help flesh out a new approach to the economics of crime. Many social economists endorse Kant's unique sense of human dignity and belief in the intrinsic worth of each human being, so it makes a convenient starting point for our burgeoning theory.[10] For instance, Lutz writes that the self-interest assumption precludes the economic agent from "approaching others as ends with intrinsic value,"[11] a clear reference to Kant's categorical imperative, and Edward O'Boyle makes use of "a humanistic philosophy of the type traced to Kant [that] starts with the premise that all humans are real, existential actualities, all having the same dignity, and all therefore equal."[12] In his critique of neoclassical law and economics, Medema writes that, among several possible approaches, a "social law and economics might begin with the presumption that . . . law must protect the basic human rights with which each individual is endowed, enforce the binding duties that exist between individuals, and in doing these, strengthen moral commitments," an approach that he identifies as Kantian.[13] Finally, Lanse Minkler has modified the standard model of economic decisionmaking to incorporate commitment, which he interprets as applicable to Kantian duty among other concepts.[14]

This chapter will begin by discussing the ethical foundations of the neoclassical model of rational choice, and explaining how they are ill-suited to the study of criminal behavior. I will then briefly explain Kant's moral system and its relationship to social economics, and outline a model in which I incorporate Kantian duties into the economic decision-making framework. I elaborate upon this model to apply specifically to criminal behavior, comparing it to the standard neoclassical economics of crime approach. We will see that the NEC assumes that the laws only affect an individual's choices through the additional cost stemming from the threatened sanction. While not denying the importance of this effect, my approach also includes the *duty* implied by the law itself, and accounts for instances (none too rare, I hope) in which people obey the law out of respect for the law, not based on a calculation of costs and benefits. Finally, I discuss how this new approach to modeling individual criminal behavior will impact the "other" side of NEC, the model of optimal enforcement, focusing on the structure of legal prohibitions and sanctions.[15]

The Ethics of *Homo Economicus* in the Neoclassical Economics of Crime

The standard model of the economic decisionmaker, or *homo economicus*, portrays him as maximally satisfying his preferences within given constraints. To the modern economist, the word "preference" is not linked to any hedonic pleasure, or any psychological state at all, but merely represents a ranking of options that can be based on whatever the agent values, whether that be happiness, honor, masochism, or the voices in his head. Due to their open-ended nature, an agent's preferences could easily contain rankings of an ethical nature. If his preferences include concern for others, he can be considered, to some extent, an altruist or, more generally, a utilitarian. If his preferences are purely self-regarding, he fits the standard representation of the self-interested decisionmaker, though this model can easily be stretched beyond any usefulness, if every possible motivation the agent could have is ultimately considered in his own interest.

In reference to the NEC literature in particular, narrowly self-interested agents are the rule.[16] Consistent with the classical utilitarianism of Cesare Beccaria[17] and Jeremy Bentham,[18] laws are seen to affect *homo economicus* only insofar as they change the costs and benefits of the options available to him: "A person commits an offense if the expected utility to him exceeds the utility he could get by using his time and other resources at other activities."[19]

Typically, behavior that is to be discouraged or deterred, that is, illegal or criminal behavior, is made more "expensive" to the agent through the imposition of penalties such as fines, imprisonment, or execution. Because the probability of detection, apprehension, and prosecution is almost always less than one, it is assumed that the agent will discount the penalty by the probability that she will "get away with it" (according to her preference for risk). Therefore, to maintain the same level of deterrence, the penalty is increased to maintain the same expected level of punishment from the agent's point of view.

To this end, criminal penalties are treated in the NEC as mere prices, as evidenced by the following quotations from leading scholars in the field: "Each crime has a price—a certain probability of a certain fine";[20] "Punishment is, at least from the criminal's standpoint . . . the price that society charges for a criminal offense"; [21] "Within the legal arena, legal rules establish prices, such as fines, community service, and incarceration, for engaging in various types of economic behavior";[22] and "The commission of most offenses results in an expenditure of effort, the possibility of an increase in the individual's wealth, and the possibility of a penalty. Aside from the penalty, the similarity between such offense decisions and labor supply decisions under uncertainty is obvious. Moreover, if the penalty is a monetary payment, *the analogy is precise*."[23] This may be a fine first approximation, and certainly one befitting economic logic, but as Robert Cooter recognizes: "The economic perspective is blind to the distinctly normative aspect of the law, viewing a sanction for doing what is forbidden merely as the price of doing what is permitted."[24]

Social economists, critical in general of the self-interest assumption in the economic model of choice, are understandably opposed to its application in decisions involving the law. As Lutz writes: "The passing of a law as such will have no effect on personal conduct but only the probability of punishment making illegal behavior more costly. . . . In other words, obedience to the law is wholly contingent upon calculations of self-interest."[25] Likewise, it is assumed that in the absence of legal sanctions, or enforcement of the laws themselves, agents would engage in whatever behavior maximizes their preferences, regardless of its illegality (or immorality). Thankfully, most people do not behave this way; in fact, many people abstain from criminal behavior even when the benefits far exceed the costs, enforcement or not, without even considering engaging in such activity. Such "irrational" decisions as these reveal a critical weakness in the economic theory of criminal behavior, which would predict far more criminal behavior than is actually observed (or presumed).[26]

The neoclassical economics of crime literature assumes that if someone *does not* commit a crime when the opportunity arises, there *must* be some hidden or "psychic" cost changing his mind, but rarely specifies what that may be. According to Isaac Ehrlich, the economic approach to crime "does not ignore the role of 'respect for the law,' penchant for violence, preference for risk and, in general, individual propensities and preferences as determinants of participation in criminal activities. But rather than rest on assumptions concerning the determinants of preference for crime, the economic approach to criminality attempts to separate preferences from objective opportunities and explore to what extent criminal behavior can be explained by the effect of opportunities, given preferences."[27] It is my position that the explanatory power of the model of individual behavior used in NEC can be improved by incorporating an ethical component, one that recognizes the moral nature of the criminal law (as well as law in general), and the effects of one's behavior on the rest of society.[28] By using the expansive approach of social economics and the moral system of Immanuel Kant, a more powerful economic model of criminal behavior will emerge, one that can account for the "irrational" obedience to the law that we observe, and make more sense of illegal behavior as well.

A New Model of Individual Behavior in the Economics of Crime

In constructing our new economic model of criminal behavior, one incorporating ethical and social concerns, I will start with a model developed elsewhere, in which Kantian duties are incorporated into the constrained preference-satisfaction framework of *homo economicus*.[29] Then I will refine the model to apply specifically to the economics of crime, emphasizing the interactions between duty, preferences, and respect for the law.

Basic Kantian Model

Kant's moral system focuses on the concept of autonomy, deriving from the essential dignity that every rational being possesses. Refuting David Hume's statement that reason is the slave of the passions, on which the economic model of choice is implicitly based, Kant elevated reason above all external and internal factors. One's reason can overrule not only influences from outside sources, such as civil and religious authority and social opinion, but also influences from within oneself, the passions Hume spoke of. Economics has adopted the first implication of autonomy in their nominal respect for consumer sovereignty and disdain for coercion and other command structures, but *homo economicus* is still beholden to his preferences, which, to compound the offense, are given a priori, not subject to reflective evaluation or judgment.

To Kant, a person must arrive at the moral law through reason alone (in order to remain autonomous), based on the dignity of all rational beings, as well as logical consistency. This moral law, which Kant regarded as merely a formalized version of the ethics of the common man, is stated as the *categorical imperative*, which can take several forms, all technically equivalent, but some more easily applied in certain circumstances. The first and perhaps best known, the Formula of Autonomy or of Universal Law, is based on consistency: "Act only according to that maxim whereby you can at the same time will that it should become a universal law."[30] The second, the Formula of Respect for the Dignity of Persons, contains the familiar prohibition against using others: "Act in such a way that you treat humanity, whether in your own person or in the person of another, always at the same time as an end and never simply as a means."[31] It is this one that is most often cited in social economics, where great emphasis is placed on treating persons as intrinsically valuable beings, not mere things. This formula also commands that we accept others' ends as our own, generating duties such as beneficence. The third, the Formula of Legislation for a Moral Community, is similar in form to the first, but emphasizes the role of a person's will in making law, not just following it: "So act as if your maxims were to serve at the same time as a universal law (for all rational beings)."[32]

More important for our purposes than the substantive nature of the categorical imperative and the duties derived from it is the nature of those duties and how moral persons must follow them. In Kant's system, in order for action to be truly moral, it must be done out of duty, not simply according to duty; the motivation behind an act determines its ethical basis. "The greatest perfection of a human being is to do his duty *from duty* (for the law to be not only the rule but also the incentive of his actions)."[33] For instance, there is a duty to not lie; if a person refrains from lying in order to gain some advantage later, whether a good job or a pleasant mate, his honesty is not moral (though it is still a good thing, generally speaking). If he is honest in hopes of securing a pleasant afterlife, it is still not a morally motivated act. Only if he refrains from lying out of duty itself is his honesty moral; this directly reflects his autonomy in the face of prudential motives, good or bad. Obviously, if our man refuses to lie even when that would benefit him greatly, we can do reasonably confident that he did so out of duty. If honesty is truly his best policy in terms of self-interest, it is difficult to tell, even for him, his true motive. Kant recognized this: "For a human being cannot see into the depths of his own heart so as to be quite certain, in even a *single* action, of the purity of his moral intention and the sincerity of his disposition."[34]

Kant described two broad types of duties, perfect (or narrow) and imperfect (or wide) duties. Perfect duties are ones that must be followed, regardless of the agent's wishes or inclinations, or of the consequences of the proscribed action. These duties are also referred to as narrow, because persons have no latitude as to how much or how little to execute them. Perfect duties are also often negative duties—do not kill, do not steal, do not lie—and chiefly serve to constrain our impulses. Imperfect duties, on the other hand, dictate general attitudes, rather than specific actions: The duty of beneficence, for example, is an imperfect duty, for it mandates merely that one adopt the attitude of helping others when able. Imperfect duties are also wide duties, because agents do have "play room" in how to execute them, and these are usually positive duties.

The key to incorporating these duties in the constrained preference-satisfaction model is to see perfect, narrow duties as duties of action (or constraints thereof), and imperfect, wide duties as duties of ends. Understanding the two types of duties this way, we can include perfect duties among an agent's constraint set, and imperfect duties among the ends represented in her preference set. Once this is done, our economic actor can maximally satisfy her "preferences" (including imperfect duties) within her constraints (including perfect duties), adhering to Kantian ethics within the standard economic model of choice.[35]

One common objection to Kant's ethics is that he demands too much: How does he expect people to live up to his various duties, and for the sake of duty at that? But Kant was much more of a realist than most give him credit for. While he certainly hoped that people could live up to their moral duties, he knew that occasionally (or even often) they would not, whether out of moral weakness or truly bad intentions. Human beings are never perfectly rational, which is why the moral law presents itself as a categorical *imperative*; our animal inclinations would not accord with the moral law without the overriding power of our will and reason. For Kant, human beings are only contingently rational or moral, reflecting weakness of will in terms of moral judgment. In economic terms, contingent rationality may be a sort of bounded rationality, which is appropriate because morality and rationality are very closely linked in Kant's system, although the weakness here is in character, not in cognitive capacity. I model contingent rationality using a probability weighting over the Kantian, duty-based objective function and the self-interested one (which may include other-regarding preferences as well). The probability weight represents the agent's moral character; the stronger his character, the higher the probability that he will act dutifully in a given situation.[36] This implies that he does not choose whether to act out of duty or self-interest, for that choice itself would have to be made according to some criterion, such as self-interest or duty, and we would be flirting with infinite regress. As I will emphasize later in our examples of potential criminal behavior, an agent's actual behavior is determined randomly, according to the probability weighting over duty and self-interest.

Application to the Economics of Crime

In this section I apply the Kantian model outlined above to criminal behavior in order to contrast it with the standard neoclassical approach. We have seen that the NEC assumes that the only way laws affect choices is through the sanctions imposed, discounted by the probability of detection, apprehension, and prosecution. This model is based purely on self-interest, and leaves little room for ethical thinking or behavior. On the other hand, the Kantian model gives us a way to integrate duties explicitly into *homo economicus*'s choice process, resulting in more elaborate decisionmaking that includes factors such as respect for the law as well as moral weakness.

Before we consider actual (imperfect) agents and legal systems, let us consider ideal Kantian ones. When we do, we face two serious problems. First, in the ideal Kantian world, laws would accord perfectly with morality as laid out in the categorical imperative. The most common examples—do not kill; do not commit battery; do not steal (all components of the criminal law in most societies)—are also clear examples of perfect duty. In the real world, however, there are many laws that do not seem to violate any perfect duties, such as victimless crimes, which will be discussed more later. Because no perfect duty seems to be violated by these actions, they would not be considered of appropriate concern for the state in Kant's view. However, Kant did say that persons have a duty to obey the laws of society, however amoral they are, unless they are in fact immoral (such as a law requiring murder, for instance). For the time being, let us assume all laws are based in morality, or at least do not prescribe immoral acts, so there is no possible moral conflict in obeying the law.

Our second problem is the behavior of the perfectly moral Kantian agent. If laws are moral in nature, and persons behave morally, then they will act in accordance with the law out of duty alone, or at least respect for the law, with no need for criminal sanctions. "If the incentive which juridical lawgiving connects with that duty, namely external constraint, were absent, the idea of duty by itself would be sufficient as an incentive."[37] A person who obeys the law purely to avoid punishment would be operating from prudential motives, not (purely) moral ones.[38] But no human being is perfectly moral, so one could say that the law and its sanctions are still useful in the case of basically good people, to help them adhere to proper behavior in times of weakness, confusion, or simple immorality. However, for a person of fine character or moral quality, the legal sanctions are superfluous; indeed, we can think whether we abstain from murder or theft because it carries a heavy penalty, or because we realize it is wrong. (I think, or rather hope, that most of us would answer the latter.)

This behavior reflects Kantian autonomy, with each person following her own moral law and acting out of duty, not simply in response to external motivation in the form of criminal sanctions. As we saw before, economists endorse a weak form of autonomy, even in the NEC, such as when they rule out factors currently in favor with sociologists, psychologists, and criminologists, like genetics, upbringing, class, environment, or brain chemistry, and instead concentrate solely on costs and benefits. If anything, economists will treat these as parameters that alter the utility function of agents, but do not directly determine whether they commit crime or not. A Kantian approach would agree with economists to a point, but would go even further, saying that none of these factors has any influence on an autonomous will, not even legal sanctions (or laws themselves).

Kantian autonomy also implies that reason overrides one's preferences, not only preferences for criminal rewards and against the accompanying sanctions, but also preferences for and against crime itself. Some scholars, such as Michael Block and John Heineke, derive a preference for honesty from their model;[39] some, such as Ehrlich, assume "psychic costs and benefits" of crime, without being more specific, but hinting that they may include guilt or excitement;[40] and finally others, such as Amitai Etzioni, try to escape the assumption of narrow self-interest by assuming moral preferences alongside, or superior to, preferences for standard goods and services.[41] Norms are another approach to modeling attitudes toward crime, but are often incorporated into preferences and/or backed by sanctions.[42] While any facet of a person's choice framework that leads to pro-social behavior is to be lauded, of course, Kant would not consider this behavior to be truly moral, because it is essentially prudential in nature. "There are many persons who are so sympathetically constituted that, without any further motive of vanity or self-interest, they find an inner pleasure in spreading joy around them. . . . In such a case an action of this kind, however dutiful and amiable it may be, has nevertheless no true moral worth."[43] If one's preferences were to change (though unlikely in standard economic models), a law-abiding person could turn to a life of crime, because his "morality" was simply a function of his preferences not "above" them like duty. "This lax or even mean way of thinking, which seeks its principle among empirical motives or laws cannot too much or too often be warned against, for human reason in its weariness is glad to rest upon this pillow."[44]

So how will we represent the common observation that decent people sometimes disregard the law? I will use the concept of the probability weighting from the last section, tailored specifically to the situation of criminal choice. As before, our overall objective function will be comprised of two parts. One part will be the standard preference ordering of *homo economicus* as normally assumed in the NEC, based on narrow self-interest. In this part of the objective function, laws will impact behavior solely through sanctions acting as prices. The other part will be the more expansive, ethical component, based on Kant's categorical imperative (representing moral and social concerns). In this part, laws (or ideally, the duties embodied therein) serve chiefly as constraints on choice, and the sanctions themselves are of no importance. This way of modeling ethical choice is significantly different from preference- or norm-based models, in that the weighting is "above" preferences as embodied in the component objective functions. When morality is represented by a preference, it can be traded off against self-interested preferences; John may prefer not to steal from his employer, but may do it if his preference for revenge (e.g., for being passed over for a promotion) becomes stronger. If we model Jim's character in his weighting over his self-interested and duty-bound "sides," we are instead representing how *likely* Jim is to embezzle funds. I will assume the "pick" between the two, according to the probability weighting, is random; if it were a choice, it would all collapse to self-interest.[45]

In this application to criminal behavior, I will consider the primary aspect of character in our Kantian model to be "respect for the law," which can be considered both generally and specifically.[46] Lutz writes that "instrumental reasoning . . . affects respect for the law" by concentrating solely on the personal costs and benefits of illegal activity and not the impacts of an agent's actions on those around him or society in general. [47] Respect for the law in general could be related to the agent's perception of the authority of law, whether this question is viewed through legal positivism (in which the law is validated by a civil authority or "sovereign") or natural law theories (in which the law itself is granted moral authority).[48] Obviously, if a person questions the validity of the law, either because she does not regard the authority as valid, or does not regard the law as rooted in morality, her weighting toward duty (disregarding Kant's dictum that all law must be obeyed out of duty) will be less. Respect for the law could also be linked to what Lon Fuller terms the "inner morality of law," properties of law such as consistency, publicity, clarity, and the absence of retroactivity.[49] If any of these properties are lacking or missing altogether, law seems less like a logical, fair system of social control, and more like a jumble of arbitrary commands, and respect for it is likely to be lacking or missing as well.

What I am calling respect for the law could also be seen as a commitment to social values or a sense of community; even if the law is seen as wrongheaded, one will be moved to obey it as a member of the larger community (rather than as duty). In their social economic model of criminal decisionmaking, Danziger and Wheeler include a "social contract tolerance index," based on

> a vector of characteristics that determine an individual's allegiance to the social contract. The greater the allegiance to the social contract, the lower the probability that the individual will engage in illegal activity. . . . These components express the socioeconomic or psychological background of the individual—his taste for risk, his level of education, his peer group relations, the cohesiveness of his neighborhood and stability of his family, his age, local labor market conditions, etc.[50]

While I will abstract away from such socioeconomic factors in favor of more essentially legal factors (though the line between them can be blurry), Danziger and Wheeler's social contract allegiance function can be easily interpreted as "respect for the law" as I am using it here.[51]

The Effect on Optimal Enforcement

We now have a model of individual decisionmaking in the context of crime, and while that is the chief focus of this chapter, it would be incomplete if I did not discuss the ramifications of this approach for determining the optimal level and method of enforcement. For as Ehrlich writes, "The approach one takes in analyzing the determinant effect of law enforcement on crime is inseparable from the approach one takes in analyzing the determinants of criminal behavior itself."[52]

Because this chapter focuses on the individual decision-making framework and not the goals of enforcement, I will take the standard goal of optimal deterrence as given, though Kantians and social economists would have disagreements with this as well.[53] Optimal enforcement is usually modeled as a Stackelberg-type game, in which the criminal's offense rate is determined as a function of punishment, and then the punishment scheme (usually severity and probability) is chosen to maximize social welfare. However, sanctions as incentives are usually considered as the only way of creating deterrence in the NEC literature; as Lutz writes, "Economists, in discussing public policy options, cannot see beyond the manipulating of *incentives* in channeling individual behavior."[54] But "if . . . there is more of some illegal activity than society is willing to tolerate, then simply increasing the punishment to some 'optimal' level will not have the desired effect if the rational maximizing assumption is incorrect."[55]

Enforcement and Deterrence

Consider an individual, Jim, whose character is represented by equal weighting (50/50) over duty and self-interest. Assume that on the self-interest side, a certain crime is welfare-improving for Jim, because the expected net benefits (without considering any possible punishment) is $100. The duty side, of course, prohibits it outright, with no consideration of any possible gain. As far as Jim is concerned, he is as likely to commit the crime as not. He does not choose whether to follow self-interest or duty; choice takes place only on the self-interest side (if that side "wins"), and the duty side allows no choice regarding immoral activities.

What penalty should the authorities set for the crime Jim may commit, if they are fully aware of his character? Let us assume the cost to the government of enforcing and imposing a penalty is equal to the value of the penalty to Jim (we can relax this later). A penalty that imposes a cost of $100 on Jim, whether in the form of a fine or short-term imprisonment, is sure to deter the crime if Jim follows his self-interest, which is the standard NEC assumption. But there is a 50 percent chance that he would never commit the crime at all, and if the penalty costs the government $100 to enforce and impose, then it would be inefficient deterrence: The authorities would be spending $100 to deter $50 worth of expected crime. It follows that they should impose a penalty of $50 (at equivalent cost to them). If Jim happens to follow self-interest, he will commit the crime, because the expected net gain is still $50; if he follows duty, he will not commit the crime regardless of the size of the punishment, but the authorities will have wasted less resources ($50 rather than $100) deterring the law-abiding side of Jim's character.[56]

Let us make the example more extreme: Consider Jane, who has a weighting of 99/1 in favor of duty. Spending resources to deter someone like her from crime, at least for all but the most serious violations, hardly seems worthwhile. The authorities are effectively concerned with deterring the self-interested side of agents, just in case they "win" in the random draw, but if the weighting on self-interest is small enough, as it is in Jane's case, the deterrence is again inefficient, not being worth the resources spent. The authorities have to deal with expectations, and someone with a 99/1 weighting has very little expectation of committing crime, and any crime that Jane may commit will be considered not worth deterring because it is so unlikely. Even if we relax the assumption of high cost to the authorities of enforcing the penalty, as long as there is any cost at all, some crimes will not be worth deterring, if the character of the potential "criminals" is known to be good and the harm from the crime is small.

According to the standard NEC crime approach, everyone is considered always to maximize self-interest, with no respect for duty, which may lead to (perhaps gross) overenforcement. In the Kantian model, persons differ in their character, some more likely to commit crime if it is in their interests, some unlikely regardless of personal gain. From the examples above, we see that, if possible, authorities should focus on deterring those most likely to commit crimes. But how to tell, without any clear way to judge character? I assumed that the authorities "knew" Jim and Jane, and realized that enforcement and punishment dollars were better spent on Jim than on Jane. In the real world, of course, this information is not easily available. As George Stigler writes:

> Indeed, the problem of determining the efficient penalty may be viewed as one in statistical inference: to estimate the individual's average, durable propensity to offend (the population value) on the basis of a sample of his observed behavior and how this propensity responds to changes in penalties. As in other sequential sampling problems, one can estimate this propensity more accurately, the longer the individual's behavior is observed.[57]

This inference could also be improved not only through length of observation, but also through depth or intrusiveness thereof, both of which would offend some people's sense of privacy and invite accusations of totalitarianism. When information is not gathered, and enforcement relies on statistical inferences that tell much about groups but little about individuals, we have profiling, which of course is very controversial and widely considered immoral. It is practiced, and accepted, to some extent now: placing more officers in more crime-ridden sections of a city, for instance. But that is different (at least in degree) from prejudging an individual based on his or her assumed group identity.[58]

Finally, our model explains the difference between prices and sanctions.[59] As mentioned earlier, the neoclassical economics of crime equates these two concepts, rendering a sanction charged for violating the law identical to the price charged for something allowed by the law. But in the model presented here, the sanction, which appears only in the self-interested part of the objective function, is backed up by duty on the other side, whereas prices appear in both. Imagine a parking space in a large city with an hourly charge of $10.[60] When considering whether or not to park there, an agent performs marginal analysis, and decides if it is worth parking in the space rather than the alternatives. Duty plays no role because there is no obvious moral aspect to the decision, and both models, NEC and Kantian/social economics, would predict the same outcome.

However, let us change the example so that the parking space is off-limits by law (reserved, close to a fire hydrant, etc.), and the penalty for parking there is $10 per hour (assume there are no further effects, such as a notation on his record). As modeled by the NEC, the decision facing the agent would be no different from the previous case; the fact that it is now an offense in the latter case is of no consequence. However, an agent modeled in the fashion described herein makes this calculation only if he has a lapse in virtue; the stronger his character, the less chance he will ever think about parking in a prohibited space. If he follows duty, the sanction is no matter; parking in the space is not allowed, and he recognizes the duty to obey that law, regardless of any benefit that may accrue to him if he violated it (a self-interested consideration). In this model, then, laws and sanctions have a distinctly different effect on the agent, as long he has some probability of acting dutifully.[61]

Respect for the Law

More important for our purposes is the issue of the weighting between self-interest and duty. To repeat, a perfectly moral agent would strictly follow the dictates of duty and would never consider committing a crime. But recognizing that people are not perfectly moral, as Kant did, we can model the possibility that agents will (unintentionally) disregard their duty and act in their narrow self-interest. To represent the unpredictability on this occurrence, I place a probability weighting between the self-interested and duty-bound objective functions, and it is that weighting which I now discuss, especially factors that can be influenced, for better or worse, by the authorities.

There is the possibility that some law-enforcement practices themselves may reduce agents' respect for the law in general. I have already discussed the normative difference between prices and sanctions, and how this model emphasizes that distinction. However, if agents themselves do not recognize it, it may lessen their respect for the law, at least those laws punishable by fines, and especially relatively small fines, such as traffic tickets. Second, even though severity and probability of punishment may be considered equally on the self-interest side (allowing for various attitudes toward risk),[62] low probability of detection and punishment may impact an individual's respect for the law. Laws that arc infrequently punished, such as littering, jaywalking, or sodomy laws, may become targets of ridicule, even though the penalties themselves may be set high enough to retain "optimal deterrence" (but at the cost of seeming disproportionate to the crime). The standard rationale for this penalty structure, of course, is that the costs of enforcing these laws is too high, rendering a low probability/high severity mix efficient, but the layman may not realize this, and instead may interpret it as lack of commitment by the authorities to those particular laws.[63]

Other issues that may affect respect for the law deal more with justice, and are reflected in criticisms of the deterrence-based, utilitarian-flavored motivation for punishment, that often denies persons their intrinsic dignity as emphasized by Kantians and social economists. Disproportionate punishment, statistical profiling, prevalence of plea bargain agreements, and rules of procedure that increase the risk of punishment of the innocent and acquittal of the guilty, all breed a cynicism that threatens to reduce overall respect for the law, and could lessen the weight given to duty in the overall objective function.[64] Subtly indicting the influence of law and economics on the criminal justice system, Herbert Morris writes:

> When law begins to be viewed as a system of social control, intent upon keeping costs down and increasing gains, rather than a system of rules to effectuate justice, the risk is inevitably run that one's sense of guilt with regard to law becomes less a factor in one's conduct. . . . As those in authority with greater frequency act to further policy rather than promote justice, their moral authority diminishes, respect for the institutions generating norms and implementing them lessens, and in its train there is a lessened regard for complying with law because it is law.[65]

The goal of devising and applying law in order to maximize efficiency or social welfare is well established among law and economics scholars, but if some regard this as dehumanizing (as Kant did, not incidentally), it may lead to a decline in respect for the law.[66]

Rather than a lack of respect for the law in general, an agent may have varying respect for certain laws; the prohibition of murder, for instance, is surely universally agreed upon, but traffic laws may be seen as more "malleable," judging from the frequency at which they are broken (and for such little reason). In this sense, a person's weighting may be a function of the criminal behavior in question; the weighting toward duty may be very strong for violent crimes and theft, and less so for stealing office supplies from work. This distinction may have nothing to do with the "size" of the crime; some may take violent crime more seriously than property crime, for instance, regardless of the amount of harm caused by each.[67]

A special case of lack of respect for specific laws may be victimless crimes, a technical term describing crimes where all persons involved are complicit in the criminal act, and there is no directly harmed victim to report the crime.[68]

The most common examples are drug use, prostitution, and gambling; in each of these cases, both the buyer and seller are guilty of criminal behavior. If persons distinguish between these laws and most crimes in which there is a directly harmed victim (such as theft and battery), decisions to pursue these behaviors will be decided by the self-interest side alone, or by both sides in parallel (with no role played by duty). This would make these laws harder to deter (in addition to the difficulty that already exists due to having no victim to report the crime). More generally, "a consequence of legal wrongdoing diverging from accepted conceptions of wrongdoing is the dilution of respect for the law's norms generally," suggesting that the increase in the number of laws, especially those that punish victimless crimes, "tends, as inflation generally does, to devaluation of the currency of laws."[69] In this way, respect for all laws could decline with increased publicity given to victimless crimes.

Clearly, an alternative route for authorities to take, rather than taking the respect for law as given, is to try to influence it. If the authorities can positively influence respect for the law among the citizenry, the crime rate and enforcement expenditures would likely fall, according to this model (and, I would think, common sense). Using the language of moral preferences rather than duties, Etzioni writes: "The policy point is that one needs to work not merely on the cost-benefit, deterrence, incentive, and police side but also on the formation of preferences side, via moral education, peer culture, community values, and mobilization of appropriate public opinion."[70] This is more easily said than done, of course, but the discussion above may offer a few suggestions, such as correcting the injustices mentioned earlier, enhancing the inner morality of the law, and evaluating victimless crimes to determine if combating them is a proper use of the coercive power of the state (and its limited enforcement resources).

Conclusion

In this chapter I have suggested a new model of individual decisionmaking regarding criminal behavior as an alternative to the standard approach in the neoclassical economics of crime literature. This new model explicitly incorporates values, a hallmark of social economics, and specifically the ethics of Immanuel Kant, which provides a common basis with social economics, due to their shared emphasis on human dignity. This model can explain more of the behavior we observe in the real world, especially "irrational" law-abiding activity in the face of net benefits from "other options." Agents in this new model recognize moral duties regarding their actions and the law, even though they may lapse in their moral judgment from time to time. This has important implications toward optimal enforcement of laws, the distinction between prices and sanctions, and efforts to enhance respect for the law among the citizenry.

I hope this is but the beginning for incorporating ethics in economic analyses of criminal behavior and enforcement. Social economics is by no means wedded to Kantian ethics, or deontological ethics in general; there are many other systems of ethics and values that can be applied to the economic study of crime, such as the classical virtue ethics of Aristotle and Aquinas, and more modern feminist and environmental ethics. Even within the standard, neoclassical approach to the economics of crime, more work can be done on examining and extending the utilitarian foundations of that model. As Jules Coleman wrote in the passage quoted at the beginning of this chapter, the legal category of crime is inherently moral, and an economic approach to studying it needs to take that into account.

Notes

I thank Margaret Oppenheimer and Nicholas Mercuro for helpful suggestions.

1. Gary S. Becker, "Crime and Punishment."

2. Jules Coleman, "Crimes, Kickers, and Transaction Structures," 165.

3. Nicholas Mercuro and Steven Medema, *Economics and the Law*, 183.

4. It should be mentioned that there is no single school of social economics, as acknowledged by Christine Rider in her presidential address to the Association of Social Economists; see Rider, "Art, Ethics, and Economics," 267. For the purposes of this chapter, personalist, humanistic, and Catholic economics are all considered to be under the broad umbrella of social economics. Steven G. Medema considers all of these (plus Kantian approaches) when contemplating a social law and economics; see Medema, "Is There Life Beyond Efficiency?" 147.

5. Mark A. Lutz, *Economics for the Common Good*, 155 (italics in original).

6. Rider, "Art, Ethics, and Economics," 263.

7. Sheldon Danziger and David Wheeler, "The Economics of Crime." See also the comments to that paper in the April 1976 issue of the *Review of Social Economy* (vol. 34, no. 1).

8. Reza Fadaei-Tehrani and Thomas M. Green, "Crime and Society."

9. Mark Lutz and Kenneth Lux, *Humanistic Economics*, 182–99; Lutz, *Economics for the Common Good*, 160–62; Medema, "Is There Life Beyond Efficiency?" From the field of socioeconomics, which shares some concerns with social economics, see the papers in Brian Forst, ed., *The Socio-Economics of Crime and Justice*, especially Llad Phillips, "Economic Perspectives on Criminality," and Graham Hughes, "The Limits of Legal Sanctions."

10. For a critical note on the relationship between social economics and Kant, see Mark D. White, "Kantian Dignity and Social Economics."

11. Lutz, *Economics for the Common Good*, 160.

12. Edward O'Boyle, "Personalist Economics," 370.

13. Medema, "Is There Life Beyond Efficiency?" 147.

14. Lanse Minkler, "The Problem with Utility."

15. There are many more aspects of the economics of crime that can also be critiqued from the viewpoint of social economics and Kantian ethics but cannot be discussed here due to space limitations, such as the justification and definition of the criminal category; the distinction between crime and tort; just and proper criminal procedure; and the purpose and justification of punishment.

16. A notable exception is Erling Eide, who incorporates norms into the agent's preference set. See Eide, *Economics of Crime*, chap. 2.

17. "Experience has shown that the common crowd does not adopt stable principles of conduct, and the universal principle of dissolution . . . cannot be avoided except by motives that have a direct impact on the senses and appear continually to the mind to counterbalance the strong impressions of individual passions opposed to the general good." Cesare Beccaria, *On Crimes and Punishments*, 7.

18. "It is the profit (that is, the expectation of the profit) of the offense that constitutes the *impelling* motive . . . by which a man is prompted to engage in the offense. It is the punishment, that is, the expectation of the punishment, that constitutes the *restraining* motive, which . . . is to act upon him in a *contrary* direction, so as to induce him to abstain from engaging in the offense." Jeremy Bentham, *The Principles of Morals and Legislation*, 179, footnote 2 (italics in original).

19. Becker, "Crime and Punishment," 176.

20. David Friedman, "Rational Criminals and Profit-Maximizing Police," 45. The passage continues (emphasis mine): "Someone willing to pay that price will commit the crime—and, from the standpoint of economic efficiency, *should*." Unfortunately, that topic is beyond the scope of this chapter!

21. Richard A. Posner, *Economic Analysis of Law*, 5.

22. Mercuro and Medema, *Economics and the Law*, 59.

23. M.K. Block and J.M. Heineke, "A Labor Theoretic Analysis of the Criminal Choice," 314 (italics added). See also W. Kip Viscusi, "The Risks and Rewards of Criminal Activity," for a similar approach, likening the criminal choice to normal occupational choice in terms of the risk/reward trade-off.

24. Robert Cooter, "Prices and Sanctions," 1523. See also George P. Fletcher, "The Fall and Rise of Criminal Theory," 278, in which he indicts law and economics and its attitude toward crime (including self-interested calculation and the interpretation of sanctions as prices) as one cause of the decline of criminal theory in the 1980s: "In the end, despite some good faith efforts, those interested in economic analysis of law simply had to ignore the complications of criminal justice."

25. Lutz, *Economics for the Common Good*, 160.

26. One could also use a transaction cost or bounded rationality argument to support general law-abiding behavior, asserting that the opportunity cost of evaluating each possible criminal opportunity is too high, but a general disposition toward, or habit of, such behavior is more efficient overall. But "prudence would seem to indicate that we not adopt an all-embracing general obligation to obey the law, but retain the ability to not adopt this policy in those cases where the costs of case-by-case assessment are not greater than the benefits." Thomas May, "On Raz and the Obligation to Obey the Law," 20.

27. Isaac Ehrlich, "The Deterrent Effect of Criminal Law Enforcement," 260–61.

28. Along the same lines, Fadaei-Tehrani and Green propose integrating "psychological, sociological, and political phenomena" into the "psychic costs and benefits" of the economic agent. See "Crime and Society," 784.

29. Mark D. White, "Can *Homo Economicus* Follow Kant's Categorical Imperative?"

30. Immanuel Kant, *Grounding for the Metaphysics of Morals*, 421 (Academy pagination).

31. Ibid., 429.

32. Ibid., 438. See Roger J. Sullivan, *An Introduction to Kant's Ethics*, chaps. 2–6, for an excellent introduction to the categorical imperative; Roger J. Sullivan, *Immanuel Kant's Moral Theory*, Part III, for a detailed summary; and H.J. Paton, *The Categorical Imperative*, for an in-depth analysis.

33. Immanuel Kant, *The Metaphysics of Morals*, 392 (emphasis in original). This principle was first introduced, though not stated as directly, in Kant, *Grounding for the Metaphysics of Morals*, 397–99 (see trans. *n*12).

34. Kant, *The Metaphysics of Morals*, 392.

35. For more details, see White, "Can *Homo Economicus* Follow Kant's Categorical Imperative?" Within a norm-based model of criminal behavior, Eide interprets some norms as limiting action (because their preference is so extreme), and others as simply influencing it, which is similar to the way we model perfect and imperfect duties, but Eide includes both in preferences. See Eide, *Economics of Crime*, 69.

36. If a normally ethical person lapses in his duty, this does not indicate that the person is evil, just somewhat lacking in virtue. If he knowingly and intentionally violates a duty, then he is evil. See Sullivan, *Immanuel Kant's Moral Theory*, chap. 9.

37. Kant, *The Metaphysics of Morals*, 220.

38. However, Thomas E. Hill recently presented an argument supporting a moral role for punishment as motivation in Kant's ethics. See T.E. Hill, "Punishment, Conscience, and Moral Worth."

39. Block and Heineke, "A Labor Theoretic Analysis of the Criminal Choice," 316.

40. Ehrlich, "The Deterrent Effect of Criminal Law Enforcement," 262.

41. Amatai Etzioni, *The Moral Dimension*.

42. For representative scholarship on norms within NEC and law and economics, see Eide, *Economics of Crime*, and Eric Posner, *Law and Social Norms*. Richard Posner and Eric B. Rasmusen emphasize the various sanctions that serve to enforce norms, including guilt and shame, but not following norms for their own sake; see Posner and Rasmusen, "Creating and Enforcing Norms." Finally, see T.J. Brennan, "The Trouble with Norms," for a critique of norm-based economic choice theories.

43. Kant, *Grounding for the Metaphysics of Morals*, 398.

44. Ibid., 426. However, Kant did hold that moral feeling could be important, not as the primary motivation to behave ethically, but as a fallback given contingent rationality. See Kant, *The Metaphysics of Morals*, 399–400, and Sullivan, *Immanuel Kant's Moral Theory*, 132–37.

45. This is especially pertinent to Posner's statement that "criminals . . . generally have the same moral beliefs as the law-abiding. They just don't want to act on those beliefs." Richard A. Posner, *The Problematics of Moral and Legal Theory*, 39. (See also footnote 58 on the same page for a curiously Kantian statement on the impossibility of knowing one's true motivation for obeying the law.)

46. See May, "On Raz and the Obligation to Obey the Law," for a discussion of general and specific obligations to obey law.

47. Lutz, *Economics for the Common Good*, 160.

48. See Jeffrie G. Murphy and Jules L. Coleman, *The Philosophy of Law*, chap. 1, for an introduction to the debate over legal positivism and natural law.

49. Lon L. Fuller, *The Morality of Law*.

50. Danziger and Wheeler, "The Economics of Crime," 117.

51. In his comment on Danziger and Wheeler's paper, Todd R. Clear derisively reduces the social contract allegiance term to "the tendency to resist temptation." He seems mainly concerned with estimation, while for our purposes, this characterization is perfectly adequate. See Clear, "Crime and Utility Maximization," 84.

52. Ehrlich, "The Deterrent Effect of Criminal Law Enforcement," 274. For a similar statement from a social economics perspective: "The knowledge of how individuals respond to different legal rules and *why they respond in the ways they do* is important, for it guides us in the design of the legal rules themselves." Medema, "Is There Life Beyond Efficiency?" 145 (emphasis added).

53. See Murphy, *Kant: The Philosophy of Right*, 119–23, for a succinct statement of Kant's retributivist justification of punishment and opposition to utilitarian emphasis on deterrence. Kant held that deterrence uses the criminal as a means to reducing the crime rate without also treating him at the same time as an end, deserving punishment for his wrongdoing independent of any net effect on society. Social economics may agree with Kant, based on this reasoning, given its ultimate grounding in human dignity, but I could find no discussions of the goals of punishment in the social economics literature.

54. Lutz, *Economics for the Common Good*, 160.

55. Medema, "Is There Life Beyond Efficiency?" 145.

56. Also, this assumes that the amount/level of deterrence has no impact on the weighting, which may not be warranted (more below).

57. George J. Stigler, "The Optimum Enforcement of Laws," 529.

58. This approach offers an alternative explanation of imposing higher penalties for repeat offenses, if the fact that such persons committed one offense reveals information about their weighting. This is as opposed to the standard NEC explanation, that higher sanctions for second offenses increases deterrence at the time of the first if the criminal is forward-looking; see A. Mitchell Polinsky and Steven Shavell, "On Offense History and the Theory of Deterrence." Posner comes closer to our reasoning: "The fact that the defendant has committed previous crimes makes us more confident that he really is guilty of the crime with which he currently is charged," lessening the risk of wrongful conviction. See Posner, *Economic Analysis of Law*, 252.

59. See Cooter, "Prices and Sanctions."

60. Coincidentally, this example is very close to the one that Becker credits with inspiring his analysis of the economics of crime; see Becker, "The Economic Way of Looking at Life," 389–90.

61. Our explanation is somewhat similar to Cooter's, though he relies on self-interest for both. In his model, an agent's marginal cost of crime is continuous in prices but discontinuous in sanctions. A substantial sanction, applied regardless of the "amount" of crime, will preclude all criminal activity for most persons, whereas prices, proportional to the amount of crime, will more likely result in interior solutions. See Cooter, "Prices and Sanctions," 1548–50.

62. See Polinsky and Shavell, "The Optimal Trade-Off Between the Probability and Magnitude of Fines."

63. Fuller writes that if, for example, "laws prohibiting the sale of contraceptives are kept on the books as a kind of symbolic act, with the knowledge that they will not and cannot be enforced, legal morality is seriously affected. This is no way to quarantine this contagion against a spread to other parts of the legal system." Fuller, *The*

Morality of Law, 153. Also see David Friedman, "Why Not Hang Them All?" for other drawbacks regarding efficient but unrealistic punishments, such as punishing all crimes by execution, with the probability of exacting the penalty scaled to the seriousness of the crime.

64. See Louis Kaplow and Steven Shavell, "Accuracy in the Determination of Liability," and John R. Harris, "On the Economics of Law and Order," as well as Stigler, "The Optimum Enforcement of Laws," 528, for views on "optimal accuracy" in determining liability. On the subject of plea bargaining, Kipnis writes, "In its coercion of criminal defendants, in its abandonment of desert as the measure of punishment, and in its relaxation of the standards for conviction, plea bargaining falls short of the justice we expect of our legal system. . . . If we are to expect our citizenry to respect the law, we must take care to insure that our legal institutions are worthy of that respect." Kenneth Kipnis, "Criminal Justice and the Negotiated Plea," 106.

65. Herbert Morris, "The Decline of Guilt," 75.

66. For critiques of the focus on efficiency in law and economics, see Ronald Dworkin, "Is Wealth a Value?" and "Why Efficiency?" and Coleman, "Efficiency, Utility and Wealth Maximization." Richard A. Posner, the chief exponent of efficiency, responds to these articles in *The Economics of Justice*, chap. 4. (See also the next chapter this volume for more on this controversy.)

67. Eide discusses a similar phenomenon with respect to differing motivation to follow norms prohibiting murder and importing excess liquor. See Eide, *Economics of Crime*, 25.

68. See Alan Wertheimer, "Victimless Crimes," for a critical discussion of victimless crimes and arguments for their decriminalization.

69. Morris, "The Decline of Guilt," 74.

70. Etzioni, *The Moral Dimension*, 242.

References

Beccaria, C. *On Crimes and Punishments* [1764], trans. David Young. Indianapolis: Hackett, 1986.

Becker, G.S. "Crime and Punishment: An Economic Approach." *Journal of Political Economy* 76 (1968): 169–217.

———. "The Economic Way of Looking at Life." *Journal of Political Economy* 101 (1993): 385–409.

Bentham, J. *The Principles of Morals and Legislation* (1781). Buffalo, NY: Prometheus Books, 1988.

Block, M.K., and J.M. Heineke. "A Labor Theoretic Analysis of the Criminal Choice." *American Economic Review* 65 (1975): 314–25.

Brennan, T.J. "The Trouble with Norms." In *Social Norms and Economic Instituions*, ed. K.J. Koford and J.B. Miller, 85–94. Ann Arbor: University of Michigan Press, 1997.

Clear, T.R. "Crime and Utility Maximization: A Note on Danziger and Wheeler." *Review of Social Economy* 34 (1976): 83–85.

Coleman, J. "Crimes, Kickers, and Transaction Structures" (1985). Reprinted in Coleman, *Markets, Morals, and the Law*, 153–65.

———. "Efficiency, Utility and Wealth Maximization" (1980). Reprinted in Coleman, *Markets, Morals, and the Law*, 95–132.

———. *Markets, Morals, and the Law*. Cambridge: Cambridge University Press, 1988.

Cooter, R. "Prices and Sanctions." *Columbia Law Review* 84 (1984): 1523–60.

Danziger, S., and D. Wheeler. "The Economics of Crime: Punishment or Income Redistribution." *Review of Social Economy* 33 (1975): 113–31.

Dworkin, R.M. "Is Wealth a Value?" *Journal of Legal Studies* 9 (1980): 191–226.

———. "Why Efficiency?" *Hofstra Law Review* 8 (1980): 563–90.

Ehrlich, I. "The Deterrent Effect of Criminal Law Enforcement." *Journal of Legal Studies* 1 (1972): 259–76.

Eide, E. *Economics of Crime: Deterrence and the Rational Offender*. Amsterdam: North-Holland, 1994.

Etzioni, A. *The Moral Dimension: Toward a New Economics*. New York: Free Press, 1988.

Fadaei-Tehrani, R., and T.M. Green. "Crime and Society." *International Journal of Social Economics* (2002) 29: 781–95.

Fletcher, G.P. "The Fall and Rise of Criminal Theory." *Buffalo Criminal Law Review* (1998) 1: 275–94.

Forst, B., ed. *The Socio-Economics of Crime and Justice*. Armonk, NY: M.E. Sharpe, 1993.

Friedman, D. "Rational Criminals and Profit-Maximizing Police: The Economic Analysis of Law and Law Enforcement." In *The New Economics of Human Behavior*, ed. M. Tommasi and Kathryn Ierulli, 43–58. Cambridge: Cambridge University Press, 1995.

———. "Why Not Hang Them All? The Virtues of Inefficient Punishment." *Journal of Political Economy* 107 (1999): S259–69.

Fuller, L.L. *The Morality of Law*. 2d ed. New Haven, CT: Yale University Press, 1969.

Harris, J.R. "On the Economics of Law and Order." *Journal of Political Economy* 78 (1970): 165–74.

Hill, T.E. "Punishment, Conscience, and Moral Worth." In *Kant's Metaphysics of Morals: Interpretative Essays*, ed. Mark Timmons, 233–53. Oxford, UK: Oxford University Press, 2002.

Hughes, G. "The Limits of Legal Sanctions." In *The Socio-Economics of Crime and Justice*, ed. Forst, 51–61.

Kant, I. *Grounding for the Metaphysics of Morals* [1785], trans. J.W. Ellington. Indianapolis: Hackett, 1993.

———. *The Metaphysics of Morals* [1797], trans. and ed., M. Gregor. Cambridge: Cambridge University Press, 1996.

Kaplow, L., and S. Shavell. "Accuracy in the Determination of Liability." *Journal of Law and Economics* 37 (1994): 1–15.

Kipnis, K. "Criminal Justice and the Negotiated Plea." *Ethics*, 86 (1976): 93–106.

Lutz, M.A. *Economics for the Common Good: Two Centuries of Social Economic Thought in the Humanistic Tradition*. London: Routledge, 1999.

Lutz, M.A., and K. Lux. *Humanistic Economics: The New Challenge*. New York: Bootstrap Press, 1988.

May, T. "On Raz and the Obligation to Obey the Law." *Law and Philosophy* 16 (1997): 19–36.

Medema, S.G. "Is There Life Beyond Efficiency? Elements of a Social Law and Economics." *Review of Social Economy* 51 (1993), 138–53.

Mercuro, N., and S.G. Medema. *Economics and the Law: From Posner to Post-*

Modernism. Princeton, NJ: Princeton University Press, 1997.
Minkler, L. "The Problem with Utility: Toward a Non-Consequentialist/Utility Theory Synthesis." *Review of Social Economy* 57 (1999): 4–24.
Morris, H. "The Decline of Guilt." *Ethics* 99 (1988): 62–76.
Murphy, J.G. *Kant: The Philosophy of Right*. Macon, GA: Mercer University Press, 1990 (reprint of 1970 original).
Murphy, J.G., and J.L. Coleman. *The Philosophy of Law: An Introduction to Jurisprudence*, rev. ed. Boulder, CO: Westview Press, 1990.
O'Boyle, E.J. "Personalist Economics: Unorthodox and Counter-Cultural." *Review of Social Economics* 59 (2001): 367–93.
Paton, H.J. *The Categorical Imperative: A Study in Kant's Moral Philosophy*. Philadelphia: University of Pennsylvania Press, 1947.
Phillips, L. "Economic Perspectives on Criminality: An Eclectic View." In *The Socio-Economics of Crime and Justice*, ed. Forst, 37–49.
Polinsky, A.M., and S. Shavell. "On Offense History and the Theory of Deterrence." *International Review of Law and Economics* 18 (1998): 305–24.
———. "The Optimal Trade-Off Between the Probability and Magnitude of Fines." *American Economic Review* 69 (1979): 880–91.
Posner, E.A. *Law and Social Norms*. Cambridge, MA: Harvard University Press, 2002.
Posner, R.A. *Economic Analysis of Law*. 5th ed. New York: Aspen Law and Business, 1998.
———. *The Economics of Justice*. 2d ed. Cambridge, MA: Harvard University Press, 1983.
———. *The Problematics of Moral and Legal Theory*. Cambridge, MA: The Belknap Press/Harvard University Press, 1999.
Posner, R.A., and E.B. Rasmusen. "Creating and Enforcing Norms, with Special Reference to Sanction." *International Review of Law and Economics* 19 (1999): 369–82.
Rider, C. "Art, Ethics, and Economics." *Review of Social Economy* 57 (1999): 263–77.
Stigler, G.J. "The Optimum Enforcement of Laws." *Journal of Political Economy* 78 (1970): 526–36.
Sullivan, R.J. *Immanuel Kant's Moral Theory*. Cambridge: Cambridge University Press, 1989.
———. *An Introduction to Kant's Ethics*. Cambridge: Cambridge University Press, 1994.
Viscusi, W.K. "The Risks and Rewards of Criminal Activity: A Comprehensive Test of Criminal Deterrence." *Journal and Law and Economics* 4 (1986): 317–40.
Wertheimer, A. "Victimless Crimes." *Ethics* 87 (1977): 302–18.
White, M.D. "Can *Homo Economicus* Follow Kant's Categorical Imperative?" *Journal of Socio-Economics*, 33 (2004): 89–106.
———. "Kantian Dignity and Social Economics." *Forum for Social Economics*, 32 (2) 2003: 1–11.

15

Economic Analysis of Tort Law

Austrian and Kantian Perspectives

Edward Stringham and Mark D. White

Introduction

How should tort law be administered? Neoclassical law and economics offers a clear answer: Tort cases should be decided so as to maximize wealth in dollar terms. Rather than needing to weigh matters of justice, morality, or rights, judges only need to decide cases based on the simple and determinate guidelines of Kaldor-Hicks efficiency. When a tort occurs, the judge simply must weigh the net costs and benefits to all parties and rule according to what maximizes wealth. In cases of positive transaction costs, when the costs imposed on the injured parties are less than the benefits that accrue to the culpable parties, we should allow the harm to continue, and vice versa. Such a system is appealing for those who believe that members of society would be better under a system of efficiency- or wealth-maximization, with little or no concern for matters of justice or rights.[1] Although the guidelines appear simple, economists in the Austrian tradition argue that the theory rests on a few questionable assumptions. Despite its apparent simplicity, the process of using efficiency to determine law raises several issues that render it nonfunctional.

The first half of the chapter outlines positive criticisms of neoclassical law and economics from the viewpoint of Austrian economics. Because Austrians believe that calculation of economic costs and benefits requires a system of property rights, we cannot use economics to determine those very property rights. But Austrian economics itself offers no normative alternative. Whereas neoclassical law and economics includes positive and normative analysis of property rights, economists in the Austrian tradition must rely on a normative theory of property rights from outside economics. The second half of the chapter outlines one such alternative, based on Kantian ethics, represented by Kantian critiques of the standard approach to tort law in law and economics scholarship. When cases are decided by notions of justice rather than efficiency, judges would not be burdened with the thorny task of calculating all the economic consequences of their decisions. Because a deontological standard does not face the same difficulties, it offers a clear substitute to the wealth-maximization standard.

Positive Criticisms of Neoclassical Law and Economics

Summary of Austrian Arguments

Austrians point to a number of problems with judging law based on economic efficiency. One theme in their critiques is that in absence of market choices, it is not clear how to determine the relevant costs and benefits necessary to render an informed decision. As Mario Rizzo explains, "Much of the efficiency-based economics of law literature sees the tort law as an attempt, however crude, to approximate the outcomes of hypothetical markets."[2] But Austrians feel that this undertaking is more easily said than done. Judges would find it too difficult to measure and compare the willingness-to-pay of the various parties involved in a particular case. Murray Rothbard writes, "In order to do so, everybody's utility scale would have to be investigated by the compensators. But from the very nature of utility scales, this is an impossibility. Who knows what has happened to anyone's utility scale?"[3] Even though neoclassical law and economics considers willingness-to-pay to be based on subjective valuation, it believes that these valuations can be known even outside of market choice. But as Austrians argue, due to the subjective nature of value, preferences can differ greatly between individuals, and, unfortunately, individuals do not have readily apparent utility functions.[4] For judges to make efficient decisions, we would need to believe that they could know individuals' preferences, which is problematic at best.

In "The Mirage of Efficiency," Rizzo argues that the case for the wealth-maximization norm rests on the unrealistic assumption of near perfect information.[5] While most economic analysis of law relies on simplified partial equilibrium models, trying to trace the effects of a law in the real world is next to impossible. "In fact, unless we can acquire a great deal of information about the interrelations between markets, we cannot know if such improvements bring us closer or further from optimality."[6] Outside of static long-run equilibrium, disequilibrium prices make measuring the efficiency of different states of the world very difficult. In the world as it exists, shadow prices are not apparent, and it is not obvious even what to count in our measurement of net wealth.[7] Prices may give us consumer valuation at the margin, but to consider net wealth we need to measure consumer surplus, and we have no way of measuring the value of inframarginal units.

Edward Stringham makes the case that judges will be unable to measure the costs and benefits associated with various outcomes.[8] Although judges can observe past prices, they are historical artifacts that do not necessarily have any relationship with current market conditions. Judges, as imperfect agents, will have a difficult time evaluating what they think various individuals are willing to pay in cases dissimilar to past events. Judges would need to predict, not what *they* would be willing to pay under different circumstances, but what *others* would be willing to pay. The problem becomes even more complicated when we realize judges have to consider all possible states of the world. To trace out the economic consequences of their decisions, judges would need to know the area under the demand curves for every imaginable circumstance.

But are judges up to this task? Walter Block has often argued that they are not.[9] Because costs are subjective, it will be extremely difficult for judges to know how much each party would be willing to pay (or bribe) to obtain various outcomes.[10] Without knowing willingness-to-pay the judges might not reach the wealth-maximizing solution. Block writes that "the judges might act 'very foolishly' and award the property rights to the wrong person. . . . Can it be expected that judges appointed largely through the political process will judge correctly (more than half the time)?"[11] If judges are unreliable in this respect, giving them discretion to decide cases based on costs and benefits will make property rights more uncertain and erratic, compromising the foundation of the market economy.[12]

In "Law Amid Flux," Rizzo gives a new perspective to the lengthy debate in neoclassical law and economics on the choice between negligence versus strict liability as a basis for accident law.[13] Under a negligence standard, the courts weigh the costs of various actions and hold individuals guilty of a tort if they are judged not to have undertaken "due care," or if the cost of their precautions was less than the expected harm from their actions.[14] Under the latter, the courts ignore precaution and other social costs and proscribe certain actions no matter who the least-cost avoider is. Although the system of strict liability is more simplistic and ignores economic consequences, Rizzo argues that the system is more attractive: "Ironically, it is precisely because we live in a dynamic world where the information needed by the 'fine-tuners' is not available that the answer must be the antiquated and static system of strict liability."[15] He argues that we cannot unambiguously test whether one law is more socially efficient than another, and that even figuring out the most basic things such as the identity of the least-cost avoider is not straightforward when conditions are constantly in flux. "A world in which technological change is permitted involves infinitely greater informational problems."[16] The least-cost avoider will vary under different cost structures, and when we are dealing with disequilibrium prices, the actual opportunity costs are only estimates. "The moral of the story is that costs are not easily measured by outside observers, especially where there is a subjective expectational component to the evaluation of forgone outputs. . . . The ability to know the extent to which market prices are correct is fundamentally an entrepreneurial skill, and the courts are not populated by entrepreneurs."[17]

Roy Cordato also stresses the problem that disequilibrium prices will not reflect the information judges need to decide their cases: "In this setting a Coasian judge faces an impossible task. He must have access to accurate information concerning foregone opportunities associated with the use of the resources under consideration. Yet disequilibrium prices will not accurately convey this information."[18] Judges should not use actual prices as an approximation for general equilibrium prices because if they were identical, the dispute already would have been resolved. As Cordato writes, "If the market generated prices are truly general equilibrium prices, there would be no problem to analyze. If the externality problem actually exists, then the apparent market prices *could not be* general equilibrium prices."[19] He argues that the efficiency norm would require judges to have perfect foresight or require them to continually reassess their decisions.[20] Instead of giving judges such challenges, Cordato supports strict liability and the "coming to the nuisance" doctrine, in which parties could not sue to block a condition, such as noise, that existed before they arrived.[21] Rather than ruling on immeasurable costs and benefits, judges would be given the simpler task of ruling on the proper ownership of titles.[22]

In "Rules Versus Cost-Benefit Analysis in the Common Law," Rizzo lodges the same arguments made about other forms of activist government policy against government activism in law. Because government judges are not omniscient and will have problems predicting the effects of different judgments, he argues that the law should not attempt to impose economic ends on society. Judges can either follow a system where they attempt to balance the societal costs and benefits of each case taken separately, possibly imposing undue costs on some individual members of society,[23] or they can follow a system that attempts to protect the autonomy of the individual through uniformly applied, established rules. Rizzo supports the latter: "The pure common law process produces abstract rules that do not impose a particular hierarchy of ends on society, but simply facilitate the attainment of various individual ends."[24] In this sense, the common law respects the goals of individuals over any social ends sought by policy makers. It resolves conflicts between members of society by balancing their respective rights and interests in order to preserve fairness or justice, not a social welfare goal that reduces individual rights and autonomy to secondary concerns.

The Problem of Economic Calculation with Undefined Property Rights

We can extend the above line of reasoning using Ludwig von Mises's arguments on the impossibility of economic calculation under socialism.[25] As Mises put forth, measurements of economic costs and benefits only make sense within a system of defined property rights and market choice. Without property rights, no meaningful prices exist, and without prices, we have no reliable way to engage in economic calculation. This brings us to a point of contention with the efficiency norm. The economic theory of property rights wishes to define rights in a way that will maximize wealth,[26] but to Austrians there is a problem of infinite regress.[27] When property rights are not well defined, willingness-to-pay is indeterminate, and thus there is no unique assignment of property rights that maximizes wealth. As Gerald O'Driscoll writes, "Maximization makes sense if we know who has what rights, and what rules govern the choice process. The suggestion that the maximization principle be used to determine the rights distribution and the legal rules is almost incoherent."[28] Under such a system, judges would be in a position of central planners engaging in nonprice resource allocation.[29]

How can willingness-to-pay determine property rights when willingness-to-pay is determined by property rights? One of the fiercest defenders of the efficiency norm in law and economics, Richard Posner, puts his finger on the dilemma:

> A related problem is that where large allocative questions are involved, as in the initial assignment of rights, the very concept of wealth-maximization becomes problematic. Since the wealth of society is the output of all tangible and intangible commodities multiplied by their market values, it is difficult to compare the wealth of two states of society in which prices are different.[30]

Because willingness-to-pay is only meaningful within a system of clearly defined property rights, we have a circularity problem of using economics to render law. We would need to know who owns the property to solve these maximization problems. Unless we assume that all people are exactly the same and would spend their money exactly the same way, the assignment of property rights will be critical for evaluating economic outcomes.

As Rizzo and Tyler Cowen point out, the problem relates to the Scitovsky

Reversal Paradox, which shows the potential incommensurability of efficiency levels.[31] In certain cases, as Tibor Scitovsky wrote, "It is impossible to decide which of the two alternative situations is more efficient; and one may get the paradoxical result that each situation is more efficient than the other."[32] This is the case when the willingness-to-pay attached to one outcome exceeds another under the current assignment of property rights, but once property rights are rearranged, the ranking is the opposite. This problem can surface if preferences vary across individuals or over time. Because changes in property rights can alter the production possibilities frontier, even in a simple two-person world we can have a situation where Andrew's preferred bundle is only attainable in state of the world *A*, and Barbara's preferred bundle is only attainable in state of the world *B*. Which state of the world is more socially efficient? The answer will depend on the distribution of property rights. When Andrew is assigned a large portion of the property rights, the net willingness to see *A* will be higher than to see *B*, but when Barbara is assigned a large portion of the property rights, the results will be the opposite.

Or consider Carl, who wishes to play basketball in the middle of the night, much to the dismay of his neighbor Donna, who wishes to sleep in quiet.[33] If Donna is rich and Carl is poor, chances are that Donna is willing to pay a lot more for quiet than Carl is willing to pay to play basketball. In this case, a quiet neighborhood is Kaldor-Hicks efficient. But if we reassign property rights so that Donna becomes poor and Carl becomes rich, as long as basketball and quiet sleep are normal goods to the respective parties, the willingness-to-pay associated with quiet will decrease and the willingness-to-pay associated with basketball will increase. Is the society with the late-night basketball richer than a society with halcyon nights? Because the different people have different preferences, the willingness-to-pay associated with the two outcomes will differ according to the assignment of property rights. As economists such as Harold Demsetz well recognize, we may not have the same outcome when wealth effects are significant.[34]

Not being able to determine the efficient outcome is an issue whenever property rights are up in the air. Consider someone who accidentally damages a statue outside the residence of a government official. Should the person who damages the statue be held liable for a tort?[35] Because Kaldor-Hicks does not evaluate the morality of the situation aside from the value of the consequences, the judge must examine willingness-to-pay and compare the cost of avoiding damaging the statue to the value of the statue. If the net willingness-to-pay attached to having the statue in place is positive, then damaging the statue is a social bad, and if the net willingness is negative (assuming the transaction costs of negotiating to remove the statue are prohibitive), then damaging the statue is actually socially beneficial. But the judge's decision will clearly be contingent on the existing assignment of property rights. In societies where dictators own a large portion of resources, we see high prices associated with such statues (both the willingness-to-pay to purchase and remove the statues would be high), but the moment property rights are rearranged away from dictators, these statues become worthless, and, as we have seen historically, they are often intentionally destroyed. When the dictator owns most of the property, the state of the world with monuments is more efficient (the willingness-to-pay attached to that outcome is higher), but when individuals own most of property, the state of the world without monuments is more efficient. Is the society with numerous statues of government officials richer than a world without? Again, we cannot answer the question unless we know the distribution of property rights; as Rizzo writes, "There is no way, then, to stand outside the law and see how it measures up against an external standard."[36]

Finally, recognizing that the Coase theorem only holds when income effects are small[37] means the economic theory of property rights only can be applied to a limited realm.[38] Although it may be possible to analyze the efficiency of small, incremental changes in property rights, we may not be able to analyze the efficiency of existing property rights. But a complete economic theory of law would have to consider all possible states of the world to calculate the global optimum for wealth. Posner writes, "If transaction costs are positive, the wealth-maximization principle requires the initial vesting of rights in those who are likely to value them most."[39] But this brings us to the conundrum: We cannot determine how much people value anything if we have an indeterminate willingness-to-pay due to not knowing who owns what. Rizzo argues that, at most, the efficiency "norm is effective in prescribing small or marginal adjustments in the law," but that "it is impossible to assign basic rights in accordance with the efficiency norm."[40] This means that we need an exogenous justification of property rights and legal rules. If law and economics does not provide the basic fundamental rules, where do they come from? And how can we ever judge that those fundamental rules are efficient? Israel Kirzner argues that economic decisionmaking, and economic analysis itself, requires a system of preexisting property rights.[41] Law cannot be determined using economic costs and benefits because those economic costs and benefits can only be meaningfully determined under an existing system of law.

A Deontological Alternative to Wealth-Maximization

How else should judges decide cases? Despite the difficulty of implementing Kaldor-Hicks efficiency, one may believe judges might as well try, for lack of a better proposal. Even though judges have limitations, they could at least do their best to render wealth-maximizing decisions. But if Austrians economists are correct in their criticisms, the problem is more fundamental.[42] It is not a question of approximating efficient outcomes, because the maximum level of wealth, much less the policy to achieve it, is often ambiguous, especially in the "hard cases" that set legal precedents. This has led some, such as Paul Rubin, to criticize Austrians as being unable to judge the efficiency of policy evaluations.[43] But accepting the Austrian criticisms need not make one a nihilist about judging the world. Murray Rothbard writes, "I conclude that we cannot decide public policy, tort law, rights, or liabilities on the basis of efficiencies or minimizing of costs. But if not costs or efficiency, then what? The answer is that only *ethical principles* can serve as a criteria for our decisions."[44] We may not be able to judge law based on efficiency, but we are capable of judging it based on other standards.

Austrian economics is a positive endeavor that does not offer or recommend particular normative ends, but it can help identify the deficiencies in certain normative proposals. The neoclassical theory of law and economics depends on information that is impossible to obtain, and ultimately relies on its own conclusions, as seen in our discussion of the circularity problems with Kaldor-Hicks efficiency. In fact, utilitarian theories in general suffer from these calculation problems, but deontological theories, such as rights-based ethical systems, do not. In such theories, legal decisions would be made based on notions of justice rather than efficiency, and judges would not face the unenviable task of calculating the economic consequences, in all possible states of the world, of all their possible actions. As Posner describes this rival view, "We are then led, in the manner of [Robert] Nozick or [Richard] Epstein, to an ethical defense of market transactions that is unrelated to their effect in promoting efficiency."[45] Admittedly, when it comes to their normative views, not all Austrians embrace theories of rights, but a large number of them do.[46] These theorists are careful to note that their normative position does not stem from economics itself, but that normative positions on property rights provide a backdrop for their economic analysis: "The choice of a particular property rights structure is beyond the realm of economic science, and has no place in positive discussions of efficiency."[47]

We do not here attempt to argue the justice of any particular deontological theory or the general concept itself, but we do hold that rights theories offer a clear alternative to welfarism, especially if one agrees merely that judges are not well suited for determining efficiency. In what follows we provide a summary of the ethics of Immanuel Kant, who specified duties that moral agents must follow and can be translated into the language of rights. We choose Kant's moral system due to its essential and obvious contrasts with many of the positions in the law and economics literature. This approach offers an alternative for those who reject the consequentialist ethics upon which neoclassical law and economics is based.

Kantian Ethics

Immanuel Kant is well known for his stand against consequentialist evaluation of moral decisions. To Kant the motivation of actions, not the consequences thereof, are of utmost importance in determining their moral status. As he wrote:

> An action done from duty has its moral worth, not in the purpose that is to be attained by it, but in the maxim according to which the action is determined. The moral worth depends, therefore, not on the realization of the object of the action, but merely on the principle of volition according to which, without any regard to any objects of the faculty of desire, the action has been done.[48]

In this sense, an attempted violation of rights would be considered just as wrong as an actual violation of rights, because the intention is the same even though the results differ. By the same token, a good act done for self-interested reasons would not be considered moral.

For an intended plan, or maxim, of action to be considered moral, it must meet two conditions: It must be based on duty, and it must also be performed out of that duty, not merely according to it. Duties are derived from the *categorical imperative*, Kant's formalization of "the moral law," which is an a priori deduction of one's reason. Kant wrote of three formulations of the categorical imperative, each emphasizing a different aspect of the moral law, but all three ideally equivalent. For our purposes, the second, the *Formula of Respect for the Dignity of Persons*, is the most useful: "Act in such a way that you treat humanity, whether in your own person or in the person of another, always at the same time as an end and never simply as a means."[49] To Kant, each rational agent has an intrinsic dignity stemming from her reason, and this dignity is not respected when anybody (including herself) uses a person simply as a means to an end. For instance, when Edith steals from Frank, she is using Frank as a means to obtaining the stolen goods for herself. If she were to treat Frank as an end and not just as a means, she would propose a transaction, and respect Frank's wishes no matter how Frank responded. This can also be interpreted as Edith's respecting Frank's right to his property, or more generally, his right not to be used merely as a means.[50]

This version of the categorical imperative directly rules out a number of actions, perhaps most importantly (and controversially) the sacrifice of a few for the benefit of the many. This holds for acts most would consider clearly ignoble, such as eradicating one group of people simply because it would increase the happiness of others, but it would also hold for acts such as saving a life at the expense of harming an innocent bystander. It also applies to less dramatic circumstances, such as property and wealth transfers, which brings the categorical imperative into direct conflict with the neoclassical approach to tort law and Kaldor-Hicks efficiency, as we shall see.

Rights and Duties

From a Kantian perspective, we find many aspects of the treatment of tort law in normative law and economics objectionable.[51] One is the treatment of rights, including property rights as well as rights in one's person, as solely instrumental to achieving efficiency. Ronald Coase uses the example of a farmer's crops harmed by a rancher's cattle, and shows that the efficient solution is identical whether the rancher is liable for the damages or not. When transaction costs are low, and property rights are clearly vested in one party or the other, the farmer and the rancher will bargain, and the party valuing it the most will purchase or retain that right. Kantians would have no objection to this, as it represents a voluntary transaction, and the brilliance of Coase's analysis lies in the conclusion that the lowest-cost solution will be reached no matter who has the property right to begin with.

It is when transaction costs are high that Kantians would disagree with Coase. In such a case, under the wealth-maximization norm, the law should award the right to the party who *would have* purchased it in an ideal bargaining context. Coase writes:

> [T]he situation is quite different when market transactions are so costly as to make it difficult to change the arrangement of rights established by the law. In such cases, the courts directly influence economic activity. It would therefore seem desirable that the courts should understand the economic consequences of their decisions and should, insofar as this is possible without creating too much uncertainty about the legal position itself, take these consequences into account when making their decisions.[52]

According to this standard, the purpose of property rights is not to ensure justice but to maximize wealth, being assigned instrumentally to produce the lowest cost outcome.

On the other hand, Kantians view rights as stemming from duties, not from any cost-benefit calculation. Posner writes, "Another objection to using

[Kantian] autonomy directly as an ethical norm . . . is that it requires an arbitrary initial assignment of rights."[53] However, rights are *not* arbitrarily assigned in a Kantian system but, rather, outlined by duties; a duty not to lie implies a right not to be lied to, and a duty not to steal implies a right not to have your property stolen.[54] We can contrast this theory of rights with neoclassical law and economics in which "the institution of rights, and particular allocations of rights, are justified only insofar as they promote social wealth more effectively than other institutions or allocations."[55] As soon as rights fail to do this, they will be disregarded in the name of efficiency; indeed, as Posner writes, "When transaction costs are prohibitive, the recognition of absolute rights is inefficient."[56] Law and economics scholars take pride in the fact that many commonly accepted rights are validated by the efficiency criterion, such as "giving a worker the right to sell his labor and a woman the right to choose her sexual partners."[57] But as Ronald Dworkin points out, such analysis uses wealth-maximization to justify rights that wealth-maximization justifies, which reveals nothing about their independent moral worth.[58] Even when wealth maximization does happen to justify certain rights, that justification could disappear with the slightest change in relative costs and benefits. Kantians believe that rights, and the duties from which they derive, are absolute as determined by the moral law. They should never be determined or "allowed" by an efficiency-based calculation, augmenting the positive Austrian arguments cited earlier.

Hypothetical Compensation

As mentioned before, Kant's mandate never to treat individuals merely as ends prevents the implementation of Kaldor-Hicks efficiency. This is primarily due to the doctrine of *hypothetical compensation*: A decision is Kaldor-Hicks efficient if the winners gain enough to compensate the losers, although the compensation need not actually take place. As such, hypothetical compensation leaves us with merely a potential Pareto improvement, and even though it may benefit others, it comes at the expense of certain individuals. Even if government attempted to compensate the victims, as long as the losers do not consent, it would be objectionable, for no one has an obligation to undergo a specific sacrifice for the greater good.

If we do not rely on hypothetical compensation, how could policy evaluation proceed? The simple solution is to rely not on hypothetical but on actual consent.[59] With any market transaction based on mutual consent, we can assume that it is ex ante utility-enhancing to the parties involved. Disregarding any third party effects, Rothbard and Jeffrey Herbener consider this a version of the Pareto principle,[60] and Anthony Kronman states it in Kantian terms: "The Pareto principle represents a moral ideal based upon respect for the autonomy of individuals and acceptance of the idea that one should always treat others as ends in themselves and not merely as means."[61] We can contrast this with a situation where parties do not have to agree, and the state reorganizes property rights to increase total welfare. In the case of hypothetical compensation, "some committed to the Kantian idea of individual autonomy would rightly feel that his moral principle had been violated, and it would not make any difference, from his point of view, that compensation could potentially be made even though it was not. *For a Kantian, the Kaldor-Hicks test has no significance.*"[62] Stringham proposes that as long we can get individuals to privately agree to law ex ante, we can have a system based on consent, arguing that this can be done in a private system similar to arbitration agreements in business.[63]

Causation

Another aspect of the economic approach to tort law with which Kantians would disagree is *reciprocal causation*.[64] In standard applications of the Coase theorem, no blame or fault is assigned to either party in a conflict, and only the efficient solution is sought. In the words of Coase, "The question is commonly thought of as one in which *A* inflicts harm on *B*, and what has to be decided is, How should we restrain *A*? But this is wrong. We are dealing with a problem of a reciprocal nature. To avoid the harm to *B* would be to inflict harm on *A*."[65] According to the normative interpretation of the Coase theorem, society should be morally indifferent between instances of harm, leaving only the relative costs of each harm to determine the efficient solution. But to a Kantian the issue is of who harmed whom, or whose rights are violated by whom: "If a person's actions will affect the persons or property of others, those actions must conform to those others' rights—that is, they must be consistent in their external effects with the equal absolute moral worth of those others as free rational beings."[66]

Richard Epstein criticizes this aspect of Coase's thought, arguing that while Coase espouses a reciprocal view of causation, his examples are stated in terms of unidirectional harm: "Coase describes each situation by the use of sentences that differentiate between the role of the *subject* of each of these propositions and the role of the *object*."[67] The harm only becomes reciprocal, Epstein explains, when the harmed party seeks legal redress: "It would be a grave mistake to say that *before* the invocation of judicial remedies the grounds of dispute disclosed reciprocal harm. . . . The notion of causal reciprocity should not be confused with the notion of redress for harm caused."[68]

In Posner's reply to Epstein, he claims that "most torts arise out of a conflict between two morally innocent activities, such as railroad transportation and farming. What ethical principle compels society to put a crimp in the latter because of the proximity of the former?"[69] But Kantians have an answer to Posner's question: rights. A farmer may have the right not to have cattle travel on his property if he homesteaded the land first or purchased it from someone who had.[70] Or the rancher company may have the right to cross lands if it homesteaded the pastures first or purchased those rights from someone who had. A Kantian judge simply must determine who is the just owner of any given right. Suppose the farmer homesteaded his land first and only later did the ranchers come to the area. Before the rancher allows his cattle to stray on the farmer's property, he should ask the farmer's permission. In a Kantian interpretation, the rancher who fails to restrain his cattle from grazing on the farmer's land is violating his duty to respect the property of the farmer. The farmer is free to sell his right to the cattle-raiser, but that right is his to begin with, and should not be assigned to the cattle-raiser by a judge just because it is worth more to him. These actions are not "morally innocent" if someone's right is violated; once this is understood, "the structure and content of the modes of rectification for infringement [of rights] will be implicit in the rights themselves."[71]

Conclusion

Determining law using efficiency is questionable in a number of ways. From a positive Austrian perspective, we can question the meaningfulness of calculating costs and benefits when property rights are undetermined. In a world with an unclear or uncertain allocation of rights, it is impossible for judges to gauge the economic effects of their decisions. From a normative Kantian perspective, we can question whether individuals should be treated merely as ends in the pursuit of efficiency and social welfare. The notions of hypothetical compensation, reciprocal causation, and the instrumental nature of rights, all essential to the analysis of tort law in neoclassical law and economics, are all inconsistent with a Kantian respect for the dignity of persons. Austrians argue that economics cannot give us a complete theory of law, and Kantians argue it should not even if it could.

What remains to be done is to provide a constructive proposal for a better way to apply economic reasoning to the study and practice of tort law, making use of the Austrian and Kantian criticisms we have outlined. Such a program would emphasize the constraints placed on judges, both to acknowledge the informational difficulties of ambitious decisionmaking and to respect the rights of individuals, more than the ends the judges would attempt to achieve.

In fact, libertarian scholars (such as Robert Nozick and Murray Rothbard[72]) may have worked the most toward this end, as many of their ideas have significant overlap with Austrian economics and Kantian ethics. But to the extent that neoclassical law and economics continues to concentrate solely on wealth-maximization, social welfare, or efficiency in its approach to tort law, it will continue to overlook the insights provided by Austrian and Kantian thinkers.

Notes

We would like to thank Rodolfo Gonzalez, Margaret Oppenheimer, and Nicholas Mercuro for helpful comments and discussion.

1. For instance, see Richard Posner, *The Economics of Justice*; David Friedman, *The Machinery of Freedom*; and Louis Kaplow and Steven Shavell, *Fairness Versus Welfare*. Kaplow and Shavell are probably the most extreme current proponents of this view, arguing that well-being should be the only criterion used in legal decisions, and any suggestion of sacrificing well-being in the interest of justice or rights to be "troubling" (8).

2. Mario Rizzo, "Law Amid Flux," 298.

3. Murray Rothbard, "Toward a Reconstruction of Utility and Welfare Economics," 236.

4. James Buchanan, *Cost and Choice*.

5. Mario Rizzo, "The Mirage of Efficiency," 641.

6. Ibid., 647.

7. Ibid., 643.

8. Edward Stringham, "Kaldor-Hicks Efficiency and the Problem of Central Planning."

9. Walter Block, "Coase and Demsetz on Property Rights," "Ethics, Efficiency, Coasian Property Rights and Psychic Income," and "Private-Property Rights, Erroneous Interpretations, Morality and Economics."

10. Block, "Ethics, Efficiency, Coasian Property Rights and Psychic Income," 87.

11. Block, "Coase and Demsetz on Private Property Rights," 114.

12. Block, "Private-Property Rights, Erroneous Interpretations, Morality, and Economics," 67, and Walter Block, "O.J.'s Defense: A *Reductio Ad Absurdum*."

13. See Steven Shavell, "Strict Liability Versus Negligence," for the orthodox treatment. For an approach to this problem based on Kantian social contract theory, see Gregory C. Keating, "A Social Contract Conception of the Tort Law of Accidents."

14. This is commonly known as the Hand Formula, first stated in Judge Learned Hand's decision in *United States v. Carroll Towing Co.*, 159 F.2d 169, 173 (2d Cir. 1947). See Richard Posner, *Economic Analysis of Law*, 179–83, for an excellent summary; and Richard Wright, "The Standards of Care in Negligence Law," for a critique (note that he mentions Hand's skepticism toward application of "his" formula, which sounds rather Austrian!).

15. Rizzo, "Law Amid Flux," 318.

16. Ibid., 307.

17. Ibid., 310.

18. Roy Cordato, *Welfare Economics and Externalities in an Open-Ended Universe*, 97.

19. Ibid., 109.
20. Ibid., 97.
21. An example would be a recording studio moving next to an airport, and then suing the airport to block its noise. See Donald A. Wittman, "First Come, First Served."
22. Cordato, *Welfare Economics and Externalities*, 100.
23. See the subsection "Hypothetical Compensation," below.
24. Mario Rizzo, "Rules Versus Cost-Benefit in the Common Law," 882.
25. Ludwig von Mises, *Economic Calculation in the Socialist Commonwealth*.
26. Richard Posner, "Utilitarianism, Economics, and Legal Theory," 109, 125–26.
27. Block, "Ethics, Efficiency, Coasian Property Rights and Psychic Income," 95.
28. Gerald O'Driscoll, "Justice, Efficiency, and the Economic Analysis of Law," 357.
29. Ibid., 359; Stringham, "Kaldor-Hicks Efficiency and the Problem of Central Planning."
30. Richard Posner, "The Ethical and Political Basis of the Efficiency Norm in Common Law Ajudication," 501.
31. Rizzo, "The Mirage of Efficiency," 650; Tyler Cowen, "The Scope and Limits of Preference Sovereignty," 254–58.
32. Tibor Scitovsky, "The State of Welfare Economics," 310.
33. Harold Demsetz ("Ethics and Efficiency in Property Rights Systems," 102) gives this example to illustrate the assignment of property rights matters when transaction costs are significant, and Block ("Ethics, Efficiency, Coasian Property Rights and Psychic Income," 86–89) discusses how we could decide who should have the rights to these activities.
34. Harold Demsetz, "Block's Erroneous Interpretations."
35. Depending on the legal system, this might be classified as a crime, but to even get to this point, we need to have a theory of crime versus torts. Murray Rothbard ("Law, Property Rights and Air Pollution," 102) argues the distinction between the two should not be made, and Bruce Benson's "Are Public Goods Really Common Pools?" shows historically that criminal law was an invention of government to generate more revenue than it could with the existing system of tort law.
36. Rizzo, "Mirage of Efficiency," 646. These issues are even more problematic when we are making income comparisons between different societies; see Amartya Sen, "Real National Income." We have to consider not just how one society would rank two social outcomes, but how two societies with different sets of preferences would compare outcomes. When price vectors, preferences, and population size in two societies differ, comparisons about which society is better off become even more awkward. As Rizzo writes in "The Mirage of Efficiency," 650: "If relative prices differ between the two societies, then the comparison of consumer surpluses is even more difficult." Cowen, in "The Scope and Limits of Preference Sovereignty," 258, adds: "Preference sovereignty can provide coherent rankings if and only if we can choose a baseline level of preferences (or wealth level) for comparing policies."
37. Demsetz, "Ethics and Efficiency in Property Rights Systems," 100.
38. Rizzo, "The Mirage of Efficiency," 651; Cowen, "The Scope and Limits of Preference Sovereignty," 267.
39. Posner, "Utilitarianism, Economics, and Legal Theory," 125.
40. Rizzo, "The Mirage of Efficiency," 651.
41. Israel Kirzner, *The Driving Force of the Market*.
42. Cowen, "The Scope and Limits of Preference Sovereignty"; Stringham, "Kaldor-Hicks Efficiency and the Problem of Central Planning."

43. Paul Rubin, "Predictability and the Economic Approach to Law," 320.

44. Rothbard, "The Myth of Efficiency," 95.

45. Posner, "The Ethical and Political Basis of the Efficiency Norm in CommonLaw Adjudication," 490.

46. For examples of those that do not embrace rights, see Henry Hazlitt, *The Foundations of Morality;* Ludwig von Mises, *Human Action;* and Leland Yeager, *Ethics as Social Science*. For those who do, see Kirzner, *The Driving Force of the Market*; Murray Rothbard, *For a New Liberty*; Hans-Hermann Hoppe, *The Economics and Ethics of Private Property*; Bryan Caplan, "The Austrian Search for Realistic Foundations," 834; Paul Cleveland, "The Failure of Utilitarian Ethics in Political Economy"; and Block, "Private-Property Rights, Erroneous Interpretations, Morality, and Economics."

47. Roy Cordato, "The Austrian Theory of Efficiency and the Role of Government," 402.

48. Immanuel Kant, *Grounding for the Metaphysics of Morals*, 399–400.

49. Ibid., 429.

50. This discussion of the categorical imperative is obviously incomplete. See Roger Sullivan, *An Introduction to Kant's Ethics*, for an overview; Roger Sullivan, *Immanuel Kant's Moral Theory*, for a detailed summary; and H.J. Paton, *The Categorical Imperative*, for an in-depth analysis.

51. Kant never discussed tort law outright; see Wright, "Rights, Justice, and Tort Law," 166.

52. Ronald Coase, "The Problem of Social Cost," 19.

53. Posner, *The Economics of Justice*, 98. For more on Kantian autonomy, see chapter 14 in this volume on a Kantian/social economics of crime.

54. The example of theft assumes the validity of property itself; we thank Margaret Oppenheimer for pointing this out. Immanuel Kant's thoughts on the institution of property can be found in *The Metaphysics of Morals*, pp. 260–70. See also Mary J. Gregor, *Laws of Freedom*, chap. 4; and Kenneth R. Westphal, "A Kantian Justification of Punishment."

55. Ronald Dworkin, "Is Wealth a Value?," 198.

56. Posner, *The Economics of Justice*, 70.

57. Ibid., 73.

58. Dworkin, "Is Wealth a Value?," 207.

59. For the consent to be just, it does require the existing set of property rights to be just to begin with.

60. Rothbard, "Toward a Reconstruction of Utility and Welfare Economics"; Jeffrey Herbener, "The Pareto Rule and Welfare Economics."

61. Anthony Kronman, "Wealth-Maximization as a Normative Principle," 235.

62. Ibid., 238 (italics added).

63. Edward Stringham, "Market Chosen Law."

64. For an Austrian statement, see Block, "Ethics, Efficiency, Coasian Property Rights and Psychic Income."

65. Coase, "The Problem of Social Cost," 96.

66. Wright, "Rights, Justice, and Tort Law," 165.

67. Richard Epstein, "A Theory of Strict Liability," 165.

68. Ibid., 165. Talcot Page makes the same point, that the notion of reciprocal harm confuses "a physical harm with the effects of a remedy" ("Responsibility, Liability, and Incentive Compatibility," 252). The concept of nonreciprocal harm may

ultimately have its roots in Aristotle's concept of "corrective justice"; see Aristotle, *Nicomachean Ethics*, section 5.5, for the original statement, and Wright, "Rights, Justice, and Tort Law," for the links between Aristotle's concepts of justice and Kant's later formulation.

69. Richard Posner, "Strict Liability," 216.

70. Rothbard, "Law, Property Rights, and Air Pollution."

71. Wright, "Rights, Justice, and Tort Law," 176.

72. Robert Nozick, *Anarchy, State, and Utopia*; Rothbard, *For a New Liberty*.

References

Aristotle. *Nicomachean Ethics*. trans., T. Irwin. Indianapolis, IN: Hackett, 1985.

Benson, B.L. "Are Public Goods Really Common Pools? Considerations of the Evolution of Policing and Highways in England." *Economic Inquiry* 32 (1994): 249–71.

Block, W. "Coase and Demsetz on Property Rights." *Journal of Libertarian Studies* 1, no. 2 (1977): 111–16.

———. "Ethics, Efficiency, Coasian Property Rights and Psychic Income: A Reply to Harold Demsetz." *Review of Austrian Economics* 8, no. 2 (1995): 61–126.

———. "O.J.'s Defense: A *Reductio Ad Absurdum* of the Economics of Ronald Coase and Richard Posner." *European Journal of Law and Economics* 3 (1996): 265–86.

———. "Private-Property Rights, Erroneous Interpretations, Morality, and Economics: Reply to Demsetz." *Quarterly Journal of Austrian Economics* 3, no. 1 (2000): 63–78.

Buchanan, J.M. *Cost and Choice: An Inquiry in Economic Theory*. Indianapolis, IN: Liberty Fund, 1999.

Caplan, B. "The Austrian Search for Realistic Foundations." *Southern Economic Journal* 65 (April 1999): 823–38.

Cleveland, P., "The Failure of Utilitarian Ethics in Political Economy." *The Journal of Private Enterprise*, 18, no. 1 (Fall 2002): 57–68.

Coase, R. "The Problem of Social Cost." *Journal of Law and Economics* 3 (1960): 1–44.

Cordato, R. "The Austrian Theory of Efficiency and the Role of Government." *Journal of Libertarian Studies* 4 (1980): 393–403.

———. *Welfare Economics and Externalities in an Open-Ended Universe: A Modern Austrian Perspective*. Boston: Kluwer Academic, 1992.

Cowen, T. "The Scope and Limits of Preference Sovereignty." *Economics and Philosophy* 9 (1993): 253–69.

Demsetz, H. "Block's Erroneous Interpretations." *Review of Austrian Economics* 10, no. 2 (1997): 101–09.

———. "Ethics and Efficiency in Property Rights Systems." In *Time, Uncertainty, and Disequilibrium: Exploration of Austrian Themes*, ed. M. Rizzo, 97–125. Lexington, MA: Lexington Books, 1979.

Dworkin, R. "Is Wealth a Value?" *Journal of Legal Studies* 9 (1980): 191–226.

———. *Taking Rights Seriously*. Cambridge, MA: Harvard University Press, 1977.

Epstein, R.A. "A Theory of Strict Liability." *Journal of Legal Studies* 2 (1973): 151–204.

Friedman, D. *The Machinery of Freedom: A Guide to Radical Capitalism.* 2d ed. LaSalle, IL: Open Court Publishing, 1989.

Gregor, M.J. *Laws of Freedom: A Study of Kant's Method of Applying the Categorical Imperative in the* Metaphysik der Sitten. Oxford: Basil Blackwell, 1963.

Hazlitt, H. *The Foundations of Morality*. Irvington-on-Hudson, NY: Foundation for Economic Education, 1994.

Herbener, J. "The Pareto Rule and Welfare Economics." *Review of Austrian Economics* 10, no. 1 (1997): 79–106.

Hoppe, H. *The Economics and Ethics of Private Property*. Boston: Kluwer Academic, 1993.

Kant, I. *Grounding for the Metaphysics of Morals* [1785], trans., J.W. Ellington. Indianapolis, IN: Hackett, 1993.

———. *The Metaphysics of Morals* [1797], trans. and ed., M. Gregor. Cambridge, UK: Cambridge University Press, 1996.

Kaplow, L., and S. Shavell. *Fairness Versus Welfare*. Cambridge, MA: Harvard University Press, 2002.

Keating, G.C. "A Social Contract Conception of the Tort Law of Accidents." In *Philosophy and the Law of Torts*, ed. G.J. Postema, 22–71. Cambridge, UK: Cambridge University Press, 2001.

Kirzner, I.M. *The Driving Force of the Market: Essays in Austrian Economics*. London: Routledge, 2000.

Kronman, A.T. "Wealth-Maximization as a Normative Principle." *Journal of Legal Studies* 9 (1980): 227–42.

———. *Human Action: A Treatise on Economics*. Auburn, AL: Ludwig von Mises Institute, 1998.

Nozick, R. *Anarchy, State, and Utopia*. New York: Basic Books, 1974.

O'Driscoll, G. "Justice, Efficiency, and the Economic Analysis of Law: A Comment on Fried." *Journal of Legal Studies* 9 (1980): 355–66.

Page, T. "Responsibility, Liability, and Incentive Compatibility." *Ethics* 97 (1986): 240–62.

Paton, H.J. *The Categorical Imperative: A Study in Kant's Moral Philosophy*. Philadelphia: University of Pennsylvania Press, 1947.

Posner R.A. *Economic Analysis of Law*. 5th ed. New York: Aspen Law and Business, 1998.

———. *The Economics of Justice*. 2d ed. Cambridge, MA: Harvard University Press, 1983.

———. "The Ethical and Political Basis of the Efficiency Norm in Common Law Adjudication." *Hofstra Law Review* 8 (1980): 487–507.

———. "Strict Liability: A Comment." *Journal of Legal Studies* 2 (1973): 205–21.

———. "Utilitarianism, Economics, and Legal Theory." *Journal of Legal Studies* 8 (1979): 103–40.

Rizzo, M. "Law Amid Flux: The Economics of Negligence and Strict Liability in Tort." *Journal of Legal Studies* 9 (1980): 291–318.

———. "The Mirage of Efficiency." *Hofstra Law Review* 8 (1980): 641–58.

———. "Rules Versus Cost-Benefit Analysis in the Common Law." *Cato Journal* 4 (1985): 865–84.

Rothbard, M. *For a New Liberty: The Libertarian Manifesto*. San Francisco: Fox and Wilkes, 1996.

———. "Law, Property Rights, and Air Pollution." *Cato Journal* 2, no. 1 (Spring 1982): 55–99.

———. "The Myth of Efficiency." In *Time, Uncertainty, and Disequilibrium: Explo-*

ration of Austrian Themes, ed. M. Rizzo, 92–98. Lexington, MA: Lexington Books, 1979.

———. "Toward a Reconstruction of Utility and Welfare Economics." In *Logic of Action I: Method, Money, and the Austrian School*, 211–55. Cheltenham, UK: Edward Elgar, 1997.

Rubin, P. "Predictability and the Economic Approach to Law: A Comment on Rizzo." *Journal of Legal Studies* 9 (1980): 319–34.

Scitovsky, T. "The State of Welfare Economics." *American Economic Review* 41 (1951): 303–15.

Shavell, S. "Strict Liability Versus Negligence." *Journal of Legal Studies* 9 (1980): 1–25.

Stringham, E. "Kaldor-Hicks Efficiency and the Problem of Central Planning." *Quarterly Journal of Austrian Economics* 4, no. 2 (Summer 2001): 41–50.

———. "Market Chosen Law." *Journal of Libertarian Studies* 14, no.1 (Winter 1998–1999): 53–77.

Sullivan, R. *Immanuel Kant's Moral Theory*. Cambridge, UK: Cambridge University Press, 1989.

———. *An Introduction to Kant's Ethics*. Cambridge, UK: Cambridge University Press, 1994.

United States v. Carroll Towing Co., 159 F.2d 169, 173 (2d Cir. 1947).

Von Mises, L. *Economic Calculation in the Socialist Commonwealth*. Auburn, AL: Ludwig von Mises Institute, 1990.

Westphal, K.R. "A Kantian Justification of Punishment." In *Kant's Metaphysics of Morals: Interpretative Essays*, ed. M. Timmons, 89–109. Oxford: Oxford University Press, 2002.

Wittman, D.A. "First Come, First Served: An Economic Analysis of 'Coming to the Nuisance.'" *Journal of Legal Studies* 9 (1980): 557–568

Wright, R.W. "Rights, Justice, and Tort Law." In *Philosophical Foundations of Tort Law*, ed. David G. Owen, 159–82. Oxford: Clarendon Press, 1995.

———. "The Standards of Care in Negligence Law." In *Philosophical Foundations of Tort Law*, ed. D.G. Owen, 249–275. Oxford: Clarendon Press, 1995.

Yeager, L. *Ethics as Social Science: The Moral Philosophy of Social Cooperation*. Cheltenham, UK: Edward Elgar, 2001.

16

Institutional Change and Economic Growth in Spain Since the Democratic Transition in 1978

Regulating Regional Self-Governance as a Key Factor

Fernando Toboso

Introduction

The institutional organization of government in Spain has undergone a radical transformation during the last twenty years. Spain has moved from a highly centralized and authoritarian political regime in which there were only two levels of government (central and local) to a democratic, three-level political system (central, regional, local).

Many changes in policy governance have taken place since 1978, including those resulting from Spain's membership in the European Union (EU), and there is no doubt that all have been influential. However, because the basic purpose of this chapter is to emphasize just once more that legal rules matter for both the total economic output produced by a country and its distribution as income among families and regions, we are not going to deal here with all of these institutional transformations. Rather, this chapter focuses on the process of institutional design by which an intermediate level of government was created in Spain. The aim is to find out how these new rules have influenced the "rise of the nation," as Mancur Olson wrote, and to deal with consequences and not with causes, though a few comments on the latter are provided.[1]

Because municipalities existed before the democratic transition and have experienced only minor changes concerning the tasks for which they are responsible—although democratic procedures have also been implemented with positive economic and distributive results—the local level of government is not addressed herein either. Our purpose is to concentrate only on the more salient features of the new institutional setting for multilevel governance created in Spain.

The chapter is an applied one. It contains both ideas and figures, the latter used mainly to provide an estimation of the magnitude of reforms and for getting straightforward comparisons with the situation characterizing traditional federal countries in general. The Länder in Germany is used as a benchmark to make qualitative and quantitative comparisons, the latter being based primarily on comparable International Monetary Fund (IMF) national account figures. Germany, a federal country that has also experienced major institutional reforms as a result of European integration and that includes a small number of regional/state governments, as is the case in Spain, has been chosen for this task. Some other federal countries might have been taken into account, but, again, the purpose here is to concentrate on the Spanish case, not to make an international comparative institutional analysis.

The argument will be conducted under the methodological rules of institutional individualism, a middle mode of explanation between holism and methodological individualism.[2] These rules allow for the incorporation into theories and models of the many formal and informal institutional aspects surrounding all human interactions and for taking into account how legal rules and social norms affect both transaction and other costs (efficiency issues) and people capacities and opportunities to get income and wealth (distributive issues). This is, then, an analysis based on a middle way institutional perspective.[3]

The chapter is organized as follows. After investigating how the decentralization process has been formally organized and the facto implemented, section 2 examines which specific tasks regional governments are responsible for and how much money they spend. In section 3, we examine which taxes, if any, are now under the control of regional governments. It also considers what other sources of income regional governments have access to for accomplishing their tasks as a consequence of a new legal framework for regional self-governance that is currently being implemented. Once these detailed investigations are completed, section 4 provides a global analysis on how the new legal rules have influenced the behavior of the agents involved and, consequently, have affected the path of economic and social growth of Spanish regions since 1980. In the concluding section, the main ideas of the chapter are emphasized and some questions about the future are posed.

The Process of Creating Regional Governments and the Decentralization of Public Tasks

When compared with recent Spanish history, the last twenty years have been, no doubt, surprising ones. Both the nineteenth and the first half of the twentieth centuries were full of unrest, recurrent political conflict, and institutional changes that ruled out further progress. By contrast, constitutional stability, democratic reforms, and per capita income and welfare growth characterize Spain's evolution since the peaceful but radical institutional transformation initiated in 1978.

The Basic Constitutional Rules for Regional Self-Governance

In the 1978 Constitution, Spain is explicitly characterized as a "state of self-governing communities" *(estado de las autonomías)* in order to demarcate it from both centralized and federal systems. Article two of the Constitution proclaims the unity of the Spanish nation and "recognizes and guarantees the right to self-governance to all *nationalities* and regions of which it is composed." Attention should be paid here to the fact that it did not just say "regions." *Nationalities*, a name that sounded unfamiliar even in the Spanish language at that time, was inserted to state explicitly that some territories were not just regions. In chapter 8, the Constitution establishes the principles, criteria, and procedures by which those rights can be made effective, but the issue of how many regional or state governments could be built was left open. In devising the distribution of political power between central and regional governments, numerous political compromises had to be reached. Although Spanish is spoken in all regions, in some of them there are people who also speak their own languages, most of which date back to the Middle Ages. Current Spanish regions also had different political institutions and kings during those ancient times. This means very much indeed; because history matters and culture transmits ideas, values, and aspirations, two nationalist parties emerged rapidly during transition in two regions or nationalities. Catalan and Basque political leaders participated from the very beginning in political negotiations that culminated with the approval of the new Constitution and its rules for multilevel governance. All this, and some other factors that cannot be addressed here,[4] explain why these rules have generated a complex and flexible system that has also evolved through time and that tends to operate very much like a competitive federal system, though in the 1978 Constitution the word "federal" was avoided.[5] Of course, Spanish political, economic, and monetary integration into the EU since 1986 has resulted in centralizing at the European level some macroeconomic policy responsibilities at the same time that other tasks were being decentralized to regional governments.

Concerning the new intermediate level of government that the Constitution allowed, seventeen autonomous communities or regional governments were finally created by a similar number of statutory laws passed in the Central Parliament from 1978–83. See Figure 16.1.

Figure 16.1 **Autonomous Communities (Regional Governments) in Spain**

Source: Ministry of Public Administrations.

The local level of government experienced no change with respect to the number of government administrations that were in existence prior to the Constitution. In Spain there are 8.098 municipalities (two of them are now autonomous cities with responsibilities similar to other regional governments), and 53 provincial governments (county councils). In an attempt to built co-operative networks at the local level, some other, local political entities (such as the so-called "metropolitan political organizations" and "political federations of cities") have nevertheless been created at the local level in all self-governing regions.

Each regional government was, and still is, formed by the two traditional branches: executive and legislative. Members of regional legislative chambers are elected through elections based on proportional representation. Executives are elected from inside the legislature. At the local level, members of municipalities are elected, but members of the remaining local governments (including provincial governments) are directly appointed by each political party according to the municipal electoral results obtained. This means that political power and budgets at the local level concentrate on municipalities and the coalitions supporting mayors.

Concerning the decentralization of tasks, a key question is, which responsibilities did the new regional governments assume? Mainly due to the diversity of historical backgrounds and aspirations of organized groups and political leaders of different regions, a compromise was reached by which two *doors* were settled for entering into regional self-governance. Article 143 of the Constitution opened a door for a low degree of regional self-governance while article 151 opened another one for those regions aspiring to a higher degree of autonomy. But because no allocation of rights was established in advance, seven regions (some considered as historic nationalities, others not) finally entered the high way of article 151 (Basque Country, Catalonia, Galicia, Navarra, Andalusia, Canary Islands, and Valencia). The other twelve regions entered the low way. Between 1979 and 1983, all statutory laws for regional self-governance were passed in the Central Parliament.

But this is not all. The complexity and flexibility of the system of multilevel governance is also due to the fact that the statutory laws were independently negotiated between the main representatives of the party—supporting the Central executive—at that time and the regional leaders that had already emerged in each region. As a result, each law is to some extent unique. Not all tasks susceptible to being decentralized actually were decentralized in all regions.[6]

This systemwide complexity and flexibility is also due to the different timing by which tasks were transferred. Of course, statutory laws fixed an initial maximum level of self-governance to be achieved. But it has been through the passing of time that those rights have been progressively decentralized, sometimes as a transfer to all regions, sometimes as a transfer to only one regional government. In the latter case, regional leaders, confident on their own capacities, were able to force the transfer in advance.

Finally, the complexity and flexibility of the system is due to the rules contained in articles 149 and 150.2. The first article establishes a list of tasks that fall exclusively under the central government's responsibility. The second article opens the possibility for the central government to delegate or cede new tasks to regional governments besides those explicitly indicated in the Constitution for the low and high ways. Because this option has been taken on several occasions, there has been much more decentralization than the one initially allowed in articles 143 and 151, and it has not yet stopped.

Some Statistical Data on the Decentralization Process

Before considering the diverse nature of tasks performed by regional governments, let us look first at some general statistics that show how decentralization has advanced rapidly since the late 1970s. Taking into account the

Table 16.1

Public Expenditure by Level of Government in Spain as a Percentage of the Total[a] (initial budgets)

	1981	1986	1996	2001
Central government	87.34	72.60	62.52	58.80
Regional governments	2.92	14.61	24.70	27.62
Local governments[b]	9.74	12.70	12.68	13.58
Total	100.00	100.00[c]	100.00[c]	100.00

Source: Ministry of Public Administrations.
[a]Expenditures coming from social security funds are attributed to the level that manage them. Each level also includes expenditures managed by their respective government agencies. Lend-Repay is not included. [b]Municipalities, provincial governments, and other local governments. [c]Approximate due to rounding.

amount of expenditures each level of government manages as a rough estimate of the said decentralization,[7] we see that regional governments in Spain are now responsible, on average, for an amount of expenditure similar to that of the German länder.

Table 16.1 shows the degree of public expenditure decentralization achieved. Three years after the approval of the 1978 Constitution, regional or state governments managed 2.9 percent of total public expenditures. Only five years later, this amount increased to 14.6 percent. After an additional twenty years, they managed 27.62 percent of total expenditure. Local government's share of total public expenditure increased from 9.7 percent to only 13.58 percent over the same period.

If we take into account the fact that total public expenditure in Spain has experienced a significant and rapid growth since transition, there is clear evidence of the high degree of decentralization achieved. Table 16.2 shows that total public expenditure amounted to a 24.9 percent of gross domestic product (GDP) in 1974 (four years before the approval of the 1978 Constitution), whereas in 1992 it amounted to 48 percent. We must also consider that Spain's GDP used for calculating the said percentages was increasing at an average annual current monetary rate of 14.6 percent during those years.[8]Although Table 16.2 shows that since 1993 total public expenditure grew at a lower rate than the rate of GDP growth, total public expenditure amounted to 0.18 billion euros in 1993, whereas in 2001 it amounted to 0.26 billion. Since 1994, Spanish GDP also has been experiencing a significant rate of growth, particularly if we compare it with that of other European countries.[9]

Although figures provided by the International Monetary Fund (IMF) are

Table 16.2

Total Public Expenditure as a Percentage of Gross Domestic Product in Spain[a] (national accounts)

1974	1980	1985	1990	1992	1993[b]	1996	2001
24.9	34.9	43.6	45.0	48.0	47.3	44.2	40.1

Source: BBVA Annual Economic Report 2001 from Interrención General de la Administración del Estado (IGAE) and Instituto Nacional de Estadística (INE) figures.

[a]Includes expenditures coming from the social security funds and the expenditures managed by government agencies. Lend-Repay is not included. [b]In 1993, there was a breakdown in tendency.

Table 16.3

Public Expenditure by Level of Government in Germany and Spain[a] (percent of the total, national accounts)

	Central	Regional/State	Local	Total
Germany, 1997	60.3	24.0	15.7	100
Spain, 1995	69.8	18.5	11.7	100

Source: IMF 2002.

[a]Expenditures coming from social security funds are attributed to the level that manage them. Each level also includes expenditures managed by their respective government agencies. Lend-Repay is not included.

updated slowly and are not completely comparable with those provided in Table 16.2,[10] they are nevertheless useful for making international comparisons. According to these figures (see Table 16.3), it is evident that the Spanish decentralization to regional governments has been high enough to place those governments closer and closer to their German counterparts. In Germany, the länder managed 24.0 percent of total public expenditure in 1997. In Spain this figure was 18.5 percent in 1995 (the most recent year accounted for in the 2002 IMF Report). Local governments in Spain are also moving closer and closer to their German counterparts.

Tasks Under the Responsibility of Regional Governments

What are the particular tasks for which regional governments in Spain are responsible? As stated previously, because the legal rules constraining the decentralization process were flexible and statutory laws were negotiated independently in each region, differences and minor quirks exist even among those who entered self-governance following the same legal route. Between

Table 16.4

Main Responsibilities by all Regional Governments in Spain

On economic sectors and infrastructures	• Agriculture, mining, and forestry • Fishing and hunting • Tourism • Roads and ports • Hydraulic and channel resources and irrigation issues • Urban planning and building • Selling activities in the region • Savings banks and other, special nonprofit credit organizations
On public services	• Primary, secondary, and higher education public services • Health public services (medical and pharmaceutical) • Social care public services • Unemployed labor services • Regional TV channels
Other	• Environmental protection • Cultural issues • Museums • Commercial thematic exhibitions • Sports

1992 and 2001, new tasks have been ceded to those autonomous communities who entered the low way, thanks to an agreement signed in 1992 by the two main political parties. This has resulted in a new approximation of low self-governance communities and high ones that render useless a much-used traditional schema[11] in which a dividing line was settled. Table 16.4 summarizes the tasks for which all regional governments are now mainly responsible for in Spain. Substantial differences still exist, however, concerning their tax responsibilities, as we will see in next section.

Table 16.4 is, of course, a general and ordered record that serves our purpose here; however, it does not show some existing differences.[12] We must also consider that in many areas, the central government "retains the right to elaborate Laws for settling the principles necessary to harmonize legal resolutions made by the Autonomous Communities, even in their own responsibility areas, when so requires the general interest" (article 150.3 of the Constitution). Though this right is being exercised moderately,[13] Nationalist party leaders in the historic regions or *nationalities* have long claimed that central harmonization legislation places unacceptable constraints on their ability to maneuver.

As one might expect, the decentralization process has not been a politically peaceful one because constitutional rules as well as the rules contained

Table 16.5

Functional Classification of Consolidated Public Expenditures by Regional Governments in Spain (initial budgets for 2002)

	Percentage of total
General public services	3.49
Public order and safety	1.37
Social security, promotion, and welfare	8.54
Health	25.08
Education	25.46
Housing and urban planning	1.97
Social assistance	2.02
Culture	2.22
Economic infrastructures	7.10
Scientific research	0.74
Information and statistics	0.06
General economic regulations	1.54
Economic regulations on productive sectors	9.72
Grants to other levels of government	3.91
Public debt interests and repayments	6.80
Total	100.00

Source: Public Finance Ministry.

in statutory laws always leave a margin for different interpretations to be made when specific policy actions are considered. Many laws and other regulatory measures passed in Central Parliament were contested in the Constitutional Court by regional governments. This is also true for many laws passed in Regional Legislative Chambers.[14]

In some areas, however, there has been no conflict, because the policies of different levels of government have complemented each other. This has been the case concerning expenditures on some cultural activities, social assistance, and local development. By looking at regional governments' budgets, it becomes obvious that money is spent on tasks that have not been subject to any formal transference. All regional budgets contain fixed allocations for expenditure on industrial policies, for research and innovation, for the creation of regional statistics and reports, and even for international relations. In Table 16.5, we can see the relative weight of these spending tasks according to budgetary figures for 2002. The public provision of health and education services stands out because it has been totally transferred to these regional governments in 2002.

In the next section we will investigate how the financial activities of those regional governments have been organized. Section 4 will focus on the consequences derived from these new legal rules.

How Much Power to Obtain Tax and Nontax Revenues Do Regional Governments Enjoy Under the New Legal Rules?

The Basic Rules Allowing Regional Governments to Get Tax Revenue

The Spanish Constitution explicitly mentions that "regions and nationalities" *should* have sufficient *financial autonomy* in order to guarantee them an appropriate degree of autonomy in exercising their functions. The 1988 Law on the Financing of the Autonomous Communities (LOFCA) defined the framework of a *general financial system* applying to all of them, except for the case of the two so-called *"foral"*[15] self-governing communities (the Basque Country and Navarra).[16] The law gives the role of coordinating and deciding on future reforms of the system to the Fiscal and Financial Policy Council (FFPC), a body composed of representatives of the central government and the regional governments.

Several reforms have been carried out since then, but the one made through Law 14 of December 27, 1996 (which reformed the LOFCA, as well as the Law of Ceding Central Taxes), represented a watershed. This law gave the regional governments a limited regulatory capacity over all the so-called ceded taxes that they had never previously enjoyed. More recently Law 7 and Law 21 (both passed on December 27, 2001) ceded new taxes as well as new regulatory capacities, as indicated in Table 16.6.

Although these ceded taxes are mainly regulated by central government, the collected yields are automatically at regional governments' disposition for their discretionary use. The revenue obtained by these regional governments is considered as their own tax revenue and is classified as such in the following Tables 16.7 and 16.8.

Besides said ceded taxes, regional governments may also create their *own taxes* according to the principles specified in the 1988 Law on the Financing of the Autonomous Communities (LOFCA). Because severe constraints are imposed,[17] few regional taxes have been created, and some of these have been declared nonconstitutional by the Constitutional Court. The taxes created by regional governments are taxes on bingo games, underemployed property, hunting preserves, water, oil-bearing fuels, and some ecological taxes. Altogether, they provide an amount of revenue much lower than the one provided by ceded taxes. According to the 2002 regional governments' budgetary figures, about 70.62 percent of their own tax revenue comes from ceded taxes. The surcharges they may add on some central taxes and others (e.g., a surcharge on personal income tax) along with the fees, rates, and prices charged for governmental services complete the regional governments' sources of own income.

Table 16.6

Taxes Totally or Partially Ceded to Spanish Regional Governments[a] and Regulatory Capacities Attributed to Those Governments

Personal income tax	Ceded 33% of the regional PIT bases. Management by central government tax agency. Regional governments may settle the *complementary tax rate structure* to be applied to the 33% of regional PIT bases. This structure must have the same intervals as the central rate structure and also be progressive. They may add new family, personal, and other deductions besides those settled by central government.
General property tax	Ceded 100% of tax revenues. Management by regional government. Regional governments may regulate the tax rate structure and the minimum property that is exempted.
Inheritance and gift tax	Ceded 100% of tax revenues. Management by regional government. Regional governments may regulate the tax rate structure and the reductions applicable on property bases.
Property transfers and stamp taxes	Ceded 100% of tax revenues. Management by regional government. Regional governments may regulate the tax rates.
Gambling tax	Ceded 100% of tax revenues. Management by regional government. Complete regulatory capacity by regional governments.
Taxes on tobacco, alcohol, and hydrofuels	Ceded 40% of tax revenues. Management by central government tax agency. No regulatory capacity by regional governments.
Taxes on electricity, motor vehicles, and retailing particular fuels	Ceded 100% of tax revenues. Management by regional government. No regulatory capacity by regional governments.
Value added tax	Ceded 35% of tax revenues. Management by central government tax agency. No regulatory capacity by regional governments.

Source: Law 14 of December 27, 1996, and Law 7 and Law 21 of December 27, 2001.
[a]Except for Basque Country and Navarra, which enjoy a special *foral* financial system.

Grants received from different sources (conditional and unconditional grants coming from several funds, investment agreements, etc.) and the income received through borrowing constitute their external sources of revenue.

Table 16.7

Revenue for Regional Governments in Spain
(percent of the total, national accounts)

	1988	1997
Grants	70.25	65.80
Own tax and nontax revenue	29.49	28.99
Borrowing	0.26	5.21
Total	100.00	100.00

Source: Government Finance Statistics Yearbook, IMF 2002.

Table 16.8

Revenue for Regional Governments in Germany
(percent of the total, national accounts)

	1988	1999 (p)
Grants	14.55	18.15
Own tax and nontax revenue	78.83	79.75
Borrowing	6.62	2.10
Total	100.00	100.00

Source: Government Finance Statistics Yearbook, IMF 2002.
(p) = Provisional.

The Relative Weight of External and Internal Sources of Revenue

The comparable figures of Table 16.7 and Table 16.8 provide us with an overall view of the relative magnitude of the income obtained from different sources by regional and state governments in Spain and Germany. It should be noted that the more updated figures provided by the 2002 IMF Yearbook only go up to 1997. Consequently, they do not register the new, own-tax revenue that Spanish regional governments will receive for 2002 and beyond as a result of the new taxes partially or totally ceded to them by the said 7 and 21 laws of December 21, 2001. These are, basically, the indirect taxes indicated in Table 16.6 in the three last rows. No regulatory capacity over them has been attributed to those governments, as indicated in the table.[18]

Table 16.7 shows that regional governments in Spain have been receiving a substantial proportion of revenue through grants that come from superior levels of government (central and European). These grants accounted for 65.8 percent of their total revenue in 1997, whereas their own tax and nontax revenue (including ceded taxes) accounted for just 28.99 percent. By con-

Table 16.9

General Government Outstanding Debt[a] in Spain by Levels of Government
(percent of the GDP national accounts)

	1991	1993	1996	1998	2002[b]
Regional government	2.7	4.5	6.2	6.2	6.2
Central government	37.3	49.7	57.6	54.9	45.6
Social security funds[c]	0.6	0.5	0.7	0.4	0.2
Local government	4.1	4.2	4.1	3.7	3.1

Source: Bank of Spain, European System of Central Banks.

[a]Securities and noncommercial loans, according to the European excessive deficit protocol.

[b]Through September.

[c]Central government decides this debt.

trast, Table 16.8 shows that grants received by the länder account for only 18.15 percent of the total revenue in 1999, whereas their own tax and nontax revenues accounted for 79.75 percent. The percentages of tax and nontax revenues are not very different for 1988 in both cases. The borrowing (deficit) figures decreasing in the Spanish case from 1988 to 1997 correspond to the increase registered in grant figures. The opposite occurred in Germany.

This global comparison allows us to state that whatever the tasks undertaken by regional governments have been during the 1980s and 1990s, Spain is more dependent upon external sources of income than is Germany (even though several taxes and tax revenues have been ceded in Spain).

This external dependency manifests also in the fact that regional governments may only vary the yields obtained from their own tax sources (ceded taxes and own taxes) in a limited way. As mentioned earlier, most of these yields come from ceded taxes that are mainly subject to central regulation. Of course, they do not participate in regulating central taxes.[19]

This financial external dependency appears even greater if we consider that the 1988 Law on the Financing of the Autonomous Communities (LOFCA) set limits to regional government borrowing as a source of income. Though these limitations have not been always respected, Table 16.9 shows how regional governments contribute to the total outstanding debt (securities and noncommercial loans) as a percentage of GDP. Roughly speaking, the central government contributes nine times more than regional governments.

The IMF figures contained in Table 16.10 show that regional governments in Spain have been contributing to the outstanding debt much less than comparable governments in Germany. Whereas the länder's contribution to outstanding debt amounted to 15.75 percent of GDP in 1997, that of the Spanish

Table 16.10

General Government Outstanding Debt[a] by Levels of Government in Spain and Germany (percent of the GDP national accounts)

	1992			1997		
	Central	Regional	All levels[b]	Central	Regional	All levels[b]
Germany	26.07	12.65	43.37	38.77	15.77	59.58
Spain	40.45	3.58	48.00	58.30	5.74	67.50

Source: Government Finance Statistics Yearbook, IMF 2002; and International Financial Statistics, IMF 2003.

[a]Securities and noncommercial loans.

[b]Including local governments.

regional governments reached only 5.74 percent. A similar gap separates the comparative figures for 1992.

So if public expenditures by regional governments in Spain have registered, as shown in the previous section, a huge rate of growth (in the total amount of money they spend in relation to the Spanish GDP and in their share of the total public expenditures), then it must be obvious from what has been shown in this section that a struggle for grants has also characterized intergovernmental relations in Spanish politics. The new financial rules have induced no competition between regional governments to attract tax bases by reducing tax rates (mainly on business), except in some minor cases affecting the two *foral* regions in the north of Spain.[20] No tax race to the bottom has occurred.

However, this new legal framework for regional government financial activities, together with the rules investigated in the previous section, has had a significant impact on regional and national politics, and consequently on economic and social growth. Before analyzing all these consequences, let us first briefly depict the main characteristics of the so-called *foral* financial system. This will provide a better understanding of what follows.

The Foral Financial Rights of Two Historic Regions or Nationalities: Basque Country and Navarra

The institutional organization of financial matters described in the previous section applies to all regional governments except for the two autonomous communities in the north of Spain that have a *foral* financial system. These two regions are characterized by the fact that they themselves regulate, manage, and collect their own taxes and those others levied in their area by the central government. This is done according to the principles and rules settled in their respective foral economic treaties, which are periodically re-agreed and passed as laws in the Central Parliament and according to international treaties signed by Spain. A fixed amount of the revenue these regional governments collect has to be transferred to the central government as a contribution to general charges. This fixed amount, or *cupo*, is settled in advance in their treaties and, because of that, it is not directly a function of tax yields.

Though some characteristics of the current *foral* financial systems for the Basque Country and Navarra already existed at the end of the eighteenth and beginning of the nineteenth century, the first written laws allowing these regions or nationalities to regulate and to manage some central taxes were completed in 1841 and 1878. The 1978 Spanish Constitution and, subsequently, the respective Autonomy Statutory Laws explicitly mention those historic rights, whose specific content for a fixed period of years must be determined by a law passed in the Central Parliament. Several *foral* economic treaty laws have been negotiated and passed since the democratic transition.[21]

Although they are formally constrained by the requirements of regional solidarity and general tax coordination and harmonization that are explicitly mentioned in the Constitution, both self-governing regions are now responsible for levying the main, direct taxes (personal income tax, corporate income tax, general property tax, inheritance and gifts tax, property transfers, and stamp taxes). For the value-added tax as well as for the other indirect taxes under their control (tax on alcoholic drinks, on tobacco, on hydrofuels, registration vehicles, etc.), European harmonization principles must be respected. In an attempt to make the tax coordination constitutional requirement operative, several criteria and rules have been settled in the *foral* treaty laws, but some degree of ambiguity remains.[22]

Because there is only an ex ante fixed amount of revenue to be transferred back to the central government, all gains obtained from better management and efforts to reduce fraud remain in the hands of the regional government. Even if tax rates have been lowered slightly and deductions increased in several taxes, compared with the tax rates and deductions that exist in the centrally regulated taxes, both *foral* regional governments get higher per capita tax revenues than those obtained by the non-*foral* regional ones. They also get higher tax revenues in relation to regional GDP.[23] Moreover, the aforementioned constitutional principles and other financial central controls do not prevent both regional governments from usually having an outstanding debt (noncommercial loans and securities) higher than the average because it is a way of allowing for higher levels of public spending.

Even if their power to tax is severely constrained, both regional governments have enjoyed not only a higher amount of per capita income than all others in recent years, but also greater financial autonomy because most of the income has been of an unconditional kind.[24]

Some Consequences of the New Legal Framework for Regional Self-Governance

From what has been indicated in the two previous sections, a conclusion follows: the new framework for regional self-governance in Spain has produced a kind of asymmetric and competitive federalist system. It is asymmetric because considerable progress has been made toward decentralizing spending responsibilities for regional governments, but only a few steps have been taken to increase their power to tax.[25] Although they are getting an increasing amount of their own tax revenue, mainly thanks to the taxes that have been totally or partially ceded to them by law, the central government has retained most regulatory capacities over these ceded taxes. The system is also a competitive one because a permanent political struggle to get more tasks and more grants has characterized the behavior of almost all political leaders and organized groups at the regional level during the period being investigated.[26]

The New Rules and Their Consequences for Political Behavior

Which consequences on the behavior of regional and central politicians might be *logically* predicted from the institutional setting previously examined? If we look at the institutionally founded literature that has been published on intergovernmental relations, two main lines of argument are prominent.

According to one of these lines, it seems reasonable to think that if the central government finances a large share of subcentral spending, members of the central government inevitably feel that they need to control the way in which the money they provide is spent. After all, they are responsible to their own taxpayers for what happens to the money they collect. It is not surprising, then, that members of central governments usually prefer specific (conditional) grants to general (unconditional) grants. The possibility of grants being cut also serves as a power mechanism that, in many cases, makes members of subcentral governments more likely to make agreements with the central government that might have been otherwise not acceptable, particularly when there are severe limitations for borrowing. If a fixed amount of money is available for grants to be allocated through bargaining among competing subcentral governments that cannot raise their own tax and nontax revenue in a significant way, it seems reasonable to predict that subcentral government leaders will have far less discretion to implement the policies they think their constituents prefer (and regional organized groups claim for) than would otherwise be the case.[27]

This may be a general case, for sure, when there is a severe budgetary constraint in the country for macroeconomic or whatever reasons and when central government leaders pay special attention to the amount of money that is transferred as grants. In fact, this is a general case concerning European democracies at the present time. But this is not what happened in Spain over the period being investigated here. Regional government leaders from all regions (sometimes called "regional barons") enjoyed much greater political power and spending autonomy than might be predicted by the kind of analysis featured above (and also by the figures presented in Table 16.7). How is it possible if grants represented around the 65 percent of the total income received by those governments on a recurring basis?

The second line of theoretical argument referred to above is more useful for understanding intergovernmental relations in Spain. The first aspect that must be taken into account is that though the said grant percentages have remained more or less stable during the period, the amount of money transferred as grants to regional governments (in total figures and in relation to GDP) has increased at a huge rate. It is, in fact, similar to the rate of growth in the total income of those regional governments and also in the rate of growth of their expenditure. As shown in Tables 16.1 and 16.2, total public expenditure amounted to 24.9 percent of GDP in 1974, whereas in 1992 it amounted to 48 percent. The regional governments' share in this huge, increasing pie also grew spectacularly from an insignificant 2.9 percent of the total to more than 25 percent during the first twelve years of decentralization. So because the central government's share of total expenditure has moved in the opposite direction (see Table 16.1), it is obvious that "regional barons" and regional governments in Spain have experienced almost no budgetary constraint during those years. Even if around 50 percent of regional government's total income usually comes from conditional appropriations linked to specific collaborative or agreed projects (see Table 6.11), regional governments have disposed of a huge and increasing amount of unconditional financial resources for pursuing their own policy objectives. The total income (conditional and unconditional, including borrowing) for which they have been responsible on an annual basis has increased more than 300 percent from 1988 to 1999 in total figures and nearly 200 percent in GDP figures (their total income amounted to a 6.45 percent of Spanish GDP in 1988, whereas in 1999 it reached 11.08 percent).

This is why a permanent struggle for tasks and for grants characterized intergovernmental relations in Spain from the 1980s until the late 1990s. This situation is very consistent with the second line of argument alluded to

Table 16.11

Conditional and Unconditional Financial Resources of Regional Governments[a] in Spain (Euros)

	Unconditional income (000)	Conditional income (000)	Total income (000)
1988	7,359,530 (45.5%)	8,807,695 (54.5%)	16,167,230 (100%)
1993	14,320,950 (39%)	22,231,055 (61%)	36,552,010 (100%)
1999	33,346,390 (53.52%)	29,323,388 (46.79%)	62,669,780 (100%)

Source: MAP.
[a]Except the two *foral* ones.

in the opening paragraph of this section. The existence of an asymmetry between spending responsibilities and tax revenue-raising capabilities of subcentral governments inevitably generates an overspending bias on the part of sub central governments. This is because the gap generated will have to be filled using a complex system of intergovernmental grants that come from upper levels of government rather than by raising regional taxes. This bias meets the favor of both organized groups and people in general because political regional representatives show themselves in regional mass media (including the public regional TV channels they are responsible for) as working hard to secure money to carry out their policies for increasing economic and social development in the region. Getting regional public infrastructures built by private building companies and paying for this with central grants received is a salient aspect of such an institutional setting.[28] The same is true for other policies subcentral governments implement in order to ensure reelection in their electoral processes. And this is what has happened in Spain because no budgetary constraint has, in fact, existed upon those governments until the latter 1990s (see Table 16.2).

A Positive Assessment of the Economic and Social Consequences Derived from the Overspending Bias

So which economic and social consequences can be attributed to the asymmetrical and competitive system for multilevel governance implemented in Spain? A negative assessment is usually made when authors analyze the overspending bias generated by the subnational tax "irresponsibility" in long-established Western democracies.[29] We want to state here, however, that in the Spanish case, and for the years investigated, the answer must be positive because of its consequences for the efficiency characteristics of the economic system and its distributive impact upon regions and families. A more comprehensive, institutional individualist analysis than those usually made is needed in order to account for the relevant aspects of the Spanish situation that, it must be emphasized, has been under a nondemocratic, centralized, and internationally isolated system of political governance during the previous forty years of transition.

In general analyses, it is usually asserted that when subcentral governments have enough power to tax their constituents for performing their tasks, these political leaders, constituents, and organized groups are all collectively forced to balance the total benefits and costs, as well as their distribution, of these government activities in a way that is not the case under a system of bargaining for central grants. There is no doubt that efficiency problems concerning the use of common-pool financial resources are higher in subcentral politics when higher is the importance of the intergovernmental grant system. When money comes from outside, less care is paid on to how it is finally spent.[30]

Because so much money has been spent by regional governments in Spain in such a short period of time (most of this money coming from external sources of revenue), those considerations are relevant here if a comparative assessment of potential, alternative uses of these public expenditures and their consequences is to be made. This is, nevertheless, a controversial task because it requires that we take into account the hypothetical alternatives existing at those years. As such, it is beyond the scope of this chapter. If this task were to be accomplished, however, it also should be taken into account that all efficiency gains obtained in the working of the polity—because of the said more balanced, and collectively reached, consideration of the benefits and costs of regional policy actions—must be compared with the efficiency losses that might also be derived from the assignment of a full power to tax to these subcentral units. Among these efficiency losses, the one derived from the generalized disregard would surely come out of the positive and negative external effects that some subcentral policies have for other neighboring regions. As it is well known, this spillover problem is partially corrected in all Western democracies by the conditional grant system.

And what about the efficiency losses derived from the increase in transaction costs that occur when persons or corporations have to fill out different tax forms for similar taxes to be paid in different regions or states?

Grants in all Western democracies also produce, in fact, beneficial impacts on regional solidarity and regional welfare because several central funds exist for allocating grants among subcentral governments according to more-or-less quantitative ratios of underdevelopment. So the equity losses generated by eliminating grants as a source of income should also be taken into account because equity is collectively assessed in positive terms as the principles of regional solidarity and redistribution usually settled in constitutions reflect.[31]

The gains derived from cutting central grants to induce a slowdown in subcentral expenditures in order to accomplish macroeconomic stabilization ratios under central government responsibility, an instrument that is in fact used, would be also lost if subcentral governments were not dependent on grants.

But, as said, the purpose of this chapter is not to deal with these and other efficiency and equity distortions that might arise as a consequence of decentralizing the power to tax to subcentral units of government.[32] And it is so because the Spanish process of institutional change whose consequences are here investigated has been very much asymmetrical with very little power to tax being transferred.

The point to be emphasized here is, however, that because more and more tasks were ceded to regional governments, and because there were so many economic and social gaps (by comparison to European democracies) to be addressed after forty years of dictatorship, this overspending bias has produced beneficial results because it has served to shorten those economic and social gaps quickly and in a more democratic and participatory way.

This overspending bias has not, however, generated an exploding situation. Total public expenditure in Spain in relation to GDP still remains under the German level. The same is true if the Spanish regional governments' expenditures are compared with the German länder.[33] And even if public expenditure on health, education, and social security by all levels of government increased very much during those years, they are still ten points lower in Spain than in Germany in relation to the GDP.[34]

The introduction of general electoral rules in 1978 has had, no doubt, a significant impact, especially with regard to the mobilization of political leaders in searching for economic and social gaps to be filled up in order to ensure reelection.[35] What the asymmetrical and competitive decentralization examined added, in this respect, was more frequent elections run by candidates that were closer to the issues to be dealt with and to the affected groups of constituents. The end result has produced greater mobilization efforts with greater efficiency to respond to the claims showing up through the regional political processes and through other existing ways for political influence.[36]

Arguments concerning innovation and experimentation in the public sector that are often invoked to support decentralization of some policy tasks also had a place in Spanish regional politics. This is because initiatives developed mainly by Catalonian governments (concerning both spending initiatives as well as organizational innovations) were imitated by other regional governments.[37] The same is true for the improved control of public-sector management that can be achieved when government ministers and their teams are only responsible for regional bureaus and not for all public administrations in the country. Activities to be supervised become fewer and closer to constituents, resulting in more effective supervision. Purposes can be achieved, in principle, with greater public-sector efficiency.[38]

Because central taxes that have been totally or partially ceded to the regional governments[39] are still managed and collected by the Central Tax Agency, and because those other taxes that are regulated and managed directly by regional governments are few and of little significance, it can be stated that no relevant transaction costs concerning tax compliance have been created as a result of the this new institutional setting, except in a case concerning the corporate income tax in the *foral* regions.

Some Related Formal and Informal Institutional Aspects

Now that the institutional, individualist story of the organization of regional self-governance in Spain and its consequences has been told, we might easily just jump to the concluding section. However, a few other formal and informal institutional factors with positive effects on the path of growth in Spain should at least be mentioned.

Concerning reforms in formal political institutions, the signing of the EU Treaties in 1986 by the central government stands out because it resulted in a new and definite step to open the Spanish economy and its sectors completely to European markets. In 1992 the Spanish economy was a part of the finally created single European market in which no protective tariffs were applied to members' reciprocal exports, many other nontariff restrictions to external trade among members were harmonized, and people and companies could freely invest in all member states. As Spain was one out of the four poorest countries in the Union, it has benefited greatly from the conditional grants distributed through European Funds for financing regional and social development projects in the poorest regions (mainly on economic and other infrastructures).[40] In fact, Spain has been the country that has benefited most since 1988 concerning its share in the total amount of distributed funds (although in per capita terms, it ranked three or four tiers down depending on the period under consideration). There is no doubt that those reforms and the financial aid received have also had positive consequences both on the rate of Spanish total economic growth and on the growth of all its regions because most of them benefited from conditional grants.[41] In Table 16.12, the Spanish gross domestic product and employment rates of growth are indicated. The surprising path of total eco-

Table 16.12

Real Gross Domestic Product and Employment Growth in Spain, 1980–2001

	1980	2001	Percentage total growth	Percentage annual average growth
Real GDP[a]	304,224	542,116	178	8.47
Employment[b]	11,887,000	15,946,000	134	6.38

Source: BBVA.
[a]GDP in real terms: 1995 prices, millions of euros.
[b]Number of persons.

nomic growth of an average annual rate 8.47 percent in real terms is a spectacular one, particularly when compared with European rates.

Table 16.13 shows that poorest regions in Spain also reduced the economic gap that separates them from the wealthiest ones in the EU in terms of regional per capita GDP. If the said distance had been just kept constant, it would have already been a successful evolution in terms of regional equity because poor regions would have surely increased the said distance if no public policy for regional development had been implemented at European, national, and subnational levels. Table 16.13 shows that those Spanish regions with the lowest real per capita GDP were able to converge to the European average level from 1988 to 1998. The seven other Spanish regions with the highest per capita GDP that are not included in the table also converged to the European average, and they did so also from below.[42] Concerning personal income distribution all over Spain, let me just say that Josep Oliver et al. conclude that this distribution is characterized by higher and higher levels of equity since 1985.[43] They also conclude that the two main factors for such an evolution must be found in the huge increase in human capital that the figures reflect and in the fact that institutional reforms and public investments in education have benefited more intensively those children from less favored families who were able to access public universities.

Although social norms and behavioral, shared principles are not the central focus of this chapter, it is useful to at least mention that the commitment problems that usually pervade some Latin American polities[44] have not been highly relevant in Spanish politics since the transition. I would dare to say that they are also less significant than in the United States if we pay attention to the literature that is being published and to the relevant, personal experiences that have been recounted.[45] Although the institutional setting implemented in Spain has led to a permanent political bargaining process between

Table 16.13

Evolution of Per Capita Gross Domestic Product in the Poorest Spanish Regions by Comparison to the European Average

	1988	1998
Galicia	57	64
Asturias	70	72
Cantabria	72	76
Castile-León	67	74
Castile-La Mancha	60	67
Extremadura	49	50
Valencia	72	77
Andalusia	55	58
Murcia	66	67
Canarias	73	77
Ceuta and Melilla	64	67
Total	64	68

Source: J. Cuadrado-Roura and T. Mancha (2003), 463.
Note: European GDP = 100.

representatives at different levels of government, and even if the Constitutional Court has been very active during the 1980s, political representatives in general[46] have paid much attention to the basic behavioral norms that become dominant in repeated and evolutionary games.[47] Of course, many political confrontations have existed between leaders from all parties and regions.[48] These confrontations also exist inside parties as is the case everywhere because any institutional reform has consequences on the participants' distribution of rights and capacities to act as well as on the current and future distribution of income and property that results.[49] However, besides all this political tension and hard bargaining, a minimum level of mutual trust has characterized the policy arena so as to minimize the said commitment problems.[50]

Because most Francoist politicians were old and were forced into retirement after the transition, the new political leaders that emerged at central and subcentral levels were those with more intensive preferences for policy activism. They did not see each other in politics just for only one legislature, and, in fact, many of them have remained in politics through these twenty years.[51] They have been forced to interact recurrently and have paid much attention to the benefits of having a reputation of trustworthiness. They were all fearful of entering a route of political confrontation similar to the one that ended with the civil war that took place from 1936 to 1939. Many of those who were political leaders during the 1980s were children during the 1930s, some with personally devastating experiences. That is another example of how history matters, not only because of the usual path-dependence arguments, but also because of its influence upon social norms and shared values and attitudes.[52]

Moreover, two political parties that are present in all regions are succeeding each other in most subcentral executives, as is the case in central government.[53] This has also introduced more stability for intertemporal agreements and policies to be carried out. In Spain these political parties are powerful, stable organizations with democratic and decentralized governance structures at the regional and local levels that are mainly financed through the central budget according to their electoral results. Therefore, the permanent bargaining to get more policy tasks and grants already mentioned has usually taken place not only under a stable and well-enforced overall institutional environment, but also under stable social and behavioral norms enforcing the pacts finally reached.[54] The decentralizing reforms implemented by the social-democratic central governments from 1982 to 1996 have not been reversed, but instead were advanced by the new Popular Party[55] central governments since then.

Of course, institutional reforms for democracy and regional self-governance in Spain benefited from the previous existence of an economy that was mainly organized under market rules, even if many policy controls and regulations were in place and had to be progressively eliminated since the very beginning, particularly after the so-called *Pactos de la Moncloa* and the central elections that took place in June 1997.[56] Many other reforms in markets and economic sectors with positive consequences took place between 1978 and 1986, but they cannot be addressed here as we cannot deal either with those economic reforms implemented since 1986 for successfully being a part of the common European market and the European Monetary Union. Let us just point out that it is in the polity where those reforms are made (this also adds new value to the Spanish system of multilevel political governance). Of course, many other organizational reforms have also been implemented in public management procedures at all public administration levels.[57]

Compared with Eastern Europe's transitions in economies that were formerly centrally planned, it must be acknowledged that the task in Spain was in fact easier because social norms, behavioral practices, and other informal institutions influencing the behavior of all economic agents in the already existing markets were much more consistent with the new, formal rules for political competition and democratic governance than was the case in the said post-Communist societies.[58]

Conclusion

Because institutional arrangements not only matter, but are key elements for determining collective action and, consequently, affecting the rise and decline of nations as Olson and others have emphasized, the arguments and figures presented herein should persuade readers that the new rules for regional self-governance implemented in Spain are the most salient issue to be taken into account when investigating the surprising path of economic and social growth experimented with since transition. An institutional individualist account of those events has been provided here in an attempt to emphasize that many formal and informal institutional aspects surrounding all human interactions may be taken into account at the same time as attention is paid to both the efficiency and distributive consequences derived from the institutional setting investigated. The analysis made ascribes, then, to a middle-way institutional perspective based on the methodological rules presented in Toboso.[59]

Although it was not called so in the 1978 Constitution, the Spanish system for multilevel governance is getting closer and closer to other federal systems. However, it may be characterized as an asymmetrical and competitive model rather than a cooperative and symmetric one. It is an asymmetric one because Spain has come a long way toward decentralizing policy tasks to regional governments, but, with the exception of the two *foral* governments, only a few steps have been taken to increase their real power to tax. The Spanish system is a competitive one because the flexibility of constitutional rules for regional self-governance and the financial system implemented have induced a permanent political struggle to get more and more policy tasks and more and more grants coming from upper levels of government. This process started in 1978 and still goes on.

The system has generated an overspending bias at the regional level because it has not been necessary to increase taxes over constituents for implementing new policy projects, but to bargain for more grants at upper levels. Although those regional governments have been enjoying an increasing amount of their own tax revenue (that will increase again in 2002 and in future years), they have been very much dependent on grants. Borrowing is also centrally controlled to a large degree, and most of their own tax revenue comes from the so-called ceded taxes over which those governments only have limited regulatory capacities. The taxes they independently regulate and manage are insignificant.

Contrary to what many general institutional analyses of intergovernmental relations predict when referring to long-established democracies, here I have tried to demonstrate that, in the Spanish case, the said new institutional structure for regional self-governance and the asymmetrical decentralization achieved has had positive consequences for the degree of efficiency characterizing the working of the economy and its sectors, and also for the degree of equity characterizing the income distribution ratios at the personal and regional levels.

Because of their consequences upon political behavior, the new rules have served to fill up most of the gap concerning economic and other infrastructures as well as social welfare services that the forty previous years of non-democratic, centralized, and internationally isolated political governance had generated. Because GDP has been increasing very much, on average, and Western, modern tax figures were also settled at the central level from the beginning of transition, a huge and increasing amount of tax revenue has been collected through the years for financing government policies at all levels. No budget constraint has, in fact, existed during the years investigated, except for some periods of significant macroeconomic disturbances. Newly elected representatives in regional legislative chambers and executives have also felt it a necessity to legitimize themselves and to provide people and organized groups with tangible results in order to ensure re-election. This has introduced a strong incentive to work hard in order to find local and regional opportunities for public action and to complete those opportunities.

The said overspending bias has not, however, had exploding consequences. As indicated, despite the huge increases registered, the total public expenditure in relation to GDP in Spain is still several points below the level of Germany, and the same is true for regional governments' expenditures if compared to that of the länder. Public expenditure on education, health, and social security and welfare in relation to the GDP in Spain is still ten points below the level reached in Germany.

Because the power to tax has mainly remained at the central level because most regional governments enjoy very few of their own taxes and only limited regulatory capacities over those that have been totally or partially ceded to them, it can be said that tax homogeneity already characterizes Spanish democratic and decentralized politics. It is also true, however, that as a consequence of both the tax particularities of the two *foral* regional governments and those regulatory capacities over ceded taxes that all other non-*foral* regions are exercising (some are not yet exercised), there is already a lower degree of regional fiscal homogeneity in Spain than in Germany.

Spain has had, it must be acknowledged, a comparative advantage if we think about transition in Eastern Europe. This is because Spain's economy was organized under market rules when the democratic transition occurred and multilevel governance was introduced. Some other informal institutions with positive effects also remained during the first twenty years of democracy here investigated, as indicated.

All this is what the analysis of the past allows us to conclude. But might these positive consequences remain for, say, another twenty years? The theoretical approach employed here, because it is a situational one, clearly conveys the idea that consequences are always situational-dependent variables. And situational circumstances (institutional and noninstitutional ones) are already being changed significantly, particularly since the late 1990s. As the gaps are more and more filled up, less and less positive value can be attributed to the overspending bias. A new external budget constraint is also in place since the late 1990s because Spain belongs to the European Monetary Union. And, finally, some sets of social norms and behavioral shared rules and attitudes that have been serving as informal rules enforcing commitment and mutual trust in the political arena are also becoming less effective. Because these shared social values and attitudes were very much influenced by past experiences (especially those linked to the civil war), they are informal institutions eroded by the passing of the time. Whether or not these very recent changes in institutional and noninstitutional circumstances may slow down, the current "rise of the nation" is an issue that transcends the scope and space assigned to this chapter.

Notes

I am grateful to Allan Schmid, Carlos Ochando, and Ian Kirkpatrick for directing my attention to some issues that needed greater thought. Tom Fiorina provided a good English editing of a previous draft that was presented at the conference "Multilevel Governance: Interdisciplinary Perspectives," organized by the Political Economy Research Center, University of Sheffield in Sheffield, June 28–30, 2001, in the United Kingdom.

1. Mancur Olson, *The Rise and Decline of Nations*. See also Olson, "Why Poor Economic Policies Must Promote Corruption" and also his posthumous book, *Power and Prosperity*.

2. See Fernando Toboso, "Institutional Individualism and Institutional Change: The Search for a Middle Way of Explanation."

3. On middle ways and bridges between different institutional analyses, see Malcom Rutherford, "The Old and the New Institutionalism"; John Groenegewen, "On Integrating Old and New Institutionalism"; Terency Hutchison, "Institutional Economics"; H. Pessali, and R. Fernández, , "Institutional Economics at the Micro Level?"; Oliver E. Williamson, "Efficiency, Power and Authority in Economic Organization"; Williamson, "The Politics and Economics of Redistribution and Efficiency"; Williamson, "Hierarchies, Markets and Power in the Economy"; and Fernando Toboso, "Explaining the Process of Change Taking Place in Legal Rules and Social Norms."

4. See Josep M. Colomer, *La Transición a la Democracia.*

5. For similar statements, see Daniel J. Elazar, "Tendencias de Desarrollo Institucional en España y en el Mundo," 21; and Gregorio Peces-Barba, "Una Lectura de la Constitución Española," 73.

6. Some of the regional leaders were in the Central Parliament and others not. For an analysis of the Basque Country case, see Colomer, *La Transición a la Democracia*, chap. 11.

7. As known, those expenditure figures only are a rough estimate of decentralization because policy tasks such as "regulating pollution of beaches" or "regulating

commercial opening and closing hours" can be tranferred to regional governments with almost no impact in their expending figures being produced because they are usually not paralleled by transferences of public workers.

8. These rates have been calculated from the figures provided in the Informe Económico Anual 2001, BBVA.

9. Whereas Spanish GDP was increasing at an average annual rate of 3.61 percent in real terms from 1996 to 2001, in Germany this rate was 1.88 percent, and in France it was 2.23 percent. These rates have been calculated from the BBVA, Informe Económico Anual 2001, and from La Caixa, *Monthly Economic Bulletin.*

10. As is indicated in both tables, Table 16.2 offers figures extracted from initial government budgets whereas Table 16.4 does so on figures based on national accounts criteria.

11. On this schema, see, for example, Robert Agranoff and Juan A. Ramos, "La Evolución Hacia una Democracia Federal en España"; Javier Suárez-Pandiello, "Fiscal Federalism in Spain"; and Antoni Castells, "The Role of Intergovernmental Fiscal Relations in Achieving Diversity and Cohesion."

12. Just as an example, it can be mentioned that only Basque Country and Catalonia have their own regional police forces. Some "high way" governments have also assumed full responsibility concerning the management of courts and tribunals of justice.

13. An illustrative example can be mentioned. Whereas regions in the high self-governance route were made responsible for public health services from the later 1980s, it has been only in 2002 that a "Central Law for health public services coordination" has been passed in Central Parliament.

14. A total of 1,579 laws, decree laws, and legislative decrees were passed in all regional legislative chambers from 1981 to 1991 in exercising their new rights. Out of the total, 120 (or 7.6 percent) were contested by central government in the Constitutional Court. A large proportion of those contested legal measures (65 percent) were elaborated in Catalonia and Basque Country legislative chambers. On the other side, of a total of 537 legal measures passed in Central Parliament from 1981 to 1991, 127 (23.6 percent) were contested by regional governments. Of the claims made to the Constitutional Court against Central legislation by regional governments, 67.7 percent were made by Basque and Catalonian governments. See Agranoff and Ramos, "La Evolución Hacia una Democracia Federal en España" 72–73.

15. *Foral* relates to the *fueros*, that is, to some traditional political privileges once awarded by a king to a city or region. The *foral* financial system of these two nationalities will be examined later.

16. Some other specific particularities affecting the Canary Islands as well as the North African cities of Ceuta and Mellilla are not relevant here.

17. Tax bases that are already subject to central government taxation cannot be taxed again, tax export effects are not allowed, and regional taxes cannot undermine the existence of a common market.

18. Because figures are not provided yet, Francisco Perez-García's "La Financiación del Estado Autonómico" has made a simulating and hypothetical estimation by which a significant increase in its own tax revenue might be predicted; however, grants will still be very significant as a financial source for most regions.

19. The Senate has less in common with the German Bundesrat even if the 1978 Constitution says that it should be organized as a territorial chamber. See Paul B. Span et al. "Cesión de Impuestos y Administración Tributaria en el Modelo Alemán

de Federalismo Cooperativo," 107; and Antonio Giménez, "Responsabilidad y Corresponsabilidad Fiscal en los Países Federales."

20. On this issue see José D. Jimenez and Pablo E. Barrilao, "Una Aproximación a la Eficiencia en la Gestión de la Agencia Estatal de Administración Tributaria"; and Alejandro Esteller, "La Eficiencia en la Administración de los Tributos Cedidos."

21. An extensive analysis of the *foral* financial system is made in José A. Arratibel's "El Sistema de Concierto y las Haciendas Europea, Estatal y Autonómica Vascas."

22. Since 1997, these formal criteria are (1) identical classification of economic activities for taxing to those used by central government; (2) the general rules and procedures published in the central general taxing law (Ley General Tributaria) must be respected; (3) no distortion in business competition or capital and labor mobility is allowed; (4) global tax pressures must be similar to the regions in the general financial system. See Carlos Monasterio and Javier Suárez-Pandiello, *Manual de Hacienda Autonómica y Local*, 258.

23. See Ignacio Zubiri, "La Capacidad Normativa de las Comunidades Autónomas Forales su Extensión al Resto de Comunidades Autónomas," 132–33.

24. Francisco Pérez-García, "La Financiación del Estado Autonómico," 64, shows that the average personal income per capita ratio in the Basque Country was 24 percent higher in 1998 than the average level of income per capita of all other non-*foral* self-governing regions. In Navarra it was 64 percent higher. See also Arratibel, "El Sistema de Concierto y las Haciendas Europea, Estatal y Autonómica Vascas"; María M. Castillo, "La Tributación de las Comunidades Autónomas"; and Antonio M. Cubero, "La Escala Autonómica del I.R.P.F."

25. Said aside the case of the two *foral* governments.

26. Although regional governments' own tax revenue will increase in 2002 and the following years because of the 2001 reform already mentioned, grants still will be a basic source of income for most regions. See Pérez-García, "La Financiación del Estado Autonómico," 58, for an estimation of the increase in own tax revenue. See also Carlos Monasterio et al., "Una Propuesta Para el 2001" for a similar, though different in substance, estimative exercise.

27. Among the many contributions dealing with those intergovernmental grants' impacts, see David King, "Public Policies in a Multilevel Government Model"; John Kincaid, "Economic Policy-making"; or Antonio Agúndez and Francisco Pedraja, "Descentralización Fiscal y Eficiencia Económica"; Monasterio et al. "Una Propuesta Para el 2001," 69, also asks themselves about the essential roles intergovernmental grants should still play in the Spanish multilevel politics for the future.

28. School buildings, port enlargements, new airports, public hospitals, industrial estates with facilities for the settlement of new firms, and new accesses and facilities for public beaches for helping to attract more tourists are some examples of these infrastructures. Emili Tortosa-Ausina, "La Distribución Provincial del Capital en España," 183, shows that the capital stock in Spain has increased 175.8 percent in real terms from 1975 to 1995, that is, at an average annual rate of 8.8 percent. See also Matilde Mas et al., *El Stock de Capital en España y sus Comunidades Autónomas*; and Mas et al., *Capitalización y Crecimiento de la Economía Española, 1970–1997*.

29. See, for example, William E. Oates, "An Essay on Fiscal Federalism," 1126; Oates, "On the Welfare Gains from Fiscal Decentralization"; Oates, *The Economics of Federalism and Local Finance*; and also Bruno S. Frey, "A Utopia?," 167. In Spain, Suarez-Pandiello, "Fiscal Federalism in Spain," 250, shares these worries.

30. See the institutional analysis on the topic contained in the classic text by Elionor Ostrom, *Governing the Commons.*

31. See Marko Küthenbürger, "Tax Competition and Fiscal Equalization."

32. We do not pay attention either to those cases in which tax competition by independent, subnational governments leads to fiscal distortions such as tax exporting, NIMBY taxation, beggar-thy-neighbor tax competition, or race to the bottom tax competition. On this see Robert P. Inman and Daniel L. Rubinfeld, "Designing Tax Policy in Federalist Economies"; M. Sato, "Fiscal Externalities and Efficiency Transfers in a Federation"; Timmoty J. Besley and Harvey S. Rosen, "Vertical Externalities in Tax Setting"; William E. Oates and Robert M. Schwab, "Economic Competition among Jurisdictions"; Oates, "An Essay on Fiscal Federalism"; or Richard Kirschgässner and Werner W. Pommerehne, "Tax Harmonization and Tax Competition in the EU."

33. According to IMF comparable figures, total public expenditure amounted to 52.67 percent of GDP in 1995, whereas in Germany they amounted to 55.4 percent in 1997. Spanish regional governments' expenditures reached 9.75 percent of Spanish GDP whereas that of the länders reached 13.35 percent for the same year.

34. See Fernando Toboso and Carlos Ochando, "Descentralización de las Responsabilidades de Gasto y Evolución de los Gastos Redistributivos en la España Democrática."

35. See Donald Wittman, "Why Democracy Produces Efficient Results."

36. Joan Subirats, "El Papel de las Comunidades Autónomas en el Sistema Español de Relaciones Intergubernamentales," 177, has calculated that, on average, each regional government is formed by around 250 new politicians, including both the elected ones in the executive or legislative tiers and the public administration high officials who are freely appointed by each executive.

37. A special report on Spain was published in the *The Economist* in December 1996. There it was written that "Spanish regions are playing a game of leapfrog, forever seeking more powers than their rivals," and that "economically, Catalonia is Spain's most successful region. . . . (It) has always been more outward-looking than other Spanish regions. And Barcelona could claim to be Europe's most successful city. A new airport, a new seafront, new roads, thriving businesses, Spain's biggest saving bank, and the 1992 Olympic games." See "Spain in Transit: A Survey," 15–16.

38. See Murray J. Horn, *The Political Economy of Public Administration*, chap. 5; Rafael Bañon and Manuel Tamayo, in "Las Relaciones Intergubernamentales en España" investigate how the remaining central administration is being reorganized because tasks and public workers are being transferred to the regional level.

39. Remember, as indicated in section 2, that the yields obtained through these ceded taxes are automatically transferred to them, but they enjoy limited regulatory capacities over these ceded taxes.

40. See Juan R. Cuadrado-Roura and T. Mancha, "Política Regional y de Cohesión," 457.

41. Some estimated, though contested, figures have been provided by the European Commission on the European Funds' contribution to the GDP growth in Spain. It has been settled at 0.7, 1.5, and 1.3 points of the said GDP real growth for 1989–1993, 1994–1999, and 2000–2006 periods. See Cuadrado-Roura and Mancha, "Política Regional y de Cohesión," 466.

42. Although during the 1960s and 1970s, some of these regiones (particularly Andalusia, Extremadura, and Castile-La Mancha) experienced a significant decrease in population figures because of costly migration (not just mobility). During the 1980s

and 1990s, population figures in regions have experienced minor changes. See Francisco Goerlich et al., "Concentración, Convergencia y Desigualdad Regional en España" for an explicit consideration of the importance of this aspect when per capita comparative figures are provided.

43. Josep Oliver and Xavier Ramos, "Anatomia de la Distribución de la Renta en España, 1985–1996"; Oliver and Ramos, "Capital Humano y Desigualdad en España, 1985–1996."

44. For the Argentinian case, see the institutional analyses by Sebastian Saiegh and Mariano Tommasi, "Why Is Argentina's Fiscal Federalism so Inefficient?" or Mariano Tommasi, Sebastian Saiegh, and Pablo Sanguinetti, "Fiscal Federalism in Argentina" to understand why the political game in Argentina does not facilitate co-operative intertemporal political exchanges.

45. Joseph Stiglitz, "Distinguished Lecture on Economics in Government," tells us about his experiences concerning problems of commitment in politics in Washington, DC. See also the very much cited works by Douglass C. North (1993); and Barry R. Weingast and William J. Marshall, "The Industrial Organization of Congess"; and Barry R. Weingast, "The Political Institutions of Representative Government." Horn, *The Political Economy of Public Administration*, 16, states that due to the fact that enacting legislators' commitments and the benefits provided to their constituents are uncertain when subsequent legislatures come, they have an incentive to protect those benefits by even attempting to implement inefficient institutional arrangements that increase the transaction costs of reversing those policies.

46. Of course, there have been some political/financial scandals, mostly related to building policies and urban development policy plans.

47. See Fernando Vega-Redondo, "Evolving Aspirations and Cooperation," and also Viktor V. Vanberg's seminal paper, "Rules and Choice in Economics and Sociology,"on individual rule-following behaviors that are deliberately chosen in economic settings because of the existing transaction costs.

48. See Colomer, *La Transición a la Democracia*, chaps. 10 and 15, for an institutional analysis of the political and military tension created by the main players during the failed military coup that took place in February 1982, or the political tension created by the successful general (not only labor) strike that took place in December 1988.

49. On the distributive consequences of institutional frameworks, see Jack Knight, *Institutions and Social Conflict*; Gary Libecap, "Distributional Issues in Contracting for Property Rights"; Allan A. Schmid, *Property, Power, and Public Choice*; Randall Bartlett, *Economics and Power*; or Avanish Dixit and John Londregan, "Fiscal Federalism and Redistributive Politics." See also Fernando Toboso and Raúl Compés, "Nuevas Tendencias Analíticas en el Ambito de la NEI."

50. On the role "mutual trust" plays in the Dutch economic miracle since the 1980s, see Frank A.G Butter,. and Robert H.J. Mosch, , "The Dutch Miracle."

51. Subirats, "El Papel de las Comunidades Autónomas en el Sistema Español de Relaciones Intergubernamentales," has calculated that half of those regional legislators repeated during the first legislatures. Though updated figures are not provided, political professionalism no doubt has increased this percentage since no temporal limitation exits at any level of government. Several presidents of regional executives and their teams have been in office—and still are—for more than twenty years.

52. See the lecture delivered by North when he received the Nobel Prize in economics in Douglass C. North, "Economic Performance Through Time," and also North, "A Transaction Cost Approach to the Historical Development of Polites and Economies."

53. In the Central Executive, the first turn took place in 1996. From 1982 to 1996, Felipe González from a social-labor democratic party (PSOE) was the president of the Central Executive. The second turn has taken place three days after March 11th, 2004.

54. On the economic consequences of stability in formal and informal institutional structures, see North, *Institutional Change and Economic Performance*, chap. 12; the lecture given at the World Bank by Oliver Williamson, "Institutions and Governance of Economic Development and Reform"; and also the innovative analysis on the consequences of legal rules by using a top-broken Edgeworth box made by Thrainn Eggertsson, *Economic Behavior and Institutions*, chap. 4.

55. Of a centrist/conservative political orientation.

56. On this, see Jose L. García-Delgado, and José M. Serrano-Sanz, "De la Primera Crisis Energética a las Elecciones del 77"; and Enrique Fuentes-Quintana, "Tres Decenios de la Economía Española en Perspectiva"; and Fuentes-Quintana, "De los Pactos de la Moncloa a la Constitución (Julio 1977–Diciembre 1978)."

57. They all have been very pro-market ones in the line of the so-called new public management. See, for example, the analysis by José M. Cabases-Hita et al., "La Eficiencia de las Organizaciones Hospitalarias" on the efficiency of public hospitals.

58. On this, see North, "Big-bang Transformations in Economic Systems"; Fernando Toboso and Raúl Compés, "La Nueva Economía Institucional y las Reformas en los Países del Este"; and Jack Winiecki, "Why Economic Reforms Failed in the Soviet System" and "Formal and Informal Rules in Post-Communist Transition."

59. Toboso, "Institutional Individualism and Institutional Change."

References

Agranoff, R., and J.A. Ramos, eds. "La Evolución Hacia una Democracia Federal en España: Un Examen del Sistema de Relaciones Intergubernamentales." In *El Estado de las Autonomías¿Hacia un Nuevo Federalismo¿* ed. R. Agranoff and J. Bañón. Bilbao: IVAP, 1998.

Agúndez, A.A., and F. Pedraja. "Descentralización Fiscal y Eficiencia Económica." *Papeles de Economía Española* 95 (2003): 24–33.

Arratibel, J.A. "El Sistema de Concierto y las Haciendas Europea, Estatal y Autonómica Vascas." *Crónica Tributaria* 92 (1999): 11–39.

Bañón, R., and M. Tamayo. "Las Relaciones Intergubernamentales en España: El Nuevo Papel de la Administración Central en el Modelo de Relaciones Intergubernamentales." In Agranoff and Bañón, *El Estado de las Autonomías*.

Bartlett, R. *Economics and Power. An Inquiry Into Human Relations and Market.* Cambridge, UK: Cambridge University Press, 1989.

Besley, T.J., and H.S. Rosen. "Vertical Externalities in Tax Setting: Evidence from Gasoline and Cigarettes." *Journal of Public Economics* 70 (1998): 383–98.

Butter, F.A.G., and R.H.J. Mosch. "The Dutch Miracle: Institutions, Networks, and Trust." *Journal of Institutional and Theoretical Economics* 159 (2003): 363–91.

Cabases-Hita, J.M., and M. Puerto López. "La Eficiencia de las Organizaciones Hospitalarias." *Papeles de Economía Españo* 95 (2003): 195–212.

Castells, A. "The Role of Intergovernmental Fiscal Relations in Achieving Diversity and Cohesion: The Case of Spain." *Environment and Planning C: Government and Policy* 19 (2001): 189–206.

Castillo, M.M. "La Tributación de las Comunidades Autónomas." *Estudios Financieros-Revista de Contabilidad y Tributación* 198 (January 1999): 27–98.

Colomer, J. *La Transición a la Democracia: el Modelo Español*. Barcelona: Anagrama, 1998.

Cuadrado-Roura, J.R., and T. Mancha. "Política Regional y de Cohesión." In *Economía de la Unión Europea,* ed J.M. Jordan. Madrid: Civitas, 2003.

Cubero, A.M. "La Escala Autonómica del I.R.P.F.: Consecuencias de la Inactividad Casi Total de las Comunidades Autónomas al Respecto." *Estudios Financieros-Revista de Contabilidad y Tributación* 188 (November 1998): 91–110.

Dixit, A., and J. Londregan. "Fiscal Federalism and Redistributive Politics." *Journal of Public Economics* 68 (1998): 53–80.

DGCHT. *La Descentralización del Gasto Público en España 1987–98*. Madrid: Ministerio de Economía y Hacienda, 1999.

Eggertsson, T. *Economic Behavior and Institutions*. Cambridge, UK: Cambridge University Press, 1990.

Elazar, D.J. "Tendencias de Desarrollo Institucional en España y en el Mundo." In Agranoff and Bañón, *El Estado de las Autonomías*.

Esteller, A. "La Eficiencia en la Administración de los Tributos Cedidos: Un Análisis Explicativo." *Papeles de Economía Españo* 95 (2003): 320–34.

Frey, B. "A Utopia? Government Without Territorial Monopoly." *Journal of Institutional and Theoretical Economics* 157 (2001): 177–86.

Fuentes-Quintana, E. "Tres Decenios de la Economía Española en Perspectiva." In *España Economía,* ed. J.L. García Delgado. Madrid: Espasa Calpe, 1989.

———. "De los Pactos de la Moncloa a la Constitución (Julio 1977–Diciembre 1978)." In *Economía Española de la Transición y la Democracia,* ed. J.L. García-Delgado. Madrid: CIS, 1990.

García-Delgado, J.L., and J.M. Serrano Sanz. "De la Primera Crisis Energética a las Elecciones del 77: Tiempo de Incertidumbre." In Garcia-Delgado, *Economía Española de la Transición y la Democracia*.

Giménez, A. "Responsabilidad y Corresponsabilidad Fiscal en los Países Federales." *Papeles de Economía Española* 83 (2000): 2–23.

Goerlich, F., M. Mas, and F. Pérez. "Concentración, Convergencia y Desigualdad Regional en España." *Papeles de Economía Española* 93 (2002): 17–31.

Groenewegen, J. "On Integrating New and Old Institutionalism: Douglass C. North Building Bridges." *Journal of Economic Issues* 29, no. 2 (June 1995): 467–76.

Horn, M.J. *The Political Economy of Public Administration. Institutional Choice in the Public Sector*. Cambridge, UK: Cambridge University Press, 1995.

Hutchison, T. "Institutional Economics: Old and New." *Journal of Institutional and Theoretical Economics* 140, no. 1 (1984): 20–33.

Informe Economico Anual. Bilbao: BBVA, 2001.

Inman, R.P., and D.L. Rubinfeld. "Designing Tax Policy in Federalist Economies: An Overview." *Journal of Public Economics* 60 (1996): 307–34.

Jiménez, J.D., and P.E. Barrilao. "Una Aproximación a la Eficiencia en la Gestión de la Agencia Estatal de Administración Tributaria." *Papeles de Economía Española* 87 (2001): 221–27.

Kincaid, J. "Economic Policy-making: Advantages and Disadvantages of the Federal Model." *International Social Science Journal* 53, no. 1 (March 2001): 85–112.

King, D. "Public Policies in a Multilevel Government Model." Madrid: IEF, 1995.

Kirschgässner, R., and W.W. Pommerehne. "Tax Harmonization and Tax Competition in the European Union: The Case of Switzerland." *Journal of Public Economics* 60 (1996): 351–71.

Knight, J. *Institutions and Social Conflict.* Cambridge, UK: Cambridge University Press, 1992.

Küthenbürger, M. "Tax Competition and Fiscal Equalization." *International Tax Public Finance* 9 (2002): 391-408.

La Caixa, *Monthly Economic Bulletin*. Several issues. Barcelona.

Libecap, G. "Distributional Issues in Contracting for Property Rights." *Journal of Institutional and Theoretical Economics* 145 (1989): 6–24.

Mas, M., F. Pérez, and E. Uriel. *El Stock de Capital en España y sus Comunidades Autónomas*. Bilbao, Spain: Fundación BBVA, 1996.

———. *Capitalización y Crecimiento de la Economía Española 1970–1997: Una Perspectiva Internacional Comparada*. Bilbao, Spain: Fundación BBVA, 2001.

Monasterio, C., and J. Suárez-Pandiello. *Manual de Hacienda Autonómica y Local.* Madrid: Civitas, 1998.

Monasterio, C., F. Alcalá, and J. Lopez-Legorda. "Una Propuesta Para el 2001: La Reforma del Sistema de Financiación de las Comunidades Autónomas de Régimen Común." In *Bases para un Sistema Estable de Financiación Autonómica*, ed. M. González- Paramo, 29–106. Bilbao: BBVA, 2001.

North, D.C. "A Transaction Cost Approach to the Historical Development of Polites and Economies." *Journal of Institutional and Theoretical Economics* 145, no. 4 (December 1989): 661–68.

———. *Institutional Change and Economic Performance.* Cambridge, UK: Cambridge University Press, 1990.

———. "Institutions, Ideology and Economic Performance." *The Cato Journal* 11, no. 3 (Winter 1992): 477–88.

———. "Institutions and Credible Commitment." *Journal of Institutional and Theoretical Economics* 156, no. 1 (1993a): 3–8.

———. "Some Fundamental Puzzles in Economic Development." In *The Economy as an Evolving Complex System,* ed. W. Arthur et al. New York: Wesley, 1993b.

———. "Economic Performance Through Time." *American Economic Review* 84, no. 3 (June 1994): 359–68.

———. "Big-bang Transformations in Economic Systems: An Introductory Note." *Journal of Institutional and Theoretical Economics* 149 (2000): 11–23.

Oates, W.E. "On the Welfare Gains from Fiscal Decentralization." *Journal of Public Finance and Public Choice* 2-3 (1997): 83–92.

———. *The Economics of Federalism and Local Finance*. Cheltenham, UK: Edward Elgar, 1998.

———. "An Essay on Fiscal Federalism." *Journal of Economic Literature* 37 (September 1999): 1120–49.

Oates, W.E., and R.M. Schwab. "Economic Competition among Jurisdictions: Efficiency Enhancing or Distortion Inducing." *Journal of Public Economics* 3 (1988): 333–54.

Oliver, J., and X. Ramos. "Anatomía de la Distribución de la Renta en España, 1985–1996: La Continuidad de la Mejora." *Papeles de Economía Española* 88 (2001a): 67–88.

———. "Capital Humano y Desigualdad en España, 1985–1996." *Papeles de Economía* Española 88 (2001b): 240–256.

———. "Why Poor Economic Policies Must Promote Corruption: Lessons from the East for All Countries." In *Institutions and Economic Organization in the Advanced Economies: The Governance Perspective*, ed. M. Baldassarri et al. London: MacMillan Press, 1998.

———. *Power and Prosperity.* New York: Basic Books, 2000.

Ostrom, E. *Governing the Commons:The Evolution of Institutions for Collective Actions.* Cambridge, UK: Cambridge University Press, 1990.

Peces-Barba, G. "Una Lectura de la Constitución Española." In *La Organización Territorial del Estado. España en Europa: Un Análisis Comparado,* ed. A. Cucó et al. Valencia, Spain: Universitat de Valencia, 2002.

Perez-García, F. "La Financiación del Estado Autonómico: Una Lectura de Veinte Años de Descentralización." In *La Organización Territorial del Estado: España en Europa; Un Análisis Comparado*, ed. A. Cucó et al. Valencia. Spain: Universitat de Valencia, 2002.

Pessali, H., and R. Fernández. "Institutional Economics at the Micro Level? What Transation Costs Theory Could Learn from Institutionalism (in the Spirit of Building Bridges)." *Journal of Economic Issues* XXIII, no. 2 (June 1999): 265–75.

Rutherford, M. "The Old and the New Institutionalism: Can Bridges Be Built?" *Journal of Economic Issues* 29, no. 2 (June 1995): 443–51.

Saiegh, S., and M. Tommasi. "Why Is Argentina's Fiscal Federalism so Inefficient? Entering the Labrynth." *Journal of Applied Economics* II, no. 1 (May 1999): 169–209.

Samuels, W., and A. Schmid, eds. *Law and Economics. An Institutional Perspective.* Boston: Kluwer-Nijhoff, 1981.

Sato, M. "Fiscal Externalities and Efficiency Transfers in a Federation." *International Tax and Public Finance* 7, no. 2 (2000): 119–39.

Schmid, A.A. *Property, Power, and Public Choice: An Inquiry into Law and Economics.* New York: Praeger, 1987.

"Spain in Transit: A Survey." *Economist,* December 14, 1996: 3–18.

Span, P.B., F. Wofgang, and I. Steinmetz. "Cesión de Impuestos y Administración Tributaria en el Modelo Alemán de Federalismo Cooperativo." *Hacienda Pública Española* 146, no. 3 (1998): 99–120.

Stiglitz, J. "Distinguished Lecture on Economics in Government: The Private Uses of Public Interests: Incentives and Institutions." *Journal of Economic Perspectives* 12 (Spring 1998): 3–22.

Suárez-Pandiello, J. "Fiscal Federalism in Spain: Decentralization: An Unfinished Task." In *Fiscal Federalism in the European Union*, ed. A. Fossati and G. Panella, 222–54. London: Routledge, 1999.

Subirats, J. "El Papel de las Comunidades Autónomas en el Sistema Español de Relaciones Intergubernamentales." In Agranoff and Bañón, *El Estado de las Autonomías.*

Toboso, F. "Explaining the Process of Change Taking Place in Legal Rules and Social Norms: The Cases of IE and NIE." *European Journal of Law and Economics* 2, no. 1 (1995): 63–84.

———. "Institutional Individualism and Institutional Change: The Search for a Middle Way Mode of Explanation." *Cambridge Journal of Economics* 25, no. 6 (November 2001a): 765–83.

Toboso, F., and R. Compés. "La Nueva Economía Institucional y las Reformas en los Países del Este: Una Primera Aproximación." In *Estudios sobre Europa Oriental,* ed. C. Juberias. Valencia, Spain: Colecció Oberta-Ciencies Socials, Universitat de Valencia, 2002.

About the Editors and Contributors

Morris Altman is Professor and Head of the Department of Economics at the University of Saskatchewan and is an Elected Fellow of World Innovation Foundation (WIF). He has recently been elected President of the Society for Advancement of Behavioral Economics (SABE) and is the new Editor of the *Journal of Socio-Economics* (Elsevier Science). Altman has published over sixty scholarly papers in behavioral economics, economic history, institutional economics, and empirical macroeconomics. Most recently he has published *Human Agency and Material Welfare: Revisions in Microeconomics and Their Implications for Public Policy* (1996), and *Worker Satisfaction and Economic Performance* (2001), with M.E. Sharpe Publishers. He is currently editing a handbook on behavioral economics for M.E. Sharpe and completing a book on Canadian economic history and another on behavioral labor economics. Also, his *Economic Growth and the High Wage Economy: Choices, Constraints and Opportunities in the Market Economy* is forthcoming.

Ann Davis received her Ph.D. in Economics from Boston College, a M.A. in Economics from Northeastern University, and her B.A. in American Studies from Barnard College. She has taught at both the University of Massachusetts at Boston and Vassar College before going to Marist College, where she is currently an Assistant Professor of Economics. Her fields of teaching and research are International, Regional, and Labor Economics. Recent publications and presentations are in institutional and gender economics. Davis is also the founding director of the Marist College Bureau of Economic Research, a position she has held since 1990. She is currently a member of the board of directors of the Dutchess County Economic Development Corporation, and a board member and chair of the Entrepreneurship Committee of Mid-Hudson Pattern for Progress. She is also a member of the Greenway Agriculture Committee, and a member of the board of the New York Main

Street Alliance. Currently in progress are studies of the high tech industry clusters in the region, both current and prospective.

Kenneth Dau-Schmidt received his Ph.D. in Economics from the University of Michigan, a J.D. in law and a M.A. in Economics from the same institution, and a B.A. in Economics and Political Science from the University of Wisconsin. He is the Willard and Margaret Carr Professor of Labor and Employment Law at Indiana University-Bloomington, and has also taught at the University of Wisconsin, the University of Cincinnati, Christian-Albrechts-Universität, Friedrich-Alexander-Universität, and Université Panthéon-Assas (Paris). His fields of teaching expertise are labor law, employment law, and the economic analysis of law. Prior to teaching, Dau-Schmidt practiced law for two years with the firm of Previant, Goldberg and Uelmen and two years as Counsel to the Labor Committee of the Minnesota House of Representatives. He is the author of three books and numerous articles on labor and employment law and the economic analysis of law. In 1991 he received the Scholarly Paper Award from the Association of American Law Schools. He has presented papers at academic conferences and law schools across the United States and in Canada and Europe. Dau-Schmidt has also been active in several national academic associations including: the American Association of University Professors, the Association of American Law Schools, the Industrial Relations Research Association, the Labor Law Group, the Law and Society Association, and the Midwest Law and Economics Association.

Amitai Etzioni is University Professor at the George Washington University. He was the founding president of the international Society for the Advancement of Socio-Economics from 1989 to 1990 and was the Thomas Henry Carroll Ford Foundation Professor at Harvard Business School from 1987 to 1989. Between 1979 and 1980 he was a Senior Adviser to the White House on domestic affairs. Etzioni is the author of twenty-two books, including *The Moral Dimension: Toward a New Economics* (1988) and *Next: The Road to the Good Society* (2001), as well as editor of the quarterly journal *The Responsive Community: Rights and Responsibilities*.

Lonnie Golden earned a Ph.D. in Economics from the University of Illinois-Urbana. He is currently Associate Professor of Economics at Penn State University, Abington College. His research primarily focuses on the economics of the labor market. In particular, it analyzes trends in working hours, overwork, labor market flexibility, and the nonstandard work force. He is coeditor of the books *Working Time: International Trends, Theory and Policy* and *Nonstandard Work: The Nature and Challenge of Changing Employment Arrangements*. His most recent research focuses on the characteristics of workers employed beyond their preferred workweek, mandatory (forced) overtime work, reforming federal and state overtime hours provisions, the distribution of formal and informal flexible work schedules among workers (funded by the Alfred P. Sloan Foundation), work schedule flexibility in organizations as an employee benefit compared with productivity enhancement tool, the changing pattern of adjustment of employment, work hours in the labor market over the business cycle, behavioral economic roots of labor supply and overwork, and compensation differentials for nonstandard and contingent workers. He has held positions on the faculty at Temple University, Penn State Delaware County, University of Wisconsin-Whitewater, and at 9to5. He serves on the editorial board of the *Review of Social Economy*.

Thomas L. Greaney is Professor of Law and Co-Director of the Center for Health Law Studies at Saint Louis University's School of Law. His publications include coauthorship of several books on health law, chapters in books, and articles in highly regarded journals, including *The Journal of the American Medical Association*, *University of Michigan Law Review*, and *Cornell Law Journal*. Before joining the faculty at Saint Louis University, he was Assistant Chief of the Department of Justice, Antitrust Division, supervising health care antitrust litigation. Greaney is coeditor in chief of the *Journal of Health Law*. He was a Fulbright Fellow in European Community competition law, Merck Visiting Scholar at Seton Hall University, a visiting professor at Universite d'Orleans in France, and Victor Kramer Fellow at Yale University. Greaney has an undergraduate degree from Wesleyan University, and a law degree from Harvard University.

Elizabeth Kruse received her Ph.D. and M.A. in Economics from the University of Massachusetts at Amherst, and her B.A. in Studio Art and Anthropology from Rutgers University. She has taught at the University of Massachusetts at Amherst and worked as an economist in the telecommunications industry. She currently works as an economist in the Office of Program Evaluation of the Internal Revenue Service. Her current research interests are telecommunications history and policy, the theory and history of institutional change, and American economic history.

Toni Lester is an Associate Professor of Law at Babson College and has also been a visiting scholar at the Stanford Center for Research on Gender, and the Wellesley College Center for Women. She writes about law, culture and society, and civil rights; her newest book is *Gender Nonconformity, Race* *and Sexuality—Charting the Connections.* Lester received undergraduate and law degrees from Georgetown University and a Ph.D. from Northeastern University.

Claude Menard received a Ph.D. in Economics and a Ph. D. in Philosophy (History of Sciences) from the University of Paris (Pantheon Sorbonne), a M.A. and a BA from the University of Montreal. He has taught at College Edouard Montpetit (Quebec), the University of Utrecht (the Netherlands) and the University of Dijon (France) before being appointed full professor in economics at the University of Paris (Pantheon Sorbonne), a position he has held since 1983. His field of teaching and research is economics of organizations and institutions and industrial organization. Menard is a founding member and a past president (2001–2002) of the International Society for New Institutional Economics (ISNIE), the founding director of the Centre for the Analytical Theory of Organizations and Markets (ATOM), and coeditor of the *Journal of Economic Behavior and Organization.* He has been a consultant for several governmental and international organizations, including the European Commission and the World Bank. He has published several books and numerous papers in international journals, mostly on the economics of organizations and institutions, but also in the history of economic thought.

Nicholas Mercuro was on the faculty of the Department of Economics and Finance at the University of New Orleans from 1976 to 1997. In 1996 Professor Mercuro was awarded the John A. Hannah Visiting Endowed Chair for Integrative Studies at Michigan State University. He accepted a universitywide professorship at Michigan State University in 1997 and in 2002 was named Professor in Residence at M.S.U.'s College of Law. Mercuro has published six books as well as authored journal articles, book chapters, and book reviews in the field of law and economics. In 1994 he founded and now serves as the series editor of a book series, *The Economics of Legal Relationships.* Throughout the 1980s and 1990s, Mercuro was a visiting professor at the Institute of Economic Theory at the University of Vienna; taught and engaged in research at the Free University of Berlin as a Fulbright Scholar; and was a Research Associate at the Erasmus Program in Law and Economics, University of Hamburg. While at M.S.U., he designed and coordinated the M.S.U. Law & Economics Program originally held in Hamburg, Germany, now located at the University of London. Recently he was awarded a grant from the French government, as Guest Professor at Institutions et Dynamiques Historiques de l'Economie, Ecole Normale Superieure de Cachan, France; in spring 2003 he was invited to the Université de Droit, d'Economie et des Sciences d'Aix-Marseille, Faculté d'Economie Appliquée, Aix en Provence, France. He received his Ph.D. degree from Michigan State University in 1977 (in Resource Development); his M.B.A. in 1970 from Seton Hall University, and in 1967 an undergraduate B.A. degree in economics from Pennsylvania State University.

Edward J. O'Boyle is Senior Research Associate at the Mayo Research Institute in West Monroe, Louisiana. In contrast to mainstream economics, which is ground in the individual as the basic unit of analysis and individualism as its philosophical foundation, O'Boyle's economics is grounded in person and personalism, which affirm human beings for their sociality as well as individuality and for the spirit dimension of their nature in addition to the material dimension. Most recently his work has turned in the direction of understanding economics as constructed on the evolution model as opposed to the cyclic model that has dominated economics for the past 100 years, and in identifying the role of classical economics in the Great Irish Famine. O'Boyle is a graduate of DePaul University and was awarded his master's and doctoral degrees in economics by Saint Louis University. He has served as a visiting professor/scholar at Poznan School of Management, National University of Ireland in Galway, Santa Clara University, Center for Economic Personalism, Santa Clara, California, and the University of Verona. He has published numerous articles in journals such as *Review of Social Economy*, *International Journal of Social Economics*, *Journal of Business Ethics*, *Monthly Labor Review*, and *Ethics and Information Technology*. In addition, O'Boyle has authored or edited six major works, including *Personalist Economics: Moral Convictions, Economic Realities, and Social Action*.

Margaret Oppenheimer is Professor of Economics at DePaul University in Chicago. From 1995 to 2001 she served as the Chair of the Department of Economics, and from 1992 to 1995 she served as the President of the Faculty Council at DePaul University. She received her undergraduate degree from Simmons College in 1967 and her Ph.D. in Economics from Northwestern University in 1974. Her areas of specialization are Labor Economics, Managerial Economics, and Economics and Gender. Some of her publications have appeared in *Managerial and Decision Economics*, *The Labor Law Journal*, *The Journal of Teaching in International Business*, and *The Journal of Sports Economics*. She is the coeditor of a volume of *The International Review of Comparative Public Policy* series titled, *Labor Markets in Transition: International Dimensions*. She has also given talks and moderated sessions on alternative approaches in Law and Economics in several different forums, including law schools, economics conferences, and the annual meetings of the Association of American Law Schools.

Warren J. Samuels is Professor Emeritus of Economics at Michigan State University. He specializes in the history of economic thought, methodology, and the economic role of government. A five-volume collection of his work was published in 1992. He is the author or coauthor of *Economics, Governance and Law: Essays on Theory and Policy* (2002); *The Economy as a Process of Valuation* (1997); *Economic Thought and Discourse in the Twentieth Century* (1993); *The Classical Theory of Economic Policy* (1966); and *Pareto on Policy* (1974). He is editor or co-editor of *Research in the History of Economic Thought and Methodology*; *Companion to the History of Economic Thought* (2003), *The Fundamental Interrelationship Between Government and Property* (1999), *Law and Economics* (1998), *Fundamentals of the Economic Role of Government* (1989), and *Law and Economics: An Institutional Perspective* (1981). His principal current research is on the use of the concept of the invisible hand.

Edward Stringham completed his dissertation under Peter J. Boettke at *George Mason University* in 2002 and is Assistant Professor at *San Jose State University*. He studies how markets can function without government law enforcement and is the author of ten articles. Recent publications appeared in *Quarterly Review of Economics & Finance*, *Managerial Finance*, and *Journal of Private Enterprise*. He was interviewed in the *Austrian Economics Newsletter* in 2002, won second prize in the Independent Institute Garvey Essay Contest in 2003, won Society for the Development of Austrian Economics Best Article Award in 2003, and won Association of Private Enterprise Education Paper of the Year Award in 2003.

Kellye Testy is the Faculty Director of the Center on Corporations, Law and Society. A frequent lecturer nationally in the areas of business and commercial law, Testy is a leading scholar in the area of corporate governance reform. She has published numerous articles and book chapters, including articles in the *California Law Review*, *Northwestern Law Review*, *Tulane Law Review*, *New York Journal of International and Comparative Law*, and *Law & Policy*, and the *Journal of Law & Contemporary Problems*. In addition to her teaching and writing activities, Testy is also active as a consultant and expert witness on a variety of corporate and securities law matters, in both state and federal court. A cofounder of the Access to Justice Institute and the founding adviser of the *Seattle Journal for Social Justice*, she earned her J.D. summa cum laude from Indiana University School of Law 1991, where she served as the *Indiana Law Journal* editor-in-chief and was a member of the Order of the Coif, a John H. Edwards Fellow and a Chancellor's Scholar. Prior to joining the faculty at Seattle University, Testy clerked for the Honorable Jesse E. Eschbach of the U.S. Court of Appeals, Seventh Circuit.

Fernando Toboso is currently a professor at the Department of Applied Economics, Univesity of Valencia, Spain, where he teaches two postgraduate courses: "Institutional Organization and Change in the Public Sector" and "Introduction to Reseach Tasks in Economics: Tools, Criteria and Methods." He is also Director of a recently created research unit on "Institutional Economics and Public Regulations" and moderator of the Spanish-speaking electronic network of scholars interested in exploring the interrelations between institutions and economics. His research interests are in methodological issues in economic analysis and with organizational structures in policy governance. In both areas he has authored several articles that have been published in the *Cambridge Journal of Economics*, the *European Journal of Law and Economics*, and the *Journal of Interdisciplinary Economics*. He has also published widely in such Spanish academic journals as *El Trimestre Económico* and *Hacienda Pública Española*. In 1985 he earned his degree in Economics with an extraordinary distinction thanks, in part, to his thesis entitled, "Mixed Economies, Power Influences, and Economic Analyses: Some Limitations of the Neoclassical Research Program." In 1990 he was awarded his Ph.D. in Economics after spending an academic year as visiting scholar at the Public Choice Center, George Mason University, Fairfax, Virginia, where he completed a dissertation: "The Methodological Foundations of the Public Choice Researh Program." He is presently working on two projects—the first is an international semminar on "Institutional Organization and Change in Policy Governance" that was held under his direction at the Internacional Menéndez Pelayo University, September 20–24, 2004, Valencia, Spain The second, in collaboration with Prof. Xosé C. Arias, is a book project (in the Spanish language—as both an author and editor) titled "Organizing Governments and Public Bureaus."

Patrick J. Welch is Professor of Economics at Saint Louis University, with secondary appointments in the Department of Public Policy Studies and School of Public Health. He is published in economics, law, business, and other journals; coauthor, with his wife, of *Economics: Theory and Practice*, an introductory text in its seventh edition, and has chapters in several edited volumes. He has also been a consultant in antitrust, market definition, and other matters, and has been twice listed in *Who's Who in Finance and Industry in the United States*. His opinions on economic matters have frequently been sought by the media, including BBC News, CNN, *U.S.A. Today*, the *Wall Street Journal*, and others. Welch is editor of *Forum for Social Economics*, and on the Board of Editors of *Review of Social Economy.* He has an undergraduate degree and master's degree in economics from Marquette University, and a doctorate in economics from the University of Pittsburgh.

Mark D. White teaches economics, including interdisciplinary courses incorporating law and philosophy, at the College of Staten Island/CUNY in New York City. His current research applies Immanuel Kant's moral and legal philosophy to economic issues and methodology, particularly in the area of law and economics. He regularly organizes conference sessions on economics and philosophy for national and regional economics associations. His recent publications include "Can *Homo Economicus* Follow Kant's Categorical Imperative?" forthcoming in the *Journal of Socio-Economics*; "Kantian Dignity and Social Economics," forthcoming in the *Forum for Social Economics*; and "Reconciling *Homo Economicus* with Dewey's Ethics," *Journal of Economic Methodology*, June 2003. He has also published on industrial organization and international trade in journals such as *Southern Economic Journal*, *Journal of Economic Behavior and Organization*, *European Journal of Political Economy*, and *Economics Letters*.

Index

W

X–Z